PROSPECTS IN INTERNATIONAL INVESTMENT LAW AND POLICY

The negotiation of a patchy but burgeoning network of international investment agreements and the increasing use to which they are put is generating a growing body of jurisprudence that, while still evolving, requires closer analytical scrutiny. Drawing on many of the most distinguished voices in investment law and policy, and offering novel, multidisciplinary perspectives on the rapidly evolving landscape shaping international investment activity and treaty-making, this book explores the most important economic, legal and policy challenges in contemporary international investment law and policy. It also examines the systemic implications flowing from frenetic recent judicial activism in investment matters and advances several innovative propositions for how best to promote greater overall coherence in rule-design, treaty use and policy-making and thus offer a better balance between the rights and obligations of international investors and host states.

ROBERTO ECHANDI is the Global Product Leader, Investment Policy, of the Investment Climate Department of the World Bank Group. He was previously the Director of the Programme on International Investment at the World Trade Institute, University of Bern.

PIERRE SAUVÉ is Deputy Managing Director and Director of Studies at the World Trade Institute, University of Bern.

PROSPECTS IN INTERNATIONAL INVESTMENT LAW AND POLICY

World Trade Forum

Edited by

ROBERTO ECHANDI

AND

PIERRE SAUVÉ

CAMBRIDGE
UNIVERSITY PRESS

CAMBRIDGE UNIVERSITY PRESS
Cambridge, New York, Melbourne, Madrid, Cape Town,
Singapore, São Paulo, Delhi, Mexico City

Cambridge University Press
The Edinburgh Building, Cambridge CB2 8RU, UK

Published in the United States of America by Cambridge University Press, New York

www.cambridge.org
Information on this title: www.cambridge.org/9781107035867

© Cambridge University Press 2013

First published 2013

Printed and bound in the United Kingdom by the MPG Books Group

A catalogue record for this publication is available from the British Library

Library of Congress Cataloguing in Publication data
World Trade Forum (15th : 2011 : Bern, Switzerland)
Prospects in international investment law and policy : World Trade Forum /
edited by Roberto Echandi and Pierre Sauvé.
pages   cm
Includes bibliographical references and index.
ISBN 978-1-107-03586-7 (hardback)
1. Investments, Foreign (International law)–Congresses.   I. Echandi, Roberto, editor of
compilation.   II. Sauvé, Pierre, 1959– editor of compilation.   III. World Trade Institute
(Bern, Switzerland)   IV. Title.
K3829.8.W67 2011
346′.092–dc23
2012043734

ISBN 978-1-107-03586-7 Hardback

CONTENTS

FIGURES

ix

TABLES

CONTRIBUTORS

MARINO BALDI, Senior Counsel, Prager Dreifuss Attorneys at law, Zurich/Bern/Brussels; former Swiss Ambassador and Trade Delegate; former Chairman of the OECD Investment Committee

YAS BANIFATEMI, Partner, Shearman & Sterling, Paris

ANDREA K. BJORKLUND, Professor at the University of California, Davis, School of Law

LAURENCE BOISSON DE CHAZOURNES, Professor, Faculty of Law, University of Geneva

TOMER BROUDE, Sylvan M. Cohen Chair in Law, Faculty of Law and Department of International Relations; Academic Director, The Minerva Center for Human Rights, Hebrew University of Jerusalem

RUDOLF DOLZER, Professor of Law, Rheinische Friedrich-Wilhelm University, Bonn

ROBERTO ECHANDI, Global Product Leader, Investment Policy, of the Investment Climate Department of the World Bank Group; former Director, Programme on International Investment, World Trade Institute, University of Bern

MICHAEL EWING-CHOW, Associate Professor, Faculty of Law National University of Singapore

MARY E. FOOTER, Professor of International Economic Law, University of Nottingham School of Law

SUSAN D. FRANCK, Associate Professor of Law, Washington and Lee School of Law

RAINER GEIGER, former Deputy Director Financial and Fiscal Affairs, Organisation for Economic Co-operation and Development

STEPHEN GELB, Director, International Investment Initiative, World Trade Institute, University of Bern; and Visiting Research Associate, Mandela Institute, University of Witwatersrand, Johannesburg

GARY CLYDE HUFBAUER, Reginald Jones Senior Fellow, Peterson Institute for International Economics

ANNA JOUBIN-BRET, Partner, Foley Hoag, Paris

BARTON LEGUM, Partner, Salans, Paris

TOBIAS A. LEHMANN, Doctoral candidate in law, University of St Gallen

CÉLINE LÉVESQUE, Associate Professor, University of Ottawa, Faculty of Law

INNA MANASSYAN, Associate, Salans, Paris

SÉBASTIEN MIROUDOT, Senior Trade Policy Analyst, Trade in Services Division, Trade and Agriculture Directorate, Organisation for Economic Co-operation and Development and Research Associate, Groupe d'Economie Mondiale, Sciences Po

THEODORE H. MORAN, Marcus Wallenberg Professor of International Business and Finance, Georgetown University and Non-Resident Senior Fellow, Peterson Institute for International Economics

PETER MUCHLINSKI, Professor in International Commercial Law, The School of Oriental and African Studies, University of London

IOANA PETCULESCU, Associate, Salans, Paris

ALEXANDROS RAGOUSSIS, Economist, Structural Policy Division, Directorate for Science, Technology and Industry, Organisation for Economic Co-operation and Development

AUGUST REINISCH, Professor of International and European Law, University of Vienna

PIERRE SAUVÉ, Deputy Managing Director and Director of Studies, World Trade Institute, University of Bern

CHRISTOPH SCHREUER, Of Counsel, Wolf Theiss Rechtsanwälte, Vienna

LAUGE N. SKOVGAARD POULSEN, Post-doctoral fellow, Nuffield College, University of Oxford, and Copenhagen Business School

DEBRA P. STEGER, Professor, University of Ottawa Faculty of Law

MARGRETE STEVENS, Consultant, King & Spalding, Washington DC

CHRISTIAN TIETJE, Dr iur, LLM (Michigan), Professor, European Law and International Economic Law, Director Institute for Economic Law and Director Transnational Economic Law Research Center, Law School, University Halle

ANNE VAN AAKEN, Professor of Law and Economics, Legal Theory, Public International Law and European Law at the University of St Gallen

JAMES ZHAN, Director, Division on Investment and Enterprise, United Nations Conference on Trade and Development

PREFACE

Launched in 1997, the World Trade Institute (WTI) annual World Trade Forum has established itself as an important hub for leading experts from academia, governments, international organisations and civil society to brainstorm, from a multidisciplinary perspective, on the new and unsettled challenges in global economic governance and to identify forward-looking solutions.

In 2010 the WTI launched the 'International Investment Initiative' (I^3), a programme aimed at promoting research, advanced training, policy advice and dialogue in the fast-moving field of international investment law and policy. The WTI thus decided that it would devote its September 2011 World Trade Forum to the most central challenges arising from the evolving landscape of international investment flows, rules and jurisprudence. The Forum's main objective was to tap into the pluridisciplinary expertise of some of the world's leading trade and investment experts and take stock of the most salient trends in cross-border investment.

This edited volume presents the results of the Forum's deliberations. As befits all such publications, the volume is the last element in a long supply chain of dedicated individuals who contributed to its timely assembly. Our first thanks are directed to the volume's contributors, both lead authors and discussants, a truly remarkable group of some of the most brilliant minds in investment law and policy. The quality of their insights made our task as editors immeasurably easier. We also owe an important debt of gratitude to the United Nations Conference on Trade and Development (UNCTAD), and in particular the Investment Division, guided by its director James Zhan, for its invaluable collaboration in helping to organise and finance both the Forum itself and the UNCTAD Experts Group Meeting that the WTI had the honour to host immediately preceding the Forum. This volume would not have been possible without the funding assistance of the Swiss National Science Foundation through its support of the WTI-anchored National Centre for Competence in Research (NCCR) on Trade Regulation. Special thanks are also owed to the Silva

Casa Foundation for its generous funding of the event. The editors are particularly indebted as well to Professor Thomas Cottier who, in his dual capacity as WTI Managing Director and Director of the NCCR Trade Regulation project, lent his full support to the Forum theme.

We also wish to extend special thanks to Margrit Vetter, Gaby Hofer, Romulo Brillo and Kätlin Pertel for their invaluable assistance in coordinating the organisation of the event; to Bertram Boie, Joel Reeves, Jin Glover and Yaxuan Chen for assisting them in this task, and to all the staff of the WTI for making everyone feel welcome in Bern during the conference. This volume would not have been possible without the dedicated work of Susan Kaplan and Kätlin Pertel in reviewing the manuscripts. Finally, our thanks go to Kim Hughes and her excellent team at Cambridge University Press for their unfailing support and strong commitment to the World Trade Forum series.

Bern, 8 August 2012

ABBREVIATIONS

AAA	American Arbitration Association
ACIA	ASEAN Comprehensive Investment Agreement
AD	anti-dumping
ADR	alternative dispute resolution
ASCM	Agreement on Subsidies and Countervailing Measures
ASEAN	Association of Southeast Asian Nations
BITs	bilateral investment treaties
BRICs	Brazil, Russia, India and China
CGD	Center for Global Development
CMMs	conflict management mechanisms
CSR	corporate social responsibility
CVD	countervailing duty
DPM	dispute prevention mechanism
DPP	dispute prevention policy
DR–CAFTA	Dominican Republic–Central America Free Trade Agreement
DSD	dispute systems design
DSU	Dispute Settlement Understanding
ECT	Energy Charter Treaty
EITI	Extractive Industries Transparency Initiative
EPZ	Export Processing Zones
EU	European Union
FCN treaties	friendship, commerce and navigation treaties
FCTC	Framework Convention on Tobacco Control
FDI	foreign direct investment
FET	fair and equitable treatment
FINSA	Foreign Investment and National Security Act (2007)
FIPA	Foreign Investment Promotion and Protection Agreement (Canada)
FIRA	Foreign Investment Review Act (Canada)
FIT	(Ontario) Feed-in Tariff
FRG	Federal Republic of Germany
FTAs	free trade agreements
FTC	Free Trade Commission (of the NAFTA)

G8	Group of Eight
G20	Group of Twenty
GATS	General Agreement on Trade in Services
GATT	General Agreement on Tariffs and Trade
GDP	gross domestic product
GRI	Global Reporting Initiative
GVCs	global supply/value chains
HDI	Human Development Index
HKIAC	Hong Kong International Arbitration Centre
IBA	International Bar Association
IBRD	International Bank for Reconstruction and Development
ICC	International Chamber of Commerce
ICJ	International Court of Justice
ICSID	International Centre for Settlement of Investment Disputes
ICSID Convention	Convention on the Settlement of Investment Disputes between States and Nationals of Other States of 1965
IFC	International Finance Corporation
IIAs	international investment agreements
IIL	international investment law
IISD	International Institute for Sustainable Development
ILC	International Law Commission
ILO	International Labour Organization
IMF	International Monetary Fund
IPAs	investment promotion agencies
IPFSD	Investment Policy Framework for Sustainable Development
IS	investment and securities
ISDS	investor–state dispute settlement
ITO	International Trade Organization
LCIA	London Court of International Arbitration
LGA	Lead Government Agency
MAI	Multilateral Agreement on Investment
M&As	mergers and acquisitions
MEA	multinational environmental agreement
MFN	most-favoured nation
MIGA	Multilateral Investment Guarantee Agency
MNC	multinational corporation
MNEs	multinational enterprises
NAFTA	North American Free Trade Agreement
NCCR	National Centre for Competence in Research
NEMs	non-equity modes
NGOs	non-governmental organisations
NPM	non-precluded measures

OECD	Organisation for Economic Co-operation and Development
OPIC	Overseas Private Investment Corporation
PCA	Permanent Court of Arbitration
PTAs	preferential trade agreements
PTIAs	preferential trade and investment agreements
RTA	regional trade agreement
SCC	Stockholm Chamber of Commerce
SCM Agreement	Agreement on Subsidies and Countervailing Measures
SD	sustainable development
SIAC	Singapore International Arbitration Centre
SMEs	small and medium-sized enterprises
SOEs	state-owned enterprises
SPS Agreement	Agreement on the Application of Sanitary and Phytosanitary Measures
SRSG	UN Special Representative of the Secretary-General on Business and Human Rights
STEs	state trading enterprises
SWEs	sovereign wealth enterprises
SWFs	sovereign wealth funds
TNCs	transnational corporations
TPP	Trans-Pacific Partnership
TRIM	trade-related investment measure
TRIMs Agreement	Agreement on Trade-Related Investment Measures
TRIPS Agreement	Agreement on Trade-Related Aspects of Intellectual Property Rights
UNCITRAL	United Nations Commission on International Trade Law
UNCTAD	United Nations Conference on Trade and Development
VCLT	Vienna Convention on the Law of Treaties
WGTI	Working Group on the relationship between Trade and Investment
WHO	World Health Organization
WIF	World Investment Forum
WTI	World Trade Institute
WTO	World Trade Organization

Introduction and overview

ROBERTO ECHANDI AND PIERRE SAUVÉ

The central contribution of international investment flows to world welfare is today beyond doubt. Today's world is one in which more goods and services are delivered to foreign markets through international production than through cross-border trade. With the dramatic growth of trade in services and the increasing fragmentation of production on a global scale, governments in developed and developing countries alike have become acutely aware of the central role that foreign investment plays in positioning their national economies in an interdependent world market and in promoting the well-being of citizens.

Over the two decades from the mid 1990s, investment has also become one of the most dynamic areas of international economic law. Such a trend stems from the negotiation of a patchy but now extensive network of international investment agreements (IIAs) around the globe and from the increasing use to which these agreements are put in addressing conflicts between foreign investors and host states.

Increasing recourse to investor–state arbitration has fuelled the development of a growing body of jurisprudence that is still evolving and has begun to attract significant scrutiny within the legal and academic communities. Heightened judicial activism in the investment field has spawned controversy within civil society, corporate and governmental circles. While many observers view the recent increase in litigation as a natural trend deriving from the development of a rule-oriented international investment regime, others consider the nature and features of investor–state arbitration increasingly ill-suited to addressing the public policy issues at stake in investor–state disputes.

Furthermore, and despite the ever closer interaction between international investment and trade, investment law has tended to evolve separately from the regulatory regime governing international trade. The failed attempt at crafting a Multilateral Agreement on Investment (MAI) in the late 1990s was very much reflective of these two 'solitudes'. Experts from these fields all too rarely interact with one another. This has fuelled an undue segmentation of these two central pillars of international economic law and policy. With trade and investment increasingly exhibiting complementary features, there is a genuine need to assess and study both phenomena in a more integrated manner and to strive to identify and exploit the natural synergies between them in legal and policy-making terms.

This volume offers a comprehensive multidisciplinary analysis of the key challenges that are reconfiguring international investment relations. Its principal value lies in our ability to bring together many of the leading economists, lawyers and political scientists to share their vast experience not only in the field of international investment law and policy, but also in that of international trade regulation, with a view to providing readers with an overarching view of the interface between these two complementary policy domains.

The volume is structured around six thematic blocks which, taken together, will provide readers with a comprehensive understanding of the main legal and policy issues confronting the international investment community. The volume takes up the following thematic areas:

- new paradigms in the economics and political economy of international investment activity;
- the interaction between international trade and investment regulation;
- the challenge of fostering greater coherence in international investment law;
- the policy-making and rule-making challenges arising from the growth in investment litigation;
- the quest for a better balance between investment protection and liberalisation and other public policy objectives; and
- the way forward for the international investment regime.

Part I of this volume focuses on new paradigms in the economics and political economy of international investment activity. The contributions provide readers with a clear vision of the evolving landscape of international investment flows and the new types of investors emerging in the international arena. Following an introductory overview of the complex environment in which cross-border activity is today unfolding, in Chapter 2, James Zhan describes the ongoing changes in the geography of foreign direct investment (FDI) flows, new investment modalities and the new types of investors dotting the global landscape. Zhan's chapter chronicles the challenges that such transformations entail for governments in their efforts to promote sustainable development. Chapter 3 by Theodore Moran centres on the analysis of emerging patterns of FDI flows and their impact on economic development. Moran alerts us to the dangers of visualising FDI as a homogeneous phenomenon. He argues that FDI comes in various forms that pose distinctive policy challenges to host countries. His chapter then advances an FDI nomenclature and discusses the advantages and challenges of each kind of FDI as a basis for policy recommendations.

Two further chapters in Part I, Chapter 4 by Sébastien Miroudot and Alexandros Ragoussis, and Chapter 5 by Lauge Poulsen, detail the challenges that stem from the changing nature of international investors. Private multinational enterprises (MNEs) are no longer the sole or dominant investors operating in the international arena. Alongside globally active firms, state-owned enterprises (SOEs) and sovereign wealth funds (SWFs) are becoming central actors in cross-border investment. Miroudot and Ragoussis' contribution offers quantitative evidence of the international expansion of public investors and investigates key policy concerns regarding the governance of SOEs, their performance and the environment in which they operate. Their empirical analysis is complemented in Chapter 5 by Poulsen's examination of some of the new issues confronting the international investment regime as a result of the increasing rise of 'state capitalism'. Poulsen's chapter assesses the extent to which the current international investment regime protects sovereign investors and the degree to which measures targeted at such investors in recent years can be deemed IIA-consistent.

The overview of the economics and political economy of international investment is completed by Chapters 6 and 7, where Gary Hufbauer and Stephen Gelb discuss the key findings advanced by Moran, Miroudot, and Ragoussis and Poulsen. While Hufbauer looks at the issue from a horizontal economics and political economy perspective, Gelb tackles the discussion from the vantage point of realities prevalent in developing countries. Both chapters show the importance of multidisciplinary analysis of the evolving influence of geography, new actors and new forms of investment on the development process.

Part II of the volume addresses the interaction between international trade and investment regulation. Chapter 8, written by Mary E. Footer, explores the relationship between trade and investment. Starting with a historical overview of the genesis of both legal regimes, Footer examines the impact of intra-firm investment flows on trade patterns. This is followed with an analysis of the economic and legal interaction between

IIAs and World Trade Organization (WTO) law and concludes with a look at possible future developments in the trade–investment relationship. Chapter 9, by Tomer Broude, starts by observing that a significant proportion of the international trade and investment flows occurring today take place through the global (or regional) supply chains of MNEs. For this reason, trade and investment are more closely tied today than ever before. Despite this increasing complementarity, Broude notes how the convergence of international trade and investment regulation remains piecemeal in character, lacking a unifying logic. Taking the differential treatment of subsidies in trade and investment as an example, he asks whether the continued distinctions between trade and investment law, rooted in historical and political causes that are no longer relevant, are still justified. Broude concludes that the time has come to end the existing legal bifurcation of trade and investment and explore the consolidation of these two fields of international economic law within a single regulatory framework.

Part II deepens Footer's and Broude's discussion of the relationship between international trade and investment through the comments and additional perspectives of Debra Steger (Chapter 10) and Christian Tietje (Chapter 11) on this complex subject. Steger acknowledges the close interaction between trade and investment, and argues that multilateralisation or integration of the trade and investment regimes into a coherent rules-based system should be an overarching goal of global governance reforms. Steger warns of the disadvantages of letting international arbitration tribunals become de facto responsible for harmonising inconsistent or incoherent systems of rules. She argues that only governments have the legitimate authority to negotiate new rules on behalf of their constituents. While recognising the ever closer interaction between trade and investment, Tietje is more cautious on the putative case for fusing trade and investment law. He argues that a close analysis of the different dimensions of the relationship between the trade and investment regimes reveals salient differences between the two legal fields. In his view, further comparative analysis is warranted. Only when the similarities and differences between trade and investment rules and legal regimes become significantly clearer may we contemplate the scope for meaningful convergence. Tietje's contribution advances a number of useful avenues of future research in this regard.

Addressing the fragmentation of the legal framework regulating international investment and the widespread perception that the still nascent jurisprudence has revealed a lack of legal consistency, Part III of the volume focuses on one of the challenges more frequently raised by investment stakeholders – whether and how to foster greater coherence in international investment law.

In Chapter 12, Andrea Bjorklund starts by addressing the question of convergence on the substantive rules and disciplines of IIAs. Her chapter challenges the notion that convergence in the substantive norms of IIAs is inherently desirable, arguing that convergence should be viewed with caution and sought in some – but not necessarily all – areas of investment law. The very notion of convergence presupposes that consensus exists over the resulting rules. She cautions that this may not be the case given the increasing diversity of constituencies that people the investment policy debate. Bjorklund argues that harmonisation might be the most desirable form of convergence given the current state of investment law, which she describes as uniformity in the interpretation of identical or virtually identical language in the same context, with suitable attention paid to different interpretations stemming from different language or even from the same language in a different context. Her contribution identifies a number of practical ways to promote such an objective.

In Chapter 13, Yas Banifatemi explores the practice of investor–state arbitration and addresses the perceived lack of consistency in the international investment law and arbitration regime. In her view, much of the criticism and commentary seems to pay insufficient attention to the structural features of the arbitral framework. She argues that the actual reasons for jurisprudential divergence are often overlooked. So too are the points of convergence. Banifatemi observes that signs of a maturing regime can be seen in the instances of emerging *jurisprudence constante*. Greater consistency may be achieved, she feels, provided the reality of what can be achieved is more clearly distinguished from prevailing myths.

Chapters 14 and 15 complement the analysis of Bjorklund and Banifatemi, featuring comments and additional perspectives from Michael Ewing-Chow and August Reinisch respectively. Both authors agree on the importance of distinguishing between convergence in the treaty-making stage from coherent interpretations of largely identical standards included in IIAs. Reinisch stresses that one of the basic functions of the law is to produce predictable outcomes and generate confidence. Accordingly, coherence should remain one of the central objectives of the *system* of investment arbitration. Without disagreeing with this view, Ewing-Chow proposes that what is needed is not consistency for consistency's sake – otherwise 'bad laws will remain bad laws'. Rather, the key is that good legal interpretations replace bad ones. Regardless of the particular perspectives of each author, the contributions by Bjorklund, Banifatemi, Ewing-Chow and Reinisch remind us that fostering coherence in a fragmented international investment regime remains a complex question. Do we want consistency in rule-making? Is such an outcome realistic or even desirable? Should we expect or wish for international tribunals promoting consistent awards given the existing variety in the contents of norms and disciplines across IIAs? And how is one to balance such issues with the need for predictability that international law should also promote? All these questions are taken up in some detail in Part III.

Part IV of the volume focuses on the policy-making and rule-making challenges arising from the recent spurt of investor–state litigation. It begins by focusing on investor–state arbitration and subsequently addresses alternative means of dispute resolution and conflict management for investors and host governments. In Chapter 16, Margrete Stevens focuses on the experience of the main venue of treaty-based investment arbitration, the International Centre for Settlement of Investment Disputes (ICSID). After documenting the considerable and sudden expansion in the ICSID caseload, she identifies ten concrete areas of operation where she suggests the ICSID could make changes with a view both to improving its day-to-day case management capabilities and to positioning itself as a stronger and more effective arbitral institution for the future. Stevens' contribution sheds light on how the ICSID could institute changes both internally and in its relationship with users in adapting to a context that is starkly different from that which prevailed at its inception half a century ago.

International investors, host governments and civil society typically disagree on many aspects related to investor–state arbitration. However, one area of possible agreement is that such litigious procedures have turned out to be slower, more costly and less predictable than originally envisaged. One of the emerging themes in this context concerns alternative means of resolving investor–state disputes. Chapter 17, co-authored by Barton Legum, Anna Joubin-Bret and Inna Manassyan, addresses the topic of mediation as an alternative to investor–state arbitration. Its co-authors describe the work undertaken by the state mediation sub-committee of the International Bar Association (IBA) to draft new rules on investor–state mediation. Chapter 18, by Roberto Echandi, introduces the concept of investor–state *conflict management* mechanisms that, among other objectives, could enable host states and investors to effectively prevent their conflicts from escalating into full-blown international disputes. After analysing the limited experience on the use of non-litigious means to resolve investor–state disputes, Echandi focuses on the political economy of investor–state disputes and proposes a conceptual framework to guide the design of protocols for the early management of investor–state conflicts. Part IV concludes with the comments of Laurence Boisson de Chazournes (Chapter 19) and Andrea Bjorklund (Chapter 20) on a menu of options for addressing the challenges arising from increased investor–state arbitration.

Part V of the volume addresses another key concern in the debate on international investment law, that of how best to promote an appropriate balance in IIAs between investment protection and other key public policy objectives. Recognising that the international investment regime is often criticised for the asymmetry it generates between the rights of investors and those of host states to adopt regulatory measures for the public good, Chapter 21, co-authored by Anne Van Aaken and Tobias Lehmann, explores economic insights into the link between foreign investment and sustainable development. The authors advance a number of interpretative arguments and techniques that could be applied to investor–state arbitration with a view to making sustainable development objectives more prominent in international adjudication. Chapter 22, co-authored by Barton Legum and Ioana Petculescu, focuses on a very concrete legal issue, addressing the potential legal impact of embedding in IIAs a clause providing for general exceptions along the lines of Article XX of the General Agreement on Tariffs and Trade (GATT). The authors ask whether the inclusion of such a clause would be compatible with the goals of investment protection treaties and whether it would enhance the existing legal framework by helping balance investor rights and the regulatory powers of the host state. Part V concludes with the comments of Céline Lévesque (Chapter 23) and Susan Franck (Chapter 24). Lévesque argues that including a general exception like that of GATT Article XX in IIAs may well limit, rather than expand, the 'policy space' sought by host governments. In Chapter 24, Franck addresses the question of balancing from a different perspective, focusing on the management of stakeholders' expectations of the international investment regime. Franck's contribution not only addresses the main points raised in Part V of the volume, but also links her analysis to the central point advanced by Echandi in Chapter 18 on the need for the current international investment regime to complement international adjudication with additional mechanisms of conflict management.

Part VI, the concluding section, looks to the future by exploring possible ways forward for the international investment regime. This part features several contributions by prominent academics and practitioners advancing novel ideas on the question of whether and how the current fragmented international investment regime could gradually evolve into a more coherent international governance system.

Part VI comprises five chapters. Chapter 25 by Christoph Schreuer focuses on the issue of coherence and consistency in international investment law. After observing that international investment law often lacks coherence and consistency in several regards, Schreuer offers a number of possible remedies. He states that some of these remedies – such as proper interpretations of most-favoured nation (MFN) clauses – are widely available, but that their effectiveness is somewhat limited. Some of the other possible remedies – such as the negotiation of a multilateral agreement on investment – which would be highly effective, appear unattainable at least for the time being. Thus, he posits that a realistic option for achieving consistency of interpretation of IIAs might be the introduction of a preliminary rulings procedure. Chapter 26 by Rudolph Dolzer focuses on the debate surrounding the issue of consistency in investment arbitration. Dolzer identifies three fundamental lines of argument, which are different in nature and lead to different solutions, namely, embracing the status quo, calling for a major regime overhaul, or improving the current regime in an incremental manner. Chapter 27 by Peter Muchlinski focuses on the key issues that, in his view, should guide the reform of the international investment regime so as to foster greater systemic coherence. Muchlinski argues that to promote such an endeavour, the reforms should take into account at least three fundamental dimensions: first, a reconsideration of the conceptual basis of IIAs, second, a discussion of the constitutional legitimacy of IIAs, and third, a recalibration of the balance of rights and responsibilities of both parties to such agreements.

As in each of the previous parts, Part VI of the volume complements the analyses undertaken with comments and additional perspectives, in this case by Marino Baldi in Chapter 28, and Rainer Geiger in Chapter 29. As the various chapters of Part VI evidence, no discernible consensus has yet to emerge globally on the best way forward for the international investment regime. However, the reflections on offer in the volume's concluding part offer a rich menu of options with which to reconfigure the new international investment agenda and guide the discussion that investment stakeholders will need to hold as part of the evolutionary process of international investment law.

The editors hope that readers will find fresh and multidimensional perspectives on the prospects of international law and policy in this volume.

The contributions we have assembled represent an attempt to combine a strong economic and political analysis with a comprehensive legal assessment of the issues confronting all investment stakeholders – governments, legal practitioners, academics, international organisations and representatives from civil society, including in the corporate world. The editors feel strongly that such multidimensionality holds the key to advancing a workable future agenda of interest to the world's increasingly diverse investment community.

PART I

Current paradigms in the economics and political economy of international investment activity

2

Investment policies for sustainable development: addressing policy challenges in a new investment landscape

JAMES ZHAN

A. Introduction

Today, the global economy is experiencing a series of investment-related challenges. The weak and fragile recovery in foreign investment and the lack of investment in productive sectors in poor countries are particularly worrisome at a time when the world is striving to deal with challenges relating to food shortage, finance and climate change, and when the development gap is widening, with the poor and marginalised being particularly affected.

Against this background, it is of particular importance to maximise the sustainable development contribution of foreign investment. Accordingly, the main challenge is to integrate foreign investment policies into national development strategies. There is a need for a systemic, holistic and systematic approach, examining the universe of national and international investment policies through the lens of specific challenges for today and tomorrow. It is time to take a fresh look at the policy regime, and to define a more comprehensive investment policy framework that effectively fosters sustainable development objectives.

This chapter will identify the main national and international challenges arising in this context. After sketching the changing landscape of global investment and identifying its sustainable development potential, it will outline national and international policy challenges associated with the objective of reaping sustainable development benefits from foreign investment. It will review recent initial policy responses, and conclude

The author would like to thank Anna Lisa Brahms for helpful suggestions and assistance. The views expressed in this chapter are those of the author and do not necessarily reflect those of the UNCTAD Secretariat or its Member States.

with a call for a more coordinated approach to addressing the key and emerging investment challenges.

B.   The changing landscape of global investment

The global investment landscape is experiencing important changes with regard to its geography and new forms of investments and investors. As to the geography of international investment flows, in 2010, for the first time, developing and transition economies absorbed more than half of the global foreign direct investment (FDI) inflows and half of the top twenty host economies for FDI were developing or transition economies. This is particularly noteworthy as FDI has become a significant source of external finance in developing countries. Moreover, developing countries (and transition economies) are increasingly becoming capital exporters. In 2010 FDI outflows from developing and transition economies increased strongly; they now account for 29 per cent of global outflows.[1]

In addition, the international investment landscape is characterised by new forms of investment. An important practical development is the increasing importance of global supply/value chains (GVCs) and non-equity modes (NEMs) of engagement of transnational corporations (TNCs), as TNCs operate in developing economies through a broadening array of production and investment models. NEM forms such as contract manufacturing and farming, service outsourcing, franchising and licensing are cases in point, as they are effectively starting to blur the line between trade and investment.

As a result, TNCs today operate internationally through three modes, which are not always mutually exclusive: FDI, trade and NEMs. Whereas FDI (i.e. the establishment of local operations directly owned and controlled by a parent company) is a 'purely' intra-firm phenomenon and trade is 'purely' inter-firm, NEMs can be both. NEMs represent long-term contractual arrangements between TNCs and local partners; the latter are formally independent (there is no equity involved), but are tied closely to the former both by virtue of being part of their global value chain/network and because of their dependence on key resources.

---

[1] UNCTAD, *World Investment Report 2011: Non-equity modes of international production and development* (Geneva: United Nations, 2011). For more recent figures, please see *UNCTAD World Investment Report 2012: Towards a new generation of investment policies* (Geneva: United Nations, 2012) and UNCTAD's quarterly Global Investment Trend Monitor, available at http://unctad.org/en/Pages/Publications/Global-Investment-Trends-Monitor-(Series).aspx

Cross-border NEM activity worldwide is significant and particularly important in developing economies. It is estimated to have generated over US$2 trillion of sales in 2010 (globally), representing up to 15 per cent of gross domestic product (GDP) in some economies. NEM exports account for 70–80 per cent of global exports in several industries. More specifically, the market for cross-border contract manufacturing and services outsourcing accounted for US$1.1–1.3 trillion and for US$330–350 billion in franchising; cross NEM-related licensing resulted in sales of US$340–360 billion. In most cases, NEMs are growing more rapidly than the industries in which they operate. Thus the growing expansion of GVCs occurring through integrated international production networks of TNCs has turned into one of the key features of globalisation.[2]

Furthermore, new forms of investors contribute to a changing landscape. First, FDI by sovereign wealth funds (SWFs) has risen in recent years, reaching US$100 billion in stock. Nevertheless, it accounts for only a small fragment (1–2 per cent) of the total assets of SWFs, valued at US$4–5 trillion.[3] The huge potential for further FDI by SWFs remains untapped. Second, the state-owned enterprises (SOEs) are increasingly becoming a source of FDI. There are at least 650 state-owned TNCs, with 8,500 foreign affiliates across the globe. While they represent less than 1 per cent of TNCs, their outward investment accounted for 11 per cent of global FDI in 2010.[4]

C.   The sustainable development potential of foreign investment

Attracting foreign investment is not an end in itself. Rather, countries aim to reap sustainable development benefits from the investment. As a source of finance for development, foreign investment can foster sustainable development in numerous ways. While benefits can materialise across all sectors of economic activities, the sustainable development contribution of foreign investment is most prominent in infrastructure, agriculture and sectors related to the green economy.

Foreign investment in infrastructure, for example, can contribute to improvements in transport capabilities, enhance communication

---

[2] UNCTAD, *World Investment Report 2011.*
[3] UNCTAD, Background note for the Sovereign Wealth Fund Round Table, UNCTAD World Investment Forum 2012, Exploring the Potential of Sovereign Wealth Funds for Investment in Sustainable Development.
[4] UNCTAD, *World Investment Report 2011; UNCTAD World Investment Forum 2012.*

capacity, facilitate logistics and modernise energy production, which in turn can advance efficiency and increase trade and economic growth.

In reality, foreign investment is a 'package' of resources, such as capital, technology, knowledge and skills, which TNCs can harness and transfer into the host country. This process can generate employment and increase fiscal revenues. By stimulating domestic demand, foreign investment can build domestic productive capacities and encourage entrepreneurship and enterprise development to supply foreign investment-receiving industries. Resultant spill-over effects can create a virtuous cycle of more domestic employment, which generates even more domestic demand and can thus lead to sustained economic growth.

In addition to foreign investment being a package of resources harnessed through FDI, TNCs are also able to leverage these resources in other ways, notably through their GVCs or networks.[5] For local partners, for instance, opportunities can arise from access to finance, technology and, most importantly, international markets. The significance of how much developing and transition countries can gain through trade and business linkages with the integrated international production networks of TNCs cannot be understated. These linkages can help strengthen the potential of the home-grown productive capacity of developing and transition countries, and improve their international competitiveness.

Similarly, integration into international production networks can have an important pro-poor dynamic, to the extent that poor or marginalised communities can link up with global or regional value chains as producers, suppliers or providers of goods or services. NEMs alone employ an estimated 14–16 million workers in developing countries.

Finally, foreign investment also offers opportunities in terms of fostering the sustainable development contribution of TNCs through socially and environmentally responsible behaviour. Corporate social responsibility (CSR) standards, although applicable to all types of enterprises, are increasingly spanning the supply chains and the integrated production networks of TNCs. In so doing, they can effectively influence the social and environmental practices of businesses worldwide.

However, NEMs, as well as FDI, pose risks for developing countries. As regards NEMs, employment in contract manufacturing, for example, can be highly cyclical and easily displaced. The value-added contribution of NEMs can appear low in terms of the value captured out of the total

---

[5] For a more detailed discussion of the benefits and challenges arising from non-equity modes (NEMs), see Chapter IV of UNCTAD, *World Investment Report 2011*.

global value chain, and developing countries may remain locked into low-value-added activities. Finally, there is the risk that TNCs may use NEMs to circumvent social and environmental standards.[6]

Hence, for TNCs (whether through NEMs or FDI) to contribute effectively to sustainable development, efforts have to be made to ensure that investors act responsibly. Measures aimed at attracting foreign investment have to be accompanied by efforts to strengthen the sustainable development facet of foreign investment. Ensuring a contribution to sustainable development therefore poses a formidable challenge for national and international investment policy-making.

D.   Policy challenges

I.   National policy challenges

Providing a balanced and effective regulatory framework for foreign investment (both FDI and NEMs) has always been a key challenge for investment policy-makers. Traditionally, the debate has focused on the establishment of a legal framework for foreign investment, which is stable, enabling and transparent. Lately, the issue of how to readjust the regulatory powers of the state in the economy has moved to the centre of discussions, partly as a result of the recent serious economic, financial and social crises around the globe.

Today, integrating foreign investment into countries' overall development strategies has emerged as the overall policy challenge. This encompasses a wide range of issues related to, among others: responsible investment and foreign investment in sensitive industries; the interaction between investment policies and industrial policies; and the overall challenge of achieving the right balance between liberalisation and regulation.[7]

1.   Ensuring responsibility and addressing sensitivities

Regulation has started to play a stronger role so as to ensure responsible investment, which reduces the negative aspects while fostering the positive social and environmental implications. In the financial sector, for example, governments have strengthened regulations following the global financial crisis. Across a number of sectors, responsible investment is

---

[6] UNCTAD, *World Investment Report 2011*.

[7] The following builds on UNCTAD, Trade and Development Board, Trade and Development Commission, Fourth session, 'Multi-year Expert Meeting on Investment for Development current policy challenges', Note by the UNCTAD Secretariat (2011).

seen as an opportunity, and regulatory efforts are made to foster investment in the poor, with the poor and for the poor (i.e. investing in projects relating to poverty alleviation, crowding in domestic investment through linkages, and producing accessible and affordable goods and services for the poor). This is supported by a trend, including in developing countries and emerging economies, towards moving from purely quantitative to more qualitative growth objectives.

Another challenge relates to foreign investment in sensitive industries. Foreign investment in agricultural production, for example, has given rise to concerns about land grab and aggravation of food shortages in host countries.[8] And foreign involvement in extractive industries has increasingly come under pressure following soaring global commodity prices. As a result, various states have rules in place or are considering new regulations to protect sensitive industries (e.g. policies aimed at strengthening local firms in sensitive industries – including mandatory joint ventures, local content requirements, nationalisations and higher tax rates).

Another set of issues at the interface between liberalisation and regulation, with a view to ensuring development benefits, relates to public or essential services.[9] With respect to services such as the provision of water, health care or education, governments face the challenge of ensuring universal access, including to the poor and marginalised members of society.[10] While aiming to increase the efficiency, accessibility and affordability of essential services,[11] policies liberalising economic activities in these sectors (including by opening them up to foreign investment) have also raised special issues of market failure and equitable distribution. Achieving an adequate balance between equity and efficiency is a core concern in ensuring sustainable development contributions from foreign investment in these sectors.

---

[8] UNCTAD, *World Investment Report 2009* (Geneva: United Nations, 2009). See also UNCTAD, Food and Agriculture Organization of the United Nations (FAO), International Fund for Agricultural Development (IFAD) and World Bank (2010), 'Principles for responsible agricultural investment that respects rights, livelihoods and resources' (PRAI).

[9] While different terminology is sometimes used (e.g. essential services, public services, service in the public interest etc.), the underlying issues are essentially the same.

[10] UNCTAD, Expert Meeting on Universal Access to Services, Note by the UNCTAD Secretariat (2006); UNCTAD, *World Investment Report 2004. The Shift Towards Services* (Geneva: United Nations, 2004).

[11] Improving access can play a crucial role in mitigating poverty and ensuring a progressive realisation of certain human rights.

2. Industrial policies – the need to manage their interaction with investment policies

Investment policies interact increasingly with industrial policies, nationally and internationally. For example, a country might restrict foreign investment to protect strategic industries. In other cases, a state may choose to give special incentives to TNCs to invest in strategic industries as this can be a source of technology and know-how. The challenge governments face here is to choose the *right* investment policy instruments and to adapt existing instruments in the face of the dynamic nature of industrial development. Horizontal policies, such as general subsidies, are often used as the basis, with the aim of improving the infrastructure of a country. The specific instruments needed depend, for example, on the business activity to be developed and the technology and skills required for it.

There is also the challenge of how to 'pick the winner', i.e. how to identify those industries or activities that already have, or possess latent, comparative advantages and benefit most from new opportunities.[12] Similarly, there is a need for governments to reduce the risk of making 'wrong' choices and wasting scarce and valuable resources. Another challenge is how to avoid a global race to the top in incentives. International coordination can help to prevent these undesirable consequences of competition and lead to synergies through economies of scale.[13]

In sum, the challenge is to manage the interaction between investment and industrial policies so that the two work together for development. Building stronger domestic productive capacity, while avoiding investment and trade protectionism, is key, as is enhancing international coordination and cooperation.[14]

3. Business facilitation and investment climates

As countries adopt and implement domestic regulations to ensure development gains from foreign investment, they also face the need to maintain an overall favourable climate towards foreign investment. Business facilitation and investment promotion measures have an important role to play in this context.

Business facilitation, for example, refers to transparency, simplification and automatisation of rules and procedures relating to enterprise creation and operation (e.g. the detailed and precise online presentation

---

[12] Also see J. Zhan, 'Making Industrial Policy Work', Project Syndicate (2011).
[13] UNCTAD, 'Multi-year Expert Meeting on Investment for Development'.
[14] UNCTAD, *World Investment Report 2011*.

of procedures that are transparent, swift and efficient). Many economies also have special business facilitation programmes, such as one-stop shop mechanisms, special economic zones and incubators. Examples of these are hi-tech zones (e.g. Electronic City in Bangalore), IT corridors (e.g. Taipei Technology Corridor) and renewable zones (e.g. Masdar City in Abu Dhabi). Finally, investment promotion policies, frequently implemented by national or regional investment promotion agencies (IPAs) and supported through the services of international investment facilitation programmes, are a common tool used to render a country more attractive to foreign investors.

Focusing business facilitation and investment promotion on key development sectors such as agriculture, infrastructure and environmentally friendly manufacture can yield particular development contributions. Policy-makers, however, need to ensure that their policies and strategies match their countries' natural resources, labour and other factor endowments. Hence, identifying their countries' competitive niche in the face of an ever-changing international division of labour and global economic setting is one of the main challenges.

4.   Liberalisation and regulation: a question of balance

Achieving the 'right' balance between investment liberalisation and avoiding a protectionist backlash through an over-emphasis on regulation is important. The annual monitoring of national investment policy changes by the United Nations Conference on Trade and Development (UNCTAD) shows that the percentage of investment regulation as opposed to investment liberalisation has grown consistently over the years and by 2010 stood at 32 per cent.[15] While some of these measures are legitimately put in place with a view to pursuing environmental, social or other public policy objectives, the risk of investment protectionism grows as restrictive measures build up.

The challenge of achieving a balance between the sovereign right to regulate and the need to avoid investment protectionism is further complicated by the difficulties encountered when attempting to draw clear borderlines between justified and unjustified reasons to restrict foreign investment, and the absence of an internationally recognised definition

---

[15] See figure III.1. in UNCTAD, *World Investment Report 2011*, p. 94. See also Joint UNCTAD-Organisation for Economic Co-operation and Development (OECD) reports on Group of Twenty (G20) investment measures and UNCTAD Investment Policy Monitors, available at: www.unctad.org/diae. For more recent figures, see *UNCTAD World Investment Report 2012: Towards a new generation of investment policies* (Geneva: United Nations, 2012).

of 'investment protectionism'. Motivations for FDI restrictions are manifold and include, for instance, sovereignty or national security concerns, strategic considerations, socio-cultural reasons, prudential policies in financial industries, competition policies, infant industry protection or reciprocity policies. In each case, countries may have very different perceptions of whether and under what conditions these reasons are legitimate. In sum, investment regulation is a must, and the key is not the quantity but the quality of regulation, that is its effectiveness and efficiency.[16]

However, countries that strengthen the regulatory environment may face a 'first mover problem', that is they risk reducing their attractiveness as a foreign investment destination compared to competing countries that apply laxer environmental or social standards. More coordination of these issues at the international level is therefore crucial in order to avoid a regulatory freeze.[17]

II. International policy challenges

International investment agreements (IIAs) can complement domestic investment promotion and facilitation policies by ensuring a stable, predictable and transparent investment climate. At the end of 2010 the IIA universe contained more than 3,000 core investment treaties, including 2,807 bilateral investment treaties (BITs) and 309 'other IIAs'.[18]

However, international investment policy-making also faces a number of challenges. As regards IIAs, these relate to a wide range of issues, including: systemic challenges arising from the network of IIAs; specific challenges associated with investor–state dispute settlement (ISDS); the lack of a clear development dimension; and concerns about policy space.

1.   Systemic challenges – a 'spaghetti bowl' of IIAs that lacks coordination with other international policies?

At the systemic level, the IIA regime is complex and confusing. With more than 3,000 core investment treaties, the universe of IIAs has become highly fragmented and complex, presenting an atomised, multilayered and multifaceted network of treaties. This 'spaghetti bowl' raises a number of practical questions and problems, notably on how the commitments

[16] UNCTAD, 'Multi-year Expert Meeting on Investment for Development'.
[17] UNCTAD, 'Multi-year Expert Meeting on Investment for Development'.
[18] For country-specific numbers of 'core international investment agreements (IIAs)' and double taxation treaties (DTTs), see UNCTAD, *World Investment Report 2011*, p. 213. For more recent figures, see *UNCTAD World Investment Report 2012*, p. 199.

interact and a how a country can best deal with numerous – potentially diverging – commitments. Questions also arise about how to address the spaghetti bowl, notably whether the increasing number of regional agreements can contribute to the disentanglement of the spaghetti strands or whether, instead of consolidation, regional approaches create an additional overlap.[19]

In sum, with thousands of treaties, numerous ongoing negotiations and multiple dispute settlement mechanisms, the IIA regime has become too large for states to handle, too complicated for firms to take advantage of, and too complex for stakeholders at large to monitor.[20]

However, despite its continuous growth, the IIA regime is still too small to cover the whole investment universe. Today's IIAs offer comprehensive cross-sectoral post-establishment protection to only two-thirds of global FDI stock and cover only one-fifth of bilateral investment relationships. While some of the FDI stock is subject to protection offered by two or more IIAs, full coverage would require another 14,100 BITs. These 14,100 treaties would cover many bilateral relationships with little propensity to investment (i.e. where FDI flows are negligible) or with little propensity to protect (e.g. between Organisation for Economic Co-operation and Development (OECD) member countries). They would, however, cover a few bilateral relationships where substantial FDI stocks exist that are not covered by any existing investment protection agreement.[21]

A further systemic challenge is that there are hardly any mechanisms for coordination between the IIA regime and other parts of the global economic system (e.g. trade, finance or competition) or other bodies of international law (e.g. international environmental law, including climate change-related, human rights or health law). This lack of coordination has manifested in recent ISDS cases, where IIAs interact with other international law, for example the so-called '*Tobacco* cases', which touch upon the relationship between IIAs and the World Health Organization (WHO) Framework Convention on Tobacco Control (FCTC).[22]

---

[19] UNCTAD, Background Note UNCTAD ad hoc Expert Group Meeting on 'Consolidation of International Investment Agreements: Disentangling the Spaghetti Bowl?', Bern, Switzerland, 8–9 September 2011, and discussions at the meeting.

[20] UNCTAD, *World Investment Report 2011*.

[21] UNCTAD, *World Investment Report 2011*.

[22] The Framework Convention on Tobacco Control (FCTC) is binding on the signatory states and obliges governments to take steps to reduce tobacco use (FCTC Part II: Objective, Guiding Principles and General Obligations). See below.

2. Investor–state dispute settlement: going beyond its original objective?

Next to the challenge of managing the complex regime of IIAs worldwide, the system is facing a growing number of ISDS cases.[23] International investment arbitration through ISDS, while designed to foster the rule of law by substituting what were considered weak or unreliable legal institutional frameworks in host countries, is increasingly exposing systemic challenges. After lying dormant for many years, a wave of treaty-based ISDS cases has recently exposed states to multi-million dollar claims, including some that touch upon public interest regulations. Protective standards enshrined in IIAs were not only used to challenge grossly unfair or manifestly arbitrary conduct by states and their organs, but also to file claims against measures aimed at preserving the environment, promoting social equality[24] or protecting public health.

A number of recent cases stand out in this regard. In April 2009 the Swedish company Vattenfall initiated a claim against Germany related to environmental restrictions imposed on a coal-fired power plant under construction near the River Elbe.[25] Whereas Vattenfall argued that the delay in issuing permits together with restrictions imposed on the use of cooling water from the river constituted a breach of the fair and equitable treatment clause of the Energy Charter Treaty, Germany maintained that the measures were legitimate environmental restrictions required by domestic and European Union (EU) law. The proceedings were suspended in 2010 and an amicable settlement was reached. Moreover, on 21 December 2011 Vattenfall sent a notice of dispute to the German Government regarding the country's nuclear phase-out.

Also of interest are the two cases challenging tobacco control measures brought against Uruguay and Australia.[26] Both cases concerned new legislation on tobacco packaging, with the investor arguing that the regulations, which were put in place to comply with the WHO FCTC, violate

---

[23] UNCTAD, 'Latest developments in investor–state dispute settlement', *IIA Issues Note Nr. 1* (2012), available at: http://unctad.org/en/docs/PublicationsLibrary/webdiaeia2012d10_en.pdf.

[24] For example, *Piero Foresti, Laura de Carli & Others* v. *The Republic of South Africa*, ICSID Case No. ARB(AF)/07/01.

[25] *Vattenfall AB, Vattenfall Europe AG, Vattenfall Europe Generation AG* v. *Federal Republic of Germany*, ICSID Case No. ARB/09/6.

[26] *FTR Holding S.A. (Switzerland), Philip Morris Products S.A. (Switzerland) and Abal Hermanos S.A. (Uruguay)* v. *Oriental Republic of Uruguay*, ICSID Case No. ARB/10/7 and *Philip Morris* v. *Australia* (UNCITRAL, 2010).

IIAs.[27] Yet the FCTC makes it mandatory to implement the obligations to control the sale and reduce the consumption of tobacco. Moreover, FCTC Article 2(1) encouraged states to introduce regulations that go beyond what was required by the Convention, even if, as stated in Article 5.3, this goes against 'commercial or other vested interests of the tobacco industry'.[28] These challenges to measures taken pursuant to the WHO Convention raise questions about coherence and consistency between different legal regimes.

Hence, today, states not only have to manage complex, lengthy and costly ISDS procedures, but also have to learn lessons from the possible constraining effects IIAs can have on domestic policy space. And today, this applies to both developing and developed countries.

Confidence in the ISDS process is further compromised by concerns related to the quality and predictability of the awards issued by tribunals: some arbitral decisions have resulted in inconsistent findings or have lacked sound reasoning, sometimes as a result of poor treaty interpretation. For example, in the cases against Argentina on grounds of the policies it adopted after the financial crisis in 2001, there have been divergent interpretations of similarly worded provisions.[29] Divergent findings by investment tribunals on similarly worded provisions can undermine legal predictability and security. Procedural concerns, including the difficulties that developing countries face in adequately responding to cases, and the lack of transparency in ISDS proceedings are starting to undermine the legitimacy of the system.

3.   The development dimension – a missing element?

Concerns have been expressed, especially by developing countries, but also by the international development community, that the current IIA regime lacks a clear development dimension. For example, it has been noted that there is no mono-causal link between the conclusion of an IIA

---

[27] See section on 'WHO Framework Convention on Tobacco Control' in T. Voon and A. Mitchell, 'Implications of international investment law for tobacco flavouring regulation', *Journal of World Investment & Trade* 12 (2011), 65–80.

[28] Available at: http://whqlibdoc.who.int/publications/2003/9241591013.pdf.

[29] See *CMS* v. *Argentina* (Award), ICSID Case No. ARB/01/8 (12 May 2005); *Enron* v. *Argentina*, ICSID, Award, Case No. ARB/01/3, 22 May 2007; *LG&E* v. *Argentina* (Decision on Liability), ICSID Case No. ARB/02/1, 3 October 2006; *Sempra* v. *Argentina* (Annulment Decision), ICSID Case No. ARB/02/16, 29 June 2010; *Enron* v. *Argentina* (Annulment Decision), ICSID Case No. ARB/01/3, 30 July 2010.

and FDI inflows. In line with their role as one among several other determinants of foreign investment, IIAs can influence a company's decision on where to invest and this impact is generally stronger for preferential trade and investment agreements (PTIAs) than for BITs. However, IIAs cannot be a substitute for domestic policies and IIAs alone can never be a sufficient policy instrument to attract FDI. Instead, the conclusion of IIAs needs to be embedded in a country's broader FDI policies, covering all determinants of foreign investment, and in a country's overall development strategy.[30]

Moreover, for the time being, IIAs mostly promote foreign investment only indirectly through the granting of investment protection and do not contain commitments by capital-exporting countries other than vague language relating to investment promotion. And while IIAs are expected to attract FDI by contributing to good governance (e.g. by fostering legal predictability, stability and transparency and by substituting what were considered weak or unreliable legal institutional frameworks in host countries with ISDS), these very aspects sometimes give rise to concerns.

Experience also shows that foreign investment does not automatically lead to developmental benefits. For liberalisation to generate such benefits, it needs to be preceded by proper regulatory and institutional frameworks. More often than not, reaping benefits requires a carefully tailored policy response to make foreign investment work for sustainable development (see above, discussion on national policies). It is therefore crucial that IIAs grant the necessary policy space to do so.

A related question is how IIAs contribute to ensuring that states get the development contribution they seek from foreign investment in return for tying their hands with an international agreement. Currently, most IIAs provide investors with rights (e.g. to bring claims against the host state before international arbitration), yet they do not impose independent obligations on investors.

An additional factor is that developing countries sometimes lack the capacity to participate fully in the evolving IIA system and may therefore risk being marginalised and left behind.

---

[30] UNCTAD, 'The Role of International Investment Agreements in Attracting Foreign Direct Investment to Developing Countries', *UNCTAD Series on International Investment Policies for Development* (2009).

E. Recent evolutions and initial responses

States have started to respond to the challenges outlined above in a number of ways. Some have started a process of terminating their agreements by denouncing them,[31] although the concrete legal consequences of this action remain unclear.[32] Others have started a review of their IIAs, sometimes combined with an effort to develop a novel model BIT. As a result, more recent treaty models, as well as some concluded treaties, are frequently characterised by new, increasingly sophisticated and precise treaty language.

That governments have become more cautious in formulating obligations and pay greater attention to formulating IIAs so as to increase precision and/or reaffirm and strengthen the states' right to regulate in the public interest can be observed in a couple of broad developments. Increasingly, the scope of the treaty is more precisely formulated. Parties are moving towards excluding certain areas of regulation from the scope of the treaty, such as taxation, financial services or government procurement. There is also a tendency to introduce general exceptions that allow more room for regulation in the areas of protecting human, animal or plant life or health, national security or prudential carve-outs. The clarification of specific obligations, such as fair and equitable treatment clauses or the precise meaning of indirect expropriation, is another broad development, in order to preserve states' right to regulate.

Furthermore, some recent agreements add specific language to ensure the protection of the environment and appropriate corporate behaviour. For instance, today countries sometimes include clauses that confirm their right to establish their own level of environmental protection, that carve out environment-related clauses from ISDS or that include language aimed at enhancing coherence between IIAs and multilateral environmental agreements.[33]

An emerging trend relates to provisions on corporate behaviour, including in areas such as environmental or social practices. Some recent treaties include clauses ranging from a simple reiteration that investors shall comply with the laws and regulations of the host countries to more

---

[31] This may be seen, for example, in the case of Ecuador, which denounced some agreements because it wished to exclude certain types of disputes from being subject to investor–state dispute settlement (ISDS).

[32] So-called 'survival clauses', included in many agreements, lock in the protective effect of the treaty for ten, or sometimes even twenty years, after termination takes effect. UNCTAD, 'Denunciation of the ICSID Convention and BITs: Impact on Investor–State Claims', *IIA Issue Note*, No. 2 (December 2010).

[33] UNCTAD, *World Investment Report 2010* (Geneva: United Nations, 2010).

elaborate provisions on anti-corruption requirements and respect for environmental and labour standards.[34]

Recent treaty practice together with the innovative approaches adopted in model BITs can offer guidance for policymakers and negotiators of future investment treaties. Yet encouraging as this development may be, there are limits to modernising and clarifying treaty content by adopting innovative approaches in newly signed IIAs. The overwhelming majority of the IIAs in existence were concluded following the traditional approach, which focused predominantly on investment protection. Even if new, more balanced, treaties are signed, investors may be able to circumvent development-friendly provisions by using unqualified most-favoured nation (MFN) clauses to claim the 'more favourable treatment' afforded to investors under older treaties.

Furthermore, there is the question whether the painstaking process of renegotiating old treaties one by one is an efficient way of clarifying provisions (e.g. it makes considerable demands on countries' capacity). A treaty-by-treaty piecemeal approach might not be the most efficient response, and there have been calls for a more coordinated and cooperative approach.

F.   Way forward

These investment-related challenges, together with today's broader debate about global economic governance, raise the question whether the policy regime – in its current form – is well equipped for playing its role in offering a reliable pillar of global economic governance, successfully promoting responsible investment, and effectively delivering on its development promise. At the national level, providing an appropriate regulatory framework for foreign investment, readjusting the regulatory powers of the state to ensure responsible investment and integrating investment policies with development policies have turned into the major challenge for policy-makers. At the international level, making IIAs work effectively for development has developed into the main objective, in the face of the spaghetti bowl of IIAs, a growing number of ISDS cases, concerns about policy space and a lack of balance between investor rights and state obligations.

While states have started to respond, including at the international level, there are limitations to modernising and clarifying IIA content

---

[34] UNCTAD, *World Investment Report 2011*, Chapter III, E. Corporate Social Responsibility.

by adopting innovative approaches in model BITs or newly signed IIAs, and hence there might be a need to explore complementary means. One option could be the proactive interpretation of agreements by states to guide tribunals towards a proper and predictable reading of IIA provisions.[35] Another could be a more coordinated effort to increase the sustainable development dimension of investment policies that goes beyond countries' individual initiatives. Multilateral engagement and joint initiatives, for example, can offer important contributions, for example, by allowing countries to share experiences and discuss best practices in addressing the above-mentioned challenges.

Multilateral consensus-building can help achieve numerous benefits. It can help identify areas of broad consensus and areas of disagreement. This in itself facilitates discussions directed at resolving potential disagreements. At a minimum, clarification of the extent of consensus in the IIA universe serves the interest of transparency and predictability. By improving – where possible – coherence between agreements, consensus-building can also improve the clarity, stability and transparency of the IIA system. If undertaken in an inclusive and participatory manner, consensus-building can also help to strengthen the development dimension and make the system more responsive to the concerns of all affected stakeholders, thereby enhancing its legitimacy and ultimately strengthening it.

By offering a platform for consensus-building and sharing of experiences and best practices, UNCTAD is working to carry forward the policy discourse about the future orientation of national and international investment policies for sustainable development. UNCTAD's Multi-year Expert Meetings on Investment for Development,[36] its Investment Commission and the biannual World Investment Forum (WIF), which has become a global centre for high-level discussion and action to harness international investment as an engine of growth and development, offer important opportunities for meeting this objective.[37]

---

[35] UNCTAD, 'Interpretation of IIAs: What States can do', *IIA Issues Note*, No. 3 (December 2011).

[36] See http://unctad.org/en/docs/ciimem3d12_en.pdf.

[37] During the World Investment Forum (WIF) 2010 which was held in Xiamen, China, both the WIF's Ministerial Round Table, with more than twenty-five ministerial-level participants, and the WIF's IIA Conference, addressed challenges and the way forward with respect to international investment policy-making. The WIF 2012 was held from 20 to 23 April 2012 in conjunction with UNCTAD XIII Ministerial Conference in Doha, Qatar. See http://unctad-worldinvestmentforum.org.

Among other matters, the 2012 WIF debated UNCTAD's Investment Policy Framework for Sustainable Development (IPFSD), which subsequently constituted the main substantive theme of the 2012 World Investment Report (WIR) entitled 'Towards a New Generation of Investment Policies'.

The IPFSD was formulated as a response to the above-described need for a systemic, holistic and systematic approach to investment policymaking and its overarching objective is to assist countries in reaping sustainable development benefits from foreign investment. The framework consists of a comprehensive guide for national and international investment policymaking: its eleven core principles first set the stage and are then converted into guidelines for national investment policies and policy options for IIAs.

With regard to national policy challenges, the IPFSD centres on the promotion and facilitation of investment, encouraging countries to maintain an overall favourable climate towards investment while adopting and implementing domestic regulations to ensure development gains from foreign investment. Among others, it offers guidelines for an investment and sustainable development strategy, investment regulation and promotion, investment-related policies and investment policy effectiveness.

With regard to international policy challenges, the IPFSD provides an array of options, covering both IIAs' substantive treaty obligations and procedural issues, such as ISDS. Options range from adjusting existing provisions, to adding new provisions and introducing special and differential treatment for future IIAs, offering a further tool for making these agreements more sustainable-development-friendly, particularly for least-developed and low-income countries.

The IPFSD thus balances investors' expectations of a stable and transparent legal framework and an attractive investment climate while preserving the regulatory powers of the state. Importantly, the IPFSD goes further than the challenges flagged in this chapter: through its comprehensive tables addressing national and international investment policies, the IPFSD provides policymakers with concrete options for placing inclusive growth and sustainable development at the heart of efforts to attract and benefit from foreign investment. Moving along with the times and technological innovations, UNCTAD formulated IPFSD as an online 'living document', offering an interactive open-source platform that enables stakeholders to exchange views and experiences.[38]

---

[38] See http://investmentpolicyhub.org.

3

Foreign direct investment and development: novel challenges

THEODORE H. MORAN

A. Overview: the argument in brief

This chapter is a response to the task set by the World Trade Forum 2011, namely to propose new economic and political-economic paradigms for the behaviour of international investors, and to identify new frontiers in the relationship between foreign direct investment (FDI) and development.

I propose to take up this assignment in immodest fashion, and explore six areas in which I shall claim to offer new perspectives and explore novel challenges in the relationship between FDI and development.

The first argument I wish to make should be the most obvious, except that it is consistently ignored by many in the economics community: FDI comes in four or five discrete forms that pose distinctive policy challenges that must be faced in order for the host country to secure the benefits and avoid harmful side-effects. These include FDI in the extractive sector, FDI in infrastructure, FDI in manufacturing and assembly (further broken down into FDI in low-skilled manufacturing and assembly versus FDI in higher-skilled manufacturing and assembly) and FDI in services. Yet the standard body of economic literature aims to find a statistically significant relationship between aggregate FDI flows and some measure of host country welfare, productivity or growth, and the most prominent modellers in the field characterise FDI as a multi-plant manufacturing phenomenon while using overall FDI flows to test their models. This leads to conclusions of questionable accuracy and dubious reliability for policy.

This chapter draws directly on T. H. Moran, *Foreign Direct Investment and Development: Launching a Second Generation of Policy Research, Avoiding the Mistakes of the First, Re-Evaluating Policies for Developed and Developing Countries* (Washington DC: Peterson Institute for International Economics, 2011).

True to this first insight, the remainder of this chapter will address the intricacies of securing benefits and avoiding damage from separate and different types of FDI.

Looking specifically at extractive sector FDI, the second argument I wish to make is that the world has made great progress in recent years in addressing 'resource curse' issues involving corrupt payments. Now, however, extractive sector investors from China, Russia, India and elsewhere may undermine these hard-won advances. What can be done to prevent extractive industry investors of all nationalities from using illicit payments to secure favourable treatment in their oil, gas and mining operations? I identify two paths to achieving this outcome.

The third argument is more tentative. In the 1990s FDI in infrastructure came to be packaged in a standard form – especially for power projects – that shifted foreign exchange risk and supply-and-demand risk almost entirely on to host authorities. By the early 2000s this form became unravelled, and investors, hosts, multilateral lending agencies and political risk insurers are still grappling with the question of what might take its place. I outline what new arrangements – and new dispute settlement procedures – might look like.

The fourth argument acknowledges that FDI in low-skill manufacturing and assembly continues to require resolute campaigns to resist sweatshop-type abuses, but points out the uncontested although largely unrecognised fact that the predominant thrust of FDI in manufacturing and assembly brings higher-skilled activities (motor vehicles and vehicle parts, industrial equipment, electronics, medical devices, and so forth) rather than garments, footwear and toys. How to attract such higher-skilled FDI so as to upgrade and diversify the host export base, while expanding backward linkages and supply chains among local firms, constitutes the new frontier for manufacturing FDI and development. But, as I point out, there are important market failures and obstacles that prevent this process from taking place naturally.

The fifth argument draws on the fourth, to highlight evidence that there are not simply labour market externalities that accrue to the host economy as manufacturing FDI moves from lower-skilled to higher-skilled activities, but labour institution externalities as well. International companies like Intel and Siemens and Toyota will not tolerate the labour strife and reputational risk that emerge from low-skilled FDI plants nearby, and may work at the zone level or national level to reinforce better labour, health and safety, and environmental standards. This insight emerges from a small number of country case studies, and requires further investigation.

The final analysis presented here lays out implications for non-governmental organisations (NGOs) and corporate social responsibility (CSR) advocates, and argues that these groups have a much more important role to play than simply pressuring foreign investors to 'give back' more to the communities and peoples living where they operate. While forming partnerships to promote greater corporate philanthropy surely has its place, NGOs and CSR advocates should refashion their agenda towards shaping and magnifying the impact of main-line FDI operations. Drawing on the materials gathered previously in this chapter, I offer some examples of what this new CSR agenda means in practical terms.

B.   Different kinds of FDI, distinctive policy challenges

FDI comes in at least four, very different, forms – FDI in extractive industries, FDI in infrastructure, FDI in manufacturing and assembly, and FDI in services. Each impacts the host economy, polity and society in such a unique fashion – and poses policy challenges of such unique character – that they cannot be lumped together for analytical purposes or rule-making.

In addition, a strong case can be made – as shown in the pages that follow – that FDI in low-skill intensive manufacturing and assembly (e.g. garments and footwear) should be separated from FDI in middle-skill intensive manufacturing and assembly (e.g. electronics, industrial equipment, motor vehicles and vehicle parts) as well.

Asking the question what is the impact of FDI on development, and then regressing aggregate FDI flows on host country growth rates, productivity measurements or welfare indicators – the predominant technique in what are considered the benchmark studies since the 1980s – jumbles together queries about the impact of FDI in Angolan oil, the impact of FDI in Indian power projects, the impact of FDI in Honduran garment export sectors, the impact of FDI in Malaysian electronics export sectors, and the impact of the spread of Walmart and Carrefour in Mexican retail services.

Yet those investigations that are commonly referred to as 'benchmark studies' of the impact of FDI on the host economy invariably use data that mix together all four categories for FDI flows and stocks, as do most other investigations. Similarly, efforts to model FDI as a single kind of phenomenon and test with data that combine radically different kinds of FDI have to be restructured. Even the most sophisticated contemporary FDI modellers all appear to characterise multinational corporations as multi-plant manufacturers, yet they use aggregate FDI data to check their models. Searching for some kind of single overall relationship between foreign investment flows and host growth, productivity or welfare obscures what may be very different kinds of effects, and hinders clear policy analysis.

This chapter maintains a proper separation among clusters of evidence, differential economic (and political-economic) impacts and distinctive policy challenges. The chapter opens with new anti-corruption threats and opportunities involving FDI in extractive industries; then turns to risk allocation dilemmas arising from FDI in infrastructure; moves on to market failures and obstacles in using FDI to move up the ladder from low-skilled to higher-skilled manufacturing activities; introduces novel evidence about the relationship between manufacturing FDI and labour market externalities and labour institution externalities; and concludes by pressing the corporate social responsibility community to refocus its agenda towards strengthening the contribution of core FDI operations in each sector, rather than simply extracting larger amounts of corporate charity.

What are the new anti-corruption threats and opportunities involving FDI in extractive industries?

C.   New forces are emerging that can be used to create a level playing field on transparency and anti-corruption for all investors in the extractive sector

An abundant natural resource base has gone from being a blessing from God – in old-style development textbooks – to a 'curse' that plagues developing countries endowed with oil, diamonds, copper, gold, iron ore, coal, nickel, bauxite and natural gas. In aggregate analysis, Sachs and Warner – following Auty – found that resource-rich developed countries had a slower economic growth rate than less resource-rich counterparts, although the correlation was subsequently shown to be highly sensitive to the time period chosen and exhibited numerous exceptions.[1]

---

[1] R. M. Auty, *Patterns of Development: Resources, Policy and Economic Growth* (London: Edward Arnold, 1994); J. D. Sachs and A. M. Warner, 'Natural resources and economic development: the curse of natural resources', *European Economic Review* 45 (2001), 827–38; G. Wright and J. Czelusta, 'The myth of the resource curse', *Challenge* 47(2) (2004), 6–38; P. Collier and B. Goderis, 'Commodity Prices, Growth and the Natural Resources Curse. Reconciling a Conundrum', *Center for the Study of African Economies*, Working Paper 276, August 2007.

Country histories reveal at least a billion dollars a year unaccounted for from the Nigerian oil sector, show diamonds financing civil war and repression, expose Chinese agents asking the Presidential Office in Angola for an official list of those who should receive bribes and who should not. Alongside these sorry country histories, however, stand counter-examples where a rich natural resource endowment has helped to fund broad-based economic and social development, in Botswana, Morocco, Malaysia, Thailand, Peru, Colombia and Chile, for example.

The difference between cases in which resource earnings – often but not exclusively generated by foreign investors – support corrupt leaders, encourage repression and civil strife, and lead to rent-seeking distortions in the host economy and cases in which resource earnings support legitimate host country developmental objectives lies principally in the degree of transparency and accountability for revenues derived from the resource base, on the one hand, and expenditures by national and local governments on the basis of those revenues, on the other, with criminal penalties for investors that can be shown to use bribes to secure favourable treatment.[2]

The period since the mid 1990s has witnessed substantial progress in combating the dynamics of resource-curse FDI. The ratification of the Organisation for Economic Co-operation and Development (OECD) Anti-Bribery Convention in 1997, followed by three phases of peer reviews, has spread anti-corruption – and increasingly vigorous enforcement – across the thirty-four OECD Member States. Since 2002 the Extractive Industries Transparency Initiative (EITI) – backed by NGOs such as Revenue Watch and the Publish What You Pay Coalition – have introduced varying degrees of increased transparency into thirty-three resource-rich countries.

Reinforcing the trend towards greater transparency in the extractive sector is the 2010 Dodd–Frank legislative requirement that oil, gas and mining companies that register with the US Securities and Exchange Commission make public all payments to all governments, plus the forthcoming European Union (EU) Transparency Directive that will mandate reporting along the same lines.

But these efforts leave OECD investors at a competitive disadvantage in relation to investors from non-OECD states such as China, Russia

---

[2] Dealing with 'Dutch disease' poses separate macroeconomic challenges involving controlling inflation, government expenditures and exchange rates. G. A. Davis and J. E. Tilton, 'The resource curse', *Natural Resources Forum* 29 (2005), 233–42.

and India. The Dodd–Frank reporting requirement, for example, should cover three of the seven largest Russian energy companies that are registered in the USA, but will not cover the four that are not. Of the sixteen largest Chinese mining companies with overseas operations, two are listed in New York and three in Hong Kong. Eleven do not have listings outside China. Two of the three largest Indian oil companies are not listed in the USA.

How can pressure be brought upon the growing numbers of Chinese, Russian, Indian and other non-OECD extractive sector investors to prevent them from undermining the hard-won advances in transparency and prevention of illicit payments? Two sources of pressure may become increasingly important.

First, a trend has emerged in investor–state arbitration that may constitute a powerful vehicle for combating corrupt payments. Over the past ten years, tribunals have shown themselves unwilling to enforce investment contracts when those contracts have been acquired through bribery.

For comparative purposes, a bottom baseline for this trend might be observed in 2000, when in *Metalclad* v. *Mexico*, despite rampant rumours of corruption and pleadings about corrupt practices, the tribunal simply chose not to address the issue of corruption.[3]

The beginnings of change appeared in 2001 in *Wena* v. *Egypt*,[4] when the Tribunal indicated in response to pleadings by Egypt that corruption of a state official could be a determining factor in deciding whether to enforce the contract, but argued that there was insufficient proof in the case at issue to consider this properly.

Moving on, in *Methanex* v. *United States* 2005,[5] the Tribunal recognised that it had the capacity to issue a finding of fact of corruption even though such allegations had not been proven in associated criminal trials. It set out an extensive discussion of the methodology for a Tribunal to follow in making such a finding, noting that a smoking gun is rarely to be found, using the analogy of connecting the dots, and going so far as to

---

[3] This analysis is derived from Working Group on Anti-Corruption, *Report of the Working Group on Anti-Corruption* (Washington DC: Center for Global Development, 2007). *Metalclad Corporation* v. *United Mexican States* (Award), International Centre for Settlement of Investment Disputes (ICSID) Case No. ARB(AF)/97/1, 30 August 2000.

[4] *Wena Hotels Limited* v. *Arab Republic of Egypt* (Award), ICSID Case No. ARB/98/4, 8 December 2000.

[5] *Methanex Corporation* v. *United States of America* (North American Free Trade Agreement (NAFTA) Award under United Nations Commission on International Trade Law (UNCITRAL) Rules), 3 August 2005.

label the pieces of evidence as dot one, dot two, and so on. Thus, although the Tribunal did not lay down a specific burden of proof to find corruption, the arbitrators nonetheless made it clear that circumstantial evidence, without using that term, is admissible, and that it is reasonable for a Tribunal to draw appropriate inferences from such evidence. While the Tribunal ruled that the evidence available to the members did not support a finding of corruption in this particular case, the arbitrators made clear that the presumption that an investor can rely upon arbitrators to enforce a contract obtained via corrupt actions is not justified.

Still more important are the two most recent cases.

In *Inceysa* v. *El Salvador*, August 2006,[6] the Tribunal both issued a finding of corruption and ruled that the fact of the corruption vitiated its jurisdiction. In this case, the Tribunal relied on a frequently used line in bilateral investment treaties (BITs), that an investment 'must be made in accordance with the law of the host country', or words to similar effect in other agreements. These words, it found, meant that an investment made through corruption was not made in accordance with law, and therefore such an investment was not within the jurisdiction of the Tribunal. As a matter of jurisdiction, therefore, the Tribunal could not hear the case.

Finally, in *World Duty Free* v. *Kenya*, October 2006,[7] the claimant readily admitted to the bribe, some two million dollars to then President Daniel Arap Moi, organised through a close business associate as an intermediary. The claimant argued, essentially, that this was the only way to do business with Kenya. This argument was rejected by the Tribunal. It held that as a matter of '*ordre publique internationale*' a case that saw the investment come into being through corruption could not be heard by the Tribunal. This expanded the reasoning of the *Inceysa* Tribunal, which had confined the reasoning to language that was found in the BIT, to a broader policy and public international law context. This is important, as not all investment agreements contain the language found in the BIT in the *Inceysa* case.

These cases show that tribunals can vitiate the right of an investor to seek remedies under international investment agreements (IIAs). They show growing acceptance of the principle – which is already widespread

---

[6] *Inceysa Vallisolenta S.L.* v. *Republic of El Salvador* (Award), ICSID Case No. ARB/03/26, 2 August 2006.
[7] *World Duty Free Company* v. *Republic of Kenya* (Award), ICSID Case No. ARB/00/7, 4 October 2006.

in domestic law – to reject the validity of any contract or permit obtained by corrupt means. Today this is widely considered to be sound law. The more difficult question is whether tribunals must so conclude. On this question there appears to be a growing movement to say that tribunals must reach this conclusion if corruption can be shown.

In analysis provided to the Center for Global Development (CGD) Working Group on Anti-Corruption, the widely recognised arbitration expert Richard Kreindler offers further support for this view.[8] Kreindler argues, in brief, that where there is some reasonable basis for believing there could be corruption, whether raised directly by a party to the arbitration or by a third party (amicus curiae for example), the Tribunal can and must exercise its responsibility to investigate, must be prepared to rule without fear or favour, and must raise and investigate the issue on its own cognisance if it has proper cause. Mere allegations of corruption cannot be enough to deprive an investor of treaty rights.

Before drawing too strong conclusions from this trend in arbitration, however, there are caveats that must be noted. Arbitral decisions are not subject to *stare decisis*; that is, while arbitrators do consider prior opinions – and there appears to be growing acceptance, as noted above, that corrupt procurement of contracts is contrary to widely accepted norms of international public policy – there is no formal process of setting and following precedent, and there cannot be until there is an appeals process that can resolve conflicting decisions by Tribunals. In addition, arbitral panels are not well equipped to pursue criminal investigations. But they do have broad plenary powers to do what is needed to ensure the proper outcome of the case. And they can, of course, always refer cases to national authorities.

How can the use of investor–state dispute settlement procedures be reinforced so as to help combat corruption? As a start is the simple need for consciousness-raising among the community of arbitrators that their responsibilities include sensitivity to the potential for corruption in the awarding of the contracts they are being asked to interpret and enforce. Accompanying this might be wider acceptance of amicus curiae interventions by civil society organisations in any given case. This enlarges the potential for identifying corruption since such organisations may have much less interest in protecting the guilty than some host governments may have.

[8] Working Group on Anti-Corruption, *Report of the Working Group on Anti-Corruption* (Washington DC: Center for Global Development, 2007).

Finally, it is vital to bring extractive sector investors of all national-ities under a common standard for disclosing payment to governments. This can be accomplished through expanding the universe of mandatory reporting for companies listed on the world's stock exchanges, in the manner of Dodd–Frank in the USA and the forthcoming Transparency Directive in the EU. These efforts can be supplemented by chan-ging the requirement that needs to be met for countries to qualify as EITI-compliant.

Currently EITI countries are given the choice of whether to disclose the revenues they receive from extractive industry investors either on a company-by-company basis or in some aggregate form. So far eleven EITI countries have chosen the former while twelve have been content with the latter (others are as yet undecided). With Dodd–Frank and EU Transparency Directive reporting of individual company payments, and EITI company-by-company disclosure of receipts, independent monitors have all the data they need to verify that investor payments are not being diverted to improper hands. But with many Chinese, Russian, Indian and other investors not covered by Dodd–Frank or EU Transparency Directive reporting requirements – plus EITI country disclosure of receipts on only an aggregate basis – there is much room for non-OECD companies to engage in illicit payments without an independent method of tracking, and some of these companies may be doing so. This leaves a gap in the monitoring of corruption, and places investors covered by Dodd–Frank or the EU Transparency Directive at a competitive disadvantage.

Fortunately there is a straightforward remedy at hand, namely to require all EITI countries to disclose extractive industry receipts on a company-by-company basis, ending the acceptability of aggregate disclos-ure, in order to be EITI-compliant. This will allow independent monitors to match what Chinese, Russian, Indian and other non-OECD investors declare they pay with what EITI country authorities report they pay, just as they can with oil, gas and mining companies listed on the major stock exchanges in the USA and Europe.

The logic of eliminating the competitive advantage currently enjoyed by Chinese, Russian, Indian and some other resource investors would sug-gest that all major extractive sector companies should endorse this switch to company-by-company disclosure for all countries that want to be EITI-compliant. The international mining firms clearly recognise that com-pany-by-company disclosure is in their own self-interest. Oddly enough, the international oil and gas firms have not yet done so. A united front of the most socially responsible extractive industry investors, backed by

NGOs such as Revenue Watch and the Publish What You Pay Coalition, should be able to change the EITI disclosure standard in short order.

D.   The period since the 1990s has exposed fundamental flaws in using FDI for infrastructure for which no workable solutions have been found

Effective participation of foreign investors in infrastructure projects is vital to developing countries. Reliable supplies of electricity, water and telecommunications repeatedly show themselves to be key components of the World Bank's 'doing business' indicators. High marks for these services, plus efficient road, port and airport facilities, are central to the growth of a robust indigenous business sector in any given developing economy, for the attraction of foreign investors in low-skilled FDI operations like garments and footwear, for the ability of individual host countries to move up from these low-skilled FDI operations to middle-skilled FDI operations like electronics, motor vehicle parts and other industrial products, and for the development of FDI supply chains and backward linkages deep into the host economy.

But it has become clear – from the Asian financial crisis of the late 1990s, through the Argentine meltdown of 2001–2002, to the international economic upheaval of 2008–2009 – that participation of foreign investors in infrastructure projects is beset by some fundamental flaws. Looking ahead, foreign investment in infrastructure requires a reappraisal of which parties should absorb risks associated with fluctuations in supply and demand for services, and with fluctuations in exchange rates.

The most serious problems have arisen in the power sector. To participate during boom times in Asian and Latin American markets, foreign investors grew accustomed to insisting – as a condition of putting capital into infrastructure – that host authorities commit themselves to purchase electricity output, and to guarantee the foreign exchange value of payments made in local currency, for years into the future. In settings where economic expansion of host countries seems unending, and forecasts show that demand for electricity will grow at 8 per cent per year (or more) as far as the eye can see, take-or-pay contracts can appear quite reasonable even when they guarantee rates of return of the order of 25–30 per cent per year in dollars to the foreign sponsors. Contemporary power project proposals in China and India – as the global economy emerges from international economic crisis in 2011 – replicate the optimistic projections that characterised the last decade of the twentieth century and the first decade of the twenty-first.

How should the costs of adjustment be apportioned, however, when the underlying assumptions for particular projects prove excessively rosy, or when economic trends in the world economy move in an adverse direction? Who should bear the risks of fluctuations in supply and demand, and the risks of fluctuations in currency values? How should contracts in this sector be enforced?

Political risk has traditionally been defined as a set of deliberate acts on the part of host authorities undertaken to change the treatment of a foreign investor. Changes in market conditions over which the host country has little or no control, which impede the host's capability to meet its obligations fall under the broader category of commercial risk.

But when host authorities find themselves incapable of fulfilling their contracts due to external changes in the international economy, investor–state arbitral panels now typically judge their performance as political acts (*unwillingness* to behave as promised) rather than commercial acts (*inability* to behave as promised).[9] More than 90 per cent of the political risk claims paid by Lloyds syndicates in the five years after the onset of the Asian financial crisis (1998–2003), according to a study by Berry, arose because a state buyer or supplier was *unable* to make good on its commitments in full and on time.[10] The formal default, concludes Berry, derived from economic misjudgement or over-commitment, not from bad faith or malicious intent on the part of host authorities. But investor–state arbitrators consistently required political risk insurers to pay breach-of-contract insurance claims during that period, and have continued to do so since. This outcome seems particularly appalling when the inability of a host country to pay for unneeded electricity results from regional financial contagion over which host authorities have no control or responsibility.

The foreign currency dimension of political risk coverage during regional financial crises has taken national and multilateral guarantee agencies by surprise. These agencies emphatically refuse to provide explicit *exchange rate protection*. But they abruptly discovered that when they offer political risk coverage to insure these take-or-pay agreements against *breach of contract*, they implicitly expose themselves to enormous

---

[9] For the origins of this interpretation by arbitration panels, see C. Berry, 'Shall the Twain Meet? Finding Common Ground or Uncommon Solutions: A Broker's Perspective' in World Bank, *International Political Risk Management: The Brave New World* (Washington DC: World Bank, 2003).

[10] *Ibid.*

currency risk, since the agreements are denominated in dollars, whereas utility payments by the local populace are made in local currency.[11]

The challenge for official political risk insurers, and for investor–state arbitration panels, is to devise a framework for dealing with investment project difficulties that arise out of international financial crises, or regional financial contagion, rather than from deliberate hostile acts on the part of host authorities. Such a framework could provide a '*force majeure*' suspension of contractual obligations during a sudden economic collapse, along the lines already visible in normal commercial relationships. In a study of twenty infrastructure projects whose terms had to be changed between 1990 and 2005, Woodhouse finds that the majority (eleven) involved a mutual 'work-out' between investor and host aimed at keeping the project viable over the longer term.[12] These eleven all featured some kind of cooperative renegotiation, including restructuring fuel supply provisions, refinancing project loans or identifying other aspects of the original contracts that could be changed by mutual agreement.

A change in how political risk insurance contracts are interpreted, and arbitrated, would have the added appeal of eliminating the element of moral hazard that is evident in the current system. International power companies covered by official political risk insurance of the vintage in the Woodhouse study behaved differently from those that were not. Investors caught in a regional economic downturn – without multilateral or national political risk coverage against breach of contract – engaged in work-outs as outlined above. In Indonesia, for example, two investors without political risk insurance coverage (Unocal and Jawa Power) agreed to a new timetable for bringing their power projects on-line as the host economy recovered, whereas an investor with political risk insurance coverage, named MidAmerica, exercised the take-or-pay requirement for a power plant whose output had no demand in order to activate its Overseas Private Investment Corporation (OPIC) claim. Current breach of contract coverage simply tempts an investor to walk away from a project once it is clear that the original assumptions were too optimistic. Worse, current breach of contract policies lead private banks that hold

---

[11] I. N. Kessides, *Reforming Infrastructure: Privatization, Regulation, and Competition.* (Washington DC: World Bank and Oxford University Press, 2004), p. 179.

[12] E. J. Woodhouse, 'Managing International Political Risk: Lessons from the Power Sector' in T. H. Moran, G. T. West and K. Martin (eds.), *International Political Risk Management: Needs of the Present, Challenges for the Future* (Washington DC: World Bank, Multilateral Investment Guarantee Agency, 2008).

a portfolio of insured infrastructure loans to withhold authorisation for restructuring the original agreement.

A new framework that pushes the parties towards a mutually acceptable work-out would broaden the context within which investor–state dispute settlement functions.[13] Instead of focusing exclusively on the narrowest dimension of contract compliance – aimed at making the foreign investor 'whole' rather than focusing on changed conditions and new opportunities when demand recovers – arbitration could take a more mediation-like form with the goal of determining how best to move forward with the interests of all parties in mind.

E. Using FDI to upgrade and diversify exports is the new frontier for international development policy

The struggle for better treatment of workers and for improvement in working conditions in the plants of foreign investors and their subcontractors in the developing world is unending at the low-skill end of manufacturing, assembly, agribusiness and horticulture.[14]

But the low-skill end is not where most FDI in manufacturing and assembly takes place. The uncontested but often unacknowledged fact is that most manufacturing FDI in developing countries flows to more advanced industrial sectors rather than to garment, footwear and other lowest-skilled operations. The predominance of FDI in more skill-intensive investor operations is growing over time.

As Table 3.1 shows, the flow of manufacturing FDI to plants in which medium-skilled operations take place – such as motor vehicles and vehicle parts, industrial machinery, medical devices, scientific instruments, electronics and electrical products, chemicals, rubber, and plastic products – is nearly *fourteen times larger* each year than the flow to low-skilled, labour-intensive operations, and has been speeding up over time. The proportion of manufacturing FDI devoted to higher-skilled activities was roughly five times larger than to lower skill-intensive activities in the period 1989–1991, but approximately fourteen times larger in the period 2005–2007.

[13] United Nations Conference on Trade and Development (UNCTAD), *Investor–State Disputes: Prevention and Alternatives to Arbitration* (New York: United Nations Publications, 2010); L. L. Riskin, J. E. Westbrook, C. Guthrie, R. Reuben, J. Robbennolt and N. A. Welsh, *Dispute Resolution and Lawyers*, 4th edn (New York: Westgroup, 2009).

[14] T. H. Moran, *Beyond Sweatshops: Foreign Direct Investment and Globalization in Developing Countries* (Washington DC: The Brookings Institution, 2002).

Table 3.1. *Manufacturing multinational corporation (MNC) operations in developing countries*

	FDI flows (millions of dollars)			FDI stocks (millions of dollars)		
	1989–1991 (annual average)	1999–2000 (annual average)	2005–2007 (annual average)	1990	1999	2007
Lowest-skilled sectors	2,837	3,100	7,487	20,766	46,864	80,545
Higher-skilled sectors	13,244	52,800	104,365	137,261	505,928	836,272

Note: For a complete breakdown by sector, see the analysis of manufacturing FDI flows and manufacturing FDI from the UNCTAD database, 2009, in T. H. Moran, *Foreign Direct Investment and Development: Launching a Second Generation of Policy Research, Avoiding the Mistakes of the First, Re-Evaluating Policies for Developed and Developing Countries* (Washington DC: Peterson Institute for International Economics, 2011).

If the stock of manufacturing FDI is used instead of the flow, the same contrast emerges: a ratio of seven to one in 1990, a ratio of ten to one in 2007 (these ratios are probably understated, moreover, since data on FDI stocks typically do not provide accurate information on reinvested earnings and allowances for accelerated depreciation that characterise the more capital-intensive higher-skilled FDI operations).

The International Labour Organization (ILO) database does not record employment in developing country industries by job classification and level of compensation. But labour market statistics support the general proposition that as skill levels increase, so do wages. Survey data from industry sectors such as motor vehicles and vehicle equipment, electronics, chemicals and industrial equipment – in comparison to garments and footwear – shows that foreign investors with higher skill-intensive operations pay their employees two to three times as much for basic production jobs, and perhaps ten times as much for technical and supervisor positions, as is paid to workers in comparable positions in lower-skilled multinational corporation (MNC) activities.

From this evidence, one cannot conclude that FDI employment in developing country manufacturing generates in the aggregate more higher-skilled jobs than lower-skilled jobs. Foreign multinational employment in more sophisticated activities is more capital-intensive (less labour-intensive) than foreign multinational employment in garments and footwear: one truck assembly export plant in Mexico may employ fewer than one thousand workers; one semiconductor export plant in Costa Rica may employ no more than 2,900 workers. One athletic footwear export plant in Vietnam may create more than 10,000 jobs.

But these data on FDI flows and stocks show that the spread of multinational corporate manufacturing around the globe provides an avenue for developing countries to move into more sophisticated sectors, and diversify their exports from these sectors, while providing employment to medium- and higher-skilled workers.

This observation takes on new significance in light of recent research showing 'what you export matters'. Developing countries that do accomplish the task of upgrading and diversifying their export base – rather than merely expanding exports in a given array of sectors – enjoy more rapid growth rates, more advanced levels of productivity, greater domestic welfare and higher standards of living than countries that are unable to do so.[15] Rapidly developing countries like China, India, Indonesia and Thailand enjoy export baskets with above-average skill-intensive goods in comparison to other countries at a similar income level.

But the task of diversifying and upgrading the export base turns out to be considerably more difficult than one might think if domestic authorities rely upon domestic economic actors alone. Even if a given country takes formidable strides in improving local doing-business indicators, an important bottleneck remains: namely the limited ability of indigenous entrepreneurs to identify and bring into existence new non-traditional activities from within the local economy (what Hausmann and Rodrik call constraints on 'self discovery').[16] This is why FDI is often the crucial ingredient needed for structural transformation. Multinational corporations possess a large stock – and a continuous flow – of novel technologies, production techniques, quality control standards and marketing procedures that might be deployed by the parent firms to new locations around the world.

---

[15] D. Hummels and P. J. Klenow, 'The variety and quality of a nation's exports', *American Economic Review* 95(3) (2005), 704–23 at 718; R. Hausmann, J. Hwang and D. Rodrik, 'What you export matters', *Journal of Economic Growth* 12(1) (March 2007), 1–25.

[16] R. Hausmann and D. Rodrik, 'Economic development as self-discovery', *Journal of Development Economics* 72 (2003), 603–33.

But how can a would-be host convince an international company to 'try out' a new production site for an activity that has never been undertaken there before, especially when the plant is likely to be intended as an integral part of the parent company's strategy to become more competitive in world markets? The kind of information the multinational manufacturer most needs to make the investment decision cannot be derived from tax rates and doing-business indicators alone, so much as from 'test-driving' the facility.

In short, the imperfection in FDI information markets resembles Akerlof's well-known conundrum of how to convince a buyer to make a large capital investment (purchase a used car) when that buyer is afraid of 'being stuck with a lemon'.[17] This requires providing reasonably credible assurances that the output of components, subassemblies or final products and services from a new plant in a novel sector can be integrated seamlessly into the parent corporation's global supplier network. The key ingredients include:

1. a competitive basic cost structure, backed by a supportive exchange rate regime;
2. access to workers, technicians, supervisors, engineers and managers with appropriate skills;
3. reasonable flexibility in adjusting the size of the workforce to reflect changing conditions of international supply and demand;
4. assurance that local affiliates can operate without losing control over technology and other business practices (enforcement of intellectual property rights, and absence of requirements to operate with a local partner);
5. reasonably reliable infrastructure for uninterrupted production (power, water) and efficient shipment (transport).

There may be coordination externalities, moreover, when these ingredients can be combined – that is, there may be a disproportionate impact in reassuring a first-mover when multiple overlapping measures can be undertaken simultaneously.

The payoff from attracting manufacturing FDI into increasingly sophisticated sectors extends beyond the direct operations of the investors themselves. As foreign investor activities move out of garments and footwear into electronics, industrial equipment, motor vehicle

[17] G. Akerlof, 'The market for "lemons": quality uncertainty and the market mechanism', *Quarterly Journal of Economics* 84(3) (1970), 488–500.

parts, medical devices and the like, the potential for backward linkages increases. Whereas multinationals take great care to avoid technology transfer in a horizontal direction – to prevent the emergence of rivals – they benefit from providing blueprints, quality control advice and advance financing to local input-providers in a vertical direction. So, as the skill intensity of FDI exports rises, the self-interest of the multinational investors in finding inexpensive and reliable suppliers in the host economy provides an important complement to the direct activities of the investors. These would-be suppliers need a business-friendly environment no less than the foreigners if they are to become competitive, grow and prosper.

Figuring out how to attract ever higher skill-intensive manufacturing FDI – while surrounding investors with reliable infrastructure, skilled labour and favourable doing-business operating conditions – is the new frontier for any host that wishes to build an internationally competitive industrial base in the developing world, especially if such a base can include supply chains reaching deep into the host economy.

For countries that are successful, an important complementary side-effect may show up in the form of labour market and labour institution externalities.

F.   There is evidence of labour institution externalities – as well as more straightforward labour market externalities – from using FDI to move into more sophisticated activities

Alongside the popular conception that most manufacturing FDI flows to lowest-skilled activities in the developing world is the conviction that – since capital is mobile and labour is fixed – multinationals will use their superior bargaining power to drive wages as low as possible.

Despite the logic of such a supposition, the data paint a different picture. The norm is closer to what Razafindrakoto and Roubaud find in the low-skilled intensive Export Processing Zones (EPZ) plants in Madagascar. They held education level, extent of professional experience, and length of tenure in the enterprise constant, and found that foreign investors in export processing zones pay 15–20 per cent more than what workers with similar qualifications received elsewhere in the economy.[18] Data from Latin America and Africa reveal a similar wage

[18] M. Razafindrakoto and F. Roubaud, 'Les entreprises franches à Madagascar: économie d'enclave ou promesse d'une nouvelle prospérité? Nouvel exclavage ou opportunité pour le développement du pays?', *Economie de Madagascar* 2 (1995), 217–48.

premium.[19] The ubiquity of the evidence led Lipsey to characterise a 'universal rule' that foreign-owned firms and plants pay higher wages than domestically owned ones.[20]

Are these wage premia more evident in richer developing countries, and less so in poorer developing countries?

Graham found exactly the opposite: compensation per indigenous employee in foreign plants in the manufacturing sector is higher, as a multiple of average compensation per employee in the host manufacturing sector, in poorer countries than in the middle-income developing countries.[21] In the middle-income developing countries, the ratio of foreign-paid wages to indigenous firm wages in manufacturing is 1.8; in the lower-income developing countries, the ratio of foreign-paid wages to indigenous firm wages in manufacturing is 2.0 – that is, twice as high as the average compensation in the host country manufacturing sector.[22]

What might explain this foreign investor wage premium? Alternative hypotheses include the possibility that foreign-owned plants are typically larger, may use different inputs and may be located in regions of higher wages overall. Lipsey and Sjoholm used an unusually detailed data set of plant and worker characteristics from almost 20,000 firms in Indonesia to separate out the relative influences.[23] Overall they found that foreign investors paid 33 per cent more for blue-collar workers and 70 per cent more for white-collar workers than did locally owned firms. Controlling for education, MNCs paid more for workers with a given education level than domestically owned firms. Controlling for region and sector, the foreign pay differential showed up as 25 per cent for blue-collar workers and 50 per cent for white-collar workers. Controlling for plant size, energy inputs per worker, other inputs per worker and proportion of female

[19] B. Aitken, A. Harrison, and R. E. Lipsey, 'Wages and foreign ownership: a comparative study of Mexico, Venezuela, and the United States', *Journal of International Economics* 40(3–4) (1996), 345–71; D. W. de Velde and O. Morrissey, 'Do workers in Africa get a wage premium if employed in firms owned by foreigners?', *Journal of African Economies* 12(1) (2003), 41–3.

[20] R. Lipsey, 'Measuring the Impacts of FDI in Central and Eastern Europe', Cambridge, MA: National Bureau of Economic Research, Working Paper 12808 (2006); A. Hijzen and P. Swaim, 'Do multinationals promote better pay and working conditions?' *OECD Observer* 269 (October 2008), 15–17.

[21] E. M. Graham, *Fighting the Wrong Enemy: Antiglobal Activists and Multinational Enterprises* (Washington DC: Institute for International Economics, 2000), pp. 93–4, Table 4–2.

[22] Graham removes salaries for foreign managers and supervisors from these calculations.

[23] R. E. Lipsey and F. Sjoholm, 'Foreign direct investment, education, and wages in Indonesian manufacturing', *Journal of Development Economics* 75(1) (2004), 415–22.

employees, the wage premium in foreign-owned establishments equalled 12 per cent for blue-collar and 22 per cent for white-collar workers. The surprise, they concluded, is that while approximately one-third of the foreign investor wage premium could be attributed to region and sector and one-third attributed to plant size and use of other inputs, one-third was left unexplained.

Flying in the face of the widespread notion that foreign investors travel to developing countries to 'exploit' local workers, or that mobile capital takes advantage of inherently fixed labour, the pleasing puzzle in the data is why multinationals pay local workers more than what is necessary to keep their plants operating efficiently.

Turning from evidence of an FDI wage premium to the question of labour market externalities, how does the spread of foreign manufacturing investment affect the wages received by workers outside the FDI plants themselves, in indigenously owned plants? Once again the unusually detailed data from Indonesia provided Lipsey and Sjoholm an opportunity to investigate whether the higher wages paid by foreign firms in their own plants lead to payment of higher wages in domestically owned companies, at least in this one country.[24] Controlling for labour force characteristics, they found a positive spillover within broad sector classifications at the national level, and a smaller (but still positive and significant) spillover within narrower sector classifications, and at the regional level.

Finally, there is interesting new evidence – potentially very valuable new evidence – showing institutional spillovers in the labour markets when the skill intensity of FDI activities rises. As the operations of foreign investors grow more sophisticated – as electronics and vehicle parts investors build plants in EPZs and industrial parks alongside garment and footwear assemblers – the former promote better worker facilities, security, transport, health and safety standards (even day care) that apply to all firms.[25] Although the evidence comes from a small sample, it includes three country histories – the Dominican Republic, the Philippines and Costa Rica – where the more skill-intensive foreign firms led the way for passage of ILO-consistent regulations at the national level (and more effective enforcement of the resulting regulations at the local level, including communal disciplining of violators) in the interest of promoting

[24] R. E. Lipsey and F. Sjoholm, 'FDI and wage spillovers in Indonesian manufacturing', *Review of World Economics* 140(2) (2004), 287–310.

[25] T. H. Moran, *Beyond Sweatshops: Foreign Direct Investment and Globalization in Developing Countries* (Washington DC: The Brookings Institution, 2002), Chapter 3.

'labour peace'.[26] This process exhibits race-to-the-top dynamics quite at variance with the race-to-the-bottom assumptions in much of the sweat-shop literature.

G.   Corporate social responsibility advocates should focus their efforts in very targeted fashion towards shaping and magnifying the impact of main-line core FDI operations

The analysis presented here provides some important guidance for how CSR advocates might play an important role in shaping and magnifying the impact of main-line core FDI operations. It is commonplace today for CSR advocates to insist that corporations that wish to establish them-selves as acting in a responsible fashion affirm that they will conduct their operations so as to follow, for example, the ten fundamental standards in the United Nations (UN) Global Compact. CSR advocates then typic-ally assert that the corporations must follow up with internal systems to promote compliance, and report results. While reporting systems vary widely, the most widely recognised template is embodied in the Global Reporting Initiative (GRI).

But the arguments introduced here earlier quickly reveal that the GRI template is far too limited.

To deal with 'resource curse' issues, the GRI prescribes, for example, that extractive sector investors should 'report the percentage of total number of management and non-management employees who have received anti-corruption training'. The recommendation that emerges from the preceding pages, in contrast, is much more specific and assert-ive: socially responsible international resource companies should use their not-inconsiderable influence when they negotiate new contracts or make follow-on investments to bring the countries where their wells and mines are located into the EITI regime, and become EITI-compliant. Then, as argued earlier, socially responsible international resource inves-tors should endorse and push for disclosure of revenue payments on a company-by-company basis in all EITI countries, thereby exposing Chinese, Russian, Indian and other investors to the same scrutiny as com-panies registered on the USA, EU or other major stock exchanges.

In the case of international investors in the manufacturing sector, I showed earlier that developing countries enjoy broader opportunities

---

[26] *Ibid.*; US Secretary of State's Award for Corporate Excellence 2009, Background mater-ials, US Embassy San Jose, June 2009.

to promote backward linkages when they succeed in attracting FDI into increasingly sophisticated operations. To take advantage of such opportunities, the GRI recommends that manufacturing multinationals report on 'how much do you buy locally'. But CSR pressures can be helpful in producing much more targeted actions on the part of these multinationals: has the socially responsible investor designated a manager to be a 'talent scout' to search out potential indigenous suppliers, or liaise with local vendor development agencies (vertical externalities)? Does the socially responsible investor take measures to provide production assistance, managerial advice and advance purchase orders to potential indigenous suppliers (a teaching externality)? Does the socially responsible investor have procedures to 'qualify' and 'certify' potential indigenous suppliers (a labelling externality)? And, does the socially responsible investor have a programme through which qualified indigenous suppliers are introduced to sister affiliates in the region (an export externality)?

With regard to influencing the doing-business milieu, the GRI protocol suggests that international corporations report on their public policy positions, and their participation in public policy development and lobbying. On the basis of the evidence presented earlier, CSR pressure should be directed specifically to pushing international corporations to improve nationwide labour institutions, such as ensuring that all members of the business associations they belong to (no matter what the skill level of their operations) operate with common and mutually acceptable human resource standards, albeit with different wage levels.

One could examine other components of corporate codes of conduct and try to translate the analysis introduced here into specific recommendations about how socially responsible investors should behave. This is a different focus from the more conventional agenda of CSR advocates to try to induce international investors to 'give back' more to the workers and communities where they are located. The objective recommended here is not to induce multinational corporations to do things – or to give money to do things – outside their sphere of core competency. Rather, the goal is to bring external pressure to enhance the impact of main-line multinational corporate activities on host country growth and welfare as sketched out in the preceding pages of this chapter.

4

Actors in the international investment scenario: objectives, performance and advantages of affiliates of state-owned enterprises and sovereign wealth funds

SÉBASTIEN MIROUDOT AND ALEXANDROS RAGOUSSIS

A. Introduction

While the demise of central planned economies and free-market reforms in developing economies have triggered massive privatisations,[1] a paradox of the period since 2000 is that the number of state-owned enterprises (SOEs) is not diminishing.[2] The main reason is that, following the example of private companies, SOEs have started to globalise. In particular, they create foreign affiliates or engage in international mergers and acquisitions to serve new markets or to improve their productivity through offshoring. With the accumulation of currency reserves in some countries, governments also have large amounts of capital to invest abroad, including in foreign equities. Sovereign wealth funds (SWFs) have been growing and now represent a non-negligible share of the world foreign

---

The authors are writing in a personal capacity. The views expressed are theirs only, and do not reflect in any way those of the Organisation for Economic Co-operation and Development (OECD) Secretariat or the member countries of the OECD.

[1] According to the World Bank's privatisation database, 8,342 large-scale privatisations (more than US$1 million) occurred between 1988 and 1999 in 108 countries. Between 2000 and 2008 the same database reports 1,859 transactions in 102 countries, available at: http://rru.worldbank.org/Privatization/.

[2] There is no comprehensive database on the basis of which the total number of SOEs could be calculated. Foreign affiliates of SOEs constitute a recent phenomenon that is not captured in earlier studies focusing on 'parent' companies (the companies directly owned by government entities). The firm-level data analysed in this paper and the estimates provided by the United Nations Conference on Trade and Development (UNCTAD) suggest that there is no significant reduction in the total number of SOEs when accounting for their affiliates.

direct investment (FDI) stock.[3] The financial crisis in 2008–2009 has also reinforced the shift of SWFs towards equity investment to diversify and broaden the types of assets they hold.[4]

SOEs and SWFs are not new, but a recent trend is their international expansion with increasing outward FDI. As new actors in the international investment regime, firms owned by governments raise a number of concerns. To begin with, host economies are not always comfortable when a foreign government becomes the owner of a 'strategic' company, as illustrated by the Dubai Ports World affair.[5] The issue goes beyond some potential anxiety on the part of the public and the government of the host country. There are sound economic concerns on the governance of SOEs and their performance, as well as on the environment in which they operate. Are the objectives of public management the same as in a private company? Are affiliates of state enterprises engaging in uncompetitive behaviour relative to private firms in the same industry? A government-owned company can receive benefits, leading to an uneven playing field in comparison with private investors and domestic firms. The economic literature has highlighted the advantage of SOEs in accessing credit, as well as the subsidies they receive, or implicit cross-subsidisation through market power on their domestic market.[6]

Moreover, the new role of SOEs in international trade and investment illustrates a trend towards state capitalism and can be regarded as a 'new mercantilism'.[7] Instead of the state trying to shield domestic

---

[3] According to UNCTAD, *World Investment Report 2011: Non-Equity Modes of International Production and Development* (New York: United Nations Publications, 2011), the share of SWF investment in cross-border mergers and acquisitions (M&As) was less than 0.5 per cent in 2004 and rose to almost 2.5 per cent in 2009 (the share became slightly lower in 2010).

[4] On the increase in equity investment from the Norwegian sovereign wealth funds, see L. C. Backer, 'Sovereign wealth funds as regulatory chameleons: the Norwegian sovereign wealth funds and public global governance through private global investment', *Georgetown Journal of International Law* 41(2) (2010), 425–500.

[5] In 2006 the acquisition of several US port facilities by Dubai Ports World was blocked by the Congress. Dubai Ports World is a subsidiary of Dubai World, a government-owned investment company from the United Arab Emirates.

[6] G. T. Qigui Liu and X. Wang, 'The effect of ownership structure on leverage decision: new evidence from Chinese listed firms', *Journal of the Asia Pacific Economy* 16(2) (2011), 254–76.

[7] I. Bremmer, 'State capitalism comes of age', *Foreign Affairs* 88(3) (2009), 40–56; R. J. Gilson and C. J. Milhaupt, 'Sovereign Wealth Funds and Corporate Governance: a Minimalist Response to New Mercantilism', Stanford Law and Economics Olin Working Paper No. 355 (2008); F. Flores-Macias and A. Musacchio, 'The return of state-owned enterprises. Should we be afraid?', *Harvard International Review* (4 April 2009).

companies from foreign competition, this new mercantilism becomes outward-oriented in the context of globalisation. The direct involvement of the state is seen as a way to ensure the expansion of domestic companies in foreign markets. Outward investment by Chinese SOEs, which has increased impressively in recent years,[8] illustrates this trend, but the phenomenon is not limited to developing countries.

Against this backdrop, the aim of this chapter is to provide quantitative evidence on the international expansion of public investors and to investigate some of the policy concerns described above in an econometric analysis. Section B sets the stage by providing definitions and by describing the legal context. Section C introduces the policy issues we address in the chapter and reviews the existing literature. Section D describes the firm-level data that we use. Section E presents the results of our analysis of the performance and behaviour of affiliates of government-owned enterprises and assesses whether the concerns are justified. Section F concludes.

B.   The international expansion of SOEs and SWFs: definitions and legal background

According to the United Nations Conference on Trade and Development (UNCTAD), there were at least 650 state-owned multinational enterprises in 2010 with more than 8,500 affiliates worldwide. The same report lists 80 SWFs at the end of 2009. SOEs and SWFs are undoubtedly key actors in today's international investment regime and a rich literature has emerged on their expansion and the policy challenges that they pose.

Before becoming investors, SOEs were already international actors through their exports and imports. Trade law, before investment law, had to deal with companies owned by governments. As a starting point, we therefore review the way the international trading system deals with SOEs. This discussion is also an opportunity to address the issue of the definition of state enterprises.

---

[8] See B. Berger, and A. Berkofsky, 'Chinese Outward Investments: Agencies, Motives and Decision-making', CASCC Briefing Paper (2009); L. K. Cheng and Z. Ma, 'China's Outward FDI, Past and Future' in R. Feenstra and S. J. Wei (eds.), *China's Growing Role in World Trade* (Chicago University Press, 2010); US–China Economic and Security Review Commission, 'Going Out: an Overview of China's Outward Foreign Direct Investment', USCC Staff Research Report (30 March 2011).

A principle in World Trade Organization (WTO) law and more generally in international law is the ownership-neutrality of rules.[9] The General Agreement on Tariffs and Trade (GATT) was developed after the Second World War in the context of a world with centrally planned economies where state ownership was the norm. Rules had to apply both to state-owned and private-owned firms. Therefore, most of the provisions found in international agreements do not distinguish between companies according to ownership. A consequence of this neutral approach is that there is generally no definition of a 'state-owned enterprise'.

However, a departure from this approach is found in GATT Article XVII. This Article includes two obligations for 'State Trading Enterprises' (STEs). The first one is to act 'in a manner consistent with the general principles of non-discrimination prescribed in the Agreement'. In particular, their purchases and sales involving imports or exports should be made 'in accordance with commercial considerations' and should 'afford the enterprises of the other contracting parties adequate opportunity, in accordance with customary business practice, to compete for participation in such purchases or sales'. The second obligation in Article XVII is a transparency requirement. Each party should notify the other parties of the products that are imported or exported by STEs and should provide information on their operations. However, there is no definition of an STE.

In 1994 an 'Understanding on the Interpretation of Article XVII' was added to the GATT. The Understanding creates a working party in charge of examining notifications of STEs on behalf of the WTO Council for Trade in Goods. The document also provides a 'working definition' for STEs:

> Governmental and non-governmental enterprises, including marketing boards, which have been granted exclusive or special rights or privileges, including statutory or constitutional powers, in the exercise of which they influence through their purchases or sales the level or direction of imports or exports.

While being more specific, the definition is still ambiguous, perhaps on purpose in order to cover different types of enterprises. Two criteria are, however, pointed out: special rights or privileges and market power. Such

---

[9] J. Ya Qin, 'WTO regulation of subsidies to state-owned enterprises (SOEs) – a critical appraisal of the China Accession Protocol', *Journal of International Economic Law* 7(4) (2004), 863–919.

criteria can be useful to characterise SOEs but 'STEs' represent a different category of firms that includes private companies with exclusive rights or monopoly rights.

More recently, the accession of China to the WTO triggered specific provisions on SOEs. Because most of the exporting companies in China are state-owned, the applicability of WTO rules raised a number of questions.[10] With respect to subsidies, the Protocol on China's accession[11] signed in 2001 introduced specific provisions for SOEs.[12] In particular, the Protocol indicates that subsidies received by SOEs should be regarded as specific in the sense of Article 2 of the Agreement on Subsidies and Countervailing Measures (ASCM) – and thus covered by the disciplines of the agreement. A list of subsidies to SOEs to be removed is also annexed to the Protocol, such as subsidies for loss-making SOEs.

Another issue discussed during the accession of China to the WTO related to investment and technology transfer. Several WTO Members requested that technology transfer should be the result of an agreement between private parties without any interference from the government.[13] While including specific provisions for SOEs, the Protocol does not provide any definition. Interestingly, only the section on subsidies mentions SOEs, whereas the provisions related to the implementation of Article XVII talk about STEs.

The General Agreement on Trade in Services (GATS) is of special interest for our topic as it comes closest to being an investment agreement under the WTO. GATS only applies to the provision of services (and not to investment per se) but includes as a mode of supply the 'commercial presence' (mode 3), which is the provision of a service through establishment. There is no reference to SOEs in GATS. GATS Article I.3 carves out services 'supplied in the exercise of governmental authority' but the definition of such services as 'supplied neither on a commercial basis, nor in competition with one or more services suppliers' does not suggest that SOEs are exempted from the disciplines of the agreement (or only in the context of pure monopolies). Disciplines on subsidies are unfortunately part of GATS 'unfinished business' and not yet negotiated. This is,

[10] G. Hufbauer, 'China as an Economic Actor on the World Stage: An Overview' in F. M. Abbott (ed.), *China in the World Trading System: Defining the Principles of Engagement* (Cambridge, MA: Kluwer Law International, 1998).

[11] World Trade Organization (WTO), Accession of the People's Republic of China, Decision of 10 November 2001, WT/L/432, 23 November 2001.

[12] See Qin, 'WTO regulation of subsidies to state-owned enterprises' for a discussion.

[13] See WTO Report of the Working Party on the Accession of China, WT/Min(01)/3.

perhaps, the reason why no special attention is given to SOEs. National treatment (Article XVII) is, however, a key non-discriminatory provision in sectors where countries take commitments and should ensure a level playing field between SOEs and private service providers, together with the most-favoured nation treatment, which is a general obligation in the agreement.

In the absence of any official definition, SOEs can be defined as firms in which the government (central, regional or local) has a controlling interest. To study their international expansion and their role in FDI, the universe of SOEs should include both parent companies and their affiliates abroad. What defines a controlling interest may differ. For example, UNCTAD defines control as a stake of 10 per cent or more of the voting power or, alternatively, as the government being the largest shareholder. However, through a 'golden share' or a blocking minority, a government can control a company without holding the majority of shares or without being the largest shareholder. This is why the Organisation for Economic Co-operation and Development (OECD) Guidelines on Corporate Governance of State-Owned Enterprises adopted in 2005 refer to enterprises where the state has a 'significant control, through full, majority, or significant minority ownership'. This is certainly the best 'working definition', although in practice the 'significant minority' might be difficult to identify. In the next section we will work with data based on majority ownership (at least 50.01 per cent of the shares or voting power).

As for SWFs, no official or universally agreed definition exists. The term itself is relatively new and, therefore, no international agreement refers to SWFs. However, an International Working Group of Sovereign Wealth Funds was created in 2008 under the auspices of the International Monetary Fund (IMF). In October 2008 this voluntary group adopted a set of principles known as the 'Santiago Principles'.[14] In an Annex of the document, they provide the following definition for SWFs:

> SWFs are defined as special purpose investment funds or arrangements, owned by the general government. Created by the general government for macroeconomic purposes, SWFs hold, manage, or administer assets to achieve financial objectives, and employ a set of investment strategies

---

[14] See J. Chaisse, J. D. Chakraborty and J. Mukherjee, 'Emerging sovereign wealth funds in the making: assessing the economic feasibility and regulatory strategies', *Journal of World Trade* 45(4) (2010), 837–75. The Santiago principles are available at: www.iwg-swf. org/pubs/eng/santiagoprinciples.pdf.

which include investing in foreign financial assets. The SWFs are commonly established out of balance of payments surpluses, official foreign currency operations, the proceeds of privatizations, fiscal surpluses, and/or receipts resulting from commodity exports.

SWFs can thus be defined as government-owned special purpose investment funds. They are established by countries such as China, Norway, Qatar, Saudi Arabia, Singapore or the United Arab Emirates (which has the largest SWF).[15] Because of natural resources or a large trade surplus, these countries have excess liquidity that has to be invested abroad.[16] SWFs represent a heterogeneous category of investors as they are set up with different objectives and are involved in a variety of financial assets, such as bonds, stocks or real estate. Even in terms of equity investment, their activities can involve minor participations, joint ventures or fully owned companies.

For the purpose of investing in stocks, SWFs often create sovereign wealth enterprises (SWEs). As these enterprises are owned by a government, they can be regarded as SOEs (and in the next section we will analyse together companies owned directly by governments and companies owned by SWFs). Some authors point out that the management of an SOE and an SWE differs.[17] Traditional SOEs were companies generally created with monopoly rights to provide services to the general population (public utilities) or companies nationalised to be part of the country's industrial policy. SWEs, by contrast, are created for financial purposes and should favour higher returns rather than political or social objectives. Their behaviour would thus be closer to private companies or closer to other private investment funds. In the future we hope we will be able to distinguish in our firm-level data affiliates of SOEs and SWFs, but this could not be done at this stage. We will hence study together all affiliates of public investors.

---

[15] In July 2011 the assets of the Abu Dhabi Investment Authority were estimated at US$627 billion (source: SWF Institute).

[16] Domestic investment would lead to inflation. In addition, for countries with natural resources the investment should offer returns to compensate for the exhaustion of these resources in the future.

[17] See L. C. Backer, 'Sovereign investing in times of crisis: global regulation of sovereign wealth funds, state-owned enterprises, and the Chinese experience', *Transnational Law & Contemporary Problems* 19(3) (2010), 3–144; A. Blundell-Wignall and G. Wehinger, 'Open Capital Markets and Sovereign Wealth Funds, Pension Funds and State-Owned Enterprises', paper prepared for the conference 'Sovereign Wealth Funds in an Evolving Global Financial System', Australian National University, Sydney, 25–26 September 2008.

C.   Three policy concerns: non-commercial objectives, poor performance and unfair advantages

The international expansion of SOEs and SWFs raises several policy concerns. In this chapter we have decided to focus on three of them and to investigate whether they are empirically justified.

I.   Non-commercial objectives of SOEs

The first policy concern related to outward investment of public investors is that, being owned by a foreign government, affiliates of SOEs could have non-commercial objectives and could present a threat to national security in the host country.[18] This would be the case, in particular, if the investment were in a sector of strategic importance to national security, such as transportation infrastructure, energy, communications or a military-related industry. An important question is whether SOEs and SWFs are independently managed with purely financial objectives (maximising returns) or whether their investment strategy is also influenced by the governments who own them and extra-economic objectives. The answer to this question might vary as, in the case of SWFs, some have delegated their management to external advisors in order to address concerns of host countries, while others are still directly managed by the governments who founded them. There are also different management practices and a different degree of involvement of the state shareholder in SOEs.

What would be the exact nature of the non-commercial objectives we evoke in this debate? While some of them might indeed be 'strategic' or 'geopolitical',[19] the literature on SOEs suggests that government-owned firms are often revenue- and employment-maximising instead of profit-maximising.[20] Social welfare cannot be absent from the agenda of

---

[18] See A. Antkiewicz and J. Whalley, 'Recent Chinese Buyout Activity and the Implications for Global Architecture', NBER Working Paper No. 12072 (March 2006) for a discussion in the case of Chinese outward investment.

[19] See C. H. Knutsen, A. Rygh and H. Hveem, 'Does state ownership matter? Institutions' effect on foreign direct investment revisited', *Business and Politics* 13(1) (2011), Article 2. The authors test whether SOEs invest less in dictatorships and countries with poor human rights protection and find the opposite: SOEs invest relatively more in countries with a high level of corruption and weak rule of law.

[20] See P. Sapienza, 'The effects of government ownership on bank lending', *Journal of Financial Economics* 72(2) (2004), 357–84; J. Whalley and S. Zhang, 'State-owned Enterprise Behaviour Responses to Trade Reforms: some Analytics and Numerical Simulation Results using Chinese Data', NBER Working Paper No. 12780 (December 2006).

managers reporting directly to the government. Atkinson and Stiglitz were the first to formalise the so-called 'social view' on SOEs, which, based on the economic theory of institutions, suggests that these enterprises are created to address market failures whenever the social benefits of their activity exceed the costs.[21]

Regarding SWFs, the debate that followed the Dubai Ports World affair focused on security and prompted a group of them to react and to adopt the Santiago Principles mentioned earlier. These twenty-four principles aim at dispelling the suspicion surrounding SWFs' investments by providing more transparency in the way the funds are managed and by introducing specific rules in their decision process. The second Principle states that the policy purpose of the SWF should be 'clearly defined and publicly disclosed'. There are then more specific rules, such as the need for an 'effective division of roles and responsibilities in order to facilitate accountability and operational independence in the management of the SWF' (Principle 6) or the requirement not to use privileged information from the state sponsor (Principle 20).

For SOEs, the OECD Guidelines on Corporate Governance of State-Owned Enterprises also emphasise transparency requirements and independence in the management. Chapter II on the 'State acting as an owner' indicates that the 'government should not be involved in day-to-day management of SOEs and allow them full operational autonomy to achieve their defined objectives'. Another key principle is that 'there should be a clear separation between the state's ownership function and other state functions that may influence the conditions for state-owned enterprises, particularly with regard to market regulation' (Chapter I).

However, guidelines and principles offer no guarantee to host economies. Countries concerned about their security are more likely to rely on safeguards when they feel threatened by the investment of a foreign government. Article XXI of GATT and Article XIVbis of GATS include such safeguards with respect to 'essential security interests'. Concerning FDI in services, it should be noted that some countries have already used their GATS schedules of commitments to maintain restrictions on foreign government ownership.[22] For example, the USA has such restrictions

---

[21] A. B. Atkinson and J. E. Stiglitz, *Lectures on Public Economics* (New York: McGraw-Hill, 1980).

[22] A. Mattoo and A. Subramanian, 'Currency undervaluation and sovereign wealth funds: a new role for the World Trade Organization', *The World Economy* 32(8) (2009), 1135–64.

for communication services (radio and television broadcasts) and insurance services (in a list of states).

II. Performance of SOEs

The second policy concern relates to the efficiency of SOEs and their affiliates. Specifically, because of their public management, SOEs and their affiliates could be less efficient and hence constitute the source of a failure, the extent of which would depend on their share of the market. The literature on privatisations generally emphasises the poor public sector performance and discusses its sources.[23] Two explanations are offered. The first is related to the lack of incentives for managers and can be described as a principal–agent problem where the government (the principal) does not monitor closely enough the manager of the firm it owns (the agent).[24] Ownership is thus the issue. A second explanation is that SOEs operate in an environment that is not conducive to efficiency. SOEs are often in non-competitive markets and receive subsidies or have access to soft loans. The specificities of this environment would explain their poor performance and should they be placed in competitive markets, their efficiency would be expected to match that of private firms. This ownership-versus-environment debate should receive new attention in the context of the internationalisation of SOEs, as their foreign affiliates are likely to be operating in more competitive environments. Should the uncompetitive environment be the primary source of inefficiency of SOEs, we would expect fewer differences between affiliates of public and private companies abroad in terms of performance.

---

[23] See A. P. Bartel and A. E. Harrison, 'Ownership versus environment: why are public sector firms inefficient?', *Review of Economics and Statistics* 87(1) (1994), 135–47; A. R. Vining and A. Boardman, 'Ownership versus competition: efficiency in public enterprise', *Public Choice* 73 (1992), 205–39; A. Schleifer, 'State versus private ownership', *Journal of Economic Perspectives* 12(4) (1998), 133–50.

[24] The lack of transparency in the management of the firm is also addressed in the Santiago Principles and OECD Guidelines on Corporate Governance of State-Owned Enterprises. Because SOEs often have specific rules for reporting financial information and are audited by the state or through an internal system of audit rather than by external independent auditors, there is the suspicion that SOE boards and managers are not controlled strictly enough. Relations with shareholders and information on the strategy of companies tend also to be less developed in the case of public investors (see Antkiewicz and Whalley, 'Recent Chinese buyout activity'). What is requested from SOEs is for them to adopt high accounting and auditing standards in line with those of listed private companies.

The sources of inefficiency of SOEs might not impact only the firm as such; they could also spill over to the performance of other private firms in the market, which forms the third policy concern discussed below.

III.   Uncompetitive behaviour of SOEs

The third policy concern from the point of view of the host economy is that foreign SOEs may benefit from unfair advantages, creating economic distortions leading to welfare losses. Capobianco and Christiansen[25] list the following privileges and immunities giving a competitive edge to SOEs:

1. outright subsidisation (through direct subsidies or indirectly through, for example, a more favourable tax regime);
2. concessionary financing and guarantees (reducing their cost of borrowing);
3. other preferential treatment by government, such as exemptions from antitrust enforcement or preference in public procurement;
4. monopolies and advantages of incumbency;
5. captive equity (rules preventing the control of the company from being transferred); and
6. exemption from bankruptcy rules and information advantages.

Some of these advantages are sometimes adopted as a compensation for specific obligations, such as the provision of universal service or constraints on pricing. But this long list of privileges and immunities suggests an uneven playing field between SOEs and private companies.

A critical question is, however, to what extent these advantages can be used by SOEs in foreign markets to the benefit of their affiliates. Any lower cost at home can certainly be used to subsidise exports or lower prices abroad in a predatory strategy. But a privileged tax status, exemptions from the application of certain laws or monopoly rights cannot easily be carried abroad by affiliates of SOEs (unless they obtain the same advantages from the host economy). Subsidisation hence arises naturally as the main policy issue when looking at the internationalisation of SOEs. In particular, subsidies and access to capital at a lower cost can be used by SOEs for cross-border mergers and acquisitions. While export subsidies

---

[25] A. Capobianco and H. Christiansen, 'Competitive Neutrality and State-owned Enterprises: Challenges and Policy Options', OECD Corporate Governance Working Papers, No. 1 (2011).

are prohibited under the WTO, the subsidisation of investment is not clearly banned by any international agreement.[26] The use of investment incentives in general has increased since 2000[27] but the trend was mainly on subsidies to attract investment (given by the host economy). FDI distortions might be even larger if subsidies are found both on inward and outward investment.

D.   A new firm-level dataset of foreign affiliates controlled by governments

In order to investigate further the three policy concerns previously described, we use a new firm-level dataset developed at the OECD where we can identify affiliates owned by SOEs and SWFs. The dataset is part of the OECD-Orbis database.

Orbis is a commercial dataset developed by Bureau van Dijk Electronic Publishing (BvDEP) that contains structural and financial information on more than 25 million companies worldwide. The OECD-Orbis database is the output of treatment of raw data provided by Bureau van Dijk to the OECD in 2011.

Each observation in the database corresponds to one account published by a firm. The financial information in the accounts is broken down into two major components: the firm's balance sheet and the profit and loss account reported for a given time period. The account is complemented by information on export turnover, on a non-systematic basis, while ownership information is available in the form of links between firms, as well as with ultimate owners.

Through the information we have on the government as ultimate owner, we are able to identify the network of foreign affiliates of SOEs. Our data includes firms that are owned by SWFs. As long as SWFs hold a majority of stakes (directly or indirectly), they are regarded as public ultimate owners and the companies they own are included in our sample of foreign affiliates of SOEs.

In order to study the performance of foreign affiliates of firms, we need comprehensive financial information on the activities of these affiliates abroad, as well as good coverage of ownership links. Neither of these two

---

[26] For a discussion of the applicability of the Agreement on Subsidies and Countervailing Measures to investment subsidies for cross-border M&A, see G. Hufbauer, T. Moll and L. Rubini, 'Investment Subsidies for Cross-Border M&A: Trends and Policy Implications', Occasional Paper No. 2, United States Council Foundation (2008).

[27] For an overview, see K. Thomas, *Investment Incentives and the Competition for Global Capital* (Basingstoke: Palgrave MacMillan, 2010).

elements is reported systematically in Orbis, therefore the full analysis is not possible for the entire sample of firms in the database. We restrict the analysis to the following countries that have SOEs: Australia, Austria, Belgium, Brazil, Bulgaria, China, Croatia, Denmark, Finland, France, Germany, Greece, Italy, Japan, Korea, Mexico, the Netherlands, Norway, Portugal, Spain, Switzerland and the United Kingdom.

We construct our sample on the basis of firms controlled by the government of one of these twenty-two countries, and operating anywhere in the world. Affiliates of SOEs are contrasted with private affiliates of firms from these twenty-two countries, also operating anywhere in the world. The sample includes 18,068 affiliates of SOEs and 438,035 affiliates of private companies. For the purpose of this empirical analysis, SOEs are defined as firms where a government (including sub-national entities) holds 50 per cent or more of the shares. This majority ownership criterion limits the number of public investors but enables us to identify firms whose management is clearly not private.

A number of treatment procedures are applied to raw data in order to eliminate duplicates, construct longitudinal series and ensure that the data conform to a minimum of quality standards for analysis.[28] Records of financial accounts in Orbis can deviate from a set of quality standards for many reasons, such as errors in data integration or false reporting. In constructing the sample used for our analysis, we exclude non-yearly accounts, or records that exhibit inconsistent dates, implausible values or unjustified shifts, in order to enhance the quality of the data therein. Moreover, we merge information on the consolidation status of the accounts with ownership links in order to eliminate observations that could be double-counted. Specifically, we choose to remove all consolidated accounts of business groups for which unconsolidated information exists within the same country–year dataset.

In terms of representativeness of the firms observed in Orbis, the unavailability of detailed financial information for relatively smaller companies, the unbalanced nature of the panels, as well as asymmetries in the coverage of different industries, could all potentially have an impact on the comparability of results to official statistics. For our regressions, we follow Deaton in not using resampling weights.[29] The author shows that

[28] For more details, see A. Ragoussis and E. Gonnard, 'The OECD-Orbis Database: Treatment and Benchmarking Procedures', OECD Statistics Working Paper (January 2012).

[29] A. Deaton, *The Analysis of Household Surveys: A Microeconometric Approach to Development Policy* (Baltimore: Johns Hopkins University Press for the World Bank, 1997).

when the sectors are homogeneous (that is, parameter estimates in the results do not vary by strata), unweighted ordinary least squares (OLS) is more efficient. When they are not, both weighted and unweighted estimators are inconsistent. In neither case is there an argument for using resampling weights in regressions.

Lastly, we introduce a size threshold of fifty employees for inclusion in our sample. Both SOEs and exporters are under-represented in samples of small firms; hence their exclusion does not involve a significant loss of information.

E.   Empirical analysis of investment strategies and performance of affiliates of public enterprises

The first question we can study with the dataset is whether the international investment patterns of SOEs differ from those of private companies. Sectoral asymmetries in the investment patterns of SOEs could be broadly considered as evidence of the existence of a security risk that was discussed in Section 2. The question is, therefore, to what extent public investors target strategic sectors.

I.   Are there asymmetries in the investment patterns of public and private firms?

There is no agreed definition of what constitutes a 'sensitive' or 'strategic' industry when it comes to foreign investment. The definition of 'essential security interests' is likely to vary from one country to another. Mattoo and Subramanian[30] give the following list of sensitive industries: communications, media, energy, financial and distribution services. Interestingly, they are all in the services sector. 'Critical infrastructures' are also generally under consideration in national security strategies. The European Union (EU) directive on the identification and designation of European critical infrastructures (2008/114/EC) lists industries in two sectors: energy (electricity, oil and gas) and transport (road, rail, air, inland waterways, ocean and short-sea shipping and ports). Other 'sensitive' manufacturing activities may come to mind, such as the manufacturing of explosives and weapons, or the defence and aerospace industry.

Acknowledging that there is no practical or objective way of creating a list of strategic industries, and taking into account the constraint of the

---

[30]   Mattoo and Subramanian, 'Currency undervaluation and sovereign wealth funds', 1153.

Table 4.1. *Share of foreign investment (capital stock) and affiliates in 'sensitive areas': SOEs versus private firms (2008)*

	SOEs	Private firms
Total number of affiliates	18,068	438,035
Number of affiliates in sensitive sectors	3,558	37,921
Share of affiliates in sensitive sectors	*19.7%*	*8.7%*
Total capital stock (billion USD)	8,067.12	7,509.17
Capital stock in sensitive sectors (billion USD)	3,823.20	2,673.60
Share of capital stock in sensitive sectors	*47.4%*	*35.6%*

agglomeration of our data at the NACE Rev. 2 4-digit level, we define 'sensitive industries' for the purpose of our analysis as the following: mining of coal and lignite (NACE Rev. 2 division 05), extraction of crude petroleum and natural gas (06), mining of uranium and thorium ores (07.21), manufacture of coke and refined petroleum products (19), manufacture of explosives (20.51), processing of nuclear fuel (24.46), manufacture of weapons and ammunitions (25.40), manufacture of air and spacecraft and related machinery (30.30), electric power generation, transmission and distribution (35.11, 35.12 and 35.13), manufacture and distribution of gas (35.21 and 35.22), water collection, treatment and supply (36), treatment and disposal of hazardous waste (38.12), construction of utility projects (42.2), land transport and transport via pipelines (49), water transport (50), air transport (51), programming and broadcasting activities (60), telecommunications (61), and financial services and insurance, except auxiliary activities (64 and 65), public administration and defence (84).

Using our dataset, we can calculate the share of investment and the number of affiliates in such sectors, comparing the results for foreign affiliates of private firms and SOEs. Table 4.1 reports such estimates for the year 2008.

Looking at the number of affiliates, state-owned affiliates tend to have a larger presence in sensitive industries. The share of public affiliates in strategic sectors comes close to 20 per cent as opposed to 9 per cent for private affiliates. When calculating the share of the capital stock in such sectors, there is also a clear bias towards SOEs: 47.4 per cent of state-owned capital is in the industries identified as sensitive, as compared to 35.6 per cent for private firms.

This is a fairly intuitive result, as SOEs (the parent companies) were historically more concentrated in sectors of public utilities and strategic

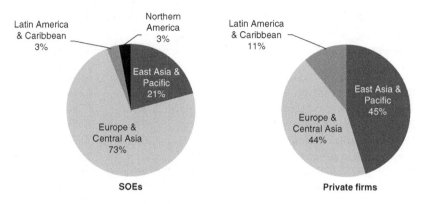

Figure 4.1. Distribution of affiliates by region: SOEs versus private firms (2008)
Source: Calculations by the authors, OECD-Orbis database.

manufacturing activities. Exclusive rights were given to SOEs in the context of regulation to achieve specific social, economic and strategic goals. Nevertheless, the concern regarding SOEs targeting more sensitive sectors takes on a different dimension when it comes to foreign expansion. And the concern is supported by the data. Another striking result from Table 4.1 is that overall there is more public capital than private capital in foreign affiliates belonging to strategic industries.[31]

Beyond differences in terms of industries, there are also contrasting investment patterns between SOEs and private companies in terms of geographical regions (Figure 4.1) and the income group of host economies (Figure 4.2). By region, the investments of SOEs tend to be concentrated in Europe and Central Asia (73 per cent), while private firms invest as much in Europe and Central Asia (44 per cent) as in the East Asia and Pacific region (45 per cent). Bearing in mind the list of countries represented in the dataset (mostly European countries with the exception of Australia, Brazil, China, Japan, South Korea and Mexico), this means that SOEs invest more in neighbouring countries than their private counterparts. New emerging markets also seem to be more attractive to private firms.[32]

---

[31] One should, however, keep in mind that we work with a sample of affiliates that may not be representative of the overall population of foreign affiliates. The bias could be in our data.

[32] A characteristic of the dataset is that little information is available on US firms; this is why Northern America has a small share of affiliates in Figure 4.1. Regions such as the Middle East and North Africa, South Asia and sub-Saharan Africa have negligible shares. Once again, the results reflect the population of firms in the dataset. Figure 4.1 is useful

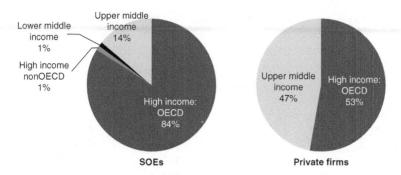

Figure 4.2. Distribution of affiliates by income group: SOEs versus private firms (2008)
Source: Calculations by the authors, OECD-Orbis database.

By income group,[33] the same differences can be identified. SOEs have a noticeably higher number of affiliates in high-income OECD countries and a lower number in upper-middle income countries (a group where the main economy is China). The share of investment between upper-middle income and high-income economies is more balanced in the case of private firms. While, generally speaking, the bulk of FDI is in high-income and upper-middle income economies, the same caveat applies to Figure 4.2; the distribution corresponds to the companies for which we have information on ownership and is not representative of all companies.

II.   How do affiliates of SOEs perform relative to affiliates of private firms?

The second concern regarding outward investment of SOEs is about the performance of their affiliates. Different variables can be studied to assess the respective performance of public and private enterprises. Using firm-level data, we can rely on the financial information we have for each firm and test persistent differences in terms of the following variables: employment, turnover, labour costs, capital stock, total factor productivity (level and growth), export turnover, export intensity, credit leverage and credit flexibility.

to compare SOEs and private firms but should not be taken as an indication of world FDI patterns.
[33] We use the World Bank classification, available at: http://data.worldbank.org/about/country-classifications/country-and-lending-groups.

Table 4.2. *Results of the econometric analysis: 'public premia'*

	No fixed effects	Year, country and industry fixed effects	Fixed effects and log of employment
Employment	1.420***	0.321***	–
Turnover	3.041***	0.615***	0.327***
Labour costs	1.764***	0.503***	0.190***
Capital stock	2.970***	0.602***	0.256***
Productivity (total factor productivity)	0.403***	0.152***	0.070***
Productivity growth	−0.006	−0.026	0.013
Export turnover	1.805***	0.320***	0.086*
Export intensity	0.731***	0	−0.013
Credit leverage	−0.080***	−0.118***	−0.126***
Credit flexibility	0.067***	0.216***	0.187***
Specification	No fixed effects	Year, country and industry fixed effects	Fixed effects and log of employment

Note: The coefficients are obtained through ordinary least square regressions with robust standard errors where the log of the variable in the first column is regressed on an SOE dummy variable. Fixed effects (years, countries and industries) are added in the second specification and the log of employment (controlling for size) in the third specification. * Significant at 10 per cent; ** at 5 per cent; *** at 1 per cent.

Table 4.2 summarises the results of the econometric analysis. Following an approach similar to Bernard *et al.*,[34] the comparison between SOEs and private firms is obtained through regressions on the log of each aggregate where the independent variable is a dummy variable that takes the value of 1 when the firm is state-owned. We add fixed effects for years, countries and industries to control for unobserved variables and, in the last specification, we add the log of employment as an independent variable to control for the size of firms. As SOEs are generally bigger, we thereby control

[34] A. Bernard, J. B. Jensen, S. J. Redding and P. K. Schott, 'Firms in international trade', *Journal of Economic Perspectives* 21(3) (2007), 105–30. The authors use these types of regressions to estimate the exporter premia in different dimensions of performance.

signed by Arab countries,[19] as well as the regional investment agreements of the Arab[20] and South-East Asian countries.[21] Yet even in the absence of such specification, sovereign investors would nevertheless tend to be covered if established under the laws of the home state[22] or if they have a seat and/or substantial business operations there,[23] which they tend to do.[24]

The analysis becomes more difficult when it comes to the International Centre for Settlement of Investment Disputes (ICSID), the most popular forum for the adjudication of investment treaty disputes. For whereas public investments were covered in the commentary to the preliminary draft of the ICSID Convention,[25] they are not mentioned anywhere in the ICSID Convention or the associated report by the Executive Directors of the International Bank for Reconstruction and Development (IBRD), which instead repeatedly speaks of *private* foreign investments.[26] So keeping in mind that the ICSID Convention is clearly *not* intended to facilitate the settlement of state-to-state disputes, Hirsch argues that only investors whose governance and activities are predominantly private should be allowed recourse to ICSID arbitration, and in borderline cases tribunals should adopt a narrow interpretation and deny jurisdiction.[27] Taking this view, SWFs or SOEs that are directly managed and/or supervised

[19] See e.g. Saudi Arabia–Austria BIT (2001), Article 3(b)(iii); Qatar–Switzerland BIT (2001), Article 1(1)(c); Kuwait–Finland BIT (1996), Article 1(iii)(b); United Arab Emirates–France BIT (1991), Article 1(2).

[20] Unified Agreement for the Investment of Arab Capital in the Arab States (1980), Amman, 26 November 1980, in force 7 September 1981, Article 1(4), available at: http://unctad.org/Sections/dite/iia/docs/compendium/en/36%20volume%202.pdf.

[21] The Association of Southeast Asian Nations (ASEAN) Comprehensive Investment Agreement, Cham-am, 26 February 2009, Article 4(e), available at: www.aseansec.org/22244.htm.

[22] E.g. Energy Charter Treaty, signed 17 December 1994, in force 16 April 1998, Article 7(2).

[23] E.g. Colombian Model BIT (2007), Article 1(1)(b).

[24] This was also the perception of several delegations, when the issue of investing state enterprises came up in the context of the negotiations over the Multilateral Agreement on Investment (MAI). See Negotiating Group on the Multilateral Agreement on Investment, 'Report to the Negotiating Group', DAFFE/MAI/DG3(96)3, 6 (1996). See also UNCTAD, *The Protection of National Security in IIAs* (Geneva: United Nations, 2009), pp. 43–4. See generally Annacker, 'Protection and admission of sovereign investment'.

[25] International Bank for Reconstruction and Development (IBRD), *History of the ICSID Convention*, 4 vols. (Washington DC: World Bank, 1970), vol. II, p. 230.

[26] W. B. Hamida, 'Sovereign FDI and international investment agreements: questions relating to the qualification of sovereign entities and the admission of their investments under investment agreements', *The Law and Practise of International Courts and Tribunals* 9 (2010), 24–5.

[27] M. Hirsch, *The Arbitration Mechanism of the International Centre for the Settlement of Investment Disputes* (The Hague: Martinus Nijhoff, 1993), pp. 64–6.

primarily by national politicians rather than external managers, for instance, might not qualify as 'a national of another contracting party' under the ICSID Convention.[28]

Yet, there have been numerous investment treaty claims pursuant to ICSID rules with state-owned or controlled companies as claimants.[29] For the most part, respondent states did not object to a public investor having access to investor–state arbitration and tribunals did not seriously address the question[30] – even though several of the claimants were arguably government agents and/or conducted essential government functions.[31] Thus far, it was only in the *CSOB* case that an ICSID tribunal had to address the matter of public investments in some detail.[32] Here, a state-owned bank was found to be a 'national' for the purpose of the ICSID Convention, as it had taken steps to act as an independent private entity and its activities were essentially commercial in nature.[33] According to the tribunal, it was thereby the function and nature of investment activities that determined the private–public distinction rather than the ownership and purpose of the entity. This conclusion relied, in part, on the widely accepted view of Aron Broches, who argued that:

> for purposes of the Convention a mixed economy company or government-owned corporation should not be disqualified as a 'national of another Contracting State' unless it is acting as an agent for the government or is discharging an essentially governmental function.[34]

---

[28] Convention on the Settlement of Investment Disputes Between States and Nationals of Other States (ICSID Convention), Washington, 18 March 1965, in force 14 October 1966, Article 25(1), available at: http://icsid.worldbank.org/ICSID/ICSID/RulesMain.jsp. On the governance structures of SWFs, see JPMorgan, 'Sovereign Wealth Funds'.

[29] See Annacker, 'Protection and admission of sovereign investment', 552–3.

[30] For an exception, where a controlling state-owned entity was not considered to be the actual party to the dispute, see *Rumeli Telekom A.S. and Telsim Mobil TelekomikasyonHizmetleri A.S.* v. *Republic of Kazakhstan* (Award), ICSID Case No. ARB/05/16, 29 July 2008. We know of one instance where a SWF has contemplated filing an investment arbitration claim: 'Temasek Loses Final Appeal against Indonesian Antitrust Law Breach Ruling', *Bloomberg*, 24 May 2010.

[31] Feldman, 'The Standing of State-Owned Entities'.

[32] *Ceskoslovenska Obchodni Banka (CSOB)* v. *The Slovak Republic* (Award), ICSID Case No. ARB/97/4, 24 May 1999. See Hamida, 'Sovereign FDI and international investment agreements'.

[33] ICSID Convention, paras. 20–21.

[34] A. Broches, 'The Convention on the Settlement of Investment Disputes between States and Nationals of Other States' in *Collected Courses of The Hague Academy of International Law*, Part II, 136 (1972), pp. 334–5. See also C. Schreuer, *The ICSID Convention: A Commentary* (Cambridge University Press, 2009), pp. 160–1.

While this test was probably not met in earlier cases involving state-owned entities (see above), the tribunal found it was in the case of *CSOB*. Whether this outcome was appropriate even under the 'Broches test' is disputed,[35] but practitioners seem comfortable with an expansive interpretation of the ICSID Convention to allow a wide range of sovereign investors as potential claimants.[36]

If future tribunals agree that this does not undermine the essential purpose of the ICSID to resolve disputes between *private* investors and host states, this will be an important development in the regulation of the internationalisation of state capitalism: a great number of SWFs and SOEs will thereby have recourse to treaty-based arbitration if they are met with restrictive measures violating obligations, such as non-discrimination, fair and equitable treatment, and expropriation without compensation. Moreover, while the majority of BITs only cover the post-establishment phase, an increasing number of states are following the practice of the USA and Canada in including comprehensive entry and establishment provisions. Although these are subject to specific exceptions, this is important as the bulk of regulatory measures targeted at sovereign investors in recent years have related to market access (see below).

C.   Sovereign investors and investment treaty obligations

If SWFs or SOEs are allowed to file investment treaty arbitrations, the often vaguely drafted investment treaties will give arbitrators considerable flexibility in determining which measures host states can take to respond to the globalisation of state capitalism. This is important, particularly with the few options for appeal enshrined in the system. As already noted by Jan Paulsson in the mid 1990s:

> [a]rbitration without privity is a delicate mechanism. A single incident of an adventurist arbitrator going beyond the proper scope of his jurisdiction in a sensitive case may be sufficient to generate a backlash.[37]

Surely it is difficult to think of more sensitive questions than those that could – and probably will – arise in the coming years involving sovereign

---

[35] Feldman, 'The Standing of State-Owned Entities'.

[36] E.g. M. Burgstaller, 'SWFS and International Investment Law' in C. Brown and K. Miles (eds.), *Evolution in Investment Treaty Law and Arbitration* (Cambridge University Press, 2011).

[37] J. Paulsson, 'Arbitration without privity', *ICSID Review – Foreign Investment Law Journal* 10 (1995), 257.

investors. And while the most effective response would be the development of a prudent jurisprudence on these questions,[38] governments would also be well advised to consider what measures they could take to ensure that sensible domestic regulation of SWFs and SOEs is not undermined by one or more 'adventurist' arbitrators.

I.   The adjudication of investment disputes involving sovereign investors

I begin with the most fundamental question, namely whether – and to what extent – sovereign investors should in fact be allowed access to treaty-based investor–state arbitration in the first place. Although the ICSID Convention may potentially permit it in many circumstances, host states may not necessarily be comfortable with allowing sovereign investors to sidetrack domestic courts in case of disputes. Some may find it difficult to see a dispute between a European government and the China Investment Corporation, for instance, as anything but a state-to-state affair. And if disputes are ultimately perceived to be between governments themselves, then surely the 'de-politicisation' (allegedly) offered by investor–state arbitration would largely be a myth.

Accordingly, host governments could consider whether sovereign entities should only be allowed to adjudicate investment treaty claims through diplomatic espousal. Such an approach would acknowledge that while the public–private distinction can be hard to draw on occasion, investor–state arbitration is not a suitable arena for what is perceived to be diplomatic disputes. An alternative option could be to allow sovereign investors access to investor–state arbitration, but only after both the home and state have given their specific consent. Inspiration here can be found in the US–Australia free trade agreement (FTA), where the two governments must agree whether an investor should be allowed to file a treaty claim.[39] For governments hesitant about giving SOEs and SWFs the same recourse to international arbitration as private investors, such an approach could be targeted at sovereign investors in particular. This would not bar SOEs and SWFs from filing investment treaty claims, yet it would be an effective barrier to sensitive claims, most of which would be left up to diplomatic negotiations or state-to-state arbitration. Finally,

---

[38] Feldman, 'The Standing of State-Owned Entities'.

[39] US–Australia Free Trade Agreement (FTA) (2004), Article 11.6, available at: www.ustr. gov/trade-agreements/free-trade-agreements/australian-fta.

treaty-drafters could specify, as indeed some investment treaties do, that in order to qualify as an investment, it has to be acquired for the purpose of economic benefits or other business purposes – that is excluding investments not made with a profit motive.[40] When it comes to SWFs, this would complement the encouragement of commercially based investment decisions in the Santiago Principles.[41]

Even if governments are generally comfortable giving sovereign investors an open door to pursue investor–state arbitration, they still need to consider whether this may require adjustments of substantive treaty protections. Recent regulatory measures concerning sovereign investors can be grouped according to three sets of concerns: security, corporate governance and home state subsidies. Below, I review each in relation to existing investment treaty disciplines.

II. Security

Some investment treaties include carve-outs for security measures. Germany's Model BIT of 2008, for instance, excludes measures taken for 'reasons of public security and order' from the national and most-favoured nation (MFN) treatment clause,[42] and the Model BITs of countries like India,[43] the USA[44] and Canada[45] include carve-outs for 'essential' security interests. Finally, a number of treaties, such as certain Russian and Mexican BITs, mention 'national' security interests.[46] Yet, since security interests typically remain undefined in investment treaties,[47] such exceptions raise questions as to what exactly essential, national or public security interests mean in practice, and which measures are necessary to protect them. Also, is it the tribunal or the adopting state which decides whether restrictive measures are in fact taken against legitimate security concerns or instead simply an example of 'hidden protectionism'?

The answer to these questions will vary depending on the treaty texts. Here one can think of a continuum.[48] At the far end of the spectrum there

---

[40] E.g. Canada–South Africa BIT, 1995, Article I(f) and I(g).
[41] IWG of SWFs, 'SWFs – Santiago Principles'; Feldman, 'The Standing of State-Owned Entities', pp. 631–4.
[42] Germany model BIT, 2009, Article 3.
[43] India model BIT, 2003, Article 12(2).
[44] US model BIT, 2004, Article 18.
[45] Canada model BIT, 2004, Article 10(4)(a) and (b).
[46] E.g. Russia–Hungary BIT, 1995, Article 2(3); Netherlands–Mexico BIT, 1998, Article 12.
[47] For an exception, see e.g. Canada–Peru BIT, 2006, Article 10(4).
[48] For a more detailed account, see UNCTAD, *The Protection of National Security in IIAs*.

is an investment treaty like the one between India and Singapore, for instance, which provides that 'any decision' taken on security grounds 'shall be non-justiciable' and the merits of such a decision are thereby not open for review by 'any arbitral tribunal'.[49] Arguably, this entirely insulates the contracting parties from arbitration claims concerning measures taken for their subjective understanding of security concerns – even if such measures were taken in bad faith.[50]

A slightly less far-reaching security carve-out is found in several BITs of the USA and Canada. While also self-judging as to what the adopting parties consider 'essential' security interests and what is 'necessary' to protect them, such carve-outs are still open to arbitral review as to whether measures have in fact been taken in good faith. So although the self-judging nature still leaves adopting states with considerable discretion, clear examples of outright protectionism are likely to result in compensation awards.

Many investment treaties with security exceptions, however, do not stipulate that they are self-judging, which leaves tribunals with greater scope to review the necessity of the measures in question. When faced with a claim, host states would therefore have to convince arbitrators that the activities of a sovereign investor were in fact a threat to security interests. This is bound to be a challenge. For while regulatory measures targeted at defence industries would often be straightforward, do concerns about financial instability also qualify as 'essential' security interests for instance? Similarly, would tribunals necessarily accept that the security exception covers measures concerning sensitive technologies in non-defence sectors, such as telecommunications or natural resources?[51] These questions are relevant for a country like the USA, since the security exceptions in several older US BITs are not explicitly self-judging.[52] Accordingly, some tribunals may find that elements of the 2007 Foreign Investment and National Security Act (FINSA) violate investment treaty

---

[49] India–Singapore Comprehensive Economic Cooperation Agreement (CECA), 2006, Article 6.12(4).

[50] A. Newcombe and L. Paradell, *Law and Practise of Investment Treaties: Standards of Treatment* (Aalpen aan den Rijn: Kluwer, 2009), p. 495.

[51] Some guidance may be found here in the Argentina cases, where economic emergencies were considered part of a country's security interests, see e.g. *LG&E v. Argentina* (Decision on Liability), ICSID Case No. ARB/02/1, 3 October 2006, para. 238.

[52] In the Argentina cases, this was subject to considerable discussion as there were some indications that the US State Department found the security exception in the US–Argentina BIT to be self-judging despite express treaty language to that effect. See e.g. A.-M. Slaughter and W. B. White, Rejoinder Opinion, 4 March 2007.

obligations by establishing excessively wide and discretionary powers of the executive in blocking *all* investments controlled by foreign governments.[53]

Finally, it is important to remember that the vast majority of BITs do *not* include security exceptions – including several signed by states with large SWFs and SOEs.[54] Here, the party adopting restrictions is left with the doctrine of necessity under customary international law, which only in the rarest of circumstances would cover regulations targeted at investments made by sovereign investors.

To sum up, particularly where security exceptions are not explicitly self-judging, or where no such exceptions exist, governments would have difficulties in making security defences for general regulatory measures targeted at sovereign investors. Investment treaty negotiators from countries with existing, or expected, regulation of sovereign investors based on security concerns should therefore consider insisting on some form of security exception in their investment treaties. Those hesitant about giving too much discretion to arbitrators to consider the legality of such measures can follow recent practice of the USA and Canada in making the clauses self-judging, perhaps with a specification that measures cannot be a disguised restriction on investment flows.[55] Alternatively, they could go further and entirely bar claims concerning regulatory measures taken for security reasons. Naturally, this latter option entails some risks of hidden protectionism, yet it does provide governments with an 'escape clause' from investment treaty disciplines, which could be politically useful if exceptionally sensitive cases have the potential to undermine the support for investment treaties as a governing institution.

III. Corporate governance

A second concern often raised about sovereign investors relates to their corporate governance. As already mentioned, state entities can have

---

[53] The Foreign Investment and National Security Act (FINSA) of 2007, Section 721(f)(8). Note that to the extent that specific provisions for investments in services and financial services are included, these could be important as well. See generally L. Hsu, 'SWFs, recent US legislative changes, and treaty obligations', *Journal of World Trade* 43 (2009), 451–77.

[54] E.g. United Arab Emirates BITs with Austria (2001) and the UK (1992), and Kuwaiti BITs with Finland (1996) and Denmark (2001).

[55] See e.g. Framework Agreement on the ASEAN Investment Area, Maketi, 7 October 1998, in force 25 May 1999, Article 13, available at: www.aseansec.org/6466.htm.

non-commercial motives for their investment activities abroad, and their structure and investment strategies tend to be non-transparent compared to many other foreign investors. To address these concerns, host states may want to impose obligations on sovereign investors in their domestic investment laws and regulations, for instance in terms of certain transparency requirements.

This would not necessarily conflict with investment treaty obligations. For apart from adhering to the laws and regulations of their host state,[56] sovereign investors may have an obligation under the 'legitimate expectations' doctrine to foresee certain regulatory changes targeted at their activities. In the *Methanex* case, for instance, the tribunal argued that the company had invested in the USA knowing that compounds posing risks to health and the environment were under constant scrutiny by authorities and thus likely to be restricted or prohibited.[57] A similar argument could be made that given the political climate in a number of Western countries, some regulatory changes concerning governance standards should be part of the legitimate expectations of sovereign investors.

Second, when it comes to allegations of non-commercial motives, the obligation to act in good faith implies that sovereign investors may be precluded from investment treaty protection if they misrepresent or conceal their nature or purpose.[58] In other words, if the worst fears of some commentators come true and an investor is used by a foreign government as a 'Trojan Horse' to destabilise the financial system of a host state, for instance, investment treaties would not protect the investor against host state interference.

In practice, however, it is difficult for host state regulators to determine the motives of sovereign investors. Also, restrictions based on vague notions of non-commercial motives could potentially conflict with standards of equity, particularly if investment treaties do not specify that investments have to be for-profit (see above). Sovereign investors could

---

[56] A number of BITs only protect investments made in accordance with national laws and regulations, including those on corporate governance, and some tribunals have asserted that this obligation exists irrespective of specific treaty provisions to that effect, e.g. *Phoenix Action Ltd* v. *Czech Republic* (Award), ICSID Case No. ARB/06/5, 15 April 2009, para. 101.

[57] *Methanex* v. *United States* (Final Award on Jurisdiction and Merits of the NAFTA Tribunal under United Nations Commission on International Trade Law (UNCITRAL) Arbitration Rules), 3 August 2005, part IV, Chapter D, p. 5, para. 10.

[58] See e.g. *Azinian* v. *Mexico* (Award), ICSID Case No. ARB(AF)/97/2, 1 November 1999.

argue – in some cases convincingly – that a range of other investors have motives other than profit when investing abroad.[59] The movement towards 'sustainable' foreign investments among pension funds, for instance, is also based on political and social rather than purely commercial considerations, yet they are not targeted by regulators.

Similarly, regulators require some disclosure of governance structure and investment plans in order to assess the motives of sovereign investors, and if not treated carefully such requirements could also conflict with investment treaty obligations. For while some tribunals have found that investors have a duty to cooperate and provide information to financial authorities,[60] others have argued that it cannot be expected as part of investors' good faith obligations to disclose long-term plans with investment projects. One tribunal stated that:

> [i]t is both unreasonable and unrealistic to posit an obligation upon an investor to disclose its ultimate objectives in making a particular investment, whether through the purchase of shares or otherwise. Ultimate objectives will ... often be highly speculative and not susceptible to precise articulation, and will be subject to change over time.[61]

Host states therefore need reasonable arguments if they wish to target sovereign investors with specific transparency requirements. SWFs and SOEs are not the only institutional investors with opaque governance structures and strategies, so if hedge funds or private equity investors are not subject to similar disclosure requirements, questions again arise about the fairness of targeting sovereign investors in particular. As noted by Rozanov:

> hedge funds are the ultimate money-making machines: seeking maximum return with minimum risk, preferably within the shortest possible time horizon. If these institutions find it advantageous to operate with minimum levels of transparency and public disclosure, then surely they do it for no other reason than to maximize profits and protect their economic interests.[62]

Also, poor records of accountability and transparency may have more to do with the corporate culture of the home state than whether or not

---

[59] A. Rozanov, 'Definitional challenges of dealing with sovereign wealth funds', *Asian Journal of International Law* 1 (2011), 249–65 at 262.

[60] See e.g. *Genin* v. *Estonia* (Award), ICSID Case No. ARB/99/2, 25 June 2001.

[61] *Saluka* v. *Czech Republic* (UNCITRAL Arbitration Partial Award), 17 March 2006, para. 232.

[62] Rozanov, 'Definitional challenges', 259.

investors are publicly controlled. This too implies that if lawmakers are not careful, national laws and regulations with specific transparency requirements for sovereign investors could come under serious scrutiny by investment arbitral tribunals for being arbitrary and/or discriminatory.

Treaty drafters could therefore consider taking steps to ensure that legitimate concerns about the corporate governance standards of sovereign investors are not undermined by arbitral tribunals. Again, the likelihood that this will happen may be small, but, given the political stakes involved, host states may not be willing to delegate too much flexibility to arbitrators to determine what is legitimate regulation of sovereign investors, and what is not.

Here, inspiration can be found from the draft model BITs of Norway and the International Institute for Sustainable Development (IISD), both of which make references to the Organisation for Economic Co-operation and Development (OECD) Guidelines for Multinational Corporations.[63] Section III of the Guidelines is particularly relevant in this context as it refers to the obligation of companies to disclose information on matters such as ownership and voting rights, intra-group relations, governance policies and enterprise objectives.[64] This, of course, would establish obligations on all foreign investors – private as well as public.

An alternative option would be explicitly to target sovereign investors by making reference to the OECD's Guidelines for Corporate Governance of SOEs[65] as well as the Santiago Principles on the structure and management of SWFs.[66] Although this has never been done before, as far as I am aware, it would further ensure that the rights granted to sovereign investors under international investment treaties are coupled with a set of obligations that have received widespread support.

Direct references to these sets of principles could make a difference in the case of investment treaty disputes. For even if the obligations only have the character of 'best efforts' – which may be necessary given their occasional ambiguity – it would send a clear signal that regulation based

---

[63] Norway draft Model BIT, preamble and Article 32; IISD Model BIT, Article 16.
[64] OECD, *OECD Guidelines for Multinational Corporations* (Paris: OECD, 2011), section III, available at: www.oecd.org/dataoecd/43/29/48004323.pdf.
[65] OECD, *Guidelines on Corporate Governance of State-Owned Enterprises* (2005).
[66] IWG of SWFs, *SWFs – Santiago Principles*, n. 8. For an assessment of the Santiago Principles, see E. Truman, 'Making the World Safe for Sovereign Wealth Funds', Peterson Institute for International Economics, 14 October 2008.

on internationally recognised standards on corporate governance should be part of the 'legitimate expectations' of sovereign investors.[67]

IV. Subsidies

Finally, the rise of sovereign investors has raised concerns about home state 'M&A' subsidies. As a starting point, it is worth recalling that, as a matter of general international law, states have the right to regulate the admission of foreign investors into their jurisdiction. Accordingly, if they wish to subject acquisitions by sovereign investors to greater scrutiny due to concerns about home state subsidies, or to block such acquisitions entirely, they are free to do so. However, particularly when investment treaties extend non-discrimination to the pre-entry stage, such measures could become subject to arbitration claims.

Most investment treaties stipulate that investments shall be promoted between the parties, but do not subject regulations and laws concerning entry and establishment to treatment and protection disciplines. So while recent decisions have been somewhat unclear as to whether investment *promotion* clauses in such treaties may in fact be enforceable,[68] it is questionable that blocking foreign acquisitions based on allegations of unfair 'M&A' subsidies by the home state could constitute violations under 'standard' BITs inspired by European models.

Yet more and more countries have followed North American practice in including legally binding liberalisation provisions in their investment treaties, particularly when they form part of broader economic integration agreements. Limitations on national and MFN treatment disciplines for the 'pre-establishment' stage are typically based on a 'negative' list approach. One such limitation tends to be subsidies and grants, which are exempt from establishment and post-establishment treatment provisions in several of the US and Canadian BITs, for instance.[69] But while this carve-out is included to prevent foreign investors from filing claims questioning various forms of financial assistance by the host state, it most

---

[67] Note that the OECD principles also overlap with principles on subsidies, as discussed below. See generally OECD, *SOEs Operating Abroad: An Application of the OECD Guidelines on Corporate Governance of State-Owned Enterprises to the Cross-border Operations of SOEs* (Paris: OECD, 2010).

[68] J. Hepburn, 'Arbitrators view treaty's "investment promotion" clause as an enforceable legal obligation, but Cuba not liable for breach in relation to treatment of health tourism venture', *IAReporter*, 4 July, 2011.

[69] E.g. Uruguay–US BIT, 2005, Article 14(5); Peru–Canada BIT, 2006, Article 9(5).

likely works both ways: if host states are allowed to distort competition by subsidising domestic investors, it is difficult to see why home states should not be allowed to subsidise their investors for going abroad. The conclusion of the tribunal in *Saluka* is worth keeping in mind:

> Financial assistance is a tool used by States to implement their commercial policies. Even though it tends to distort competition and to undermine the level playing field for competitors, States cannot be said to be generally bound by international law to refrain from using such a tool.[70]

While these comments addressed whether the fair and equitable treatment standard prohibited state aid (which it did not according to the tribunal), they imply that 'M&A' subsidies are not illegal under investment law except if explicitly stated in treaty provisions. Attempts to block acquisitions by foreign investors due to concerns about home state subsidies could therefore potentially violate liberalisation provisions in investment treaties. Accordingly, investment treaty negotiators could consider whether it is time to incorporate treaty language explicitly addressing the possibility of penalising unfair investment subsidies.

As this will be new territory for the investment treaty regime, governments would be well advised to tread carefully. One option is to follow the prudent set of principles suggested by Hufbauer and his collaborators.[71] The first is that in the interest of transparency, foreign investors should disclose all subsidies received three years before the takeover bid. Among these, subsidies can only be 'actionable' if they (i) have involved capital provided below market terms; (ii) sum up to 5 per cent or more of the acquisition, and (iii) a bona fide rival has been involved in the bidding. Finally, since analyses of whether the subsidies actually had an impact on a specific bid are likely to take months, a per se approach is favoured where the mere existence of the subsidy is what is relevant rather than its (alleged) effect on the market.[72]

---

[70] *Saluka Investments BV* v. *Czech Republic* (Permanent Court of Arbitration (PCA) Partial Award under UNCITRAL Arbitration Rules), 2006, para. 445.

[71] Hufbauer *et al.*, 'Investment Subsidies for Cross-Border M&A'.

[72] Note that a similar approach is taken in the WTO with respect to export subsidies. Following these rules, disciplines on investment subsidies could also potentially be narrowed down further by specifying that M&As cannot be blocked based on subsidy concerns, if the subsidies were not contingent on foreign acquisitions in law or in fact (cf. provision on export subsidies in the WTO Agreement on Subsidies and Countervailing Measures, Article 3). Naturally, if the firm fails to disclose sufficient information to rule out this possibility, then this should be taken into account by tribunals when considering the legality of a blocked acquisition.

This would imply that when a private investor makes a bona fide bid for an acquisition, the host state is free to block competing bids from SOEs, SWFs or investors with significant subsidies (i.e. 5 per cent of the acquisition or more). The host state is not allowed, however, to block bids from investors with non-significant subsidies, nor is it allowed to block bids from subsidised or sovereign investors if they have no bona fide rivals (subject to security or sector-specific exceptions). These principles could potentially be included in investment treaties with liberalisation provisions, either as a side agreement or as part of reservation schedules.

D. Conclusion

Since 2000 Western states have attempted to strike a balance between open investment regimes and prudent regulation of sovereign investors in the public interest. Now the question arises how to couple these efforts with legal obligations on the international plane. With multilateralism all but abandoned by most major industrial powers, investment treaties provide the most realistic platform for this purpose. The task is all the more pressing, as current investment treaty obligations have the potential to conflict with attempts to regulate sovereign investors.

The chances of such a conflict may be slim, provided governments avoid a protectionist backlash. Also, one should not exaggerate the propensity of sovereign investors to file investment treaty claims, as their leaders in China, the United Arab Emirates and Saudi Arabia, for example, would thereby risk further political opposition to their acquisitions abroad. However, governments, which otherwise support investment treaty arbitration as an adjudicative system, should recall that even a single controversial case could aggravate the growing political backlash against the investment treaty regime in some corners of the world – or even foreign investments in general. And in recent years the rise of sovereign investors have been one of the most politicised and sensitive developments in the international investment regime.

Host states may therefore want to consider whether it is a welcome development that arbitrators seem so keen on expanding the jurisdictional scope of investment treaty arbitration to cover sovereign investment activities.[73] Given the politics involved, how much flexibility should arbitrators have in determining what is legitimate regulation of the (re-)

---

[73] Feldman, 'The Standing of State-Owned Entities'.

emergence of state capitalism and what is not? This is likely to become a key question in future investment treaty negotiations. For instance, if ongoing talks with China pursued by both the USA and the European Union result in actual negotiations, they could provide a useful starting point to establish 'hard' legal disciplines for the international governance of sovereign investors. Renegotiations, or reinterpretations,[74] of existing investment treaty obligations could be another important avenue for exploration.

The irony is obvious. Current investment treaty standards have their roots in the colonial era, where Western sovereign – or quasi-sovereign – trading companies were heavily involved in establishing international legal standards to protect their investments abroad.[75] Today the tables are turning and Western countries may have to adjust some of these standards when playing host to sovereign investors from the developing world.

---

[74] On the much-overlooked role of investment treaty interpretation by state parties, see A. Roberts, 'Power and persuasion in investment treaty interpretation: the dual role of states', *American Journal of International Law* 104 (2010), 179–225.

[75] A. Anghie, *Imperialism, Sovereignty, and the Making of International Law* (Cambridge University Press, 2005).

6

Reflections on the current paradigms of international investment activity

GARY CLYDE HUFBAUER

A. Introduction

The contributions by Moran, Poulsen and Miroudot and Ragoussis in this volume represent the frontier of economic research on international investment. They also provide a springboard for future research. The purpose of this short note is to summarise the main points of these chapters and suggest themes for further work.

B. Foreign direct investment and development: novel challenges

In his chapter, Moran contends that researchers should classify foreign direct investment (FDI) into at least four different categories, and that one category – FDI in manufacturing – could be further subdivided into low-skilled activities and medium-skilled and high-skilled activities. 'Benchmark' studies that lump all FDI together do not, in Moran's view, accurately estimate its impact on growth and productivity and do not lead to appropriate recommendations for host country policies.

It is unclear whether further econometric analysis will challenge or validate Moran's taxonomy. Future research should address whether control variables to distinguish different categories of FDI can detect a meaningful difference in the impact of FDI on key economic variables, such as growth and productivity. As a competing taxonomy, perhaps control variables that distinguish between host countries could better explain differences in the growth and productivity outcomes associated with FDI rather than the industry character of the FDI.

Moran's policy recommendations vary for each of the four different categories of FDI. Some of these recommendations are very tasty, others need spice and some cause indigestion.

I.   Extractive industries: corruption

The recommendation for company-by-company transparency is very tasty as it stands. Adding a 'whistle-blower reward' would add spice. The reward should be paid by the offending company, in an amount equal to the corrupt payment. The award should be paid to any person (or persons) who could demonstrate to a specially constituted tribunal, by clear and convincing evidence, that a corrupt payment had been made. I am troubled by the suggestion that an arbitration tribunal can nullify a company's treaty rights based on mere evidence of a corrupt payment. In my view, the criminal threshold of 'beyond a reasonable doubt' should be required. If a lower evidentiary standard becomes the norm, some countries might 'salt' their investment contracts with questionable side payments (e.g. to specially recommended lawyers, engineers or consultants) so that, at a later date, treaty rights can be nullified.

II.   Infrastructure FDI: take-or-pay and foreign exchange clauses

In the 1990s some Latin American and Asian countries were clearly over-optimistic in their demand projections for electricity and other infra-structure, and over-confident in their currency pegs. They entered into contracts that could not be fulfilled after the Asian crisis, but were, in some cases, subject to bilateral investment treaty (BIT) arbitration or Overseas Private Investment Corporation (OPIC)-style insurance. Moran's recommendation that future infrastructure contracts should be wary of these clauses is reasonable. However, the suggestion that existing clauses should be voided by arbitrators or insurers is troubling. A key feature of invest-ment contracts is to assign risk between parties. Commercial certainty requires that the losing party must be obliged to pay up.

III.   Using FDI to diversify and upgrade exports

Moran's recommendations to upgrade manufacturing activity are sound. However, equal attention paid to services is missing. Manufactured exports will not be the path to prosperity for the next generation of emer-ging countries. Nor will manufactures be the source of huge employ-ment gains for workers leaving the rural sector. On the other hand, better services can be a gigantic source of productivity and employment. FDI in service sectors is the new and promising frontier for emerging countries.

IV. *Advice for corporate social responsibility advocates*

Moran's menu is sensible. However, it is unclear whether sensible recommendations meet the demands of corporate social responsibility (CSR) advocates – especially those who want to slice big chunks from the corporate body.

C. Investment treaties and the globalisation of state capitalism

In his chapter Poulsen provides a detailed and sophisticated appraisal of how state-owned enterprises (SOEs) and sovereign wealth funds (SWFs) fit within the existing legal regimes for FDI – regimes which were largely designed for private FDI. The opening question is whether investment provisions in BITs and free trade agreements (FTAs) even apply to SOEs and SWFs. If these provisions do apply, do the SOEs and SWFs have the same recourse to arbitration mechanisms as private firms?

The somewhat surprising answer to these questions is that, for the most part, SOEs and SWFs enjoy the same treaty and arbitration rights as private investors. When BITs were drafted and the International Centre for the Settlement of Investment Disputes (ICSID) was established, no one foresaw the rapid rise of SOEs and SWFs.

Security exceptions in existing legal regimes are an obvious feature which might be invoked more frequently against SOEs and SWFs than against private firms. Self-judgment of security decisions is written into some BITs, but not all. Corporate governance and subsidies are other trouble spots for SOEs and SWFs, but at best these subjects are lightly regulated by existing BITs and FTAs.

After examining the existing legal regimes, Poulsen considers how rules in the Western world might evolve in light of fast growth in the overseas investment activities of SOEs and SWFs – particularly enterprises based in emerging countries and oil states. Now that the wealth tables have turned, and more investment is flowing from emerging countries to the Organisation for Economic Co-operation and Development (OECD) nations, Poulsen suggests that governance and subsidy issues will receive more attention. He also suggests that new rules are more likely to be written in bilateral and regional agreements than in a multilateral framework.

I agree with Poulsen's assessment and suggestions. Two other areas of tension exist which require examination. First, in addition to explicit subsidies by way of equity and debt capital, SOEs often enjoy the implicit advantage of low home country corporate taxation. By contrast, large private corporations that compete with SOEs typically pay high corporate taxes. Some SOEs may fritter away their tax advantage by overstaffing or through obsolete technology, but others will be models of efficient enterprise. Unless tax burdens on large private corporations are significantly reduced – a hard political task when the United States, European Union (EU) and Japan are swamped by fiscal deficits – tax differences are likely to become a new source of tension.

Second, if Reinhart and Rogoff are correct,[1] and the USA and Europe face a decade of slow growth due to high fiscal deficits and huge public debt burdens, they are likely to court FDI more energetically, no matter the source. This is especially true of US states and EU Member States. Emerging countries and oil states may use this new eagerness to turn the tables in BIT and FTA negotiations. Emerging countries may attempt to negotiate language that limits asset freezes on security grounds, ensures compensation and narrows the 'policy space' of Western nations with respect to inward FDI.

D.   Actors in the international investment scenario

In their chapter, Miroudot and Ragoussis describe their large-scale database of SOEs, and how they carried out a comparative analysis between the foreign operations of SOEs and private firms, controlling for industry and country characteristics. This in itself is a major achievement. In addition, the authors uncover interesting results regarding the similarities and differences between the two populations.

Given the overlap between 'sensitive' industries and the fields of operation for British and French SOEs, their higher concentration in sensitive sectors abroad is not a big surprise. Differences in FDI destination, by region and host country income level, are not large.

From a host country standpoint, higher employment and higher labour costs of SOE affiliates abroad are desirable characteristics, especially in these difficult times. Lower export intensity is, however, an unfavourable feature.

The most interesting similarities between the two populations are the extent of leverage and the amount of interest paid as a percentage of debt. From a statistical standpoint, the SOEs have no advantage over private

---

[1] C. M. Reinhart and K. S. Rogoff, Peterson Institute for International Economics, 'A decade of debt policy', *Policy Analyses in International Economics* 95 (September 2011).

firms. This does not exclude individual instances of subsidised SOE activity, but the finding does suggest that subsidised credit is not widespread for SOEs based in Britain and France. Whether the same finding would characterise SOEs based in emerging countries such as Brazil, India and China remains to be determined.

With their database, the authors might be able to investigate two additional aspects: tax payments (corporate, payroll and value added tax (VAT), among others) and labour turnover. Furthermore, expanding the database used by Miroudot and Ragoussis would be a worthwhile project for the OECD. Enlisting cooperation from statistical authorities in additional countries – especially less advanced OECD members such as South Korea, Mexico and Turkey – would allow for more robust comparisons between SOEs and private firms. An even greater advance would be coverage of Brazil, India and China, although the difficulty of enlisting statistical cooperation from these countries may be formidable.

A useful addition to the text of future FTAs and BITs might be a requirement that the authorities collect company-level data of the sort gathered by the authors of this chapter, and make it available for statistical analysis. Far too little is known about the characteristics of corporate operations abroad, whether private firms or SOEs.

7

A Southern perspective on the existing investment landscape

STEPHEN GELB

This chapter focuses primarily on Moran's contribution, which proposes a new paradigm for foreign investors' behaviour and its impact on host economy development, although the issue of investors with significant state ownership focused on by Miroudot and Ragoussis and by Poulsen is also discussed.[1]

Moran's main point is that foreign investors should be distinguished by sector rather than analysed at the aggregate national level, given the very different impact on the host economy, and therefore distinct policy implications. He examines foreign direct investment (FDI) in three major sectors, disappointingly ignoring services. He argues that the growing presence of investors from emerging Asian economies in the extractive industries in other developing economies jeopardises improvements to governance in the latter. He argues, secondly, that the interpretation of 'political risk' in infrastructure projects, which includes the consequences of international economic crises, is too broad and places an excessive burden on host country governments while favouring foreign investors in disputes. And he argues that in relation to manufacturing, developing countries should focus their efforts on attracting FDI into high-skill more capital-intensive sub-sectors rather than low-skill 'sweatshop' assembly activities.

I fully agree with Moran that aggregate FDI flows and stocks tell us little about the content and causality of the impact of FDI, except in terms of macroeconomics and the balance of payments – the contribution of FDI flows to filling the savings and foreign exchange 'gaps' – where there is little distinction between direct and indirect investment inflows. In terms of growth and productivity improvements where foreign *direct* investment

---

[1] See chapters by Moran, Miroudot and Ragoussis, and Poulsen in this volume.

makes a difference – technology and skills enhancements, linkages with domestic firms in the host economy, provision of a wider range of goods and services than would otherwise be available in the host economy – aggregate FDI data tells us practically nothing. I share Moran's bemusement about economists who keep doing regressions using aggregate FDI data to make claims about FDI impact that simply do not stand up to scrutiny, given faulty data and often spurious causality. Demonstrations of growth and productivity impact of FDI require examination of *processes* rather than relying on statistical data that reflect *outcomes*.

While I go along with Moran in this critique, the question arises of whether more detailed firm-level data is available, especially in developing countries. Most often it is not, at least not at the fine-grained level needed. Miroudot's and Ragoussis' very useful regression analysis of investment by state-owned enterprises (SOEs), confirming the preconception about SOEs' focus on employment and output rather than profitability, shows the value of using firm-level data rather than national-level data. But the authors were able to obtain detailed data for only three large European countries, so their results do not really shed much light on the group of firms that evidently motivates their research, and that of Poulsen – SOEs from emerging market economies.

Moran is right to emphasise sectoral distinctions, though his point is an old one. But he asserts rather than justifies his position. I would argue that one, indeed *the*, major reason is that sectoral characteristics are fundamental determinants of foreign investors' ownership advantages and of host countries' location advantages, to use the terms of Dunning's Ownership–Location–Internalization (OLI) conceptual framework.[2] Ownership advantages reflect the sources of investors' economic rents and their strategies to increase appropriation of rents at the expense of competitors and rivals. Location advantages of the host economy are the features that attract specific groups of foreign investors, and enable the host government to ensure that the foreign entry results in some net benefit to the host country, that is, to ensure that the host economy obtains some share of the economic rent generated by the investment. Both sets of advantages vary according to sector, and together they shape the impact of FDI in the host economy.

Even though it overlaps in part with sectoral distinctions, a useful distinction can still be drawn between market-seeking and resource-seeking

---

[2] See J. Dunning and S. Lundan, *Multinational Enterprises and the Global Economy*, 2nd edn (Cheltenham: Edward Elgar, 2008).

motives of investors, the latter being further divided into natural
resources, cost-reducing resources and strategic assets. Moran eschews
these distinctions, yet they are a crucial aspect of the difference between
extractive (resource-seeking) and infrastructure (market-seeking) FDI.
In terms of manufacturing FDI this distinction is also critical, as host
economy linkages and spillovers are likely to vary. Of course, some
projects may be both market- and resource-seeking, and the markets targeted are likely to extend beyond the host economy to focus on its region,
or even other regions. Nonetheless, linkages and spillovers are likely
to be different and more substantial in market-seeking projects than
resource-seeking ones, which are more focused on producing inputs that
feed into production processes elsewhere.

The market-seeking versus resource-seeking distinction is usefully
employed by Miroudot and Ragoussis in their econometric analysis
to explain the different export performances of state-owned and private firms. They also distinguish between 'sensitive' and other sectors,
the former (all in services) reflecting host country national security and
cultural concerns. It is surprising, though, that the list of sensitive sectors used in their data analysis[3] excludes, for example, transport, even
though the authors explicitly mention Dubai Ports World's abandoned
entry to the United States, and also mining, where 'national interest'
was used by the Canadian government to prevent BHP Billiton's takeover of Potash Corp. of Saskatchewan. Both of these cases illustrate the
sometimes blurred line between security concerns (and indeed economic
regulation broadly) and FDI protectionism, common in services sectors,
because market failure is more prevalent than in goods production.

Host governments should be concerned about the possibility of
foreign-owned SOEs or sovereign wealth funds entering their economies
with non-commercial (i.e. political) agendas. But Miroudot and Ragoussis
and Poulsen all imply that anxiety in the West about this issue – focused
particularly on the BRICs (Brazil, Russia, India and China) as home countries, and within the BRICs, particularly on China – may be exaggerated.
The critical issue, as Poulsen argues, is 'the function and nature of the
investment activities' rather than ownership, that is, what is the SOE's
motive for outward investment? Is it acting as an agent of its government

[3] Pierre Sauvé pointed out at the World Trade Forum that the list, taken from Mattoo and
Subramanian (2008), has a very Indian 'feel'. A. Mattoo and A. Subramanian – The World
Bank Development Research Group, 'Currency Undervaluation and Sovereign Wealth
Funds: A New Role for the World Trade Organization', Policy Research Working Paper
4668 (2008).

(whatever the level of the government's shareholding), or is it acting as an independent entity, as a private corporation does? This emphasises the need for a better definition of SOEs in terms of the size of the state's shareholding, as argued by Poulsen and Miroudot and Ragoussis. Miroudot and Ragoussis use a threshold of 50 per cent to define an SOE, in contrast to the United Nations Conference on Trade and Development (UNCTAD)'s 10 per cent.[4] But much more important than the size of the public ownership stake is the need to assess the content and nature of their home state's influence (or lack thereof) over SOE investor strategy and behaviour. The Orbis database used by Miroudot and Ragoussis for their econometric analysis includes subnationally owned enterprises as SOEs. But do subnational governments necessarily have a common political agenda with each other and with their national government? Many Chinese SOEs are owned not by the central state, but by subnational governments, competing intensely with each other for growth, often subverting central government objectives and strategies. Yet discussion of Chinese outward FDI most often takes all SOEs (whomever their owners) to be part of a coordinated 'grand strategy' of the Chinese central state.[5]

The concerns may be legitimate to the extent that they focus on national security (subject to the caveat above regarding protectionism), but are less so with regard to the supposed commercial advantages that home governments provide to their SOEs. Common standards should be applied when examining credit availability and subsidies. Ultimately, it comes down to whether or not firms – especially banks – have a soft budget constraint. As seen in the wake of the global financial crisis, the latter are not found only in 'new investor' countries, but also in Western countries. And the foreign aid budgets of many OECD countries are rife with 'tied aid' conditions, tantamount to subsidies, and even those countries eschewing such conditions began to do so only recently.

The stereotypes of SOE and SWF investors are matched by stereotypes, in Moran's discussion, of foreign investors in developing countries and of the host economy itself. The investor is implicitly assumed to be a 'Northern' multinational corporation (MNC) with a global lead in technology and good practice, for example from the Midwest in the USA or the *Mittelstand* in Germany, while the host economy is taken to be a

---

[4] United Nations Conference on Trade and Development (UNCTAD), *World Investment Report 2011* (Geneva: UNCTAD, 2011).
[5] The *World Investment Report 2011* does not make this mistake, excluding subnationally owned SOEs from its measure of outward FDI by Chinese SOEs: Table 1.9, p. 31.

middle-income country already heavily involved in global value chains. Both these 'straw men' are wrong.

Looking first at the host economy, many low-income countries and even middle-income countries in Africa are barely 'in the game' to receive FDI – they have not been able to attract much low wage/low skill 'sweatshop' FDI, let alone more skill- and capital-intensive foreign producers. These countries arguably need *more* sweatshops to absorb their low-skilled unemployed and underemployed labour, a point which applies even to South Africa with de facto unemployment well over 30 per cent, and much higher in smaller towns. Moran is right to worry about the upgrading potential and permanence of low-skill, low-wage FDI, but it is not clear that it is either possible or desirable to 'leapfrog' to higher skill, more capital-intensive manufacturing FDI, as suggested by Moran. Many countries lack the necessary capabilities and competencies to do so. But even if they have the necessary attributes, 'leapfrogging' may not be desirable – it is important first to absorb labour outside the formal economy (whether in rural or urban areas) into low-skill, low-wage employment to avoid a situation where a capital-intensive industrial sector co-exists with high unemployment. For example, Kenya has the beginnings of auto assembly, but the country still needs investment in low-tech consumer goods production such as clothing and shoes.

There is also implicit archetyping of the investors. In the case of Kenyan autos, the investors are Chinese – Foton and Chery – both state-owned, relatively young corporations which are not technological leaders with *global* advantages in this sector, but imitators who nonetheless have ownership advantages in the Kenyan (and African) market. There are very few OECD home country manufacturing firms in skill- and capital-intensive sectors in Africa, at least outside South Africa, and little evidence that firms of this sort are looking at Africa as potential production locations at present. OECD firms considering investing in Africa are likely to be in services or natural resource extraction. It is Asian firms that are most likely to invest now in light manufacturing sectors in Africa, where low-wage, low-skill workers are required. Indeed there is an important opportunity now to attract more Chinese firms in light manufacturing sectors, as the Chinese economy shifts to a new growth model with wages and other costs rising and the exchange rate appreciating, both of which will make outward FDI more attractive for Chinese manufacturers/assemblers. African countries should seize this opportunity, *pace* Moran.

Finally, it is worth touching on Moran's important point about FDI's potential externalities for host economy institutional and governance reform in the labour market. This issue is not new – it was a mainstay in the debate about disinvestment from apartheid South Africa in the 1970s, for example – but it is not often emphasised. Moran's discussion perhaps reflects too much faith in multinationals acting 'autonomously' to achieve labour stability. Often pressure on multinationals is needed from home governments and especially Western non-governmental organisations (NGOs) and consumers, to improve labour market conditions in affiliates (and social and environmental conditions). And it also ignores the political environment in the host country, which is crucial. Many local actors – elements of business, government officials, trade unions, even NGOs – benefit from the status quo, and these groups are likely to resist change. But without some minimum level of support from host country actors, political change or institutional reform is likely to be unsustainable.

PART II

The interaction between international trade and investment regulation

8

On the laws of attraction: examining the relationship between foreign investment and international trade

MARY E. FOOTER

A. Introduction

This chapter advances the proposition that foreign investment is drawn to international trade like a moth to the flame and that this mutual attractiveness has become stronger with the passage of time. Traditionally, both foreign investors and traders have sought specific terms and conditions for commercial access to overseas markets, combined with certain guarantees as to the level of treatment they could expect from a host state. Neither was indifferent to the protection offered by the rule of law in the global economy.[1] This is no less so today.

The only thing that has changed is that large transnational corporations (TNCs) or multinational enterprises (MNEs) have become the key players in global product chains with an emphasis increasingly on services-based foreign direct investment (FDI) and a shift away from international production, based on traditional raw materials, towards manufacturing.[2] As a result, MNEs have become increasingly flexible in the location of their production or business activities and consequently in their market access. They may therefore 'treat FDI and exporting as alternatives in

---

[1] The rule of law is essential for participation in the global economy; see S. D. Franck, 'The legitimacy crisis in investment treaty arbitration: privatizing public international law through inconsistent decisions (2004–2005)', *Fordham Law Review* 73 (2005), 1521–626 at 1524, cited in L. Y. Fortier, 'Investment and the Rule of Law: Change or Decline?' in R. McCorquodale (ed.), *The Rule of Law in International and Comparative Context* (London: British Institute of International and Comparative Law, 2010), p. 128.

[2] P. Muchlinski, *Multinational Enterprises and the Law*, 2nd edn (Oxford University Press, 2007), p. 22.

their product sourcing and market access strategies',[3] combining them to their maximum advantage. With this in mind, the aim of the chapter is to explore the underlying relationship between FDI and international trade. The remainder of the chapter is organised as follows.

Section B sketches the historical context of the investment–trade relationship in bilateral and multilateral terms. Section C discusses the impact of intra-firm investment flows on patterns of trade and the effect of international investment agreements (IIAs) on multilateral trade. Section D examines the mutual attractiveness of foreign investment and international trade in the domain of dispute settlement, beginning with a brief overview of some General Agreement on Tariffs and Trade (GATT)/ World Trade Organization (WTO) disputes where foreign investment has left its imprint on trade. It then picks up on the proposition that the spread of a global network of bilateral investment treaties (BITs), and similar investment instruments in free trade agreements (FTAs), may entice foreign investors to challenge host states for breaches of WTO law, as part of their commitment to provide an enabling legal and regulatory environment for FDI. Another possibility is that investment arbitration tribunals may be attracted to the idea of either 'referencing' WTO law in their decisions or using it in an interpretative context. The chapter concludes in section E with a prognosis as to how the relationship between foreign investment and international trade may develop.

B. The nexus between international investment and trade: historical context

For decades states have sought to regulate FDI within the context of a broader trade or commercial treaty regime. Beginning with treaties of friendship, commerce and navigation (FCN treaties) through the failed Havana Charter for an International Trade Organization (ITO)[4] and eventually – to some extent – in the WTO,[5] foreign investment and international trade have enjoyed a familiar linkage. The relationship between these two

---

[3] S. Picciotto, 'Linkages in international investment regulation: the antinomies of the Draft Multilateral Agreement on Investment', *University of Pennsylvania Journal of International Economic Law* 19(3) (1998), 731–68 at 744.

[4] For details of the stillborn International Trade Organization (ITO) see J. H. Jackson, *The World Trading System* (Cambridge, MA: The MIT Press, 1997), pp. 36–7.

[5] The World Trade Organization (WTO)'s founding instrument is the Agreement Establishing the World Trade Organization, Marrakesh, 15 April 1994, in force 1 January 1995, 1867 UNTS 154; 33 ILM 1144 (1994).

areas of economic activity has been endorsed by developments at the Organisation for International Economic Co-operation and Development (OECD),[6] in the United Nations (UN) General Assembly and the United Nations Conference on Trade and Development (UNCTAD).[7] Since the 1990s the nexus between investment and trade has only increased in the context of regional integration agreements, such as the North American Free Trade Agreement (NAFTA),[8] or functional integration agreements like the Energy Charter Treaty (ECT),[9] each of which has a self-contained chapter or a section on international investment.

I. Flirting with the co-existence of bilateralism and multilateralism: FCN treaties, the Havana Charter and the GATT

FCN treaties and similar types of bilateral treaty instruments, which are commercial in the broadest sense of the word, have often laid the foundations for agreement between states. These so-called treaties of establishment were designed to protect natural and legal persons, their interests and their properties in a country other than their own.[10] They contained fundamental principles on access, non-discrimination, security and due process, many of which have retained their place in modern BITs.[11]

Such FCN treaties, grounded on principles of equity and fair treatment, appear to be a far cry from the type of trade concession that typically formed the basis of a bargaining process in international commerce, as

---

[6] The Organisation for Economic Co-operation and Development (OECD) is an economic grouping of twenty-four mostly industrialised countries. It was established as a reconstituted organisation (as successor to the Organisation for European Economic Co-operation or OEEC of 1948) by treaty of 14 December 1960, 888 UNTS 179.

[7] The United Nations Conference on Trade and Development (UNCTAD) was established pursuant to UNGA Res. 1785, 17 U.N. GAOR, Supp. 17, at 14, U.N. Doc A/5217 (1963) and UNCTAD Final Act, U.N. Doc. E/Conf. 46/141, vols. 6–8 (1964). It became an official organ of the United Nations (UN) General Assembly by means of G.A. Res. 1995, 19 U.N. GAOR, Supp. 15, at 1, U.N. Doc. A/5815 (1965).

[8] North American Free Trade Agreement between the Government of Canada, the Government of the United Mexican States and the Government of the United States of America (NAFTA), 13 December 1993, in force 1 January 1994, 32 ILM 289 (1993).

[9] Final Act of the European Energy Charter Conference, 12 December 1994, AF/EECH, reprinted in (1995) 34 ILM 373; for an extensive discussion of the provisions of the Energy Charter Treaty (ECT), see T. W. Wälde (ed.), *The Energy Charter Treaty: An East–West Gateway for Investment and Trade* (London: Kluwer Law International, 1996).

[10] H. Walker, Jr, 'Modern treaties of friendship, commerce and navigation', *Minnesota Law Review* 42 (1957–1958), 805.

[11] K. J. Vandevelde, *Bilateral Investment Treaties* (Oxford University Press, 2010), p. 21.

exemplified by the GATT 1947.[12] Nevertheless, what foreign investment and international trade have in common is the search for a reconciliation between the need for 'positive, universally tenable rules' and the need to provide some 'moderation and a spirit of accommodation'.[13]

This idea lay at the heart of the work of the Preparatory Committee (Prepcom) of the UN Conference on Trade and Employment that completed work on a founding Charter for an ITO,[14] which was presented to a specially convened conference in Havana at the end of 1947.[15] Chapter III of the Havana Charter for an ITO, entitled 'International Investment for Economic Development and Reconstruction', contained some rules on FDI, although there was an underlying tension between investment and trade that centred on the economic sovereignty of individual states.[16]

Article 12 of the Havana Charter specifically recognised the importance of both public and private forms of international investment in promoting economic development and reconstruction.[17] When it came to admitting FDI, Members of the ITO were to undertake the dual obligations to 'provide reasonable opportunities ... and adequate security for existing and future investments' and 'to give due regard to the desirability of avoiding discrimination as between foreign investments'.[18] At the same time the Havana Charter contained no specific obligations granting access to foreign investment. Instead, Members undertook to provide for consultation and negotiation of bilateral and multilateral investment instruments on the matter.[19] Additionally, ITO Members would retain the right to take

---

[12] Final Act Adopted at the Conclusion of the Second Session of the Preparatory Committee of the United Nations Conference on Trade and Development, 30 October 1947, 55 UNTS 188 (1947), containing the General Agreement on Tariffs and Trade (GATT) and the Protocol of Provisional Application, in force 1 January 1948 (GATT 1947).

[13] Walker, 'Modern treaties', 810.

[14] Report of the Second Session of the Preparatory Committee of the United Nations Conference on Trade and Employment, UN Doc. E/PCT/186 (Geneva, 1947).

[15] The Final Act and Related Documents of the United Nations Conference on Trade and Employment, Havana, Cuba, 21 November 1947 to 24 March 1948 (Final Act of the Havana Conference), included the draft Charter for the International Trade Organisation (Havana Charter), UN Doc. ICITO/1/4 (1948).

[16] Report by the Secretariat of the United Nations Conference on Trade and Development (UNCTAD), *The Outcome of the Uruguay Round: an Initial Assessment – Supporting Chapters to the Trade and Development Report* (UNCTAD Secretariat Report 1994), 1994, UNCTAD/TDR/14 (Supplement), p. 136ff. for an overview of foreign investment and the trading system under the Havana Charter.

[17] Havana Charter, Section III, Article 12.1(a).

[18] Havana Charter, Article 12.2(a) (i) and (ii).

[19] Havana Charter, Article 12.2(b).

safeguard measures to ensure that inward FDI would not interfere in their internal affairs and domestic policies, and they alone would determine the terms and conditions for its entry and establishment.[20]

There was also an explicit recognition in the Havana Charter that bilateral and multilateral agreements on investment could promote and protect FDI by the nationals of capital-exporting Members in other capital importing Members.[21] The Havana Charter therefore endorsed the status quo in investment treaty-making in the immediate post-Second World War era, which was founded upon a system of FCN treaties. Had the Havana Charter entered into force, it would have led the way for a treaty-based system of investment alongside Members' international trade obligations but it would not have promoted the specific integration of FDI in the ITO.

With the failure of the project for an ITO the international community was left with the GATT 1947 and its annexed tariff schedules. The GATT 1947 marked the successful conclusion of an unparalleled exercise in tariff cutting, combined with rules to protect the value of those bound tariffs, but it never had any rules on foreign investment. Instead, the GATT represented a paradigm shift from bilateral to multilateral treaty-making in international trade while foreign investment continued to regulate a system of FCN-type treaties, later leading to a series of BITs.

A few sporadic decisions adopted by the GATT Contracting Parties in the 1950s dealt with issues of foreign investment. One of them was aimed at encouraging donor and recipient countries to conclude bilateral and multilateral investment agreements to stimulate the international flow of capital.[22] Throughout the 1960s and 1970s the relationship between investment and trade at the multilateral level was inconsequential and remained so until 1981. It was a broader-based GATT policy initiative, known as the Consultative Group of Eighteen,[23] that eventually took up the challenge

---

[20] Havana Charter, Article 12.1(c)(i) and (ii).

[21] Havana Charter, Article 12.1(d).

[22] Resolution of the Contracting Parties of 4 March 1955 on 'International Investment for Economic Development', (1955) BISD 3S/49, 50; see UNCTAD Secretariat Report 1994, p. 136.

[23] The Consultative Group of Eighteen was established by Decision of the GATT Council of 11 July 1975, GATT Doc. L/4204, BISD 22S/15, later confirmed by means of a further Decision of the Contracting Parties, 22 November 1979, being the 'Mandate of the Consultative Group of Eighteen', GATT Doc. L/4869, BISD 26S/289–290; see further Note by the GATT Secretariat, 9 June 1987, GATT Doc. MTN.GNG/NG14/W/5 and M. E. Footer, *An Institutional and Normative Analysis of the World Trade Organization* (Leiden: Martinus Nijhoff/Brill, 2006), pp. 122–3.

of dealing with 'investment performance requirements' and 'investment incentives', both of which were considered to be closely linked to export and import substitution requirements. However, the Consultative Group of Eighteen failed to reach any consensus on the trade-related effects of either of these two investment measures.[24]

II.　The emergence of BITs and the seduction of multilateralism

Meanwhile international investment law developed further by means of a plurality of reciprocal, mutually enforcing bilateral treaties and a series of international investment contracts between investors and host state governments, the latter most often in the form of concession contracts for the exploitation of oil, gas and mineral resources. With the end of colonialism in many parts of the world and the emergence of a large number of newly independent, but economically underdeveloped states,[25] many capital-exporting countries entered into 'newer-style' FCN treaties with developing, capital-importing states. These bilateral treaties were based on the assumption that they would lead to an increase in FDI, which would benefit developing host states through the 'multiplier effect' brought about by an injection of capital, human resources and transfer of technology.[26] This proved not always to be so in the case of FCN treaties as well as later BITs.[27]

Post-Second World War FCN treaties typically addressed diverse aspects of the trade and investment relationship that emphasised 'favourable conditions' and 'non-discrimination', embodied in the most-favoured nation (MFN) and national treatment standards. They also imposed on host states the obligation not to expropriate without

---

[24] Report of the Consultative Group of Eighteen to the Council of Representatives, L/5210, (1981) BISD 28S/71, 75–6.

[25] Vandevelde, *Bilateral Investment Treaties*, pp. 42–3; examples include the friendship, commerce and navigation treaty (FCN treaty) practice of the United States with countries like China, Ethiopia, Iran, Israel and a host of European countries, details of which are found in Walker, 'Modern treaties', 805–6 and 809–12, where he discusses the scope and coverage of FCN treaties.

[26] W. M. Reisman and R. D. Sloane, 'Indirect expropriation and its valuation in the BIT generation', *British Yearbook of International Law* 74 (2003), 115–50 at 116.

[27] M. Hallward-Driemeier, 'Do Bilateral Treaties Attract FDI? Only a Bit ... and They Could Bite', World Bank Policy Research Working Paper No. 3121, World Bank, Washington DC (2003), reproduced in K. P. Sauvant and L. E. Sachs, *The Effect of Treaties on Foreign Direct Investment: Bilateral Investment Treaties, Double Taxation Treaties, and Investment Flows* (Oxford University Press, 2009), pp. 715–24.

compensation.[28] One of the first capital-exporting states to forge ahead with its own BITs programme was the Federal Republic of Germany (FRG).[29] However, the FRG–Pakistan BIT of 1959[30] was more like earlier FCN treaties, as is evident from its inter-state character, with only inter-state and no investor–state dispute settlement clauses. Effectively, it meant that an investor had to rely on diplomatic protection from the home state nationality in espousing any claim brought under the BIT.

Attempts were made to put FDI on a multilateral treaty basis in the 1950s[31] but it was not until the OECD adopted a Convention on the Protection of Foreign Property in 1967[32] that new developments occurred. This novel instrument gave investors from OECD Member countries the right to take up any FDI complaint against a host state before an international arbitration tribunal without recourse to the diplomatic protection of their home state. Contemporaneously, the idea of investor–state arbitration had emerged as one of the key provisions in the adoption of the Convention on the Settlement of Investment Disputes between States and Nationals of Other States of 1965 (ICSID Convention).[33] Increasingly, from the 1980s onwards, capital-exporting states were prepared to conclude BITs that provided for ex ante host state consent to investor–state arbitration.[34] It became commonplace in BITs to offer a choice of alternative fora for resolving investment disputes using the International Centre for Settlement of Investment Disputes (ICSID), ad hoc arbitration with United Nations Commission on International Trade Law (UNCITRAL)

---

[28] Vandevelde, *Bilateral Investment Treaties*, pp. 50–1.

[29] R. Dolzer and C. Schreuer, *Principles of International Investment Law* (Oxford University Press, 2008), p. 19.

[30] Treaty between the Federal Republic of Germany (FRG) and Pakistan for the Promotion and Protection of Investments, Bonn, 25 November 1959, in force 28 April 1962 (1963) 457 UNTS 23.

[31] Dolzer and Schreuer, *Principles of International Investment Law*, p. 18 and see generally A. V. Lowe, 'Changing Dimensions of International Investment Law' in W. Shan, P. Simons and D. Singh (eds.), *Collected Courses of the Xiamen Academy of International Law* (Leiden: Martinus Nijhoff, 2008).

[32] OECD Convention on the Protection of Foreign Property (1967), reproduced in 7 ILM 117 (1968).

[33] Convention on the Settlement of Investment Disputes Between States and Nationals of Other States (ICSID Convention), 575 UNTS 159, (1965) 4 ILM 524, Washington DC, 18 March 1965, entered into force 14 October 1966.

[34] C. Schreuer, 'The Dynamic Evolution of the ICSID System' in R. Hofmann and C. Tams (eds.), *The International Convention on the Settlement of Investment Disputes (ICSID): Taking Stock after 40 Years*. Schriften zur Europäischen Integration und Internationalen Wirtschaftsordnung, 7 (Baden-Baden: Nomos, 2007), p. 20.

Arbitration Rules[35] or International Chamber of Commerce (ICC) Arbitration Rules.[36]

The 'newer' generation of BITs also developed a more sophisticated understanding of the 'favourable conditions' necessary for FDI. Henceforth, the investor–host state relationship has been based on 'an effective *normative* framework: impartial courts, an effective and legally restrained bureaucracy' and a measure of transparency in decision-making by public authorities, all of which form part of the international rule of law.[37] It means that the host state must maintain an adequate administrative and regulatory framework and an enabling legal environment for FDI.[38] We return to this issue in section C.I.

In the mid 1990s a group of OECD Members were seduced by the idea of a multilateral regime for investment. Spurred on by developments in the Uruguay Round and the conclusion of the tripartite NAFTA with a section on investment (Chapter 11), negotiations started at the OECD in 1995 on a Multilateral Agreement on Investment (MAI).[39] The intention was to create a comprehensive multilateral framework for all types of international investment with high standards for liberalising investment protection.[40] It also sought to establish effective dispute settlement procedures, both at the state-to-state level, modelled on the WTO and NAFTA panel system, and through investor–state arbitration. MAI panels, unlike WTO ones, would be allowed to grant direct, pecuniary compensation, or restitution in kind. Consistent with the practice of BIT treaty-making, investor–state dispute settlement under the MAI provided for investment arbitration using the ICSID, UNCITRAL Arbitration Rules or the ICC Arbitration Rules. Only OECD Member countries were involved

---

[35] United Nations Commission on International Trade Law (UNCITRAL) Arbitration Rules, adopted by UN General Assembly Resolution 31/98 on 15 December 1976.

[36] International Chamber of Commerce (ICC) Rules of Arbitration, in force 1 January 1998, available at: www.iccarbitration.org.

[37] Reisman and Sloane, 'Indirect expropriation', 117.

[38] These requirements approximate to three of the World Bank's six governance indicators, namely Government Effectiveness, Regulatory Quality and Rule of Law; see further Worldwide Governance Indicators (Washington DC, 2009), available at: http://info.worldbank.org/governance/wgi/index.asp and D. Kaufmann, A. Kraay and M. Mastruzzi, 'The Worldwide Governance Indicators: Methodology and Analytical Issues', Draft Policy Research Working Paper (Washington DC: World Bank, 2010).

[39] Details about the draft Multilateral Agreement on Investment (MAI), and the draft text up until 1998, are available at: www.oecd.org/document/35/0,3343,en_2649_33783766_1894819_1_1_1_1,00.html.

[40] Picciotto, 'Linkages in international investment regulation', 742–3.

in the negotiation of the MAI but it was intended that the final agreement would be open for adherence by *all* states, including non-OECD Members.

A series of drafts were produced, but negotiations stalled when the French Government withdrew its support for the MAI in 1998 and any attempt to negotiate further was abandoned. There was principal disagreement among OECD Members on matters such as the over-broad definition of investor and investment, protection against expropriation, and the dispute settlement provisions. A further aspect of the negotiations exercise was its asymmetrical character. OECD Member countries backed the development of strong pro-investor rules on FDI, which alienated many non-OECD Members, the majority of which were developing countries and which felt duty bound to attend the negotiations as observers. The failure of the MAI was also due to the internationally coordinated campaign against it.[41] The issue of multilateral investment rules then shifted to the WTO where the topic of investment had already made landfall, as we shall see in the next section.

III.   Renewing the bilateral and multilateral relationships
between investment and trade: the WTO and other
forms of economic integration

The relationship between investment and trade is readily determinable in the WTO regulation of services trade. When it comes to balance of payments statistics, governments have traditionally recorded their services transactions between residents and non-residents alongside other foreign exchange receivables, including returns from FDI, royalties and other non-resident transactions, or so-called 'invisibles'. During the Uruguay Round the provision of the services in the General Agreement on Trade in Services (GATS)[42] was also defined in terms of resident/non-resident transactions, with the addition of the supply of services through a foreign affiliate or commercial presence abroad. This became known as 'mode 3 – commercial presence'.[43]

---

[41] *Ibid.*, 749.
[42] General Agreement on Trade in Services (GATS), 15 April 1994, in force 1 January 1995, Marrakesh Agreement Establishing the World Trade Organization, Annex 1B, The Legal Texts: The Results of the Uruguay Round of Multilateral Trade Negotiations, 1869 UNTS 183; 33 ILM 1167.
[43] GATS, Article I:2(c).

The GATS envisages a right of establishment in its definition of 'commercial presence', which means 'any type of business or professional establishment'.[44] It may include 'the constitution, acquisition or maintenance of a juridical person' or 'the creation or maintenance of a branch or a representative office' within the territory of a Member for the purpose of supplying a service.[45] Where the GATS differs from some other investment-type instruments, including the NAFTA, is that where a WTO Member has granted market access by means of a positive listing of sectors and sub-sectors in mode 3 – commercial presence, the right of establishment only applies to those 'positive' commitments (so-called 'positive listing'). This is then combined with the 'negative listing' of any non-conforming measures that a WTO Member wishes to maintain in a scheduled sector or sub-sector for mode 3.[46] In other words, it is not a general right of establishment, subject to a 'negative list of exclusions', as is the case under Chapter 11 NAFTA that simply lists only those sectors and areas that are excepted from coverage.[47]

However, from a balance of payments perspective, the supply of a service by an entity resident in the consumer's territory is a transaction between residents and is therefore *not* recorded as a trade transaction.[48] Instead, it is characterised as an investment. Since the provision of services abroad usually requires some sort of commercial presence, that is through the subsidiary, or branch, of a company or through an agency, it will be a form of FDI in a host state.

The link between investment and trade is even more obvious when one looks at those GATS provisions under which Members have made specific commitments with respect to market access and national treatment.[49] Market access is usually coupled with a guarantee of national treatment to be accorded in respect of all measures 'affecting' the

---

[44] GATS, Article XXVIII(d).

[45] GATS, Sections (1) and (2).

[46] UNCTAD, *Preserving Flexibility in IIAs: The Use of Reservations*, UNCTAD Series on International Investment Policies for Development (New York: United Nations Publications, 2006), p. 25.

[47] See the 'negative list of exclusions' in Annexes 1, 2 and 3 to NAFTA, which fall into three categories: sectoral, reciprocal and 'tit for tat'; see further G. C. Hufbauer and J. J. Schott, *NAFTA Revisited: Achievements and Challenges* (Washington DC: Peterson Institute, 2005), pp. 201–3.

[48] M. E. Footer and C. George, 'The General Agreement on Trade in Services' in P. MacRory, A. Appleton and M. Plummer (eds.), *The World Trade Organization: Legal, Economic and Political Analysis* (Aspen: Springer, 2005), p. 825.

[49] Article XVI GATS (market access).

supply of services in the sectors inscribed in the Schedules of Services Commitments, and subject to any conditions or qualifications set out therein.[50]

It is obvious that the conditions upon which access to a particular market is granted, and the type of treatment that is guaranteed under mode 3 supply, is exactly the same as that covered by investor protection clauses under many BITS, which specifically control the entry and/or establishment of foreign investors and investment.[51] In fact, there is considerable overlap between some BITs and the GATS. This became apparent immediately after the entry into force of the GATS when many WTO Members chose to list specific sectoral commitments under mode 3 in accordance with their domestic laws on FDI and/or their bilateral treaty obligations.[52]

Many WTO Members either bound an existing situation (so-called 'standstill') or else removed certain existing restrictions on market access ('rollback').[53] Others maintained 'permitted' limitations that were inconsistent with Article XVI GATS (so-called market access limitations).[54] The latter included such matters as limitations on the type of legal entity through which a service could be supplied, or limitations on equity participation in a corporate or business entity, 'in accordance with [a Member's] laws and regulations'. There were also other territorial limitations and restrictions on the basis of nationality for both services and service suppliers. Both limitations are usually found in relation to the 'controlled entry' model of admission and establishment of foreign investment and investors, which is common to the majority of BITs and some regional investment agreements.[55]

---

[50] Article XVII GATS (national treatment). This approach to investment-type service commitments in the GATS is known as the 'selective liberalization model', which is slightly more open than the 'controlled investment model' described below in the text; see 'Admission and Establishment', Chapter 4, in UNCTAD, *International Investment Agreements: Key Issues* (UNCTAD, Admission and Establishment) (New York: United Nations Publications, 2004), vol. II, p. 150.

[51] J. W. Salacuse, *The Law of Investment Treaties* (Oxford University Press, 2010), p. 102.

[52] R. Adlung, P. Morrison, M. Roy and W. Zang, 'FOG in GATS Commitments: Boon or Bane', World Trade Organization: Staff Working Paper, ERSD-2011–04 (March 2011), pp. 10–11. The Working Paper is significant in that the analysis only deals with mode 3 supply, i.e. commercial presence, which is the mode of supply most analogous to FDI.

[53] Footer and George, 'The General Agreement on Trade in Services', pp. 859–60.

[54] Article XVI:2 GATS.

[55] UNCTAD, Admission and Establishment, pp. 148–50.

The other obvious link between investment and trade is the Agreement on Trade-Related Investment Measures (TRIMs Agreement),[56] which was negotiated in the Uruguay Round. It seeks to prevent the trade-restrictive and distorting effects that some investment measures may have on trade in goods. Strongly influenced in its conception by the GATT panel decision in *Canada – Foreign Investment Review Act* (FIRA),[57] Article 2.1 of the TRIMs Agreement bans any trade-related investment measure (TRIM) that is inconsistent with the national treatment standard of Article III GATT 1994[58] or the prohibition on quantitative restrictions in Article XI GATT 1994.[59] It uses an 'illustrative list' approach to define what is meant by TRIMs. Broadly summarised they include what are known as 'performance requirements': local purchasing and local content requirements; trade-balancing requirements; foreign exchange restrictions; and export performance requirements.[60]

Some states like the United States and Canada favour the admission and establishment of FDI on the basis of the national treatment standard and/or MFN at both the pre- and post-establishment stage.[61] What amounts to 'a right of admission, albeit limited in scope'[62] may nevertheless be subject to the right of each party to the BIT to adopt or maintain certain exceptions falling within certain sectors, sub-sectors or activities, listed in a separate Annex.[63]

Additionally, more recent BITs like the 2012 US Model BIT or the Canadian Model Foreign Investment Promotion and Protection Agreement (FIPA) contain provisions stating that performance

[56] Agreement on Trade-Related Investment Measures (TRIMs Agreement), 15 April 1994, in force 1 January 1995, Marrakesh Agreement Establishing the World Trade Organization, Annex 1A, The Legal Texts: The Results of the Uruguay Round of Multilateral Trade Negotiations 143 (1999), 1868 UNTS 186.

[57] GATT Panel Report, *Canada – Administration of the Foreign Investment Review Act* (*Canada – FIRA*), L/5504, BISD 30S/140, adopted 7 February 1984.

[58] Article XI GATT 1994, 15 April 1994, Marrakesh Agreement Establishing the World Trade Organization, Annex 1A, The Legal Texts: The Results of the Uruguay Round of Multilateral Trade Negotiations (1999) 17, 1867 UNTS 187, 33 ILM 1153 (1994).

[59] Article III GATT 1994.

[60] Article 2.2 TRIMs and Annex to the TRIMs Agreement.

[61] Articles 3(1) and 4(1) of the Treaty between the Government of the United States of America and the Government of [Country] Concerning the Encouragement and Reciprocal Protection of Investment (2012 US Model BIT), available at: www.state.gov/documents/organization/18837.pdf; Articles 3(1) and 4(1) of the Agreement between Canada and … for the Promotion and Protection of Investments (Canada Model FIPA), available at: http://italaw.com/documents/Canadian2004-FIPA-model-en.pdf.

[62] Dolzer and Schreuer, *Principles of International Investment Law*, p. 89.

[63] Article 14, 2012 US Model BIT and Article 7, Canadian Model FIPA.

requirements, of the type contained in the illustrative list of the TRIMs Agreement, must not be imposed by the host state as a condition for the establishment, expansion or maintenance of investments. Similar prohibitions on performance requirements are taken up in individual investment chapters in some FTAs, for which the NAFTA[64] serves as a model. Dolzer and Schreuer have suggested that 'issues of competing jurisdiction and of consistency would arise if such measures were to be challenged both before the WTO dispute settlement system and before a tribunal with a jurisdictional basis in a BIT'.[65] This issue is considered further in section D.II.

The linkage between international investment and trade was revisited early on in the life of the WTO at the First Ministerial Conference held in Singapore in 1996 when Ministers decided to establish the Working Group on the relationship between Trade and Investment (WGTI).[66] Its task was merely analytical and exploratory. No new rules or commitments were to be negotiated without the specific consensus of WTO Members.

Following the abandonment of the MAI negotiations in 1998 it was anticipated that the matter would be taken up at the WTO. At Doha, Ministers recognised the case for a multilateral framework to secure 'transparent, stable and predictable conditions for long-term cross-border investment, particularly foreign direct investment'.[67] It was therefore agreed that negotiation would take place *after* the Fifth Ministerial Conference 'on the basis of a decision to be taken, by explicit consensus, at that Session on modalities of negotiations'.

However, the WGTI could not agree on how to address the concerns of developing country Members who did not want see their right to regulate FDI curtailed, including the right to apply TRIMs and other performance measures, in pursuit of their development needs.[68] Due in part to a group of developing countries, which firmly rejected the launch of negotiations on investment and other so-called 'Singapore issues', the

---

[64] Article 1106 NAFTA.

[65] R. Dolzer and C. Schreuer, *Principles of International Investment Law*, 2nd edn. (Oxford, 2012).

[66] First WTO Ministerial Conference, Singapore, 9–13 December 1996, 'Ministerial Declaration', WT/MIN(96)/DEC, 18 December 1996, para. 20.

[67] Fourth WTO Ministerial Conference, Doha, 9–14 November 2001, 'Ministerial Declaration', WT/MIN(01)/DEC, 20 November 2001, para. 20.

[68] Muchlinski, *Multinational Enterprises and the Law*, pp. 669–73 and M. L. de Sterlini, 'The Agreement on Trade-Related Investment Measures' in P. MacRory, A. Appleton and M. Plummer (eds.), *The World Trade Organization: Legal, Economic and Political Analysis* (Aspen: Springer, 2005), pp. 477–8.

issue became polarised at the Cancún Ministerial Conference.[69] The meeting concluded without any consensus on taking the work of the WGTI forward in the form of a multilateral agreement on trade and investment.[70]

Subsequently there has been a closer relationship between international investment and trade not because of, but in spite of, multilateralism. This has manifested itself in various ways. For example, since the late 1980s there has been a movement among some states to desert the classical BIT, which addresses only FDI issues, in favour of the negotiation of investment provisions in the context of FTAs.[71] The first of these was the USA–Canada Free Trade Agreement of 1988,[72] which formed the basis for the conclusion of the NAFTA in 1993, including Chapter 11[73] with its own investment regime and separate system of investment arbitration.

The trend towards the incorporation of investment provisions in FTAs has continued unabated, beginning with the USA, which has entered into a number of them.[74] Japan too has adopted a similar policy course, with a series of economic partnership agreements (EPAs).[75] Other Asian countries have followed Japan's lead.[76] In addition, older forms of regional economic integration such as the Association of Southeast Asian Nations (ASEAN)[77] have developed fully-fledged investment instruments.[78]

---

[69] Fifth WTO Ministerial Conference, Cancún, 10–14 September 2003.

[70] De Sterlini, 'The Agreement on Trade-Related Investment Measures', p. 5 and pp. 15–17.

[71] Dolzer and Schreuer, *Principles of International Investment Law*, p. 25.

[72] Free Trade Agreement between Canada and the United States of America, concluded at Ottawa/Washington DC and Palm Springs, 4 October 1988, in force 1 January 1989, 27 ILM (1988) 281.

[73] Chapter 11 NAFTA.

[74] See for an example the Agreement on the Establishment of a Free Trade Area between the United States and Singapore, Washington DC, 6 May 2003, in force 1 January 2004, and others at the Office of the United States Trade Representative, available at: www.ustr.gov/trade-agreements.

[75] See for example the Agreement between Japan and the Republic of Indonesia for an Economic Partnership, Jakarta, 20 August 2007, in force 1 July 2008, available at: www.mofa.go.jp/region/asia-paci/indonesia/epa0708/index.html.

[76] Salacuse, *The Law of Investment Treaties*, p. 103.

[77] The Association of Southeast Asian Nations (ASEAN) was established on 8 August 1967 in Bangkok, Thailand, with the signing of the Bangkok Declaration by Indonesia, Malaysia, Philippines, Singapore and Thailand, since when Brunei Darussalam, Vietnam, Laos PDR, Myanmar (Burma) and Cambodia have joined; for details of the ASEAN Charter, including revisions, see www.asean.org.

[78] ASEAN Comprehensive Investment Agreement (ACIA), Cha-am, Thailand, 26 February 2009, in force 29 March 2012, available at: www.asean.org.

There are reportedly some 295 forms of regional agreements, primarily aimed at trade but with substantive chapters or additional protocols on investment.[79]

C.   Mapping the interlinkages between FDI and trade flows

What does all of this mean in terms of the relationship between investment and trade? The linkages that are discussed in this section are those that affect the way in which our global economy operates. Increasingly, much investment is intra-firm investment and it is having a discernible effect on patterns of trade in terms of exports of final goods as well as parts and components. Sometimes there is an 'internal' aspect to this relationship where WTO membership or accession leads to accelerated domestic reform by the host state in areas such as trade facilitation (border and customs procedures), enhanced transit, technical standards and services infrastructure. Similarly, WTO Membership brings about regulatory and other policy reforms.[80] Linked to this is the effect that BITs and investment instruments in FTAs may have on trade flows. Despite scepticism in some quarters, the empirical evidence reveals a strong correlation between FDI by means of such investment instruments and multilateral and regional trade flows.

I.   The impact of intra-firm investment flows on the pattern of trade

At the distance of more than half a century we tend to forget that the post-Second World War era ushered in the rise of the TNC or MNE, eventually leading to the 'the rise of foreign direct investment by MNEs to current levels'.[81] This was accompanied by the unprecedented importance of MNEs in international production, initially based on raw materials but increasingly geared towards manufacturing and, in the modern era, combined with 'services based FDI, and the development of major regional free trade and investment liberalisation regimes, alongside the establishment of the WTO'.[82]

---

[79] UNCTAD, *World Investment Report 2009* (Geneva, 2009).

[80] B. Kaminski and B. Javorick with the assistance of F. Ng, 'Linkages between Foreign Direct Investment and Trade Flows' in H. Broadman (ed.), *From Disintegration to Reintegration: Eastern Europe and the Former Soviet Union in International Trade* (Washington DC: World Bank, 2005), Chapter 7.

[81] Muchlinski, *Multinational Enterprises and the Law*, p. 9.

[82] *Ibid.*, p. 15 and especially p. 20.

There has been a tendency in the literature to assume that firms choose either to supply foreign markets through exports or through the establishment of production facilities. However, there is evidence to suggest that in fact there is a high degree of complementarity between FDI and trade.[83] This has come about as a result of the growing fragmentation of production by MNEs and middle-size firms combined with the emergence of distribution networks that span the globe. The phenomenon is known as 'production fragmentation'.

It translates into the global diffusion of production and an increased international trade in final goods and parts and components. Additionally, IT and other new technologies have led to dividing the value chains of certain industries, like car manufacturing, into smaller functional units. Their main activities are performed by foreign subsidiaries or else they are subcontracted out to independent suppliers.[84]

Production fragmentation offers developing countries in particular the opportunity to join global production chains by specialising in the labour-intensive fragment of the manufacturing process in which they have a comparative advantage. They thereby move from supplying small, local markets to accessing bigger foreign markets.[85] Global diffusion of production also leads to increased international trade in final goods, as well as in parts, components or accessories (so-called 'intermediate goods').[86] It also tends to lead to greater integration in the production and marketing arrangements of MNEs.

A further aspect of this trend is that foreign firms may have a profound effect on a host country's participation in international trade. In other words, the injection of foreign capital into a manufacturing process, or a particular industry, may lead to more export-orientated activity by domestic firms. The establishment of a commercial presence, in particular through foreign ownership, is also likely to lead to increased prospects for exports.[87]

A recent study by the WTO shows how a mixture of infrastructure services, tariffs, FDI, cheaper technology and lower transportation costs all

---

[83] UNCTAD, *UNCTAD: World Investment Report 1996: Investment, Trade and International Policy Arrangements* (New York and Geneva: United Nations, 1996).

[84] Kaminski and Javorick, 'Linkages between Foreign Direct Investment and Trade Flows', p. 339.

[85] *Ibid.*

[86] This is perhaps best exemplified by the computer and car manufacturing industries in their supply of assembly plants.

[87] Kaminski and Javorick, 'Linkages between Foreign Direct Investment and Trade Flows', p. 362.

affect the trading environment and the international exchange of goods. This leads to increased market access, an expansion in cross-border links between firms and an increase in the trade in intermediate goods.[88] From the WTO study, which focuses on the Southeast Asian market, MNEs are the driving force behind the trend to 'offshore' not only manufacturing but also other parts of their business activities, including related activities like accounting.[89]

Already in the second half of the 1990s, following the entry into force of the WTO, it was estimated that about one-third of world trade involved MNEs in intra-firm trade.[90] That percentage is significantly higher today. However, this development has another aspect. MNEs have become more sensitive to the investment environment in which they operate. It has become easier too for them to relocate geographically in response to any number of variables, ranging from changes in the cost of production or market access, to a difference in regulatory conditions or simply a change in the perceived risks bound up with a particular investment.[91]

Where the relationship between investment and trade really reveals itself is in the changing nature of sources of capital investment. Empirical studies show that official flows of capital, that is governmental or institutional support, may act as a powerful stimulus for the host state to enact domestic reforms. However, it is private capital flows that respond most to governance reform measures, including those associated with trade facilitation. For the centrally planned economies of Eastern and Central Europe and some of the Central Asian Republics it has been shown that there is a positive correlation between the size of inward investment flows and the dismantling of many centrally planned economies. Most significantly where host states have accelerated the reform process, provided an effective legal and regulatory framework for investment and have adopted measures to stem corruption and enforce property rights, FDI flows have been higher.[92]

---

[88] WTO, the Institute of Developing Economies (IDE-JETRO), *Trade Patterns and Global Value Chains in East Asia: From Trade in Goods to Trade in Tasks* (Geneva: WTO Secretariat, 2011).

[89] *Ibid.*, p. 55.

[90] UNCTAD, *World Investment Report 2002: Transnational Corporations and Export Competitiveness* (Geneva: United Nations Publication, 2002).

[91] Kaminski and Javorick, 'Linkages between Foreign Direct Investment and Trade Flows', p. 340.

[92] *Ibid.*, p. 367. Kaminski and Javorick actually describe the impact of such reforms on FDI flows in terms of governance indicators, using the World Bank's Governance Indicators database, for which see above note 38.

When it comes to FDI by MNEs in manufacturing and production facilities aimed at export, there are various associated costs. These crucially
include a good trade-facilitating infrastructure with a well-functioning
customs administration. There is also a requirement for good transit links
provided by efficient transportation systems and communications networks. Finally, adherence to internationally recognised technical standards and processes such as certification and conformity assessment will
also raise costs.

Additionally, for some sectors where a highly-skilled workforce is
needed for the supply of a service, for example telecommunications or
computing, the quality of a host state's services infrastructure and links
may play a key role. Some of the empirical work in this areas reveals that
where states have committed to regulatory and governance reforms, often
arising out of their accession to the WTO (or in the case of some Central
and Eastern European states their accession to the European Union (EU)),
and have acquired an effective *normative* framework, as noted in section
B.II, they are more likely to attract inward FDI.[93]

II.   *The effect of international investment agreements on*
international trade and vice versa

Another important factor to consider when mapping the inter-linkages
between FDI and trade flows is the effect, if any, BITs and stand-alone
investment chapters, sections or protocols, which are found in some FTAs,
have on trade flows and vice versa. Despite scepticism in some quarters,[94]
the empirical evidence reveals a correlation between FDI flows, by means
of such investment instruments, and multilateral and regional trade
flows.

One reason for this is that the signing of a BIT by a particular host state
may lead to further economic integration. This can be measured by looking at whether export trade associated with MNE activity rises after a BIT
has been signed. It is also possible to measure whether the rise in export
trade occurs relative to the adherence to one or more regional FTAs. From
the study by Swenson, based on trade flows between 1975 and 2000, BITs
appeared to have the greatest effect on trade facilitated by MNEs. This is
particularly true when it comes to trade in capital goods, that is manufactures, and products that can be differentiated on the basis of their country

---

[93] *Ibid.*, pp. 369–73.
[94] Hallward-Driemeier, 'Do Bilateral Treaties Attract FDI?'.

of origin.[95] The signing of a BIT often signals a form of investment liberalisation that is linked to trade rather than trade liberalisation for its own sake, as happens in the case of multilateral trade under the WTO or a regional arrangement.

Perhaps where the evidence of the effect of a BIT on trade has proven most effective is the presence of a treaty instrument that provides a commitment by the host state to a set of investor protection standards and to third-party international dispute settlement. The presence of a BIT helps to reduce uncertainty among potential investors, most of which are MNEs.[96] To a certain extent this corroborates the findings in the previous section where a host state has enacted a number of strategic market-orientated legal and regulatory reforms in order to attract export-orientated investment.

Conversely, there also appears to be a connection between some international trade and investment agreements, such as FTAs with stand-alone investment chapters, sections or protocols, and their ability to attract FDI flows. However, the extent to which such FTAs are capable of increasing investment flows may depend upon the strength of certain investor protection provisions in those agreements, such as standards of treatment and third-party dispute settlement.

While a number of studies have examined the impact of BITs and investment chapters in FTAs on FDI flows,[97] Berger et al.[98] concentrate on the extent to which such agreements offer broad liberalisation commitments associated with market access. What they examine is the extent to which a regional trade agreement (RTA) with an investment chapter, as opposed to an ordinary BIT, may attract FDI. This depends upon whether the RTA offers national treatment at the pre-establishment stage and whether there is a form of non-discriminatory and effective dispute settlement at the post-establishment stage.

---

[95] D. L. Swenson, 'Bilateral Investment Treaties and International Integration', University of California, Davis and NBER, August 2008, 23, available at: www.econ.ucdavis.edu/faculty/dswenson/BITsIntegration08.pdf.

[96] See Vandevelde, Bilateral Investment Treaties, who refers to the use of a BIT as a commitment mechanism that encourages FDI because it removes a degree of uncertainty about a particular host state.

[97] See the collection of essays that brings together a wide variety of previously published material on the matter, edited by Sauvant and Sachs, The Effect of Treaties on Foreign Direct Investment.

[98] A. Berger, M. Busse, P. Nunnenkamp and M. Roy, 'Do Trade and Investment Agreements Lead to More FDI? Accounting for Key Provisions Inside the Black Box', WTO Staff Working Paper, ERSD-2010–13, September 2010.

Their findings reveal that the most positive impact on FDI flows occurs where there is an FTA with a stand-alone investment instrument like Chapter 11 of the NAFTA, which adopts a negative list of exclusions[99] and which is coupled with guarantees of national treatment at the pre-establishment stage. In other words, liberal admission rules in FTAs promote bilateral investment. When it comes to dispute settlement the presence of investor–state arbitration clauses in both types of agreement plays a more minor role. Berger *et al.* find that strong dispute settlement provisions in FTAs are not necessarily associated with stronger bilateral investment flows any more than under a BIT. Thus, it appears that the impact of this aspect of investment law on trade may be more apparent than real. It is to this issue that we turn next.

D. The mutual attractiveness of investment and trade in dispute settlement

We have seen that investment had very little or no role to play in the GATT 1947 despite some decisions of the GATT Contracting Parties and a failed policy initiative by the Consultative Group of Eighteen in the 1970s. The same cannot be said of the GATT dispute settlement system. Section D.I briefly examines how one GATT panel decision affected the outcome of the Uruguay Round negotiations on TRIMs and how subsequent WTO panel decisions have responded to similar measures taken by WTO Members as host state governments in the field of FDI.

Alongside this development, there are several challenges in the field of dispute settlement arising from the ongoing relationship between investment and trade, which centre on multiple and/or parallel proceedings in different fora and are addressed in section D.II. To what extent, if at all, does the spread of a global network of IIAs lead to investors bringing complaints against host states for breaches of WTO law? Where this has already happened, how have investment arbitration tribunals reacted to such complaints, based on existing WTO law and jurisprudence?

---

[99] For details on the 'negative list of exclusions' in NAFTA Chapter 11 at fn. 47. It may well be that BITs, such as the one between the USA and Uruguay, for which see Treaty Between the Government of the United States of America and the Oriental Republic of Uruguay Concerning the Encouragement and Reciprocal Protection of Investment, 4 November 2005, 44 ILM 268, may eventually prove to have the same effect.

I. Investment law and policy issues in GATT/WTO dispute settlement

In the GATT era a direct challenge was mounted to the investment legislation of one of the Contracting Parties. The FIRA[100] Panel related to a complaint by the USA against Canada's Foreign Investment Review Act or FIRA,[101] which required foreign investors to give written undertakings that they would favour the purchase of Canadian goods over imported goods and called on them to meet certain export performance requirements. When the Panel was established by the GATT Council several delegates doubted the panel's competence to deal with the matter since it involved investment, which was not a GATT activity. They presumed that the Panel would limit itself to dealing only with those investment issues that fell within the 'four corners of the GATT'.[102] As parties to the dispute, the USA and Canada agreed that the matter concerned neither the FIRA itself nor Canada's right to regulate the entry and expansion of FDI but the consistency of the required purchase and export undertakings under the FIRA.[103]

The panel subsequently found the local purchasing requirements violated the national treatment standard[104] under Article III:4 GATT 1947 (and also Article III:5 GATT 1947)[105] but not the prohibition on quantitative restrictions in Article XI:1 GATT 1947[106] because 'local purchasing undertakings do not prevent the importation of goods as such.'[107] However, it did not find that Canada had acted inconsistently with its GATT obligations in allowing certain foreign investment to be subject to the export of specific amounts in proportion to production, that is product mandating. There was quite simply 'no provision in the General Agreement which [forbade] requirements to sell goods in foreign markets in preference to the domestic market'.[108]

The FIRA panel addressed only two TRIMs, namely local purchasing requirements and product mandating, but left unaddressed other

---

[100] *Canada – FIRA* Panel Report, above n. 57.
[101] Canada: Foreign Investment Review Act, 1973, 12(5) ILM (1973) 1136–1153.
[102] *Canada – FIRA* Panel Report, para. 1.4.
[103] *Ibid.*, para. 3.3; see further T. S. Shenkin, 'Comment – Trade-related investment measures in bilateral investment treaties and the GATT: moving toward a multilateral investment treaty', *University of Pittsburgh Law Review* 55 (1993–1994), 541–606 at 562.
[104] *Ibid.*, paras. 5.12 and 5.13.
[105] Paras. 4 and 5 of Article III GATT 1947.
[106] Para. 1 of Article XI GATT 1947.
[107] *Canada – FIRA* Panel Report, para. 5.14.
[108] *Ibid.*, para. 5.18.

undertakings required by the Canadian legislation for foreign investors. These included the requirements: (a) to set up a purchasing division in a Canadian subsidiary or (b) to manufacture goods and components locally that would otherwise be imported, and (c) to require Canadian participation in the investment enterprise.[109]

Under the TRIMs Agreement requirement (b) would currently be caught by the ban on 'local content requirements'.[110] However, an MNE with a local subsidiary, whose investment activity comprised the production for export, might be required to comply with certain product-mandating requirements in accordance with the 'laws and regulations' of the host state. This would not be a contravention of the TRIMs Agreement unless the product-mandating requirements were linked to investment incentives (a much under-studied phenomenon) designed to encourage direct exports to particular countries. Where this could lead to some WTO Members being favoured over others the measure would be a violation of the MFN principle.

The FIRA Panel has left its mark on WTO jurisprudence, although mostly as to whether the commitment by a private actor (in this case an investor) to a particular course of action constitutes a 'requirement' within the meaning of Article III:4 GATT 1994.[111] Claims of a violation of Article 2.1 TRIMs in certain WTO disputes have been dismissed because the infringing measure was already in violation of Article III:4 GATT 1994.[112]

The only case in which a trade-related investment measure has been successfully challenged under the TRIMs Agreement was *Indonesia – Autos*[113] where the Panel examined the Indonesian Car Programme 1993 and 1996, which was designed to develop local manufacturing capacity for finished motor vehicles and parts and components. The panel, in

---

[109] UNCTAD Secretariat Report 1994, p.138.

[110] Article 1(a) of the Illustrative List in the Annex to the TRIMs Agreement.

[111] For example, WTO Panel Report, *Japan – Measures Affecting Consumer Photographic Film and Paper* (*Japan –Film*), WT/DS44/R, adopted 22 April 1998, para. 10.51 and WTO Panel Report, *Canada – Certain Measures Affecting the Automotive Industry* (*Canada – Autos*), WT/DS/139/R and WT/DS/142R, adopted 19 June 2000, para. 10.73.

[112] As in *Canada – Autos*, where the Customs Valuation Agreement (CVA) requirements provided for in the Motor Vehicles Tariff Order (MVTO) 1998 and the Special Remission Order (SRO) were in violation of Article III:4 GATT 1994. Therefore, the panel did not find it necessary to rule that they were inconsistent with Article 2.1 of the TRIMs Agreement, para. 10.91.

[113] WTO Panel Report, *Indonesia – Certain Measures Affecting the Automobile Industry* (*Indonesia – Autos*), WT/DS/54/R, WT/DS554/R, DSD59/R, DS64/R, adopted, 23 July 1998.

examining whether the measures in question were 'investment measures' reviewed the legislative provisions relating to these measures. To begin with it found that 'the broad term "investment measures" indicates that the TRIMs Agreement is not limited to measures taken specifically in regard to *foreign* investment'. And moreover, 'internal taxes advantages or subsidies are only one of many types of advantages that can be construed as advantages tied to a local content rule, which is a principal focus of the TRIMs Agreement'.[114]

Indonesia also argued that the local content requirements of its car programmes did 'not constitute classic local content requirements within the meaning of the *FIRA* Panel ... because [it] left companies free to decide from which source to purchase parts and components'.[115] The Panel, however, dismissed this argument, finding there was 'nothing in the text of the TRIMs Agreement to suggest that a measure is not an investment measure simply because a Member decides not to characterise the measure as such or on the grounds that the measure is not explicitly adopted as an investment regulation'.[116] It went on to find that the local content was a TRIM that violated Article 2.1 TRIMs Agreement.[117]

II. The attraction of WTO law and jurisprudence for investment arbitration

As we have already seen in the preceding sections of this chapter, since the mid 1990s participation of MNEs in global product chains, and an emphasis on services-based FDI, has resulted in a move away from production based on traditional raw materials towards manufacturing and production facilities aimed at export markets. Alongside this development there has been a spread in the global network of BITs, and similar investment instruments in FTAs, known collectively as IIAs. These investment instruments may provide investors with a jurisdictional basis to challenge host states for breaches of WTO law where they have failed to bring their laws and regulations into conformity with their WTO obligations.

This has led to the suggestion that in future there could be issues of 'competing jurisdiction and consistency' where the domestic law or policy of the host state might give rise to a TRIM, or a similar measure, being

---

114 *Ibid.*, para. 14.73.
115 *Ibid.*, para. 14.90.
116 *Ibid.*, para. 14.91.
117 *Ibid.*, paras. 14.72–14.91.

'challenged both before the WTO dispute settlement system and before a tribunal with its jurisdictional basis in a BIT',[118] that is there is the possibility of double jeopardy and double recovery. One such area of contention could be, as Dolzer and Schreuer point out, 'the admissibility of (export) performance requirements only applying to foreign investors [which] remains to be clarified under the standard of national treatment.'[119] Currently, this latter issue is being tested in the case of *Mesa Power Group v. Canada*,[120] brought under Chapter 11 NAFTA.

Taking the example of the TRIMs Agreement in the preceding section, we have already seen a challenge under the WTO Dispute Settlement Understanding (DSU)[121] against Indonesia's use of a local content rule in its Car Programme in the case of *Indonesia – Autos*. However, a foreign investor might also be able to challenge the consistency of a host state's regulatory measures under the investor–state dispute settlement provisions of a BIT, or a similar investment treaty instrument in an FTA, claiming a breach of national treatment (including performance requirements), the fair and equitable treatment standard or even expropriation. Similarly – and perhaps somewhat exceptionally – a foreign investor might seek to challenge the consistency of a host state's regulatory measures with its specific WTO obligations in an investment arbitration forum.[122]

In international dispute settlement there is no bar to bringing a complaint at the inter-state level in the DSU for a breach of a WTO obligation and subsequently, or in parallel, at the investor–state level before an investment arbitration tribunal against the same government as the host state. Thus, following a finding under the DSU by a panel (and possibly the Appellate Body) that a particular measure is WTO-inconsistent, it can lead to a recommendation that the offending measure be withdrawn by the government of the WTO Member concerned. Subsequently, or

---

[118] Dolzer and Schreuer, *Principles of International Investment Law*, p. 92.

[119] *Ibid.*

[120] *Mesa Power Group, LLC v. Government of Canada (Mesa Power v. Canada)*, Notice of Intent to Submit a Claim to Arbitration under Section B of Chapter 11 of the North American Free Trade Agreement, 6 July 2011.

[121] Understanding on Rules and Procedures Governing the Settlement of Disputes (DSU), Marrakesh, 15 April 1994, in force 1 January 1995, Marrakesh Agreement Establishing the World Trade Organization, Annex 2, The Legal Texts: The Result of the Uruguay Round of Multilateral Trade Negotiations (1999) 354,1869 UNTS 401, 33 ILM 1226 (1994).

[122] G. Verhoosel, 'The use of investor-state arbitration under bilateral investment treaties to seek relief for breaches of WTO law', *Journal of International Economic Law* 6(2) (2003), 493–506 at 495.

concurrently, a complaint can be filed against the same government as the host state for the infringement of a protection standard under a BIT or an investment chapter in an FTA on the grounds that the measure is 'unfair, inequitable or discriminatory and/or amounts to expropriation'.[123] If proven, this can lead to the award of monetary compensation or damages against the host state government.

There are a several advantages for the investor in mounting such a challenge. First, there is scope for a broad array of domestic regulatory measures beyond the TRIMs Agreement that could give rise to a challenge concerning the conformity of those measures with WTO obligations. One only needs to think of other 'covered agreements',[124] such as the GATS, the Agreement on the Application of Sanitary and Phytosanitary Measures (SPS Agreement)[125] or the Agreement on Trade-Related Aspects of Intellectual Property Rights (TRIPS Agreement),[126] all of which oversee behind the border measures in the form of laws and regulations. Alternatively, such a domestic measure might be characterised as a form of subsidy under the Agreement on Subsidies and Countervailing Measures (SCM Agreement).[127]

Second, the attraction of using investment arbitration to challenge a WTO-inconsistent measure by a host state is that a private party can use the investor–state dispute settlement system under a BIT, or an FTA investment instrument such as NAFTA Chapter 11, without having to resort to the diplomatic protection of the home state. Third, under international law the injured party, that is the foreign investor, may choose the most appropriate remedy. In the field of investment arbitration such a remedy is not limited to withdrawal of the measure as it would be under

---

[123] *Ibid.*

[124] The term 'covered agreements' refers to the scope of WTO jurisdiction *ratione materiae*. See Article 3.2 of the DSU.

[125] Agreement on the Application of Sanitary and Phytosanitary Measures (SPS Agreement), Marrakesh, 15 April 1994, in force 1 January 1995, Marrakesh Agreement Establishing the World Trade Organization, Annex 1A, The Legal Texts: The Results of the Uruguay Round of Multilateral Trade Negotiations (1999) 70, 1867 UNTS 493.

[126] Agreement on Trade-Related Aspects of Intellectual Property Rights (TRIPS Agreement), 15 April 1994, in force 1 January 1995, Marrakesh Agreement Establishing the World Trade Organization, Annex 1C, The Legal Texts: The Results of the Uruguay Round of Multilateral Trade Negotiations 320 (1999), 1869 UNTS 299, 33 ILM 1197 (1994).

[127] Agreement on Subsidies and Countervailing Measures (SCM Agreement), Marrakesh, 15 April 1994, in force 1 January 1995, Marrakesh Agreement Establishing the World Trade Organization, Annex 1A, The Legal Texts: The Results of the Uruguay Round of Multilateral Trade Negotiations (1999) 275, 1867 UNTS 14.

the DSU but usually consists of monetary compensation, and occasionally restitution in kind.

A recent example of a domestic measure[128] being impugned concurrently under the DSU and before an investment arbitration tribunal is the Ontario Feed-in Tariff (FIT)[129] programme for renewable energy, which is currently the subject of a WTO panel and a NAFTA Chapter 11 complaint against the Government of Canada. In the WTO dispute of *Canada – Renewable Energy*[130] Japan is claiming that the FIT measures, which provide for the purchase by the Ontario Power Authority from four Ontario-based wind/solar power manufacturing facilities[131] of electricity generated from renewable resources, at rates established under twenty-year term contracts, violates Articles 3.1(b) and 3.2 SCM since the measures can be construed as a subsidy.[132] Additionally, the FIT

[128] It should be recalled that a number of the so-called 'Softwood Lumber' disputes between Canada and the USA between 2001 and 2004 have been considered in both the WTO dispute settlement system (e.g. *United States –Preliminary Determinations with Respect to Certain Softwood Lumber from Canada* (*US – Softwood Lumber III*), WT/DS236; *United States – Final Countervailing Duty Determination with respect to Certain Softwood Lumber from Canada* (*US – Softwood Lumber IV*), WT/DS257; *United States – Final Dumping Determination on Softwood Lumber from Canada* (*US – Softwood Lumber V*), WT/DS264; and *United States – Investigation of the International Trade Commission in Softwood Lumber from Canada* (*US – Softwood Lumber VI*), WT/DS277) and under NAFTA Chapter 11 (e.g. *Pope & Talbot* v. *Government of Canada* (*Pope & Talbot* v. *Canada*) (Award on Merits, Award on Damages), 10 April 2001, (2002) 122 ILR, 352 and 31 May 2002, 41 ILM 1347 (2002) and *Canfor Corporation and Terminal Forest Products Ltd.* v. *United States of America* (*Canfor et al.* v. *USA*) (Decision on Preliminary Question [of Jurisdiction]), 6 June 2006).

[129] The legal basis for Ontario's Feed-in Tariff (FIT) Programme is Section 25.35 of the Electricity Act, S.O. 1998, c. 15, Sched. A as amended by the Ontario Green Energy and Green Economy Act 2009, S.O. 2009, c.12, Schedule A; for further details and commentary see M. E. Streich, 'Green energy and Green Economy Act, 2009: A "FIT"-ing policy for North America?', *Houston Journal of International Law* 33(2) (2011), 419–52.

[130] *Canada – Certain Measures Affecting the Renewable Energy Generation Sector* (*Canada – Renewable Energy*), WT/DS412/R and *Canada – Measures Relating to the Feed-In Tariff Program*, WT/DS462/R, joint panel report, 19 December, 2012.

[131] The Purchase Power Agreements between the Ontario Power Authority (OPA) are with a South Korean consortium, led by Samsung C&T Corporation, which has agreed to build four wind and solar power manufacturing facilities in Ontario with a combined power-generating capacity of 2.6 gigawatts by 2016. In exchange the OPA has guaranteed the Samsung consortium energy prices, preferential access to the transmission system and CDN$437 million in incentives tied to the timely completion of the manufacturing facilities.

[132] A subsidy in the sense of Article 1.1 of the SCM Agreement; in this case the subsidy is considered by the Complainant to be a specific subsidy within the meaning of Article 2.3 SCM; see *Canada – Renewable Energy*, Request for the establishment of a Panel, WT/DS412/5, 7 June 2011.

measures are discriminatory in the sense of Article III:4 GATT 1994[133] because they accord less favourable treatment to imported equipment for renewable energy generation facilities than is accorded to like equipment originating in Ontario. The measures also contravene Article 2.1 TRIMs Agreement because they are contingent on the use of equipment for renewable energy-generating facilities produced in Ontario over equipment imported from other WTO Members, that is there is a local content requirement.[134]

In the recent investment complaint of *Mesa Power* v. *Canada*, an American investor has brought a complaint against the Government of Canada, as the host state, challenging the same FIT measures. By awarding wind power contracts to domestic companies and subsidiaries of a non-NAFTA party,[135] Mesa Power, as the foreign investor, considers that the Ontario Power Authority has acted unfairly and has abused its powers and the (award) process thereby contravenes various NAFTA provisions inter alia Article 1101 (national treatment), Article 1103 (MFN treatment) and Article 1105 (international law minimum standard of treatment), as does the 'buy local' contract requirements, which qualify as a prohibited export performance requirement under Article 1106 NAFTA.[136] Arguably the host state, Canada, has failed to maintain an adequate regulatory framework and an enabling environment for FDI that is free from bias, is non-discriminatory and is not prejudicial to an investor's legitimate expectations.

However, where the WTO and the NAFTA Chapter 11 cases differ is that while the measure in dispute is the same, that is the FIT programme on renewable energy generation, the identity of the foreign investor or trading company behind each is different. Both the WTO dispute and the NAFTA investment arbitration not only reveal the strong underlying relationship between foreign investment and international trade but also

---

[133] Article III GATT 1994, reflects the principle of non-discrimination with respect to internal laws and regulations under the national treatment standard.

[134] Article 2.1 TRIMs Agreement, refers to an 'Illustrative List' of TRIMs, which appears at the end of the TRIMs Agreement and the measure invoked is considered to be in violation of the prohibition in 1(a), which refers to 'local content', which is the same measure that was found to be WTO-inconsistent in the case of *Indonesia – Autos*.

[135] For details of the award of the Purchase Power Agreements to the local subsidiaries of a South Korean consortium, led by Samsung C&T Corporation in 'like circumstances', see above note 135. In the case of *Mesa Power* v. *Canada*, Boulevard Associates Canada, Inc., a local company, which is also placed in like circumstances, is considered to have received more preferential treatment from the OPA.

[136] See above n. 8, for detailed coverage of NAFTA provisions.

pit both against environmental concerns and the right of the host state, Canada, to pursue a particular form of industrial policy.

It could also lead to the question of whether the foreign investor, Mesa Power, might be able to challenge the consistency of Canada's regulatory measures with its specific WTO obligations through investment arbitration. While not yet specifically at issue in the *Mesa Power* v. *Canada* dispute, the investor has invoked Article 1105 NAFTA, which states that parties shall 'accord to investments of investors of another Party treatment *in accordance with international law*'.[137] Some commentators have read Article 1105 NAFTA as providing a 'gateway for the incorporation of WTO disciplines into that provision'.[138] However, in practice no NAFTA investment tribunal has considered that it has jurisdiction to incorporate WTO law into Article 1105 NAFTA by referencing 'international law' in this way.

Methanex v. *USA*[139] is undoubtedly the dispute that sets the bar for any consideration of a host state's violation of the GATT 1994, or indeed any other WTO obligation, in an investor–state dispute. Methanex in its complaint against the USA, concerning the California State ban on the use of MTBEs (an oxygenate and source for octane in the production of gasoline) on environmental grounds, was challenged before a NAFTA investment tribunal on the basis that the ban constituted a substantial interference with, and a taking of, Methanex's investment in its wholly owned US facility. The Tribunal was not persuaded by Methanex's argument that the action by the Californian authorities violated numerous provisions of the GATT.[140] It was of the view that Article 1131 NAFTA does not create any such jurisdiction because the tribunal's jurisdiction is necessarily limited by Articles 1116 and 1117 NAFTA.

It went on to state that: '[T]here is no specific "envoi" to the GATT in any of the provisions of Section A, namely Articles 1102 [National Treatment], 1105 [Minimum Standard of Treatment] and 1110 [Expropriation and Compensation] in respect of which Methanex alleged breaches by the USA'.[141] Recalling the decision in the *OSPAR* arbitration (*Ireland* v. *United*

---

[137] Article 1105(1) NAFTA.
[138] Verhoosel, 'The use of investor-state arbitration under bilateral investment treaties', 503.
[139] NAFTA Tribunal under United Nations Commission on International Trade Law (UNCITRAL) Arbitration Rules, *Methanex Corporation* v. *United States of America* (*Methanex* v. *USA*) (Final Award of the Tribunal on Jurisdiction and Merits), 9 August 2005.
[140] *Ibid.*, para. 4.
[141] *Ibid.*, para. 5.

Kingdom),[142] the Tribunal was of the view that to interpret Article 1131(1) NAFTA in this way would be an unwarranted transformation of the NAFTA "'into an unqualified and comprehensive jurisdictional regime, in which there would be no limit *ratione materiae* to the jurisdiction of a tribunal established under" Chapter 11 NAFTA'.[143]

Where the Tribunal was prepared to modify its position was in drawing upon WTO jurisprudence in interpreting substantive NAFTA provisions, such as the national treatment provision in Article 1102 NAFTA, which formed part of the complainant's submission in *Methanex*. This is consistent with the approach taken by other NAFTA tribunals in cases such as *S D Myers v. Canada*,[144] *Pope & Talbot v. Canada*[145] and *Feldman v. Mexico*[146] where a test for 'like circumstances' was developed. Each of those tribunals drew upon WTO jurisprudence as a guide to construing 'like circumstances' in national treatment cases, although the final test is very different from that applied to 'like products' under the GATT.[147]

Accordingly, the Tribunal in *Methanex* believed that it 'may derive guidance from the way in which a similar phrase in the GATT has been

---

[142] This is a reference to the arbitral award in *Dispute Concerning Access to Information under Article 9 of the OSPAR Convention (Ireland v. United Kingdom)*, Permanent Court of Arbitration (PCA), Final Award, 2 July 2003, 42 ILM 118, at 1136, para. 85.

[143] *Methanex v. USA*, para. 5.

[144] *S D Myers v. Government of Canada* (First Partial Award), 13 November 2000 (2001) 40 ILM 1408, paras. 243–246 with reliance on the Appellate Body's reasoning over 'like products' in the Appellate Body Report, *Japan –Taxes on Alcoholic Beverages (Japan – Alcoholic Beverages II)*, WT/DS38/AB/R, adopted 1 November 1996.

[145] *Pope & Talbot v. Canada* (Award on Merits), 10 April 2001 (2002) 122 ILR 352, paras. 45–63 and 68–69 with reliance on the WTO Panel Reports in: WTO Panel Report, *European Communities – Regime for the Importation, Sale and Distribution of Bananas (EC – Bananas III)*, WT/DS27/R, adopted 22 May 1997 and WTO Panel Report, *European Communities – Measures Affecting Asbestos and Asbestos-Containing Products (EC – Asbestos)*, WT/DS135/R, adopted 18 September 2000 as well as the GATT Panel Report, *United States – Measures Affecting Alcoholic and Malt Beverages (US – Alcoholic and Malt Beverages)*, DS23/R, BISD 39S/206, adopted 19 June 1992, and GATT Panel Report, *United States Section 337 of the Tariff Act of 1930 (US – Section 337 of the Tariff Act 1930)*, L/6439, BISD 36S/345, adopted 7 November 1989. The Tribunal noted that in the GATT context national treatment was reviewed for its effect on the 'modification of conditions of competition' rather than 'less favourable treatment', as applied in the investment context.

[146] *Marvin Roy Feldman Karpa v. United States of Mexico* (Award), ICSID Case No. Arb(AF)/99/1, 16 December 2002 (2003) 18 ICSID Review-FILJ 488, para. 165, with reference to Article III GATT concerning the issue of 'like circumstances'.

[147] N. DiMascio and J. Pauwelyn, 'National treatment in trade and investment: worlds apart or two sides of the same coin?' *American Journal of International Law* 102(1) (2008), 71–2.

interpreted in the past'. It went on to state, however, that it would not treat GATT/WTO jurisprudence as 'binding precedent' but merely as persuasive authority.[148] This position has been endorsed in later decisions, as for example in *Canfor Corporation et al* v. *USA*,[149] where the Tribunal was asked to consider the US Byrd Amendment as largely 'non-compliant with the WTO Anti-dumping[150] and Subsidies and Countervailing Measures[151] Agreements'. In *Canfor* the Tribunal was of the view that: 'the findings of WTO panels and its Appellate Body … constitute relevant factual evidence which the Tribunal can and should appropriately take into account' when deciding the investment dispute.[152]

When it comes to interpreting exceptive clauses in a BIT there have also been investment arbitration awards, such as the one in *Continental Casualty* v. *Argentina*[153] where the Tribunal interpreted an investment treaty provision on the basis of WTO jurisprudence. It concerned the construction of the concept of 'state of necessity' in Article XI of the Argentina–USA BIT and in customary international law, which was considered by reference to the necessity test imported from Article XX GATT jurisprudence.[154] Instead of interpreting the customary international law rule on the state of necessity, as codified by the International Law Commission (ILC) in Article 25 of the draft ILC Articles on State Responsibility,[155] the Tribunal took the view that Article XI of the Argentina–USA BIT was derived from a parallel model clause in US FCN treaties, which in turn reflected the formulation of wording in Article XX GATT 1947.[156]

The Tribunal therefore considered it more appropriate to have reference to GATT/WTO case law, which had dealt extensively with 'the concept

---

[148] *Marvin Roy Feldman Karpa* v. *United States of Mexico*, para. 6.

[149] *Canfor et al.* v. *USA*, paras. 274–346 deal with the Byrd Amendment.

[150] Agreement on Anti-dumping and Countervailing Measures, Marrakesh, 15 April 1994, in force 1 January 1995, Marrakesh Agreement Establishing the World Trade Organization, Annex 1A, The Legal Texts: The Result of the Uruguay Round of Multilateral trade Negotiations (1999) 191,1867 UNTS 493.

[151] SCM Agreement, above n. 131.

[152] *Canfor et al.* v. *USA*, para. 327.

[153] *Continental Casualty Company* v. *The Argentine Republic* (*Continental Casualty* v. *Argentina*) (Award), ICSID Case No. ARB/03/9, 5 September 2008.

[154] *Ibid.*, paras. 192–195.

[155] Responsibility of States for Internationally Wrongful Acts, 2001, text adopted by the International Law Commission at its 53rd Session, 2001, reproduced as an annex to General Assembly Resolution 56/83 of 12 December 2001 (ILC Draft Articles on State Responsibility).

[156] The Tribunal was no doubt led down this 'interpretative path' by one of the arbitrators, Professor Giorgio Sacerdoti, a former Member of the WTO Appellate Body.

and requirements of necessity in the context of economic measures derogating to ... obligations contained in GATT, rather than [referring] to the requirement of necessity under customary international law'. It drew in particular on *Korea - Beef*[157] in determining that the word 'necessary' in Article XX(d) GATT 1994 was not 'limited to that which is "indispensable" or "of absolute necessity" or "inevitable"'.

Instead, other measures might fall within its ambit and in fact the term 'necessary' referred to 'a range of degrees of necessity that could be measured along a continuum'.[158] Additionally, in determining whether a measure, which is 'not necessary' may nevertheless be 'indispensable', it applied the process of 'weighing and balancing' various factors, again on the basis of *Korea - Beef* and confirmed in later WTO jurisprudence.[159] Finally, basing itself on *US - Gambling*[160] and *Brazil - Retreaded Tyres*[161] the Tribunal determined that a measure is not necessary if another treaty-consistent or less inconsistent measure is 'reasonably available' as an alternative measure.[162] This approach by the Tribunal in *Continental Casualty* v. *Argentina*, which involved the importation of the concept of necessity under Article XX GATT into investor–state arbitration, has been criticised in the scholarship.[163]

Similarly, other investment arbitration tribunals have explicitly rejected the idea that WTO jurisprudence is relevant for interpreting specific investment treaty provisions. For example, in the case of *Occidental* v. *Ecuador*[164] the Tribunal believed that the plain language as well as the object and purpose of the national treatment provision in the Ecuador–USA BIT, as opposed to GATT/WTO law, were markedly different. It was particularly keen to strike down the notion that a competition-based

[157] WTO Appellate Body Report, *Korea - Measures Affecting Imports of Fresh, Chilled and Frozen Beef (Korea - Beef)*, WT/DS161/AB/R, adopted 10 January 2001.
[158] *Continental Casualty* v. *Argentina*, para. 193, with reliance on *Korea - Beef*, para. 161.
[159] *Korea - Beef*, para. 194.
[160] WTO Appellate Body Report, *United States - Measures Affecting the Cross-Border Supply of Gambling and Betting Services (US - Gambling)*, WT/DS285/AB/R, adopted 20 April 2005, para. 308 (with reference to Article XIV GATS).
[161] WTO Panel Report, *Brazil - Measures Affecting Imports of Retreaded Tyres (Brazil - Tyres)*, WT/DS332/R, adopted 12 June 2007, para. 7.211.
[162] *Continental Casualty* v. *Argentina*, para. 195.
[163] J. E. Alvarez and T. Brink, 'Revisiting the Necessity Defense: Continental Casualty v. Argentina', IILJ Working Paper 2010/3, Finalized 04/14/10, *Yearbook on International Investment Law & Policy (2010–2011)* (New York: Oxford University Press, 2012).
[164] *Occidental Exploration and Production Company* v. *The Republic of Ecuador* (Award), LCIA Case No. UN3467, 1 July 2004, 12 ICSID Reports 59, para. 175.

reading of the national treatment standard in the BIT could have any relevance in the particular context of this dispute.[165]

What does emerge from the practice of investment arbitration awards tribunals is that they make a clear distinction between WTO law as applicable law under IIAs, when an investor seeks to challenge a WTO-inconsistent measure by the host state, and GATT/WTO law as relevant interpretative context, in the sense of Article 31(3)(c) of the Vienna Convention on the Law of Treaties (VCLT).[166] This Article provides that the treaty interpreter, which in this case is the arbitral tribunal, shall take into account 'any relevant rules of international law applicable in the relations between the parties'.[167] Indeed, NAFTA arbitral tribunals appear to have little difficulty in referring to WTO jurisprudence as persuasive authority for the purposes of interpreting NAFTA Chapter 11, as is evident from a number of arbitral awards,[168] although owing to the lack of precedent or a *jurisprudence constante* in investment arbitration there is no need for other investment tribunals, such as under the ICSID, to follow this lead. Thus, it might be true to say, on the basis of a number of NAFTA decisions, that WTO jurisprudence holds a certain attraction for investment arbitration tribunals but the incorporation of WTO law by reference does not.

E.   Possible future developments in the investment–trade relationship

If we look back at the relationship between investment and trade since the end of the 1940s we observe that it has been one of twists and turns. It has navigated a course between attempts at bringing bilateral and multilateral investment issues under the aegis of an international organisation (the stillborn ITO) in the immediate post-Second World War era to partially addressing trade and investment issues in the WTO, by way of the OECD and the UN General Assembly. Alongside this activity, and in tandem, there has emerged an investment regime, which is based on more than 1,800 validly enforceable BITs, and other investment instruments in a growing number of FTAs.

---

[165] *Ibid.*
[166] Vienna Convention on the Law of Treaties (VCLT), Vienna, 23 May 1969, in force 27 January 1980, A/Conf.39/27 / 1155 UNTS 331 / 8 *ILM*679 (1969) / 63 AJIL 875 (1969).
[167] Article 31(3)(c) VCLT.
[168] Verhoosel, 'The use of investor–state arbitration under bilateral investment treaties', fn. 122, 503 and relevant cases.

We have also noted the increasingly close linkages between FDI and trade, especially when it comes to the impact of intra-firm investment flows on the pattern of trade. This has come about largely as a result of production fragmentation, based on the global diffusion of production and increased international trade in final goods, parts and components. Perhaps the biggest change in terms of interlinkages has been the interaction of BITs, and more significantly investment chapters in FTAs, with FDI flows that are linked to broader-based market access and trade liberalisation. The pre-eminent example here is the NAFTA although there are an increasing number of such trade and investment-type agreements.

The challenge for the future lies in better understanding how the interaction between FDI and international trade is unfolding and whether the renewed relationship between these two areas of economic activity can ever lead to greater convergence in rule-making, standard-setting and the settlement of investment and trade disputes. So far, in GATT/WTO jurisprudence there has been little inclination to move beyond the subject matter of covered agreements and this is unlikely to change.

However, WTO panels and the Appellate Body could draw some lessons from investment arbitration by looking at the way in which some arbitral tribunals have gone about interpreting and applying 'rules of international law' in the sense of Article 31(3)(c) VCLT,[169] in particular where it concerns rules of customary international law. Thus, certain matters such as the rules on attribution, which lie at the heart of the law of state responsibility, and are so critical to the determination of host state liability in investment disputes, could provide guidance on how to deal with issues of attribution in WTO dispute settlement.[170] The jurisprudence on various treaty-based defences, raised before investment arbitration tribunals, could offer guidance to WTO panels and the Appellate Body when interpreting exceptive clauses or concepts such as a state of necessity, including 'economic necessity'. Similarly, the application by investment arbitration tribunals of broader principles of international law, such as good faith, equity and the doctrine of legitimate

---

[169] Some scholars have considered this reference to 'any relevant rules of international law' in interpreting treaty text to be a principle of 'systemic integration' and one that addresses issues of 'fragmentation'; see further C. McLachlan, 'Investment treaties and general international law', *International and Comparative Law Quarterly* 57(1) (2008), 361–401.

[170] See for a scholarly contribution, S. M. Villalpando, 'Attribution of conduct to the state: how the rules of state responsibility may be applied within the WTO Dispute Settlement System', *Journal of International Economic Law* 5(2) (2002), 393–420.

expectations, which have traditionally been invoked before investment arbitration tribunals when interpreting the fair and equitable treatment standard, might provide guidance to WTO decision-makers. However, the limits to WTO dispute settlement, as ever, rest on the reluctance of panels and the Appellate Body to broaden their interpretative boundaries.

Conversely, where investment arbitration tribunals have drawn on GATT/WTO jurisprudence in reaching final awards the practice has been mixed and frequently inconsistent. There are important reasons for this that are to do with the structural variations between investor–state arbitration and WTO dispute settlement.[171] Such variations arise from the different *ratione personae* (investor–state versus inter-state dispute settlement), private versus public decision-makers (party-appointed private arbitrators versus ad hoc panellists/Appellate Body Members), retrospective versus prospective remedies and the nature of those remedies (monetary compensation versus compensatory adjustments and/or rebalancing of concessions).

There are also limits on the extent to which WTO jurisprudence can be brought into investment arbitration. The principles of treaty interpretation that apply in respect of each of these dispute settlement *fora* may stem from the same source, that is the VCLT or its customary international law usage, but nevertheless their application in practice should be more than merely an opportunistic cross-referencing exercise. Thus there is no good reason to believe that the fundamental rules on matters such as non-discrimination, MFN and even exceptive clauses, which appear on their face to unite the legal regimes underpinning FDI and international trade, are necessarily the same in their evolution or their application. Taking this a step further, there is no reason to adduce the wholesale importation of WTO law by reference into investment arbitration awards for the reasons stated by the Tribunal in *Methanex*.[172]

[171] Alvarez and Brink, 'Revisiting the Necessity Defense', p. 18.
[172] *Methanex* v. *USA*, paras. 5–6.

Investment and trade: the 'Lottie and Lisa' of international economic law?

TOMER BROUDE

A. Introduction

In Erich Kästner's *Das Doppelte Lottchen*[1] (literally, 'The Double Lotties', translated into English under the title *Lottie and Lisa*[2]) Lisa's hair is curly, Lottie's hair is braided, but otherwise they look alike. This is not surprising because they are in fact identical twins, separated at a very young age following an unfortunate divorce, each of them subsequently being raised by one of their parents, and developing different characters. When chance brings the nine-year-old Lisa and Lottie together at summer camp, they recognise their common heritage and decide to trade places, so each of them can meet their previously unknown (other) parent. The cheerful ending – decidedly optimistic, for a children's novel initially published in 1949 Germany – has the twin girls and their parents reunited as a family. The charm of the original story has persisted throughout the ensuing decades as the inspiration of several children's films, including Disney's *The Parent Trap*.[3]

In many ways, Kästner's Lottie and Lisa are analogous to the two major branches of international economic law – international trade regulation and investment protection law. As economic and social phenomena, international trade and investment are inextricably linked. Yet like

The author wishes to thank Roberto Echandi, Mary Footer, Debra Steger, Christian Tietje and the participants of the World Trade Forum for their helpful comments.

[1] E. Kästner, *Das Doppelte Lottchen: Ein Roman für Kinder* (Hamburg: Cecilie Dressler, 1949).
[2] E. Kästner, *Lottie and Lisa: A Novel for Children* (London: Jonathan Cape, 1950).
[3] The first version from 1961 was remade in 1998 with Lindsay Lohan playing the role of the twins; see www.imdb.com/title/tt0055277/ and www.imdb.com/title/tt0120783/.

twins separated at birth, the regulation of these economic areas has been entrusted to discrete legal systems, with different characteristics. There are clear historical and political economy reasons for the development of the bifurcation of the regulatory fields, but these reasons should no longer be dispositive and the existing legal separation is difficult to justify in today's globalised economy. Indeed, in spite of this functional and regulatory separation, in practice international trade and investment are more closely tied to each other now than ever before. Had the need (or opportunity) arisen today to draw up an international system of international economic law from scratch, it is unlikely that trade and investment would have been treated so separately.

This chapter takes the general view that it is time to seriously consider a consolidation of the two fields, similar to the family reunion of Lottie and Lisa and their parents. More precisely, the call is not merely to contemplate how to somehow reconcile the procedural and substantive technicalities of international trade and investment law, a formidable challenge in itself,[4] but rather more ambitiously to reconceive (for lack of a better word) the two fields as one. This does not mean that the more individual characteristics of trade and investment should be disregarded or abandoned; far from it, there are significant differences between the twins. But ideally they should be sensitised to each other, rationalised and consolidated.

In section B I will provide a stylised account of the separation of regulation of the twins' upbringing despite the enduring high degree of chromosomal identity between them. In section C I will describe the circumstances that now agitate for reconnection. In section D, I will examine, as a case study, a particular and relatively compartmentalised issue area of international economic concern – the regulation of subsidies – demonstrating the overlaps and gaps between trade aspects and investment issues, in order to concretise the claim that continuing to regulate international trade and investment separately is problematic and difficult to justify. Section E closes with some brief forward-looking conclusions.

---

[4] See, e.g. N. DiMascio and J. Pauwelyn, 'Non-discrimination in trade and investment treaties: worlds apart or two sides of the same coin', *American Journal of International Law* 102(1) (2008), 48–89; J. Kurtz, 'The use and abuse of WTO law in investor–state arbitration: competition and its discontents', *European Journal of International Law* 20(3) (2009), 749–71e.

B.   Degrees of separation: a narrative of the trade–investment divide

The fundamental questions that drive international trade regulation (in short: 'who sells what, where?')[5] and investment protection law (similarly simplified: 'who invests where, how?') are deeply and conceptually linked. At the meta-level, at least, both areas are concerned with the efficient international allocation of resources. Adam Smith's 'invisible hand' and David Ricardo's comparative advantage are not only theories of international trade – the international mobility of goods (and services) – but also theories of investment, because they may be concomitantly understood as explanations of investor responsiveness to market returns from manufacturing activities (i.e. the decision to invest in production of cloth or wine). The goals of trade law[6] and investment law,[7] with all their nuances, are strikingly similar, ultimately concerned with the facilitation of economic efficiency through international economic activity.

Yet at the same time it is true that (like identical twins) the two questions are analytically separable. Smith, Ricardo and many other theorists of trade,[8] while advocating a reduction of barriers to the free movement of goods, have often assumed that the capital investments necessary for the production of goods are a local rather than international resource,

---

[5] This is not to imply that trade law guarantees market share, but it protects market access and competitive conditions that determine international trade patterns.

[6] Whether understood as a restraint of protectionism, or a restraint of terms-of-trade manipulation, the ultimate goal of trade law is efficiency. For discussion, see D. H. Regan, 'What are trade agreements for? Two conflicting stories told by economists, with a lesson for lawyers', *Journal of International Economic Law* 9(4) (2006), 951–88.

[7] The main goals of international investment law are the protection of foreign investment, the liberalisation of investment flows and foreign investment promotion. Arguably, all these goals are served by restraining governmental intervention with the aim of economic efficiency. See J. W. Salacuse and N. P. Sullivan, 'Do BITs really work? An evaluation of bilateral investment treaties and their grand bargain', *Harvard International Law Journal* 46 (2005), 67–130. Whether these goals are effectively achieved – or even desirable – is the subject of much debate. See generally M. Sornarajah, *The International Law on Foreign Investment*, 3rd edn (New York: Cambridge University Press, 2010), pp. 47–60; and L. E. Sachs and K. P. Sauvant, *The Effect of Treaties on Foreign Direct Investment: Bilateral Investment Treaties, Double Taxation Treaties, and Investment Flows* (Oxford University Press, 2009).

[8] E.g. the Heckscher–Ohlin factor proportions theorem assumes that capital is an endowment of a state and that there is no capital movement between states; but see A. Wood, 'Give Heckscher and Ohlin a chance!', *Weltwirtschaftliches Archiv* 130(1) (1994), 20–49, arguing that the empirical inaccuracy of the Heckscher–Ohlin theorem is derived from the fact that capital is in fact internationally mobile.

derived within the jurisdiction of production (international trade without international investment). Conversely, rent-seeking transnational investors find national markets that are protected from international competition in trade to be particularly attractive for investment purposes (international investment without international trade).[9] In short, one can liberalise international trade separately from international investment, and vice versa, even though it would make sense to do both together, given the strong relationship between them, and their common meta-goals.

Indeed, at the post-Second World War cradle of international economic law – in London, Washington DC, at Bretton Woods and Havana – it would have been eminently sensible to draw up an international legal system that would regulate and liberalise both trade and investment, but historical circumstances – and mainly the wrong reasons, as in many separations – agitated towards estrangement. In trade, the scars of *inter bellum* beggar-thy-neighbour protectionist policies, the desire to restructure Transatlantic commercial relations and the needs of the European powers, led by Great Britain, to maintain their unbalanced economic relations with their (soon-to-be-former) colonies,[10] led to the creation of a multilateral trading arrangement characterised by 'enlightened mercantilism',[11] albeit in the stunted institutional form of the General Agreement on Tariffs and Trade (GATT). In contrast, in investment no such necessity for either liberalisation or protection was identified by international policy- and law-makers, certainly not in the multilateral context. Consequently, the 1948 Havana Charter included only hortatory language relating to investment,[12] which never found its way into binding law. The need for international legal regulation of investment – specifically the protection

---

[9] Indeed, this has been associated with some import-substitution programmes in developing countries, based on foreign direct investment (FDI), as well as with so-called 'tariff-jumping' FDI. See T. H. Moran, *Foreign Direct Investment and Development: The New Policy Agenda for Developing Countries and Economies in Transition* (Washington DC: Peterson Institute for International Economics, 1998), pp. 36–8.

[10] The issue of 'imperial preferences' was central to the negotiations that led to the General Agreement on Tariffs and Trade (GATT). See D. A. Irwin, P. C. Mavroidis and A. O. Sykes, *The Genesis of the GATT* (Cambridge University Press, 2008).

[11] Enlightened mercantilism prefers increased exports over imports, but overall, increased international movement of goods is a good thing. See P. Krugman, 'The move toward free trade zones', *Federal Reserve Bank of Kansas City Economic Review* 5 (1991), 5–24 at 15; and K. Bagwell and R. W. Staiger, 'GATT-Think', NBER Working Paper No. 8005, November 2000, 41, available at: www.nber.org/papers/w8005.

[12] P. C. Mavroidis, 'Regulation of Investment in the Trade Regime: From ITO to WTO' (Mimeo, 2011, on file with author), 3–4.

of investments – did not emerge until well into the post-colonial era, in a predominantly North–South bilateral context, and in privileged economic sectors largely unregulated by international trade law at the time (such as infrastructure and extractive industries);[13] but by then the parenting of the two daughters – the regulation of trade and investment, Lottie and Lisa – had been effectively divided.

Separation was surely accepted as divorce, at least when in the early 1980s a GATT dispute settlement panel faced with investment-related claims based on GATT law told it like it was (though not as it should have been): 'The purpose of Article III:4 is not to protect the interests of the foreign investor but to ensure that goods originating in any other contracting party benefit from treatment no less favourable than domestic goods.'[14] The premier multilateral regulatory arrangement in international economics was concerned with goods, not with investment; the GATT was home to Lottie, but not to Lisa. Efforts aimed at reconciliation between the alienated siblings – in the World Trade Organization (WTO) Agreement on Trade-related Investment Measures (TRIMs)[15] and in its Working Group on Trade and Investment – were feeble, and insignificant in their outcomes.[16] The attempt to provide the international regulation of investment a home of its own as a Multilateral Agreement on Investment (MAI) under the auspices of the Organisation for Economic Co-operation and Development (OECD) proved disastrous,[17] leaving the field of investment open to fragmented regulation by thousands of

---

[13] See Sornarajah, *The International Law on Foreign Investment*, p. 21: '[i]t was only after the dissolution of empires that the need for a system of protection of foreign investment came to be felt by the erstwhile imperial powers, which now became the exporters of capital to the former colonies and elsewhere.'

[14] See GATT Panel Report, *Canada – Administration of the Foreign Investment Review Act*, L/5504–30S/140, adopted 7 February 1984, para. 5.9 and also para. 6.5: '[T]he national treatment obligations of Article III of the General Agreement do not apply to foreign persons or firms but to imported products.'

[15] World Trade Organization (WTO) Agreement on Trade-related Investment Measures (TRIMs Agreement), Marrakesh, 15 April 1994, in force 1 January 1995, Marrakesh Agreement Establishing the World Trade Organization, Annex 1A, The Legal Texts: the Results of the Uruguay Round of Multilateral Trade Negotiations, 1868 UNTS 186.

[16] See P. Sauvé, 'Multilateral rules on investment: is forward movement possible?', *Journal of International Economic Law* 9(2) (2006), 325–55.

[17] For the most advanced draft Multilateral Agreement on Investment (MAI), see Organisation for Economic Co-operation and Development (OECD), DAFFE/MAI(98)7/REV1, 22 April 1998; on the MAI and its demise, see P. Muchlinski, 'The rise and fall of the Multilateral Agreement on Investment: where now?', *The International Lawyer* 34(3) (2000), 1033–53.

bilateral investment treaties (BITs).[18] The enduring absence of a 'World Investment Organisation' stands in stark contrast to trade's robust multilateral system, bringing to mind that other children's novel about similar youngsters trading places – Mark Twain's *The Prince and the Pauper*,[19] in which one physically identical child gains institutional strengths that far outshine those of the other.

C.   Come together, right now? Contemporary convergence

Regulatory treatment of trade and investment therefore seems formally distinct and removed, but genetic realities prevail. The separation brought about by historical factors and political economy as described above has led investment and trade law to develop as discrete legal systems with distinct formal characteristics. Trade law is founded upon the Bretton Woods multilateral ideal, with highly technical and elaborate rules, enforceable mainly through state-to-state dispute settlement. Investment law, in contrast, is based on a web of BITs establishing general principles of conduct, and enforced by investor–state arbitration. The logic of both systems, however, is market and welfare driven – even if the markets, and welfare, can be different.

These characteristics have accentuated the general market liberalisation aspects of trade law while emphasising the protection of private activity in investment law. This has led some commentators to argue that the goals of the two fields are in fact differentiated – that trade law is concerned with 'overall efficiency' whereas investment law relates to the protection of 'individual rights'.[20] However, this argument would appear to confuse the functionalities of the law with its ultimate goals, which remain shared – that is, the goal of economic efficiency and consequent welfare through liberalised international economic activity.

Furthermore, these differences are quite superficial. For example, trade law today is hardly less fragmented (by an increasing number of preferential trade agreements (PTAs)) than investment law.[21] It is broadly

---

[18] For the United Nations Conference on Trade and Development (UNCTAD) database of bilateral investment treaties (BITs) in force, see www.unctadxi.org/templates/DocSearch____779.aspx.

[19] See M. Twain, *The Prince and the Pauper: A Tale for Young People of All Ages*, 1st American edn (Boston: James R. Osgood and Company, 1882). This too became a Disney film, with Mickey Mouse in the starring role; see www.imdb.com/title/tt0100409/.

[20] DiMascio and Pauwelyn, 'Non-discrimination in trade and investment treaties'.

[21] For an indicative survey (now out of date) see R. Fiorentino, L. Verdeja and C. Toqueboeuf, 'The Changing Landscape of Regional Trade Agreements: 2006 Update', WTO Discussion Paper (Geneva: WTO Publications, 2007).

acknowledged that international trade law indirectly protects individual rights of private economic operators,[22] and that state-to-state disputes are representative of agglomerated private claims.

Moreover, in today's world international trade and investment are strongly linked, perhaps more than ever. Few traders are not interested in international investment, and few investors are not interested in international trade. Indeed, at least half of world trade occurs between affiliates of multinational enterprises, that is between corporations that maintain concurrent trade and investment relations.[23] According to some statistics, FDI 'has become more important than trade for delivering goods and services to foreign markets'.[24]

This reflects a fundamental shift in business models that affects both trade and investment patterns. In the not-too-distant past 'multinational corporations' merely invested in manufacturing that was physically close to foreign markets; this still happens, but today 'globally integrated enterprises' 'are investing more to change the way they supply the entire global market'.[25] Corporations that once would have been considered as 'national champions' now invest in local foreign subsidiaries not only to overcome trade barriers and to increase market access abroad, but also rely to a large extent upon global supply chains built on foreign suppliers and subsidiaries – even competing brands.[26]

Such shifts in the ways of doing international business have inevitably affected – even reshuffled – the old political economies of trade and investment upon which the legal systems were established. Conventional national economic lines have been blurred, standing traditional relationships on their head. A Finnish corporation (Nokia) invested in New York can ask the United States government to impose import restrictions against foreign goods imported by a US corporation (Apple).[27] US labour

---

[22] Most eloquently stated in WTO Panel Report, *United States – Sections 301–310 of the Trade Act of 1974 (US – Section 301 Trade Act)*, WT/DS152/R, adopted 22 December 1999, paras. 7.77–7.78.

[23] European Commission, 'Towards a Comprehensive European International Investment Policy', Communication from the Commission to the Council, The European Parliament, The European Economic and Social Committee and the Committee of the Regions, COM(2010)343 Final, 7 July 2010, 3, available at: http://trade.ec.europa.eu/doclib/docs/2011/may/tradoc_147884.pdf.

[24] See K. P. Sauvant, 'New sources of FDI: the BRICs – outward FDI from Brazil, Russia, India and China', *Journal of World Investment and Trade* 6 (2005), 639–709.

[25] S. J. Palmisano, 'The globally integrated enterprise', *Foreign Affairs* 8(3) (2006), 127–37 at 130.

[26] See, e.g. P. K., 'Slicing an Apple: How Much of an iPhone is Made by Samsung?', *The Economist*, 10 August 2011. The answer to the question is approximately 26 per cent.

[27] See N. Becker, 'Nokia, Apple Patent Feud Continues', *Wall Street Journal*, 30 December 2009.

unions can petition for safeguards to be imposed against imports from China produced by subsidiaries of their own American employers.

Furthermore, the post-colonial North–South constellation that was responsible, at least in part, for the separation of trade law and investment regulation is now largely irrelevant. The multilateral trading system is no longer effectively dominated by the USA and the European Union (EU), as the gallery of trade powers changes and expands to include developing countries, both small and large. Most importantly perhaps, states traditionally thought of as exclusively capital-importing have become capital exporters,[28] with many of the manufacturing enterprises of the global 'North' owned by investors from the global 'South'.[29] Today's global economy can no longer be thought of as asymmetrical in any clear-cut or meaningful systemic manner. Rather, it is a complex patchwork of transnational networks and interests not defined by any particular political pattern.

Trade and investment law have also both raised very similar concerns regarding their effects on important areas such as human rights, labour rights and the environment – the 'trade and ...' problem,[30] mirrored by the 'investment and ...' problem.[31] With respect to both trade and investment, the criticism is that the economic logic underlying their regulation takes precedence over non-economic interests and concerns. The critics do not draw significant distinctions between trade law and investment regulation, and rightfully so.

Overall, despite their formal divorce, trade and investment have strongly converged since the 1990s. This convergence (or reunion) has been manifested most strongly in the rules governing international service provision and in the field of dispute settlement. With respect

---

[28] Sauvant, 'New sources of FDI'.

[29] Examples abound: e.g. Swedish automobile manufacturer Volvo owned by the Chinese Zhejiang Geely Holding Group. See K. Bradsher, 'Ford Agrees to Sell Volvo to a Fast-Rising Chinese Company', *New York Times*, 28 March 2010, available at: www.nytimes.com/2010/03/29/business/global/29auto.html.

[30] The literature relating to this difficulty is vast. See, e.g. D. P. Steger, 'Afterword: The "trade and ..." conundrum – a commentary', *American Journal of International Law* 96(1) (2002), 135–45.

[31] See M. Hirsch, 'Interactions between Investment and Non-Investment Obligations in International Investment Law' in C. Schreuer (ed.), *Oxford Handbook of International Law on Foreign Investment* (Oxford University Press, 2008); M. Hirsch, 'The Interaction between International Investment Law and Human Rights Treaties: A Sociological Perspective' in T. Broude and Y. Shany (eds.), *Multi-sourced Equivalent Norms in International Law* (Cambridge: Hart Publishing, 2011).

to services, mode 3 of the General Agreement on Trade in Services (GATS)[32] relates to the provision of services through commercial establishment and is in essence a discipline of liberalising investment. Accordingly, the very same economic activity – for example a financial enterprise establishing a subsidiary in a foreign country – if it both satisfies a pertinent definition of 'investment' and is considered a service, may be covered by both trade law and investment law.[33] The potential importance of this normative overlap is growing, especially because trends point to increased FDI in services sectors.[34]

With respect to dispute settlement, it is telling that despite the very different characters of the state-to-state dispute settlement system of the WTO and the investor–state system of investment arbitration, in several cases the same fact pattern has led to litigation in both.[35] In the Softwood Lumber saga, the complexity of overlapping litigation – involving WTO and North American Free Trade Agreement (NAFTA) trade cases as well as NAFTA Chapter 11 investment arbitration, prompted the parties to arrive at a special agreement (the 'Softwood Lumber Agreement') entailing a waiver of both state and private claims, transferring the entire issue to the London Court of International Arbitration,[36] representing an ad hoc consolidation of trade and investment regulation. Furthermore, cases that are at root trade disputes have been brought before investment tribunals (so far unsuccessfully),[37] in the hope that this crossover will lead

---

[32] General Agreement on Trade in Services (GATS), Marrakesh, 15 April 1994, in force 1 January 1995, Marrakesh Agreement Establishing the World Trade Organization, Annex 1B, The Legal Texts: the Results of the Uruguay Round of Multilateral Trade Negotiations, 1869 UNTS 183; 33 ILM 1125, 1167.

[33] See B. D. Meester and D. Coppens, 'Mode 3 of the GATS: A Model for Disciplining Measures Affecting Investment Flows?' (Mimeo, 2011, on file with author).

[34] United Nations Conference on Trade and Development (UNCTAD), World Investment Report 2004 – The Shift to Services (New York: United Nations, 2004), Chapter III.

[35] See J. Pauwelyn, 'Editorial comment: adding sweeteners to Softwood Lumber: the WTO–NAFTA "spaghetti bowl" is cooking', Journal of International Economic Law 9(1) (2006), 197–206.

[36] See L. Guglya, 'The interplay of international dispute resolution mechanisms: the Softwood Lumber controversy', Journal of International Dispute Settlement 2(1) (2011), 175–207.

[37] See NAFTA tribunal (under United Nations Commission on International Trade Law (UNCITRAL) Arbitration Rules), In re Consolidated Canadian Cattle Claims (Award on Jurisdiction), 28 January 2008, paras. 143 and 147, available at: www.state.gov/documents/organization/99954.pdf. The investment claim brought by Canadian cattlemen for compensation due to import restrictions related to mad cow disease was rejected at the jurisdictional stage, when the arbitral panel determined that the claimants were not considered investors in the respondent state.

to financial compensation for trade restrictions, whether in violation of trade law[38] or not. Dispute settlement promises to continue to be a principal meeting place for trade and investment law; it is, for example, only a matter of time before most-favoured nation and 'umbrella' clauses are used by creative litigants to transpose trade law to investment cases and vice versa.

The convergence of trade and investment has even led to an institutional consolidation of decision-making within governments. In some cases this is simply by administrative fiat – with trade bureaucracies like the Office of the US Trade Representative or Foreign Affairs and International Trade Canada (DFAIT) seized of both trade and investment negotiations and litigation. In the case of the European Union, the integration of trade and investment policy-making has required a complex internal process of transferral of investment treaty-making powers from the Member State level to the Union level of the Common Commercial Policy. One cause for this amalgamation is certainly an understanding that trade and investment policy must go together.[39] Similar overlaps now exist in the private legal sector and also among judicial decision-makers, with WTO panellists and indeed Appellate Body members occasionally serving as investment arbitrators. Nowadays, practitioners and scholars of trade law and investment protection law not only view the same world from their office windows, they also occupy the same offices.

In sum, it is evident that despite their initial separation, the regulation of trade and the law of investment have inevitably gravitated towards each other, drawing on their common genetic make-up. However, this convergence is far from being true consolidation. Rather, it is piecemeal and unplanned, lacking a unifying logic. The overlaps already mentioned – in services regulation, in dispute settlement – are full of confused links and gaps. In the next section, I will delve into another area in which incoherence between trade and investment concerns and regulations is apparent – the field of subsidies.

---

[38] G. Verhoorsel, 'The use of investor–state arbitration under bilateral investment treaties to seek relief for breaches of WTO law', *Journal of International Economic Law* 6 (2003), 493–506.

[39] See M. Bungenberg, 'The Politics of the European Union's Investment Treaty Making' in T. Broude, M. L. Busch and A. Porges (eds.), *The Politics of International Economic Law* (Cambridge University Press, 2011).

D. Gaps between trade and investment regulation: the case of subsidies

Highly reflective of the separation between trade and investment law discussed above, the landscape of the international legal regulation of subsidies at the global level is striking in its unbalanced approach towards subsidies related to trade and those related to investment. This is problematic from a general economic perspective because the concerns raised by subsidies with respect to trade are different from the concerns relating to investment, although they are complementary and both have implications for economic welfare.[40] Nevertheless, the trade system has taken precedence over investment – one twin emerging as stronger than the other.

From the perspective of international trade theory, the main issue relating to subsidies is that they might distort international trade in relation to comparative advantage (and, in an imperfect world, in relation to market access commitments).[41] The concern is therefore generally in respect to the relative position of goods and services in international and domestic markets. 'Subsidies are not negative for international trade *per se*. Only government measures that affect the production of goods or their marketing conditions can have a harmful effect on trade.'[42]

In contrast, the chief systemic concerns raised by subsidies in the investment field are twofold. The first concern is unbridled international competition over FDI that would lead to inefficient over-investment both nationally and at the aggregate international level. Even in the 1990s it was noted that '[f]ew countries compete for foreign investment without any form of subsidies today',[43] and this is certainly still the

---

[40] For a more detailed discussion of gaps between the regulation of subsidies in investment and trade, and the rationale of such regulations, see T. Broude, 'Interactions between Subsidies Regulation and Foreign Investment, and the Primacy of the International Trade Regime' in Z. Drábek and P. C. Mavroidis, *Regulations of Foreign Investment: Challenges for International Harmonization*, vol. XXI: World Scientific Studies in International Economics (Singapore: World Scientific, 2012).

[41] See A. O. Sykes, 'Subsidies and Countervailing Measures' in P. F. J. Macrory, A. E. Appleton and M. G. Plummer (eds.), *The World Trade Organization: Legal, Economic and Political Analysis*, volume II (New York: Springer, 2005).

[42] See G. E. Luengo Hernández de Madrid, *Regulation of Subsidies and State Aids in WTO and EC Law* (Dordrecht: Kluwer, 2007).

[43] See M. Blomström and A. Kokko, National Bureau of Economic Research, 'The Economics of Foreign Direct Investment Incentives', NBER Working Paper 9489, February 2003, referring to UNCTAD, *Incentives and Foreign Direct Investment*, Current Studies, Series A, No. 30 (New York: United Nations, 1996).

case.[44] To the extent that inward FDI is thought of as a contribution to domestic economic growth,[45] governments are willing to go to great lengths to secure FDI, either for specific projects or across the board.

The second subsidy concern regarding investment relates not to the fear that subsidies will attract excessive FDI, but that they will deter it by discriminating in favour of domestic investors. Where a market failure is apparent, local firms also need to be incentivised or subsidised to invest in particular sectors, and this might cause some discrimination against FDI (unintentionally or otherwise). In other cases, however, returns on investment could be high enough that a government might be coaxed to reserve investment incentives, in whole or in part, to domestic investors, providing them with anticompetitive rents. This would be inefficient in allocative terms if the investment might have been more welfare-enhancing for a foreign investor, or if the domestic investor would have made a better comparative return in another investment sector or in another country. To be sure, in the not too distant past the national investment promotion regimes of developed countries were mostly tilted *against* foreign investment,[46] and as the current proliferation of investment protection arbitrations attests, national measures in many jurisdictions still have a tendency to discriminate against and exclude foreign capital (or at least to be perceived as doing so by foreign investors).

Subsidies therefore raise significant efficiency-related concerns but they are different with respect to the separated twins of trade and investment. The existing international regulatory environment, however, deals only with the trade concerns, not those of investment. In the trade arena, the WTO Agreement on Subsidies and Countervailing Measures (SCM),[47] in

[44] See also C. P. Oman, *Policy Competition for Foreign Direct Investment: A Study of Competition among Governments to Attract FDI* (Paris: OECD, 1999); and K. Bjorvatn and C. Eckel, 'Policy competition for foreign direct investment between asymmetric countries', *European Economic Review* 50(7) (2006), 1891–907.

[45] For doubts on this matter, see G. H. Hanson, 'Should Countries Promote Foreign Direct Investment?', UNCTAD, G-24 Discussion Paper no. 9, UN Doc. UNCTAD/GDS/MDPB/G24/9 (New York: United Nations, 2001).

[46] E.g. Canada's investment regime, which was highly protectionist and discriminatory in the 1960s and 1970s, requiring between 1974 and 1984 a specific review of all foreign investment under the Foreign Investment Review Act (FIRA) (see Oman, *Policy Competition for Foreign Direct Investment*, p. 74).

[47] Agreement on Subsidies and Countervailing Measures (SCM Agreement), Marrakesh, 15 April 1994, Marrakesh Agreement Establishing the World Trade Organization, Annex 1A, The Legal Texts: the Results of the Uruguay Round of Multilateral Trade Negotiations 275 (1999), 1867 UNTS. 14. Rules on subsidies also appear in the WTO Agreement on Agriculture but they will not be dealt with here.

conjunction with other trade rules and the WTO's robust dispute settlement system, provides a detailed system of rules on the legality of subsidies,[48] an effective system of adjudication and enforcement regarding harmful subsidies, as well as an elaborate system of 'self-help' against them in the form of countervailing duty (CVD) law.[49] In contrast, international investment law arguably contains no particularly significant rules dedicated to the regulation of subsidies and investment incentives. This is, of course, reflective of the absence of a multilateral regulatory agreement on investment, and the fragmentation of investment protection law in general.

Since 1976 the OECD has had in place a Declaration on International Investment Incentives and Disincentives,[50] which provides only a very loose consultative framework with respect to cases in which a Member considers that 'its interests may be adversely affected by the impact on its flow of international direct investments of measures taken by another Member country which provide significant official incentives and disincentives to international direct investment'. This pales in comparison to the SCM's sophisticated mechanisms with respect to subsidies and CVD, and has not been resorted to meaningfully.[51] The failed OECD-sponsored MAI, in its most advanced draft from 1998,[52] included specific language on investment incentives, but much of it was in square brackets, and some negotiating states took the position that this language was simply unnecessary. The draft article that was discussed would have applied the principles of transparency, national treatment and most-favoured nation (MFN) treatment to incentives for inward FDI, and would have recognised the capacity of non-discriminatory investment incentives to distort capital flows and investment decisions. The latter issue would, in any case,

---

[48] Not only in the GATT and SCM Agreement, but also in the TRIMs Agreement, which inter alia prohibits certain measures granting an advantage (such as a subsidy) contingent on a trade-related performance requirement. See United Nations (UN), *UNCTAD Series on Issues in International Investment Agreements, Incentives*, UNCTAD/ITE/IIT/2003/5, 2004, pp. 23–5.

[49] See, in detail, M. Matsushita, P. C. Mavroidis and T. J. Schoenbaum, *The World Trade Organization: Law, Practice, and Policy* (Oxford University Press, 2006), Chapter 10.

[50] OECD, 'International Investment Incentives and Disincentives', Second Revised Decision of the Council, May 1984, in OECD, 'Declaration and Decisions on International Investment and Multinational Enterprises: Basic Texts', DAFFE/IME(2000)20, 8 November 2000, 35.

[51] OECD, 'The OECD Declaration and Decisions on International Investment and Multinational Enterprises: 1991 Review' (1992).

[52] Muchlinski, 'The rise and fall of the Multilateral Agreement on Investment'.

have been deferred for subsequent negotiations,[53] but of course all this was not to be.

Indeed, with most of the international regulation of investment relegated to the global web of BITs, the treatment of subsidies in investment law is inconsistent and undeveloped. Many BITs do not mention subsidies at all, leaving open the question of whether subsidies may be challenged as infringements of national treatment or MFN treatment, while other BITs – especially investment chapters in PTAs – explicitly carve out subsidies from these disciplines.[54] Moreover, the majority of BITs regulate only 'post-establishment' phases of investment, so that they are significantly constrained from addressing the problem of investment incentives discriminating ex ante against FDI,[55] and indeed only with difficulty may they be used to address the problem of international competition over FDI through inefficient subsidisation.

The task of regulating subsidies at the global level therefore falls largely to the SCM Agreement and to WTO law. This regime is, quite naturally, geared towards addressing the concerns raised by subsidies with respect to international trade. In fact, a critical analysis of the SCM regime demonstrates significant gaps in its capacity to address investment concerns in subsidies regulation. Thus, for example, the general definition of 'subsidy' under Article 1 SCM Agreement – comprising a 'financial contribution' and a 'benefit' to the recipient – is indeed broad enough to cover investment incentives and investment-related subsidies quite generally. A government interested in stimulating private investment by providing government capital in any form, for whatever reason, would almost certainly find itself subject to SCM disciplines, possibly running afoul of them – even if the subsidy were efficient in investment terms. If the investment incentive were deemed necessary in the face of a bona fide market failure,[56] it would by definition require the government to grant

---

[53] For the most advanced Multilateral Agreement on Investment, see Organisation for Economic Co-operation and Development (OECD), Negotiating Group on the Multilateral Agreement on Investment, The Multilateral Agreement on Investment Draft – Consolidated Text, DAFFE/MAI(98)7/REV1, 22 April 1998; on the MAI and its demise, see P. L. Muchlinski, 'The Rise and Fall of the Multilateral Agreement on Investment: Where now?' 34(3) *The International Lawyer* (2000), 1033–53.

[54] See, e.g., NAFTA, Article 1108.7(b); 2004 United States (US) Model Bilateral Investment Treaty (BIT), Article 14.5(b), available at: www.state.gov/documents/organiza-tion/117601.pdf; Canada Model BIT, Article 9.5(b), available at: http://italaw.com/documents/Canadian2004-FIPA-model-en.pdf.

[55] See *UNCTAD Series on Issues in International Investment Agreements*, p. 18.

[56] Market failure in private investment can arise for a wide range of reasons. With respect to investment in innovation, for example, causes vary among sectors, including, e.g.,

funding – in the form of direct finance, loan guarantees, credit or even equity capital – at terms better than those available on the commercial market in the absence of governmental support, thus being caught in the definition of 'benefit'.[57] Of course, this would also be the case if the subsidy were granted in less benign circumstances, in the absence of market failure, in order to protect domestic investors or to inefficiently attract FDI. Thus, the definition of 'benefit' in the SCM Agreement and its focus on market value of inputs does not provide any meaningful tools to distinguish between subsidies that are problematic from an investment perspective and those that are not.

As another example, the categories of subsidies regulated by the SCM Agreement pay no attention to the chief concerns that investment regulation has with respect to subsidies (i.e. over-incentivisation and discrimination). The category of 'prohibited subsidies' comprising subsidies contingent upon export performance and/or domestic content is delineated by trade concerns that do not necessarily correlate with investment-related issues. Thus, neither an inefficient financial incentive for FDI nor a discriminatory measure designed to deter FDI would be caught by the prohibition, if it were not made contingent upon export performance or on domestic content. Conversely, an export-contingent subsidy or domestic requirement-based subsidy could be prohibited under the SCM, even if it were indifferent to the source of private investment in the firm supported by it. Indeed, existing WTO findings of export-contingency subsidies are oblivious to such questions.[58]

'Countervailable subsidies' under Part VSCM – those that may be faced with CVD – are also clearly focused on trade-based government subventions; Part V SCM is an elaboration of Article VI:3 GATT[59] that limits

---

financial market transaction costs facing SMEs; risk associated with standards for new technology; limited appropriability of generic technologies; small firm size, high risk etc. See S. Martin and J. T. Scott, 'The nature of innovation market failure and the design of public support for private innovation', *Research Policy* 29 (2000), 437–47.

[57] See WTO Panel Report, *Canada – Measures Affecting the Export of Civilian Aircraft* (*Canada – Aircraft*), WT/DS70/R, adopted 14 April 1999, paras. 9.112–3; 'a financial contribution will only confer a "benefit", i.e., an advantage, if it is provided on terms that are more advantageous than those that would have been available to the recipient on the market' (upheld in WTO, Appellate Body Report, *Canada – Measures Affecting the Export of Civilian Aircraft* (*Canada – Aircraft*), WT/DS70/AB/R, 2 August 1999, paras. 157–8).

[58] See, e.g., WTO Appellate Body Report, *European Communities and Certain Member States – Measures Affecting Trade in Large Civil Aircraft* (*EC – Airbus*), WT/DS316/AB/R, adopted 18 May 2011, para. 703.

[59] Part V Subsidies and Countervailing Measures Agreement begins with Article 10, the title of which is 'Application of Article VI of GATT 1994'. Article VI GATT and the SCM

the use of CVD to direct or indirect bounties or subsidies granted 'on the manufacture, production or export' of products and is therefore only concerned with production and export subsidies, whether they have an effect on investment or not.

The category of 'actionable subsidies' – that although not prohibited per se, may provide the basis for state-to-state WTO dispute settlement – depends on the subsidy causing 'adverse effects to the interests of other Members' (Article 5 SCM Agreement). The term 'adverse effects' encompasses three alternative occurrences: (a) 'injury' to a domestic industry; (b) nullification or impairment of benefits, especially with respect to tariff bindings; and (c) serious prejudice to interests. Ultimately, all three alternatives focus on trade effects, rather than on potential investment effects such as over-subsidisation or discriminatory exclusion of FDI. Injury, as set out in detail in Article 15 SCM, is a term relating to 'subsidized *imports*' and the 'domestic market for like *products*' and 'domestic *producers*' (emphases added). These are all trade-based terms. Similarly, nullification or impairment of benefits relating to tariff bindings under Article II GATT are concepts relating exclusively to trade, telling us nothing about the investment-efficiency of the subsidy. And finally, 'serious prejudice', a term originally derived from Article XVI GATT and the Tokyo Round Subsidies Code,[60] is limited by Article 6.3 SCM to cases in which a subsidy affects imports, prices or market share – all trade output terms, not referring to the potentially no less adverse effects of subsidies on the flows of investment. In other words, in this area as well, a subsidy significantly influencing investment might not be considered 'actionable' if it did not affect trade, and in the reverse, a subsidy might be 'actionable' even when it has no appreciable impact on investment.

There are other such gaps that demonstrate that the WTO subsidies regime is entirely divorced from investment concerns; I elaborate on these elsewhere.[61] The WTO regime does not apply to 'non-specific' subsidies, despite their potential distortive effects on FDI. The remedies provided by the WTO subsidies regime are calibrated with trade effects, not

---

Agreement are considered in WTO jurisprudence as parts of an 'inseparable whole'. See WTO Panel Report, *Brazil – Measures Affecting Desiccated Coconut (Brazil – Desiccated Coconut)*, WT/DS22/R, adopted 17 October 1996, para. 241.

[60] Agreement on the Interpretation and Application of Articles VI, XVI, and XXIII of the GATT, 12 April 1979, in force 28 October 1981, 31 UST 513, BISD 26th Supp. 56.

[61] See Broude, 'Interactions between Subsidies Regulation and Foreign Investment', section 4.

investment; and subsidies in services sectors are not clearly regulated in the WTO, despite their strong link to FDI flows.

E. Conclusion: time to consolidate

The analysis of the question of subsidies regulation is, I believe, merely demonstrative of the overall relationship between the twins of trade law and investment law. Despite the family resemblance of Lottie and Lisa – after all, both trade and investment have similar concerns (complementary and cumulative) relating to the economic efficiency effects of subsidies – in practice, only those concerns associated with international trade are taken into account in a meaningful regulatory manner. And although trade and investment have in practice become so strongly interlinked, the institutional regulatory family separation persists.

From a policy perspective, it seems difficult to justify a continued bifurcation. Looking again to subsidies, one wonders if it makes any sense to effectively proscribe subsidies that influence the physical movement of goods, assuming their inefficiency, while at the same time, at least by default, allowing subsidies that create an inefficient global allocation of investment resources. Much the same could be said about other specific areas of regulation – discriminatory treatment of goods and services compared to discriminatory treatment of investment; the treatment of intellectual property as a trade-related issue when it is no less related to international investment; increased access to goods and services markets when access to capital markets remains constrained; incongruous limitations on trade and investment-related measures based on the same 'non-economic' considerations; differences between regional trade arrangements and regional investment structures. The list goes on.

The regulation of trade and investment has been separated for historical and political reasons. These causes are no longer relevant, either to economic theory or to contemporary international economics. It makes little sense to continue the separation of trade and investment today, any more than Lisa and Lottie should have grown up apart.

10

International trade and investment: towards a common regime?

DEBRA P. STEGER

A. Real world versus legal world

As both Mary Footer and Tomer Broude have noted, in the real world of business and government policy-making, trade and investment are inextricably linked and interwoven. Footer notes, in particular, that 'There has been a tendency in the literature to assume that firms choose either to supply foreign markets through exports or through the establishment of production facilities. However, there is evidence to suggest that in fact there is a high degree of complementarity between FDI and trade'.[1] For multinational enterprises (MNEs), intra-firm trade in goods and services is becoming increasingly more important. Footer also describes how production fragmentation has led to integrated trade and investment decisions on the part of MNEs and small and medium-sized enterprises (SMEs) from both developed and developing countries.[2]

Government policy-makers, recognising that businesses do not separate trade and investment into different silos, frequently design government measures with both policy objectives in mind. Examples include measures taken to attract foreign investment in the automobile industry by providing a tariff exemption on imports of automobiles from the same companies abroad[3] and a feed-in tariff programme designed to provide incentives for foreign and domestic investment in renewable energy generation projects.[4]

---

[1] M. Footer, 'On the Laws of Attraction: Examining the Relationship between Foreign Investment and International Trade', Chapter 8 of this volume.

[2] *Ibid.*

[3] World Trade Organization (WTO) Panel Report, *Canada – Certain Measures Affecting the Automotive Industry* (*Canada – Autos*), WT/DS139/142/R, adopted 19 June 2000.

[4] WTO, *Canada – Certain Measures Affecting the Renewable Energy Generation Sector* (*Canada – Renewable Energy*), DS/WT412/R, DSWT426/R, circulated 19 December 2012.

While to an economist, business person or policy-maker, movement of goods, services and foreign direct investment should logically be covered in the same agreement, history has not allowed this to happen. Instead, there is the international trade regime comprising the World Trade Organization (WTO) Agreement that deals with trade in goods, trade in services, trade-related intellectual property rights and trade-related investment measures as well as more than 320 preferential trade agreements (PTAs), some of which have investment chapters. Separately, governments have negotiated around 3,000 international investment agreements to protect their investors. Attempts to negotiate multilateral rules on investment, first in the Organisation for Economic Co-operation and Development (OECD) and later in the WTO, both failed and the Doha Development Round itself has stalled, raising doubts as to the ability of the multilateral system to negotiate new rules. In the meantime, the major players, such as the European Union (EU), the United States and China, have embarked on a strategy of negotiating new PTAs with their key trading partners as well as a host of new bilateral investment agreements to pursue their national interests. Their recent actions call into question the strength and long-term viability of the multilateral trading system, the WTO, as well as the possibility of integrating trade and investment rules into one, coherent, multilateral system.

B. Trade and investment: separate or together?

Despite their early common origins in friendship, commerce and navigation treaties, history has left us with legally separate regimes for trade and investment. There are reasons for this. 'The trade regime is an interstate construct focused on the macro-issues of market access and trade opportunities to increase overall welfare; the investment regime, in contrast, is centered on the micro-issues of attracting and protecting investments made by individual investors.'[5] Since the 1990s, there has been some progress to integrate trade and investment rules in trade agreements, in particular in the WTO General Agreement on Trade in Services (GATS) and in PTAs negotiated by the USA and Canada, starting with the North American Free Trade Agreement (NAFTA), which have included investment chapters with pre-establishment market access provisions.

---

[5] N. DiMascio and J. Pauwelyn, 'Nondiscrimination in trade and investment treaties: worlds apart or two sides of the same coin?', *American Journal of International Law* 102(1) (2008), 48–89 at 56.

Both Footer and Broude eloquently describe the real world intercon-
nections between trade and investment flows and decisions of business
and government policy-makers. Footer, however, appears resigned to
accept the legal status quo of international trade and investment agreements as they are, and to trust that investment arbitration tribunals
will make good use of their powers to use international law to bring
some measure of coherence and consistency to the two legally separate
systems. Broude, on the other hand, argues that it no longer makes economic sense to maintain two separate fields of law for trade and investment, and he explains how the rules of the WTO Agreement on Subsidies
and Countervailing Measures (SCM Agreement) are designed to apply to
measures affecting trade in goods rather than to programmes designed to
encourage foreign direct investment. He maintains that there have been
some strong signs of convergence, in particular, by the inclusion of mode
3 'commercial presence' as a form of trade in services in the WTO General
Agreement on Trade in Services (GATS), which he states 'is in essence a
discipline of liberalising investment'.[6] He also states that there has been
convergence between trade and investment in dispute settlement in that
private investors are increasingly bringing claims under NAFTA Chapter
11 and similar investor–state arbitration provisions based on the same
government measures that are also the subject of state-to-state disputes
under the WTO.[7] Footer also acknowledges the growing propensity for
investor–state claims relating to the same government measures that have
also been the subject of WTO disputes.[8]

Surprisingly, neither author proposes a reintegration of trade and
investment rules in a strong, multilateral rules-based treaty or warns
against the serious risks to legitimacy from continuing along the path
of separate trade and investment treaty regimes. For all of the business,
economic and policy reasons that they espouse, multilateralisation or
integration of the trade and investment regimes into a coherent rules-
based system should be the overarching goal. With the continuing proliferation of international investment agreements and preferential trade
agreements, and the exponential increase in investor–state arbitration,
the risks of fragmentation, incoherence and inconsistencies in interpretations of the rules are growing. On the positive side, however, there
appear to be opportunities for plurilateralisation of investment rules with

[6] T. Broude, 'Investment and Trade: The "Lottie and Lisa" of International Economic Law?',
    Chapter 9 of this volume.
[7] *Ibid.*
[8] Footer, 'On the Laws of Attraction'.

the EU obtaining competence over investment in the Lisbon Treaty and the current plurilateral free trade negotiations taking place in Asia, South America, Africa and the Trans Pacific Partnership.

C. Government measures are not designed solely for trade or investment purposes

From a policy perspective, governments often have multiple objectives when they are designing subsidy programmes, particularly in relation to major new strategic initiatives. As a result, their measures are usually very complex and difficult to characterise as simply relating to trade in goods, trade in services, or investment. A government may design a subsidy programme for economic policy reasons including innovation, competitiveness, research and development, productivity, industrial policy and job creation without specifically considering the programme's effects on trade. However, the SCM Agreement requires that government measures be broken down and analysed according to certain legal constructs that the governments may not have had in mind when they designed their measures.

This is particularly relevant for complex subsidy programmes. In *Canada – Autos*,[9] for example, the Government of Canada had provided a tariff exemption for imports of motor vehicles and parts from companies that had manufacturing plants in Canada and that had maintained certain ratios of production to sales in Canada as well as certain levels of Canadian value-added in the year of importation as compared with a base year. This measure was found to be a prohibited export subsidy under Article 3.1(a), but not a prohibited domestic content subsidy under Article 3.1(b) of the SCM Agreement. It was also found to violate national treatment under Article III:4 of the General Agreement on Tariffs and Trade (GATT) 1994 and most-favoured nation (MFN) under Article I of the GATT 1994. In its essence, however, complex though this programme was, it was an incentive to foreign motor vehicle companies to establish manufacturing plants in Canada. It was an investment subsidy programme implemented by means of a tariff exemption. It had effects on trade in goods and was therefore examined under the GATT and the SCM Agreement, but its fundamental policy purpose was to attract foreign direct investment.

---

[9] WTO Panel Report, *Canada – Certain Measures Affecting the Automotive Industry* (*Canada – Autos*), WT/DS139/142/R, adopted 19 June 2000; WTO Appellate Body Report, *Canada – Autos*, WT/DS139/142/AB/R, adopted 19 June 2000.

The Ontario Feed-In Tariff Program was designed to encourage foreign as well as domestic investment in renewable energy generation sources. One of the major benefactors of that programme is the Korean company, Samsung. The programme has been challenged in the WTO under the SCM Agreement and the GATT 1994.[10] This is another example of a measure that a government imposed for several policy reasons, including to encourage foreign direct investment. But other WTO Members have alleged that it constitutes a prohibited domestic content subsidy under Article 3.1(b) of the SCM Agreement and a violation of national treatment under Article III:4 of the GATT 1994. However, the Ontario Government ostensibly did not take the measure with trade in goods in mind; it argues that its objectives were protecting the environment and encouraging investment in renewable energy sources.

D.   There is more in the WTO on investment than meets the eye

The WTO is not strictly about market access; it is also about rules. While it is true that the Annex 1A agreements, such as the GATT 1994, the SCM Agreement and the Agreement on Trade-Related Investment Measures (TRIMs Agreement), relate to trade in goods and the Annex 1B agreement, the GATS, relates to trade in services, the terms 'relating to' or 'affecting' trade in goods or services have been interpreted very broadly in GATT and WTO jurisprudence.

As was demonstrated in *Canada – Administration of the Foreign Investment Review Act*,[11] Article III:4 of the GATT 1994 applies to trade-related investment measures. The WTO TRIMs Agreement confirms the applicability of GATT Article III:4 and prohibits specific performance requirements. However, Article III:8 of the GATT 1994 exempts direct subsidies from the national treatment obligation.

The GATS applies to investment measures through mode 3 (commercial presence). Both Broude and Footer agree with most commentators that the GATS is a multilateral agreement that provides disciplines on the supply of 'trade in services' through the mode of 'commercial presence'. However, footnote 8 to Article XVI:1 also establishes that where a WTO Member has made market access commitments in a specific sector under

---

[10] WTO, *Canada – Renewable Energy*. See above, note 4.
[11] General Agreement on Tariffs and Trade (GATT) Panel Report, *Canada – Administration of the Foreign Investment Review Act (Canada – FIRA)*, L/5504, BISD 30S/140, adopted 7 February 1984.

either mode 1 (cross-border) or mode 3 (commercial presence), if movement or transfers of capital are also essential to the supply of the specific services, the Member is committed to allow those movements or transfers of capital.

I. Subsidies

With respect to subsidies, in particular, there is more in the WTO agreements with respect to investment than might be obvious at first glance. Where subsidy programmes affect trade in services in the commercial presence mode, they will be subject to the general MFN obligation in Article II[12] and, in sectors where specific commitments have been made, the market access obligations under Article XVI or national treatment obligations under Article XVII. Thus, although there have been unsuccessful negotiations on subsidy disciplines under the GATS within the WTO as mandated by Article XV, pending any results in those negotiations, the status quo is that the obligations of the GATS apply to subsidy measures relating to trade in services. Therefore, government subsidy programmes related to trade in services are subject to the MFN obligation in Article II of the GATS, and to the extent that a Member has made specific commitments relating to certain services sectors under mode 3 (commercial presence) for market access or national treatment, then those subsidy programmes could also be subject to market access or national treatment obligations under the GATS. As a result, investment incentive programmes for services sectors could be covered by some of the GATS obligations depending upon the facts and the commitments made by the Member concerned.

The definition of 'subsidy' in Article 1 and the requirements with respect to 'specificity' in Article 2 of the SCM Agreement relate to enterprises not production of goods per se. A programme that meets the definition of 'subsidy' and is 'specific' is not necessarily proscribed by the Agreement. Further examination is required to determine whether the programme is a prohibited subsidy under Part II or an actionable subsidy under Part III of the Agreement.

At issue in a WTO subsidy dispute is usually a complex government programme designed for investment, research and development, competitiveness, industrial policy and other objectives. It may, or may not, be made available only to domestic enterprises. Article III:8 of the GATT

---

[12] WTO Appellate Body Report, *Canada – Autos*. See above, note 9.

1994 was presumably intended as an exception from the national treatment obligation for a simple reason: why should taxpayers pay subsidies to foreign enterprises from their tax dollars? The SCM Agreement recognises that subsidy programmes designed to attract foreign investment could have adverse effects on trade. Programmes that were intended by governments to provide incentives for foreign direct investment can be examined by WTO panels under the GATT 1994 and the SCM Agreement because they can have effects on trade.[13] In *Canada – Autos*, the Canadian investment incentive for foreign enterprises to establish manufacturing plants in Canada, effected through a tariff exemption on imports of automobiles, was found to be inconsistent with Canada's obligations under the MFN and national treatment provisions of Articles I and III:4 of the GATT 1994 as well as the export subsidy prohibition of Article 3.1(a) of the SCM Agreement.[14]

It is worth noting that, in the investment chapters of PTAs negotiated by the USA, subsidies or grants provided by parties or state enterprises have been excluded from the application of important obligations. For example, in the NAFTA the national treatment and MFN obligations do not apply to 'subsidies or grants provided by a Party or a state enterprise, including government-supported loans, guarantees or insurance'.[15]

II.   Is history changing?

Integrating trade and investment into a multilateral agreement may not be a utopian dream. They are integrated as chapters in a growing number of PTAs. Following the trend set by the NAFTA, the USA and Canada have included investment chapters with pre-establishment obligations and investor–state arbitration in their PTAs. The goal of investment

---

[13] See, for example, WTO Panel Report, *Canada – Autos*, see note 9 above; WTO Panel Report, see note 4 above.

[14] *Canada – Autos*.

[15] North American Free Trade Agreement (NAFTA), Article 1108(7)(b). The United States continued with this language in the free trade agreement with Central America and the Dominican Republic, the USA–CAFTA–DR Free Trade Agreement, signed 5 August 2004, Article 10.13(5), available at: www.ustr.gov/trade-agreements/free-trade-agreements/cafta-dr-dominican-republic-central-america-fta/final-text; and in the USA–Korea Free Trade Agreement (FTA), signed on 30 June 2007, approved by the US Congress on 12 October 2011, Article 11.12(5), available at: www.ustr.gov/trade-agreements/free-trade-agreements/korus-fta/final-text. See also an exception for existing measures relating to subsidies or grants in Article 11.5(6) in regard to minimum standard of treatment.

chapters in these PTAs is not solely protection of investments but also market access. Starting with Canada, the EU will negotiate investment chapters in its PTAs. The Trans Pacific Partnership Agreement, if it is successful, will most likely follow the US or Canadian model for the investment chapter.

After the Multilateral Agreement on Investment negotiation debacle, investment was agreed as part of the WTO Doha Development Round agenda, but it was withdrawn at Cancún along with other Singapore issues because of the objections of developing countries. However, after experience with investor–state arbitration (in particular, countries such as Argentina, which have had a number of cases brought against them), developing countries may change their minds and come to realise that a multilateral, rules-based agreement would be in their interest.

III.   Is investment arbitration the cure or the curse?

Footer maintains that there is 'no bar' in international dispute settlement to a state bringing a dispute in the WTO and an investor bringing a claim under an international investment agreement relating to the same measure 'concerning the conformity of those measures with WTO obligations'.[16] However, on minimum standard of treatment, the NAFTA Free Trade Commission (the Parties) adopted a binding interpretation of Article 1105 in 2001, which clarified that 'in accordance with international law' means 'customary international law minimum standard of treatment of aliens' and that a breach of another international agreement or of another provision of the NAFTA does not establish a breach of Article 1105.[17] This interpretation has been codified in subsequent PTAs concluded by the USA and Canada. Given the different nature and purpose of WTO obligations from the principles of minimum standard of treatment of aliens or expropriation, for example, it is unlikely that there will be much cross-pollination between these specific trade and investment norms.

Nicholas DiMascio and Joost Pauwelyn have demonstrated in a leading article how a common treaty-based principle of non-discrimination – national treatment – has been interpreted differently in the WTO and

---

[16] Footer, 'On the Laws of Attraction'.
[17] NAFTA Free Trade Commission, *Notes of Interpretation of Certain Chapter 11 Provisions*, 31 July 2001, available at: www.international.gc.ca/trade-agreements-accords-commerci aux/disp-diff/NAFTA-Interpr.aspx?lang=en&view=d.

NAFTA Chapter 11 cases given the different object and purpose of the investment chapter of the NAFTA and the GATT.[18] However, they also show how there has been some small sign of possible evolution in the WTO Appellate Body's interpretation of key elements of the national treatment principle that (if it continues) may lead to greater convergence over time.[19]

Investors attempting to bring WTO or trade-related claims before investment tribunals have not met with success, precisely because although the provisions of international investment agreements may be vague, they were not intended to incorporate, whether as applicable law or by interpretation, other treaties with different purposes and objectives. The WTO Agreement does not constitute customary international law in relation to minimum standard of treatment of aliens or expropriation. Therefore, using investment arbitration as a method to apply and interpret WTO law should not be a reliable method for substantive convergence of the two fields. The rules under NAFTA Chapter 11, except possibly the obligations on national treatment and performance requirements, are not similar enough to warrant reference to WTO cases even for interpretive guidance purposes.

More worrisome is that investment tribunals are ad hoc, appointed to hear individual cases, and there is no guarantee that their decisions will be consistent or coherent. To date, none of the claims brought by investors concerning WTO-related matters have been successful. But one cannot predict what ad hoc tribunals will do in the future. Putting one's trust in ad hoc investment tribunals to be the guardians of international law responsible for the convergence of trade and investment law will only compound the current lack of consistency and coherence in investment tribunal awards and add serious legitimacy concerns. Ad hoc investment tribunals have neither the legal authority nor the administrative capacity to make complex economic policy decisions relating to allocation of global resources or to apply WTO law.

Despite the ambitions of some claimants, as Footer notes in her discussion of the NAFTA Chapter 11 cases to date, the tribunals have unanimously found that they have no jurisdiction to hear claims based on WTO

---

[18] DiMascio and Pauwelyn, 'Nondiscrimination in trade and investment treaties', 58–79, see note 5 above.

[19] DiMascio and Pauwelyn favour the trend toward convergence and the Appellate Body's latest interpretations. *Ibid.*, 82–8. See also WTO Appellate Body Report, *United States – Measures Affecting the the Production and Sale of Clove Cigarettes* (US – Clove Cigarettes) WT/DS406/AB/R, adopted 24 April 2012; Panel Report, *US – Clove Cigarettes*, WT/DS406/R, adopted 24 April 2012.

legal obligations as applicable law. However, some have been willing to entertain arguments involving WTO cases as guidance in interpreting NAFTA provisions. This is hardly a basis on which to ground hopes of convergence of trade and investment norms for the future. The fundamental problem is one of legitimacy – the rules were negotiated by sovereign governments. These rules were intended for different purposes, and it should not be left to ad hoc tribunals, in particular, under investor–state arbitration, to be responsible for harmonising inconsistent or incoherent systems of rules. That responsibility lies with the states that negotiated the treaties. For legitimacy and accountability reasons, ad hoc tribunals comprising private commercial arbitrators should not decide delicate, complex policy issues relating to efficient allocation of global resources and WTO law.

E.   Conclusion

For businesses and policy-makers, trade and investment are two sides of the same coin; they are inextricably linked. International legal regimes, however, are spinning into greater fragmentation as the number of preferential trade agreements and bilateral investment treaties with investor–state arbitration mechanisms continues to increase. The multilateral system is at risk as the Doha Round has stalled, and WTO Members have turned instead to negotiating bilateral and plurilateral agreements. Dispute settlement, however, continues unabated, both in the WTO and under international investment agreements. With the proliferation of investment arbitration cases under different fora being heard by ad hoc tribunals, there are risks of inconsistent and incoherent awards, raising concerns that this may threaten the legitimacy of the systems themselves.

The question arises of how to encourage greater convergence and coherence of trade and investment rules, so that they reflect economic realities and make policy sense. Should we accept the treaties as they are, and put the onus on the dispute settlement systems to bring greater convergence between the trade and investment realms? Is it fair to ask private investors to bring claims based on sound economic policy bases and/or ad hoc tribunals to decide complex public policy issues? Is it an appropriate role for either investment tribunals or WTO panels to 'fill gaps' or 'make law' by invoking international law other than the provisions before them? Only governments have the legitimate authority to negotiate new rules (based on policy) on behalf of their citizens. The ultimate goal, therefore, should be the multilateralisation of trade and investment rules into a coherent policy framework.

11

Perspectives on the interaction between international trade and investment regulation

CHRISTIAN TIETJE

A. Introduction

The excellent chapters on the relationship between international invest-ment law and trade by Mary Footer and Tomer Broude both wrap up a discussion that is not at all new – Softwood Lumber[1] was decided quite some time ago – but still lacks analytical clarity. As a substantial amount of scholarly writing and some dispute settlement practice already exists, the main challenge while discussing investment law and trade is how to add substantially new aspects to the discussion. This is obviously a chal-lenge the two authors had to cope with. This chapter is divided into two sections: the first highlights some aspects of the chapters by Footer and Broude. In section II, I will add some thoughts on what, in my opinion, is the necessary further thinking concerning trade and investment.

B. Basic structure of the chapters by Footer and Broude

In her chapter Footer takes a strong historical perspective. This makes sense and is even necessary. In fact, the historical origins of the current legal regimes on trade and on investment are too often neglected. Most important, as described by Footer in her paper, are treaties of friendship, commerce and navigation (FCN).[2] However, it would be worth looking even more closely at specific provisions of FCN and other trade agreements namely those of the nineteenth century. It is amazing how sophisticated

---

[1] For details see J. Pauwelyn, 'Adding sweeteners to Softwood Lumber: the WTO–NAFTA spaghetti bowl is cooking', *Journal of International Economic Law* 9 (2006), 197–206.

[2] For an overview see A. L. Paulus, 'Treaties of Friendship, Commerce and Navigation' in R. Wolfrum (ed.), *Encyclopedia of Public International Law*, available at: www.mpepil.com.

the regulations were at that time and how much of the wording chosen in the nineteenth century is still in use today. For example, Article XX of the General Agreement on Tariffs and Trade (GATT), a provision that is increasingly discussed in the investment context, uses almost identical wording to that used in the nineteenth century.[3]

Moreover, Footer gives a comprehensive account of the developments in the area of trade and of investment after the Second World War, namely with regard to the failed Havana Charter, the exclusively trade-focused GATT 1947, the importance of developments in the Organisation for Economic Co-operation and Development (OECD) and the emergence of bilateral investment treaties (BITs) as the most important shift from multilateralism to bilateralism in investment law. However, one important systemic aspect could be underlined more clearly: modern investment law has, in contrast to trade law, been developed because of the shortcomings of traditional public international law with regard to the protection of interests of private economic actors. Most important in this regard is the *Anglo-Iranian Oil Company Case*[4] as a direct background to the development of BITs and the International Centre for Settlement of Investment Disputes (ICSID) Convention. The case demonstrates that diplomatic protection and other means used in traditional public international law are not suited for enforcing commercial contracts, even if one of the contracting partners is a state.[5]

A second important issue highlighted by Footer concerns the importance of multinational enterprises (MNEs) as – so to speak – actors integrating international investment and international trade. I have two comments on this. The first is more of a question: the chapter highlights the consequence of what is known as 'production fragmentation' or 'global production chains' for the complementarity between foreign direct investment (FDI) and trade. I wonder whether this is true for both greenfield investment and mergers and acquisitions (M&As). Even though the picture changed somewhat after the crisis of 2007–2009, M&As for a long

---

[3] A comprehensive analysis is provided by F. Bayer, *Das System der deutschen Handelsverträge von 1853 und 1914: völkerrechtliche Prinzipien und ihre Gemeinsamkeiten mit dem heutigen Weltwirtschaftsrecht* (Berlin: BWV Berliner Wissenschafts-Verlag, 2004).

[4] International Court of Justice, *Anglo-Iranian Oil Co. Case (United Kingdom v. Iran)*, ICJ Reports 1952, 93.

[5] See the analysis by C. Tietje, K. Nowrot and C. Wackernagel, 'Once and forever? The Legal Effects of a Denunciation of ICSID', University of Halle (2008), pp. 16ff.

time represented the majority of the value of international investment.[6] The second point concerning MNEs and the interdependence of investment and trade relates to the contradictions that arise in this regard. Broude in his chapter highlights such contradictions with reference to the example of subsidies. Practically, I would say that there is an even more important example – anti-dumping (AD) law. Consider the example of the anti-dumping investigations by the European Union (EU) concerning energy-saving light bulbs from China. In this case, the application for an anti-dumping investigation was filed by Osram, a German company. Osram products represent more than 25 per cent of EU market share in energy-saving light bulbs. However, Philips objected to the application. Philips products represent more than 50 per cent of EU market share. However, more than 70 per cent of this market share is imported products from China, produced in China in a production facility of the Philips company. The crucial question in this case was whether Philips had to be considered a 'community producer' in terms of EU AD; this would have entitled Philips to object to the initiation of an AD investigation by the European Commission.[7] This example shows that the increase in global investment might lead to a conflict of interests with regard to trade law issues. Moreover, the increase in global investment as a phenomenon of globalisation might even challenge traditional concepts of trade law, namely in the area of trade defence instruments.

Turning finally, with regard to Footer's chapter, to dispute settlement, I have two additional points: first, while discussing and perhaps criticising the fact that arbitral tribunals do not take World Trade Organization (WTO) law fully into account, but only within the limited scope of Article 31(3)(c) Vienna Convention on the Law of Treaties (VCLT), one must remember that a tribunal in investment arbitration – as in any arbitration – is not a court and has limited competencies. The tribunal's competencies are determined by the parties, including the applicable law.[8] This is similar to the limitation of the WTO dispute settlement to 'covered agreements' in the sense of Article 1(1) of the Dispute Settlement

---

[6] See United Nations Conference on Trade and Development (UNCTAD), *World Investment Report 2011* (Geneva: United Nations, 2011), pp. 10ff, available at: www.unctad-docs.org/files/UNCTAD-WIR2011-Full-en.pdf.

[7] For a detailed analysis see C. Tietje and B. Kluttig, 'The definition of community industry in EU antidumping law', *Global Trade and Customs Journal* 3 (2008), 89–98.

[8] See, e.g., J. Collier and V. Lowe, *The Settlement of Disputes in International Law: Institutions and Procedures* (Oxford University Press, 1999), pp. 198ff.

Understanding (DSU).[9] Second, in 2011 at least two Section 301/302 petitions in the United States concerning investment law issues were recorded. In a petition in May 2011, individuals requested that the Trade Representative initiate a Section 301 investigation with respect to alleged expropriations without adequate compensation by the Government of the Dominican Republic.[10] In August 2011 it was made public that the US company Azurix's planned to file a 301 petition with the US government with regard to the non-payment by Argentina of an ICSID award.[11] These are interesting developments relating to how trade law instruments are used to enforce investment law.

Let me now turn to the chapter by Broude, who makes, at least in certain respects, very similar points to those made by Footer. He also draws attention to the historical development and to the current factual situation, both of which demonstrate the interdependence of trade and investment. However, although both chapters go in the same direction, Broude is more explicit on the point that there is hardly any difference between trade law and investment law. Both are, in his words, *Das doppelte Lottchen* – the Lottie and Lisa – of international economic law. I will not go into a discussion on the different personalities of Lisa and Lottie, who, even though they are twins, have a quite different character and personality. However, I am sceptical as to whether the 'family reunion' of trade and investment is a realistic and convincing option. Rather, it would seem more fruitful to try to analyse the existing and non-existing relationships between the two regimes of international economic law (law of international finance being the third pillar). In this regard it would appear necessary to differentiate between different dimensions of the overall topic. I would suggest at least the following dimensions:

- overall rationale of the two regimes: individual rights guarantees versus general welfare considerations;
- bilateral versus multilateral approaches;
- rules collision versus rule modification;

---

[9] On 'covered agreements' see e.g. World Trade Organization (WTO), *Appellate Body Report, Guatemala – Anti-Dumping Investigation Regarding Portland Cement From Mexico (Guatemala – Cement)*, WT/DS60/AB/R, adopted 25 November 1998, para. 64.

[10] United States Trade Representative (USTR), 'Petition Under Section 302 on Alleged Expropriations by the Dominican Republic, Decision not to Initiate Investigation', *Federal Register* 76(136) (2011), 41857–41858.

[11] International Institute for Sustainable Development (IISD), 'Azurix petitions the USTR on enforcement of award against Argentina', *Investment Treaty News Quarterly* (2011).

- rules collision versus harmonised interpretation;
- broad versus narrow interpretation and application of jurisdictional clause in trade and investment regimes.

Without going into an extensive discussion of the issues mentioned, it is plausible to assume that a close analysis of these different dimensions would reveal legally important differences between trade law and investment protection law. It is the task of lawyers to work on differences like these. Moreover, only when we are clear about the details of similarities and differences between rules and legal regimes may we move on to criticism and/or making suggestions for improvements. Thus, instead of trying to flip to the last page of the story, it seems necessary to tell the story in detail from the beginning.

C. Some further thoughts

Let me conclude with some thoughts based on, but going beyond three issues in relation to the chapters of Footer and Broude, namely, rule of law, de facto modification of legal concepts and regulatory competition.

First, it would appear worthwhile to study the impact of both trade and investment law on the proliferation of the rule of law. This has to be done, not separately for each of the two legal regimes, but from a comparative perspective. It will be interesting to see how both regimes contribute to and are influenced by the rule of law idea. Some studies in this regard have already been conducted,[12] but a comprehensive analysis from a comparative perspective is still lacking.

Second, as indicated, we seem to have not only the situation of rule collision concerning trade and investment law, but possibly even situations of rule modification. To demonstrate, corporate social responsibility (CSR) and related concepts play an increasingly important role in international investment law. One of the highly debated issues concerning CSR and investment law has been the so-called investment nexus. Via the requirement of an investment nexus, a national enterprise or MNE

---

[12] With regard to trade law, see e.g. E.-U. Petersmann, 'Multilevel judicial governance of international trade requires a common conception of rule of law and justice', *Journal of International Economic Law* 10 (2007), 529–51. On investment law, see e.g. E.-U. Petersmann, 'International rule of law and constitutional justice in international investment law and arbitration', *Indiana Journal of Global Legal Studies* 16 (2009), 513–33; S. W. Schill, 'Fair and Equitable Treatment under Investment Treaties as an Embodiment of the Rule of Law', IILJ Working Paper 2006/6, Global Administrative Law Series, available at: www.iilj.org/oldbak/working%20papers/20066SchillxGAL.htm.

would be bound to CSR standards with regard to economic relationships with enterprises in countries that have not committed themselves to CSR standards only if there was some kind of investment involved. As a consequence of the investment nexus, it has usually been hard to determine CSR in global supply chains. This changed with the 2011 update to the OECD Guidelines for Multinational Enterprises from May 2011.[13] There is no longer an investment nexus in the 2011 update. Instead, a due diligence obligation has been established concerning any activity of any enterprise within a supply chain. Thus, even in a case without any investment involved, a company may be obliged not to undertake certain import activities with a global supply chain because of CSR considerations.[14] As a consequence, the crucial point is that, subject to due diligence requirements, there is no longer any freedom of importation in the sense of Article XI:1 of the GATT. Indeed, the 2011 OECD Guidelines de facto modify the content of Article XI:1 of the GATT in the sense of establishing conditionality of free market entry. This is done without any investment nexus.

Third, and finally, I wish to question the general proposition that there is a need to merge trade law and investment law. Would we not overburden the system? Do we really have identical or at least highly similar underlying concepts of the two regimes which would make them suitable for a merger? What is wrong with having the two legal regimes compete in the sense of searching for the best regulatory approach? I leave these questions, together with the other issues I have put forward, open to further discussion.

---

[13] Organisation for Economic Co-operation and Development (OECD), *Guidelines for Multinational Enterprises* (2011 edn), 25 May 2011, available at: www.oecd.org/datao-ecd/43/29/48004323.pdf.

[14] For details see B. H. Melgar, K. Nowrot and W. Yuan, 'The 2011 Update of the OECD Guidelines for Multinational Enterprises: Balanced Outcome or an Opportunity Missed?' University of Halle (2011), pp. 26ff.

PART III

The challenge of fostering greater coherence in international investment law

12

Practical and legal avenues to make the substantive rules and disciplines of international investment agreements converge

ANDREA K. BJORKLUND

A. Introduction

Convergence is defined as 'movement directed toward or terminating in the same point'.[1] At the point of convergence one would have uniformity, with all currents coalescing. The idea of convergence also encompasses notions of harmonisation, predictability and consistency, all of which are generally viewed as favourable traits in investment law and policy. Yet whether uniformity is desirable depends largely on whether one agrees with the rule that emerges, and even on whether one agrees that there should be a uniform rule in a particular area. Thus, the first thing I want to do is challenge the idea that convergence in the substantive rules and disciplines of international investment agreements (IIAs) is necessarily desirable. I suggest that convergence should be viewed with caution and sought in some but not all areas of investment law.

Given that conclusion, the second question is where convergence should be sought. Is convergence desirable in the investment laws adopted by various states? Would it be helpful in the investment agreement provisions detailing the concessions the treaty parties make to open various sectors of their economy to foreign investment? Is uniformity desirable in the usual protections offered to foreign investors, including national treatment and most-favoured nation (MFN) treatment? Is it desirable in the investor–state arbitration process itself, including in arbitral decision-making? Finally, assuming that *some* degree of uniformity is desirable in *some* of the aforementioned areas, what are the avenues that might best achieve such convergence?

[1] Oxford English Dictionary (online edition, 2011), available at: www.oed.com/.

B.   Is convergence in the substantive rules and disciplines of IIAs desirable?

Seeking uniformity in the rules governing international investment seems reasonable on the surface. It would be likely to foster predictability and certainty, characteristics that many allege investment law lacks.[2] It would streamline dispute settlement by eliminating some of the more common jurisdictional objections – if there were one uniformly agreed-upon definition of 'investment' or 'investor', for example, regardless of the context in which it was used, two frequent jurisdictional disputes could be minimised if not avoided altogether.[3]

More penetrating scrutiny, however, reveals that achieving uniformity would entail significant costs and might not yield commensurate benefits. Achieving uniformity would require compromise from those with sometimes strongly differing opinions; in such cases often no one is happy with the resulting middle ground. In addition, preserving state 'regulatory space' is a concern that embraces not just freedom to craft protective internal regulations but also freedom to accord different protections in different treaties. Uniformity in investment treaties undermines the very freedom to vary their international obligations that states might prefer to guard. Four issues serve to illustrate some of the hazards of uniformity and the obstacles to achieving it; no doubt there are others.[4]

The first question is how the uniform rule comes into effect. Who makes the rule? How is it agreed on? There is some danger that the state or group of states with greater political power will formulate a rule that suits them, and that those that are less politically powerful will have less

[2] See G. van Harten, *Investment Treaty Arbitration and Public Law* (Oxford University Press, 2007); M. Waibel, A. Kaushal, K.-H. L. Chung and C. Balchin (eds.), *The Backlash Against Investment Arbitration: Perceptions and Reality* (Alphen aan den Rijn: Kluwer Law International, 2010); S. Franck, 'The legitimacy crisis in investment arbitration: privatizing public international law through inconsistent decisions', *Fordham Law Review* 73 (2005), 1521–625; H. Mann, 'Civil Society Perspectives: What Do Key Stakeholders Expect from the International Investment Regime?' in J. E. Alvarez, K. P. Sauvant *et al.* (eds.), *The Evolving International Investment Regime: Expectations, Realities, Options* (Oxford University Press, 2011).

[3] See A. K. Bjorklund, 'The emerging civilization of investment arbitration', *Penn State Law Review* 113 (2009), 1269–300 at 1273–86.

[4] See L. Mistelis, 'Is Harmonisation a Necessary Evil? The Future of Harmonisation and New Sources of International Trade Law' in I. Fletcher, L. Mistelis and M. Cremona (eds.), *Foundations and Perspectives of International Trade Law* (London: Sweet & Maxwell, 2011), p. 3, paras. 1–048 and 1–049 (describing pitfalls related to harmonisation of international commercial law and trade regulation).

influence but will be compelled by circumstances to accept the rule. The failure of the Multilateral Agreement on Investment (MAI) is at least partially attributable to the fact that it was drafted by the Organisation for Economic Co-operation and Development (OECD) and was going to be opened for signature by non-OECD Member States only after the text was relatively final.[5] Similarly, most of the states with active model bilateral investment treaty (BIT) programmes are relatively highly developed and are often accused of imposing their views on states with relatively less bargaining power.

The second question is the content of the rule. In contrast to the problem identified above, it is also possible that negotiations will result in consensus about only the most general version of the rule – a least common denominator at a high level of abstraction – which will be likely to lead to significant differences in interpretation once it is applied, thereby defeating the purpose of uniformity. One could imagine a provision requiring payment of compensation in the event of expropriation with no clarifying language about when, if ever, regulatory measures amount to expropriation, due to an inability to agree on a more particular rule. Alternatively, but illustrative of the same problem, the universally agreed-upon rule could be so innocuous as to serve as no effective commitment at all. Again using expropriation as an example, one could imagine a provision excluding any possibility of compensation for a government measure that does not outright transfer title in the property to the host-state government. Although such a provision would not altogether be without effect, most of the expropriations alleged to have occurred over the past thirty or more years have been of the indirect or creeping sort,[6] and those arguments would no longer be open to investors. A side effect of this type of uniformity could be to continue the trend towards shoehorning many claims

---

[5] See, e.g., M. Sornarajah, *The International Law on Foreign Investment*, 2nd edn (Cambridge University Press, 2004), p. 295; Public Citizen, 'The Alarming Multilateral Agreement on Investment (MAI) Now Being Negotiated at the OECD', Public Citizen's Global Trade Watch Backgrounder, available at: www.citizen.org/trade/article_redirect. cfm?ID=5625. For a more general discussion of the perceived legitimacy of rules applicable to those with allegiances to different, though at times overlapping, communities, see H. G. Cohen, 'Finding international law, Part II: Our fragmenting legal community', *New York University Journal of International Law and Politics* 44 (2012), 1049–107.

[6] A. Reinisch, 'Expropriation' in P. Muchlinski, F. Ortino and C. Schreuer (eds.), *Oxford Handbook of International Investment Law* (Oxford University Press, 2008) pp. 420–51; A. K. Hoffmann, 'Indirect Expropriation' in A. Reinisch (ed.), *Standards of Investment Protection* (Oxford University Press, 2008). Investors have not necessarily succeeded in their claims of indirect expropriation. Reinisch 'Expropriation', pp. 451–6; Hoffmann, 'Indirect Expropriation', pp. 167–70.

alleging wrongful measures into the rubric of fair and equitable treatment violations[7] (assuming such an obligation was included in the hypothetical uniform treaty). Views on whether this would or would not be a desirable outcome might differ; fair and equitable treatment is one of the standards of treatment that gives the most discretion to arbitrators and thus might be less conducive to predictability than would more narrow and specialised obligations.[8]

The third potential drawback is the limitation on freedom of choice by home and host governments. In ratifying any investment agreement a state cedes some sovereignty; if there is only 'one rule' available, or if all rules inevitably are interpreted to mean the same thing, regardless of the language states put into their agreements, their freedom of action is thereby limited.

Two current hot topics in investment arbitration illustrate this concern. The first is treaty shopping. Some treaties have very broad investor 'standing' provisions that permit investors to route their investments through subsidiaries in a state that has an investment treaty with the state hosting the investment.[9] By virtue of those treaties states may find themselves according protections to investors from states with whom they do not have treaties and with whom they have no desire to have a treaty. This observation does not seek to excuse states from obligations they entered into freely, if not always thoughtfully – it simply points to a tool that can help to achieve uniformity but that has not been warmly welcomed. The second is the use of the MFN clause to import 'better' treatment, including preferential procedural provisions, into the basic treaty. In its most anodyne form an MFN clause might be used to strike a procedural formality found in the basic treaty, thus making the basic treaty resemble more closely the third-party treaty.[10] The *Maffezini* tribunal outlined several

---

[7] T. J. Grierson-Weiler and I. Laird, 'Standards of Treatment' in P. Muchlinski, F. Ortino and C. Schreuer (eds.), *Oxford Handbook of International Investment Law*, pp. 287–90, 299–301.

[8] The fluidity of the fair and equitable treatment standard is one of the reasons it is so controversial. Yet the gradual accretion of case law has given it greater predictability. M. Kinnear, 'The Continuing Development of the Fair and Equitable Treatment Standard' in A. K. Bjorklund, I. A. Laird and S. Ripinsky (eds.), *Investment Treaty Law: Current Issues III* (London: British Institute of International and Comparative Law, 2009), pp. 223–6.

[9] See, e.g., G. Kahale, III, 'The new Dutch sandwich: the issue of treaty abuse', 48 *Columbia FDI Perspectives* (10 October 2011); D. Burriez, 'Le *treaty shopping* procedural d'incorporation dans le contentieux arbitral transnational,' *ICSID Review – Foreign Investment Law Journal* 25 (2010), 394–408.

[10] This was the use to which the most-favoured nation (MFN) clause was put in the *Maffezini* decision. The tribunal decided that the primary treaty's requirement that an investor

procedural matters that could not be affected by the MFN clause due to their specially negotiated nature.[11] The tribunal thus evinced a desire to preserve the authority of different states to negotiate special deals as between themselves, although the difficulty in discerning which matters should fall into that category was one of many reasons the *Maffezini* decision was criticised.

The potential for muscular use of an MFN clause might be said to argue in favour of a negotiated uniformity. The MFN clause can cause disuniformity – if interpreted broadly it might permit an investor to create a so-called 'Frankenstein' treaty comprising bits and pieces gleaned from different treaties and bearing no resemblance to any treaty actually negotiated.[12]

Finally, one should be wary of embracing too readily promised-land goals that cannot be reached. Even the most perfectly formulated rule, uniform and universally applicable, might be interpreted differently by different decision-makers, or even differently by the same decision-makers depending on context. Thus, to the extent that convergence is sought in answer to the problems posed by inconsistent application of a rule as inherently discretionary as fair and equitable treatment (as illustrated by the *Lauder* and *CME* cases), one might be disappointed. Moreover, some rules defy perfect exposition, or, as Paulsson puts it,

---

seek relief in local courts for eighteen months prior to submitting a claim to international arbitration could be bypassed because the secondary treaty imposed no such limitation and thus afforded more favourable treatment to investors submitting claims under that treaty. *Emilio Agustín Maffezini* v. *The Kingdom of Spain* (Award), International Centre for Settlement of Investment Disputes (ICSID) Case No. ARB/97/7, 25 January 2000, paras. 54–61.

[11] These included circumstances when the parties had specifically conditioned their consent to arbitration on a fundamental rule of international law, such as requiring that local remedies be exhausted or that investors elect either local or international remedies; when they selected a specific forum, such as ICSID; or when they had agreed to a highly specialised system of dispute resolution with particularised procedural rules, such as the North American Free Trade Agreement (NAFTA) Chapter 11. *Maffezini*, para. 63. The tribunal also generally provided that the MFN clause not be used 'to override public policy considerations that the contracting parties might have envisaged as fundamental conditions for their acceptance of the agreement'. *Maffezini*, para. 62.

[12] See, e.g., *Plama Consortium Limited* v. *Republic of Bulgaria* (Decision on Jurisdiction), ICSID Case No. ARB/03/24, 8 February 2005, para. 219: 'a host state which has not specifically agreed thereto can be confronted with a large number of permutations of dispute settlement provisions from the various BITs which it has concluded. Such a chaotic situation – actually counterproductive to harmonization – cannot be the presumed intent of the Contracting Parties'; R. Teitelbaum, 'Who's afraid of Maffezini? Recent developments in the interpretation of most-favoured-nation clauses', *Journal of International Arbitration* 22 (2005), 225–38.

'resolution by abstraction'.[13] To the extent convergence is sought with respect to a principle that seems to defy complete and coherent exposition – how one distinguishes a compensable regulatory taking from an incidental and non-compensable incursion into a property right, for example – the disappointment is likely to be even more profound.

The foregoing might suggest that I am opposed to convergence in investment law and policy. Such is not the case. But convergence should be sought only when appropriate, and mindful of the preceding limitations. The most desired type of convergence given the current state of investment law might be termed harmonisation, or agreement along different frequencies – uniformity in the interpretation of identical or virtually identical language in the same context, with suitable attention paid to different interpretations stemming from different language or even from the same language in a different context. The harmonisation approach would provide greater predictability and consistency while nonetheless honouring differences in the commitments states have made.

C.   Where should convergence be sought?

Several candidates for uniformity in investment law present themselves. Let me highlight six.

Municipal investment laws. IIAs usually contain promises by a state to alter or amend its municipal investment laws in ways that favour investors who are nationals of the treaty counterparty. Often states make different commitments in different economic sectors. It is common, for example, for a state to place limits on the amount of foreign investment in the telecommunications sector, or in the aviation sector, or in areas of significant national importance, such as the oil industry.[14] Should every state have

---

[13] J. Paulsson, 'Avoiding Unintended Consequences', in K. P. Sauvant (ed.), *Appeals Mechanism in International Investment Disputes* (Oxford University Press, 2008), p. 244. Paulsson lists the identity of compensable regulatory measures, abuse of power, minimum standards of fairness, denials of justice and discrimination as areas that elude resolution by abstraction.

[14] In the NAFTA, Mexico reserved to the state the right to perform exclusively, and to prevent the establishment of investments, in the areas of petroleum, other hydrocarbons and basic petrochemicals, electricity, nuclear power, postal services, railroad transportation and a few other sectors. North American Free Trade Agreement, Canada–Mexico–United States, 17 December 1992, 32 ILM 605, Annex III, Schedule of Mexico. Saudi Arabia and Jamaica ratified the ICSID Convention, but notified the Secretariat that their agreement excluded natural resources disputes. See N. Schrijver, *Sovereignty Over Natural Resources: Balancing Rights and Duties* (Cambridge University Press, 1997), p. 186 and n. 49.

the same levels of permissible participation? It is at least arguable that states might have good reason for permitting different levels of participation depending on their history, their interest in protecting domestic industries, their national security interests and the like. Market liberalisation commitments reflect assessments about core sovereignty interests that can and should vary from state to state.

Exceptions. Investment treaties contain exceptions and reservations. Should all treaties contain identical exceptions and reservations, or should those vary from treaty to treaty? Canada famously included a cultural industries exception in the North American Free Trade Agreement (NAFTA), which dated from the earlier Canada–United States Free Trade Agreement (FTA).[15] Should all states have a cultural industries exception, or only those that feel strongly about their cultural industries? The cultural industries exception in the NAFTA applies only as between Canada and the USA and Canada and Mexico; the USA and Mexico have no similar obligation as between themselves.[16] Some of Canada's newer treaties, including its Model Foreign Investment Promotion and Protection Agreement (FIPA) of 2003, have a general exceptions clause that is virtually identical to Article XX of the General Agreement on Tariffs and Trade (GATT).[17] Should all treaties have a similar provision? The USA has included in its most recent treaties a self-judging essential security exception whose very invocation, it suggests, precludes a tribunal

---

[15] NAFTA, Article 2106 and Annex 2106. Annex 2106 actually provides that any measure adopted or maintained by Canada with respect to cultural industries be governed by the provisions of the Canada–USA Free Trade Agreement.

[16] M. Kinnear, A. K. Bjorklund and J. F. G. Hannaford, *Investment Disputes Under NAFTA: An Annotated Guide to NAFTA Chapter 11* (Alphen aan den Rijn: Kluwer Law International, 2006; 2008 and 2009 update), 1108.22.

[17] Agreement Between Canada and … for the Promotion and Protection of Investments (2003), Article 10, General Exceptions:

> Subject to the requirement that such measures are not applied in a manner that would constitute arbitrary or unjustifiable discrimination between investments or between investors, or a disguised restriction on international trade or investment, nothing in this Agreement shall be construed to prevent a Party from adopting or enforcing measures necessary:
>
> (a) to protect human, animal or plant life or health;
> (b) to ensure compliance with laws and regulations that are not inconsistent with the provisions of this Agreement; or
> (c) for the conservation of living or non-living exhaustible natural resources.

The Canadian Model Foreign Investment Promotion and Protection Agreement (FIPA) was approved by the Cabinet in 2003 and was made public in 2004. Copy on file with the author.

from exercising jurisdiction.[18] In other words, the decision to raise the self-judging exception is subject to no review at all, not even whether or not it has been invoked in good faith. Should every treaty contain such a robust exception?[19] If they did, one would have achieved uniformity but diminished the level of protection offered to a degree many might think undesirable. Moreover, the interpretation tribunals will actually give to the language remains to be seen.

Substantive investment treaty obligations. Most investment treaties contain similar obligations. The provisions requiring national treatment, MFN treatment, fair and equitable treatment and full protection and security, and free transfer of currency, as well as those prohibiting expropriation without payment of compensation are relatively standard.[20] They are not, however, identical. Notable areas of divergence include broad or narrow MFN clauses, including clauses that explicitly extend MFN protection to dispute settlement and many others that are silent on the question;[21] provisions extending to investors' promises regarding the minimum standard of treatment and others extending the protection

---

[18] USA–Peru FTA, 12 April 2006, Article 22.2, n. 2: 'For great certainty, if a Party invokes Article 22.2 in an arbitral proceeding initiated under Chapter Ten (Investment) or Chapter Twenty-One (Dispute Settlement), the tribunal or panel hearing the matter shall find that the exception applies.' Available at: www.ustr.gov/trade-agreements/free-trade-agreements/peru-tpa/final-text.

[19] See, e.g., S. Schwebel, 'The United States 2004 Model Bilateral Investment Treaty: an exercise in the regressive development of international law', *Transnational Dispute Management* 2 (2006), available at: www.transnational-dispute-management.com/article.asp?key=780; J. E. Alvarez, 'The Evolving BIT', *Transnational Dispute Management* 7 (2010), available at: www.transnational-dispute-management.com/article.asp?key=1542.

[20] See generally A. Newcombe and L. Paradell, *Standards of Treatment* (Alphen aan den Rijn: Kluwer Law International, 2009), pp. 121–479 (discussing most frequently included substantive standards of treatment); C. McLachlan, L. Shore and M. Weiniger, *International Investment Arbitration: Substantive Principles* (Oxford University Press, 2007), pp. 25–43.

[21] The United Kingdom (UK) Model bilateral investment treaty (BIT), for example, provides in Article 3(3), that: 'for the avoidance of doubt it is confirmed that the treatment provided for in paragraphs (1) and (2) above shall apply to the provisions of Article 1 to 11 of this Agreement', which expressly includes the dispute settlement provisions found in Article 8. See Y. Banifatemi, 'Most-Favoured-Nation Treatment in Investment Arbitration' in A. K. Bjorklund, I. A. Laird and S. Ripinsky (eds.), *Investment Treaty Law: Current Issues III* (London: British Institute of International and Comparative Law, 2009), p. 272. On the other hand, the Canada–Peru FTA provides in Annex 804.1: 'For greater clarity, treatment "with respect to the establishment, acquisition, expansion, management, conduct, operation and sale or other disposition of investments" referred to in paragraphs 1 and 2 of Article 804 does not encompass dispute resolution mechanisms, such as those in Section B, that are provided for in international treaties or trade agreements.' United

encompassed in a stand-alone fair-and-equitable-treatment standard;[22] and expropriation provisions that are very broadly formulated and appear to include any manner of indirect expropriation, and those that attempt to exclude regulatory takings.[23] Some treaties contain provisions, such as umbrella clauses, that others do not, and some such clauses are formulated differently, and possibly confer different protections, than do others.[24] Would it be better if identical language in different treaties were

Nations Conference on Trade and Development (UNCTAD), *Most-Favoured-Nation Treatment: A Sequel* (Geneva: United Nations Publications, 2010), p. 86. Most do not address the issue. UNCTAD, *Most-Favoured-National Treatment*, pp. 37–8.

[22] For a discussion of the relationship between the minimum standard of treatment and fair and equitable treatment, see Kinnear, 'The Continuing Development of the Fair and Equitable Treatment Standard', pp. 220–3.

[23] Compare NAFTA Article 1110(1), which provides 'No Party may directly or indirectly nationalize or expropriate an investment of an investor of another Party in its territory or take a measure tantamount to nationalization or expropriation of such an investment ("expropriation") except:

(a) for a public purpose;
(b) on a non-discriminatory basis;
(c) in accordance with due process of law and Article 1105(1); and
(d) on payment of compensation in accordance with paragraphs 2 through 6

and Annex B13(1) of the 2003 Canadian Model FIPA:
The Parties confirm their shared understanding that:

(a) Indirect expropriation results from a measure or series of measures of a Party that have an effect equivalent to direct expropriation without formal transfer of title or outright seizure;
(b) The determination of whether a measure or series of measures of a Party constitute an indirect expropriation requires a case-by-case, fact-based inquiry that considers, among other factors:
   (i) the economic impact of the measure or series of measures, although the sole fact that a measure or series of measures of a Party has an adverse effect on the economic value of an investment does not establish that an indirect expropriation has occurred;
   (ii) the extent to which the measure or series of measures interfere with distinct, reasonable investment-backed expectations; and
   (iii) the character of the measure or series of measures;
(c) Except in rare circumstances, such as when a measure or series of measures are so severe in the light of their purpose that they cannot be reasonably viewed as having been adopted and applied in good faith, non-discriminatory measures of a Party that are designed and applied to protect legitimate public welfare objectives, such as health, safety and the environment, do not constitute indirect expropriation.'

[24] See K. Yannaca-Small, 'What about this "Umbrella Clause"?' in K. Yannaca-Small (ed.), *Arbitration Under International Investment Agreements: A Guide to the Key Issues*

interpreted to mean the same thing? Probably, assuming the interpretation adopted was 'correct'.[25] Would it be better if all treaty provisions were identical? Not necessarily, and one's view would be likely to depend on one's satisfaction with the uniform standard.

Procedural provisions in investment treaties. One could similarly focus on areas of convergence and divergence in the procedural aspects of investment agreements, or even of international arbitration generally.[26] One area that has received a great deal of attention is the difference between so-called no-U-turn and fork-in-the-road clauses.[27] Some treaties permit the commencement of local proceedings and their subsequent abandonment in favour of international proceedings; others state that a claimant should elect which avenue of relief to pursue initially and, at least on one theory, prohibit the claimant from seeking redress in another tribunal.[28] A similar issue pertains to the procedural hurdles investors must surmount before submitting a claim. Some treaties require that investors pursue local remedies for eighteen months before commencing an international arbitration, whereas others contain explicit or implicit

(Oxford University Press, 2010); A. C. Sinclair, 'The Umbrella Clause Debate' in A. K. Bjorklund, I. A. Laird and S. Ripinsky (eds.), *Investment Treaty Law: Current Issues III* (London: British Institute of International and Comparative Law, 2009).

[25] The lack of formal system of precedent or appellate body with the ability to issue binding decisions means that the progress towards a correct (or at least widely accepted as correct) decision is less linear than in a traditional hierarchical system. See generally A. K. Bjorklund, 'Investment Treaty Arbitral Decisions as *Jurisprudence Constante*' in C. B. Picker, I. D. Bunn and D. W. Arner (eds.), *International Economic Law: The State and Future of the Discipline* (Oxford: Hart Publishing, 2008); G. Kaufmann-Kohler, 'Arbitral precedent: dream, necessity or excuse?', *Arbitration International* 23 (2007), 357–78; C. Schreuer and M. Weiniger, 'A Doctrine of Precedent?' in P. Muchlinski *et al.* (eds.), *Oxford Handbook of International Investment Law* (Oxford University Press, 2008).

[26] Gabrielle Kaufmann-Kohler has suggested that the arbitration community has created an informal but dense layer of procedural rules, norms and guidelines that govern arbitration. G. Kaufmann-Kohler, 'Global Implications of the U.S. Federal Arbitration Act: The Role of Legislation in International Arbitration', *ICSID Review – Foreign Investment Law Journal* 20 (2005), 339–56 at 350–1. Chester Brown makes a more extensive argument about the development of dispute settlement norms across tribunals in his outstanding book. C. Brown, *A Common Law of International Adjudication* (Oxford University Press, 2007).

[27] See Kinnear *et al.*, *Investment Disputes Under NAFTA*, 1121.10–1121.12; A. R. Parra, 'The Initiation of Proceedings and Constitution of Tribunals in Investment Treaty Arbitrations' in K. Yannaca-Small (ed.), *Arbitration Under International Investment Agreements: A Guide to the Key Issues* (Oxford University Press, 2010), pp. 109–10.

[28] See A. K. Bjorklund, 'Private rights and public international law: why competition between international courts and tribunals is not working', *Hastings Law Journal* 59 (2007), 241–307 at 296–8, 300–4 (discussing lack of identity of cause of action to support a *res judicata* finding in cases where investors have first sought relief in local fora).

waivers of the local remedies rule and do not require any initial attempt to resolve a grievance locally.[29] Some treaties (and the International Centre for Settlement of Investment Disputes (ICSID) Arbitration Rules) include frivolous claims provisions that permit respondents to seek early dismissal of cases brought against them, whereas others do not.[30] Some treaties, notably the post-NAFTA IIAs concluded by Canada and the USA, require the publication of awards and other relevant documents, including memorials and pleadings; others do not.[31] The more recent US and Canadian treaties also explicitly permit intervention by *amici curiae*, under appropriate circumstances; others do not.[32] Should identical provisions be interpreted identically? Probably, subject to the same caveats included above. Should all treaties contain identical provisions? Perhaps not.

Arbitral tribunal decisions. Many concerns around the idea of uniformity have to do with real or apparent inconsistencies in arbitral decisions. The *CME* and *Lauder* cases are among the first and most famous examples. One tribunal found that the Czech Republic had breached the treaty's fair and equitable treatment obligation and awarded significant damages in favour of the investor; the other tribunal found, based on identical facts,

---

[29] See, e.g., William S. Dodge, 'National courts and international arbitration: exhaustion of remedies and res judicata under Chapter Eleven of NAFTA', *Hastings International and Comparative Law Review* 23 (2000), 357–83 at 374; George K. Foster, 'Striking a balance between investor protections and national sovereignty: the relevance of local remedies in investment treaty arbitration', *Columbia Journal of Transnational Law* 49 (2010), 201–67 at 211–15.

[30] See, e.g., ICSID Rules of Procedure for Arbitration Proceedings (Arbitration Additional Facilities Rules) Chapter VIII, Article 45(6) (2006) ('Unless the parties have agreed to another expedited procedure for making preliminary objections, a party may, no later than 30 days after the constitution of the Tribunal ... file an objection that a claim is manifestly without legal merit'); 2004 US Model Bilateral Investment Treaty (BIT), Article 28(4)–28(6); Treaty Between the United States of America and the Oriental Republic of Uruguay Concerning the Encouragement and Reciprocal Protection of Investment, Article 28(4)–28(6), 25 October 2004.

[31] See generally A. J. Menaker, 'Piercing the Veil of Confidentiality: The Recent Trend Towards Greater Public Participation and Transparency in Investor–State Arbitration' in K. Yannaca-Small (ed.), *Arbitration Under International Investment Agreements: A Guide to the Key Issues* (Oxford University Press, 2010), pp. 131–9; C. Knahr, 'Transparency, third party participation and access to documents in international investment arbitration', *Arbitration International* 23 (2007), 327–56; Bjorklund, 'The Emerging Civilization of investment arbitration', 1288–90.

[32] Menaker, 'Piercing the Veil of Confidentiality', pp. 140–53; E. Obadia, 'Extension of proceedings beyond the original parties: non-disputing party participation in investment arbitration', *ICSID Review – Foreign Investment Law Journal* 22 (2007), 349–79.

that there was no breach.[33] The differences in these decisions did not stem from differences in the applicable legal standards, nor did they depend on differences in interpretation of the applicable legal standard. Rather, they depended on different applications of the law to the facts of the case.[34] Other decisions have in fact diverged with respect to different interpretations of the identical legal standard: examples include the definition of investment under the ICSID Convention;[35] the interpretation to be given the minimum standard of treatment under Article 1105 of the NAFTA;[36] whether the essential security clause in the Argentina–USA BIT imports

[33] S. Alexandrov, 'On the Perceived Inconsistency of Investor–State Jurisprudence' in J. E. Alvarez and K. P. Sauvant *et al.* (eds.), *The Evolving International Investment Regime: Expectations, Realities, Options* (Oxford University Press, 2011), p. 66 (noting the difference in outcome depending on the two tribunals' different approach to the attribution of the acts of a private individual to the state).

[34] J. Paulsson, 'The Practitioner's Perspective on the Need for Reform: "Hâtez-vous Lentement"' in A. Fijalkowski (ed.), *International Institutional Reform: 2005 Hague Joint Conference on Contemporary Issues of International Law* (The Hague: TMC Asser Press, 2005) pp. 299–300; Alexandrov, 'On the Perceived Inconsistency of Investor–State Jurisprudence', pp. 60–3.

[35] Compare *Fedax* v. *Venezuela*, ICSID Case No. ARB/96/3 (Decision of the Tribunal on Objections to Jurisdiction) (11 July 1997) and *Salini Costruttori S.p.A. and Italstrade S.p.A.* v. *Morocco* (Decision on Jurisdiction), ICSID Case No. ARB/00/4, 23 July 2001 with *Biwater Gauff (Tanzania) Limited* v. *United Republic of Tanzania* (Award), ICSID Case No. ARB/05/22, 24 July 2008. See also J. D. Mortenson, 'The meaning of "investment": ICSID's *travaux* and the domain of international investment law', *Harvard International Law Journal* 51 (2010), 257–318; C. Schreuer *et al.*, *The ICSID Convention: A Commentary*, 2nd edn (Cambridge University Press, 2009), Article 25; D. Krishan, 'A Notion of Investment' in T. Weiler (ed.), *Investment Treaty Arbitration: A Debate and Discussion* (New York: Juris Publishing Inc., 2008); E. Cabrol, 'Pren Nreka v. Czech Republic and the notion of investment under bilateral investment treaties: does "investment" really mean "every kind of asset"?' in K. P. Sauvant (ed.), *Yearbook on International Investment Law & Policy 2009/2010* (New York: Oxford University Press, 2010).

[36] Compare *Merrill & Ring Forestry L. P.* v. *Canada* (Award), United Nations Commission on International Trade Law (UNCITRAL), ICSID-administered case (NAFTA), 31 March 2010, para. 213 (the Tribunal finds that the applicable minimum standard of treatment of investors is found in customary international law and that, except for cases of safety and due process, today's minimum standard is broader than that defined in the *Neer* case and its progeny. Specifically this standard provides for the fair and equitable treatment of alien investors within the confines of reasonableness. The protection does not go beyond that required by customary law, as the FTC has emphasised. Nor, however, should protected treatment fall short of the customary law standard) with *Glamis Gold Ltd.* v. *United States of America* (Award), UNCITRAL (NAFTA) 14 May 2009, para. 616 ('The fundamentals of the *Neer* standard thus still apply today: to violate the customary international law minimum standard of treatment codified in Article 1105 of the NAFTA, an act must be sufficiently egregious and shocking – a gross denial of justice, manifest arbitrariness, blatant unfairness, a complete lack of due process, evident discrimination, or a manifest lack of reasons – so as to fall below accepted international

the customary international law standard of necessity;[37] and whether MFN clauses permit claimants to seek application of more favourable procedural provisions as well as more substantive legal protections.[38] Should one expect a uniform interpretation in all of these cases? Is the first decision inevitably to be followed? What if certain decisions were viewed as wrong, or even unwise? Does coherence triumph over correctness?

I and others have written elsewhere about the gradual development of investment law jurisprudence.[39] Without a hierarchical system topped by a tribunal that can issue authoritative, binding decisions, the fits-and-starts progress towards a more uniform jurisprudence is not surprising. Investors and states might want more certainty against which to measure their conduct, both before and after a dispute commences. Yet given the lack of agreement about a number of areas of the law, inherently imprecise standards such as the obligation to provide fair and equitable treatment, and the necessarily divergent appreciation of the facts of any

standards and constitute a breach of Article 1105(1)'). The *Glamis Gold* tribunal acknowledged that the world community's appreciation of what might constitute egregious or shocking treatment has changed.

[37] Compare J. E. Alvarez and K. Khamsi, 'The Argentine Crisis and Foreign Investors' in K. P. Sauvant, *Yearbook on International Investment Law & Policy 2008/2009* (New York: Oxford University Press, 2009); J. E. Alvarez and T. Brink, 'Revisiting the Necessity Defense: Continental Casualty v. Argentina', *Yearbook On International Investment Law & Policy 2010/2011* (New York: Oxford University Press, 2011); A. K. Bjorklund, 'Economic Security Defenses in International Investment Law', *Yearbook on International Investment Law & Policy 2008/2009* (New York: Oxford University Press, 2009); R. Dolzer and C. Schreuer, *Principles of International Investment Law* (Oxford University Press, 2008), p. 167; A. Reinisch, 'Necessity in international investment arbitration – an unnecessary split of opinions in recent ICSID cases?', *Journal of World Investment & Trade* 8 (2007), 191–214 (pro conflation) with W. Burke-White and A. von Staden, 'Investment protection in extraordinary times: interpreting non-precluded measures provisions', *Virginia Journal of International Law* 48 (2007), 307–410; J. T. Kurtz, 'Adjudging the exceptional at international investment law: security, public order and financial crisis', *International and Comparative Law Quarterly* 59 (2010), 325–71; C. Binder, 'Changed Circumstances in Investment Law: Interfaces Between the Law of Treaties and the Law of State Responsibility with a Special Focus on the Argentine Crisis' in C. Binder *et al.* (eds.), *International Investment Law for the 21st Century: Essays in Honour of Christoph Schreuer* (Oxford University Press, 2009); A. Stone Sweet, 'Investor–state arbitration: proportionality's new frontier', *Law and Ethics of Human Rights* 4 (2010), 47–76; C. McLachlan, 'Investment treaties and general international law', *International and Comparative Law Quarterly* 57 (2008), 361–401 at 390–1 (anti-conflation).

[38] Banifatemi, 'Most-Favoured-Nation Treatment'; UNCTAD, *Most-Favoured-Nation Treatment.*

[39] Bjorklund, 'Investment Treaty Arbitral Decisions'; Kaufmann-Kohler, 'Arbitral precedent'; Schreuer and Weiniger, 'A Doctrine of Precedent?'

given case, it would be too much to expect a high degree of uniformity too quickly.

Integrating the obligations of states and investors. Investment treaties are criticised for their asymmetry: they impose obligations on states without exacting corresponding commitments from investors; and for their narrow focus: they address investment protections, often without specifying how those correlate with a state's other obligations. These problems are sometimes overstated; investment treaties are an attempt to redress the power enjoyed by the state precisely because of its sovereign authority. Without a treaty the state enjoys asymmetrical power vis-à-vis the investor. Moreover, there are various techniques to take into account obligations that exist outside the boundaries of the treaty but are nevertheless applicable. The obligations of investors arise under the fair and equitable treatment standard as tribunals assess whether the investor's conduct has triggered the state's actions, or consider the obligation to pay damages and any compensating set-off.[40] It is possible that closely connected counterclaims might be brought by host states against investors.[41] Existing interpretive tools – notably Article 31(3)(c) of the Vienna Convention on the Law of Treaties – can help investment treaty tribunals to integrate the dispersed and disparate obligations of states.[42]

Notwithstanding these existing tools, concluding more symmetrical agreements that in themselves take into account the rights and obligations of investors, as well as the varied rights and obligations of states, would be a more streamlined way to ensure a balance between investor

---

[40] P. Muchlinski, 'Caveat investor?: the relevance of the conduct of the investor under the fair and equitable treatment standard', *International & Comparative Law Quarterly* 55 (2006), 527–57.

[41] See J. Crawford, 'Treaty and contract in investment arbitration', *Arbitration International* 24 (2008), 351–74; A. K. Hoffmann, 'Counterclaims by the respondent state in investment arbitrations', *SchiedsVZ, Heft* 6 (2006), 317–20; A. K. Bjorklund, 'Mandatory rules in international investment law', *American Review of International Arbitration* 18 (2008), 175–204. But see *Spyridon Roussalis* v. *Romania* (Award), ICSID Case No. ARB/06/1, 7 December 2011.

[42] See C. McLachlan, 'The principle of systemic integration and Article 31(3)(c) of the Vienna Convention', *International & Comparative Law Quarterly* 54 (2005), 279–320. U. Kriebaum, 'Privatizing human rights: the interface between international investment protection and human rights', *Transnational Dispute Management* 3(5) (December 2006), available at: www.transnational-dispute-management.com/article.asp?key=947; C. H. Brower II, 'Obstacles and pathways to consideration of the public interest in investment treaty disputes' in K. P. Sauvant (ed.), *Yearbook on International Investment Law & Policy 2008–2009* (New York: Oxford University Press, 2008); A. van Aaken, 'Fragmentation of international law: the case of international investment protection', *Finnish Yearbook of International Law* 17 (2008), 91–130.

protection and state regulatory authority, and would help to alleviate concerns about asymmetrical agreements that on the surface give too much power to investors. Bringing together into one document balanced rights and responsibilities, and directives to decision-makers regarding the relationship the states sought to establish between varying obligations, would be a most helpful type of convergence.

D.   Avenues to bring about convergence

Assuming convergence in at least some aspects of international law and policy is desirable, how might it be achieved? Some of these avenues already exist, and in at least some cases have been employed so as to achieve consistency.

One avenue leading towards convergence comprises textual uniformity. The broadest convergence would be achieved were there to be a new multilateral investment agreement; less ambitious but more achievable plurilateral initiatives might evidence progress towards convergence and might result in pockets of uniformity. The second avenue involves interpretive techniques and the establishment of institutions such as an appellate body, which might prove effective even in the absence of a multilateral or plurilateral approach.

I.   Textual convergence

Multilateral agreement. The most obvious avenue to achieve convergence is to negotiate a multilateral agreement, along the lines of the GATT. Given the failure of the MAI, and given the difficulties that the Doha Round of GATT negotiations, which for a time included an investment component, is facing, the political difficulties in achieving such a result seem currently insurmountable.[43]

---

[43] Yet some have suggested that the climate is becoming more hospitable for negotiating a multilateral agreement on investment. R. Geiger, 'Multilateral Approaches to Investment: The Way Forward' in J. E. Alvarez and K. P. Sauvant *et al.* (eds.), *The Evolving International Investment Regime: Expectations, Realities, Options* (Oxford University Press, 2011), pp. 172–3; J. Zhan, J. Weber and J. Karl, 'International Investment Rulemaking at the Beginning of the Twenty-First Century: Stocktaking and Options for the Way Forward' in J. E. Alvarez and K. P. Sauvant *et al.* (eds.), *The Evolving International Investment Regime: Expectations, Realities, Options* (Oxford University Press, 2011), pp. 205–10; W. Shan, 'Towards a balanced liberal investment regime: general report on the protection of foreign investment', *ICSID Review – Foreign Investment Law Journal* 25 (2010), 421–97 at 477–9.

There are practical difficulties too. The large number of extant investment agreements – more than 2,900[44] – complicates matters. How do you fit the existing treaty regime into a multilateral regime? There would have to be widespread agreement to jettison existing treaties and sign on to the new multilateral agreement. One would also have to address the thorny problem of the rights that investors might seek to assert under the 'old' treaties, assuming they were more favourable than the provisions contained in the 'new' treaty.[45] Shifting to a multilateral approach could also be achieved by waiting for existing treaties to expire and not renewing them, but that would take a long time. Still, with sufficient will it could be done.

Plurilateral initiatives. One avenue that might lead towards convergence, but that would fall short of actual uniformity, is the conclusion of plurilateral treaties, often by states in defined geographical regions. This approach is most evident in the European Union's assertion of competence over investment in the Lisbon Treaty.[46] Another prominent example is the negotiations for the Trans-Pacific Partnership, which includes an investment chapter.[47] It is true that negotiations for a Free Trade Area of

---

[44] This number was accurate as of the end of 2008. UNCTAD, *Recent Developments in International Investment Agreements 2008 – June 2009* (Geneva: United Nations Publications, 2009) (reporting 2,676 bilateral investment treaties (BITs) and 273 international investment agreements (IIAs)).

[45] Whether or not investors enjoy rights independent of their home states has come up in a number of contexts, including in the Mexican corn sweetener cases. *Archer Daniels Midland et al.* v. *Mexico* (Award), ICSID Case No. ARB(AF)/04/05, 21 November 2007, paras. 161–180; *Archer Daniels Midland et al.* v. *Mexico* (Concurring Opinion of Arthur Rovine), ICSID Case No. ARB(AF)/04/05, 21 November 2007; *Corn Products International* v. *Mexico* (Decision on Responsibility), (Separate Opinion of Andreas F. Lowenfeld), ICSID Case No. ARB(AF)/04/1, 15 January 2008, paras. 161–179. See generally Bjorklund, 'Private rights and public international law'; B. L. Smit Duijzentkunst, 'Treaty rights as tradeable assets: can investors waive investment treaty protection?', *ICSID Review – Foreign Investment Law Journal* 25 (2010), 409–20.

[46] M. Bungenberg, 'Going Global? The EU Common Commercial Policy After Lisbon' in C. Hermann and J. P. Terhechte (eds.), 2010 *European Yearbook of International Law* (Berlin: Spring-Verlag, 2010), pp. 135–51; Rudolf Dolzer (Chapter 26 in this volume).

[47] Trans-Pacific Partnership (TPP) Fact Sheet, 'Enhancing Trade and Investment, Supporting Jobs, Economic Growth and Development: Outlines of the Trans-Pacific Partnership Agreement' (12 November 2011), available at: www.ustr.gov/about-us/press-office/fact-sheets/2011/november/outlines-trans-pacific-partnership-agreement ('The investment text will provide substantive legal protections for investors and investments of each TPP country in the other TPP countries, including ongoing negotiations on provisions to ensure non-discrimination, a minimum standard of treatment, rules on expropriation, and prohibitions on specified performance requirements that distort trade and investment. The investment text will include provisions for expeditious, fair,

the Americas are moribund, but the Lisbon Treaty and the Trans-Pacific Partnership have given new life to plurilateralism.

Model agreements. Another route less comprehensive than an MAI but which might be achievable would be the widespread adoption of a 'model agreement', such as the one proposed by the International Institute for Sustainable Development.[48] The OECD is considering the feasibility of sponsoring a similar initiative.[49]

This approach has to some degree already been implemented by states with robust model investment agreements: NAFTA Chapter 11, and the experiences states had under it, had a heavy influence on the 2003 Canadian Model FIPA and the 2004 US Model BIT; those agreements in turn have influenced more than a dozen investment agreements that might well be termed the NAFTA's progeny.[50]

Each of the textual solutions proposed above illustrates some of the problems outlined earlier. The first was, who makes the rules? Who would wield the pen in the drafting of a multilateral agreement, of a plurilateral agreement, or of a model agreement? As far as a multilateral agreement is concerned, one suspects that existing agreements would have a strong influence on the content of any text. To the extent that those provisions are deemed to favour capital-exporting countries, that bias might survive to inhabit any multilateral agreement. On the other hand, given increasing concerns about the asymmetry in existing treaties and the fact that many historically capital-exporting countries are now capital-importing countries as well, there is some potential for greater balance in treaty drafting. In addition, the rapidly mounting number of investment cases is effectively illustrating the pluses and minuses of existing provisions. The first MAI was sponsored by the OECD and negotiated against a backdrop of very few investment cases. Any new MAI would be negotiated

and transparent investor-State dispute settlement subject to appropriate safeguards, with discussions continuing on scope and coverage. The investment text will protect the rights of the TPP countries to regulate in the public interest').

[48] H. Mann *et al.*, *IISD Model International Agreement on Investment for Sustainable Development – Negotiators' Handbook* (International Institute for Sustainable Development (IISD), 2005), available at: www.iisd.org/publications/pub.aspx?pno=686.

[49] A. Gurria, 'The Global Economy and the Global Investment Agenda: An OECD Perspective' (10 March 2010), available at: www.oecd.org/document/0/0,3746,en_2649_34529562_44775040_1_1_1_34529562,00.html.

[50] See F. Bachand and E. Gaillard (eds.), *Fifteen Years of NAFTA Chapter 11 Arbitration* (New York: Juris, 2011); S. Puig and M. Kinnear, 'NAFTA Chapter Eleven at fifteen: contributions to a systemic approach in investment arbitration', *ICSID Review – Foreign Investment Law Journal* 25 (2010), 225–67.

with much more knowledge on the part of all those involved. Plurilateral agreements also suggest great potential in this regard. Model agreements drafted by the historic capital-exporting countries might change – certainly the 2004 US Model BIT has been criticised for its alleged retrenchment in protection of foreign investors[51] – although one wonders whether they would change enough to satisfy critics.

The second question is what would be the content of the rules contained in the instrument? I have suggested above several areas in which agreement on the rule might be problematic. What definition of investment would draw agreement from a significant majority of countries? Would it require a contribution to economic development? How would that be measured? Would unlawful expropriation entitle a claimant to a different amount of compensation than a lawful expropriation? Would there be a self-judging national security exception? All of these matters could and presumably would be dealt with in negotiations, but it is far from clear that everyone would be satisfied with the result; in fact, one of the few things that one could say for sure is that everyone would *not* be satisfied with the result. This is true for any of the above options.

The third issue identified above was the effects on state autonomy – on sovereignty, if you will. What kinds of limits on foreign investment would states be able to maintain in the face of convergence towards a single treaty? Would there be a regional agreements provision, like that found in the World Trade Organization (WTO), which would result in yet another kind of 'spaghetti-bowl' structure? A separate question is whether all investment agreements *should* in fact look alike. Should investment agreements involving resource-rich states, in which the investment is very likely a hundred-million-dollar multi-year non-moveable obsolescing bargain, involve the same promises towards investors as investment agreements involving human-capital rich states, in which the initial commitment of capital is likely to be much less and the investment is likely to be much more portable in the event the investor finds more fertile soil elsewhere?[52] Should all states open themselves to investment in all sectors, notwithstanding their idiosyncratic interests? These are problems, but are the kinds of problems faced by treaty negotiators all the time, and thus

---

[51] Schwebel, 'The United States 2004 Model Bilateral Investment Treaty'; Alvarez, 'The Evolving BIT'.

[52] A. K. Bjorklund, 'Improving the International Investment Law and Policy System: Report of the Rapporteur' in J. E. Alvarez and K. P. Sauvant *et al.* (eds.), *The Evolving International Investment Regime: Expectations, Realities, Options* (Oxford University Press, 2011), pp. 231–2.

should be surmountable given sufficient will on the part of the negotiating parties.

The fourth issue addressed above was the 'promising something you cannot deliver' question. Certainly a single agreement would contain a uniform text. Plurilateral agreements would result in pockets of uniformity. A drawback to the 'model agreement' approach is the potential for small but potentially significant divergences in the implementation of each individual agreement. These differences could, perhaps, be overcome by some of the interpretive approaches outlined below. Yet even if one had a single uniform text, differences in interpretation might well ensue, depending on the steps taken to achieve interpretive harmonisation as discussed below. That being said, if one had a uniform text, or even a few uniform texts, one would by definition have more convergence than one finds in the more than 2,900 extant treaties.

II.   Interpretive convergence

In the absence of textual convergence, textual variations might be overcome by tribunal decision-making.[53] The two existing techniques that best exemplify this process are the application of the MFN principle to harmonise procedural obligations in various treaties and the *jurisprudence constante* evidenced in some areas by the gradual coalescence of approach around a single interpretation.[54] Indeed, Schill has persuasively pointed to the most-favoured nation provision and the interpretive conventions adopted by tribunals as ways that investment law has been multilateralised even in the absence of a global agreement.[55] Another interpretive approach that would lead to greater harmony is the establishment of an appellate body.[56]

MFN treatment. The most famous, or infamous, application of the MFN principle has been to achieve convergence in procedural provisions in different treaties. This approach has not been without criticism and,

---

[53] For a more in-depth discussion of specific interpretive techniques, see the contribution to this volume by Banifatemi (Chapter 13).

[54] See the discussion at pp. 345–6; G. Kaufmann-Kohler, 'Is Consistency a Myth?' in Y. Banifatemi (ed.) *Precedent in International Arbitration* (Huntington, NY: Juris Publishing, 2007), 137, 147.

[55] S. W. Schill, *The Multilateralization of International Investment Law* (Cambridge University Press, 2009).

[56] See, e.g., K. Yannaca-Small, 'Annulment of ICSID Awards: Limited Scope But is There Potential?' in K. Yannaca-Small (ed.), *Arbitration Under International Investment Agreements: A Guide to the Key Issues* (Oxford University Press, 2010), pp. 626–33.

incidentally, the practice with respect to MFN clauses that do not specify their applicability to procedural provisions has not itself been uniform. Although some differences in language – broad versus narrow phraseology – help to explain the differences in approach adopted by different tribunals, they do not explain all of them. Ignoring differences in language tends to result in convergent decisions, whereas giving effect to differences in language leads towards divergent results but recognises states' sovereign rights to negotiate MFN provisions with differing scopes and procedural hurdles to submitting investment claims that might vary from treaty to treaty. And the fact that different tribunals have different approaches to the same or virtually identical MFN clauses illustrates the illusive nature of perfect interpretation.

Jurisprudence Constante. Investment law has no formal system of precedent. To the extent that multiple consistent decisions on the same topic gradually accrete into an accepted approach towards a particular legal provision or towards the application of a particular law, there might be said to be a *jurisprudence constante.*

This method has some advantages, but is slow. Moreover, it is likely to be less successful, or even slower, for those areas in which there is less agreement as to the appropriate norm.[57] And to the extent there is disagreement, disparate decisions lend force to criticisms of incoherence. The definition of investment is an excellent example. For some time there seemed to be a general coalescence (subject to criticism, of course) around the so-called *Salini* test.[58] Yet a subsequent decision in the *Biwater Gauff* case has challenged this apparent consensus, as has subsequent scholarship.[59]

Letting law develop through tribunal decision-making is subject to criticism with respect to who is making the rules. To the extent tribunals are implementing the rules agreed to in treaties negotiated to protect the interests of capital-exporting states they might be said to be perpetuating those rules. To the extent apparently divergent principles coalesce, they could be said to be watering down stronger rules or giving too much force to weaker rules (e.g., the customary international law of necessity and an independent essential security clause coalescing into proportionality;[60]

---

[57] Kaufmann-Kohler, 'Arbitral Precedent', 372

[58] Mortenson, 'The meaning of "investment"', 286.

[59] *Biwater Gauff (Tanzania) Ltd* v. *United Republic of Tanzania* (Award), ICSID Case No. ARB/05/22, 24 July 2008; Mortenson, 'The meaning of "investment"', 280–96.

[60] See, e.g., A. Reinisch, 'Necessity in investment arbitration – an unnecessary split of opinions in recent ICSID Cases?', *Journal of World Investment and Trade* 8 (2007), 191–214 at 201; Bjorklund, 'Economic Security Defenses', p. 487.

the minimum standard of treatment converging with fair and equitable treatment[61]).

Appellate body. Another interpretive mechanism is the possibility of establishing an investment law appellate body along the lines of the WTO Appellate Body. This would be easiest and most effective if it accompanied a multilateral agreement. The ICSID's raising of the matter during the period 2000–2010 and its cold reception by many states has stalled any progress on it in that sphere;[62] the USA does not appear to be pursuing the establishment of an appellate body as foreseen in multiple US investment agreements.

Setting aside practical difficulties, having a single body to which all investment tribunal decisions could be appealed would tend to lead to interpretive uniformity. Even assuming that such a tribunal would have more than three people, that is assuming that not every appellate body decision would be issued by the same three judges, there would still be greater potential for a uniform approach by members of the same judicial body. Procedures including circulation of opinions among all of the judges, or even the provision for *en banc* review, could help to achieve uniformity. That uniformity would be maximised if there were a formal system of hierarchy such that appellate body decisions were *stare decisis.*

Decisions by an appellate body established by a multilateral agreement would enjoy a good deal of presumptive legitimacy. The 'who makes the rule' question would be minimised, assuming a truly multilateral agreement that would take into account the interests of developing as well as developed countries, of capital-importing as well as capital-exporting economies and the like. Even discrete appellate bodies established pursuant to different plurilateral agreements would be likely to enjoy significant prestige, although the potential for different strands of decision-making would be greater. Should one be in a position of having different appellate bodies established for individual agreements, as was apparently envisaged in the USA–Chile FTA, the potential for divergence would be much higher.[63] One would have potentially competing 'authoritative'

---

[61] See, e.g., *Merrill & Ring Forestry L.P.* v. *Canada* (Award), UNCITRAL, 31 March 2010, paras. 183–213 (discussing evolution of the minimum standard of treatment).

[62] Yannaca-Small, 'Annulment of ICSID Awards', pp. 628–32.

[63] Annex 10-H of the Chile–USA FTA, which entered into force in 2004, apparently envisages a bilateral mechanism:

Possibility of a *Bilateral* Appellate Body/Mechanism
   Within three years after the date of entry into force of this Agreement, the Parties shall consider whether to establish a *bilateral* appellate body or similar mechanism

pronouncements about different questions. There might be strands of thought that would eventually converge, but the process would probably be much slower.

The content-of-the-rule question would not necessarily be solved by the establishment of an appellate body, but it might be minimised. An appellate body would decide cases that establish precedent, rather than the slower-to-coalesce *jurisprudence constante*. Precedent fosters legal certainty, and also helps to develop law and to 'facilitate the unity of the law'.[64] One might hope that a multilateral agreement would contain obligations that clarify some of those questions that have bedevilled the investment law field. But, even if that were the case, other issues would be sure to arise. An appellate body might issue a ruling about a hotly contested issue with which half or more of those reading would disagree. Requiring that decision to be followed by all subsequent tribunals risks concretising an approach that turns out to be undesirable. This can happen in municipal law, too, but given the degree to which many issues in investment law remain contentious, premature hardening of interpretations is risky.

The potential for appellate body decisions to have an effect on states' deliberate decisions to make differentiated choices about what obligations they are undertaking would also arise in the context of plurilateral agreements and, to an even greater extent, in the context of model agreements that have been implemented with small or large variations. If, hypothetically, there were a European investment agreement and a European appellate body, one can imagine an appellate body established under the Trans-Pacific Partnership Agreement viewing the European Union (EU) body's decisions as persuasive authority, even if the treaty language were slightly different. The same tendency might be even more pronounced if

to review awards rendered under Article 10.25 in arbitrations commenced after they establish the appellate body or similar mechanism [emphasis added].

Annex 10-F of DR – CAFTA, on the other hand, which entered into force for the first members in 2006, refers only to an appellate mechanism, and more clearly leaves the door open to establishing one appellate body to serve a number of different agreements:

Appellate Body or Similar Mechanism

1. Within three months of the date of entry into force of this Agreement, the Commission shall establish a Negotiating Group to develop an appellate body or similar mechanism to review awards rendered by tribunals under this Chapter. Such appellate body or similar mechanism shall be designed to provide coherence to the interpretation of investment provisions in the Agreement.

[64] See J. Klabbers, 'Precedent and principles', *Turku Law Journal* 3 (2001), 71–83 at 75.

one had multiple appellate bodies established under multiple agreements. On the other hand, small differences in language might be read to require significant differences in interpretation simply because of the fact of the difference. This might or might not be more respectful of actual sovereign choice, but it would lead to divergence rather than convergence.

The final category identified above is the 'perfection' category. Establishing an appellate body would solve some but not all problems with respect to investment law. It is possible that the pluses outweigh the minuses, but an appellate body alone cannot impose agreement about which substantive norms and which procedural protections a treaty ought to include. Vague standards such as fair and equitable treatment almost certainly will be applied differently in different contexts, whether it is an appellate body or a tribunal that is engaged in the decision-making. Those standards that defy abstraction, such as the appropriate way to assess regulatory takings, are unlikely to be magically clarified by an appellate body when they have not been definitively established by the highest courts of multiple states or by multiple international tribunals.

E.   Conclusion

The title of this chapter is *practical* and legal avenues to make the substantive rules and disciplines of IIAs converge. The most beneficial convergence would be best achieved were the world community to negotiate an MAI that included an appellate body entrusted with the ability to issue precedential decisions. Such a result would certainly be legal, but given the political situation in the world today it hardly seems practical. The second best option for convergence would appear to be plurilateral agreements that establish pockets of uniformity.

One should be wary of premature convergence. Establishing an appellate body whose decisions are precedential in the absence of a multilateral agreement might be especially risky given the lack of consensus about key issues in investment law. Ralph Waldo Emerson famously remarked that 'A foolish consistency is the hobgoblin of little minds'.[65] It is better to be inconsistent but sometimes correct rather than consistent but always wrong. Convergence sought solely for the sake of convergence is

---

[65] R. W. Emerson, *Essays: Self Reliance* (First Series, 1841). The entire quote reads, 'A foolish consistency is the hobgoblin of little minds, adored by little statesmen and philosophers and divines.'

a hobgoblin we should avoid. Yet harmonisation of different strands of thought might be achievable and desirable.

Absent global negotiations resulting in universally agreed-upon rules, one might strive for harmonic convergence – uniform understandings along different wavelengths. Choosing between two or three or even more options would permit treaty negotiators to choose the level of protection they seek but with some assurance of what that choice means.

Furthermore, one needs to have a realistic assessment of what international investment agreements, and the settlement of disputes arising under them, can achieve. Convergence, or even consistency, will not by itself render international investment agreements legitimate in the eyes of their critics. It would remove one pillar of criticism, but might well erect others. Attempts to achieve convergence would be likely to sharpen the focus on the lack of agreement about the nature of the rights that investment agreements ought to protect and on the tension between a march towards uniformity and a state's desire to protect its regulatory space in the manner best suited to it. There is no single right answer to how this balance should be achieved, and there is no magic formula that can answer the question in any of the millions of scenarios that might present themselves.

One of the aims of investment law, both with respect to liberalising the domestic investment regime and to internationalising dispute settlement, was to depoliticise the investor–state relationship by taking the politics out of decision-making. The extent to which this has been achieved is debatable;[66] the extent to which it is desirable or even possible, given the compromises inherent in state regulation and the politically charged issues that frequently surround investment policy, is also open to question.[67] If investor–state arbitral tribunals are viewed as exercising public regulatory power in a manner that does not respect the multiple interests states must balance in regulating those doing business within their regulatory purview, no amount of uniformity or harmonisation will salve concerns about legitimacy. Yet states have agreed to refer decision-making under investment treaties to international tribunals, and some of those

---

[66] See A. K. Bjorklund, 'Sovereign immunity as a barrier to the enforcement of investor–state arbitral awards: the re-politicization of investment disputes', *American Review of International Arbitration* 21 (2010), 211–41 at 239–40.

[67] See S. W. Schill, 'System-building in investment treaty arbitration and lawmaking', *German Law Journal* 12 (2011), 1083–110; B. Choudhury, 'Recapturing public power: is investment arbitration's engagement of the public interest contributing to the democratic deficit?', *Vanderbilt Journal of Transnational Law* 41 (2008), 775–832 at 782–9.

decisions will have important political repercussions. Investment arbitration can thus be viewed as another forum in which discussions about conflicting policies occur,[68] and those discussions are likely to continue, and to continue to be controversial, no matter what kind of uniformity investment rules have achieved.

---

[68] Jan Klabbers suggests embracing, rather than disdaining, 'politics': 'For politics is of course not just warfare by other means (though it is that too, perhaps). What politics also is, is open and honest debate about how best to organize our lives together, which values to uphold, and how to treat each other and ourselves in proper fashion … If we stop thinking of politics as the precursor of war by other means, and instead start to employ a richer notion of politics as facilitation our common lives and our common future, then we might not feel too depressed about not being able to find enlightenment in a realm beyond the political.' Klabbers, 'Precedent and principles', 82.

13

Consistency in the interpretation of substantive investment rules: is it achievable?

YAS BANIFATEMI

A. Introduction

With the accelerating pace of the development of international investment law, tension seems to be growing between the requirement that each dispute be resolved on the basis of the relevant investment treaty, whose application and interpretation is the duty of the arbitral tribunal constituted to settle that dispute, and the desire to achieve consistency in the interpretation of the law. In the words of the International Court of Justice (ICJ), 'justice of which equity is a manifestation … should display consistency and a degree of predictability.'[1] At the same time, consistency can only be achieved within the ambit of the same or substantially the same substantive rules.

Indeed, there has been much ado about a perceived lack of consistency in the international investment law and arbitration regime. The phrase 'legitimacy crisis' is often heard.[2] Yet, much of the criticism and commentary seems not to take into consideration the structural framework of the regime (section B). Often the actual reasons for divergence are overlooked. So too are the points of convergence. This is not to say that unhappy instances of inconsistent case law do not exist. They do and merit consideration, to the extent, in particular, that they may reflect policy issues.

The author wishes to thank Ilija Mitrev-Penusliski for his valuable assistance during the preparation of this chapter.

[1] *Continental Shelf (Libyan Arab Jamahiriya/Malta)*, Judgment, ICJ Reports 1985, p.13, para. 45.

[2] See S. D. Franck, 'The legitimacy crisis in investment treaty arbitration: privatizing public international law through inconsistent decisions', *Fordham Law Review* 73 (2004–2005), 1521–625. See also M. Waibel, A. Kaushal, K.-H. L. Chung and C. Balchin (eds.), *The Backlash Against Investment Arbitration* (Alphen aan den Rijn: Kluwer Law International, 2010).

Consistency and inconsistency should thus be viewed in context (section C). Yet again, signs of maturity of the regime can be seen in the instances of emerging *jurisprudence constante*. Greater consistency may be achieved, provided the reality of what can be achieved is discerned from the myth (section D). Each of these propositions will be addressed in turn.

B.   Treaty interpretation by arbitral tribunals: the unavoidable framework

To the extent that it borrows from both international law and arbitration law, investment arbitration is subject to the substantive framework imposed by international law as regards the rules of treaty interpretation (section I below) and the structural framework imposed by arbitration as a decentralised system (section II below). It is against the background of these constraints that the question of consistency in investment arbitration must be viewed.

I.   *The substantive framework imposed by international law: the rules of treaty interpretation as codified in Article 31 of the Vienna Convention on the Law of Treaties (VCLT)*

Arbitral tribunals refer almost systematically to the canons of treaty interpretation found in the VCLT, which largely reflect customary international law.[3] A recent empirical study shows that thirty-five of ninety-eight decisions by investor–state tribunals constituted under the auspices of the International Centre for Settlement of Investment Disputes (ICSID) rendered from 1 January 1998 to 31 December 2006 made explicit reference to the VCLT, with 'an increase in references toward the end of the period examined'.[4]

Pursuant to Article 31 of the VCLT, the interpretation of international treaties, including investment treaties, centres on the text of the treaty, namely 'the ordinary meaning of the terms of the treaty in their context and in light of [the treaty's] object and purpose'. Only if such interpretation leaves the meaning ambiguous or obscure, or leads to a result that is manifestly absurd or unreasonable, can one resort to the supplementary

---

[3] See, for example, *Tokios Tokelés* v. *Ukraine* (Decision on Jurisdiction), International Centre for Settlement of Investment Disputes (ICSID) Case No. ARB/02/18, 29 April 2004, para. 27.

[4] O. K. Fauchald, 'The legal reasoning of ICSID tribunals – an empirical analysis', *European Journal of International Law* 19(2) (2008), 301–64 at 314.

means of interpretation set forth at Article 32 of the VCLT, chiefly the preparatory works of the treaty and the circumstances of its conclusion.

If the primary rules of interpretation focus on the text, context, and object and purpose of a given treaty, one may assume that, by definition, the interpretation of each treaty will be individualised.[5] An additional factor of individualisation in treaty interpretation is that for each dispute a single arbitral tribunal is constituted ad hoc, with a degree of discretion in the interpretation exercise. In this context, why is consistency expected? Such an expectation seems to stem from the fact that different arbitral tribunals employ the same interpretative tools to interpret the same or similarly drafted substantive rules. Can there be an objective and right interpretation in every instance?

In addition to the substantive framework of the interpretation rules imposed by international law, the structural framework imposed by arbitration law also accounts for the varying (and some would say inconsistent) interpretation of similar or similarly drafted provisions in investment treaties.

II. The structural framework imposed by arbitration law: a decentralised system

Today the regime of international investment law consists of more than 3,000 international investment agreements, by far the greatest portion of which are bilateral investment treaties (BITs) concluded between two states and binding only on those states.

Each investor–state dispute arising out of a BIT or a multilateral investment agreement is decided by a different arbitral tribunal specifically constituted for the purpose of settling that particular dispute and composed of jurists coming from different legal cultures. While most BITs have very similar procedural and substantive provisions, an arbitral tribunal's interpretation of those provisions is binding only on the parties to

---

[5] The use of the VCLT's interpretation tools in the case of similar or similarly worded provisions may yield different results as a result of difference in context, object and purpose, preparatory works or subsequent party agreements or practice in the application of the respective treaties: see *Methanex Corporation* v. *United States of America* (Final Award under North American Free Trade Agreement (NAFTA) and United Nations Commission on International Trade Law (UNCITRAL) Arbitration Rules), 3 August 2005, para. 16 (citing the holding of the International Tribunal for the Law of the Sea (ITLOS) in the *Mox Plant Case*).

the dispute and only in respect of the particular case.[6] Thus, each arbitral tribunal engages in a one-off interpretation with no precedential value other than for the parties.

This is an inherent quality of the regime, much like that of the ICJ as set out in Article 59 of the ICJ Statute: 'The decision of the Court has no binding force except between the parties and in respect of that particular case.' And while the ICJ is not bound by its own previous decisions, it often relies on and refers to them, seeking good cause when it is asked to do otherwise. As the ICJ noted in *Case Concerning Land and Maritime Boundary between Cameroon and Nigeria*:

> It is true that, in accordance with Article 59, the Court's judgments bind only the parties to and in respect of a particular case. There can be no question of holding Nigeria to decisions reached by the Court in previous cases. The real question is whether, in this case, there is cause not to follow the reasoning and conclusions of earlier cases.[7]

In investment arbitration, arbitral tribunals cannot search in their own jurisprudence for a previous interpretation of the same or a similarly drafted provision. An investment treaty tribunal has no previous jurisprudence of its own. However, despite the absence of a system of precedent in international arbitration,[8] the decisions of arbitral tribunals are replete with references to previous decisions of other arbitral tribunals. As the *El Paso* v. *Argentina* Tribunal noted, for example:

> It is, nonetheless, a reasonable assumption that international arbitral tribunals, notably those established within the ICSID system, will generally take account of the precedents established by other arbitration organs, especially those set by other international tribunals.[9]

---

[6] See, for example, NAFTA Article 1136(1) ('An award made by a Tribunal shall have no binding force except between the disputing parties and in respect of the particular case'). See also *AES Corporation* v. *the Argentine Republic* (Decision on Jurisdiction), ICSID Case No. ARB/02/17, 26 April 2005, para. 23 (holding that a decision by an ICSID tribunal is only binding on the parties to the dispute and that there is no rule of precedent that applies in the ICSID system).

[7] *Land and Maritime Boundary between Cameroon and Nigeria* (*Cameroon* v. *Nigeria*), Preliminary Objections (*Nigeria* v. *Cameroon*), Judgment, ICJ Reports 1999, p. 31, para. 28.

[8] On this question generally, see Y. Banifatemi (ed.), 'Precedent in International Arbitration', *IAI Series on International Arbitration No. 5* (Huntington: Juris Publishing, 2008).

[9] *El Paso Energy International Company* v. *the Argentine Republic* (Decision on Jurisdiction), ICSID Case No. ARB/03/15, 26 April 2007, para. 39. See also decisions referred to below under section D.III.

The structural framework of the international investment regime is thus marked by *a multiplicity of treaties*, which, while containing similar standards, or sometimes similarly drafted provisions, vary in wording; and *a multiplicity of arbitral tribunals*, constituted only for a specific case and whose decisions do not constitute a precedent, neither vis-à-vis subsequent decisions rendered pursuant to the same treaty nor vis-à-vis subsequent decisions rendered pursuant to a similar treaty. Importantly, there exists no standing judicial body of a higher instance to review the decisions of arbitral tribunals, and which, if need be, could harmonise the interpretation of investment treaty provisions or bring consistency to the body of international investment jurisprudence. There is no hierarchy of courts in international arbitration. In the ICSID system, arbitral awards are reviewed by ad hoc committees with limited review powers and which, like arbitral tribunals, are constituted only for the specific case at hand. Nor does such a higher instance exist outside the ICSID system, where limited review takes place before domestic courts.

The result, to borrow from James Crawford (in turn quoting Lord Tennyson), is that decisions in investor–state disputes are a true 'wilderness of single instances'.[10] It is perhaps a wilderness of single instances that are not unaware of each other.

It is only within this dual framework that one may raise the question of whether consistency and predictability may be achieved, or are even desirable.

C. Consistency and inconsistency in context

To better understand to what extent consistency may be achieved in the interpretation of investment treaties, it may be useful to review certain instances in which different tribunals have interpreted the same provision of the same treaty (section I below) and similarly drafted provisions or similar treaty mechanisms in different treaties (section II below).

I. *Interpretation of the provisions of the same treaty by different tribunals: is consistency required?*

With the conclusion of multilateral investment treaties such as the North American Free Trade Agreement (NAFTA), the Energy Charter

---

[10] J. Crawford, 'Similarity of Issues in Disputes Arising under the Same or Similarly Drafted Investment Treaties' in *IAI Series on International Arbitration* No. 5; Banifatemi, 'Precedent in International Arbitration', 99.

Treaty (ECT) and the Dominican Republic–Central America Free Trade Agreement (DR–CAFTA), the opportunities for different arbitral tribunals to provide their own interpretation of the same provision of the same treaty have increased. Article 17(1) of the ECT is an example.

In the case of BITs, those opportunities are understandably fewer, although certainly not non-existent, as the decisions by tribunals applying the same treaty provisions in cases with 'repeat' players, such as Argentina, amply show. Article XI of the United States–Argentina BIT provides an example.

Each example will be examined in turn.

1.   Denial of Benefits

To date, four tribunals constituted under the ECT have tackled the 'Denial of Benefits' clause contained at Article 17(1). Significantly, when they have had to interpret the provision, all tribunals have provided a consistent interpretation.[11] One of these tribunals – *Petrobart* – did not in fact interpret this provision.

Article 17(1) ECT reads:

> Each Contracting Party reserves the right to deny the advantages of this Part [Part III] to:
>> (1) a legal entity if citizens or nationals of a third state own or control such entity and if that entity has no substantial business activities in the Area of the Contracting Party in which it is organized ...;

In the cases where this provision came into play, the interpretative issues were: (i) whether under Article 17(1), Contracting Parties can only deny to investors the advantages of Part III of the ECT (the substantive investment protections) or whether they can also do so with respect to the advantages of Article 26 of Part V (the right to bring a dispute to arbitration); (ii) whether Article 17(1) operates as an automatic denial of certain treaty benefits when its conditions are met, or whether a Contracting Party must in fact exercise that right; (iii) whether the exercise of the right under Article 17(1) has prospective or retrospective effect; (iv) what a 'third state' for the purposes of Article 17(1) is; and (v) who bears the burden of establishing that an investor is 'own[ed]' or 'control[led]' by nationals or citizens of a third state.

---

[11] These are the *AMTO, Plama, Petrobart* and *Yukos*-related tribunals. For the purposes of this discussion the tribunals constituted in each of the three *Yukos*-related arbitrations are considered to be a single tribunal.

The tribunals that tackled the first four issues converged in deciding that: (i) Contracting Parties can only deny to investors the advantages of Part III of the ECT and not the advantages of Article 26 of Part V; (ii) Article 17(1) confers a reservation of right to the Contracting Parties, and such a right must be expressly exercised; (iii) an exercise of the right to deny benefits can only have prospective effect and not retrospective effect; and (iv) a 'third state' for the purposes of Article 17(1) is a state that is not a Contracting Party to the ECT.

For example, on the first issue, the tribunal constituted in the *Yukos*-related arbitrations referred explicitly to the holding in *Plama* and agreed:

> 440. However, insofar as those arguments are deemed to address the question of whether the Tribunal has jurisdiction to pass upon the merits of the claims of Claimant, they are not on point. That is because Article 17 specifies – as does the title of that Article – that it concerns denial of the advantages of 'this Part,' *i.e.*, Part III of the ECT. Provision for dispute settlement under the ECT is not found in 'this Part' but in Part V of the Treaty. Whether or not Claimant is entitled to the advantages of Part III is a question not of jurisdiction but of the merits. Since Article 17 relates not to the ECT as a whole, or to Part V, but exclusively to Part III, its interpretation for that reason cannot determine whether the Tribunal has jurisdiction to entertain the claims of Claimant.
>
> 441. The holding of the tribunal in *Plama* v. *Bulgaria* is on point:
>
> Article 26 provides a procedural remedy for a covered investor's claims; and it is not physically or juridically part of the ECT's substantive advantages enjoyed by that investor under Part III … This limited exclusion from Part III for a covered investor, dependent on certain specific criteria, requires a procedure to resolve a dispute as to whether that exclusion applies in any particular case; and the object and purpose of the ECT, in the Tribunal's view, clearly requires Article 26 to be unaffected by the operation of Article 17(1).
>
> 442. This Tribunal finds the reasoning of the *Plama* tribunal on this point convincing and adopts it.[12]

On burden of proof, two tribunals diverged. The *Plama* Tribunal held that the burden of establishing ownership or control by a citizen or national of a third state falls on the claimant.[13] The *AMTO* Tribunal held that,

---

[12] *Hulley Enterprises Limited* v. *The Russian Federation* (Interim Award on Jurisdiction and Admissibility), Permanent Court of Arbitration (PCA) Case No. 225, 30 November 2009, paras. 440–442 (internal footnotes omitted).

[13] *Plama Consortium Limited* v. *Bulgaria* (Decision on Jurisdiction), ICSID Case No. ARB/03/24, 8 February 2005, para. 82.

following the *onus probandi actori incumbit* maxim, the burden of proof rests on the party advancing the allegation, which in the case of Article 17(1) was the respondent state.[14]

Bearing in mind that the last of these issues is not strictly a matter of interpreting the provision, but one of appropriate allocation of burden of proof, it is noteworthy that the existing case law on Article 17(1) ECT is a clear example of consistency. It remains to be seen if the identical interpretation achieved by the various ECT tribunals will be preserved.[15] Presumably, as the decisions of arbitral tribunals do not bind subsequent tribunals, future encounters with Article 17(1) may lead to divergent results. At the same time, one may consider that when a similar interpretation in relation to the same provision is achieved over and over again, subsequent tribunals would need compelling reasons to depart from such an interpretation. The unanimous call for consistency would indeed be unheard if this consistent reasoning were to be challenged in the future by the parties in other ECT cases.

2.   Article XI of the USA–Argentina BIT

To date, in five cases brought against Argentina in the aftermath of its economic crisis, five tribunals constituted under the USA–Argentina BIT – the *CMS, LG&E, Enron, Sempra* and *Continental Casualty* Tribunals – faced Argentina's defence based on Article XI of that BIT. Article XI of the USA–Argentina BIT reads:

> This Treaty shall not preclude the application by either Party of measures necessary for the maintenance of public order, the fulfillment of its obligations with respect to the maintenance or restoration of international peace or security, or the protection of its own essential security interests.

Essentially, Argentina claimed that Article XI allows it to take the measures of which the investors complained, even if those measures were otherwise inconsistent with the treaty. In their interpretation of this provision, and of the legal issues arising out of it, as well as its application to the facts, the findings of the five tribunals were consistent in relation to certain issues and divergent on others. Four of the five decisions were

---

[14] *Limited Liability Company AMTO* v. *the Ukraine* (Final Award), Stockholm Chamber of Commerce (SCC) Case No. 080/2005, 26 March 2008, paras. 64–65.

[15] For example, some authors have argued that the exercise of the right to deny benefits could have retrospective effect. See L. A. Mistelis and C. M. Baltag, 'Denial of benefits and Article 17 of the Energy Charter Treaty', *Penn State Law Review* 113 (2009), 1301–21 at 1320–21.

subject to annulment proceedings, with two being eventually annulled specifically in relation to their holdings on Article XI.

The principal issues that arose in relation to the interpretation of Article XI were: (i) whether Article XI is a self-judging clause; (ii) whether economic crises fall within the scope of Article XI; and (iii) whether Article XI precludes the application of the treaty to measures that fall within the scope of that provision or whether Article XI precludes the wrongfulness of such measures, and, in that context, what is the relationship between Article XI and the customary international law defence of necessity.

All five tribunals held that Article XI applies to economic crises, although there was disaccord as to the gravity of the crisis required to trigger the provision, *CMS* seemingly setting a very high threshold – a total collapse of the economy. Similarly, there was unanimity that Article XI is not a self-judging clause.

The third issue, however, gave rise to inconsistent interpretation. The *CMS*, *Enron* and *Sempra* Tribunals – all three chaired by the same president – first examined Argentina's defences under the rules of customary international law on necessity as arguably codified in Article 25 of the International Law Commission (ILC) Articles. All three tribunals held that the economic crisis in Argentina did not meet the high threshold of Article 25 and then cursorily dealt with Article XI of the BIT. After finding that Article XI was not a self-judging provision, the tribunals held that the analysis of the rules of customary international law on necessity applied to or informed the analysis of Article XI and, having already decided the issue previously, did not proceed any further (in *CMS* this was done implicitly). The result of the tribunals' conflating Article XI of the BIT and Article 25 of the ILC Articles was that the former, like the latter, would operate to preclude wrongfulness.

The *LG&E* Tribunal, on the other hand, started its analysis with Article XI, distinguishing it from customary international law and, without extensive legal analysis, decided that the Argentinean crisis met the standard. According to the Tribunal, Article XI excused Argentina from liability for the period of the crisis.[16] In further contrast to the previous decisions, in *Continental Casualty* the Tribunal held that if Article XI were triggered, it would in fact preclude the application of the

---

[16] *LG&E Energy Corp., LG&E Capital Corp., LG&E International Inc.* v. *the Argentine Republic* (Decision on Liability), ICSID Case No. ARB/02/1, 3 October 2006, paras. 226–261.

treaty to those measures falling within the scope of that provision; in other words, if Article XI applied, there would be no breach of the treaty (as opposed to there being an excuse from liability, i.e., a preclusion of wrongfulness).[17]

The *CMS*, *Enron* and *Sempra* awards drew criticism from the ad hoc committees constituted to review them. While the sections on Article XI in the decisions of the *Enron* and *Sempra* Tribunals are strikingly similar, and in bottom-line terms not different from that of the *CMS* decision, the three ad hoc committees adopted three different approaches in their analyses of those decisions. The *CMS* ad hoc committee stated that, given its limited powers of review, it could not find an annullable error in the Tribunal's application of the law (thus there being no manifest excess of powers under Article 52(1)(b) of the ICSID Convention). Yet it went out of its way to note that the Tribunal's interpretation of Article XI was 'erroneous'[18] and that Article XI of the BIT and Article 25 of the ILC Articles adopted different regimes:

> Article XI is a threshold requirement: if it applies, the substantive obligations under the Treaty do not apply. By contrast, Article 25 is an excuse which is only relevant once it has been decided that there has otherwise been a breach of those substantive obligations.
>
> Furthermore Article XI and Article 25 are substantively different. The first covers measures necessary for the maintenance of public order or the protection of each Party's own essential security interests, without qualifying such measures. The second subordinates the state of necessity to four conditions. It requires for instance that the action taken 'does not seriously impair an essential interest of the State or States towards which the obligation exists, or of the international community as a whole', a condition which is foreign to Article XI. In other terms the requirements under Article XI are not the same as those under customary international law as codified by Article 25, as the Parties in fact recognized during the hearing before the Committee.[19]

In contrast, the *Enron* ad hoc committee did not make any pronouncements on whether or not the Tribunal had accurately identified the law in relation to Article XI, but found annullable errors. According to the committee, the Tribunal had failed to properly apply customary international

---

[17] *Continental Casualty Company* v. *the Argentine Republic* (Award), ICSID Case No. ARB/03/9, 5 September 2008, paras. 163–164.

[18] *CMS Gas Transmission Company* v. *the Argentine Republic* (Decision of the ad hoc Committee on the Application for Annulment by the Argentine Republic), ICSID Case No. ARB/01/8, 25 September 2007, paras. 129–136.

[19] *Ibid.*, paras. 129–130.

law and, consequently, treaty law (since the Tribunal's findings in respect of the former were the basis of its findings in respect of the latter).[20]

Finally, the *Sempra* ad hoc committee took yet another view: it decided that, in conflating the analyses required under customary law and treaty law and then proceeding only with the former, the Tribunal had in fact failed to apply the applicable law, namely Article XI, which amounted to a manifest excess of powers within the meaning of Article 52(1)(b) of the ICSID Convention.[21]

Not only did the five tribunals interpret Article XI differently, but the three ad hoc committees took three different approaches to the findings in the three of those awards that followed largely the same analysis. This set of decisions elicited various reactions in the community, commentators hastening to condemn the system on account of what they perceived to be its inherent defect – an important lack of consistency. In that context, Argentina's protests were perhaps understandable, although they were voicing the political challenges Argentina was facing in complying with a decision that awarded more than one hundred million dollars to the investor and in which the ad hoc committee had been found to have erred on the law.[22] Leaving aside the politically charged context of the Argentinean economic crisis, from a purely legal perspective one may find some merit in the fact that the decision reached by the *CMS* Tribunal was not considered to be a precedent and that the varying (or inconsistent) decisions allowed a diverse case law putting into perspective the issues of international law as regards the distinction between Article XI as a clause precluding the application of the substantive obligations under the treaty and rules of customary international law in relation to the exoneration of state responsibility.

II.   Interpretation of the same type of substantive protection or treaty mechanism: is consistency desirable?

More frequently, arbitral tribunals are asked to interpret provisions drafted similarly to provisions in other treaties that have already been

---

[20] *Enron Corporation Ponderosa Assets, L.P* v. *the Argentine Republic* (Decision on the Application for Annulment of the Argentine Republic), ICSID Case No. ARB/01/3, 30 July 2011, paras. 400–405.

[21] *Sempra Energy International* v. *the Argentine Republic* (Decision on the Argentine Republic's Application for Annulment of the Award), ICSID Case No. ARB/02/16, 29 July 2010, paras. 186–228.

[22] W. Burke-White, 'The Argentine financial crisis: state liability under BITs and the legitimacy of the ICSID system', *Asian Journal of WTO & International Health Law and Policy* 3 (2008), 199–234 at footnote 90.

interpreted by other tribunals. In this context, differences in wording, the manner in which parties argue their case, or the varying legal trend or more general context, have led to both convergent and inconsistent interpretation. Three examples are worthy of note: fair and equitable treatment provisions, most-favoured nation (MFN) clauses and umbrella clauses.

1. Fair and equitable treatment

While arbitral tribunals have uniformly recognised that the application of the fair and equitable treatment standard greatly depends on the wording of the relevant provision and on the facts of the specific case, the case law suggests that several 'sub-standards' or 'components' of the fair and equitable treatment standard have emerged.

The determination of the content of the fair and equitable treatment standard by the Tribunal in *Bayindir* v. *Pakistan* illustrates the point. The Tribunal first noted that 'customary international law and decisions of other tribunals may assist in the interpretation of this provision'. This was particularly pertinent in that case 'given that Article 4(2) of the [applicable treaty] simply state[d] a general obligation of fair and equitable treatment'.[23] The Tribunal then agreed with the claimant's identification of 'the different factors which emerge from decisions of investment tribunals as forming part of the FET standard'.[24] Referring to a number of previous decisions, it then enumerated some of these factors:

> the obligation to act transparently and grant due process, to refrain from taking arbitrary or discriminatory measures, from exercising coercion or from frustrating the investor's reasonable expectations with respect to the legal framework affecting the investment.[25]

Another area of convergence in arbitral case law is that bad faith on the part of the host state is not required for a finding of unfair and inequitable treatment. The *Siemens* Tribunal found that it emerged from a review of the case law that:

> except for *Genin*, none of the recent awards under NAFTA and *Tecmed* require bad faith or malicious intention of the recipient State as a necessary element in the failure to treat investment fairly and equitably, and that, to the extent that it has been an issue, the tribunals concur in that customary international law has evolved. More recently in *CMS*, the

---

[23] *Bayindir Insaat Turizm Ticaret Ve Sanayi A.S.* v. *Islamic Republic of Pakistan* (Award), ICSID Case No. ARB/03/29, 27 August 2009, para. 176.

[24] *Ibid.*, para. 178.

[25] *Ibid.* (footnotes omitted). See also *Biwater Gauff (Tanzania) Ltd.* v. *United Republic of Tanzania* (Award), ICSID Case No. ARB/05/22, 24 July 2008, para. 602.

tribunal confirmed the objective nature of this standard 'unrelated to whether the Respondent has had any deliberate intention or bad faith in adopting the measures in question'. Of course, such intention and bad faith can aggravate the situation but are not an essential element of the standard.[26]

At the same time, possible divergence on some of the remaining issues is to be expected. For example, does the legitimate expectations component of the standard include reasonable reliance on implicit representations made by the host state? Does the standard require proactiveness on the part of the host state vis-à-vis the legal and business environment it accords to investments?[27]

On the whole, the jurisprudence on the fair and equitable standard 'shows a clear progression over time towards more exacting requirements imposed on the host state'.[28] Tribunals have done much to develop the law and have done so largely in agreement, despite (or perhaps because of) the high degree of malleability of the text in fair and equitable treatment provisions.

2. MFN treatment

The interpretation of the standard of MFN treatment, on the other hand, has given rise to a split between tribunals as to whether investors, through the MFN clause of the basic treaty, can avail themselves of the more favourable dispute resolution mechanisms contained in third-party treaties.

Two approaches have essentially emerged on this question: the *Maffezini* and the *Plama* approaches, although a closer look at these decisions shows that the two are not irreconcilable.[29] In *Maffezzini*, the Tribunal decided that the MFN treatment could extend to the dispute

---

[26] *Siemens A.G. v. Argentina* (Award), ICSID Case No. ARB/02/8), 6 February 2007, para. 299.

[27] See, for example, *MTD Equity Sdn Bhd. & MTD Chile S.A. v. Republic of Chile* (Decision on Annulment), ICSID Case No. ARB/01/7, 21 March 2007, paras. 65–71 (agreeing with some criticisms of the *Tecmed* Tribunal's interpretation of the fair and equitable treatment standard as requiring that the state pursue a variety of proactive measures and noting that 'the extent to which a State is obliged under the fair and equitable treatment standard to be pro-active is open to debate').

[28] G. Kaufman-Kohler, 'Arbitral precedent: dream, necessity or reality', *Arbitration International* 23(3) (2007), 357–78 at 372 (referring to the findings of a study by Professor C. Schreuer).

[29] See Y. Banifatemi, 'The Emerging Jurisprudence of the Most-Favored-Nation Treatment in Investment Arbitration' in A. Bjorklund, I. A. Laird and S. Ripinsky (eds.), *Investment Treaty Law: Current Issues III* (London: British Institute of International and Comparative Law (BIICL), 2009).

resolution mechanism, allowing the investor to circumvent the 18-month negotiation period, unless there exist 'policy considerations that the contracting parties might have envisaged as fundamental conditions for their acceptance of the agreement in question'.[30] The *Plama* Tribunal held that, unless the parties to a treaty specifically agreed that the MFN provision may extend to dispute resolution mechanisms, investors could benefit only from the more favourable substantive protections in other treaties.[31]

Thereafter, tribunals seem to have broadly followed one approach or the other, including in cases where investors have relied on the MFN provision in the basic treaty to benefit from the broader arbitration provision in a third treaty when the dispute resolution clause of the basic treaty is limited to the determination of the amount or mode of compensation in the event of an expropriation. An analysis of the case law shows that the divide is more specifically on the question whether the concept of 'treatment' includes access to arbitration, that is whether dispute resolution arrangements constitute a 'substantive' right that benefits from the MFN treatment or if it is a 'procedural' right excluded from such benefit.

The Tribunal in *Wintershall*, after reviewing what it termed 'a welter of inconsistent and confusing *dicta* of different tribunals, ("case-law")',[32] sided with *Plama* and its progeny to reject the applicability of the MFN clause to dispute settlement provisions.[33] Interestingly, a prior decision in *Siemens* based on the same treaty – a decision the *Wintershall* Tribunal was not only aware of, but which it explicitly analysed – had reached the opposite result.[34]

On the other hand, in *Renta 4* the Tribunal noted that an appraisal of the numerous decisions regarding the MFN treatment revealed that 'a *jurisprudence constante* of general applicability is not firmly established. It remains necessary to proceed BIT by BIT.'[35] While it considered that 'there is no ... legal rule to say that "treatment" does not encompass the

---

[30] *Emilio Agustín Maffezini* v. *Spain* (Decision on Objections to Jurisdiction), ICSID Case No. ARB/97/7, 25 January 2000, para. 62.

[31] *Plama Consortium Limited* v. *Bulgaria* (Decision on Jurisdiction), ICSID Case No. ARB/03/24, 8 February 2005, paras. 183–227.

[32] *Wintershall Aktiengesellschaft* v. *the Argentine Republic* (Award), ICSID Case No. ARB/04/14, 8 November 2008, para. 189.

[33] *Ibid.*, paras. 160–196.

[34] *Siemens A.G.* v. *Argentina* (Decision on Jurisdiction), ICSID Case No. ARB/02/8, 3 August 2004, paras. 102–103.

[35] *Renta 4 S.V.S.A et al.* v. *Russian Federation* (Award on Preliminary Objections), SCC Case No. 24/2007, 20 March 2009, para. 94.

host state's acceptance to international arbitration',[36] it found that by its terms the MFN treatment in that particular basic treaty did not extend to dispute settlement but was limited to fair and equitable treatment.

Going a step further on the basis of the broad formulation of the MFN clause at hand, the majority in *Impregilo* found that the term 'treatment' would be 'in itself wide enough to be applicable also to procedural matters such as dispute settlement'.[37] The majority reviewed the case law on the issue of whether MFN extended to dispute settlement and noted that it must 'attach special weight to the wording of the MFN clause, which extends its scope to "all other matters regulated by this Agreement"'.[38] It noted that in *Berschader*, the Tribunal had found that, 'despite the fact that the MFN clause covered "all matters", this [was] insufficient to make the clause applicable to dispute settlement'.[39] The majority concluded that it was:

> unfortunate if the assessment of these issues would in each case be dependent on the personal opinions of individual arbitrators. The best way to avoid such a result is to make the determination on the basis of case law whenever a clear case law can be discerned. It is true that, as stated above, the jurisprudence regarding the application of MFN clauses to settlement of disputes provisions is not fully consistent. Nevertheless, in cases where the MFN clause has referred to 'all matters' or 'any matter' regulated in the BIT, there has been near-unanimity in finding that the clause covered the dispute settlement rules. On this basis, the majority of the Tribunal reaches the conclusion that Impregilo is entitled to rely, in this respect, on the dispute settlement rules in the Argentina–US BIT and that the case cannot be dismissed for non-observance of the requirements in Article 8(2) and (3) of the Argentina–Italy BIT.[40]

---

[36] *Ibid.*, para. 101.

[37] *Impregilo S.p.A.* v. *Argentine Republic* (Award), ICSID Case No. ARB/07/17, 21 June 2011, para. 99. For a contrary view, in a situation in which the BIT did not cover 'all matters' and where the Tribunal found that 'treatment' as used in that BIT did not apply to dispute settlement, see *ICS Inspection and Control Services Limited (United Kingdom)* v. *The Republic of Argentina* (Award on Jurisdiction), PCA Case No. 2010–9, 10 February 2012.

[38] *Impregilo S.p.A.* v. *Argentine Republic* (Award), ICSID Case No. ARB/07/17, 21 June 2011, paras. 103–107.

[39] *Ibid.* para. 106.

[40] *Ibid.*, para. 108. Arbitrator Stern took exception to the majority's views and submitted a dissenting opinion 'to try to explain why, in principle, an MFN clause cannot import, in part or in toto, a dispute settlement mechanism from a third party BIT into the BIT which is the basic treaty applicable to the dispute'. She argued that an MFN clause could only apply to 'the rights that an investor can enjoy' and not to 'the fundamental conditions for the enjoyment of such rights, in other words, the insuperable conditions of access to the rights granted in the BIT', such as the requirement to attempt to have the case settled in

In light of this diverging case law and the strong views expressed in the various awards and dissenting opinions, one may wonder whether the debate merely reflects a technical divergence as regards the interpretation of the word 'treatment' or if, in reality, what is at stake is the views one may have as to the degree of protection that ought to be recognised for the investors in investment treaties and investment arbitration. In other words, the divergence in the case law on the effect of MFN clauses may more easily illustrate arbitral or doctrinal activism than difficulties in the textual interpretation of the relevant provisions.

3. Umbrella clauses

The effect of umbrella clauses has given rise to even more diverse interpretations. The split between the SGS v. Pakistan and the SGS v. Philippines Tribunals on the issue of whether, through the operation of an umbrella clause, arbitral tribunals may rule on breaches of contract as breaches of a treaty, is well known: the former denied that an umbrella clause may have that effect, restricting its application to exceptional circumstances only,[41] while the latter held that the host state's failure to observe 'binding commitments, including contractual commitments' would be in breach of the umbrella clause, and thus a breach of the treaty.[42]

Thereafter, a third and more restrictive approach emerged. After reviewing the prior case law, the El Paso Tribunal took the findings in SGS v. Pakistan as a basis, adding that an umbrella clause will only apply to contractual commitments into which the host state itself has entered in its sovereign capacity.[43] The Tribunal found support in the treaty's definition of an investment dispute, which included disputes relating to 'investment agreements' or 'investment authorizations', which, the Tribunal opined, was what the umbrella was referring to.[44] Another example is provided by the BIVAC decision. The Tribunal in that case noted that the SGS cases were 'irreconcilable' and decided to follow the reasoning of the SGS v. Philippines Tribunal. Curiously, even after it had found the two cases

---

the local courts for eighteen months: Concurring and Dissenting Opinion of Professor B. Stern, 21 June 2011, para. 16 and para. 47.

[41] SGS Société Générale de Surveillance S.A. v. Islamic Republic of Pakistan (Decision on Jurisdiction), ICSID Case No. ARB/01/13, 6 August 2003, paras. 163–174.

[42] SGS Société Générale de Surveillance S.A. v. Republic of the Philippines (Decision on Jurisdiction), ICSID Case No. ARB/02/6, 29 January 2004, paras. 113–129.

[43] El Paso Energy International Company v. The Argentine Republic (Decision on Jurisdiction), ICSID Case No. ARB/03/15, 27 April 2006, paras. 70–82.

[44] Ibid., para. 81.

irreconcilable and followed *SGS* v. *Philippines*, the Tribunal in *BIVAC* attempted to distinguish the matter at hand from *SGS* v. *Pakistan* on the basis of the location of the umbrella clause in the treaty.[45]

Disagreement also exists as to whether, in a situation where the contract has been concluded by a legal entity separate from the host state, the lack of privity between the state and the investor (or the investment) operates to automatically defeat the claim under the umbrella clause, or if the customary rules of international law on attribution ought to be applied. The *Hamester* decision illustrates the divide in the case law while also providing an example where no attempt has been made to distinguish the two lines of cases. In that case, the Tribunal followed several decisions supporting that privity of contract is required. Noting the contrary view and maintaining its opposition without further analysis, the Tribunal held that even if the rules on attribution were to be applied, in that particular case the entity's execution of the contract was not attributable to the state.[46]

Today the state of the law on umbrella clauses is nothing less than scattered. Here too, in the same way as the effect of MFN clauses, the divergence is not simply a textual one in relation to the different texts whose interpretation has been provided; there are also clear divergences in opinion on the level of protection (or, conversely, level of responsibility for the host state) that investment treaties should ensure. As the *BIVAC* Tribunal noted:

> We recognise in particular that there is no *jurisprudence constante* on the effect of umbrella clauses, that the subject is one on which legal opinion is divided, that the relationship between commercial and sovereign acts of government is not free from difficulty, and that each particular clause falls to be interpreted and applied according to its precise wording and the context in which it is included in a BIT.[47]

It is therefore not surprising that issues such as the effect of an MFN clause or the effect of an umbrella clause have been at the heart of the recent debates in investment arbitration. These are the questions that

---

[45] *Bureau Veritas, Inspection, Valuation, Assessment and Control, BIVAC B.V.* v. *Republic of Paraguay* (Decision of the Tribunal on Objections to Jurisdiction), ICSID Case No. ARB/07/9, 29 May 2009, paras. 134–142.

[46] *Gustav F W Hamester GmbH & Co KG* v. *Republic of Ghana* (Award), ICSID Case No. ARB/07/24, 18 June 2010, paras. 342–348.

[47] *Bureau Veritas, Inspection, Valuation, Assessment and Control, BIVAC B.V.* v. *Republic of Paraguay* (Decision of the Tribunal on Objections to Jurisdiction), ICSID Case No. ARB/07/9, 29 May 2009, para. 141.

crystallise most effectively, in reference to state consent, the question of what limits, if any, should be assigned to the jurisdiction of arbitral tribunals in investment arbitration. Leaving aside doctrinal debates, however, and focusing on arbitral decisions as the sole determining element, the question is whether consistency in arbitral case law is achievable at all.

D. Achieving greater consistency: myth and reality

Various alternatives have been advanced in practice to promote greater consistency in investment arbitration:

- a centralised treaty interpretation mechanism (section I below);
- authentic treaty interpretation by the contracting parties to the treaty (section II below); and
- the development of a *jurisprudence constante* in investment treaty arbitration (section III below).

A closer look at these alternatives shows that, in reality, systemic consistency may not always be achievable or even desirable.

I.   Centralised treaty interpretation: is it achievable or desirable?

One of the proposals aimed at promoting greater consistency in investment arbitration is the introduction of a centralised or institutionalised treaty interpretation mechanism. Examples include a model following the Free Trade Commission (FTC) of the NAFTA, the introduction of an appellate body and proposals for an evolving role to be played by the ICSID's ad hoc committees.

1.   The NAFTA's FTC

The NAFTA's principal institution in charge, inter alia, of the application of the agreement is the FTC, a body comprising cabinet-level representatives of the NAFTA's contracting parties. The FTC also 'resolve[s] disputes that may arise regarding [the NAFTA's] interpretation or application' (Article 2001(2)(c)).

The FTC's interpretation of the treaty is binding on NAFTA tribunals (Article 1131(2)). In entrusting the FTC with authoritative interpretation of the treaty, the NAFTA contracting parties have arguably created a mechanism through which they can more conveniently control the development of the law in relation to that treaty.

An FTC-like mechanism may prove to be a powerful tool in achieving consistency – in line with the parties' intent – in the case law on a specific treaty. If at all achievable, the introduction of such a mechanism by parties contracting to a treaty could be more easily conceived in the multilateral than the bilateral setting. Arguably, it could conclusively resolve inconsistencies in the case law by binding prospective tribunals to a certain interpretation of a treaty.

However, the experience with the NAFTA's FTC has not been without controversy. In 2001, at a time when in at least one arbitration proceeding claims under Article 1105 (minimum standard of treatment) of the NAFTA were pending, the FTC issued an interpretation in which it provided an authoritative interpretation of that provision.[48] This interpretation caused an upheaval in the NAFTA community. In this respect, the opinion expressed by Sir Robert Jennings in the *Methanex* arbitration is worthy of mention as regards the propriety of an interpretation for purposes of a pending proceeding:

> It would be wrong to discuss these three-party 'interpretations' of what have become key words of this arbitration, without protesting the impropriety of the three governments making such an intervention well into the process of arbitration, not only after the benefit of seeing the written pleadings of the parties but also virtually prompted by them. In the present case, without asking for leave, one of the actual Parties to the arbitration has quite evidently organized a démarche intended to apply pressure on the tribunal to find in a certain direction by amending the treaty to curtail investor protections. This is surely against the most elementary rules of due process of justice.[49]

Sir Robert's words illustrate the difficulties arising out of an institutionalised interpretation in the context of pending proceedings when the outcome of the proceedings could be determined by that interpretation. At the same time, should this avenue be adopted in relation to specific treaties, it may not be realistic, given the proliferation of disputes in practice, to require that such interpretations be precluded while the cases in which the provision subject to interpretation is operative are pending. In addition, an interpretation provided by the contracting parties may be

---

[48] See Notes of Interpretation of Certain Chapter 11 Provisions (NAFTA Free Trade Commission, 31 July 2001), available at: www.international.gc.ca/trade-agreements-accords-commerciaux/disp-diff/NAFTA-Interpr.aspx?lang=en&view=d).

[49] *Methanex Corporation* v. *United States of America* (Second Opinion of Sir Robert Jennings), Arbitration under NAFTA and UNCITRAL Arbitration Rules, Q.C., 6 September 2001, 4–5.

relevant to the intention of those parties at the time when they entered into the treaty, provided, however, that certain procedural and due process safeguards are put in place to preserve the rights of all parties, including those of the investor.

2.   The introduction of an appellate body

The establishment of an appellate body is an option advocated by some but mistrusted or even flatly dismissed by others. Having entertained the idea in 2004, when it considered amending its rules, the ICSID ended up not pursuing this option further.[50]

At first sight, a permanent appellate body composed of eminent jurists in the field could presumably serve to bring more consistency and predictability. The main criticism, however, is that this would almost inevitably turn investment treaty arbitration into a permanent two-tier process, much like that of the World Trade Organization (WTO), countering the essence of arbitration – finality of the award.[51]

In addition, there is no guarantee that an appellate body would always render decisions that are correct as a matter of law or are not subject to criticism. This is all the more so given that the structural framework of arbitration law would essentially remain unchanged, namely that the appellate body would provide interpretations in relation to different treaties in different cases, as opposed to a single repeat instrument, such as the WTO instruments. The question is then what the purpose and function of an appellate body is supposed to be: to provide the 'correct' interpretation of the law (even if the case law in its majority goes in a different direction), or to achieve a definitive response on debated issues when there is a split in the case law? Hardly any particulars have been provided on these difficult questions by those who advocate the creation of an appellate mechanism in investment arbitration. The same holds true for the practical impediments to the creation of an appellate body, which are overwhelming given the structure of the system as it stands, namely a decentralised system based essentially on a network of countless treaties setting bilateral relations and providing for the resolution of disputes by individual tribunals constituted for each individual dispute.

---

[50] See ICSID Secretariat, 'Possible Improvements of the Framework for ICSID Arbitration', Discussion Paper, American Society of International Law – Proceedings of the 103rd Annual ASIL Meeting, 22 October 2004, available at: https://icsid.worldbank.org.

[51] See Y. Banifatemi, 'Mapping the Future of Investment Treaty Arbitration as a System of Law – Remarks', American Society of International Law – Proceedings of the 103rd Annual ASIL Meeting (2010), 323.

3.   Can there be a control function for ICSID
ad hoc committees?

Lastly, commentators have looked into the possibility of having ICSID ad hoc committees play a role in the harmonisation of international investment law.[52]

Should ad hoc committees help harmonise international investment law? For example, was the *CMS* ad hoc committee correct to 'clarify certain points of substance on which, in its view, the Tribunal had made manifest errors of law'?[53] Arguably, the decision of the Tribunal in *Continental Casualty*, rendered after the *CMS* annulment decision, explicitly followed the approach preferred by the *CMS* ad hoc committee. However, is the role of an ad hoc committee to provide guidance for future tribunals in relation to questions of law, as also professed by the *CMS* ad hoc committee, or is it to exercise its review of the award in light of the limited and strict grounds provided at Article 52 of the Washington Convention?[54]

Alternatively, should ICSID appoint the same ad hoc committee members from a small pool of international law experts who will (explicitly or implicitly) be entrusted with the function of controlling the developments in the law and, accordingly, its consistency? Three limitations exist in this respect. First, the powers of the ad hoc committee members are too limited to perform such a function. Second, even if these bodies had broader competencies, the ad hoc nature of their decisions and the lack of precedent in the system are likely to lead to the same splits in jurisprudence as is the case for arbitral tribunals. The approach adopted by the ad hoc committees in the *CMS*, *Enron* and *Sempra* cases more than hint at this outcome. Finally, a number of investment treaty decisions are rendered outside the ICSID system, for which there is no equivalent review

---

[52] See C. Knahr, 'Annulment and its Role in the Context of Conflicting Awards' in M. Waibel, A. Kaushal, K.-H. L. Chung and C. Balchin (eds.), *The Backlash Against Investment Arbitration* (Alphen aan den Rijn: Kluwer Law International, 2010); M. Reisman, 'Reflections on the Control Mechanism of the ICSID' in E. Gaillard (ed.), *IAI Series on International Arbitration No. 6: The Review of International Arbitral Awards* (Huntington: Juris Publishing, 2010).

[53] *CMS Gas Transmission Company* v. *the Argentine Republic* (Decision of the *ad hoc* Committee on the Application for Annulment by the Argentine Republic), ICSID Case No. ARB/01/8, 25 September 2007, para. 45.

[54] For a critical view, see Y. Banifatemi 'Defending Investment Treaty Awards: Is There an ICSID Advantage?' in A. J. van den Berg (ed.), *50 Years of the New York Convention*, *ICCA Congress Series No. 14* (Dublin: Kluwer Law International, 2009). See also Reisman, 'Reflections on the Control Mechanism of the ICSID System'.

mechanism, and, consequently, about whose potential inconsistency the ICSID's ad hoc committees will be powerless to do anything.

II. Authentic treaty interpretation by contracting states: is it achievable or desirable?

Authentic treaty interpretation by the contracting parties to a treaty may be viewed as both a legitimate and a more practicable mechanism to achieve consistency in investment treaty interpretation. Two methods exist in this respect: recourse to the *travaux préparatoires* of a treaty, and the possible intervention of the investor's home state in the course of arbitration proceedings to provide its interpretation of the treaty under review.

1. Resorting to a treaty's drafting history

The drafting history of a treaty, when available, may provide a useful tool to the parties in relation to the interpretation of specific treaty provisions. In fact, the *travaux préparatoires* are more often than not referred to by the parties. As the *Malaysian Salvors* ad hoc committee stated:

> Courts and tribunals interpreting treaties regularly review the *travaux préparatoires* whenever they are brought to their attention; it is mythological to pretend that they do so only when they first conclude that the term requiring interpretation is ambiguous or obscure.[55]

This is especially true as regards the negotiating history of the Washington Convention, which is widely referred to by parties and tribunals alike.[56]

However, it must not be overlooked that the *travaux préparatoires* are a supplementary means of treaty interpretation and can only be resorted to if the conditions in Article 32 of the VCLT are met. In other words, there will be no need to venture beyond the primary rule of treaty interpretation in Article 31. In this respect, for example, the Tribunal in the *Yukos*-related arbitrations found no need to venture into the drafting history

---

[55] *Malaysian Historical Salvors, SDN, BHD v. The Government of Malaysia* (Decision on the Application for Annulment), ICSID Case No. ARB/05/10, 16 April 2009, para. 57. For a contrary view, see W. M. Reisman and M. H. Arsanjani, 'Interpreting treaties for the benefit of third parties: the "salvors' doctrine" and the use of legislative history in investment treaties', *American Journal of International Law* 104 (2010), 597–604.

[56] C. Schreuer, 'Diversity and Harmonization of Treaty Interpretation in Investment Arbitration' in M. Fitzmaurice, O. Elias and P. Merkouris (eds.), *Treaty Interpretation and the Vienna Convention on the Law of Treaties: 30 Years On* (Leiden: Martinus Nijhoff, 2010), p. 138.

of the ECT in relation to the interpretation of Article 45 of the treaty on provisional application:

> The Tribunal does not consider that its interpretation of Article 45 resulting from the application of the general rule of interpretation leads to a result which is manifestly absurd or unreasonable. Nor has the Tribunal found that its interpretation of Article 45 according to Article 31 of the VCLT 'leaves the meaning ambiguous or obscure'; quite the contrary. The Tribunal recognizes that, in practice, tribunals and other treaty interpreters may consider the *travaux préparatoires* whenever they are pleaded, whether or not the text is ambiguous or obscure or leads to a manifestly absurd or unreasonable result.[57]

Leaving aside the conditions in which the negotiating history of a treaty may be resorted to, it remains true that, where the negotiating history of a treaty is available, it may provide useful assistance to the tribunals in their interpretation task. However, three factors should be kept in mind. First, BITs rarely have published or even recorded workable *travaux préparatoires*.[58] Second, in the case of multilateral treaties, the treaty interpreters may be confronted with a bottomless record of unilateral statements evidencing the preference of one party, as opposed to the intent of all parties. In such cases, the negotiating history may be particularly informative when it reveals the position of a respondent state: even if the positions specifically taken by that state do not reflect the common intention of the drafting parties, it may reflect at the very least the intention of that particular state and be relevant to the tribunal when the position of that state is precisely what is at stake. The third factor is the tribunals' discretion to determine the evidentiary value of the evidence before them, and therefore to assess and determine the weight to be given to individual evidence related to the negotiating history of a treaty.

More generally, when the negotiating history sheds light on the meaning to be given to a specific provision, it is stating the obvious that the resulting interpretation will relate only to the treaty at hand. In other words, any consistency achieved through the negotiating history of a treaty, especially in the case of multilateral treaties, will bring about consistency in relation to that treaty only; it will not lead to systemic consistency, even

---

[57] *Hulley Enterprises Limited* v. *The Russian Federation* (Interim Award on Jurisdiction and Admissibility), PCA Case No. 225, 30 November 2009, para. 268.

[58] This was the case in the *Aguas del Tunari, S.A.* v. *Bolivia* arbitration. See *Aguas del Tunari, S.A.* v. *Bolivia* (Decision on Jurisdiction), ICSID Case No. ARB/02/3, 21 October 2005, para. 274.

if the provision being interpreted has a wording similar to that of a different treaty.

2. Intervention of the home state as *amicus curiae*

In addition to the drafting history of a treaty, another tool may be considered for the purposes of harmonised interpretation, particularly in the context of BITs, namely the juxtaposition of the contracting parties' views on the interpretation of a treaty in the course of a dispute.

Thus, when a respondent state offers its views on the manner in which a BIT provision ought to be construed, particularly when in doing so it resorts to its own materials evidencing the contracting parties' intent in relation to that provision, the tribunal may consider offering the investor's home state the opportunity to offer the other contracting party's views in the form of an *amicus curiae* brief.[59] This does not mean that the tribunal should be provided with yet another pleading on issues such as the state of the case law or the doctrine on the provision (the parties' pleadings ought to suffice for this purpose), but rather with the authentic view of the home state as to the contracting parties' intention, supported by contemporaneous documentation and/or witness testimony. The home state's views may be of particular significance when the documentation evidencing the intention of the contracting parties is not available to the investor.

This mechanism has been considered by United Nations Commission on International Trade Law (UNCITRAL) in its ongoing works on the formulation of a legal standard on transparency in investment arbitration. In particular, UNCITRAL has specifically looked into the issue of *amicus curiae* briefs provided by the investor's home state on issues of treaty interpretation. As highlighted by Working Group II:

> It was observed that two possible types of amicus curiae should be distinguished and perhaps considered differently. The first type could be any third party that would have an interest in contributing to the solution of the dispute. A second type could be another State party to the investment treaty at issue that was not a party to the dispute. It was noted that such State often had important information to provide, such as information on *travaux préparatoires*, thus preventing one-sided treaty interpretation.

---

[59] In that sense, the proposed mechanism is not unlike that provided for in Article 63 of the ICJ Statute, which in paragraph 1 provides that '[w]henever the construction of a convention to which states other than those concerned in the case are parties is in question, the Registrar shall notify all such states forthwith' and in paragraph 2 that '[e]very state so notified has the right to intervene in the proceedings; but if it uses this right, the construction given by the judgment will be equally binding upon it'.

In response, it was said that an intervention by a non-disputing State, of which the investor was a national, could raise issues of diplomatic protection and was to be given careful consideration. It was suggested that third parties who could contribute to the resolution of the dispute could be identified and invited by the arbitral tribunal to assist it. The home State of the investor could be one such third party.[60]

At the fifty-third session of the Working Group, it was observed that a State Party to the investment treaty that was not a party to the dispute could also wish, be invited, or have a treaty right to make submissions. It was noted that such State(s) often had important information to provide, such as information on the travaux préparatoires, thus preventing one-sided treaty interpretation (A/CN.9/712, para. 49).[61]

The existence of such a mechanism, in particular if it is given as a power to the arbitral tribunal on its own motion, may prevent situations similar to that which arose in *SGS* v. *Pakistan* in the aftermath of the decision on jurisdiction in relation to the effect of an umbrella clause. In that case, Switzerland, the investor's home state, wrote to ICSID, noting the Tribunal's decision with 'a great deal of concern' and asking why its view had not been sought during the proceedings. Switzerland further clarified its intention in relation to the umbrella clause at the time of the treaty's conclusion, namely that this type of provision is 'intended to cover commitments that a host state has entered into with regard to specific investments of an investor or investment of a specific investor, which played a significant role in the investor's decision to invest or to substantially change an existing investment'.[62] However, by then Switzerland's intervention could achieve nothing more than airing the state's disgruntlement at the decision, whereas an intervention in the course of the proceedings may have shed some light on the Tribunal's consideration of the meaning and *raison d'être* of the umbrella clause in the Switzerland–Pakistan BIT.

---

[60] UNCITRAL, Forty-Fourth Session, 'Report of Working Group II (Arbitration and Conciliation) on the Work of its Fifty-third Session (Vienna, 4–8 October 2010)', UN Doc. A/CN.9/712, para. 49.

[61] UNCITRAL, Forty-Fourth Session, 'Report of Working Group II (Arbitration and Conciliation) on the Work of its Fifty-fifth Session (Vienna, 3–7 October 2011)', UN Doc. A/CN.9/736, para. 78.

[62] Note on the Interpretation of Article 11 of the BIT between Switzerland and Pakistan in the light of the Decision of the Tribunal on Objections to Jurisdiction of ICSID in Case No. ARB/01/13 *SGS Société Générale de Surveillance S.A.* v. *Islamic Republic of Pakistan*, attached to the Letter of the Swiss Secretariat for Economic Affairs to the ICSID Deputy-Secretary General dated 1 October 2003, published in 19 *Mealey's International Arbitration Report* E3 (February 2004).

Thus, the possibility of inviting the investor's home state to air its views in relation to an interpretation unilaterally provided by the host state (also the respondent state in the arbitration) may assist tribunals in determining the common intention of both parties at the time of conclusion of the bilateral treaty in relation to a specific provision whose interpretation is sought. In terms of propriety, this mechanism arguably does not raise the same issues as those raised by Sir Robert Jennings in relation to the interpretation provided by the FTC: the home state's intervention would serve the purpose of providing contemporaneous evidence on the negotiation of the treaty, which by definition is available to the respondent state but not to the investor, and, as highlighted by the works of UNCITRAL, avoiding 'one-sided treaty interpretation'.

Here too, however, the intervention of the investor's home state cannot assist arbitral tribunals beyond the specifics of a particular treaty, and would thus potentially serve to bring consistency in respect of the jurisprudence in relation to a particular BIT only.

III.   Arbitral tribunals' reliance on 'precedents': the development of a jurisprudence constante in investment treaty arbitration

As already emphasised, the structural design of the system, namely its decentralisation, is an inescapable impediment to systemic consistency. The tools for achieving consistency are thus largely treaty-specific. At the same time, the system is not blind to harmonisation and uniformity. Certain other factors must be taken into account.

The age of the system must not be overlooked: investment arbitration is still in its adolescence. While, since the 1950s, multiple generations of investment arbitrations have succeeded, the case law until the late 1990s was scarce. The beginning of the twenty-first century, however, has witnessed a veritable flood of investment treaty decisions, in parallel with an exponential growth of the community of investment arbitration practitioners and commentators. Awareness of the law in this field has never been more acute. As a result, the system is maturing by the day – parts of it at a slower pace. In that context, some inconsistency is inevitable.

Inconsistency is also part of the system because that may be what the parties wish. While commentators and other observers call for consistency as a manner to predict the law, investors and host states, when they are parties to an arbitration, may wish to safeguard their opportunity to fully argue their case, even if this means arguing their case differently from the solutions that have been adopted in practice. This is inherent to the absence of precedent in international arbitration. The example of Argentina, which could argue *de novo* – and win – its case in *Continental Casualty* in relation to Article XI of the USA–Argentina BIT, following the *CMS* decisions, perfectly illustrates this point. In this context, inconsistency may in fact help the development of the law.

Against this background, it is worthwhile remembering that arbitral tribunals generally view their function as entailing the development of the law. The Tribunal in *SGS v. Philippines* noted in this respect:

> In the Tribunal's view, although different tribunals constituted under the ICSID system should in general seek to act consistently with each other, in the end it must be for each tribunal to exercise its competence in accordance with the applicable law, which will by definition be different for each BIT and each Respondent State. Moreover there is no doctrine of precedent in international law, if by precedent is meant a rule of the binding effect of a single decision. There is no hierarchy of international tribunals, and even if there were, there is no good reason for allowing the first tribunal in time to resolve issues for all later tribunals. It must be initially for the control mechanisms provided for under the BIT and the ICSID Convention, and *in the longer term for the development of a common legal opinion or* jurisprudence constante, *to resolve the difficult legal questions* discussed by the *SGS v. Pakistan* Tribunal and also in the present decision.[63]

The *ADC v. Hungary* Tribunal was of the same view:

> It is true that arbitral awards do not constitute binding precedent. It is also true that a number of cases are fact-driven and that the findings in those cases cannot be transposed in and of themselves to other cases. It is further true that a number of cases are based on treaties that differ from the present BIT in certain respects. However, *cautious reliance on certain principles developed in a number of those cases, as persuasive authority, may advance the body of law, which in turn may serve predictability in the interest of both investors and host states.*[64]

The Tribunal in *Saipem v. Bangladesh*, later followed by the *Pey Casado* Tribunal, similarly held that:

> it must pay due consideration to earlier decisions of international tribunals. It believes that, subject to compelling contrary grounds, it has a

---

[63] *SGS Société Générale de Surveillance S.A.* v. *Republic of the Philippines* (Decision on Jurisdiction), ICSID Case No. ARB/02/6, 29 January 2004, para. 97, emphasis added.
[64] *ADC Affiliate Limited and ADC & ADMC Management Limited* v. *Republic of Hungary* (Award), ICSID Case No. ARB/03/16, 2 October 2006, para. 293, emphasis added.

duty to adopt solutions established in a series of consistent cases. It also believes that, subject to the specifics of a given treaty and of the circumstances of the actual case, it has a duty to seek to contribute to the harmonious development of investment law and thereby to meet the legitimate expectations of the community of States and investors towards certainty of the rule of law.[65]

In other words, it is in the arbitral tribunals' 'duty to seek to contribute to the harmonious development of investment law' and it is in their development of a *jurisprudence constante* that one may find the main tool to address inconsistency in investment arbitration.[66]

Thus, it is to be hoped that what will *not* be followed are analyses – no matter how persuasive and no matter how distinguished the jurists making them – of treaties whose structure, wording and context, while at first glance similar, are materially different from the structure, wording and context of the treaties being interpreted. It is also to be hoped that arbitrators will not forget that their primary duty is that of settling the dispute at hand (as argued) between the parties, and that they will not flirt with the audience at large with superfluous *dicta* or dissenting opinions designed at 'making law'.

Ultimately, consistency and predictability may be nothing more than the result of what can be called a 'Darwinian approach': an expectation that, over time, poor attempts to develop and harmonise the law will be less influential and will not be followed up, and that high-quality interpretations and reasoning will have longer lines of progeny.

---

[65] *Saipem S.p.A.* v. *The People's Republic of Bangladesh* (Decision on Jurisdiction and Recommendation on Provisional Measures), ICSID Case No. ARB/05/07, 21 March 2007, para. 67. See also *Victor Pey Casado and President Allende Foundation* v. *Republic of Chile* (Award), ICSID Case No. ARB/98/2, 8 May 2008, para. 119 ('Avant de procéder à l'examen de ces conditions, le Tribunal tient à préciser qu'il n'est pas lié par les décisions et les sentences CIRDI rendues antérieurement. Le présent Tribunal estime toutefois qu'il se doit de prendre en considération les décisions des tribunaux internationaux et de s'inspirer, en l'absence de justification impérieuse en sens contraire, des solutions résultant d'une jurisprudence arbitrale établie. Tout en tenant compte des particularités du traité applicable et des faits de l'espèce, le Tribunal estime aussi devoir s'efforcer de contribuer au développement harmonieux du droit des investissements et, ce faisant, de satisfaire à l'attente légitime de la communauté des Etats et des investisseurs quant à la prévisibilité du droit en la matière').

[66] On *jurisprudence constante*, see A. K. Bjorklund 'Investment Treaty Arbitral Decisions as *Jurisprudence Constante*' in C. Picker, I. Bunn and D. Arner (eds.), *International Economic Law: the State and Future of the Discipline* (Oxford: Hart, 2008), p. 265. See also Banifatemi, *IAI Series on International Arbitration No. 5*.

14

Coherence, convergence and consistency in international investment law

MICHAEL EWING-CHOW

A. Introduction

Before I begin my discussion, I think we should first attempt to understand what we mean by the terms coherence, convergence and consistency. While I am aware of the limitations of lexicons, they are a natural place to start. The Oxford English Dictionary Online[1] defines coherence as 'logical connection or relation; congruity, consistency'. Convergence is 'the action or fact of converging; movement directed toward or terminating in the same point'. Finally, consistency is defined as 'the quality, state, or fact of being consistent; agreement, harmony, compatibility'. All three terms can be used to describe physical natures or systemic characteristics. Allow me then to begin with the physical as a metaphor for the metaphysical.

B. Coherence

This World Trade Forum was appropriately held in Bern where Albert Einstein had his 'Annus Mirabilis' in 1905. In that year, Einstein published four articles that contributed substantially to the foundation of modern physics and also radically changed our understanding of space, time and matter. The first of these articles published in the scientific journal *Annalen der Physik* was titled 'On a Heuristic Viewpoint Concerning the Production and Transformation of Light', in which Einstein theorised for the first time that light could be described as being composed of discrete quanta rather than continuous waves. This earned Einstein the Nobel Prize in Physics in 1921. Later, in 1924, Satyendra Nath Bose would use this theory to create the mathematics behind the Bose–Einstein statistics

---

[1] The Oxford English Dictionary, available at: www.oed.com/.

that were eventually used to predict the existence of Bose–Einstein condensates in which atoms are all coherent (i.e. at the same quantum state). One way to obtain these coherent condensates is to supercool the matter.

However, this discussion is not about physics. It is about the law. Legal rules and procedures operate in a complicated, messy and heated environment and not under theoretical or laboratory conditions. As legal realists we understand that the complex network of actual facts, the political, social and cultural considerations and even the individual adjudicators of a dispute affect the outcome and the ostensible reasoning. Yet if theorists in other fields involving networks such as communications and transport have applied the Bose–Einstein statistics to their modelling, we can perhaps apply the physics definition of the term coherence to international investment arbitration law.

Coherence in physics is a property of waves that enables stationary interference either temporally or spatially. Two waves can come together to constructively create a larger wave or subtract destructively from each other to form a smaller wave. If waves are of equal strength but exactly out of phase, they cancel each other out. Irregular patterns, however, ensue when waves have multiple amplitudes and occur in different phases. This is indeed the 'choppy waters' we find ourselves in when we attempt to make sense of the many international investment arbitration (IIA) awards.[2]

At this stage, we should ask ourselves whether we should indeed be discomfited by the apparent chaos we observe when the awards made rely on different texts and facts and are not binding on any later tribunal. In fact, it would be startling and perhaps even unnatural if we were to observe a complete convergence of rules and perfect consistency in such a situation. Allow me to expand on this.

C. Convergence of substantive rules

A complete convergence of rules may occur in a thought experiment[3] suggested by Rawls in his book *A Theory of Justice*[4] to consider a social contract created when all parties are subjected to a veil of ignorance. However, later even Rawls himself modified his assumption of two common principles of justice or a common original position that all people would find

---

[2] See, e.g., J. R. Weeramantry, 'The future of past awards in investment arbitration', *ICSID Review* 25 (2010), 111–24 at 112–15.
[3] Like those favoured by Einstein.
[4] J. Rawls, *A Theory of Justice* (Cambridge, MA: Harvard University Press, 1971).

themselves in.[5] Many have further argued that even in the original position, different levels of risk aversion and of morality would be likely to exist.[6] This lack of uniformity at the level of the utility of the rules would increase exponentially once the veil of ignorance is lifted. Rawls therefore suggested that 'overlapping consensus' might be obtained by the method of 'public reason giving' – justifying a particular position by way of reasons that people of different moral or political backgrounds could accept.[7]

So it is with international investment law – the rules are less than uniform because they are aimed at different objectives. DiMascio and Pauwelyn suggested that harmonised multilateral rules were needed for trade because of the dangers of trade diversion but that this was not the case for investment rules.[8] This is true mainly because few investment regimes provide for pre-establishment rights, thus preventing distortions in mode 3 of trade in services (commercial presence).[9] Moran's new book[10] on the different dynamics of foreign direct investment (FDI) opines that even with regard to utility reasoning, different forms of investment rules will need to be developed to fit different types of FDI.

Attempts to create a uniform multilateral treaty on investment such as the Organisation for Economic Co-operation and Development (OECD) Multilateral Agreement on Investment (MAI) and the proposal for the inclusion of investment as one of the Singapore Issues in the World Trade Organization (WTO) Doha Development Agenda have all failed. Basically, in the absence of a concern for trade diversion, we may agree that we like the idea of convergence but we do not know where we want to converge towards. Bjorklund emphasises this point in Chapter 12 of this book and I find myself in complete agreement.

Perhaps, rather than defining coherence as moving towards a common point, we could describe coherence as logical, orderly and

---

[5] J. Rawls, *Justice as Fairness: A Restatement* (Cambridge, MA: Belknap Press, 2001).

[6] See, e.g., R. Nozick, *Anarchy, State and Utopia* (New York: Basic Books, 1974) and more recently A. Sen, *The Idea of Justice* (Cambridge, MA: Harvard University Press, 2009).

[7] J. Rawls, *Political Liberalism* (Cambridge, MA: Harvard University Press, 1993).

[8] N. DiMascio and J. Pauwelyn. 'Nondiscrimination in trade and investment treaties: worlds apart or two sides of the same coin?', *The American Journal of International Law* 102(1) (January 2008), 48–89.

[9] If pre-establishment rights were provided and market access scheduled, these investment agreements would create the General Agreement on Trade in Services (GATS) plus preferential treatment for those covered by the investment agreement.

[10] T. H. Moran, *Foreign Direct Investment and Development: Launching a Second Generation of Policy Research: Avoiding the Mistakes of the First, Reevaluating Policies for Developed and Developing Countries* (Washington DC: Peterson Institute for International Economics, 2011).

aesthetically consistent. Such a definition would not require us to define a static goal but rather a dynamic process of refinement and improvement of the rules. We would need to examine the transparency, legitimacy and institutional issues involved in the drafting, application and amendment of such rules rather than the substantive text of the rules themselves.

The WTO, when faced with the proliferation of preferential trade agreements (PTAs), did not attempt to harmonise those PTAs or limit them. Instead, an institutional system known as the Transparency Mechanism was set up to monitor, report and comment on these PTAs. In so doing, a certain institutional convergence in the way PTAs should be constructed and textually manifested could emerge over time. Wittgenstein may have argued that a word like 'chair' does not have a fixed characteristic but rather chairs are recognised by having a number of significant 'family resemblances'.[11] Derrida may have further emphasised this open-textured nature of words with his theory of deconstructive *différance*.[12] Nonetheless, both Wittgenstein and Derrida acknowledged the relational aspect of textual epistemology.[13]

Thus, the work of the United Nations Conference on Trade and Development (UNCTAD) in publishing and explaining new developments in IIAs and arbitral awards is perhaps one step towards such a relational convergence if not necessarily a textual one.[14] The focus should not be on making all rules uniform, but rather perhaps explaining to the stakeholders and reasoning with them so as to create 'overlapping consensus' in the Rawlsian sense.

D. Consistency in interpretation

I will be provocative here. While the idea of consistency is an attractive one for many lawyers, I think such an attraction is misguided, if

---

[11] See generally L. Wittgenstein, *Philosophical Investigations* (Oxford: Basil Blackwell Ltd, 2001.)

[12] See generally J. Derrida, *Speech and Phenomena and Other Essays on Husserl's Theory of Signs*, trans. D. B. Allison (Evanston, IL: Northwestern University Press, 1973); *Différance. Margins of Philosophy*, translated by Alan Bass (Chicago and London: Chicago University Press, 1982); and *Positions*, translated by A. Bass (University of Chicago Press, 1971).

[13] Notes 11 and 12 above.

[14] See United Nations Conference on Trade and Development (UNCTAD), 'International Investment Agreements', available at: http://unctad.org/en/pages/DIAE/International%20Investment%20Agreements%20(IIA)/International-Investment-Agreements-(IIAs).aspx.

not dangerous. We do not want consistency for consistency's sake. Otherwise bad laws will remain bad laws. In perhaps its most famous case, *Brown v. Board of Education*,[15] the United States Supreme Court overturned a consistent interpretation of the Equal Protection Clause which upheld the legality of 'separate but equal' laws. The Supreme Court therefore overturned a consistent but bad (both morally and in terms of policy) interpretation and made segregation illegal under the US Constitution. We should encourage good legal interpretations to replace bad ones.

Yet we are uncomfortable as lawyers if such radical changes occur all the time, even if they are changes for the better. At the back of our minds we despair about how we should advise our clients, how we should plead in the courts and, if we are adjudicators, how we should justify our results.

Einstein himself was ill at ease with the Heisenberg Uncertainty Principle, and this fundamental limit on the ability to ascertain with accuracy simultaneously the position and momentum of a particle caused Einstein to famously remark, 'God, does not play dice with the Universe.' Einstein believed instead that this was only a provisional uncertainty and that some 'hidden variable' remained to be discovered that would resolve the problem.

Again, I would ask whether we would need such certainty. Instead of certainty I would propose the less rigid term of predictability. While Banifatemi suggests in Chapter 13 of this book that there is an emerging *jurisprudence constante*,[16] I would respectfully submit that it depends on the level of scrutiny. At the macro level, this assertion is true. However, as stated before, and Banifatemi's chapter also illustrates this, the text and the factual context often result in divergence at the micro level. That said, I believe we still are within the realm of predictability. The problem often lies in the textual reasoning in the awards, which attempts to explain why a specific claim succeeded or failed. With different adjudicators and a multiplicity of texts, it is hardly surprising that textual inconsistency is apparent in the awards. In the unique situations of similar text and similar facts, such as Article XI of the USA–Argentina BIT cases, Banifatemi suggests that the jurisprudence is still developing.

Indeed, Banifatemi concludes by explaining that there is a 'Darwinian Approach' to consistency and predictability in that over time 'quality

---

[15] *Brown v. Board of Education of Topeka*, 347 U.S. 483 (1954).
[16] Y. Banifatemi, 'Consistency in the Interpretation of Substantive Investment Rules: Is It Achievable?', Chapter 13, p. 200.

interpretations and reasonings will have longer lines of progeny'.[17] I agree with this in areas where the issue has been the subject of many cases over a long enough period. If one looks at nature, the diversity of species reflect that a Darwinian process does not necessarily lead to consistency of results in any one particular period. Instead, various species exist at any one time occupying the same niche, and only over time would there be extinction caused by competition and adaptation to changing environmental factors. In the context of investment arbitration, this is also true; as more clarity in the indirect expropriation standard developed, investors began to pursue fair and equitable treatment claims. The old story of a vendor of swords and shield is relevant in this context. The story is told that in a crowded market, a man heard a vendor laud the strength of the sword he was selling for its ability to cut through every shield. So he bought the sword. Walking away he heard the same vendor entice buyers to buy his shield as it could block every sword.

So at a particular period in time, how should we deal with uncertainties caused by the slowly evolving process?

E. Conclusion

One way that physicists attempt to create coherence from a light source emitting waves of different amplitudes and wavelengths is to focus and filter. A non-coherent source of light is first passed through a pinhole aperture to create spatially coherent waves and then passed through a wavelength filter to create a wave form that is both spatially and temporally coherent.

Perhaps lawyers can learn from this approach as well. Despite the many criticisms[18] of the WTO Dispute Settlement System, most lawyers will agree it is a relatively stable, fairly predictable and largely coherent system. The WTO has several relative advantages over IIA: (1) there is a single text; and (2) there is a single supporting institutional structure. This allows it to focus the inquiry and filter out noise.

While it would be unlikely and perhaps even inappropriate for a single text to be proposed for international investment law, perhaps the relational epistemology created by increased understanding of the multiple texts

---

[17] Ibid., p. 414.
[18] See, e.g., M. R. Williams, 'Pirates of the Caribbean (and beyond): developing a new remedy for WTO non-compliance', George Washington International Law Review 41 (2009), 503–40.

and awards will move us towards similarity if not uniformity. Regional agreements like the Association of Southeast Asian Nations (ASEAN) Comprehensive Investment Agreement (ACIA)[19] have become the template for intra-Asian agreements just as the North American Free Trade Agreement (NAFTA) has been a model for agreements with NAFTA members.[20]

Further, while some arbitrators are cautious about substantive inputs[21] from the relevant arbitral secretariats, it should be noted that one major feature of the WTO's dispute settlement system is the careful stewardship of the texts by the WTO Secretariat. The WTO Secretariat legal staff provides substantive support to panellists and to the Appellate Body members. While secretariats often have the most continuity and familiarity with the texts and the issues, the difference between stewardship of a multilateral single text[22] for the benefit of all Members and the more ad hoc nature of international investment arbitrations should not be too easily dismissed. Nonetheless, careful calibrations and refinement of the support given by the relevant secretariats can perhaps be initiated without unduly undermining the independence of the arbitrators. Already the provisions of NAFTA Articles 1128 and 1131, permitting individual state parties to provide their input or joint commissions to issue binding interpretation, would suggest that we have already crossed the Rubicon on this issue.[23] The challenge is not a philosophical one but a practical one of balancing the interests of the parties.

---

[19] Association of Southeast Asian Nations (ASEAN) Comprehensive Investment Agreement (ACIA), Cha-am, 26 February 2009, available at: www.aseansec.org/documents/ASEAN%20Comprehensive%20Investment%20Agreement%20%28ACIA%29%202012.pdf.

[20] E.g. compare ASEAN ACIA, UNCTAD, 'International Investment Agreements', with Agreement on Investment under the Framework Agreement on Comprehensive Economic Cooperation Among ASEAN Member Countries and the Republic of Korea, Kuala Lumpur, signed 13 December 2005, available at: www.fta.gov.sg/akfta/ak%20investment%20agreement%20(signed).pdf.

[21] E.g., *Vivendi II* v. *Argentina* (Additional Opinion of J. H. Dalhuisen), ICSID Case No. Arb./97/3, 30 July 2010; *Vivendi II* v. *Argentina* (Decision on Argentine Republic's Request for the Annulment of the Award Rendered), ICSID Case No. Arb./97/3, 20 August 2007, available at: http://italaw.com/documents/VivendiSecondAnnulmentDecision.pdf.

[22] J. E. Alvarez, 'Revisiting the Necessity Defense: Continental Casualty v. Argentina', Institute for International Law and Justice (IILJ) Working Paper 2010/3.

[23] North American Free Trade Agreement between the Government of Canada, the Government of the United Mexican States and the Government of the United States of America (NAFTA), 13 December 1993, in force 1 January 1994, 32 ILM 289 (1993), available at: www.nafta-sec-alena.org/en/view.aspx?conID=590.

In any case, it should be noted that we are still in the early days of the evolution of international investment arbitration.[24] Trade dispute settlement in the General Agreement on Tariffs and Trade took more than fifty years to develop into the current WTO system. If one were to draw a single lesson from the WTO, it is this – it is the journey and not the destination that most shapes our understanding and ultimately the evolution of the system.

[24] See J. C. Thomas and M. Ewing-Chow, 'The maturation of investment treaty arbitration', *ICSID Review* 25 (2010), 3–20 at 17–20.

15

The challenge of fostering greater coherence in international investment law

AUGUST REINISCH

With the coming of age of investment arbitration, manifest through the exponential increase of awards since the end of the 1990s, the fact that this 'system of investment arbitration' is not a system at all, but rather the sum of individual arbitration decisions based on either – ever fewer – contractual arbitration clauses or in most cases on international investment agreements (IIAs) – so-called treaty arbitration – has made evident that there is a true risk of fragmentation and incoherent outcomes.[1] Some spectacular cases have clearly demonstrated that there is potential for disagreement between arbitrators to the extent that the same factual circumstances may be assessed in a totally contradictory way on the basis of practically identical bilateral investment treaty (BIT) standards.[2] It is immediately apparent that this kind of lack of coherence may seriously

---

[1] See my contribution to the *liber amicorum* Hafner: A. Reinisch, 'The Proliferation of International Dispute Settlement Mechanisms: The Threat of Fragmentation vs. the Promise of a More Effective System? Some Reflections from the Perspective of Investment Arbitration' in I. Buffard, J. Crawford, A. Pellet and S. Wittich (eds.), *International Law between Universalism and Fragmentation – Festschrift in Honour of Gerhard Hafner* (Leiden: Martinus Nijhoff, 2008).

[2] See the investment law cause célèbre in this regard, the *CME* and *Lauder* cases: *Re An UNCITRAL Arbitration, Lauder* v. *The Czech Republic*, 3 September 2001, 9 ICSID Reports 66; 14 World Trade and Arbitration Materials (2002), 35, and *Re UNCITRAL Arbitration Proceedings, CME Czech Republic BV* v. *The Czech Republic* (Partial Award), 13 September 2001, 9 ICSID Reports 121, 14 World Trade and Arbitration Materials 109 (2002). See also C. N. Brower and J. K. Sharpe, 'Multiple and conflicting international arbitral awards', *Journal of World Investment and Trade* 4 (2003), 211–22; A. Reinisch, 'The use and limits of res judicata and lis pendens as procedural tools to avoid conflicting dispute settlement outcomes', *The Law and Practice of International Courts and Tribunals* 3 (2004), 37–77; A. Reinisch, 'The Issues Raised by Parallel Proceedings and Possible Solutions' in M. Waibel, A. Kaushal, K.-H. L. Chung and C. Balchin (eds.), *The Backlash against Investment Arbitration: Perceptions and Reality* (Alphen aan den Rijn: Kluwer Law International, 2010).

diminish the appeal of investment arbitration because it will decrease the confidence of potential claimants, as well as respondents, in a predictable form of dispute settlement.

In that sense the need for greater coherence is immediately evident. Where investment tribunals are called upon to apply and interpret largely identical standards, litigants expect roughly uniform outcomes. That is a basic requirement of the law's function to produce predictable outcomes and to generate confidence. It is thus not surprising that such considerations are resorted to when an argument is made in support of the relevance of 'precedents' in investment arbitration.[3]

However, the topic here is broader than a mere reflection on the need for and methods of fostering coherence in applying already existing investment law. As rightly pointed out by Andrea K. Bjorklund in Chapter 12, one should debate equally the desirability of greater coherence of investment law at a preliminary stage, that is at the stage of shaping substantive rules, through investment treaty-making. Clearly, states may have different preferences as to what they want to see included as protected investments, how far they are ready to define indirect expropriation, what meaning and scope they wish to give to a most-favoured nation (MFN) clause, or what level of protection they deem appropriate under fair and equitable treatment. Here the appeal of greater coherence is much less evident. Thus, the means for achieving such coherence, ideally through a multilateral investment agreement, are less likely to be pursued in the future. Nevertheless, it would be useful to reconsider the potential of more uniform rules, possibly on a regional level, where the desirability of more coherent investment rules has been properly identified. It may be one of the virtues of the new investment powers of the European Union (EU) within its Common Commercial Policy[4] that the adoption of EU

---

[3] See A. K. Bjorklund, 'Investment Treaty Arbitral Decisions as *Jurisprudence Constante*' in C. Picker, I. Bunn and D. Arner (eds.), *International Economic Law: The State and Future of the Discipline* (Oxford: Hart, 2008). See also G. Kaufmann-Kohler, 'Arbitral precedent: dream, necessity, or excuse', *Arbitration International* 23(4) (2007), 357–78; A. Reinisch, 'The Role of Precedent in ICSID Arbitration' in C. Klausegger, P. Klein, F. Kremslehner *et al.* (eds.), *Austrian Arbitration Yearbook* (Vienna: C. H. Beck, Stämpfli & Manz, 2008); A. Rigo Sureda, 'Precedent in Investment Treaty Arbitration' in C. Binder, U. Kriebaum, A. Reinisch and S. Wittich (eds.), *International Investment Law for the 21st Century. Essays in Honour of Christoph Schreuer* (Oxford University Press, 2009).

[4] See also M. Bungenberg, 'Going Global? The EU Common Commercial Policy After Lisbon' in C. Hermann and J. P. Terhechte (eds.), *European Yearbook of International Economic Law* (Heidelberg: Springer, 2010); J. Griebel, 'Überlegungen zur Wahrnehmung der neuen EU-Kompetenz für ausländische Direktinvestitionen nach Inkrafttreten des Vertrags von Lissabon', *Recht der Internationalen Wirtschaft* (2009); M. Krajewski,

investment treaties or investment rules within broader trade agreements will increase the substantive coherence of investment law quite significantly where common standards will replace the different BIT standards of individual Member States.

Recognising this justified caveat – that is that the desirability of common rules may indeed be questioned at the law-making stage – it still appears that, at the level of applying investment rules, coherence remains one of the central objectives of the 'system' of investment arbitration.

Banifatemi reminds us that, in practical terms, coherence may be difficult to achieve by investment tribunals since they have to decide individual cases on the basis of specific investment treaties. Indeed, BIT standards, diverging slightly in their texts, often give rise to endless *e contrario* v. *per analogiam* arguments, and the parties and tribunals are torn between respecting the wording of the specific treaty (and the intentions of the respective contracting parties) and the quest to contribute to a meaningful body of investment law that extends beyond the individual case.

Only where the latter view prevails, or in the case of deciding on the basis of identical treaty provisions, do more elaborate techniques to secure coherence, like the creation of an appellate mechanism in investment arbitration[5] or the idea of creating the possibility to make something like a 'preliminary reference' to an investment court,[6] seem worthy of discussion. In the great majority of investment arbitrations based on different, but often substantially similar treaties, the ideal of coherence can be pursued only if investment tribunals display reasonable respect

---

'External trade law and the constitution treaty: towards a federal and more democratic common commercial policy?', *Common Market Law Review* 42 (2005), 91–127; A. Reinisch, 'The Division of Powers Between the EU and its Member States "After Lisbon"' in M. Bungenberg, J. Griebel and S. Hindelang (eds.), *European Yearbook of International Economic Law – Special Issue: International Investment Law and EU Law* (Heidelberg: Springer, 2011); C. Tietje, 'Die Außenwirtschaftsverfassung der EU nach dem Vertrag von Lissabon', *Beiträge zum Transnationalen Wirtschaftsrecht* No. 83 (2009).

5 'Possible Improvements of the Framework for ICSID Arbitration', Discussion Paper of the ICSID Secretariat dated 26 October 2004. See also B. Legum, 'Options to Establish an Appellate Mechanism for Investment Disputes' in K. Sauvant (ed.), *Appeals Mechanism in International Investment Disputes* (Oxford University Press, 2008); D. Gantz, 'An appellate mechanism for review of arbitral decisions in investor–state disputes: prospects and challenges', *Vanderbilt Journal of Transnational Law* 39 (2006), 39–76; C. Tams, 'An Appealing Option? The Debate about an ICSID Appellate Structure' in C. Tietje, G. Kraft and R. Sethe (eds.), *Beiträge zum Transnationalen Wirtschaftsrecht* No. 57 (2006).

6 See C. Schreuer, 'Preliminary Rulings in Investment Arbitration' in K. Sauvant (ed.), *Coherence and Consistency in International Investment Law* (Oxford University Press, 2008).

towards the views of other tribunals.[7] This may ultimately lead to a *jurisprudence constante*[8] that will foster the confidence of the users of the system of investment arbitration and thus the system itself.

Ultimately, one should not forget that confidence in investment arbitration will also depend on the quality of the awards. In this respect, it is too easy to chastise arbitrators for outcomes with which one disagrees.[9] Instead, the entire investment arbitration community should be called upon to ensure the quality of arbitral awards. This starts with the parties' and their counsels' responsibilities in connection with selecting arbitrators and making well-reasoned submissions, and extends beyond the arbitral decision-making process itself to moderation and self-restraint of annulment committees and national courts when asked to set aside or to refuse enforcement of awards.

---

[7] See in this respect *ADC Affiliate Limited and ADC & ADMC Management Limited* v. *Republic of Hungary* (Award), ICSID Case No. ARB/03/16, 2 October 2006, para. 293 ('It is true that arbitral awards do not constitute binding precedent. It is also true that a number of cases are fact-driven and that the findings in those cases cannot be transposed in and of themselves to other cases. It is further true that a number of cases are based on treaties that differ from the present BIT in certain respects. However, cautious reliance on certain principles developed in a number of those cases, as persuasive authority, may advance the body of law, which in turn may serve predictability in the interest of both investors and host States').

[8] See, in particular, A. K. Bjorklund, 'Investment Treaty Arbitral Decisions as *Jurisprudence Constante*'.

[9] See, for instance, *CMS Gas Transmission Company* v. *The Argentine Republic* (Decision on Annulment), ICSID Case No. ARB/01/8, 25 September 2007.

PART IV

The policy- and rule-making challenges arising
from the growth in investment litigation

16

ICSID at the crossroads: some thoughts and recommendations for improving the dispute settlement system

MARGRETE STEVENS

A. Introduction

The explosive growth of cases brought under bilateral investment treaties (BITs) since the late 1990s has affected both arbitration practitioners and the institutions that administer the cases, most of all the International Centre for Settlement of Investment Disputes (ICSID or Centre) which is part of the World Bank Group. At the end of the 1990s there were eight pending cases before ICSID; 10 years later there were 44 pending cases; by 2008 that number had doubled to more than 100. As of late 2011, the number of disputes before ICSID was approaching some 150 pending cases.[1]

The considerable and quite sudden expansion in the case-load has been a major challenge to ICSID since there were few indications in the late 1990s that this would happen. While budgets were eventually increased, enabling more staff to be hired, many in the arbitration world felt that the institution was simply reacting to external developments. At the same time, the magnitude of claims grew, cases became more complex and costly, and took longer to resolve, and tribunal findings became more vulnerable to challenge. This suggests that ICSID and the investor–state dispute settlement system as a whole are at a crossroads, calling for an

Ms Stevens is a consultant in King & Spalding's Washington DC, office, where she works with the firm's International Arbitration Practice Group. The views expressed in this article are personal to the author and do not necessarily represent the views of King & Spalding or its clients. Ms Stevens served at the International Centre for Settlement of Investment Disputes (ICSID) as counsel and senior counsel from 1989 to 2007.

[1] See ICSID Website/Pending Cases, available at: http://icsid.worldbank.org/ICSID/ FrontServlet?requestType=GenCaseDtlsRH&actionVal=ListPending.

in-depth look at the strains on the system and the formulation of a broad set of reforms.

In a sense, the growth in the number of cases is old news. The proliferation of treaty consents, combined with greater awareness in the business and legal community of the possibility of bringing claims against states for breaches of investment treaty standards, has opened a large and visible legal terrain of investment arbitration which is here to stay. The opportunity to look forward and examine what can be done to improve the system as we move on from here is therefore welcome. The focus of my discussion will be on ICSID, not only because institutional arbitration under the Convention on the Settlement of Investment Disputes between States and Nationals of Other States (ICSID Convention) has become the preferred way of settling investment disputes but also because of the leadership role that ICSID can play in the continued elaboration of the overall investment dispute settlement system.

To the extent that ICSID has been the 'gold standard' of investor-state arbitration, it has had a difficult recent past. At the very time the case-load was exploding, ICSID went through a decade during which it was deprived of continuity, stability and accountability, let alone prudent succession-planning, most of all reflected in the high turnover at the top: four different Secretaries-General, over a ten-year period, interspersed with a similar number of acting assignments, all of whom were essentially new to the field.[2] This situation has improved in some respects in the last few years, and it may therefore be a particularly good time to consider what sort of reforms might enhance the system henceforth.

With this in mind, I have identified ten areas of operation where I believe that ICSID could make changes, both to improve its day-to-day case management capabilities and to position itself as a stronger and more effective arbitral institution for the future. Some of the suggestions are limited in scope and could be implemented without a great deal of time and cost. Other proposals will require a significant commitment of resources. Some of the suggestions can be carried out by ICSID alone, while others will need the collaboration and approval of the World Bank. All of the suggestions, alone but more often in combination, have the potential to augment the standing of ICSID as the pre-eminent institution for the administration of investment disputes.

---

[2] Following Ibrahim Shihata's retirement in 2000, there followed Ko Yung Tung (2000–2003), Roberto Dañino (2003–2006), and Ana Palacio (2006–2008). Since June 2009, Meg Kinnear has served as Secretary-General.

B. A framework for change: ten suggestions

I. The ICSID Panel of Arbitrators

My first point concerns the ICSID Panels of Conciliators and Arbitrators, specifically the Panel of Arbitrators, as that is the Panel most often relied upon. It will be recalled that Article 3 of the ICSID Convention provides that ICSID shall maintain a Panel of Conciliators and a Panel of Arbitrators. Article 13(1) provides that each Contracting State may designate to each Panel four persons who may but need not be its nationals. Article 13(2) provides that the Chairman may designate ten persons to each Panel. Article 14 sets out the requirements that must be met by designees to the Panels and further stipulates that 'competence in the field of law shall be of particular importance in the case of persons on the Panel of Arbitrators'. Article 15 provides that Panel members shall serve for renewable periods of six years, and that Panel members shall continue in office until their successors have been designated. Finally, Article 16 provides that a person may serve on both Panels.

Regulation 21 of ICSID's Administrative and Financial Regulations deals with the establishment of the Panels. The Regulation requires that the Secretary-General invite Contracting States to make Panel designations whenever a State has the right to make one or more such designations. The Regulation also requires the Secretary-General to maintain lists which from time to time must be shared with all Contracting States, and which must be made available to any State or person. In practice, ICSID regularly reminds Member States of their right to make appointments and of the importance of the Panels; and the Panels of Conciliators and Arbitrators are revised whenever a State notifies the Centre of changes to its designees. The most up-to-date list is available on the ICSID's website in the section containing Official Documents.[3]

As of 20 August 2011, 101 out of 147 ICSID Contracting States had availed themselves of the opportunity to make designations to the Panel of Arbitrators, designating a total of 353 names. The Panel, as is widely recognised, plays a critical role in the functioning of the ICSID dispute settlement system, in particular in regard to the constitution of tribunals where the parties have failed to agree on the presiding arbitrator. In these circumstances the ICSID Convention ensures that the appointment can

---

[3] See ICSID website/Official Documents/Panels, available at: http://icsid.worldbank.org/ ICSID/FrontServlet?requestType=ICSIDDocRH&actionVal=MembersofPannel.

be made by the Chairman of ICSID's Administrative Council (in effect, the President of the World Bank). When the Chairman is called upon to make such an appointment, the arbitrator must be selected from the Panel of Arbitrators. The requirement that calls for selection from the Panel also applies to the constitution of ad hoc committees formed, also by the Chairman, to decide on annulment applications.[4]

On the face of it, one would think that some 350 names would ensure that the selection process in individual cases would be underpinned by ample choices among qualified candidates. Reality shows a different picture. Looking back over the Panel appointments made in a two-year period between 2009–2011, it becomes clear that only about 10 per cent of the 353 panel designees receive appointments as presiding arbitrator or ad hoc committee members, evidencing repeat appointments of a small cluster of experienced, well-known arbitrators. A second group of panel designees are clearly viewed as qualified arbitrators and have served in proceedings but, following positions taken on specific legal issues in particular cases, appear no longer to be seen as viable candidates for presiding arbitrator or ad hoc committee appointments. The large number of designees who are not called upon show that more than four-fifths of the Panel members are not thought to have the requisite experience.

An additional problem affecting the Panel of Arbitrators concerns the relative paucity in the number of designations. As mentioned above, 101 ICSID Contracting States have made appointments to the Panel, demonstrating that only two-thirds of ICSID's membership have contributed to the Panel. Moreover, of the 101 countries that have made designations, almost half, or 47, have let their designations expire. While the designations under the Rules are still valid,[5] expired designations nevertheless send an unavoidable signal of absence of diligence in ensuring that the available information is current.[6] More than 25 per cent of all designations expired more than five years ago, meaning that the individual was put on the panel more than eleven years ago, before the surge in treaty-based investment disputes.

The above described issues show not only that the Panel is not the resource it ought to be, but points to a larger, more fundamental problem, namely that many Contracting States are not sufficiently attentive

---

[4] See Convention on the Settlement of Investment Disputes between States and Nationals of Other States, Washington DC, 18 March 1965, in force 14 October 1966, 575 UNTS (ICSID Convention), Article 38, Article 40, and Article 52(3).
[5] ICSID Convention, Article 15(1).
[6] *Ibid.*, Article 15(3).

to the demands on the dispute settlement system created by the proliferation of investment treaties and the ensuing dispute activity. The fact that
only two-thirds of ICSID Contracting States have made appointments
is evidence of this problem. Instead of a possible Panel of Arbitrators of
576 designees, there are only 353. While numbers alone will not solve the
problem, as can be seen from the existing situation, there is every indication that improving the Panels should be considered a priority.

The conclusion that the Panel is not fulfilling the role in the system that
the drafters had envisioned is easily drawn, and as the case-load expands,
and as we continue to examine ways and means to manage time and cost,
as well as questions of conflicts, challenges and broader concerns with
legitimacy issues, the importance of a well-functioning Panel becomes
crucial.

My suggestion on this issue is for ICSID to embark on a focused, high-
level campaign with national authorities as well as with the Administrative
Council to draw attention to the critical needs of the institution as it dis-
charges it responsibilities in the appointment process. The campaign
should emphasise that the Chairman's ability to make sound and qualified appointments depends upon the quality of ICSID Panels, and all
ICSID Contracting States ought to contribute to this endeavour. In this
connection it would be helpful to call attention to Article 13(1) of the
ICSID Convention, which provides that panel members do not need to be
nationals of the designating state. The effectiveness of the ICSID system
is destined to suffer if the pool of arbitrators available to ICSID remains
artificially small and lacking in recognised experience.

II. Training

My second suggestion concerns the need to recognise the value of training as a contributing element to meeting the challenge of improving the
Panel of Arbitrators. While for many years ICSID has collaborated with
the American Arbitration Association (AAA) and the International
Chamber of Commerce (ICC) in the organisation of the Annual Joint
Colloquium, and while ICSID staff, including the Secretary-General, are
frequent and generous contributors to countless conferences, workshops
and seminars organised by other organisations, the Centre has on the
whole stayed away from in-house training.[7] One idea might be to consider

---

[7] In a two-year period from 2009 to 2011, ICSID held two seminars in Washington DC.

hosting bi-annual seminars of a few days' duration for newly appointed designees to the Panel of Arbitrators. ICSID could take on the organisational role and make presentations on the broader tenets of ICSID jurisprudence as well as the work of ICSID annulment committees, and more experienced arbitrators could be invited to speak on topics ranging from how to manage an ICSID case, to how to deal with procedural issues.

Training sessions of this kind would allow newly appointed designees to make meaningful contact with the Centre and other colleagues in the sphere of investment arbitration; the Centre, in turn, would be afforded the opportunity to meet Panel members who, short of a recommendation from reliable sources, would otherwise stand little chance of becoming 'a known quantity'. Such training sessions would not in and of themselves constitute a commitment to being appointed, but one could envisage that seminars of this kind, over a period of time, would foster increased knowledge of the ICSID system and its requirements, and contribute to new channels of communication with users in parts of the world that today have little or no meaningful representation among the jurists who are giving shape to international investment law.

A further possibility, as ICSID continues to publish the *ICSID Review – Foreign Investment Law Journal*, would be to invite recently appointed Panel members to contribute with comments or articles on relevant topics, efforts that would allow Panel designees to develop their profile and build their reputation within the circles of the investment arbitration community.

III.   Appointment of arbitrators by ICSID

My third suggestion calls for an improvement in the procedure currently followed by ICSID where the Chairman is requested to make the appointment of the presiding arbitrator. The arbitration rules provide that before such appointments are made, the Chairman shall consult with both parties as far as possible. The rules also require that where the Chairman has been requested to make such appointments, he or she is to use his or her best efforts to comply within thirty days after receipt of the request.[8]

---

[8] ICSID is currently working to make such appointments within a six-week time frame.

There is a tension between proceeding with such appointments in an expeditious manner and soliciting opinions on proposed names from the parties to the proceeding, which often leads to delays. The larger problem in the appointment procedure, however, stems from the limited number of viable candidates available for individual cases, as discussed above. The fact that ICSID, for most presiding arbitrator appointments, can muster only three names gives the parties very limited opportunity to evaluate different profiles, let alone come to an agreement on the best possible candidate. In the absence of real consultations, the procedure more often than not results in appointments that one or both parties reluctantly endorse if at all.

As ICSID considers ways and means to improve the dispute settlement system, including steps to enhance the Panel of Arbitrators, I would suggest that putting in place an appointment procedure that to a greater extent seeks both parties' satisfaction with a given appointment, ought to be an important goal. It should be recognised that the investor–state dispute settlement system makes it particularly difficult to identify arbitrators who occupy the desirable middle ground. States, for the most part, are understandably anxious that arbitrators be knowledgeable in the area of public international law. Investors, not unexpectedly, look to arbitrators who are well versed in business and commercial law. Claimants look to arbitrators who have a reputation for dealing with cases with speed and efficiency – attributes of less concern to respondents. Because parties therefore identify different backgrounds, attributes and reputations as desirable, it becomes particularly important that the consultation process is expanded and that the presiding arbitrator is someone who is recognised as qualified by both sides. Taking into account that this process should not become an exercise in delaying the constitution of the tribunal, the suggestion is for ICSID to offer parties ten names, in one round, as opposed to the current three. The list of proposed names should be accompanied by an invitation to the parties to rank the arbitrators in order of preference, indicating whether any of the proposals are unacceptable. This method is generally followed by the Permanent Court of Arbitration (PCA) when the Court acts as appointing authority in United Nations Commission on International Trade Law (UNCITRAL) proceedings brought under bilateral investment treaties, and gives both sides a more realistic opportunity to come to an agreement on the proposed candidates.

IV. Explanatory notes to the arbitration rules

My fourth suggestion is a call for an update of the annotated version of the Regulations and Rules adopted by the Administrative Council. Under Article 6 of the ICSID Convention, the Administrative Council shall adopt the administrative and financial regulations of the Centre; the rules of procedure for the institution of proceedings; and the rules of procedure for conciliation and arbitration proceedings. The first Regulations and Rules, which came into force on 1 January 1968, were accompanied by a set of Explanatory Notes. The Notes, which were last reissued in 1975, were prepared by the Secretariat, and only a few copies are still in circulation. The Notes 'do not constitute part of the Rules and have no legal force'; however, at the time of their issuance, the Administrative Council considered that the Notes might be useful to the parties to proceedings.[9] I would suggest that with the expansion of the case-load, including the need for the system to absorb many new players, not only from among states and investors, but also from the ranks of arbitrators and counsel, issuing a new set of Explanatory Notes would be a useful contribution to the operation and understanding of the procedural rules of the ICSID system. Another reason is that with an increased number and greater turnover of tribunal secretaries, a more pronounced need has arisen to record procedural precedence. An updated version of the Notes would explain best practice in matters of arbitral procedure, as procedural law has developed in the thirty-five years since the first Notes were issued.

For example, the arbitration rule calling for an ICSID proceeding to have two distinct phases, namely a written procedure followed by an oral one, is no longer primarily relevant to the principal proceeding on the dispute itself. Instead, it has become increasingly common for the rule also to apply to subsidiary parts of the proceeding including provisional measures, objections to jurisdiction, document production and other evidentiary issues, the disqualification of counsel and to provisional stays of enforcements of awards.[10] In a similar vein, the rule on the written procedure calling for a memorial, counter-memorial, a reply and a rejoinder, makes no mention that post-hearing briefs and post-hearing reply briefs have in recent years become part of the standard case procedure.[11]

---

[9] See ICSID Regulations and Rules, Introductory Note, ICSID/4/Rev.1.
[10] See ICSID Arbitration Rule 29.
[11] *Ibid.*, Rule 10.

The above-mentioned developments as regards pleadings show how cases, especially under investment treaties, have consistently become more complicated and voluminous. These developments, I suggest, ought to be reflected and explained in a commentary to the rules, not least because the procedural developments have had considerable impact on the duration and cost of investment arbitration, which should be assessed in that light.

A second reason for issuing an updated version of the Explanatory Notes is that several formal amendments have been introduced to the ICSID rules of procedure over the years. The amendments include the changes introduced in 1984, 2003 and 2006.

The 1984 amendments made three substantive changes to the arbitration rules. The first was to allow for pre-hearing conferences that could be held by the parties to stipulate uncontested facts or to discuss an amicable settlement of the dispute. The second change confirmed that interim measures of protection could only be sought from national courts if the parties had so agreed. The third change allowed ICSID to publish excerpts from the legal holdings of an award, without seeking the consent of the parties.[12]

The 2003 amendments sought in particular to make certain provisions more flexible, avoiding unnecessarily rigid deadlines regarding the appointment and disqualification of arbitrators. While the 1968 and 1984 rules had mandated that the Chairman make his or her decisions within thirty days after receiving the request or the proposal, the 2003 rules provided that the Chairman should use his or her best efforts to comply with such requests or proposals within thirty days of receipt. In recent years, the thirty-day time limit has been eroded, and it might be useful to explain the background to the 2003 amendment in new Explanatory Notes, to make clear that the change was introduced to avoid a rigid deadline, but not to allow such decisions regularly to take much longer, even several months.[13]

The 2006 amendments introduced the most recent changes to the ICSID rules of procedure. The changes to the arbitration rules concerned preliminary procedures, the publication of awards, access of third parties and disclosure requirements of arbitrators. Some of the background to these most recent changes may be found in discussion and working

---

[12] See A. R. Parra, 'Revised Regulations and Rules', *News From ICSID* 2(1) (1985), 4–6.
[13] ICSID is currently working to make such appointments within a six-week time frame.

papers of the ICSID Secretariat, available on the ICSID website in the News Release section.[14]

The above record shows that procedural developments in cases, as well as a series of formal amendments to the rules, have over a period of some twenty-five years introduced significant changes to the original text and to the application of the arbitration rules. The original Explanatory Notes may still provide assistance in regard to some provisions, but for the most part one would have to supplement such commentary with information from a variety of other sources, to the extent that such material is available or can be found.

My suggestion on this point is, therefore, to consolidate all relevant information regarding the rules in a new set of Notes, to ensure that all users, counsel, arbitrators and ICSID staff have access to the same background information on the rules that govern the arbitral procedure.

V.   Ethics rules

My fifth suggestion concerns a set of ethics rules to govern counsel conduct in proceedings brought under the ICSID Convention. Such rules would ensure that counsel and parties are subject to similar standards of conduct when appearing before ICSID tribunals. This concern would seem particularly pertinent in the ICSID context where there is no requirement that a party be represented by a lawyer.[15]

The question of applicable ethics rules can be examined in three different contexts: one problem presents itself when opposing counsel subject to different national ethics rules appear before an international arbitral tribunal. The different national rules may lead to what has been termed an uneven playing field: some national rules may work to the advantage of one side, while the comparable national rule may do the opposite for the other side. One of the most frequently cited examples concerns pre-testimonial

---

[14] See, 'Possible Improvements of the Framework for ICSID Arbitration', ICSID Secretariat Discussion Paper, October 2004, available at: http://icsid.worldbank.org/ICSID/FrontS ervlet?requestType=ICSIDPublicationsRH&actionVal=ViewAnnouncePDF&Announc ementType=archive&AnnounceNo=14_1.pdf. See also 'Suggested Changes to the ICSID Rules and Regulations', ICSID Secretariat Working Paper, 12 May 2005, available at: http://icsid.worldbank.org/ICSID/FrontServlet?requestType=ICSIDPublicationsRH&a ctionVal=ViewAnnouncePDF&AnnouncementType=archive&AnnounceNo=22_1.pdf.

[15] See ICSID Arbitration Rule 18 and Explanatory Note 18(B), which provides that '[i]t is not mandatory that a party select a lawyer to act on its behalf, though self-interest should ensure that parties will select representatives of acknowledged competence in the law'.

preparation of a witness. In general, common law systems consider it legitimate to prepare a witness, while civil law systems on the whole do not permit communication with witnesses prior to trial. In international arbitration it is now common practice for a potential witness to be questioned by counsel about the facts of the dispute, and for counsel to assist in the presentation of testimony, given that tribunals generally require the parties to submit written witness statements.[16]

Another question concerns the issue of who may appear as a fact witness since legal systems take different approaches in regard to whether a person affiliated with a party to the dispute may appear as a witness. The common law approach allows for this kind of testimony while civil law systems often do not. In international arbitration it is generally accepted that any person can testify as a fact witness, and this approach is followed in the International Bar Association (IBA) Rules on the Taking of Evidence.[17]

Considering another element of advocacy in international arbitration, one commentator has pointed out that legal systems vary in their consideration of what constitutes 'truthful' conduct by lawyers. United States lawyers are recognised as having a wider margin of possible construction of the law, without consideration as to whether such construction will ultimately prevail. In contrast, civil law systems take a less permissive view in regard to creative arguments, tending towards a limitation on what sort of argument can be made. In international arbitration, a custom has developed that allows for some creativity but that nevertheless must be reasonable and not fall within the realm of overzealous advocacy.[18]

A second problem arises when the same counsel is subject to more than one set of national ethics rules, resulting in the application of 'double deontology'. Sometimes, for example, the same counsel may be subject to conflicting rules. Alternatively, counsel may have to comply with rules which are unfamiliar, in some cases because of the location of the arbitration hearings. Perhaps reflecting these concerns, an ICSID tribunal has

[16] See D. Bishop and M. Stevens, 'The Compelling Need for a Code of Ethics in International Arbitration: Transparency, Integrity and Legitimacy' in A. J. van den Berg (ed.), *Arbitration Advocacy in Changing Times, ICCA Congress Series, 2010 Rio Volume 15* (The Hague: Kluwer Law International, 2011), p. 394.

[17] Bishop and Stevens, 'The Compelling Need for a Code of Ethics'. See also Article 4 of the IBA Rules on the Taking of Evidence in International Arbitration, May 2010, available at: www.ibanet.org/Publications/publications_IBA_guides_and_free_materials.aspx.

[18] See K. Rogers, 'Fit and function in legal ethics: developing a code of conduct for international arbitration', *Michigan Journal of International Law* 23 (2002), 341–423 at 361.

recently pointed out the risk of 'inconsistent or indeed arbitrary outcomes' if decisions are made by national bodies.[19]

The third context in which the question of applicable ethics rules may be examined stems from the fact that, alongside existing national ethics rules, international arbitration has developed its own customs and practice in regard to a range of procedural issues.[20]

The need for international arbitration ethics rules is evident in the recent decisions of three ICSID tribunals that were called on to rule on requests to have one of the parties' legal representatives disqualified from appearing in the arbitral proceeding. Two cases involved a relationship with one of the arbitrators that was claimed to threaten the integrity of the tribunal.[21] A third case concerned alleged access to confidential information of one of the counsel.[22] One tribunal found an inherent power to disqualify counsel;[23] one tribunal speculated that *if* an inherent power existed, it could only be exercised rarely and in exceptional circumstances;[24] and one committee found that it had not only the power but also the duty to deal with a request for disqualification.[25] In one decision the tribunal said that:

> For an international system like that of ICSID, it seems unacceptable for the solution to reside in the individual national bodies which regulate the work of professional service providers, because that might lead to inconsistent or indeed arbitrary outcomes depending on the attitudes of such bodies, or the content (or lack of relevant content) of their rules. It would moreover be disruptive to interrupt international cases to ascertain the position taken by such bodies.[26]

The second tribunal called for counsel to present his client's case 'in due compliance with the applicable rules of professional conduct and

---

[19] See *Hrvatska Elektroprivreda d.d. v. Republic of Slovenia* (Tribunal's Ruling on the Participation of a Counsel) (hereinafter *Hrvatska* Decision), ICSID Case No. ARB/05/24, 6 May 2008, para. 23.

[20] See Bishop and Stevens, 'The Compelling Need for a Code of Ethics', p. 6, available at: www.josemigueljudice-arbitration.com/xms/files/02_TEXTOS_ARBITRAGEM/01_Doutrina_ScolarsTexts/ethics/ethics_in_int_arb_-_icca_2010_-_bishop.pdf.

[21] See generally *Hrvatska* Decision. See also *The Rompetrol Group N.V. v. Romania* (Decision on the Participation of Counsel) (hereinafter *Rompetrol* Decision), ICSID Case No. ARB/06/3, 14 January 2010.

[22] See Unpublished Decision of ICSID Annulment Committee (2008) (hereinafter Unpublished Annulment Committee Decision).

[23] See *Hrvatska* Decision, para. 33.

[24] See *Rompetrol* Decision, para. 25.

[25] See Unpublished Annulment Committee Decision, para. 37.

[26] See *Hrvatska* Decision, para. 23.

ethics'.[27] In the third case, where the parties had made extensive reference to different national rules on legal ethics, as well as the Council of Bars and Law Societies of Europe Code, the Committee said that:

> This material is valuable to the extent that it reveals common general principles which may guide the Committee. But none of it directly binds the Committee, as an international tribunal. Accordingly, the Committee's consideration of the matter is not, and should not be, based upon a nice reading of any particular code of professional ethics, applicable in any particular national jurisdiction. Such codes may vary in their detailed application. Rather, the Committee must consider what general principles are plainly indispensable for the fair conduct of the proceedings.[28]

Legitimacy often evokes notions of good governance and predictability. Particularly in arbitrations involving states, these are hallmarks of a system that users recognise as being capable of providing procedural fairness. While the system may not be broken, it lends itself to criticism, at a minimum for being archaic. Applicable ethics rules are difficult to identify, tensions are not readily resolved, and experienced practitioners – both among counsel and arbitrators – may have a considerable advantage over newcomers to the field. Moreover, the sanctions that inappropriate – or unethical – counsel conduct may invite from tribunals are far from clear. This could, as has been the case in the past, involve an award of costs. More recently, however, tribunals have also been asked to disqualify counsel, raising the question of whether a tribunal has the power and duty to deny a party the legal representation of its choice, and if so, on what grounds.

As noted by Bishop,[29] 'Lack of clarity as to which ethical rules apply, the existence of conflicting rules and obligations, the non-transparency and increased size [monetary value] of many proceedings', and complexity of claims, 'combined with greater public scrutiny', creates a dangerously unstable foundation. Other areas of arbitral practice, for example with respect to challenges to arbitrators, show the importance of the arbitral system being able to police itself. In a similar vein, ICSID arbitration ought to be able to articulate and enforce standards for counsel's conduct on the basis of clear rules of general application.[30]

---

[27] See *Rompetrol* Decision, para. 19.
[28] See Unpublished Annulment Committee Decision, para. 41.
[29] D. Bishop. 'Ethics in International Arbitration. Keynote Address', International Council for Commercial Arbitration (ICCA) Conference, Rio, 2010 (www.arbitration-icca.org/media/0/12763302233510/icca_rio_keynote_speech.pdf).
[30] See Bishop and Stevens, 'The Compelling Need for a Code of Ethics', pp. 406–7.

VI. ICSID Users' Committee

A major effort to improve the Panel of Arbitrators, in-house ICSID training for new Panel members, the possible issuance of a set of amended
Explanatory Notes to the procedural rules, and the elaboration of a set
of ethics rules, are all time-consuming and difficult endeavours which
may not be quickly implemented given the existing ICSID staffing levels. To this end, my sixth suggestion is to revisit an idea first put forward
by V. V. Veeder some years ago, which is for ICSID to establish a Users'
Committee.[31]

Article 3 of the ICSID Convention provides that the Centre shall
have an Administrative Council and a Secretariat. Article 4 provides
that the Administrative Council shall be composed of one representative of each Contracting State. The provision also stipulates that in
the absence of a contrary designation, each governor and alternate
governor of the World Bank appointed by a Contracting State shall be
ex officio its representative and its alternate respectively. Most countries have refrained from making contrary designations and as a rule
it is the Finance Minister of a Contracting State who serves on the
ICSID Administrative Council. The Report of the Executive Directors
on the ICSID Convention notes that the principal functions of the
Administrative Council are the election of the Secretary-General and
the Deputy Secretary-General, the adoption of the budget of the Centre
and the adoption of administrative and financial regulations and procedural rules.[32]

Article 9 of the Convention provides that the Secretariat shall consist
of a Secretary-General, one or more Deputy Secretaries-General and
staff. The functions of the Secretary-General, which are also addressed
in the Executive Directors' Report, are largely centred on the performance of a variety of administrative functions as legal representative, registrar and principal officer of the Centre. Regulation 10 of the
Administrative and Financial Regulations deals with the appointment
of ICSID staff members, providing that appointments may be made
directly or by secondment. Regulation 12 provides that ICSID staff act
solely under the direction of the Secretary-General. The Secretariat

---

[31] See V. V. Veeder, 'Why bother and why it matters: ICSID', *Institute for Transnational
Arbitration* 20(3) (2006), 1.
[32] See Report of the Executive Directors on the Convention on the Settlement of Investment
Disputes between States and Nationals of Others States, Article 19.1.

currently employs a team of some thirty staff: nine counsel and senior counsel, seven consultants and some fifteen administrative staff.[33]

While the Centre therefore enjoys a straightforward administrative structure, it lacks the benefit of a board or a court consisting of high-profile arbitration specialists to guide the Centre in the administration of its services. Such bodies, it may be recalled, are common features of other arbitral institutions and include, for example, the Court of the London Court of International Arbitration (LCIA); the International Court of Arbitration of the International Chamber of Commerce (ICC); and the standing boards of arbitration institutions such as the American Arbitration Association (AAA), the Arbitration Institute of the Stockholm Chamber of Commerce (SCC), the Singapore International Arbitration Centre (SIAC) and the Hong Kong International Arbitration Centre (HKIAC).

With respect to ICSID, informal sounding boards do exist and ICSID staff, as may be expected, regularly have the opportunity to discuss arbitration matters with sitting tribunal members, and with a host of other practitioners in the context of conferences, seminars and the Annual Joint Colloquium. The exchanges that are feasible in such contexts are, however, not structured to provide ICSID with the kind of support that might contribute to identifying and addressing issues of institutional concern. Discussions are also not particularly transparent.

In his 2006 keynote address at the ITA Workshop in Dallas, V. V. Veeder explained that the English Commercial Court's Users' Committee had played a positive role for some forty years in the operation of the Court, noting that the Committee 'is purely advisory; [that] it has no powers; and [that] it has no legal or constitutional basis'.[34] The Committee meets four times a year to discuss with the Commercial Judges topics of concern and reform regarding the Court's services. Its members are all professional users of the Court from England and abroad – barristers, solicitors, foreign lawyers and parties – and its membership fluctuates widely. In recent years the Users' Committee has been involved in specific projects. Different working parties have been constituted to consider improved business processes; the possibility of amending certain rules; and providing an assessment of how the 1996 Arbitration Act has worked since it was brought into force.[35]

---

[33] See ICSID, ICSID Annual Report (2010), available at: http://icsid.worldbank.org/ICSID/FrontServlet?requestType=ICSIDPublicationsRH&actionVal=ViewAnnualReports#.

[34] See Veeder, 'Why Bother and Why it Matters: ICSID'.

[35] *Ibid.*

V. V. Veeder reminded us in 2006 that ICSID's users have 'a wealth of ideas or responses to offer to ICSID based on practical experience'. As part of the catalogue of suggestions that I have been asked to come forward with, I recommend the establishment of an ICSID Users' Committee. The Committee could be composed of representatives of states and investors, as well as counsel and arbitrators. There could be bi-annual meetings, organised by ICSID and held in connection with the suggested training seminars, or in conjunction with the Annual Joint Colloquium.

VII. Mediation and mediators

Many of the cases that are brought to ICSID, as may be recalled, result in settlements. Of the 226 cases that ICSID lists as concluded as of 20 August 2011, close to 40 per cent have been settled before the rendition of an award.

Recognising that many ICSID disputes have the potential to be resolved through non-arbitral procedures, ICSID ought to consider whether the Centre could play a more proactive role in promoting settlements.[36] ICSID could, for example, initiate confidential consultations with parties that have settled their dispute, to gather information as to what procedures have proven effective in obtaining settlements on agreed terms, and distribute such information among its users.

The Centre could also provide parties and tribunals with information at the first session of the tribunal as to how Rule 21 of the Arbitration Rules might be used in arbitration proceedings, for example as a 'mediation window'. Another step that could be considered would be to offer the good offices of the Secretary-General as appointing authority in ad hoc mediations, as well as in conciliations conducted under the UNCITRAL Rules. And finally, ICSID could offer administration of mediation proceedings under the Investor–State Mediation Rules that are currently being drafted under the auspices of the IBA.

VIII. Case surveys

My eighth suggestion is brief and can be implemented quite easily. I propose that ICSID embraces the use of a case evaluation form, to be

---

[36] See M. Stevens, 'Investor–State Mediation: Observations on the Role of Institutions' in A. Rovine (ed.), *Contemporary Issues in International Arbitration and Mediation – The Fordham Papers 2009* (The Hague: Martinus Nijhoff, 2010).

completed by parties, counsel and arbitrators at the conclusion of each proceeding. The form, similar to the one that the ICC uses on completion of a proceeding, would solicit opinion and feedback on the process administered by ICSID.

Specifically, the form would invite answers to questions concerning case-related work undertaken by the Secretariat, the financial aspects of the proceeding, time, and the overall quality of the service provided by ICSID as compared to alternative venues and institutions. The answers to these questions might in many cases be available to the Secretariat without asking parties, counsel and arbitrators to evaluate the process, and it could be argued that there is no need to record what is already known. On completion of a case, the Secretariat is generally aware of whether a case has left participants in the proceeding content with the process, and an opinion on time and cost can be formed with reference to what is average.

The form should go beyond these questions, however, and ask participants for their comments, observations and suggestions on any aspect of the ICSID arbitration system. Inviting constructive thoughts and practical ideas would provide ICSID with useful tools to re-evaluate best practice on a continuous basis, and it could introduce changes as necessary. The evaluation form would also ensure that such feedback was obtained more consistently and not only where participants are either profoundly dismayed or particularly pleased with aspects of the proceeding, in which cases they often take it upon themselves to inform the Secretariat of their views without invitation.

Finally, the administration of a case evaluation form would contribute to project an institutional outlook that signals concern with the satisfaction of its users, remaining open to criticism channelled in an appropriate way. While in the past, with significantly fewer cases, it was quite feasible for the Deputy Secretary-General to be available for consultations with parties to proceedings regarding shortcomings in the administration of cases, both during the pendency of proceedings and at their conclusion, this has become much more difficult as the case-load has grown. As the case-load continues to expand, and as the number of different tribunal secretaries rise, with some, unavoidably, discharging their duties with more experience than others, it becomes even more important to record and synthesise experience in an organised, even-handed manner. Feedback obtained through evaluation forms could also be assessed in collaboration with the above suggested Users' Committee. While maintaining the confidentiality of individual assessments and cases, an aggregated summary of evaluations should be provided in the ICSID's Annual Report.

IX. Appointment of one or more Deputy Secretaries-General

My ninth suggestion concerns the organisation of the ICSID Secretariat. As mentioned above, ICSID has a simple administrative structure consisting of the Administrative Council and the Secretariat. As also mentioned above, Article 9 of the ICSID Convention provides that the Secretariat shall consist of a Secretary-General, one or more Deputy Secretaries-General, and staff. Article 10(1) provides that the Secretary-General and any Deputy Secretary-General shall be elected by the Administrative Council by a majority of two-thirds of its members on the nomination of the Chairman. Article 10(3) provides that during the Secretary-General's absence or inability to act, and during any vacancy of the office of the Secretary-General, the Deputy Secretary-General shall act as Secretary-General. If there is to be more than one Deputy Secretary-General, the Administrative Council shall determine in advance the order in which they shall act as Secretary-General.

As may be recalled, the ICSID Secretariat remained small in number for the first three decades of the Centre's existence. The first Deputy Secretary-General was not appointed until 1999 and served for a full six-year term (from 1999 to 2005). The second Deputy Secretary-General served from 2007 until early 2011.

When the second Deputy Secretary-General stepped down in 2011, the Secretary-General announced that ICSID had no immediate plans to fill the Deputy Secretary-General's position, and that instead 'a flat structure of six teams' would be part of a new management and decision-making strategy.[37]

This decision ought to be reconsidered for several different reasons. The first is ICSID's significant pending case-load, which as of 24 August 2011 consisted of 131 cases. Tribunals or ad hoc committees had been constituted in 104 of the cases; and in the remaining 27 cases, the Secretariat was in the process of supervising the constitution of the tribunal. With this extensive case-load, including ongoing responsibility for the timely constitution of tribunals, it would seem prudent to assign to more than one person transparent, supervisory responsibilities to ensure efficiency, accountability and seamless administration. Case administration,

---

[37] 'DIAC Hires ICSID Deputy Head', Global Aritration Review (10 August 2011).

especially when it comes to time-sensitive matters, would benefit from the election of one or more Deputy Secretaries-General who would act for the Secretary-General when the latter is not available.

The call for a Deputy Secretary-General can also be supported with respect to some of the work carried out by the Secretary-General in other areas that are not case-related, namely in regard to the administrative interactions of the Secretariat with the World Bank. This is an area of ICSID's operations that at times is somewhat opaque to the outside world, and for the most part of far less public interest than that of the case administration side. However, in areas of human resources, general services including office allocation, travel, hearing and conference organisation, procurement matters, resource allocation, accounting, auditing and trust funds management, ICSID works in close collaboration with different departments within the Bank, and must follow Bank rules and procedures. While less visible to the outside world, this area of ICSID's activities similarly requires involvement of senior staff, both in regard to day-to-day management and with respect to policy-oriented issues, for example the staffing and financing of the Secretariat.

The number of cases and the considerable scope of administration within the framework of the rules and procedures of the World Bank Group suggest portfolios for two Deputy Secretaries-General: one who would be responsible for case administration and one whose area of responsibility would be administrative matters as they relate to the Secretariat operating within the World Bank Group.

My suggestion to appoint two Deputy Secretaries-General is not based only on the considerable amount of complex work with which the Secretariat is charged. A third reason for adding the Deputy Secretary-General level to the management structure of ICSID stems from the need to have more than one senior ICSID staff member, that is the Secretary-General, who can be an effective interlocutor with senior staff in other parts of the Bank as well as with the members of the Administrative Council. For example, the suggestion that steps must be taken to improve the quality of the Panel of Arbitrators is premised on the Secretariat being in a position to engage with the Council at a sufficiently senior and experienced level. In this regard it is important to recall that Deputy Secretaries-General are, as is the case with the Secretary-General, elected by the Administrative Council and therefore enjoy a level of recognition, stature and confidence in the eyes of ICSID Contracting States that is less likely to be bestowed upon more junior Secretariat staff.

The final reason to appoint a Deputy Secretary-General is perhaps the most important. It would meet the need to ensure continuity so that an ICSID Secretariat lawyer will automatically be able to act as Secretary-General in the absence of the Secretary-General, if the Secretary-General was unable to act or during any vacancy of the office of the Secretary-General. Without the appointment of a Deputy Secretary-General, there is no mechanism in place that ensures seamless management of an arbitration specialist in the event that the Secretary-General becomes unavailable, whether temporarily or permanently. I would suggest that this situation be addressed as a matter of urgency with the World Bank, which would have to approve any promotion and added remuneration that, in all likelihood, would accompany one or more appointments to the position of Deputy Secretary-General.

X. ICSID and compliance with awards rendered under the ICSID Convention

My tenth suggestion concerns the enforcement of ICSID awards. I have included this issue in the discussion because the continued success of the institution will to a large extent depend on whether ICSID awards are reliably complied with. No amount of reform or institutional change can make up for the erosive effect of parties' failure to comply with awards. In regard to the enforcement of ICSID Convention awards, Article 54, as is well known, requires each Contracting State of the Convention to recognise an award rendered pursuant to it as binding, and to enforce the pecuniary obligations imposed by the award as if it were a final judgment of the state's court. However, as regards the enforcement of awards against states, Article 54 is not the principal provision of the ICSID Convention. This is set forth in Article 53 of the ICSID Convention, which requires each party to 'abide by and comply with the terms of the award'. In regard to the Contracting State party to the dispute, a failure to abide by and comply with the award is a violation not only of its undertaking to arbitrate but also of an international treaty obligation.

In recent years non-compliance with ICSID awards has for the first time become a concern to the entire dispute settlement system. In particular, Argentina's position on the requirements of the Convention and continued failure to meet its payment obligations have strained the dispute settlement mechanism. The problem, of course, has immediate impact on the award creditor, who after years of arbitration is faced with the need to find new avenues to pursue its claim. However, the damage brought about by non-compliance with awards also extends to the institution, to the extent that failure by states to meet payment obligations undermines the most important and innovative provisions established by the ICSID Convention.

My suggestion in this regard is for ICSID to launch a high-profile campaign to draw attention to this development. One step would be to include in the Centre's Annual Report a list of outstanding awards. ICSID's users, I suggest, would also welcome an account in the ICSID Annual Report of the position taken by the World Bank itself in regard to debtors' failure to comply with an award. This is particularly so given that breach of the constituent treaty of one of the five organisations that make up the World Bank Group ought, automatically, to have Group-wide repercussions.

C. Conclusion

The starting point for the suggestions put forward in this discussion was the acceptance that major shifts have taken place since 2000 in ICSID's responsibilities. No longer a quiet backwater of the World Bank Group, ICSID, and the World Bank itself, must embrace the reality of a large and growing case-load. This encompasses claims that often concern hundreds of millions of dollars, in aggregate amounting to a sizeable fraction of the total annual lending programme of the World Bank Group as a whole; proceedings that with increasing frequency lead to submissions of annulment applications; heightened concerns with conflicts of interest, leading to challenges to arbitrators and issues respecting counsel conduct; and of emerging resistance in some quarters to complying with the provisions of the Convention respecting the enforcement of awards. ICSID is concerned with process and not with the outcome of disputes. That, of course, is the responsibility of arbitrators. The line between process and outcome, however, is not always as easily drawn as one would think, but together they underpin ICSID's legitimacy. Solid outcomes that will be respected by the parties and the international arbitration community depend on competent, well-considered appointments, including meaningful consultations and more systematic feedback from users as processes unfold.

While the Panel designations are the responsibility of the ICSID Contracting States, it is for the ICSID Secretariat to articulate the pressing need for Member States to ensure that this resource works well, so that the Chairman can make appointments with justified confidence.

As ICSID moves forward, the question must be posed whether an organisation of this kind is well served by relying on one person alone with formal responsibilities at management level. The answer, for reasons set out above, is an unequivocal no – the span of control is too great. 'ICSID at the crossroads' refers to the choices that present themselves at this point: to continue, more or less, as the saying goes, with business as usual. Or to institute change both internally and in ICSID's relationship with its users; change that would mark the beginning of a new era as ICSID approaches its fiftieth anniversary in 2016.

17

Rules for investor–state mediation: draft prepared by the International Bar Association State Mediation Subcommittee

BARTON LEGUM, ANNA JOUBIN-BRET
AND INNA MANASSYAN

The State Mediation Subcommittee of the International Bar Association (IBA) Mediation Committee has prepared a draft set of rules specifically to address disputes and conflicts arising between foreign investors and sovereign states that host their investment.

Following from the meetings of the State Mediation Subcommittee at the Buenos Aires, Madrid and Vancouver annual meetings of the IBA, a draft set of rules for investor–state mediation (the 'Draft Set of Rules') was prepared and presented at the Dubai annual meeting and is open for further input and discussion.

This Draft Set of Rules was prepared against the background of a significant increase in investor–state disputes arising from international investment agreements for the promotion and protection of foreign investment. Although the majority of these treaties provide for an amicable settlement period of three or six months to allow the parties to seek to settle the dispute amicably through negotiation, conciliation or mediation, empirical evidence shows that these alternative means to settle a conflict with an investor are seldom used to their best advantage. With the proliferation of investor–state cases, however, stakeholders have begun to look more closely into alternative approaches available under the treaties or proposed by relevant institutions, as it is felt that international arbitration should not be the only means available to settle a dispute arising from an investment.

On the occasion of earlier IBA annual meetings, the State Mediation Subcommittee reviewed the specificities of investor–state disputes and the often-expressed desire of the parties for swift, cost-effective and final settlement of the disputes while at the same time preserving the long-term link between the investor and the host state. Some basic elements that could foster a mediated settlement of investment disputes while providing clear guidance to the parties were identified and discussed. The Subcommittee highlighted a general lack of awareness by parties and practitioners and three main obstacles that are repeatedly raised by states' representatives, investors and practitioners. The first obstacle is the lack of a specific set of rules adapted to investor–state mediation that could provide sufficient flexibility to the parties seeking to mediate a conflict or a dispute while also offering predictability as to the steps and rules applicable to the process. A second issue perceived as an obstacle to mediation is that there is no roster or a pool of potential mediators that could be drawn upon by the parties to intervene successfully in investor–state cases. The third is the absence of a national framework encouraging mediation of investment disputes.

The State Mediation Subcommittee tasked itself with the preparation of a draft set of rules that could be used by state representatives and investors wishing to engage in mediation at whatever stage of a conflict or dispute. To this end, the Subcommittee established a working group composed of several drafting committees (the 'Working Group'). As it was initially conceived to find a common denominator for differing perspectives on the investor–state mediation process in the prospective Rules, the Working Group has comprised representatives of various stakeholders, including state entities, mediation institutions and practitioners in the field, evenly mingled within each of the drafting committees.

It was agreed that the proposed Rules should be drafted in simple and concise terms, to provide the parties with practical guidance without complicating the process. It was felt that mediation rules should not duplicate existing arbitration or conciliation rules, that they should minimise time and costs and that they should be available to parties at any stage of a conflict or a dispute, including while an arbitration procedure is pending.

The overarching guiding principle for drafting this set of Rules was to make them accessible to and useable by a wide range of end-users, to provide flexibility and simplicity to the parties, but at the same time predictability and legitimacy to the process.

The Draft Set of Rules propose guidelines for the commencement and the termination of a mediation process, for the conduct of mediation, for the appointment and the role of a mediator (or co-mediators), for privacy and confidentiality of the mediation and for related issues such as costs.

It was proposed to give the Draft Set of Rules a broad scope of application, in line with the drafting guidelines. The reference to 'investment-related differences and disputes' is meant to allow parties to use the prospective Rules in a variety of situations and instances arising from the relationship between investors and states. The Draft Set of Rules may be used for any kind of differences and disputes and at different stages of a dispute, whether it has already materialised or at the early stage of a difference or a conflict. In this regard, Article Two of the proposed Draft Set of Rules, which sets out the general outline for commencement of a mediation process, provides for a flexible procedure and the possibility to initiate mediation under the prospective Rules prior to or concurrently with domestic court or arbitration proceedings. The guiding principle was to provide for a minimum degree of formality to begin the mediation process so as to facilitate recourse to this means of dispute settlement by parties.

At the same time, members of the Working Group felt it necessary to provide the parties with predictable and clear guidelines as to the process of designation, resignation and replacement of the mediator or co-mediators. They feature under Articles 3 to 6 of the Draft Set of Rules. Recourse to co-mediators was considered an interesting feature in the investor–state context, where the element of trust and acceptability is essential to the success of the process. Co-mediation creates further possibilities of combining mediators' distinct skills and backgrounds.

Albeit different from the arbitration context, and to facilitate the parties being well informed about the choice of a mediator, prior to accepting his or her appointment a mediator shall disclose any personal interest or other potential conflicts in the difference or dispute in a statement of independence and availability, a model of which is attached to the Draft Set of Rules as Appendix A. This Appendix also seeks to ensure that availability of the mediator is disclosed from the outset. Parties are also encouraged to agree upon the mediator's disclosed hourly rates or fees from the beginning of the proceedings.

The procedure for designation of a mediator provided in the Draft Set of Rules seeks to meet the need to ensure that the parties are comfortable and fully engaged in the process while at the same time reducing possible and unnecessary delays in the procedure. The bottom-line principle is that, in any event, the parties have full responsibility and freedom to engage in a mediation process and designate a mediator. However, it was felt that some support could be useful for the party wanting to launch the mediation and to ensure that the other party can make an informed decision about its participation. To this end, the Working Group designed two fallback possibilities to support the party wanting to launch the mediation process:

(1) a designating authority can be chosen by the parties in cases where the parties fail to agree on a mediator; and
(2) the Secretary-General of the Permanent Court of Arbitration shall select a designating authority in cases where the parties fail to agree on it. In addition, and always in order to ensure a swift and efficient outcome of the designation procedure, the Draft Set of Rules provides a set time limit.

Similar simple and clear-cut rules are proposed for the resignation and replacement of a mediator in Article 5 of the Draft Set of Rules. It was also decided to follow the same approach with regard to settlement and termination of the mediation (Articles 11 and 12) where the consensual and party-driven nature of mediation is underlined. Any party has the full discretion to settle or to withdraw from the mediation process at any time, as well as to agree on the terms and conditions of such a decision.

In the same spirit and for practical purposes, the Working Group chose to emphasise the importance of a first mediation management conference to be conducted by the mediator (or co-mediators). Within strict timelines, the background of Article 9 is to give the mediation process a chance, and allow both parties to participate in this first and essential step and to make an informed decision on whether they wish to continue with mediation to settle the difference or the dispute at hand.

An interesting feature of the Draft Set of Rules is the possibility for institutional support to the mediation process or more generally the possibility for an arbitration and mediation institution to be involved. There was general agreement that given the consensual and ad hoc nature of mediation, the Draft Set of Rules should allow the parties and the mediator(s) to seek the support and the intervention of an institution where appropriate and authorised by the parties.

It was further discussed and then agreed by the Working Group that the prospective Rules will provide for the conduct of mediation and the role of the mediator in broad terms. While the mediator is authorised to make decisions pertaining to the conduct of the mediation in order to move the process towards its conclusion, the powers of the mediator remain strictly within the limits of the agreement of the parties.

Two distinctive features of the Draft Set of Rules in the particular context of investor–state disputes relate to confidentiality of documents and information as well as the confidentiality and privacy of the process.

The Draft Set of Rules originally proposed a default rule that information provided to the mediator by any one of the parties is not, unless otherwise indicated, confidential vis-à-vis other parties to the mediation and therefore the mediator may disclose information received from one party to any other party to the mediation. However, there was broad consensus in favour of a confidentiality rule, unless the mediator is expressly authorised to disclose said information. The Working Group also crafted broad privacy and confidentiality provisions, tailored to the specific needs of investor–state mediation, in order to satisfy the need for transparency that arises when a state is involved in such a procedure.

The Draft Set of Rules was presented and discussed at the annual meeting of the IBA in Dubai in November 2011. The feedback received before and during the presentation was very positive and constructive and it is foreseen that the Draft Set of Rules will be circulated widely among interested stakeholders to generate comments and views about an instrument that, once adopted, could be useful for states and investors in mediation of conflicts and in avoiding having to resort to a more costly and intrusive dispute settlement process, such as international arbitration, where the relationship between the investor and the host state may be adversely affected.

The draft set of rules can be viewed on: www.ibanet.org/LPD/Dispute_Resolution_Section/Mediation/Default.aspx.

18

Complementing investor–state dispute resolution: a conceptual framework for investor–state conflict management

ROBERTO ECHANDI

A. Introduction

Two decades of investor–state litigious activity have revealed the limitations of existing investor–state arbitration procedures. These procedures do not fully satisfy the interests of either the foreign investors or the host states when it comes to ensuring the effective implementation of international investment agreements (IIAs), and the optimal functioning of the international investment regime.[1] Both investors and states consider existing investor–state dispute settlement (ISDS) processes too costly, too slow and too indeterminate.[2] Further, some stakeholders have cautioned that increased litigation curtails the possibility of developing long-term harmonious relationships between foreign investors and host states.[3] Such an outcome is contrary to one of the key objectives that IIAs are supposed to promote, that is the creation of a political and economic environment in host states conducive to fostering increasing investment inflows.

Against this background, and considering the success that alternative dispute resolution (ADR) mechanisms have had in other contexts, various investment stakeholders have started to advocate the consideration

---

[1] For the purposes of this chapter, the 'international investment regime' is understood to be the network of international agreements of various kinds comprising rules and disciplines on investment, mainly but not exclusively bilateral investment treaties (BITs) and investment chapters in preferential trade agreements (PTAs).

[2] J. J. Coe Jr, 'Toward a complementary use of conciliation in investor–state disputes: a preliminary sketch', *Journal of International Law and Policy, University of California, Davis* 12 (2005), 7–46.

[3] United Nations Conference on Trade and Development (UNCTAD), *Investor–State Disputes: Prevention and Alternatives to Arbitration*. UNCTAD Series on International Investment Policies for Development (New York: United Nations, 2010), E.10.II.D.11.

of non-litigious means of resolving investment-related disputes arising between investors and host states.[4] Interestingly, in addition to investor-state arbitration, most IIAs include provisions calling on both investors and host states to settle their disputes amicably. Further, the international investment regime provides for different institutions, such as the International Centre for Settlement of Investment Disputes (ICSID), and rules, such as the United Nations Commission on International Trade Law (UNCITRAL), which offer investors and host states the opportunity to use ADR mechanisms other than arbitration to solve their differences. These include fact-finding, mediation and conciliation. Yet, in practice, such ADR mechanisms have rarely been used in the context of treaty-based investor–state disputes.[5]

This chapter analyses the variables that could explain the limited use of ADR as a means to solve treaty-based investor–state disputes, and argues that a critical factor explaining this situation is that ADR techniques have so far been conceived exclusively as alternative *dispute resolution* processes. ADR techniques such as mediation or conciliation have been visualised as alternative procedures for attempting to resolve a conflict that has already escalated into a full-blown dispute under an applicable IIA. This chapter argues that the hybrid private–public nature of treaty-based investor–state disputes has many implications that do not arise in the purely private and commercial context. In addition to other critical political effects, these implications make it extremely difficult for ADR to replace investor–state arbitration as a dominant means of dispute settlement. Thus, this chapter proposes a new conceptual approach to dealing with investor–state conflict, by developing a dispute prevention framework that would enable investors and governments to manage their treaty-based conflicts before they escalate into disputes under IIAs.

This chapter argues that after almost two decades of experience with investor–state arbitration, the international investment regime can no longer afford to leave all problems arising between investors and host states to be exclusively addressed through *dispute resolution procedures*.

---

[4] Coe, 'Toward a complementary use of conciliation in investor–state disputes'; B. Legum, 'The difficulties of conciliation in investment treaty cases: a comment on Professor Jack C. Coe's "Towards a complementary use of conciliation in investor–state disputes: a preliminary sketch"', *Mealey's Arbitration Report* 21(4) (2006), 72; reprinted in *Mediation Committee Newsletter* (International Bar Association) 27 (2006), 2.

[5] In its forty-five year history, the International Centre for Settlement of Investment Disputes (ICSID) has only reported six cases where conciliation procedures have been initiated. See http://icsid.worldbank.org/ICSID/FrontServlet?requestType=ICSIDDocR H&actionVal=CaseLoadStatistics. See also UNCTAD, *Investor–State Disputes*.

It is necessary to complement these procedures with effective investor–state *conflict management* mechanisms, enabling host states and investors to effectively prevent their problems from escalating into full-blown investor–state disputes – thus the reference to investor–state dispute prevention. The problem is that, currently, the institutional infrastructure required to enable such investor–state conflict management mechanisms to develop is practically non-existent. The main focus of this chapter is therefore to provide an initial contribution towards filling this gap.

Following on from this introduction, this chapter has four further sections. Section B explains the different approaches to dispute resolution identified by conflict theory, placing particular emphasis on interest-based processes and the advantages that their use can offer to the parties involved. Section B presents an overview of the use of amicable means for dispute resolution in the international investment regime, and explains the main factors identified by the literature that attempts to explain their limited utilisation in the context of treaty-based disputes between foreign investors and host states.

Section C focuses on the elaboration of the incipient concept of conflict management in the context of investor–state relations. In particular, on the basis of conflict theory and the theoretical background used by dispute systems design (DSD), this section will explain the distinction between the concepts of 'conflict' and 'dispute', and will address the practical implications of such a distinction for the purposes of developing protocols for avoidance of investor–state disputes. Section D will explain how the notion of investor–state conflict management can be translated into policies and specific investor–state conflict management mechanisms enabling disputes to be avoided. This section also provides a preliminary sketch of the essential elements of a standard protocol for investor–state conflict management. Last, but not least, Section E draws conclusions, placing the technical discussion in the broader context of the evolution of international investment law.

B. The search for interest-based alternatives to investor–state arbitration

There is growing interest in the literature in exploring the feasibility of using non-litigious dispute resolution to resolve investor–state disputes. A growing body of scholarship has started to explore the application of ADR techniques such as conciliation and mediation to the investor–state context.[6] Recent academic writings have also suggested a more systematic and holistic approach by applying DSD to investor–state arbitration.[7] These proposals are based on the common idea that adjudication should not be visualised as the exclusive means of settling disputes between international investors and host states. Further, such literature recognises the significant potential benefits of applying interest-based dispute resolution methods to investor–state disputes. Given its important implications, the concept of interest-based resolution and its relationship with other approaches to dispute settlement is discussed below.

I. Interest-based dispute resolution and its advantages

According to the approach used by the parties in attempting to resolve their disputes, dispute resolution theory classifies the universe of dispute resolution processes into three broad categories. First, the parties involved in a quarrel may attempt to settle their disagreements by determining who is more powerful, 'power-based resolution'; second, by determining

---

[6] Coe, 'Toward a complementary use of conciliation in investor–state disputes'; J. Coe Jr., 'Should Mediation of Investment Disputes Be Encouraged, and, If So, by Whom and How?' in A. W. Rovine (ed.), *Contemporary Issues in International Arbitration and Mediation: The Fordham Papers* (2009); J. Coe Jr. 'Settlement of Investor–State Disputes through Mediation – Preliminary Remarks on Processes, Problems and Prospects', in D. Bishop (ed.), *Enforcement of Arbitral Awards Against Sovereigns* (Huntington, NY: Juris, 2009); U. Onwuamaegbu, 'The role of ADR in investor–state dispute settlement: the ICSID experience', *News from ICSID* 22(2) (2005), 12–14; Legum 'The difficulties of conciliation in investment treaty cases, 1–3; J. Salacuse, 'Is there a better way? Alternative methods of treaty-based, investor–state dispute resolution', *Fordham International Law Journal* 31 (2007), 138–85; M. Clodfelter, 'Why Aren't More Investor–State Treaty Disputes Settled Amicably?' in UNCTAD, *Investor–State Disputes: Prevention and Alternatives to Arbitration II*, Proceedings of the Washington and Lee University and UNCTAD Joint Symposium on International Investment and Alternative Dispute Resolution, 29 March 2010, Lexington, Virginia, USA (New York: United Nations, 2011) UNCTAD/WEB/DIAE/ IA/2010/8; T. W. Wälde, 'Pro-active mediation of international business and investment disputes involving long-term contracts: from zero-sum Litigation to Efficient Dispute Management', *Transnational Dispute Management* 1(2) (2004), available at: www.transnational-dispute-management.com/article.asp?key=110; T. Weiler and F. Baetens (eds.), *New Directions in International Economic Law. In Memorium Thomas Wälde* (Leiden: Martinus Nijhoff, 2011).

[7] Dispute system design (DSD) is not a dispute resolution in itself. 'Rather, it is the intentional and systematic creation of an effective, efficient and fair dispute resolution process based upon the unique needs of a particular system ... [by] analyzing existing patterns of disputing, creating new processes, and implementing and evaluating the new system to improve its efficacy.' S. Franck, 'Integrating investment treaty conflict and dispute settlement design,' *Minnesota Law Review* 92 (2007), 161–230 at 178.

who is right, 'rights-based resolution'; or third, by reconciling their interests – what is also called 'interest-based resolution'.[8]

From a historical perspective, probably the oldest approach to resolving conflicts and disputes at all levels of human interaction has been through recourse to power. The exercise of power entails the capacity of one party to the dispute to compel another party to behave in a manner in which it would not willingly behave otherwise.[9] Such power can be either physical, social, economic or political. As the relative power of each of the parties involved in a dispute may not always be clear to the other(s), power-based resolution often entails power contests. Such power contests may range from totally peaceful means – such as taking a vote to measure political power or organising a strike to demonstrate economic power – to the threat or actual use of force.

A second approach to resolving disputes is to rely on some independent standard with perceived legitimacy or fairness to determine who is right. This is 'rights-based' resolution.[10] Although they can derive from socially accepted patterns of behaviour, rights typically derive from the applicable legal system. The development of laws or contracts, either at the national or international level, is the main source for rights, which act as the legitimate standard according to which the disputes are resolved. The problem is that determining the scope and content of a particular right is often not easy. Rights are seldom crystal clear and a particular right cannot be assessed in isolation, but must be looked at in relation to other existing rights which may apply to the same situation, and which may even be conflicting. Thus, rights-based dispute resolution often entails the need for adjudication, understood as an impartial and independent third party to examine the applicable rights to a given situation and determine the outcome of the dispute.[11]

A third approach to resolving disputes is to rely on the reconciliation of the different interests of the parties involved in a conflict, known as 'interest-based' dispute resolution. Interest-based dispute resolution processes promote constant and interactive communication among the parties to allow them to reach an agreement. Such processes could entail

[8] W. Ury, J. Brett and S. Goldberg, *Getting Disputes Resolved: Designing Systems to Cut the Costs of Conflict, The Program on Negotiation at Harvard Law School* (Cambridge, MA: Harvard, 1993); S. Smith and J. Martinez, 'An Analytic framework for dispute systems design', *Harvard Negotiation Law Review* 14 (2009), 123–169.

[9] Ury et al., *Getting Disputes Resolved*, p. 7.

[10] Ibid.

[11] Ibid.

direct negotiations among the parties to the dispute or the intervention of a third party, which intervenes as a facilitator, either through conciliation, mediation or other techniques.

In practice, interest-based processes such as negotiation, conciliation or mediation rarely focus exclusively on the interests of the parties involved. Negotiation seldom takes place in a vacuum. In practice, negotiation often takes place in the shadow of the law or in the shadow of power. Thus, some negotiations focus on determining who is right, such as when the negotiating parties compete to prove that their position has greater merit. Other negotiations take place in the shadow of a determination of who is more powerful, such as when nations exchange threats and counter-threats. Other negotiations involve a mix of all these variables.[12] Thus, in the process of resolving a dispute, the attention of the parties involved may shift from interests to rights to power and back again to interests. As further explained in Section II, this is particularly relevant in the context of investor–state disputes.

Differentiation between power-based, interest-based and rights-based dispute resolution provides a very useful framework for understanding various key aspects of the political economy of international investment. First, it enables us to understand the relationship between foreign investors and host states through history and to value the advantages of a rule-oriented investment regime over power-based dispute resolution.

Historically, before foreign investors had the possibility of submitting a claim to international arbitration under an IIA, when confronted with a dispute with the host state, investors only had two possibilities. One was to submit a claim to the courts of the host state. As foreign investors often did not trust local courts, the second possibility was to invoke the diplomatic protection of their own governments. Throughout the nineteenth and early twentieth centuries, diplomatic protection was a common way to deal with investment-related disputes. In many instances, the abuse of diplomatic protection led to 'gun-boat diplomacy' and other power-oriented manifestations in disputes with developing countries.[13]

As mentioned in the introduction to this chapter, even though the development of the web of IIAs since the 1990s has led to many challenges – including significant economic and political costs for governments and investors, as they are involved in rising numbers of

---

[12] *Ibid.*
[13] J. Cable, *Gunboat Diplomacy 1919–1979: Political Applications of Limited Naval Force* (London: Macmillan, 1981).

investor–state arbitration cases – it is also true that such trends reflect an evolution towards rights-based dispute resolution. Clearly, with the proliferation of IIAs and the development of a growing body of jurisprudence on international investment law, international investment relations have become increasingly 'rule oriented', moving away from the traditional 'power oriented' relationships that historically prevailed in the international investment setting. Investment relations are increasingly being governed by rules and principles included in conventional instruments of international law rather than by political or economic might.[14] Under most circumstances, rule-oriented adjudication is clearly preferable to power-oriented resolution of investment-related disputes.

A second practical implication of unveiling the distinction between power-oriented, interest-based and rights-based dispute resolution in the context of international investment relations is that this distinction also enables investment stakeholders to see clearly that rights-based international adjudication, such as ISDS, is not the only possible way to resolve investor–state disputes. Furthermore, as the high economic and political costs of ISDS have become more evident, the pressure to find alternative means of dispute resolution has increased. Thus, the distinction between power-based, rights-based or interest-based dispute resolution also helps to reveal the enormous potential benefits of the interest-based approach to foster more stable and satisfactory investor–state relationships.

Recent literature has recognised many of the potential advantages that fostering interest-based processes could have in the context of investor–state disputes. The first is that such processes are based on the negotiation of mutually acceptable solutions by the parties themselves. Thus, not only can the parties to the dispute exert much greater control over the problem-solving process, but also – and unlike in a zero-sum adjudication of rights – successful interest-based ADR, such as direct negotiation, conciliation or mediation, leads to win–win settlements where none of the parties to the dispute end up being a loser. Thus, reconciling interests tends to generate a higher level of mutual satisfaction with the outcomes than solving disputes on the basis of determining rights or power. This is particularly important for maintaining productive relationships in the long term, which are crucial in the investor–state context. A more pragmatic and yet critical aspect of interest-based ADR is that agreements

---

[14] J. Jackson, *The World Trading System: Law and Policy of International Economic Relations* (Cambridge, MA: MIT Press, 1997); S. Franck, 'Development and outcomes of investment treaty arbitration', *Harvard International Law Journal* 50(2) (2009), 435–89.

secured by negotiation have the advantage that, given their consensual nature, they are self-executing and enforcement problems do not arise.[15]

Last, but not least, one of the most obvious advantages of interest-based or amicable dispute resolution processes over investor–state arbitration is that they could save the parties significant time, money and energy. As previously explained, the use of investor–state arbitration entails significant political and economic costs, not only in terms of resources consumed or destroyed, but also in terms of opportunities lost for both investor and host states.[16] Given its multiple advantages, it is worth reviewing how the international investment regime deals with interest-based dispute resolution and the experience gained in its application.

II. Interest-based dispute resolution in the current international investment regime

There is no data available to appraise the frequency and rate of success or failure of any preliminary amicable consultations that hypothetically could be taking place between investors and host states and that

---

[15] P. K. Yu, 'Toward a Nonzero-Sum Approach to Resolving Global Intellectual Property Disputes: What We Can Learn from Mediators, Business Strategists, and International Relations Theorists', Cardozo Law School Jacob Burns Institute for Advanced Legal Studies Working Paper Series No. 46 (2002); M. Reisman, 'International Investment Arbitration and ADR: Married but Best Living Apart' in UNCTAD, *Investor–State Disputes: Prevention and Alternatives to Arbitration II, Proceedings of the Washington and Lee University and UNCTAD Joint Symposium on International Investment and Alternative Dispute Resolution*, 29 March 2010, Lexington, VA, USA (New York: United Nations, 2011), UNCTAD/WEB/DIAE/IA/2010/8, p. 22.

[16] Despite their multiple advantages, it should be stressed that interest-based dispute resolution methods may not always be appropriate – or even desirable. For instance, in cases where there are significant asymmetries of power among the disputing parties, rights-based adjudication – or at least negotiations in the shadow of law – may be more appropriate than purely interest-based negotiation, as the application of the law may have an important effect on levelling the playing field among non-equals: C. Costantino and C. Sickles-Merchant, *Designing Conflict Management Systems* (San Francisco: Jossey-Bass, 1996). Moreover, there may be situations where the interests of the parties, or at least of one of them, may be better served by achieving complete victory in the dispute – an outcome that could only be reached by rights-based adjudication (Yu, 'Toward A Nonzero-Sum Approach'). Such a situation would arise when one of the parties needs to set a precedent to clarify certain legal issues, or to establish a certain reputation. In the investor–state context, this would be the case of a dispute involving the clarification or assertion of the right of the host state to regulate in favour of key public policy objectives In such a situation, interest-based dispute resolution may not be the most appropriate alternative because of the need of the government to set a clear precedent and signal to its constituents its authority to regulate legitimate public policy objectives.

never escalate to the investor–state litigation phase. Some experts have suggested that a significant number of disputes between investors and host states may currently be channelled through early amicable settlement, as the number of disputes that actually reach the litigation stage through investor–state arbitration is minimal in the light of the huge magnitude and level of integration of current international investment flows.[17] Such a line of argument is persuasive. However, the lack of reliable empirical data may also hide trends going in the opposite direction. It may also be possible that, given the high costs associated with investor–state arbitration, a significant number of disputes may simply not be finding any legal outlet for resolution under the international investment regime. Finally, both trends may well be taking place, as they are not incompatible.

However, the available information suggests a puzzling trend regarding the use of consensual means of dispute resolution in the context of investor–state investment controversies. Empirical evidence shows that consensual settlements of disputes between investors and governments are taking place, not in the context of the application of available interest-based ADR procedures, which have rarely been used, but rather in the context of investor–state arbitration proceedings. For instance, ICSID statistics show that, in 2011, 39 per cent of all registered ICSID cases, the majority of which are treaty-based disputes, have been settled or otherwise discontinued by the parties before the arbitration tribunal has rendered a final award.[18] Further, by early 2010, the United Nations Conference on Trade and Development (UNCTAD) estimated that at least 55 of the 357 then known treaty-based investor–state arbitration disputes had been settled.[19] This trend raises two questions. First, if in the context of investor–state relations, non-litigious means of dispute resolution have so many advantages, how is it that ADR mechanisms are rarely used as alternatives to investor–state arbitration? Second, which variables explain

---

[17] Reisman, 'International Investment Arbitration and ADR', p.22.
[18] International Centre for the Settlement of Investment Disputes (ICSID), *The ICSID Caseload Statistics, 2010* (Montréal, Québec: ICSID, 2011) available at: http://icsid.world-bank.org/ICSID/FrontServlet?requestType=ICSIDDocRH&actionVal=CaseLoadStatistics.
[19] Although there is no detailed information yet regarding disputes submitted to ad hoc arbitration under the United Nations Commission on International Trade Law (UNCITRAL) or to other venues, experts have argued that there is no reason to suppose that the trends regarding settlement of disputes in the context of other arbitration fora would be very different. Clodfelter, Why Aren't More Investor–State Treaty Disputes Settled Amicably?, p. 38; UNCTAD, *Investor-State Disputes: Prevention and Alternatives to Arbitration II.*

why consensual settlements tend to occur in the context of investor–state arbitrations? We address these two questions below.

In general, recourse to means that constitute an alternative to investor–state arbitration is frequently enshrined in IIAs. These treaties often require the parties to a dispute to first seek amicable settlement through negotiations and consultations conducted seriously and in good faith, and only when such negotiations and consultations fail should international arbitration be considered. Furthermore, to ensure that the parties to the dispute actually do make an effort to settle their disputes amicably, most IIAs also provide for 'cooling-off' periods – intervals which, depending on the applicable treaty, vary between three and six months from the submission of the notice of intent for arbitration until the arbitration procedure actually starts. Despite these general references, most IIAs do not include provisions specifically referring to – and even less mandating – the use of interest-based ADR procedures as alternatives to investor–state arbitration. Nevertheless, being inherently voluntary processes, nothing in IIAs prevents investors and host states engaged in a dispute from opting for interest-based ADR, which is at their disposal thanks to various international instruments and institutions that regulate the ADR procedures in detail. In the patchy legal framework constituting the international investment regime, there are multiple sets of rules that in principle could be referred to or used to conduct ADR in the investor–state context. Probably the most relevant would be the rules set up under the ICSID Convention and ICSID Additional Facility, the UNCITRAL conciliation rules and the International Chamber of Commerce (ICC) ADR rules. It should be noted, however, that, of these, only the ICSID rules were specifically designed to apply in the context of investor–state disputes.[20]

In practice, the use of the ADR rules referred to above for resolving treaty-based investment disputes arising between investors and host states has been extremely limited. For instance, in the case of the ICSID, from 1965 – when the ICSID Convention was negotiated – until 2011 there were only six cases submitted for conciliation under the ICSID rules.[21]

---

[20] In addition to arbitration, the ICSID Convention contains the Rules of Procedure for Conciliation Proceedings that could be applied to resolve disputes involving ICSID Member States themselves and investors from ICSID Member States. Further, the Additional Facility of ICSID also envisages conciliation and fact-finding procedures that could apply in situations where either party to the dispute is not a member of ICSID or where the issue at stake is not entirely related to investment (Onwuamaegbu, 'The role of ADR in investor–state dispute settlement', 12).

[21] 'ICSID Caseload Statistics, 2010', available at: http://icsid.worldbank.org/ICSID/FrontServlet?requestType=ICSIDDocRH&actionVal=CaseLoadStatistics.

Further, up to 2011 not a single case had been submitted under the ICSID Additional Facility fact-finding rules.[22]

Thus, despite most IIAs containing language encouraging consensual means of dispute resolution and the availability of various procedural venues for ADR, interest-based ADR has not been used in practice – and consequently is neither visualised by investors nor host states – as an effective alternative to treaty-based investor–state arbitration. Considering the widespread encouragement of consensual ISDS in the texts of IIAs, the relative lack of recourse to mediation or conciliation is puzzling. Although still in its embryonic stage, a survey of the literature sheds light on the various factors that can explain the limited use made of interest-based ADR to attempt to resolve treaty-based investor–state disputes.

Several variables have been proposed by scholars to explain the relatively limited recourse to interest-based ADR.[23] One way of assessing these different factors is to distinguish between three broad categories. First, there are those determinants resulting from the relative novelty of the idea of interest-based dispute resolution in the investor–state context. Second, there are those structural factors which are related to the particular nature of treaty-based investor–state disputes. And third, there are the difficulties with using interest-based dispute resolution stemming from the lack of clarity and the evolving nature of international investment law. We explain each of these three categories below.

1. Barriers related to the novelty of interest-based conflict resolution in the investor–state context

Regarding the first category, experts have pointed out that from the outset, especially in Western countries, the legal culture tends to conceive of litigation as the natural way to solve legal disputes, and investor–state ones are no exception.[24] Thus, to start with, in the context of the evolving international economic law, neither investors nor host states have naturally considered interest-based ADR as the first option when a dispute arises. The focus of attention has been international adjudication, in particular investor–state arbitration. Consequently, the knowledge of,

---

[22] *Ibid.*
[23] Coe, 'Toward a complementary use of conciliation in investor–state disputes'; Coe, 'Settlement of Investor–State Disputes through Mediation, p. 52; Onwuamaegbu, 'The role of ADR in investor–state dispute settlement', 14; Legum, 'The difficulties of conciliation in investment treaty cases', 3; Salacuse, 'Is there a better way?', 138; Clodfelter, 'Why Aren't More Investor–State Treaty Disputes Settled Amicably?', p. 40.
[24] Franck, 'Integrating investment treaty conflict and dispute settlement design'.

familiarity with, and predisposition to use ADR among investment stake-holders – both investors and host governments – is still limited. The lack of practice and the non-binding nature of ADR fuels perceptions that interest-based resolution is ineffective, and ultimately may be a waste of time and resources. Further, other experts have also blamed the limited use of ADR to resolve investor–state disputes on the features of some of the ADR rules themselves. It has been pointed out that existing ADR rules need to be adjusted to make them more flexible, informal and easy to administrate. It has been argued that currently, some of them entail processes that may be as long, formal and almost as costly as arbitration, and yet they do not lead to a binding, enforceable award. Last, the literature has recognised that if ADR is to become more common in the investor–state context, it will be necessary to have a readily identifiable pool of experts with both mediation skills and a solid background in international investment law, and such a combination is not easy to find.

This state of affairs generates a vicious cycle. On the one hand, the lack of knowledge, familiarity and confidence of investment stakeholders that ADR is an effective option for resolving treaty-based investment disputes contributes to preventing the development of an adequate infrastructure – both institutionally and in terms of human resources – to efficiently use ADR in the investor–state context.[25] Consequently, it is difficult to generate greater familiarity, better perceptions and more confidence in the ability of interest-based processes to apply efficiently to treaty-based disputes arising between international investors and host states.

The incipient nature of interest-based processes in investor–state ADR should also be put into perspective. The use of investor–state arbitration is a relatively recent phenomenon. Indeed, it was not until the mid 1990s that its use began to increase. Thus, the international community is just starting to cope with investor–state arbitration and the multiple challenges it poses. Within this context, it should not be surprising that the international investment regime has not yet fully developed the infrastructure necessary to enable interest-based processes to become an effective vehicle to address investor–state conflict. It should be noted, however, that assessing the prospects for the development of such infrastructure requires a full understanding of the nature of the investor–state conflict.

---

[25] Some scholars also point out that such perceptions are fuelled by some legal practitioners who do not necessarily have all the incentives to promote the use of ADR (T. Wälde, 'Mediation/Alternative Dispute Resolution in Oil, Gas and Energy Transactions: Superior to Arbitration/Litigation from a Commercial and Management Perspective' (1985), available at: www.dundee.ac.uk/cepmlp/journal/html/Vol13/article13–8.pdf).

In this regard, and as previously stated, the second set of factors explaining the limited recourse to interest-based ADR relate precisely to the peculiar private–public nature of treaty-based investor–state disputes.

2. Barriers related to the private–public nature of treaty-based investor–state disputes

The limited use of interest-based ADR to settle treaty-based investment disputes between foreign investors and host states also relates to variables that go way beyond lack of knowledge and infrastructure, and stem from the very structure of these disputes. As Clodfelter clearly points out, '[t]he public nature of the parties and the measures in most investor-state disputes makes them very different from commercial disputes'.[26] The circumstance that one of the parties is a sovereign state, combined with the fact that claims challenge public measures that often relate to key public policy objectives, generates complex dynamics that discourage governments from seeking consensual settlement of investor–state disputes. The various explanations offered by the specialised literature may be summarised under three sets of factors which are explained below.

First, governments are complex organisations. Authority is allocated among numerous agencies, which also operate at different administrative levels. Thus, even assuming that within the administration there is a clear chain of command to deal with investor–state disputes – which often is not the case – making major decisions tends to be slow and cumbersome. Furthermore, the decision and the terms of settlement of an investment dispute may lead to intra-departmental disagreements, which may in turn be coloured by intra-governmental politics. In those conditions it is not easy for government officials to undertake the risk and effort of negotiating a settlement that may later be challenged or may not be respected by another governmental agency. Such a situation does not arise when there is a binding international award settling the dispute.

Second, governments operate within the boundaries of local administrative laws. Thus, participation in ADR entails the existence of an agency with the legal authority to negotiate with investors, represent the host state in these negotiations, reach a settlement of the dispute – including authorisation to use taxpayers' money to compensate for damages – and have the means to make the terms of the settlement binding and effective vis-à-vis the other agencies of the administration. Although increased litigation activity has led some states to set up intra-governmental structures

---

[26] Clodfelter 'Why Aren't More Investor–State Treaty Disputes Settled Amicably?', p. 40.

to deal efficiently with investor–state arbitration – and such structures could also be instrumental for ADR – the legal authorisation to use public funds to comply with the resolution of an international arbitration tribunal usually does not extend to the use of public funds to reach consensual settlements with foreign investors.

Third, and more importantly, governments are politically accountable entities. At every level intra-governmental and external constituencies constantly scrutinise government officials and hold them accountable for their actions. A voluntary settlement of an investor–state dispute holds the possibility that the government could be held accountable for having conceded – or appearing to have conceded – many serious charges. A settlement may be perceived as a recognition by the government that the state had violated its international legal obligations. Furthermore, a settlement may also be seen as the government conceding responsibility for applying a regulatory measure that many domestic sectors may consider not only appropriate but also fully legitimate under domestic and even under international law. As Clodfelter clearly states: 'investor–state disputes commonly refer to public values, often involving scrutiny of actions of public authorities in the execution of their public duties or to advance policies stated in the law – disputes of this nature … implicate deep seated values concerning sovereignty, sovereign reputation and the basic role of the State in managing economic affairs.'[27]

The extremely sensitive political consequences that a voluntary settlement of an investor–state dispute may entail are just part of the story. Governments will also have to respond to their constituencies on the terms of the settlement reached, and be ready to justify why a particular investor receives a particular treatment relative to other foreign or national investors.

Further, governments settling investor–state disputes through ADR would also have to justify the use of taxpayers' money, and the amount needed, to pay the compensation usually claimed by the investor as a result of the damage caused. From a political perspective, using fiscal resources to redress a claim made by a foreign transnational corporation (TNC) – no matter how legitimate the claim – is not an easy sell for any government. Any domestic political actor may argue that instead of making a transfer in favour of a foreign investor, the cash could have been used to finance other public policy priorities, such as education and health. Negotiating the payment of damages in the absence of adjudication is also

---

[27] Ibid.

a very sensitive issue because of the risk of allegations of collusive corruption schemes set up between the government and the investors when
agreeing the amount of compensation to be paid. Thus, it is one thing
for a government to use scarce fiscal resources only to the extent necessary to legally comply with an international obligation. In this case, the
resulting compensation will be determined not by the government and
the affected investor, but rather by an independent international tribunal,
which will bear the political cost of making such decision. It is another
thing for a government to accept a mutually agreed compensation payment, the amount of which could be questioned by anyone in the political
setting of the host state.

In sum, when attempting to reach a mutually agreed solution to an
investor–state dispute through ADR, governments are confronted with
too many and too sensitive political risks. As these risks may be easily
avoided by resorting to adjudication, it seems natural that the use of ADR
to settle investor–state disputes would be limited.

Within this context, before having to assume the political costs associated with a voluntary settlement of a controversial investor–state dispute,
governments often find it more politically convenient to let an international tribunal assume the political cost of making a decision.[28] As the
arbitration award is legally binding, it is easy for governments to shield
themselves from the controversy generated by the content of the award,
an award from which they can dissociate themselves and even criticise,
and yet comply with it as a result of the need to respect a decision enacted
by a legitimate tribunal under international law.

3.   Barriers related to the lack of clarity and evolving nature of international investment law

Given the recent development of international investment law, any
interest-based process of investor–state dispute resolution is likely to
take place in the shadow of the law. Clearly, no party to a dispute will
ever agree voluntarily to settle a particular dispute if in the end a negotiated agreement entails higher costs and less favourable conditions than

---

[28]   As Reisman accurately points out: 'This seems especially to be the situation with respect
to governments in international investment law disputes. Indeed, in States in which there
are active political oppositions waiting for an opportunity to pounce on the incumbents
for having "betrayed" the national patrimony by settling with an investor, modalities
other than transparent third-party decisions can undermine or even bring down governments and destroy personal careers.' Reisman, 'International Investment Arbitration
and ADR', p. 26.

would otherwise be obtained through adjudication. In this regard, the more predictable the likely outcome of a rights-based dispute resolution process, the easier it will be for the parties to ponder the benefits of using rule-based negotiation approaches to resolve their disputes.

The problem is that, contrary to other international economic law contexts like the World Trade Organization (WTO), where a single dispute settlement system interprets a single set of agreements, the current international investment regime not only comprises several thousand similar and yet different IIAs, but also is based on a decentralised dispute settlement approach. Similar provisions are included in myriad agreements, which in turn can be potentially interpreted by a multiplicity of arbitral tribunals. Within this context, it is not surprising that decisions of arbitral tribunals regarding the scope of IIAs and the content and breadth of their key substantive standards have not been consistent. The need to foster greater consistency and coherence in the jurisprudence of international investment arbitration tribunals has been widely discussed in the investment literature.[29] Further, lack of consistency in investment case law has also been considered by many experts to be one of the fundamental factors limiting the potential for amicable settlement in investor–state cases.

> Negotiations need to occur by bargaining in the shadow of the law, which means it is necessary for both parties to properly assess the relative strengths and weaknesses of their own and the opponent's cases … But the ability of the parties in many investor–state cases to make such assessments is severely impaired by the fact that, on these key issues, tribunals follow disparate paths to decision and bring about very different outcomes … On a wide range of [both jurisdiction and substantive protection] issues, there is significant uncertainty about how an arbitral tribunal will rule. Consequently, a party's probabilities of success often cannot be reliably estimated and neither party can get a true picture of what it may be giving up or gaining through a 'negotiated' conclusion to the dispute.[30]

4.   Summary

The analysis of the three sets of variables explained above helps us to explain why so far the use of interest-based ADR has been so limited in the context of treaty-based investment disputes. Furthermore, that analysis

---

[29]   On the issue of coherence and consistency in international investment law, see the contributions by Schreuer, Dolzer, Muchlinski, Bjorklund, Ewing-Chow, Banifatemi and Reinisch in this volume.

[30]   Clodfelter, 'Why Aren't More Investor–State Treaty Disputes Settled Amicably?', p. 41.

also sheds light on why, in practice, consensual settlements have tended to be limited to the contentious context of investor–state arbitration.

To be able to settle disputes, governments need to be in a position to clearly and objectively demonstrate to their political constituencies that settling the dispute is a better alternative for the host state than waiting for the arbitral tribunal to render a final award. Such an outcome would be achieved by demonstrating at least two critical points: first, that unless there was a settlement, the arbitral tribunal would be likely to hold the state liable for breach of an international legal obligation, and/or second, that the terms and effects of a negotiated settlement would lead to a more convenient outcome for the state than the terms derived from an adverse award rendered by the tribunal. In other words, for governments to be politically able to settle a dispute, they need to objectively show to their constituents the potential international liability derived from a state measure, and the opportunity cost of letting such liability be declared by an arbitration tribunal rather than solving the problem amicably.

This chapter argues that, in many cases, a solution to this conundrum can be found by addressing the investor–state conflict at an earlier stage, before the conflict degenerates into a full-blown dispute under an IIA. In this sense, this chapter argues that it is necessary to complement *dispute resolution procedures* with dispute prevention policies and mechanisms that enable host states and investors to *manage* their conflicts before they escalate into investment disputes under an IIA.

C.   Developing the concept of investor–state conflict management: a basis for protocols for dispute avoidance

I.   *The distinction between 'conflict' and 'dispute' and its application to the investment context*

Most of the time, in all contexts – and the field of international investment law and policy is no exception – there has been a trend to use the terms 'conflict' and 'dispute' interchangeably. Both terms are used to refer to a difference or a problem between the parties in a relationship. However, conflict theory and DSD literature make a clear conceptual distinction between these two terms, and such differentiation turns out to be critical for creating protocols for the avoidance of investor–state disputes.

For DSD practitioners the terms conflict and dispute are not synonymous. While conflict is a process, a dispute is just one of the typical by-products of conflict. 'Conflict is the process of expressing dissatisfaction, disagreement, or unmet expectations with any organizational interchange; a dispute is one of the products of conflict ... [w]hereas conflict is often ongoing, amorphous, and intangible, a dispute is tangible and concrete – it has issues, positions, and expectations for relief.'[31]

This approach visualises a dispute at the end of a 'continuum'. A dispute stems from a process of degradation, whereby a state of agreement among the parties to a relationship devolves into the identification of a problem, then to a conflict arising from that problem, and then to a dispute arising from that conflict. Thus, a conflict is a problem unattended, and a dispute is an unattended conflict that has evolved into a 'defined, focused disagreement, often framed in legal terms'.[32] This sequential distinction has two important corollaries.

The first is that problems and conflicts are inherent to all levels of human interaction; thus, conflict is unavoidable. Instead, disputes can be prevented if conflict is successfully managed and dealt with before it escalates into a focused disagreement expressed in legal terms and entailing expectations of relief. Second, relationships are dynamic rather than static and they evolve over time and according to the circumstances. As conflicts are an inherent part of relationships, they are also dynamic, and evolve with time. Once an unattended conflict has degenerated into a dispute, the approaches necessary to resolve the difference also vary. Thus, DSD literature also makes the distinction between the concepts of 'conflict management', and 'dispute resolution'. Conflicts are managed. Disputes are resolved. Let us develop this point further.

In the initial period of the conflict management stage, dissatisfaction or disagreement is somewhat shapeless, and thus there is a wide array of options the parties can use to deal with the situation. Conflict management processes attempt to address the interests of the parties involved in the conflict, and in this way attempt to eliminate or substantially reduce the source of dissatisfaction or disagreement. As will be further explained below, the fact that a dispute does not yet exist promotes an environment that is more conducive to the success of interest-based processes. Once a conflict has evolved into a dispute, the situation is quite different. There is a defined and focused disagreement. When the dispute is framed in legal terms – as in the context of treaty-based investment disputes – the conflict has evolved to the point where one party has formulated a claim that an action of another is not only illegal, but that it has also inflicted damage,

---

[31] Costantino and Sickles-Merchant, *Designing Conflict Management Systems*, p. 5.
[32] Smith and Martinez, 'An analytic framework for dispute systems design'.

entitling the affected party to seek a concrete expectation of relief, often expressed in terms of compensation. Thus, in the end both conflict management and dispute resolution are different approaches to dealing with the different degrees of maturity of a conflict.

1.   The investor–state conflict continuum

In the context of the relationship between a foreign investor and the host state, conflicts appear when the parties express dissatisfaction, disagreement or unmet expectations in their relationship. In a world where economic activity in most countries tends to be highly regulated, and thus leads to a high level of interaction between foreign investors and the authorities of host states, the possibilities for conflict are present every day.

To perform almost any economic activity, foreign investors require permits, licences or authorisations from public authorities of the host state. Administering concessions for public services, granting all sorts of permits, applying tax, health or any other type of regulations are just some examples of tasks performed by public agencies that deal with foreign investors on a daily basis. The risk for treaty-based investment disputes between foreign investors and host states is considerably higher than in other contexts for two important reasons.

First, norms and disciplines included in IIAs have quite a broad scope of application, and tend to apply to all measures that a state might take and affect an investment owned or controlled by an investor covered under the agreement. Second, states consist of a conglomerate of governmental agencies. These agencies – which can be part of the national, regional or sub-regional administration – may be bureaucratic, have different policy priorities, and even different attitudes with respect to foreign investment; yet all of them are equally bound by the norms and disciplines of IIAs. Thus, the possibility of a conflict arising between a foreign investor and the host state is very high, as various agencies can take different measures – even contradictory ones – with respect to a given foreign investment. In numerous countries red tape and contradictory requirements for obtaining authorisations or licences are a common source of irritation – and thus, conflict – to any person interacting with the public administration.

Furthermore, the possibility of conflict in the context of investor–state relations is often exacerbated, as a significant number of the agencies that enact measures affecting the economic activity of foreign investors are not familiar with the obligations included in IIAs. Given the wide scope of application of IIAs, and the fact that foreign investment can take place in almost any sector of economic activity, the agencies involved in the negotiation of IIAs tend not to overlap with the numerous agencies that can enact measures affecting the effective implementation of the agreements. These variables help to explain why limited information, communication and coordination – and perhaps even open disagreements – between public agencies are often at the root of conflicts between foreign investors and host states. Moreover, these same variables also explain why, in the context of investor–state relationships, a significant number of conflicts are often not effectively managed and descend into full-blown investment disputes. In many countries the first the authorities competent to deal with investor–state disputes hear about a treaty-based investment conflict is when they receive from the investor a formal notice of intent to submit a claim to arbitration.

In practice, the existence of a conflict manifests when an investor expresses dissatisfaction or concern to an authority of the host state as a consequence of the adoption of or failure to adopt a particular measure. In many countries the agency adopting the measure may not be familiar with the rules and disciplines of IIAs, or may even ignore the existence of these agreements. Once the investor raises the problem – usually with the agency that adopted the measure being challenged – the problem may or not be solved. In the latter situation the lack of resolution may stem from various factors, ranging from simple bureaucratic inertia or red tape, to a disagreement between the agency and the investor regarding the problem. Such disagreement may be related to the legality or convenience of the measure or to the impact that the contested measure may or may not have on the investor.

When confronted with a problem raised by an investor – either a domestic or a foreign one – the public character of the agency concerned requires its actions to be viewed within the framework of the applicable body of administrative law. The degree of flexibility provided to the agency by the domestic administrative laws to use interest-based processes may vary from country to country. However, regardless of the degree of flexibility available, because of the public nature of the measures at issue and the agency involved, any negotiation will certainly occur in the shadow of the law. In this regard, it is very likely that the agency concerned would assess the problem raised by the investor exclusively in terms of its field of competence and policy priorities, rather than in terms of the potential liability derived from an IIA. Further, even if the norms and obligations of the IIA are taken into consideration at this stage, the general and vague language used in most agreements raises complex interpretation issues

that may be difficult for any public agency to deal with without specialised legal advice.

If the problem remains unresolved, time will pass, and the disagreement and the investor's non-conformity will continue. Further, as a consequence of the application or the contested measure, damages may be
inflicted on the investor. The conflict will continue to ferment until the
investor, motivated by the economic cost generated by the unmanaged
conflict, will seek legal assistance and explore the alternatives for obtaining redress. If at this stage the attempts to resolve the conflict amicably
have not rendered any particular positive result, it is likely that the lawyer
assisting the investor will advise the affected investor to consider resort
to investor–state arbitration under the IIA, and then formally present the
competent authorities of the host state with a notice of intent to submit a
claim to arbitration. Figure 18.1 illustrates the continuum in the evolution of an investor–state dispute.

As Figure 18.1 illustrates, by the time the investor submits a notice of
intent to arbitrate, the conflict will have crystallised into a dispute. The
unattended conflict will have evolved into a defined, focused disagreement, framed in clear legal terms and requiring a particular form of
relief, that is a request for compensation for the damages generated by
the actions of the government. This determination regarding the moment
when the conflict evolves into a dispute is particularly relevant, as in the
investor–state context the political economy of conflict management is
likely to be quite different from the political economy of dispute resolution. This point is further developed in section 2.

2.   The practical implication of distinguishing between conflict management and dispute resolution: overcoming the barriers for amicable solutions to investment-related problems

This chapter argues that, in the context of investor–state relations, one
of the most important practical implications of making the distinction
between conflict management and dispute resolution is that such differentiation enables us to understand the scenario where interest-based
problem-solving techniques, which are different from adjudication, may
be more likely to be politically feasible. As explained above, by the time
the conflict has crystallised into a dispute, the dynamics of the unresolved
conflict between the investor and the host state will probably generate a
situation in which various structural factors – in particular those related
to the hybrid private–public nature of the dispute – play against enabling

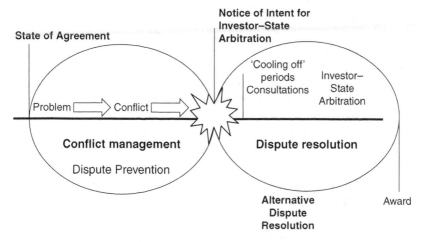

Figure 18.1.   The conflict 'continuum' in the investment context
Source: Author.

the parties to reach a negotiated settlement. However, here we argue that most of these critical barriers apply only once an investor–state dispute has come into existence, and thus they do not hold in situations where the conflicts have not yet crystallised into disputes under the applicable IIA. Let us develop this assertion further.

From the perspective of the host state, when a foreign investor submits a legal claim to investor–state arbitration, that very action has at least four very sensitive political implications. First, there is an open challenge against a measure which may be pursuing legitimate public policy objectives. This may lead to an outcry from several sectors that may not only wish to defend the measure, but may also oppose having any foreign investor second-guessing domestic legislation in foreign tribunals. If the investor–state conflict were properly managed at an early stage, interest-based processes could create value for both parties, and focus the discussion on *how the application* of the measure could still pursue its public policy objectives and yet simultaneously prevent the inconveniences that have led the conflict with the investor to arise in the first place. Thus, the challenge to the public measure, and the political cost associated with such a challenge, could be prevented.

Second, an investor–state claim also entails the openly public allegation by the investor that the host state is violating its international obligations.

To some degree, such an allegation represents a 'harassment' effect for the accused sovereign state, leading to defensive attitudes being adopted by government officials who find it difficult to recognise any such breach – even assuming that the violation was actually happening and that they privately knew about it. Again, if an interest-based solution to the problem were found – even if it was the result of negotiations under the shadow of the law – the investor would never submit a claim to arbitration, and thus a public allegation of a breach of any international obligation would never arise in the first place.

Third, an investor–state claim also entails the request of the investor for compensation, usually of significant amounts of money. In addition to compensation, any payment entails an additional political cost for the host state associated with having to pay a foreign investor – often a transnational corporation – large amounts of fiscal resources that could otherwise have been spent on public projects critical for the development of the country. Avoiding the economic and political costs of arbitration is one of the most evident and politically attractive potential advantages of appropriate management of the investor–state conflict. Early management of the conflict could easily prevent any significant damage being inflicted on any of the parties involved in the conflict. Further, the conflict could be resolved through solutions that may not require the use of public fiscal resources at all.

Fourth, the submission of a treaty-based claim to investor–state arbitration also means that dispute will be brought before a foreign tribunal, which will enact a binding decision on the parties. Having an arbitration tribunal resolving the dispute often leads to claims of violations of sovereignty and lack of legitimacy of the adjudication process. If properly managed, the investor–state conflict would never reach the dispute resolution stage, and thus there would never be an arbitration tribunal adjudicating. A further key feature of interest-based procedures is that they would allow the parties themselves to keep control of the process of managing their conflict. Even if the parties requested the assistance of a third party to help them reach an agreement – for instance through the use of preventive ADR techniques – the inherently voluntary nature of these processes ensures the total control of the parties.

In sum, the practical implication of making the distinction between investor–state dispute resolution and investor–state conflict management is that such differentiation can overcome some of the structural barriers associated with the private–public nature of investment disputes, which make it very difficult for investors and host states to use non-litigious approaches to address their grievances. That is why experts have rightly recognised that 'the best chance to resolve a dispute between a foreign investor and a government agency is likely before the investment dispute becomes a dispute under an investment treaty.'[33]

II. The two fundamental dimensions of dispute prevention

In addressing the structural difficulties acting as disincentives for amicable resolution of investor–state disputes, we referred to three broad categories of barriers. First, those related to the lack of the necessary infrastructure to enable interest-based conflict resolution in the investor–state context. Second, barriers related to the private–public nature of investor–state disputes, and third, barriers related to the lack of clarity and evolving nature of international investment law. In the last section we explained how the barriers related to the private–public nature of investor–state disputes can be overcome by managing the conflict before it escalates into a dispute under the applicable IIA. The two remaining categories of barriers to interest-based processes shed light on two areas that require attention to foster effective prevention of treaty-based investor–state disputes.

In this regard, it is worth noting that the prevention of investor–state disputes could be visualised as comprising two broad dimensions: a 'substantive' and a 'procedural' one. From a substantive point of view, prevention of investor–state disputes has a strong link with the level of clarity and precision of provisions in IIAs. Simply stated, the more clear and precise the obligations of IIAs, the less need for the parties applying the agreement to elucidate their application in specific practical situations. The problem is that in the context of IIAs, and in particular in the case of bilateral investment treaties (BITs) negotiated before the first investor-state disputes arose, several rights and obligations have been drafted in terms that are too general and vague.

Evidence shows that, since 2000, a significant number of investor-state disputes have arisen as a result of the lack of clarity of certain key substantive provisions of IIAs.[34] The number of issues submitted to

---

[33] Legum, 'The difficulties of conciliation in investment treaty cases', 3.

[34] The fact that a significant number of IIAs contain substantive provisions that have required clarification is evidenced not only by increased ISDS activity, but also by the impact that litigation has had on investment rule-making. Recent studies have documented how, since 2000, escalation in ISDS has led various states to redraft their IIAs to clarify several provisions and address some of the shortcomings revealed during the first years of investor–state litigation (UNCTAD, *Bilateral Investment Treaties 1995–2006:*

international arbitration tribunals for clarification is significant. With more than 390 treaty-based cases brought to investor–state arbitration by the end of 2010,[35] international arbitration tribunals have dealt with numerous issues that range from the clarification of what constitutes a covered investment for purposes of the application of an IIA, to clarifying the content of various standards of protection and treatment included in those agreements, for example fair and equitable treatment, national treatment and most-favoured nation (MFN) treatment, and the protection against unlawful expropriation.[36] Further, and as explained in section C.II.3, the variety in the specific formulation of the various standards of treatment and protection and the lack of clarity regarding the breadth and content of rights and obligations in IIAs has also been exacerbated by inconsistent jurisprudence.

Within this context, the relevant question for purposes of developing the protocols for avoiding investor–state disputes is: what could be done to foster greater clarity in the negotiation and interpretation of rules and obligations of IIAs? A complete answer to this question would clearly go beyond the scope of this chapter, as it would necessitate addressing myriad critical challenges affecting the patchy and extensive framework of IIAs that constitute the basis of contemporary international investment law. To a great extent, the other chapters in this volume precisely address those challenges. Further, options for better negotiation and greater coherence in the interpretation of IIAs have already been explored in the literature.[37] Thus, apart from flagging for the reader this dimension of the general notion of dispute prevention, this chapter focuses on the other more critical dimension of the concept.

In addition to the substantive considerations referred to above, the concept of dispute prevention also has a 'procedural' dimension. From this vantage point, dispute prevention entails a more concrete and tangible outcome, that is the development of the infrastructure necessary to

Trends in Investment Rulemaking (New York: United Nations, 2007) E.06.II.D.16; UNCTAD, *Investor–State Dispute Settlement And Impact On Investment Rulemaking* (New York: United Nations, 2007), pp. 71–87.

[35] UNCTAD, 'Latest Developments in Investor-state Dispute Settlement', *IIA Issues Note*, No. 1, March 2011.

[36] UNCTAD, *Bilateral Investment Treaties 1995–2006*; UNCTAD, *Investor–State Dispute Settlement And Impact On Investment Rule Making*, pp. 71–87.

[37] In addition to the extensive work produced by academia, UNCTAD has published numerous documents on this particular issue, which are available at: http://unctad.org/en/Pages/DIAE/International%20Investment%20Agreements%20(IIA)/Publications.aspx.

provide investors and host governments with the opportunity to manage their conflicts well before they escalate into full-blown disputes under the IIAs. Such infrastructure would clearly entail specialised human resources and capacity-building. However, the term infrastructure here mostly refers to the basic, underlying legal and institutional framework required to develop an investor–state conflict management system. In this regard, we propose here that such infrastructure may be developed through a series of policies and mechanisms, which in this context we denominate as investor–state dispute prevention policies (DPPs) and conflict management mechanisms (CMMs).

D. Creating the infrastructure for management of investor–state conflicts

I. Dispute prevention policies (DPPs)

In the literature and practice of international investment law and policy, dispute prevention is still a relatively new and unexplored idea. It has been preliminarily conceptualised as the action of 'minimizing potential areas of dispute through extensive planning in order to reduce the number of conflicts that escalate or crystallise into formal disputes'.[38] On this basis, DPPs can be defined as any course of action adopted and pursued by one or more governments, specifically aimed at preventing investor–state conflicts arising under IIAs from escalating into full-blown disputes under those agreements. The problem with this concept is that it is too general. Like any other area of public policy, DPPs can take a wide variety of forms and approaches. Further, DPPs can be implemented at the domestic and at the international level.

Governments may unilaterally design and implement DPPs at the domestic level through programmes promoting best administrative practices among their own agencies. For instance, governments may promote capacity-building on the content and potential impact of IIAs, or to develop better protocols for communication and coordination among the different state agencies dealing with foreign investors.

Second, governments may also seek an international concerted approach to designing and implementing DPPs. State-to-state cooperation can take numerous forms and approaches. For instance, states may agree on mechanisms to enable the parties to clarify the scope and

[38] UNCTAD, *Investor–State Disputes: Prevention and Alternatives to Arbitration*, p. xiv.

content of treaty provisions, or to negotiate effective incentives to induce both investors and governments to undertake conflict management processes seriously and in good faith before any notice of intent for arbitration is submitted.

II. Conflict management mechanisms (CMMs)

As part of the implementation of DPPs, governments may go a step further and design concrete procedural mechanisms, established either by law or contract, to enable investors and host states to step in early to manage investment-related conflicts and prevent dispute escalation, that is CMMs. Here we propose a typology distinguishing between two main categories of CMMs. The first category would comprise ad hoc CMMs resulting from the direct negotiation by the parties involved in a given relationship and embodied in a contract, and thus they are denominated as *contractual* dispute prevention mechanisms (DPMs). The second category of CMMs would comprise those investor–state conflict management mechanisms embedded within the institutional structure of the host state. Here these are denominated as *institutional* CMMs.

1. Contractual CMMs

Contractual CMMs would have to be negotiated by the investor and the host state well before any conflict arose, most probably in the context of the negotiation of an investment contract. In this scenario, the idea would be that, in addition to the substantive rights and obligations governing the investment relationship, the contract could include specific provisions prescribing procedures for managing any future conflicts with the explicit purpose of avoiding escalation to litigation. The use of contractual CMMs is a widespread practice in private contracts; thus, the notion is not really new. The novelty would be to envisage such practices in the investor–state context as part of the infrastructure required to establish an investor–state conflict management system.

In the investor–state context, contractual CMMs could either consist in mechanisms enabling the parties to consult directly among themselves to manage any conflict which may arise during the implementation of the contract, or could provide a particular problem-solving technique to allow a third party to assist in managing the conflict. The latter situation would entail the use of *preventive* ADR. Although originally envisaged to apply in situations where a dispute has already crystallised, studies published in the literature have recognised the application of ADR problem-solving techniques as methods to assist in the management of conflicts.[39] Dispute resolution boards, mediation, fact-finding or early neutral evaluation are just some of the preventive ADR techniques to which the parties to a contract could agree well before a conflict arises.

At least in theory, contractual CMMs have the advantage of enabling the parties involved in the potential conflict to tailor the mechanisms to fit the particular needs of their relationship. However, the main limitation of this kind of CMM is that, as already said, they would probably apply exclusively in situations where the relationship between the investor and the host state was regulated by a contract.

2. Institutional CMMs

Institutional CMMs can be defined as investor–state conflict management mechanisms institutionalised within the structure of the public administration of the host government. Unlike contractual CMMs, institutional CMMs would in principle apply horizontally to all investments, regardless of whether or not they are governed by an investment contract.

Empirical data reveals that around half the cases submitted to investor–state arbitration under IIAs do not arise from measures adopted at the central or national levels of government – the levels at which IIAs are negotiated. Rather, evidence shows that a significant number of investor-state disputes tend to arise with respect to measures adopted by municipal or provincial governments or by state agencies in charge of specific sectors of the economy.[40] Thus, institutional CMMs may be particularly useful in dealing with investment-related conflicts stemming from the application of inconsistent policies and measures by different government agencies – in particular, inconsistencies which could entail the liability of the host state under an IIA.

As a result of the increase in the use of investor–state arbitration and the associated costs, since 2000 an increasing number of governments have started to explore ways of being better prepared to handle disputes. Literature documenting these incipient administrative practices is scant.[41] However, such writings provide clear evidence of a critical fact:

---

[39] Constantino and Sickles Merchant, *Designing Conflict Management Systems*.

[40] S. Franck, 'Empirically evaluating claims about investment treaty arbitration', *North Carolina Law Review* 92 (2007), 1–87.

[41] UNCTAD, *Investor–State Disputes: Prevention and Alternatives to Arbitration*; UNCTAD, 'Latest Developments in Investor–State Dispute Settlement'; D. A. Pawlack and J. A. Rivas, 'Managing Investment Treaty Obligations and Investor–State Disputes: A Guide For Government Officials', in T. E. Carboneau and M. H. Mourra (eds.), *Latin*

that a number of governments are aware of the increase in investor–state litigation activity and are reacting by attempting to improve their administrative practices. Further, the early experiences with investor–state dispute preparedness also shed light on some of the key elements that standard protocols for institutional CMMs should include. Procedures for intra-governmental information, coordination and decision-making with respect to grievances raised by investors are some of the issues that various governments – especially those with experience as defendants in investor–state arbitration – have addressed and for which they have developed best practices which can inform the development of institutional CMMs.[42]

In addition to policies on dispute preparedness, some countries have also started to focus specifically on the exploration of mechanisms to prevent investor–state disputes. Given the novelty of the topic, and the non-existence of standard protocols for designing and implementing institutional CMMs, it is not surprising that so far the experience has been limited to very few countries. In these cases the dispute prevention initiatives have tended to be framed within the context of aftercare services provided by investment promotion agencies. The best-known example in this regard is the case of the Office of the Foreign Investment Ombudsman in the Republic of Korea.[43] In 2010 Russia also announced the creation of an Investment Ombudsman Office.[44] The experience of most governments regarding institutional CMMs certainly deserves further research. The scant literature has provided only a preliminary and casuistic description of the few best practices so far developed by a limited number of countries.[45] The conceptual framework developed in this chapter purports to be a preliminary contribution towards organising such research.

American Investment Treaty Arbitration: The Controversies and Conflicts (Leiden: Kluwer Law International, 2008).

[42] UNCTAD, *Investor–State Disputes: Prevention and Alternatives to Arbitration*.

[43] UNCTAD, 'Latest Developments in Investor–State Dispute Settlement'.

[44] 'In 2010 the President decided to establish the office of investment ombudsman to investigate complaints submitted by foreign investors. Per the President's directive, the Russian Government adopted a decision in August last year that an investment policy department will be set up at the Economic Development Ministry, and such a department was established.' Commentary by First Deputy Prime Minister Igor Shuvalov following the meeting with investment ombudsmen in federal districts, 2 August 2011. Official Site of the President of Russia, available at: http://eng.news.kremlin.ru/ref_notes/62/print.

[45] UNCTAD, *Investor–State Disputes: Prevention and Alternatives to Arbitration*.

On the basis of the analysis presented here, we offer a preliminary sketch of the essential elements that a standard protocol for the development and implementation of institutional CMMs should contain. This sketch does not claim to represent a design for a particular form of institutional CMM. The design of a specific conflict management system has to be undertaken, on a case-by-case basis, by the relevant investment stakeholders in a particular country. Thus, to propose a 'one size fits all' institutional CMM would clearly be inappropriate. Rather, the identification of the essential structural elements of institutional CMMs is intended to provide a framework that will permit stakeholders to create their own adaptive conflict management solutions, and apply these principles and approaches to their own specific political, legal and economic contexts.

Clearly, in most countries the appropriate development of institutional CMMs would be likely to entail the implementation of a comprehensive programme. Such a programme would have to be geared towards adjusting and modernising parts of the host state's public administration infrastructure to enable investment stakeholders to manage investor–state conflicts early on. As illustrated by Figure 18.2, we propose that a protocol for further research and implementation of institutional CMMs should comprise at least seven fundamental elements.

First, the preparation of a comprehensive investment stocktaking process represents the point of departure of any well-conceived national strategy for institutional CMMs. The purpose of an investment stocktaking process is to allow government authorities to obtain a clear diagnosis on three fundamental aspects:

- There should be clear identification of the concrete international legal obligations undertaken by the country through the different IIAs. Many countries have many IIAs in force, each with similar, but not identical, rules and disciplines. Through invocation of MFN, some investors may attempt to accumulate the guarantees provided by these different agreements.
- The stocktaking process should also lead to a clear profile of the main features of the foreign investment existing in the host country.
- The stocktaking analysis should also assess the different kinds of problems, conflicts and disputes known to have arisen between foreign investors and governmental authorities.

Thus, a complete investment stocktaking process should comprise at least three key components: a regulatory audit, an empirical analysis of

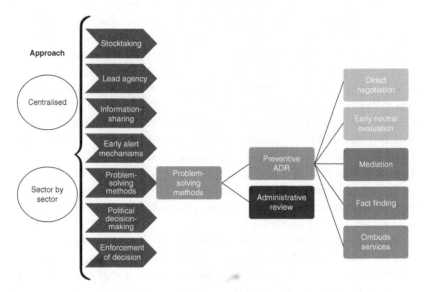

Figure 18.2. Institutional investor–state conflict management mechanisms
Source: Author.

investment stock and flows into the country, and a record of the investor–state conflict history of the country.[46]

Second, there should be an institutional structure clearly identifying the competent government agency in charge of implementing the CMMs. There is a clear consensus in the literature on the importance of having a lead agency within the government with the competence to coordinate the management of investor–state conflicts and disputes.[47] Further, experts agree that it is critical that the lead agency be provided with the necessary resources and political and legal authority to fully engage with the affected investor in conflict management processes.

Third, protocols for the development of institutional CMMs should also include efficient techniques for intra-governmental information-sharing. Information-sharing should enable the lead

---

[46] Pawlack and Rivas, 'Managing Investment Treaty Obligations and Investor–State Disputes; UNCTAD, 'Investor–State Disputes: Prevention and Alternatives to Arbitration', *UNCTAD Series on International Investment Policies for Development* (New York: United Nations, 2010).

[47] Legum, 'The difficulties of conciliation in investment treaty cases'; Pawlack and Rivas, 'Managing Investment Treaty Obligations and Investor–State Disputes'; UNCTAD, *Investor–State Disputes: Prevention and Alternatives to Arbitration*.

agency to coordinate the diffusion of relevant information to those agencies more likely to generate or to become involved in investment-related conflict. Information-sharing may involve substantive information on the contents and breadth of the obligations included in the different IIAs. It should also entail informing the highest possible number of governmental departments about the existence and purpose of the institutional CMMs in the host state, so that the departments know who to contact if they are doubtful about the consistency of their measures with IIAs or if a conflict with a foreign investor arises. In this regard, the role of the lead agency becomes critical, as it would act as the focal governmental contact point for the other agencies in all matters related to the application and implementation of IIAs.

Fourth, protocols for the development of institutional CMMs should also include early alert mechanisms. These mechanisms would enable the lead agency to learn about the existence of an investment-related conflict as early as possible. As previously explained, timing is a key variable in preventing a conflict from crystallising into a dispute under an IIA. Indeed, only by detecting the conflict early enough will institutional CMMs have a chance to operate.

Fifth, institutional CMMs must also envisage different problem-solving methods for the parties to use when seeking an interest-based solution to the conflict. Although the difference may be quickly resolved through administrative review by the host state of the measure generating the conflict, protocols on institutional CMMs should also provide the possibility for the affected investor and the host state to use preventive ADR techniques to manage their conflict. Mediation, fact-finding, early neutral evaluation or ombuds services are just some of the preventive ADR techniques that could be useful.[48] Even in the conflict management phase, government officials may still require the 'political cover' that only the participation of an independent expert third party could provide. We should recall that, to be able to find an amicable solution to a conflict, governments may always be asked to clearly and objectively demonstrate to their political constituencies that resolving the conflict is a better alternative for the host state than proceeding to litigation. The opinion of an independent expert may be critical to achieve this result.

Sixth, once the problem-solving process has enabled the parties to find a solution to the conflict, it is paramount that this solution receives the

---

[48] UNCTAD, *Investor–State Disputes: Prevention and Alternatives to Arbitration*.

approval of the appropriate political authority of the host state and the investor. Such high-level political endorsement would guarantee that the measure providing a solution to the problem would be effectively implemented. If such mechanisms are not clearly included in the proto-cols for institutional CMMs, there is the risk that the consensual solution to the conflict agreed by representatives of governments and investors may subsequently be ignored or not respected by one of the many other agencies of the government or even by higher hierarchical levels of the enterprise involved in the conflict.

Last but not least, and closely related to the aspect referred to above, the seventh essential element that should be included in a standard proto-col for the development of institutional CMMs is effective enforcement mechanisms to enable the decision resolving the conflict to actually stick, and be effectively implemented. Such mechanisms would prevent a con-flict, which in principle was resolved, from later escalating into a full-blown dispute as a result of the lack of compliance with the terms of the solution agreed by any of the parties.

E.   Conclusions

The significant escalation in the use of investor–state arbitration since 2000 has revealed a series of shortcomings of the existing ISDS system that risk eroding the legitimacy of the whole international investment regime. Although not all investment stakeholders share the same diagno-sis, there is a point on which most of them agree: existing dispute settle-ment procedures have turned out to be too expensive – both in economic and political terms – as well as being too slow and too indeterminate. Thus, the literature has started to explore the use of other non-litigious means of resolution for treaty-based disputes arising between investors and host states.

This chapter has explained how empirical evidence shows that con-sensual settlement of disputes between investors and host states is tak-ing place, not in the context of the application of existing ADR rules but rather, almost exclusively, within the context of investor–state arbitration proceedings. We have also unveiled the factors that explain this trend. After analysing the political and legal barriers, which in practice have prevented the use of interest-based approaches in the context of investor–state disputes, we have found that most of those obstacles do not apply in situations where the conflict has not yet crystallised into a dispute under an applicable IIA. Within this context, we have proposed a conceptual framework for the prevention of investor–state disputes based on the critical distinction between the notions of *dispute resolution* and *conflict management*.

Further, the dispute prevention framework develops the concepts of dispute prevention policies and conflict management mechanisms. Such policies and mechanisms would represent the fundamental infrastructure for enabling investment stakeholders to design, in a given context, a conflict management system. The rationale of such a system would be to enable host states and investors to effectively manage and resolve their conflicts before they escalate into full-blown investor–state arbitration disputes. Clearly, the conceptual framework developed in this chapter is just an initial step towards prevention of investor–state disputes. Research and policy in this new area of international investment law is just beginning, as is the potential usefulness of the conceptual framework to assist in organising those endeavours.

In the current interdependent world, the search for alternatives to investor–state dispute resolution entails much more than a procedural discussion. In fact it raises a profound philosophical question: what should the parameters of governance orienting the evolution of the international investment regime be?

The differentiation between power-based, rights-based and interest-based dispute resolution used in the context of conflict theory is quite useful when translated to the context of the historical evolution of international investment relations and international investment law in particular. Whereas investor–state investment disputes used to be predominantly resolved through diplomatic protection – an approach that in practice led to power-based dispute resolution – with the proliferation of IIAs and the increase in investor–state arbitration the trend has shifted towards rights-based dispute resolution.

Thus, international investment relations have become increasingly 'rule-oriented' rather than being 'power oriented', in the sense that they have become increasingly governed by rules and principles included in conventional instruments of international law rather than by political and economic might.[49] In general, this should be considered a positive development for both international and domestic investment

---

[49] Jackson, *The World Trading System*, p. 109; Franck, 'Development and outcomes of investment treaty arbitration'.

governance.[50] However, the legalisation of international investment relations is also exerting strong pressures on host countries' administrations, leading various political actors to resist these pressures, and to challenge the legitimacy of the current international investment regime. Within this context, it is not surprising that a significant share of the literature on international investment law has recently focused on how this regime – and ISDS procedures in particular – should be revisited and adjusted to properly respond to the realities of the twenty-first century.[51]

No one could argue that the current international investor–state arbitration mechanisms in IIAs do not need to be improved – there may be, however, significant disagreements as to what kind of improvements to make and how they should be implemented. However, regardless of this discussion, this chapter has demonstrated that any serious attempt to modernise the international investment regime should be made bearing in mind that, to perform its function properly, the regime can no longer afford to leave all problems arising between investors and host states to be exclusively addressed through adjudication.

After almost two decades of experience with investor–state arbitration, the time has come for the international investment regime to complement *dispute resolution* procedures with *conflict management* mechanisms. There are several justifications for this assertion. First, this chapter has explained how, in principle and from many vantage points, consensual solutions to investor–state conflict would be much more efficient than adjudication. We have made reference to the views among investment stakeholders that such procedures have turned out to be too costly – both in economic and in political terms – too slow and too indeterminate. Second, the exclusive reliance on adjudication as a means to manage investor–state conflict is generating such high economic and political costs that the legitimacy of the international investment regime is being corroded. This is a serious problem if we take into account how central the

---

[50] Today no one could seriously argue that power-based dispute resolution should predominate in international economic relations.

[51] Some governments have even taken a more radical reactive approach in response to the increase in investor–state litigation. While some, like the government of Australia, have started to refrain from continuing to negotiate investor–state dispute settlement provisions in IIAs, others, such as some South American countries, have even taken steps to withdraw from international conventions regulating those procedures. It may be too early to tell whether these decisions will represent a trend or will remain isolated instances, but what seems clear is that such policies go in the direction of returning to an era where investor–state conflict was resolved through diplomatic protection.

relations between investors and host states have become within current international economic dynamics. As Reisman clearly points out:

> The popular demand to increase national wealth and, through some form of distribution, to expand economic and other life opportunities for all citizens, is a universal feature of modern political life. *That this demand can be met solely by autochthonous national development is no longer seriously argued.* Responsible officials at the national level, knowing that positive development now requires a constant flow of incoming and outgoing investment, *have little choice but to participate in the making and applying of international investment law.*[52]

It is time to conceive the application of international investment law as going beyond litigation. After evolving from power-based to rule-based dispute settlement, it is time for the international investment regime to evolve, and to incorporate interest-based conflict management mechanisms. The conceptual framework developed in this chapter is an attempt at an initial contribution to guide further research and policy in this new potential dimension of international investment law.

[52] Reisman, 'International Investment Arbitration and ADR', p. 25 (emphasis added).

19

The growth in investment litigation: perspectives and challenges

LAURENCE BOISSON DE CHAZOURNES

In their chapters, Margrete Stevens and Roberto Echandi have both advanced some thought-provoking ideas on investor–state dispute settlement. A few points raised by their contributions will be addressed below.

Let me first refer to the proposal for having rules of ethics for counsel acting before International Centre for Settlement of Investment Disputes (ICSID) tribunals and supposedly also before other investment tribunals. Although I consider that it is important to have a set of international rules of ethics governing counsel, as well as rules of ethics governing arbitrators and experts, I would be cautious about making it a sort of *lex specialis* in the investment area. We should have a *lex professionalis* that is closely modelled on similar rules that also apply to international courts and tribunals and reinforce systemic integrity.[1]

I would like to refer to the recently adopted International Law Association (ILA) *Hague Principles on Ethical Standards for Counsel Appearing before International Courts and Tribunals*, which concern counsel in ICSID and other dispute settlement proceedings to which a state is party. These Principles constitute an attempt to establish minimal common standards of conduct for counsel in international fora. They were intended to stimulate discussion in the international community of lawyers and practitioners and to encourage further developments.[2] Having been involved in the drafting process of these rules, I believe that

---

[1] See, e.g., Chapter 4 of the Regulations of the International Criminal Court ('Counsel Issues and Legal Assistance'); the Code of Conduct for European Lawyers (produced by the Council of Bars and Law Societies of Europe); and the ongoing work of the IBA Arbitration Committee's Task Force on Counsel Ethics, www.ibanet.org/Article/Detail.aspx?ArticleUid=610bbf6e-cf02–45ae-8c3a-70dfdb2274a5.

[2] See P. Sands, 'Introduction to the ILA Hague Principles on Ethical Standards for Counsel Appearing before International Courts and Tribunals', *The Law and Practice of International Courts and Tribunals* 10(1) (2011), 1–5.

the Principles have greatly benefited from an exchange of knowledge concerning counsels' experiences and the practices of various courts and tribunals.[3] In this context I believe that, if it is necessary to have a specific set of rules in the investment field, investment arbitration should draw from this experience in other international dispute settlement fora.

However, while we should not isolate ICSID, we should still take into account its peculiarities. ICSID is one of the institutions of the World Bank Group, and much of the desired change and restructuring would have to rely on World Bank decision-makers for its implementation. There is thus a need to raise the profile of the Centre within the World Bank Group. In this respect, it is interesting to note that in the reports produced in the context of the last round of Bretton Woods reforms (catalysed in large part by the initiative of the Group of Twenty (G20)), no mention was made of ICSID. This need to strengthen ICSID within the World Bank Group is particularly timely, as the World Bank – and not just the International Finance Corporation (IFC) and Multilateral Investment Guarantee Agency (MIGA) – is increasingly involved in activities linked to the private sector. The World Bank and the ICSID clearly have a common interest in strengthening the capabilities of the latter, particularly the solidity and fairness of its procedures.

A second issue with a similar thrust concerns the enforcement of awards. Stevens' chapter reminds us of Articles 53 and 54 of the ICSID Convention. Obviously, these provisions do not have the legal persuasiveness that they should. There is room for creativity so as to ensure better compliance with ICSID awards, and ways to strengthen compliance should be explored.

There, too, inspiration could be drawn from other fora for ensuring compliance with awards. It is interesting in this context to note the initiatives that the United Nations (UN) Secretary-General and other UN bodies took to ensure compliance with the decisions of the International Court of Justice (ICJ) through the establishment of mixed commissions or the sending of observers. The President of the World Bank as well as the Administrative Council of ICSID might be inspired to develop similar initiatives. These initiatives could, inter alia, allow for the monitoring of compliance with awards. At present, there is no such monitoring system. The practice of the World Trade Organization (WTO) could also

---

[3] See Study Group on the Responsibility of International Organisations, 'Report of the Seventy-Fourth Conference (Held in The Hague, 15–19 August 2010)', *International Law Association Reports of Conferences* 74 (2011), 956–60.

provide some insights in this respect, if one considers its surveillance mechanism.[4]

Another avenue that could be explored is the establishment of a group of 'friends of ICSID'. Many international organisations have established such groups to help them confront the future. With this, I mean a group of state representatives or a group of people with a high profile on the international scene – working or not with the World Bank – and possibly with a connection to the ICSID dispute settlement practice. Such a group could devise new ways of thinking about the importance of ensuring the viability of ICSID in the long term and about ensuring compliance with arbitration decisions in particular.

The third point I would like to raise concerns the 'finality' of an award. Echandi alludes to this point in an *a contrario* manner when discussing the sensitive political consequences of voluntary settlement through diplomatic means. He rightly reminds us that, for political reasons, it is often easier to permit an independent international tribunal to take decisions in the last resort. This relieves states of the responsibility to resolve disputes through negotiations and to face the domestic political consequences arising from the concessions inevitably made in the process. This behaviour pattern is also familiar in other dispute settlement fora, such as the WTO and the ICJ.

In this context, the investor–state dispute prevention concept that was introduced has great virtues. Obviously, there is a need for better coordination in the way governments internally manage and respond to investment decisions and issues. This can be achieved through the development of dispute prevention policies. In particular, the creation of 'focal points' within host state governments – to which parties can turn when difficulties arise – could prevent conflicts from evolving into legal disputes. Here I would refer to the so-called Internal Market Problem Solving System (SOLVIT) system introduced by the European Commission to take some pressure off the normal infringement procedure against Member States. In this system a Member State citizen or business that alleges a public authority's misapplication of internal market law can submit its case to its local SOLVIT centre, which generally proposes a resolution within ten weeks.[5]

---

[4] See Article 21 of the Understanding on Rules and Procedures Governing the Settlement of Disputes, Annex 2 of the World Trade Organization (WTO) Agreement, available at: www.wto.org/english/tratop_e/dispu_e/dsu_e.htm#21.

[5] Internal Market Problem Solving System (SOLVIT) website, http://ec.europa.eu/solvit/site/about/index_en.htm.

Now turning to the internationally concerted mechanisms that Echandi proposed, they raise a challenging paradox or an 'open dialectic'. In an area where encouraging private sector foreign investment through direct access to remedies used to be an article of faith, more and more interstate mechanisms are now proposed for consultation and conciliation purposes. This emerging interstate trend has the colour of diplomatic protection without the content. Owing to the risk of politicisation of investment disputes that states' intervention carries, safeguards should be considered to ensure that these mechanisms do not create hurdles to investor remedies. Principles of global administrative law, such as the principles of accountability and openness, might be able to play the role of procedural safeguards.[6] Principles of comity may also play a role in this context.

My fourth point is that alternative dispute resolution (ADR) techniques have positive features that should also be promoted in investment disputes. They play both a preventive and a remedial role. As suggested by both authors, there is room to persuade the stakeholders of the advantages of ADR. In the first place, Echandi has rightly targeted the economic costs, but he has also mentioned the political and social costs attached to international litigation. In this context, ADR imposes lighter burdens. However, there would be a need to work more on the social aspects of ADR and their acceptance by groups of concerned citizens. There might be a need for more transparency in order to involve all stakeholders in the decisions. More access to information may encourage greater use of ADR, as it would contribute to broadening the acceptance of ADR's legitimacy.

I would like to end by noting that neither Stevens nor Echandi has referred to the need to establish an appeal mechanism or a *Cour de Cassation* in the field of investment dispute resolution. Discussion of 'finality' might extend beyond the rendering of an award. I do not have a settled view on this issue, but looking once more to other dispute settlement fora, one can note a trend towards embracing two-tiered judicial mechanisms in judicial fora in which non-state parties have access. Can the legitimacy of the investment dispute settlement system escape discussion of this issue?

---

[6] On these principles, see B. Kingsbury, N. Krisch and R. B. Stewart, 'The emergence of global administrative law', *Law and Contemporary Problems* 68(3) (2005), 16–61.

20

Different approaches to address challenges arising from increased investor–state litigation

ANDREA K. BJORKLUND

The international community is continually seeking to perfect dispute settlement. Whether institutional or ad hoc, arbitration has been the preferred way to resolve disputes between states and, in recent years, between states and private individuals. Arbitration permits disputing parties to avoid courts that might be biased in favour of one of them, and avoids jurisdictional restrictions imposed by municipal laws on sovereign immunity. In addition arbitration, at least in its ideal form, offers a cheaper and faster alternative to fully-fledged litigation. Yet arbitration, whether commercial or investor–state, has now come to resemble its more formal rival, litigation. Long-drawn-out American-style discovery, no-holds-barred cross-examination, and voluminous pleadings at both the jurisdictional and merits stages all feature in arbitration.[1] Concerns about inequality of arms between the parties to an investor–state dispute and more generally about the cost, complexity and torpor of the investor–state dispute settlement process in particular have also prompted thinking about change.

International investment arbitration is thus ripe for improvement.[2] There is no shortage of problems subject to reform proposals. The two chapters discussed below tackle divergent issues – modification of an existing institution versus the creation of an entirely new process. Their

---

[1] See T. Stipanowich, 'Arbitration: the new litigation', *Illinois Law Review* 1 (2010), 1–59; A. K. Bjorklund, 'The emerging civilization of investment arbitration', *Penn State Law Review* 113 (2009), 1269–300.

[2] In 2007 Columbia's Vale Center on Sustainable International Investment Law hosted a symposium on 'What's Next in International Investment Law and Policy? Improving the International Investment Law and Policy System'. Papers from that conference are published in J. E. Alvarez and K. P. Sauvant (with K. G. Ahmed and G. Vizcaíno), *The Evolving International Investment Regime: Expectations, Realities, Options* (Oxford University Press, 2011).

approaches are appropriately different: Margrete Stevens suggests modest but potentially powerful modifications to the functioning of that now-venerable institution, the International Centre for Settlement of Investment Disputes (ICSID), while Roberto Echandi has designed a new conceptual framework that, if implemented, would forestall investor–state dispute settlement by identifying and resolving burgeoning conflicts before they could blossom into fully-fledged disputes.

Stevens draws on her intimate knowledge of ICSID to suggest practical improvements to the workings of that institution. Of her ten suggestions, no fewer than four relate specifically to decision-makers. They encompass increasing the availability and variety of arbitrators appointed by ICSID, enhancing their training and their interaction with users of the system, and placing more emphasis on the appointment of trained mediators to ICSID's panel of conciliators. She also suggests formalising the feedback ICSID receives from its constituency by implementing case surveys, republishing and updating the explanatory notes to ICSID's arbitration rules, appointing one or more Deputy Secretaries-General, promulgating ethics rules to govern counsel arbitrating ICSID cases, and using the World Bank to encourage recalcitrant states to pay ICSID awards. Finally, she suggests establishing an ICSID 'users' group', comprising representatives of states and investors, as well as counsel and arbitrators, who would consult regularly with the ICSID Secretariat to ensure timely and free communication among interested entities.

Echandi's focus is an ambitious attempt to establish a framework to *prevent*, rather than resolve, disputes and which could be implemented in any country. His proposal has to overcome the barriers to dispute prevention that exist in the multi-headed hydra that is government in many states. To that end, he has formulated a set of dispute prevention policies for governments to adopt and, further, a set of dispute prevention mechanisms to facilitate the actual implementation of those policies. These are flexible enough to be implemented notwithstanding differences in governmental structure. Intra-governmental information-sharing is one key component of this strategy; another is ensuring that the information be transmitted to those officials with the authority to engage in conflict prevention procedures. He perceptively identifies the divide that too often exists between the agency with knowledge and potential involvement in the simmering conflict and the agency that might have knowledge of the potential liability the state would face vis-à-vis an applicable international investment agreement and, perhaps, a more objective assessment of the relative responsibility for the brewing problems.

Relatively few investment disputes are settled; formal alternative dispute resolution mechanisms are novel to governments, which in addition lack the will to settle for some of the same reasons that dispute prevention mechanisms have to be implemented carefully to overcome the difficulties posed by dispersed governmental authority. In addition to the barrier posed by bureaucratic complications, Echandi notes the barriers to the settlement of disputes inherent in the 'private/public' nature of the investment regime. Governmental decision-making is often slow, is subject to local administrative laws, and is done by politically accountable entities. Indeed, this last issue is often viewed as insurmountable – how does one ensure that those with the political authority to settle a dispute have the will to exercise that authority. In all too many cases an official might find it more politically expedient to postpone making decisions for which he would be accountable by letting an investor–state arbitration take its typically cumbersome, time-consuming course. In the event of a decision adverse to his government, if he still occupies the same position, he can blame the arbitral body. By proposing a conflict prevention mechanism, which in Echandi's framework would obviate the need for formal settlement talks (or arbitration), the problem of political calculation that subverts the possibility for settlement could be avoided.

A third significant barrier to the settlement of disputes is the lack of clarity about the obligations states have in international investment agreements. Settlement negotiations are facilitated when liability is clear; closer cases tend to lead to a more adversarial outcome, whether in litigation or arbitration.

By forestalling the coalescence of a dispute, Echandi's framework would bypass the barriers to settlement and bypass the expense and contentiousness of arbitration. Successful implementation of his proposals would facilitate a continued cooperative relationship between an investor and a host government. It would not foreclose all investor–state dispute settlement, but might dampen or avert some disputes.

Both sets of proposals should be taken seriously by the constituencies to which they are addressed. Stevens' proposals are first and foremost directed to the ICSID Secretariat itself, but to implement some of the proposals the Secretariat would need the support of its Member States. Echandi's proposals need to be implemented by states themselves. States and ICSID ought to take Stevens' proposals seriously; a relatively modest expenditure of resources could yield significant results. ICSID, as the premier investment arbitration institution, has an interest in continually striving to improve the services it provides, including the quality of the arbitrators it appoints and leveraging its association with the World Bank to ensure the enforcement of arbitration awards rendered under the ICSID Convention.

Investor–state dispute settlement is not going to disappear; its inclusion in more than 2,900 investment agreements ensures its survival. But investor–state dispute settlement is not and should not be the only method of resolving disputes; the United Nations Conference on Trade and Development (UNCTAD) has recently suggested alternatives to arbitration[3] and Echandi goes one step further in his creative, thoughtful, and potentially highly effective proposal that states take steps to ensure that they are well placed to assess and respond to problems even before they ripen into disputes. His proposals are a recipe for good governance that could help states resolve problems with private entities, whether they be foreign or domestic investors. Moreover, the dispute prevention mechanism could serve multiple purposes; in addition to conflict prevention it might also be able to facilitate settlement, if warranted, or to ensure a coordinated and well-thought-out strategy in responding to arbitration were a claim to be filed. Thus, a state's investment in a dispute prevention mechanism could pay dividends many times over.

[3] UNCTAD, *Investor–State Disputes: Prevention and Alternatives to Arbitration* (Geneva: United Nations, 2010).

PART V

The quest for an adequate balance between investment protection and liberalisation and other public policy objectives

21

Sustainable development and international investment law: a harmonious view from economics

ANNE VAN AAKEN AND TOBIAS A. LEHMANN

A. Introduction

At first sight, the goals of IIL and economic development should be perfectly aligned. After all, IIL developed after the International Centre for Settlement of Investment Disputes (ICSID) Convention[1] was negotiated under the auspices of the World Bank. The World Bank would not have had a mandate for negotiation had it not been for the goal of development. It is less clear, however, whether IIL also fosters sustainable development (SD). This chapter sets out to develop a conceptual understanding of IIL that includes economic insights. Whereas in trade law economic insights have been widely applied, even in application of the law, this is true to a much smaller extent in IIL. Furthermore, the political economy rationale has been explored in trade law, but not in IIL. This chapter aims at filling this gap by surveying the economic insights into the link between foreign direct investment (FDI) and SD and suggesting appropriate interpretive arguments and places (jurisdictional phase v. merits phase) in investment arbitration. Coupling IIL and economic insights might help not only to ground IIL firmly in the goals it pursues, but also to change to treaty-making and treaty interpretation by putting them on an evidence basis.

First, in section B, we will clarify what we mean by SD, since the term is still unclear and its definition disputed. Then we explore the economic

We gratefully acknowledge the help in style editing provided by the Institute for Advanced Study Berlin. This chapter was written during the author's stay at the Institute and we gratefully acknowledge all the support from the staff. We would also like to thank our commentator, Susan Franck, at the World Trade Forum in Bern, September 2011 for her very constructive comments. Gratitude is also due to the participants in the discussion.

[1] Convention on the Settlement of Investment Disputes between States and the Nationals of Other States, Washington DC, 18 March 1965, in force 14 October 1966, 575 UNTS 159.

insights into the assumed causal link between international investment agreements (IIAs) and foreign direct investment (FDI) as well as between FDI and economic growth. Last but not least, we will discuss the correlation between growth as measured by gross domestic product (GDP) and welfare indices such as the Human Development Index (HDI). This will inform us about the empirical insights into the relationship between IIAs and SD, which is discussed in section C. In section D we will develop our own political economy model, based on the one used in trade theory, and discuss the presumed insights into the impact of IIAs on the 'good governance' of host states, since both are crucial for understanding the development impact of IIAs. Although treaty-drafting would be the best way to integrate SD into IIL, changes are achieved very slowly by this means. Therefore, section E offers suggestions as to how treaty interpretation of IIAs can be used to foster the goal of SD, based on the economic insights. Section F concludes the chapter.

B.   The concept of sustainable development

Economic growth and development theories have a long and controversial history but they are closely connected to SD.[2] SD is traditionally understood, as defined in the Brundtland Report, as development that 'implies meeting the needs of the present without compromising the ability of future generations to meet their own needs'.[3] A consensus has arisen that economic growth alone is not enough. Rather, the economic, social, and environmental aspects of any action are interconnected and have to be viewed together. Considering only one of them at a time might lead to errors in judgement and 'unsustainable' outcomes.[4] Thus, at the core of SD are three pillars: society, the economy and the environment. People and their rights, habitats and economic systems are interrelated. 'A society (or communities within a larger society) that faces unrest, poverty and disease will not develop in the long term: social well-being and economic well-being feed off each other, and the whole game depends on a

---

[2] For an overview and new developments, see, e.g., J. Y. Lin, 'New structural economics: a framework for rethinking development', *The World Bank Research Observer* 26 (2011), 193–221, available at: http://wbro.oxfordjournals.org/content/26/2/193.full.pdf+html.

[3] United Nations General Assembly, 'Report of the World Commission on Environment and Development', General Assembly Resolution 42/187, 11 December 1987, available at www.un.org/documents/ga/res/42/ares42–187.htm and Brundtland Report, *Our Common Future* (Oxford University Press, 1987), p. 43.

[4] T. Strange and A. Bayley, 'Sustainable Development: Linking Economy, Society, Environment', *OECD Insights* (2008), p. 25.

healthy biosphere in which to exist.'[5] There are thus many human rights relevant to SD, especially those included in the International Covenant on Economic, Social and Cultural Rights,[6] such as the right to health. We will follow the approach proposed by the Organisation for Economic Co-operation and Development (OECD) and take a broader view of SD, thus including not only environment but also good governance and rule of law. As the OECD acknowledges, governance and regulatory factors, too, can impede or hinder sustainability.[7]

This observation has been confirmed by empirical studies, which find that institutions, including legal institutions, are crucial for economic development (and for other aspects of development).[8] An integrationist approach seems to be the state of the art, the consensus being that capital investment (let alone FDI investment) is insufficient for economic development and even more so for SD.[9]

C. Empirical insights into investment and development

Economics as a discipline informs us on the question of whether, how and under what circumstances FDI is beneficial for host countries. Economic writings have expressed many different viewpoints on FDI. Let us start again with the purely economic rationale of IIAs, including the empirical evidence relevant to the theory. The classical theoretical causal chain assumed by treaty makers (and classical economic textbooks) is that IIAs[10] foster FDI, FDI leads to economic growth, and growth leads to enhanced welfare of the population. The assumed causation from IIAs and FDI to enhanced welfare is not an unequivocal one, although the assumption often seems to be that not only investment as such, but also FDI contributes

---

[5] *Ibid.*, p. 27. See U. Beyerlin, 'Sustainable Development' in R. Wolfrum (ed.), *Max Planck Encyclopedia of Public International Law* (Oxford University Press, 2009): online edition, for an overview of SD in international law, available at: www.mpepil.com/subscriber_ article?script=yes&id=/epil/entries/law-9780199231690-e1609&recno=2&searchType= Quick&query=sustainable+development.

[6] International Covenant on Economic, Social and Cultural Rights, opened for signature 16 December 1966, in force 3 January 1976, 993 UNTS 3.

[7] Strange and Bayley, 'Sustainable Development'.

[8] M. J. Trebilcock and R. J. Daniels, *Rule of Law Reform and Development. Charting the Fragile Path of Progress* (Cheltenham: Edward Elgar, 2009), p. 12.

[9] B. Levy and F. Fukuyama, 'Development Strategies: Integrating Governance and Growth' World Bank Policy Research Working Paper Series (2010), available online at SSRN: http://ssrn.com/abstract=1547635.

[10] Including bilateral investment treaties (BITs) as well as investment chapters in economic partnership agreements.

to growth. It is precisely this belief, coupled with immense and some-times costly efforts to attract FDI, that has triggered extensive research by academics, mainly economists. We now know that some of these causal assumptions are empirically fragile or that the assumed causal link works only under certain circumstances.

The empirical evidence on the correlation of the first relationship between IIAs and FDI is mixed.[11] Although many studies have been undertaken since 2000, no consensus on the causation from IIAs to FDI has been reached. Furthermore, the positive relationship between FDI and growth is empirically shaky.[12] The empirical results on the positive spillovers of FDI have been mixed and depend very much on the sector and type of FDI (everything else being equal). The value added by FDI is usually assumed to be better technological or management know-ledge, thereby leading to enhanced productivity (which is the key driver for growth).[13] It is also found that complementary activities of domestic firms are enhanced through FDI, for example by the demand of multi-national enterprises (MNEs) for intermediaries: this can be the expansion of upstream industries that induce additional demand from MNEs for

---

[11] See M. Hallward-Driemeier, 'Do Bilateral Investment Treaties Attract FDI? Only a Bit ... and They Could Bite', World Bank Policy Research Working Paper No. WPS 312 (2003), available at: http://wdsbeta.worldbank.org/external/default/WDSContentServer/IW3P/IB/2003/09/23/000094946_03091104060047/Rendered/PDF/multi0page.pdf; J. Tobin and S. Rose-Ackerman, 'When BITs have some bite: the political-economic environment for bilateral investment treaties', *Review of International Organizations* (2010), 1–32; E. Neumayer and L. Spees, 'Do bilateral investment treaties increase foreign direct invest-ment to developing countries?' *World Development* 33 (2005), 1567–85; J. W. Salacuse and N. P. Sullivan, 'Do BITs really work? An evaluation of bilateral investment treaties and their grand bargain', *Harvard International Law Journal* 46 (2005), 67–130; J. Webb Yackee, 'Do bilateral investment treaties promote foreign direct investment? Some hints from alternative evidence', *Virginia Journal of International Law* 51 (2010), 397–441. Usually more relevant are: market potential, market growth, RTAs (for hub and spoke), general conditions of investment, human capital (skills), resources etc. See UNCTAD, *World Investment Report* (New York: UNCTAD, 2003). For a summary of the empirical findings, see UNCTAD, *The Role of International Investment Agreements in Attracting Foreign Direct Investment to Developing Countries* (Geneva: United Nations, 2009).

[12] There is not even a theoretical consensus on the relationship between FDI and growth; rather one can distinguish three positions: the Washington Consensus; sceptics; and dirigisme resurrected. For a recent survey, see M. Irandoust, 'A survey of recent devel-opments in the literature of FDI-led growth hypothesis', *Journal of World Investment & Trade* 11 (2010), 275–91.

[13] For an overview of the empirical studies, see for example T. Moran and E. Graham and M. Blomström, 'Introduction and Overview' in T. Moran, E. Graham and M. Blomström (eds.), *Does Foreign Direct Investment Promote Development?* (Washington DC: Institute for International Economics, 2005).

local input and transfer expertise to suppliers (e.g. quality control, management techniques). There is no empirical evidence that an increased variety of inputs benefits downstream industries (e.g. through better technological input, like computers) – probably because this availability depends more on the trade regime, that is, the import openness of the host country. Consequently, there is more likely to be a positive effect in the services industry, as services are more local and frequently non-tradable or not readily tradable (e.g. telecommunications, banking and electricity). Also, there are wage spillovers, since MNEs usually pay higher wages, thus benefiting workers in foreign firms. Finally, as for the relationship between growth (usually measured as a change in GDP) and welfare, there is usually a correlation,[14] but if one accepts the view that welfare is better measured by the HDI (which in addition to GDP includes social indicators like education and health), a more differentiated picture emerges.[15] However, HDI can be equated with SD only to a certain extent, since SD also includes public goods such as the environment. There is thus only a partial overlap.

D.   The neglected variable: institutions

There is no longer any doubt that institutions are important for economic development as well as for SD. Law and development research has illuminated, in particular, the nexus between the rule of law and development. This cannot be extensively discussed here.[16] Suffice it to say that this nexus is no longer in question, although the details are controversial. We would like to focus here on the discussion on the spillover effects of IIAs on 'good

---

[14] M. Todaro and S. Smith, *Economic Development*, 9th edn (Boston: Addison Wesley, 2006), pp. 57–63. In many cases there are significantly different ratings, depending on whether one takes GDP or HDI.

[15] This concerns only the measurement. Clearly, there is an economic as well as a philosophical discussion on what constitutes human welfare. See A. K. Sen, *Development as Freedom* (Oxford University Press, 1999); A. K. Sen, *Commodities and Capabilities*, 4th edn (Delhi: Oxford University Press, 1999); A. K. Sen, 'Utilitarianism and welfarism', *Journal of Philosophy* 76 (1979), 463–89; A. K. Sen and B. Williams (eds.), *Utilitarianism and Beyond* (Cambridge University Press, 1982); A. K. Sen, 'Equality of What?' in A. K. Sen (ed.), *Choice, Welfare and Measurement* (Cambridge, MA: Harvard University Press, 1997).

[16] For overviews, see K. W. Dam, *The Law–Growth Nexus: The Rule of Law and Economic Development* (Washington DC: Brookings Institution, 2006); M. J. Trebilcock and K. E. Davis, 'The relationship between law and development: optimists versus skeptics', *American Journal of Comparative Law* 56 (2008), 895–946; Trebilcock and Daniels, *Rule of Law Reform and Development*, pp. 1–57.

governance' of the host states and the political economy rationale for concluding IIAs, since both seem important for the interpretation of IIAs.

I. *The possible impact of IIAs on host state institutions*

One idea raised by lawyers and taken up by economists and political scientists is that investment protection also contributes to the host states' 'good governance' and rule of law standards: 'Standards of due process and good governance required for FDI may spill over into domestic law and may set new standards also for the domestic legal system.'[17] At first glance, this would seem to provide a rationale for interpreting IIAs strictly in order to have as much spillover effect as possible. The idea behind this complementary view is that international law may help to improve national institutions, helping nationals (or foreign investors) to put pressure on their governments and helping governments to bind themselves. Drawing on the seminal book by Albert O. Hirschman,[18] one can distinguish exit, voice and loyalty as individual responses to the decline in a state's governance. If the international investor can easily exit from national administration of justice, no pressure will be put on the government by foreign investors – and local investors will not benefit. A complementary effect is thus not to be expected.

Although there is little empirical evidence available yet, one empirical study found no support for fostering good governance through IIAs;[19] rather, a crowding-out effect was found, resulting from the decision to bypass domestic courts. Another study also tested the influence of bilateral investment treaties (BITs) on institutional quality and did not find any direct influence of this kind.[20] Nevertheless, a certain minimum level of institutional quality is needed for IIAs to attract FDI.[21] There are, thus, complicated interaction effects.

[17] P. Muchlinski, F. Ortino and C. Schreuer, 'Preface' in P. Muchlinski, F. Ortino and C. Schreuer (eds.), *The Oxford Handbook of International Investment Law* (Oxford University Press, 2008), p. v.

[18] A. O. Hirschman, *Exit, Voice and Loyalty* (Cambridge, MA: Cambridge University Press, 1970).

[19] T. Ginsburg, 'International substitutes for domestic institutions: bilateral investment treaties and governance', *International Review of Law and Economics* 25 (2005), 107–23.

[20] J. P. Sasse, *An Economic Analysis of Bilateral Investment Treaties* (Wiesbaden: Gabler, 2011), pp. 160–9.

[21] Tobin and Rose-Ackerman, 'When BITs have some Bite', finding that BITs cannot entirely substitute for an otherwise weak investment environment. Rather, countries must have the necessary domestic institutions in place that interact with BITs to make these international commitments credible and valuable to investors.

II. The political economy question

The rationales that have traditionally been advanced to explain why developing countries enter into IIAs viewed the state as a unitary (benevolent) actor.[22] However, once we equate welfare with the notion of sustainable development, which we understand as including governance, the benevolent state approach is no longer appropriate as it excludes by definition several relevant aspects (e.g. rule of law, anti-corruption and participation). One possible remedy is to use a political economy approach, which recognises that the government (politician) may not maximise national economic welfare (as is implicitly assumed in the benevolent state approach), but instead its own welfare.[23] In the following, we focus solely on representative democracies – where an elected government acts on behalf of the citizens. This approach views regulations as being set by an incumbent government maximising its *political support*, that is its probability of re-election, and thus makes it possible to explain why regulations may favour consumers despite the better lobbying of producers.[24] It has been applied to trade policy formulation, but to the best of our knowledge not yet to negotiations on investment agreements. We attempt to remedy this shortcoming by applying the conceptual framework developed by Grossman and Helpman to IIA negotiations.[25] In their framework, the probability of re-election depends positively on the aggregate social welfare of voters and total political contributions. Political contributions can only be made by an organised interest group, namely a group of citizens sharing some common interest (e.g. firms, workers or consumers) that is organised. These interest groups make offers of political contributions to

---

[22] See A. T. Guzman, 'Why LDCs sign treaties that hurt them: explaining the popularity of bilateral investment treaties', *Virginia Journal of International Law* 38 (1998), 639–88; B. Simmons, Z. Elkins and T. Guzman, 'Competing for capital: the diffusion of bilateral investment treaties, 1960–2000', *Illinois Law Review* 1 (2008), 265–304; Ginsburg, 'International substitutes for domestic institutions'; and S. Montt, *State Liability in Investment Treaty Arbitration: Global Constitutional and Administrative Law in the BIT Generation* (Portland: Hart Publishing, 2009).

[23] Also suggesting a political economy rationale are: Trebilcock and Daniels, *Rule of Law Reform and Development*, p. 38ff., the reason that 'so many developing countries are either unwilling or unable to adopt strong rule of law institutions [might be the consequence of] political economy-based impediments'.

[24] S. M. Olson, *The Logic of Collective Action* (Cambridge, MA: Harvard University Press, 1971).

[25] G. M. Grossman and E. Helpman, 'Protection for sale', *American Economic Review* 84 (1994), 833–50 at 838, under the assumption that 'voters are more likely to re-elect a government that has delivered a high standard of living'.

the incumbent government conditional on the policies it chooses. Political contributions help politicians in future elections and thus increase their chances of being re-elected. Consequently, the economic efficiency of a given policy is in general not a concern – only the re-election probability associated with it.

Several empirical observations also support our view that the political economy framework is the appropriate one for analysing investment policies. A discussion of the empirical evidence regarding the impact of domestic groups on policy formation is beyond the scope of this chapter and we will solely focus on investment policies.[26] Kenneth J. Vandevelde, the United States chief BIT negotiator during the 1980s, notes that one of the reasons the USA did not exclude existing investments from the BIT (as repeatedly requested by other countries) was that this would have led to opposition by existing investors.[27] He thus explicitly acknowledges the relevance of a country's internal dynamics for the design of IIA policies, at least in the USA. More recently, domestic politics appear to have been central to Australia's decision to withdraw from investor–state international arbitration.[28] And finally, a recent empirical study focusing on tax incentives that aim at attracting FDIs suggests that domestic politics is a strong driver in FDI-related policies.[29] The study's main finding is that above-average[30] FDI incentives increase the probability of re-election – strongly supporting a political economy approach to the formulation of FDI policies. These results, however, hold true only when voters believe that the investment will create new jobs. This may be true for reductions in tax liabilities for new investments, but clearly not for all FDIs (e.g. not for FDIs in relation to strategic takeovers). Furthermore, the study is a partial equilibrium analysis because it neglects the impact of such policies on political contributions. Taking into account the indirect effect of

---

[26] For an overview, see D. C. Mueller, *Public Choice III* (Cambridge University Press, 2003), pp. 350–3.

[27] K. J. Vandevelde, *US International Investment Agreements* (New York: Oxford University Press, 2009), p. 111: 'the Senate would be less likely to give its … consent to a BIT lacking the enthusiastic support of existing investors.'

[28] K. Tienhaara and P. Ranald, 'Australia's rejection of investor–state dispute settlement: four potential contributing factors', *Investment Treaty News* 1(4) (2011), 6–7: '[t]he ALP has a minority government and is reliant on the support of some independents and Greens … the need to retain this support is likely to strengthen [its] position against ISDS.'

[29] N. M. Jensen and E. J. Malesky, 'Pass the Bucks: Investment Incentives as Political Credit-Claiming Devices. Evidence from a Survey Experiment', Working Paper Series (2010), available at: http://ssrn.com/abstract=1669771.

[30] Better incentives than competitors, i.e. countries with which one competes to attract FDIs.

political contribution on re-election may yield a different net effect if the policies adversely affect the local firms' profits. Both shortcomings are relevant here.

In the following, we roughly sketch the structure of the type of political economy model we have in mind and then compare its predictions for developed countries to the United States' position with respect to IIAs during the 1980s. We focus on two countries, a developed and a developing one. Each country is composed of firms and voters. Ownership represents a negligible proportion of the total voting population: the voting population is thus solely composed of individuals who are both workers in a specific industry and consumers. We further assume that there are only two types of firms (two sectors), manufacturing and services, each comprising an organised interest group (i.e. each country has two lobbies). FDI inflows in each sector increase competition and even carry the risk of crowding out local firms in that sector. FDI flows from developed to developing countries are accompanied by wage and productivity spillovers (this is not true in the opposite direction). Investments in under-developed industries yield additional demand for upstream industries (this is true for both sectors) and yields increased input variety for downstream industries (mainly true for services). Whether IIAs actually cause FDIs is irrelevant – only whether voters and firms *believe* this is so matters. IIAs mitigate the risk for investors by stabilising the investment environment through the provision of a neutral dispute resolution mechanism in the form of an extra-jurisdictional institution.[31] Consequently, if capital is held by foreigners, IIAs may restrict the policy space of the host country by potentially subjecting some policies to compensation (hereinafter: regulatory cost). This restriction directly affects the voters' welfare. Finally, we assume that the perceived expected regulatory cost is a function of past lawsuits and awards: the perceived cost converges to the true cost as the number of lawsuits and awards increases.[32]

Let us now turn to the model predictions for a developed country. During the 1980s and early 1990s the likelihood of FDI inflows from developing to developed countries was rather low because of the developing

---

[31] Ginsburg, 'International substitutes for domestic institutions', 108; K. J. Vandevelde, 'The economics of bilateral investment treaties', *Harvard International Law Journal* 41 (2000), 469–502 at 488 and 499.

[32] See for a confirming empirical study: L. N. Poulsen and E. Aisbett, 'When the Claim Hits: Bilateral Investment Treaties and Bounded Rational Learning', Crawford School Research Paper No. 5 (2011), available online at SSRN: http://ssrn.com/abstract=1899342.

countries' small stock of capital. Consequently, even if individuals in developed countries were to believe that IIAs promote FDIs, there should not be any opposition as IIAs could still be thought of as roughly neutral in terms of employment creation, regulatory cost and increased domestic competition.[33] Hence, the only relevant variables are workers and firms in industries which either already have investments abroad or which intend to invest there. Although we cannot deduce from our model whether firms' foreign investment decisions would be affected by IIAs,[34] we can see that firms with already existing investment may be willing to support IIAs in order to protect their positions. Workers will oppose IIAs if they believe that they lead to jobs being moved abroad. The model thus suggests that firms were the driving force behind the IIA negotiations of developed countries and that the only potential opposition would have come from workers. This is indeed what we observed for the USA: the business community played a major role in the creation of the BIT programme;[35] the main interest of the USA was to 'protect existing investment';[36] and negotiators from developed countries were very keen to point out the lack of evidence that BITs cause FDIs (which can, and should, be understood as a means to avoid opposition by domestic workers anxious not to lose their jobs).[37]

Despite the aforementioned empirical studies suggesting that IIAs may in the past not have led to positive institutional spillovers, we hold that this does not exclude them. Insofar as the probability of re-election is positively related to FDI inflows, the politician will seek to increase foreign

---

[33] Put differently, the associated deadweight loss equals zero: G. Becker, 'Toward a more general theory of regulation: comment', *Journal of Law and Economics* 19 (1976), 245–8 at 246.

[34] This would require augmenting the model with a theory for why firms invest abroad. See, for example, the OLI framework: J. Dunning, 'Trade, Location of Economic Activity and the MNE: A Search for an Eclectic Approach' in B. Ohlin, P. Magnus Wijkman and P.-O. Hesselborn (eds.), *The International Allocation of Economic Activity: Proceedings of a Nobel Symposium held at Stockholm* (London: Macmillan, 1977), p. 395.

[35] K. J. Vandevelde, 'A Brief History of International Agreements' in K. P. Sauvant and L. E. Sachs (eds.), *The Effect of Treaties on Foreign Direct Investment: Bilateral Investment Treaties, Double Taxation Treaties, and Investment Flows* (Oxford University Press, 2009), p. 32.

[36] K. J. Vandevelde, 'The BIT program: a fifteen-year appraisal', *American Society of International Law Proceedings* 86 (1992), 532–40 at 534; and Vandevelde, *US International Investment Agreements*, p. 110: 'the primary interest of the United States in negotiating BITs was to protect existing investment.'

[37] Vandevelde, *US International Investment Agreements*, p. 110: 'US negotiators were candid about the lack of evidence that the BITs actually would attract new investment.'

investments. If there is furthermore a presumption that this can be done by increasing the expected profits of foreign investors (e.g. through risk reduction) and if the protection provided by IIAs partially depends on domestic institutions, for example by requiring exhaustion of local remedies, then the politician will have incentives to improve the quality of local institutions in order to reduce risk – and thus alleviate the possibly substitutive effect that IIAs may have on domestic institutions.[38] Hence the political economy model suggests IIAs should not be disregarded as a potential tool for institutional reform.

E. A possible way forward

If institutions matter for (sustainable and economic) development and IIAs form part of the relevant institutional framework, then the problem of how to draft or interpret IIAs comes to the fore.[39] This assumes that IIAs can be good governance tools and thus contribute to SD, if drafted or interpreted accordingly. The proper way of aligning SD and IIL is by appropriate treaty-drafting. The USA and Canada have been at the forefront in this area. But for the time being, since most treaties are in force as they are, it is more interesting to focus on how to integrate SD into law application.[40] Although there are many possibilities for integrating the concept of SD into law application, space restrictions limit us to a few suggestions.

[38] Note that this cannot reduce the political risk as much as international arbitration because of the government's commitment problem ('dynamic inconsistency problem'). See, for example, Guzman, 'Why LDCs sign treaties that hurt them', 658ff.; Ginsburg, 'International substitutes for domestic institutions', 113; A. van Aaken, 'Primary and Secondary Remedies in International Investment Law and National State Liability: A Functional and Comparative View' in S. Schill (ed.), *International Investment Law and Comparative Public Law* (Oxford University Press, 2010), p. 721.

[39] We abstract from investment contracts in this chapter. They are nevertheless a crucial link between investment and development. Clearly, e.g., stabilisation clauses can be, depending on how they are drafted and interpreted, an impediment for development. See J. Ruggie and International Finance Corporation, 'Stabilization Clauses and Human Rights. International Finance Corporation' (2008), available at: www.ifc.org/ifcext/media.nsf/Content/Stabilization_Clauses_Human_Rights; R. Howse, 'Freezing Government Policy: Stabilization Clauses in Investment Contracts', *Investment Treaty News* (2011), available at: www.iisd.org/itn/2011/04/04/freezing-government-policy-stabilization-clauses-in-investment-contracts-2/.

[40] But see, e.g., K. von Moltke, 'International Investment and Sustainability: Options for Regime Formation' in K. Gallagher and J. Werksman (eds.), *The Earthscan Reader on International Trade and Sustainable Development* (London: Earthscan, 2002), p. 347, for options on treaty-drafting.

I.   *The object and purpose of IIAs*

The preamble of the World Trade Organization's (WTO's) Marrakesh Agreement[41] famously contains 'Sustainable Development' as a purpose. No such thing is found in most IIAs;[42] they usually refer only to development or to economic development, although this has been changing recently.[43] There is consensus that a preamble serves as one means for the teleological interpretation of treaties. Teleological interpretation is not meant to give *contra legem* discretion to arbitrators, but it is also theoretically unsustainable in the case of IIAs to argue that the text is clear; IIAs belong to the most vaguely formulated treaties in international law and teleological interpretation is thus needed.[44] There is no great debate, however, on the degree to which this interpretation may be dynamic in the sense that not only the purpose, but also current economic insights, including empirical findings, can be applied. We will discuss this in the following.

Finding the object and the purpose of a treaty is not an easy task. Several questions arise for a law interpreter: what is the meaning of the object and purpose, how are they to be identified, what is the relationship between the object and the purpose, how can the different stated purposes of a treaty be balanced, how are the object and the purpose to be interpreted, and whether and how should social science be taken into account when interpreting the object and the purpose? Often there

---

[41] Marrakesh Agreement Establishing the World Trade Organization, 15 April 1994, in force 1 January 1995, 1867 UNTS 154.

[42] But the reference is to be found in free trade agreements (FTAs), e.g. the Australia–Chile FTA: 'Implement this Agreement in a manner consistent with sustainable development and environmental protection and conservation.'

[43] See K. Gordon and J. Pohl, 'Environmental Concerns in International Investment Agreements: A Survey', Working Papers on International Investment (2011), No. 2011/1, OECD Investment Division, available at: www.oecd.org/daf/investment, for an overview on the development of treaty provisions relating to the environment. Ninety per cent of the newer treaties have some kind of reference to it; some of them speak of 'sustainable development' in their preamble: *ibid.* pp. 12ff.

[44] It is well known from legal theory that in order to construct the ordinary meaning of a term, precisely these other interpretational methods are needed. As stated early on in S. Jennings and A. Watts (eds.), *Oppenheim's International Law Vol. I (Peace)* (London: Longman, 1992), p. 1267: 'The finding whether a treaty is clear or not is not the starting point but the result of the process of interpretation.' Generally for interpretive methods in international law, see among others R. K. Gardiner, *Treaty Interpretation* (Oxford University Press, 2008); Jennings and Watts (eds.), *Oppenheim's International Law Vol. I (Peace)*, pp. 1266ff.

are several, possibly conflicting stated purposes.[45] So either possible trade-offs arising between these purposes should be admitted (and balanced in the merit phase) or other conflict solutions should be found. Several issues have to be acknowledged. First, the object should not be confounded with the purpose. Second, for interpretation, the purpose is more important than the object. And third, there might be different layers of purposes, just as in a decision matrix there are sometimes complex means/end relationships. Depending on what level one examines, an end might become a means.[46] In IIAs these layers may be the protection of investors' rights, the promotion of investment, economic development or welfare, understood as SD. Put differently, the object of the treaty may be investor protection, while the underlying purpose is (sustainable) development.

We believe that it is questionable whether the only purpose of IIAs is the protection of investment, even though citations abound in tribunals' decisions that state that the purpose of a BIT is the protection of the investments, for example 'The Tribunal shall be guided by the purpose of the Treaty as expressed in its title and preamble. It is a treaty "to protect" and "to promote" investments ... It is to create favourable conditions for investments and to stimulate private initiative.'[47] It seems almost undisputed that the purpose of the BIT is (solely) the protection of the investment. In the view of some tribunals, IIAs are instruments for the maximisation of investor protection and, accordingly, uncertainties about ambiguous treaty provisions should be resolved in favour of foreign investors.[48]

---

[45] K. J. Vandevelde, 'Treaty interpretation from a negotiator's perspective', *Vanderbilt Journal of Transnational Law* 21 (1988), 281–311 at 288ff.

[46] Seminal: G. Myrdal, 'Das Zweck-Mittel-Denken in der Nationalökonomie', *Zeitschrift für Nationalökonomie* 4 (1933), 305–29.

[47] *Siemens A.G. v. The Argentine Republic* (Decision on Jurisdiction), ICSID Case No. ARB/02/8 (3 August 2004) para 81. Very clearly also Vandevelde, 'Treaty interpretation from a negotiator's perspective', 299.

[48] See, e.g., *SGS Société Générale de Surveillance S.A. v. Republic of the Philippines*, ICSID Case No. ARB/02/6 (29 January 2004), para. 116: 'It is legitimate to resolve uncertainties in its interpretation so as to favour the protection of covered investments.' See also *Noble Ventures, Inc. v. Romania*, ICSID Case No. ARB/01/11 (12 October 2005), para. 52 (concerning the teleological interpretation of an umbrella clause: 'The object and purpose rule also supports such an interpretation. While it is not permissible, as is too often done regarding BITs, to interpret clauses exclusively in favour of investors, here such an interpretation is justified').

Not only is it already questionable whether the *only* purpose of IIAs is the protection of investment,[49] but also whether this actually is a purpose: most preambles reveal that protection of investment is more a means to an end, that is welfare, development or prosperity (of home and host states).[50] The US Model BIT 2004,[51] the Swiss Model BIT[52] and the Norwegian Draft Model BIT (discarded),[53] for example, state that prosperity is the goal,[54]

---

[49] See also *Saluka Investments BV* v. *Czech Republic* (Partial Award), UNCITRAL (17 March 2006), para. 300: 'The protection of foreign investments is not the sole aim of the Treaty, but rather a necessary element alongside the overall aim of encouraging foreign investment and extending and intensifying the parties' economic relations. That in turn calls for a balanced approach to the interpretation of the Treaty's substantive provisions for the protection of investments, since an interpretation which exaggerates the protection to be accorded to foreign investments may serve to dissuade host States from admitting foreign investments and so undermine the overall aim of extending and intensifying the parties' mutual economic relations.'

[50] J. W. Salacuse, *The Law of Investment Treaties* (Oxford University Press, 2010), p. 114: 'A careful reading of investment treaty preambles reveals these long-term objectives ["economic cooperation", "economic development", or "mutual prosperity"]'.

[51] 'Recognizing that agreement upon the treatment to be accorded such investment will stimulate the flow of private capital and the *economic development* of the Parties; Agreeing that a stable framework for investment will maximize effective utilization of economic resources and *improve living standards ... Desiring to achieve these objectives in a manner consistent with the protection of health, safety, and the environment, and the promotion of internationally recognized labor rights*' (emphasis added).

[52] 'Recognizing the need to promote and protect foreign investments with the aim to foster the economic prosperity of both States'. It also includes it in a number of FTAs in the preamble. But Switzerland also uses the annex of its treaties to refer to SD. In the Switzerland–El Salvador BIT, e.g., it says: 'It is understood that, in conformity with the principles set forth in these articles [on investment promotion, protection and non-discrimination], the concepts of sustainable development and environmental protection are applicable to all investments.'

[53] 'Recognizing that the promotion of sustainable investments is critical for the further development of national and global economies as well as for the pursuit of national and global *objectives for sustainable development*' (emphasis added).

[54] The International Centre for Settlement of Investment Disputes (ICSID) was created in 1965 under the auspices of the World Bank with the goal of fostering flows of private capital to developing countries ('international cooperation for economic development'); see the Preamble of the ICSID Convention. For the ICSID Convention, see C. Schreuer, *The ICSID Convention. A Commentary on the Convention on the Settlement of Investment Disputes Between States and Nationals of Other States* (Cambridge University Press, 2001), preamble, para. 11: 'The ICSID Convention's primary aim is the promotion of economic development.' *Ibid.*, Article 25, para. 88: 'Therefore, it may be argued that the Convention's object and purpose indicate that there should be some positive impact on development.' Similarly, Prosper Weil invokes the purpose of the ICSID Convention in his dissenting opinion in *Tokios Tokeles* v. *Ukraine* (Decision on Jurisdiction), ICSID Case No. ARB/02/18 (29 April 2004).

and some commentators have followed this approach.[55] Environmental concerns are also increasingly being expressed in the preamble.[56] Also, the broad purpose of the ICSID Convention is to establish an effective means of settling disputes that, by providing security for FDI in developing countries, will promote the capital flows (means) needed for economic development in the developing world (end). The ICSID Convention was set up under the auspices of the World Bank[57] not primarily to protect private property as such, but to foster development.[58] One may well argue, therefore, that the object and purpose of the investment regime is broader: it is (sustainable) development.

There are counter-arguments, coming foremost from the treaty negotiators of capital-exporting countries,[59] namely that IIAs are concluded to protect foreign investors abroad. There are several arguments against investment protection being the sole purpose. First, if there is no veil of ignorance as to who is exporting capital and who is importing capital, the latter country cannot be expected to want also to protect foreign property since one would need to assume that it is altruistic, not an easily justifiable assumption. Why would a state conclude a treaty to protect foreigners just for the sake of protecting foreigners? We know of no theory of international relations or international law assuming altruistic states. It seems that since both countries need to agree to the IIA, they have differing

---

[55] N. DiMascio and J. Pauwelyn, 'Nondiscrimination in trade and investment treaties: worlds apart or two sides of the same coin?,' *American Journal of International Law* 102 (2008), 48–89.

[56] Gordon and Pohl, *Environmental Concerns in International Investment Agreements*, p. 24. The authors also say that states may assume that the interpretational space given to arbitrators is not used to come to grips with environmental concerns and 'while growing awareness of environmental threats has arguably driven the increasing use of environmental language in IIAs, the set of issues that are explicitly mentioned in IIAs as well as the underlying paradigms of environmental protection appear to penetrate the investment treaty community slowly, if at all'.

[57] See also the Articles of Agreement of the International Bank for Reconstruction and Development, World Bank, Article 1 (i), available at: http://web.worldbank.org/WBSITE/EXTERNAL/EXTABOUTUS/0,,contentMDK:20049557~menuPK:63000601~pagePK:34542~piPK:36600~theSitePK:29708,00.html: 'To assist in the reconstruction and development of territories of members by facilitating the investment of capital for productive purposes.'

[58] Preamble of the ICSID Convention: 'Considering the need for international cooperation for economic development, and the role of private international investment therein.' This states a clear means–end relationship. See also C. Schreuer, L. Malintoppi, A. Reinisch and A. Sinclair, *The ICSID Convention. A Commentary*, 2nd edn (Cambridge University Press, 2008), paras. 11 *et seq.*: 'The Convention's primary aim is the promotion of economic development.'

[59] Vandevelde, 'A Brief History of International Agreements'.

purposes in mind; consequently, investment protection can surely not be the sole purpose. Second, the veil of ignorance concerning capital flows is becoming thicker: former capital-importing states have become capital exporters (e.g. Russia, India, China and Brazil). Third, outward FDI may negatively impact the home country's development: repatriation of profits may lead to increased market power and welfare losses; or possibly have negative effects on domestic employment due to reduced exports.[60] Thus, one needs at least to assume a double purpose, that is investment protection plus development. Furthermore, former capital exporters are now in need of capital as well. We therefore submit that development is a purpose for both contracting states. The purpose of IIAs must be seen as contributing to the welfare or prosperity of home and host states by means of investment protection and promotion.

It seems puzzling that tribunals could mistake the means (investment) for the end (development) when identifying the purpose of a treaty. There is only one likely reason why tribunals take the protection of investment as the purpose of an IIA: they must assume that there is an unproblematic and unconditional (causal) link from the protection of investors in IIAs to growth and development and that protection of investors can therefore be used as a proxy for development. In other words, if protection of FDI and development are so closely connected that protection of FDI almost equals development, then it does not matter which of the two is taken as the purpose of an IIA. As the *Amco* Tribunal held: 'To protect investments is to protect the general interest of development and of developing countries.'[61] However, as we have seen above, this assumption is empirically shaky, and tribunals should take this shakiness into account when interpreting an IIA.

Our point here is not that the assumed relationship does not exist, but rather that one needs to take a more cautious and differentiated approach from the one investment tribunals have usually taken. Investment protection does not equal development and therefore cannot be taken as a 'proxy' purpose. Rather, the first layer, investment protection, is the object of the treaty, investment promotion an intermediary purpose, and development the ultimate purpose of an IIA. Accepting this may lead to different approaches being taken in the interpretation of IIAs.

---

[60] For an overview of the empirical studies see A. Kokko, 'The Home Country Effects of FDI in Developed Economies', EIJS Working Paper Series No. 225 (2006), p. 1, available at: http://swopec.hhs.se/eijswp/abs/eijswp0225.htm: 'outward FDI is beneficial to the investing firm, but ... the effects on the home country vary.'

[61] *Amco Asia Corporation and others* v. *Republic of Indonesia* (Decision on Jurisdiction) ICSID Case No. ARB/81/1 (25 September 1983), 23 ILM 351 (1984), para. 23.

Furthermore, the question arises whether 'development' has now evolved to mean SD, especially in light of the aforementioned empirical insights. Whereas the traditional rule affirms that the treaty has to be interpreted in the light of the law in force at the time the treaty was concluded, the other rule would require that the interpretation be guided by the rules of international law in force at the time the treaty is applied.[62] Much depends on the treaty language. A term itself may not be static, but evolutionary, for example 'expropriation'.[63] Also, the object and purpose of a treaty may hint that interpretation should take into account progressive development.[64] Thus, just as the general exceptions in Article XX GATT are intended to adjust to the situation as it develops over time[65] and the International Court of Justice interprets international treaties dynamically,[66] IIL would be more open to interpretation in line with the economic insights into SD if the second approach to intertemporality were taken. If one also accepts that SD is evolving into a customary law principle,[67] then it should also be used as a principle in investment arbitration, not only by the WTO, where it is expressly written in the preamble.

[62] International Law Commission, 'Fragmentation of International Law: Difficulties Arising from the Diversification and Expansion of International Law. Report of the Study Group of the International Law Commission, finalised by Martti Koskenniemi' (13 April 2006), A/CN.4/L.682, para. 475. In *Aegean Sea Continental Shelf (Greece v. Turkey)*, Judgment, ICJ Reports 1978, p. 32, the ICJ applied the presumption that a generic term is 'intended to follow the evolution of the law and to correspond with the meaning attached to the expression by the law in force at any given time'.

[63] International Law Commission, 'Fragmentation of International Law', para. 478 (a), using expropriation as one example.

[64] *Gabčíkovo-Nagymaros Project (Hungary/Slovakia)*, Judgment, ICJ Reports 1997, p. 76, paras. 132–147, where the Court states that the treaty is not static, but open to adaptation to emerging norms of public international law.

[65] WTO Appellate Body Report, *United States – Import Prohibition of Certain Shrimp and Shrimp Products (US – Shrimp)*, T/DS58/AB/R, DSR 1998:VII, adopted 12 October 1998, 2795–2796, para. 130: 'From the perspective embodied in the preamble of the WTO Agreement, we note that the generic term "natural resources" in Article XX (g) is not "static" in its content or reference but is rather "by definition, evolutionary".'

[66] In *Aegean Sea Continental Shelf (Greece v. Turkey)*, p. 32, the ICJ applied the presumption according to which a generic term is 'intended to follow the evolution of the law and to correspond with the meaning attached to the expression by the law in force at any given time'. Likewise, the Inter-American Court has identified as part of the 'corpus juris of human rights law' the principle that 'human rights treaties are living instruments whose interpreters must consider changes over time and present-day conditions': *Consular Assistance*, Advisory opinion of 1 October 1999, Int-Am CHR Series A, No. 16, 256ff., paras. 114–115.

[67] *Gabčíkovo-Nagymaros Project (Hungary/Slovakia)*, paras. 140–141 and *Pulp Mills on the River Uruguay (Argentina v. Uruguay)*, Provisional Measures Order of 13 July 2006, ICJ Reports 2006, p. 113, para. 80, as well as *Pulp Mills on the River Uruguay (Argentina v. Uruguay)*, Judgment of 20 April 2010, ICJ Reports 2010, p. 54, para. 177: 'the balance

II.   Jurisdiction or merits: where to consider sustainable development?

There has been an ongoing dispute about the proper place for 'development' in the interpretation of IIAs. One of the most controversial issues is the element of jurisdiction *ratione materiae* 'investment' in Article 25 ICSID Convention and whether it entails development as well as its interaction with the investment definitions in IIAs if a dispute is adjudicated under the ICSID Convention. Is development an integral part of the definition of investment?[68]

The first problem is whether to choose the so-called 'double-keyhole' approach by which the investment definition of both the ICSID Convention and the IIA must be fulfilled cumulatively,[69] or whether the IIA with its usually broader definition 'trumps' the Convention. The second problem is whether the criteria usually attributed to an 'investment' are just interpretive tools or necessary conditions to find an 'investment'.[70] The third problem concerns the criteria. The famous 'Salini' test identifies the following elements as being indicative of an investment, for the purpose of the ICSID Convention: (a) a contribution, (b) a certain duration over which the project is implemented, (c) a sharing of operational risks, and, most controversially,[71] (d) a contribution to the host state's development.[72] It is this last element that we would like to discuss.

Even though there are good arguments for why development should play a role in investment disputes, especially if the case is adjudicated under the ICSID Convention, it does not make sense from an economic point of view

---

between economic development and environmental protection that is the essence of sustainable development.' Yet, this is strongly disputed; see Beyerlin, 'Sustainable Development', para. 15 *et seq.*

[68] As in *Malaysian Historical Salvors SDN, BHD* v. *Malaysia* (Decision on Jurisdiction), ICSID Case No. ARB/05/10 (17 May 2007).

[69] R. Dolzer and C. Schreuer, *Principles of International Investment Law* (Oxford University Press, 2008), pp. 61ff.; P.-E. Dupont, 'The notion of ICSID investment: ongoing "confusion" or "emerging synthesis"?', *Journal of World Investment & Trade* 12 (2011), 245–72 at 251.

[70] E. Gaillard, 'Identify or Define? Reflections on the Evolution of the Concept of Investment in ICSID Practice' in C. Binder, U. Kriebaum, A. Reinisch and S. Wittich (eds.), *International Investment Law for the 21st Century. Essays in Honour of Christoph Schreuer* (Oxford University Press, 2009).

[71] See *Malaysian Historical Salvors, SDN. BHD* v. *Malaysia* (Decision on the Application for Annulment), ICSID Case No. ARB/05/10 (16 April 2009), para. 80.

[72] *Salini Constuttori SPA and Italstrade* v. *Morocco* (Decision on Jurisdiction), ICSID Case No. ARB/00/4 (23 July 2001), paras. 50–58.

to integrate 'development' at the jurisdictional stage of the proceedings. It is impossible for a tribunal to decide whether a certain investment contributes to (economic) development or not.[73] There is no dispute in economic theory that it can take quite a long time before an investment begins to generate profits or output. Just think about pharmaceutical firms and their research and development of drugs, but the same could be true for natural resource extraction. The question then arises of the time at which one determines whether the investment contributes to development or not: the time of the original investment, the time the dispute arose, the time of filing the case, the time of deciding the case, or some other time? The term investment is future-oriented. So could it be that the tribunal would need to decide whether the original investment would have contributed to development in future times, for example in thirty years?

Furthermore and even more important: if it is accepted that SD, instead of purely economic development, should guide a tribunal's interpretation, there are difficult balancing decisions to be made, since there are usually trade-offs to consider. For example, in the mining sector environmental regulations as well as labour and other human rights and governance issues, are to be taken into account to a greater extent. These decisions have to be made primarily by the host state. Tribunals can contribute to SD by taking into account these trade-offs by balancing decisions in the merit phase, for example when interpreting the concept of indirect expropriation or fair and equitable treatment; it is not a question quickly decidable in the jurisdictional phase.

Finally, there is another problem relevant to the SD discussion, which is the question of whether the investment is made or owned in accordance with the law of the host state, and if not, whether this would disqualify it from meeting the 'investment' definition. Here, the problem of

---

[73] Similarly, *Phoenix Action, Ltd.* v. *Czech Republic* (Award), ICSID Case No. ARB/06/5 (15 April 2009), para. 85: 'It is the Tribunal's view that the contribution of an international investment to the development of the host state is impossible to ascertain – the more so as there are highly diverging views on what constitutes "development". A less ambitious approach should therefore be adopted, centered on the contribution of an international investment to the economy of the host State, which is indeed normally inherent in the mere concept of investment as shaped by the elements of contribution/duration/risk, and should therefore in principle be presumed.' Also *Alpha Projektholding GmbH* v. *Ukraine* (Award), ICSID Case No. ARB/07/16 (8 November 2010), which muses that including development 'invites a tribunal to engage in a post hoc valuation of the business, economic financial and/ or policy assessments that prompted the claimant's activities.' The tribunal is to think that the subjective plans of the claimant are decisive. It must be an objective assessment, since an investor is badly placed to judge the development of the host country.

corruption comes to the fore.[74] Again, from an economic perspective it makes no sense to consider this aspect in the jurisdictional phase because that would imply an 'all or nothing' solution for the investment contract. The host state could then easily avoid any obligation resulting from a contract tainted by corruption; it could thus profit from its own violation of national or international law. We would prefer to follow other proposals which take a differentiated approach in the merit phase, where the contract can be modified or adapted depending on the exact circumstances.[75]

III. Proportionality

IIL is being increasingly criticised, mainly because it is regarded as not taking other areas of special international law sufficiently into account – it is read in 'clinical isolation'.[76] How can tribunals find harmonious interpretation between investment law and non-investment law that codifies SD norms? The discussion on the means of integrating SD goals and IIL has centred partly on the use of the proportionality principle.[77] To our knowledge, the first tribunal to use the proportionality test in indirect expropriation was the *Tecmed* v. *Mexico* Tribunal.[78] It thereby referred to the European Court of Human Rights.[79]

States may explicitly take general environmental or human rights-inspired measures to fulfil their international or constitutional obligations even though there are no special norms for this in their respective IIA. Here, arbitral tribunals have considerable scope to interpret the

---

[74] H. Raeschke-Kessler and D. Gottwald, 'Corruption' in P. Muchlinski, F. Ortino and C. Schreuer (eds.), *The Oxford Handbook of International Investment Law* (Oxford University Press, 2009); J. G. Lambsdorff, 'Causes and Consequences of Corruption: What do We Know from a Cross-Section of Countries?' in S. Rose-Ackerman (ed.), *International Handbook on the Economics of Corruption* (Cheltenham: Edward Elgar, 2006).

[75] Lambsdorff, 'Causes and Consequences of Corruption', especially pp. 598ff.

[76] To paraphrase the WTO Appellate Body Report, *United States – Standards for Reformulated and Conventional Gasoline (US–Gasoline)*, WT/DS2/AB/R, adopted 29 April 1996, para. 17.

[77] See A. van Aaken, 'Fragmentation of international law: the case of international investment law', *Finnish Yearbook of International Law* 17 (2008), 91–130.

[78] *Tecnicas Medioambientales TECMED S.A.* v. *United Mexican States*, ICSID Case No. ARB (AF)/00/2 (29 May 2003), para. 122: '[T]he Arbitral Tribunal will consider, in order to determine if they are to be characterized as expropriatory, whether such actions or measures are proportional to the public interest presumably protected thereby and to the protection legally granted to investments, taking into account that the significance of such impact has a key role upon deciding the proportionality.'

[79] See, e.g., *James and Others* v. *the United Kingdom*, 98 Eur. Ct. H.R. (ser. A) (1986); *Lithgow and Others* v. *United Kingdom*, 102 Eur. Ct. H.R. (ser. A); *Matos e Silva, Lda. and Others* v. *Portugal*, Eur. Ct. H.R., Reports of Judgments and Decisions 1996-IV, 1114, § 86.

provisions of IIAs in a way that balances SD goals and investor protection, especially if the state has taken a non-discriminatory measure.[80] The most prominent and most frequently used protective provisions are indirect expropriation and 'fair and equitable treatment'. They require investment tribunals to identify the proper reference points for assessing the fairness and equity of measures adopted or maintained by host states. These norms, as very indeterminate legal terms, also constitute openings for the consideration of human rights norms or environmental protection under Article 31(3)(c) Vienna Convention on the Law of Treaties (VCLT). In the case of indirect expropriation, tribunals may not apply the 'sole effects' doctrine but may also include the purpose of the regulatory measure.[81] They may thereby include a state's potential environmental obligations or human rights obligations as a reasonable purpose for the national measure in question. Furthermore, in the context of fair and equitable treatment, the reference points for judging the fairness and equitableness of a measure could include special areas of international law. Thus a balancing of conflicting values – investor protection versus environment and human rights – would be carried out on the international level and by international tribunals.

In the act of balancing, it is also necessary to take into account that, from an economic point of view, investors are the better risk bearers, since they may insure the risks.[82] This argument may not hold true for all circumstances but should be considered when balancing legitimate expectations of investors. Not all of their expectations are legitimately burdening the state with risks of regulation.

IV.   Other norms of IIAs

A good example of good governance mechanisms for development is the 'rule of law' principle. As used by the World Bank,[83] it is not applied in

---

[80] Van Aaken, 'Fragmentation of international law'.

[81] The US Model BIT of 2004 requires exactly this when it states in its Annex B on expropriation: '[e]xcept in rare circumstances, nondiscriminatory regulatory actions by a Party that are designed and applied to protect legitimate public welfare objectives, such as public health, safety, and the environment, do not constitute indirect expropriations.'

[82] L. Kaplow, 'An economic analysis of legal transitions', *Harvard Law Review* 99 (1986), 509–617, arguing that it is not efficient to compensate private actors for regulatory change. They are in a better position to insure themselves, e.g. against currency risks. For a discussion on the Argentinian cases, see A. van Aaken, 'Zwischen Scylla und Charybdis: Völkerrechtlicher Staatsnotstand und Internationaler Investitionsschutz', *Zeitschrift für vergleichende Rechtswissenschaft* 105 (2006), 544–69.

[83] See the World Bank's website describing its programmes on governance: http://web. worldbank.org/WBSITE/EXTERNAL/WBI/EXTWBIGOVANTCOR/0,,menuPK:1740 542~pagePK:64168427~piPK:64168435~theSitePK:1740530,00.html.

fighting corruption but also in building the institutional (administrative and judicial) capacity of states. The rule of law has become a development policy.[84] This includes not only the judiciary but also the administrative branch, with a special view to procedures. Can IIL, as Dolzer said, be a tool for the development of good governance in host countries?[85] As IIL stands today, it basically allows foreign investors an opt-out from the municipal legal system.[86] We submit that in the context of IIAs, one should not be too eager to dismiss the mixture of national proceedings and international arbitration provided for in the treaties, because there may well be public policy considerations behind all of them. If foreign investors can exit national judicial proceedings too easily, pressure on the local administration of justice might be weaker than otherwise.[87] This calls for a different interpretation of the local-courts-first requirement, examining the waiting periods and the extensive use of the most-favoured nation clause in procedural matters,[88] more so since empirical studies show that court proceedings in most countries are much faster than assumed by investment tribunals and thus their arguments do not hold empirically.[89]

F.   Conclusion

IIL, just like international trade law, has an economic rationale. IIL has been very slow to take up economic reasoning in its application. Furthermore, for a long time treaty-making was based on the very simple assumption of classical economic textbook wisdom on how to achieve economic development. This is insufficient if it is desirable that the state of the art in economics is taken into account. The good news is that if empirical research and institutional economics or law and development

---

[84] G. Barron, 'The World Bank & Rule of Law Reform', LSE Working Paper No. 05–70, (2005), available at: www2.lse.ac.uk/internationalDevelopment/pdf/WP70.pdf. For the international movement on the rule of law, see T. Carothers, 'The rule of law revival', 77 *Foreign Affairs* 95 (1998), 95–106.

[85] R. Dolzer, 'The impact of international investment treaties on domestic administrative law', *Journal of International Law and Politics* 37 (2005), 953–72 at 972.

[86] Van Aaken, 'Primary and Secondary Remedies in International Investment Law'.

[87] Extensively: *ibid.*

[88] *Ibid.*

[89] See the numbers of the Lex Mundi Project, a joint project of international law firms, available at: www.lexmundi.com. These are subjective indicators generated by questionnaires sent to practitioners.

literature are taken into account, the sometimes opposing goals of IIL and SD seem much better aligned. Although conflicts may still arise, there are several interpretive methods that can help to find a suitable balance. These should be used in combination with the insights from SD studies. This chapter is meant to be a first step towards outlining a more general conceptual approach to integrating economics into IIL, and it is hoped it will show that this approach could help to achieve SD.

22

GATT Article XX and international investment law

BARTON LEGUM AND IOANA PETCULESCU

A. Introduction

The investment law regime has sometimes been criticised for an asymmetry between investors' rights and the right of states to adopt regulatory measures for the public good. Some scholars and non-governmental organisations (NGOs) have asked whether a general exception should be introduced to international investment agreements (IIAs), to allow public authorities to safeguard legitimate interests of the community. The major source of inspiration for this proposal has been Article XX of the General Agreement on Tariffs and Trade (GATT), which provides a list of regulatory measures that may be adopted by World Trade Organization (WTO) Members consistent with their GATT obligations to foster free trade. The text of the Article reads as follows:

> Subject to the requirement that such measures are not applied in a manner which would constitute a means of arbitrary or unjustifiable discrimination between countries where the same conditions prevail, or a disguised restriction on international trade, nothing in this Agreement shall be construed to prevent the adoption or enforcement by any contracting party of measures:
>
> (a) necessary to protect public morals;
> (b) necessary to protect human, animal or plant life or health;
> (c) relating to the importations or exportations of gold or silver;
> (d) necessary to secure compliance with laws or regulations which are not inconsistent with the provisions of this Agreement, including

Barton Legum is a partner in Salans' Paris office and head of the firm's investment treaty arbitration practice. From 2000 to 2004 he served as Chief of the NAFTA (North American Free Trade Agreement) Arbitration Division in the Office of the Legal Adviser, United States Department of State. Ioana Petculescu is an associate in Salans' Paris office. She holds a PhD in public international law and focuses on international arbitration. The authors are grateful to Cherine Foty, an intern in Salans' Paris office, for her valuable research assistance.

those relating to customs enforcement, the enforcement of monopolies operated under paragraph 4 of Article II and Article XVII, the
protection of patents, trade marks and copyrights, and the prevention of deceptive practices;

(e) relating to the products of prison labour;

(f) imposed for the protection of national treasures of artistic, historic
or archaeological value;

(g) relating to the conservation of exhaustible natural resources if such
measures are made effective in conjunction with restrictions on
domestic production or consumption;

(h) undertaken in pursuance of obligations under any intergovernmental commodity agreement which conforms to criteria submitted to
the CONTRACTING PARTIES and not disapproved by them or
which is itself so submitted and not so disapproved;

(i) involving restrictions on exports of domestic materials necessary to
ensure essential quantities of such materials to a domestic processing
industry during periods when the domestic price of such materials
is held below the world price as part of a governmental stabilization
plan; Provided that such restrictions shall not operate to increase the
exports of or the protection afforded to such domestic industry, and
shall not depart from the provisions of this Agreement relating to
non-discrimination;

(j) essential to the acquisition or distribution of products in general or
local short supply; Provided that any such measures shall be consistent with the principle that all contracting parties are entitled to an
equitable share of the international supply of such products, and that
any such measures, which are inconsistent with the other provisions
of the Agreement shall be discontinued as soon as the conditions giving rise to them have ceased to exist. The CONTRACTING PARTIES
shall review the need for this sub-paragraph not later than 30 June
1960.[1]

---

[1] General Agreement on Tariffs and Trade (GATT), Marrakesh, 15 April 1994, in force
1 January 1994, Marrakesh Agreement Establishing the World Trade Organization,
Annex 1A, Legal Instruments – Results of the Uruguay Round, 1867 UNTS 187, available
at: www.wto.org/english/docs_e/legal_e/gatt47_02_e.htm. For a transposition of this
provision in European Union (EU) law, see Article 36 of the Treaty on the Functioning
of the European Union, Lisbon, 13 December 2007, in force 1 December 2009, 2008 OJ
C 115/47, available at: http://eur-lex.europa.eu/LexUriServ/LexUriServ.do?uri=OJ:C:200
8:115:0047:0199:en:PDF: 'The provisions of Articles 34 and 35 shall not preclude prohibitions or restrictions on imports, exports or goods in transit justified on grounds of public
morality, public policy or public security; the protection of health and life of humans,
animals or plants; the protection of national treasures possessing artistic, historic or
archaeological value; or the protection of industrial and commercial property. Such prohibitions or restrictions shall not, however, constitute a means of arbitrary discrimination
or a disguised restriction on trade between Member States.' See also Article 2101 of the

This chapter considers whether such a 'general exceptions' clause is compatible with the goals of investment protection treaties and whether it could add anything to the already existing legal framework balancing investors' rights and the regulatory powers of the state. After summarising the current state of legal literature (section B), we will consider state practice (section C). We will then draw a comparison between justifications under the customary international law rules on the protection of aliens and GATT Article XX exceptions (section D). Finally, a discipline-by-discipline analysis of the relevance of such a 'general exceptions' clause allows us to reach a conclusion with respect to value added to international investment law (section E).

B.   Positions expressed in legal literature

In recent years a number of authors have considered what balance may best be struck between principles regarding the protection and promotion of foreign investment and rules concerning the protection of human rights, the environment, health and safety policy objectives. Protecting public health, labour and environmental concerns requires, in the opinion of some commentators, the introduction in treaties of provisions making reservations or exceptions for those concerns.[2] Recent state practice shows

---

NAFTA, San Antonio, 17 December 1992, in force 1 January 1994, available at: www. nafta-sec-alena.org/en/view.aspx?conID=590: '1. For purposes of: (a) Part Two (Trade in Goods), except to the extent that a provision of that Part applies to services or investment, and (b) Part Three (Technical Barriers to Trade), except to the extent that a provision of that Part applies to services, GATT Article XX and its interpretative notes, or any equivalent provision of a successor agreement to which all Parties are party, are incorporated into and made part of this Agreement. The Parties understand that the measures referred to in GATT Article XX(b) include environmental measures necessary to protect human, animal or plant life or health, and that GATT Article XX(g) applies to measures relating to the conservation of living and non-living exhaustible natural resources. 2. Provided that such measures are not applied in a manner that would constitute a means of arbitrary or unjustifiable discrimination between countries where the same conditions prevail or a disguised restriction on trade between the Parties, nothing in: (a) Part Two (Trade in Goods), to the extent that a provision of that Part applies to services, (b) Part Three (Technical Barriers to Trade), to the extent that a provision of that Part applies to services, (c) Chapter Twelve (Cross-Border Trade in Services), and (d) Chapter Thirteen (Telecommunications), shall be construed to prevent the adoption or enforcement by any Party of measures necessary to secure compliance with laws or regulations that are not inconsistent with the provisions of this Agreement, including those relating to health and safety and consumer protection.'
[2] See S. Ganguly, 'The investor-state dispute mechanism (isdm) and a sovereign's power to protect public health', *Columbia Journal of Transnational Law* 38 (1999), 113–68 at 166.

some movement towards inclusion of such clauses, as demonstrated in section C below.

Noting the evolution of state practice, authors have pointed out that '[w]ith the inclusion of interpretative statements, general exceptions clauses and new preambular language, investment treaties are undergoing a significant reorientation'.[3] Such reorientation is meant to ensure, these authors argue, that arbitral tribunals will in the future take greater account of non-investment policy objectives when interpreting new-generation agreements and will find a better way to balance such objectives with the goals of investment protection.

Referring to non-precluded measures (NPM) provisions limiting the applicability of investor protection under certain IIAs in exceptional circumstances, some authors have argued that arbitral tribunals should show much more deference to the states' powers when interpreting these provisions. Taking as an example the 'margin of appreciation' doctrine developed by the European Court of Human Rights,[4] they emphasise that:

> the more a particular dispute implicates questions of quasi-constitutional nature and the more disconnected the tribunal from the particular societies impacted, the more appropriate it becomes for the tribunal to utilize an interpretive approach such as the margin of appreciation, that gives some deference to the first-order determinations of government policy by the state itself ... Both because the state may be better positioned to assess the situation and possible policy responses and due to the uncertainties that often affect the policy-making space, the development of a margin of appreciation in NPM assessments would allow tribunals to engage in a substantive review while preserving for states some of the freedom of action they sought through the inclusion of an NPM clause.[5]

---

[3] S. A. Spears, 'The quest for policy space in a new generation of international investment agreements', *Journal of International Economic Law* 13 (2010), 1037–75 at 1071.

[4] The doctrine of the 'margin of appreciation' is used by the European Court of Human Rights (ECtHR), inter alia, when determining whether a state's interference with the right to property protected by Article 1 of Protocol No. 1 to the European Convention on Human Rights (ECHR) is justified in the public interest. In general terms, it means that the state is allowed a certain measure of discretion, subject to European supervision, when it takes legislative, administrative, or judicial action in the area of a Convention right. See D. J. Harris, M. O'Boyle, E. P. Bates and C. M. Buckley, *Harris, O'Boyle & Warbrick – Law of the European Convention on Human Rights*, 2nd edn (Oxford University Press, 2009), pp. 11–13.

[5] W. W. Burke-White and A. von Staden, 'Investment protection in extraordinary times: the interpretation and application of non-precluded measures provisions in bilateral investment treaties', *Virginia Journal of International Law* 48 (2008), 307–410 at 372–3. See also B. Choudhury, 'Recapturing public power: is investment arbitration's engagement of the

Suggested approaches for reviewing state regulatory measures in the context of investment law also include the 'least restrictive alternative' approach, as developed in United States constitutional practice and jurisprudence and by the WTO Appellate Body in the international trade law context,[6] the doctrine of 'necessity' developed by the European Court of Justice, the 'proportionality' analysis first developed by some national administrative and constitutional courts and the 'reasonable nexus to rational government policies' standard developed by some investor–state tribunals in the context of the non-discrimination standard found in bilateral investment treaties (BITs).[7]

Common to all these opinions is that these new approaches to states' power to regulate in the public interest are desirable to preserve or enhance the legitimacy of the investment law regime and, notably, of the International Centre for Settlement of Investment Disputes (ICSID) system.

C. Review of state practice

As pointed out in legal writings, state practice has made some steps in recent years towards including various 'general exceptions' clauses, permitting states to set aside treaty benefits in exceptional circumstances when public concerns are at stake. These GATT Article XX-like provisions condition the exceptions on fulfilment of certain requirements specified in the *chapeau*, which are aimed at 'avoiding abuse or illegitimate use of the exceptions to substantive rules'.[8]

Our review of bilateral investment agreements and free trade agreements (FTAs) containing investor protection provisions identified four categories of approaches.

The first category includes instruments expressly incorporating GATT Article XX and/or General Agreement on Trade in Services (GATS) Article XIV. This is the case of certain FTAs covering investment matters. For example the China–New Zealand FTA contains a general exception

---

public interest contributing to the democratic deficit?', *Vanderbilt Journal of Transnational Law* 41 (2008), 775–832 at 775ff.

[6] See Burke-White and von Staden, 'Investment protection in extraordinary times', 346: 'In US practice, the state is allowed to take an action that burdens citizens' rights if it furthers an essential state interest, but only if it is the least restrictive alternative available to achieve a particular goal.'

[7] See Spears, 'The quest for policy space', 1048–9.

[8] World Trade Organization (WTO) Appellate Body Report, *United States - Standards for Reformulated and Conventional Gasoline (US - Gasoline)*, WT/DS2/AB/R, adopted 20 May 1996, para. 25.

in its Article 200(1), which makes express reference to both Article XX of the 1994 GATT and to Article XIV of the GATS, and applies to the Agreement's Chapter 11 on Investment. It states: 'For the purposes of this Agreement, Article XX of GATT 1994 and its interpretive notes and Article XIV of the GATS (including its footnotes) are incorporated into and made part of this Agreement, mutatis mutandis.'[9]

This FTA also clarifies that the exception applies, among others, to 'environmental measures necessary to protect human, animal or plant life or health'.

The second category is that of agreements that, without making express reference to GATT Article XX, were clearly inspired by it and include a similar, general list of exceptions. For example, recent Asian investment treaties – such as the ASEAN Comprehensive Investment Agreement (ACIA) or the Association of Southeast Asian Nations (ASEAN) agreements on investment under the Framework Agreement on Comprehensive Economic Cooperation with Korea and China (AKIA and ACHIA) – have an exceptions provision similar to GATT Article XX.[10]

Article 18 of the Singapore–Jordan BIT also contains a list of exceptions on the same model:

> Subject to the requirement that such measures are not applied in a manner which would constitute a means of arbitrary or unjustifiable discrimination, between the Parties where like conditions prevail, or a disguised restriction on investments in the territory of a Party by investors of the other Party, nothing in this Treaty shall be construed to prevent the adoption or enforcement by a Party of measures:
>
> (a) necessary to protect public morals or to maintain public order;
> (b) necessary to protect human, animal or plant life or health;
> (c) necessary to secure compliance with laws or regulations which are not inconsistent with the provisions of this Treaty including those relating to:

---

[9] China–New Zealand Free Trade Agreement (FTA), Beijing, 7 April 2008, in force 1 October 2008, available at: www.chinafta.govt.nz/1-The-agreement/2-Text-of-the-agreement/index.php. See also Article 168 (General Exceptions) of the Agreement between Japan and Mexico for the Strengthening of the Economic Partnership, Tokyo, 17 September 2004, in force 1 April 2005, available at: www.mofa.go.jp/region/latin/mexico/agreement/agreement.pdf; and Article 1601 of the Australia–Thailand FTA, Bangkok, 5 July 2004, in force 1 January 2005, available at: www.dfat.gov.au/fta/tafta/tafta_toc.html.

[10] See M. Ewing-Chow and K. Prasad, 'Creating policy space? The inclusion of the general exception in the ASEAN Comprehensive Investment Agreement and the ASEAN China FTA Investment Chapter', forthcoming in *Transnational Dispute Management* (cited with the authors' permission).

    (i) the prevention of deceptive and fraudulent practices or to deal with the effects of fraud on a default of contract;

    (ii) the protection of the privacy of individuals in relation to the processing and dissemination of personal data and the protection of confidentiality of individual records and accounts;

    (iii) safety;

(d) imposed for the protection of national treasures of artistic, historic or archaeological value;

(e) relating to the conservation of exhaustible natural resources if such measures are made effective in conjunction with restrictions on domestic production or consumption.[11]

In similar, although not identical, terms, Article 24(2)(b) of the 1994 Energy Charter Treaty (ECT) provides that:

> Part III of the Treaty [Investment Promotion and Protection] shall not preclude any Contracting Party from adopting or enforcing any measure
>
>   (i) necessary to protect human, animal or plant life or health;
>
>   (ii) essential to the acquisition or distribution of Energy Materials and Products in conditions of short supply arising from causes outside the control of that Contracting Party, provided that any such measure shall be consistent with the principles that
>
>   (A) all other Contracting Parties are entitled to an equitable share of the international supply of such Energy Materials and Products; and
>
>   (B) any such measure that is inconsistent with this Treaty shall be discontinued as soon as the conditions giving rise to it have ceased to exist; or
>
>   (iii) designed to benefit Investors who are aboriginal people or socially or economically disadvantaged individuals or groups or their Investments and notified to the Secretariat as such, provided that such measure
>
>   (A) has no significant impact on that Contracting Party's economy; and
>
>   (B) does not discriminate between Investors of any other Contracting Party and Investors of that Contracting Party not included among those for whom the measure is intended, provided that no such measure shall constitute a disguised restriction on Economic Activity in the Energy Sector, or arbitrary or unjustifiable

[11] Jordan–Singapore bilateral investment treaty (BIT), Amman, 16 May 2004, in force 22 August 2005, available at: www.worldtradelaw.net/fta/agreements/JorSing_BilInvTreaty. pdf. See also Article 33 of the FTA between the European Free Trade Association (EFTA) states and Singapore, Egilsstadir, 26 June 2002, in force 1 January 2003, available at: www.efta.int/~/media/Documents/legal-texts/free-trade-relations/singapore/ EFTA-Singapore%20Free%20Trade%20Agreement.pdf.

discrimination between Contracting Parties or between Investors or other interested persons of Contracting Parties. Such measures shall be duly motivated and shall not nullify or impair any benefit one or more other Contracting Parties may reasonably expect under this Treaty to an extent greater than is strictly necessary to the stated end.[12]

The exception clause in the ECT is tailored to the specific subject addressed by the treaty – the energy sector. Moreover, the first paragraph of Article 24 expressly indicates that it 'shall not apply to Articles 12, 13 and 29' regarding compensation for losses, expropriation and interim provisions on trade-related matters, respectively.

The third category refers to certain instruments that contain additional specific clauses or provisions which are generally aimed at promoting a specific legitimate interest, such as the environment or labour rights or cultural and linguistic diversity.[13]

Such additional clauses have often been inserted in the preambles of investment agreements, in order to promote further categories of objectives, such as internationally recognised labour standards[14] and the furtherance of sustainable development.[15] For example, Article 11 of the Canadian Model BIT states:

> The Parties recognize that it is inappropriate to encourage investment by relaxing domestic health, safety or environmental measures. Accordingly, a Party should not waive or otherwise derogate from, or offer to waive or otherwise derogate from, such measures as an encouragement for the

---

[12] Energy Charter Treaty (ECT), Lisbon, 17 December 1994, in force 16 April 1998, available at: www.encharter.org/fileadmin/user_upload/document/EN.pdf.

[13] See Article 1(6) of the French Model BIT (2006), available at: www.unctad.org/sections/dite/iia/docs/Compendium//en/131%20volume%205.pdf: 'Nothing in this agreement shall be construed to prevent any contracting party from taking any measure to regulate investment of foreign companies and the conditions of activities of these companies in the framework of policies designed to preserve and promote cultural and linguistic diversity.'

[14] See the Preamble of the United States Model BIT (2004), available at: www.state.gov/documents/organization/117601.pdf: 'Desiring to achieve these objectives in a manner consistent with the protection of health, safety, and the environment, and the promotion of internationally recognized labor rights.' See also the Preamble of the USA–Turkey BIT, 29 September 1999, in force 11 February 2000, *Official Gazette of the Government of Turkey* No. 23961, 11 February 2000: '12. Recognizing the significance to both countries' economic welfare of working toward the observance and promotion of internationally recognized core labor standards based on the principles underlying core ILO Conventions.'

[15] See the Preamble of the USA–Turkey BIT: '13. Desiring to ensure that trade and environmental policies are mutually supportive in furtherance of sustainable development.'

establishment, acquisition, expansion or retention in its territory of an investment of an investor. If a Party considers that the other Party has offered such an encouragement, it may request consultations with the other Party and the two Parties shall consult with a view to avoiding any such encouragement.[16]

Unlike the first two categories, provisions in this category are framed not necessarily as a general exception, but instead as rules of construction or non-operative text.

Finally, a fourth category may be envisaged, which encompasses public order exception clauses and therefore constitutes a limited form of general exception. Some US BITs include provisions allowing the state to adopt measures considered necessary to maintain public order, sometimes combined with other general exceptions that may or may not be directly related, including 'essential security interests' exceptions.[17]

D.   Comparative analysis of customary international law defences and GATT Article XX

In light of the developing state practice mentioned above, it is useful to consider relevant justifications under customary international law and compare them to those contained in GATT Article XX. Such an analysis may provide a basis for assessing whether a GATT Article XX-type

---

[16] Canada Model BIT (2004), available at: http://italaw.com/documents/Canadian2004-FIPA-model-en.pdf. See also Article 12 of the US Model BIT (2004), Article 1114 of the North American Free Trade Agreement (NAFTA) and Article 74 of the Agreement between Japan and Mexico for the Strengthening of the Economic Partnership.

[17] See Article XI of the USA–Argentina BIT, Washington, 14 November 1991, in force 20 October 1994, available at: www.unctad.org/sections/dite/iia/docs/bits/argentina_us.pdf: 'This Treaty shall not preclude the application by either Party of measures necessary for the maintenance of public order, the fulfillment of its obligations with respect to the maintenance or restoration of international peace or security, or the Protection of its own essential security interests.' See also Article 24(3) of the ECT: 'The provisions of this Treaty other than those referred to in paragraph (1) shall not be construed to prevent any Contracting Party from taking any measure which it considers necessary: (a) for the protection of its essential security interests including those (i) relating to the supply of Energy Materials and Products to a military establishment; or (ii) taken in time of war, armed conflict or other emergency in international relations; (b) relating to the implementation of national policies respecting the non-proliferation of nuclear weapons or other nuclear explosive devices or needed to fulfil its obligations under the Treaty on the Non-Proliferation of Nuclear Weapons, the Nuclear Suppliers Guidelines, and other international nuclear non-proliferation obligations or understandings; or (c) for the maintenance of public order. Such measure shall not constitute a disguised restriction on Transit.'

'general exceptions' clause would materially impact the existing investment treaty legal regime.

The 1961 Draft Convention on the International Responsibility of States for Injuries to Aliens (also known as the 1961 Harvard Draft),[18] which was generally intended to reflect and codify customary international law, classifies certain acts and omissions of states causing damage to an alien as 'wrongful' (Article 3) except where there is a 'sufficient justification' (Article 4) for the conduct. A 'sufficient justification' is defined as '[t]he actual necessity of maintaining public order, health, or morality in accordance with laws enacted for that purpose' (Article 4(2)). However a justification will be insufficient where 'the measures taken against the injured alien clearly depart from the law of the respondent State or unreasonably depart from the principles of justice or the principles governing the action of the authorities of the State in the maintenance of public order, health, or morality recognized by the principal legal systems of the world'.[19]

---

[18] See L. B. Sohn and R. R. Baxter, 'Responsibility of states for injuries to the economic interests of aliens', *American Journal of International Law* 55 (1961), 545.

[19] Sohn and Baxter, 'Responsibility of States for Injuries'. See also United Nations Conference on Trade and Development (UNCTAD), *UNCTAD Series on Issues in International Investment Agreements: Taking of Property* (New York: United Nations Publications, 2000), p. 12: 'In customary international law, there is authority for a number of limitations or conditions that relate to [inter alia] the requirement that there should be no discrimination'; Article 11(a)(ii), Convention Establishing the Multilateral Investment Guarantee Agency, Washington, 11 October 1985, in force 12 April 1988, 24 ILM 1605 (1985), indicating that covered risks concerning expropriations may include 'any legislative action or administrative action or omission attributable to the host government which has the effect of depriving the holder of a guarantee of his ownership or control of, or a substantial benefit from, his investment, with the exception of non-discriminatory measures of general application which the governments normally take for the purpose of regulating economic activity in their territories'; A. Newcombe and L. Paradell, *Law and Practice of Investment Treaties: Standards of Treatment* (Alphen aan den Rijn: Kluwer Law International, 2009), p. 358: '[A] state does not incur responsibility for the legitimate and *bona fide* exercise of sovereign police powers subject to … an analysis of proportionality and reasonableness'; *ibid.*, p. 363: 'A significant consideration in assessing police power regulations … is the proportionality between the harm that the government measure aims to address and its effect on the investor, in light of the investor's legitimate investment-backed expectations'; *Saluka Investments BV v. the Czech Republic* (Partial Award), 17 March 2006, para. 255, available at: http://italaw.com/documents/Saluka-PartialawardFinal.pdf: 'It is now established in international law that States are not liable to pay compensation to a foreign investor when, in the normal exercise of their regulatory powers, they adopt in a non-discriminatory manner *bona fide* regulations that are aimed at the general welfare.' See also *Chemtura Corporation v. Government of Canada* (United Nations Commission on International Trade Law [UNCITRAL] [NAFTA] Award), 2 August 2010, para. 266,

Another important statement of customary international law, the Restatement Second of the Foreign Relations Law of the United States adopted by the American Law Institute in 1965, confirms these exceptions, providing that 'conduct attributable to a state and causing damage to an alien does not depart from the international standard of justice indicated in §165 if it is reasonably necessary for' any of the following purposes: 'the maintenance of public order, safety, or health',[20] 'the enforcement of any law of the state (including any revenue law) that does not itself depart from the international standard',[21] 'in order to control the value of currency or to protect the foreign exchange resources of the state'[22] or 'to conserve life or property in the case of disaster or other serious emergency'.[23]

Moreover, as indicated by the commentary to the American Law Institute's Restatement Third of the Foreign Relations Law of the United States, it is also an accepted principle of customary international law that where economic injury to non-nationals results from a bona fide, non-discriminatory regulation within the police powers of the state, compensation is not required:

> A state is not responsible for loss of property or for other economic disadvantage resulting from bona fide general taxation, regulation, forfeiture for crime, or other action of the kind that is commonly accepted as within the police power of states, if it is not discriminatory.[24]

---

available at: http://italaw.com/documents/ChemturaAward.pdf: 'Irrespective of the existence of a contractual deprivation, the Tribunal considers in any event that the measures challenged by the Claimant constituted a valid exercise of the Respondent's police powers. As discussed in detail in connection with Article 1105 of NAFTA, the [Pest Management Regulatory Agency of Canada] took measures within its mandate, in a non-discriminatory manner, motivated by the increasing awareness of the dangers presented by lindane for human health and the environment. A measure adopted under such circumstances is a valid exercise of the State's police powers and, as a result, does not constitute an expropriation.'

[20] American Law Institute, *Restatement of the Law Second, The Foreign Relations Law of the United States* (Washington DC: American Law Institute Publishers, 1965), para. 197, Police Power and Law Enforcement.

[21] Restatement Second of Foreign Relations Law, §197. Police Power and Law Enforcement.

[22] Restatement Second of Foreign Relations Law, §198, Currency Control.

[23] Restatement Second of Foreign Relations Law, §199, Emergencies.

[24] American Law Institute, *Restatement of the Law Third, The Foreign Relations Law of the United States* (Washington DC: American Law Institute Publishers, 1987), para. 712. See also *Saluka Investments BV* v. *the Czech Republic* (Partial Award), 17 March 2006, paras. 254 and 262 (footnotes omitted): 'In the opinion of the Tribunal, the principle that a State does not commit an expropriation and is thus not liable to pay compensation to a dispossessed alien investor when it adopts general regulations that are "commonly accepted as within the police power of States" forms part of customary international law today.'

A comparison between the subject of measures covered by the customary international law justification and those of GATT Article XX shows that the exemptions resulting from the former correspond only in part to the list provided by the latter. Customary international law limits the exceptions to the general maintenance of public order, safety, health and morality, whereas the list in GATT Article XX is visibly more extensive and somewhat different. For example, in addition to the protection of 'animal or plant life or health', GATT Article XX includes 'the protection of patents, trade marks and copyrights, and the prevention of deceptive practices', 'national treasures of artistic, historic or archaeological value', and 'conservation of exhaustible natural resources', among others.

As scholars have noted, 'international law addresses trade and investment separately and regulates them in ways that are dramatically different.'[25] As explained in legal literature, international trade is governed by multilateral instruments within the WTO framework, whereas international investment is mostly subject to bilateral instruments, the Multilateral Agreement on Investment (MAI) having failed to be adopted. WTO rules are numerous and complex, while foreign investment is protected by a smaller set of principles, mostly derived from customary international law.[26] It is therefore logical that GATT Article XX, born from a different context and addressing some similar concerns from a different perspective, may or may not be adapted to the specific disciplines imposed by investment treaties.

E. Relevance of 'general exceptions' clauses for the investment law regime

An evaluation of the suitability of GATT Article XX in the investment context is best made by considering the impact of such an exception on

---

[25] N. DiMascio and J. Pauwelyn, 'Nondiscrimination in trade and investment treaties: worlds apart or two sides of the same coin?', *American Journal of International Law* 102 (2008), 48–89 at 48.

[26] *Ibid.*, 48ff. The authors also emphasise that, in the trade regime, the actors are exclusively states that are by definition on an equal footing, and any change in the regime must be made by mutual consent. In contrast, there is an asymmetrical relationship between a private investor and the host state. WTO law knows a state-to-state enforcement mechanism where the normal remedy is compliance; in investment law, investors can sue states in international arbitration and the normal remedy is compensation. Finally, another noteworthy difference between trade and investment relates to their relative degrees of risk and involvement in domestic affairs: if a trade deal fails, the company may still be able to ship the goods elsewhere; if an investment deal fails, the money invested is most likely gone.

each of the principal investment disciplines. As demonstrated below, such an analysis shows that for many disciplines GATT Article XX would have little impact – and the impact it would have is not necessarily consistent with that which proponents of Article XX advocate.

I. National treatment

Both international trade and international investment regimes prohibit in general discrimination based on nationality. The vast majority of IIAs contain national treatment provisions.

However, GATT Article XX contains an 'exception to the exception' restricting its application to measures that are 'not applied in a manner which would constitute a means of arbitrary or *unjustifiable discrimination* between countries where the same conditions prevail' (emphasis added). As a result, under GATT/WTO law certain forms of discrimination may be 'justifiable'.

In contrast, the investment regime does not generally permit 'justifiable' discrimination. It is true that differential treatment may amount to discrimination only when domestic and foreign investments or investors are in the same situation or are placed 'in like circumstances' as clarified by certain agreements.[27] Thus, the national treatment standard is a relative one.[28] However, there are significant differences between the international trade and international investment regimes in this respect. Not only are the objectives of the principle of non-discrimination different in GATT/WTO law from those in international investment law,[29] but

[27] See NAFTA Article 1102: 'Each Party shall accord to investors of another Party treatment no less favorable than that it accords, in like circumstances, to its own investors with respect to the establishment, acquisition, expansion, management, conduct, operation, and sale or other disposition of investments.'

[28] Newcombe and Paradell, *Law and Practice of Investment Treaties*, pp. 148–9: 'The legal analysis involves a comparison between the host state's treatment of domestic and foreign investors or domestic and foreign investments. Unlike an absolute or minimum standard of treatment provision (e.g. expropriation and fair and equitable treatment), the national treatment standard does not have any intrinsic substantive content. The required standard of treatment depends on the treatment of the applicable treaty-defined comparator.'

[29] DiMascio and Pauwelyn, 'Nondiscrimination in trade and investment treaties', 66–7: '[I]n the GATT/WTO, national treatment has two functions. First, it protects tariff reductions against circumvention by way of discriminatory internal measures. Second, and over time more importantly, it assures equal competitive opportunities between imports and domestic production by eliminating origin-based internal measures, which are politically disruptive and economically inefficient ... BITs were originally concluded in order to go beyond national treatment and, contrary to the trade regime, not to make national treatment a central legal principle.'

investment arbitration tribunals have often refused to apply the 'like circumstances' test adopted by the WTO dispute settlement bodies.[30]

Indeed, where discrimination is established, a derogation is generally rejected by the investment law regime. From a policy perspective, the situations in which it might be 'justifiable' to treat investments differently

[30] NAFTA tribunals have held the test under Article 1102 to be separate and distinct from that under GATT Article III(4) and not to be confused therewith. They have also recognised the need not to make expressions used in different contexts and treaties interchangeable in spite of their similarity. See *Methanex Corporation* v. *United States of America* (Final Award of the Tribunal on Jurisdiction and Merits), UNCITRAL, 3 August 2005, Part IV, Chapter B), available at: http://italaw.com/documents/Methanex FinalAward.pdf, para. 35: 'In fact, the intent of the drafters to create distinct regimes for trade and investment is explicit in Article 1139's definition of investment'; *Cargill, Incorporated* v. *United Mexican States* (Award), ICSID Case No. ARB(AF)/05/2, 18 September 2009, available at: http://italaw.com/documents/CargillAwardRedacted. pdf, para. 193: 'The Tribunal accepts that "like circumstances" in Article 1102 has to be interpreted on its own terms. Article 1102 requires that no less favourable treatment be provided when foreign investors and domestic investors are in "like circumstances". It does not refer to "like products" and there cannot be an automatic transfer of GATT law relating to "like products" to the Article 1102 term "like circumstances"'; *Merrill & Ring Forestry L.P.* v. *Government of Canada* (Award), UNCITRAL, International Centre for Settlement of Investment Disputes (ICSID) Administrated, 31 March 2010, available at: www.international.gc.ca/trade-agreements-accords-commerciaux/disp-diff/ merrill.aspx?lang=en&view=d, para. 86: 'The Tribunal is mindful of the need not to make expressions used in different contexts and treaties interchangeable in spite of their similarity, as is the case of "like products" under GATT Article III:4. WTO panels and other tribunals have been extremely careful not to interpret expressions or concepts used in specific provisions in the light of the use of those or similar expressions in other contexts. This care is also appropriate in respect of the Investor's argument of identifying the meaning of "in like circumstances" of Article 1102 with under Articles 1405 or 1505'. See also DiMascio and Pauwelyn, 'Nondiscrimination in trade and investment treaties', 75–6: 'In sum, every major interpretation of the "in like circumstances" or "in like situations" language in the national treatment provisions of investment agreements has rejected the trade law emphasis on alteration of the conditions of competition (the "competition test") in favor of a test that focuses on whether an alleged discrimination is effectively based upon nationality rather than some other policy reason (the "regulatory context" test). The tests devised by investment tribunals have differed along several important factors. Most apparently, the tribunals have taken various positions on the breadth of the domestic investments to be compared. At one extreme, the Occidental tribunal compared all foreign and domestic exporters. At the other extreme, the Methanex tribunal compared only identical foreign and domestic exporters. The majority have fallen between these two extremes, comparing foreign and domestic investments in the same business or economic sector based upon the presumption that such investments raise similar public policy concerns'; Ewing-Chow and Prasad, 'Creating policy space?': 'Generally under NAFTA as long as there is some rational nexus or reasonable relationship between the measure and the policy not based on nationality, which is shown by the host state in rebuttal to the determination of "the in like circumstances" the tribunals have not found a breach of Article 1102.'

based on nationality of ownership appear to be relatively few. One may take the example of an outbreak of mad cow disease. It may be justifiable for a state to prevent beef imports from a country affected by the disease under international trade law. But it is difficult to imagine any reasonable justification for a state to treat investments differently in this situation solely on the basis of the nationality of their ownership.

Hence, a GATT Article XX-like provision would appear unnecessary in IIAs because the application of the national treatment obligation in the investment context prohibits any differential treatment between investments owned by domestic and foreign investors, subject only to such measure- and sector-specific exceptions as may be negotiated for a particular agreement. The exception for 'justifiable' discrimination in GATT Article XX would appear to be neither necessary nor desirable in the investment context.

II.   Fair and equitable treatment

The international standard mostly invoked by foreign investors is the fair and equitable treatment (FET) standard. The obligation of the parties to investment agreements to accord to each other's investments 'fair and equitable treatment' has been given various interpretations by government officials, arbitrators and scholars. The meaning of the standard may not necessarily be the same in all the treaties in which it appears and may not always be synonymous with the minimum standard of treatment in customary international law. The proper interpretation may depend upon the specific wording of a particular treaty, its context, negotiating history or other indications of the parties' intent.[31] By way of example,

---

[31] See Organisation for Economic Co-operation and Development (OECD) Directorate for Financial and Enterprise Affairs, 'Fair and Equitable Treatment Standard in International Investment Law', Working Papers in International Investment Number 2004/3, September 2004, available at: www.oecd.org/dataoecd/22/53/33776498.pdf, p. 1. See also *Biwater Gauff (Tanzania) Ltd.* v. *United Republic of Tanzania* (Award), ICSID Case No. ARB/05/22, 24 July 2008, available at: http://italaw.com/documents/Biwateraward.pdf, paras. 590–591: 'In the Arbitral Tribunal's view, as noted by Schreuer and Dolzer, caution must be exercised in any generalised statement about the nature of the "fair and equitable treatment" standard, since this standard finds different expression in different treaties. For example, some treaties (such as the BIT here) simply refer to "fair and equitable treatment". Others include express language treating this standard as an element of the general rules of international law (e.g. the French model treaty), or list this standard alongside the rules of international law. Given the wording of Article 2(2) of the BIT here, the Arbitral Tribunal sees force in the argument that the Contracting States here ought to be taken to have intended the adoption of an autonomous standard.'

arbitral tribunals have from time to time articulated the content of FET provisions as including, among others, the prohibition of a conduct that would be 'arbitrary, grossly unfair, unjust, idiosyncratic, discriminatory, or lacking in due process' and the obligation of the state to 'respect procedural propriety and due process'.[32]

There is today substantial jurisprudence asserting that the protection of the investor's legitimate expectations as to stability and predictability of the legal and regulatory framework is also an essential element of the FET standard. This jurisprudence considers more than the foreign investor's subjective expectations.[33] Tribunals have stated that such expectations must be reasonable and must take into account the equally legitimate right of the state to regulate domestic matters in the public interest.[34]

The *chapeau* to GATT Article XX makes clear that it does not apply if the measure is arbitrary or is a 'disguised restriction on international trade [here, investment]'. Given the content of the fair and equitable treatment, there appears to be general congruence between the exception to GATT Article XX and the FET standard. Since it is difficult to imagine a measure that would be a violation of the FET standard and that would not also be viewed as arbitrary under GATT Article XX, it does not seem that

---

[32] *Rumeli Telekom A.S. and Telsim Mobil Telekomunikasyon Hizmetleri A.S. v. Kazakhstan* (Award), ICSID Case No. ARB/05/16, 29 July 2008, available at: http://italaw.com/documents/Telsimaward.pdf, para. 609. The Tribunal's definition of the FET standard also encompassed the obligation of the state to act in a transparent manner and in good faith.

[33] See T. T. Pham, 'International investment treaties and arbitration as imbalanced instruments: a re-visit', *International Arbitration Law Review* 13(3) (2010), 81–95 at 89: 'In sum, the protection of investor expectations, itself being a broad concept, is nevertheless limited in its scope. The protection is at the same time restricted by the need to maintain a reasonable degree of regulatory flexibility on the part of the host state to take legislative action in the public interest. The consideration of "reasonableness" of the protection of investor expectations can now be seen as a specific application of the more general notion of balance between the protection of investor confidence and host state's regulatory powers.'

[34] *Parkerings-Compagniet AS v. Republic of Lithuania* (Award), ICSID Case No. ARB/05/8, 11 September 2007, available at: http://italaw.com/documents/Pakerings.pdf, para. 332: 'It is each State's undeniable right and privilege to exercise its sovereign legislative power. A State has the right to enact, modify or cancel a law at its own discretion. Save for the existence of an agreement, in the form of a stabilisation clause or otherwise, there is nothing objectionable about the amendment brought to the regulatory framework existing at the time an investor made its investment. As a matter of fact, any businessman or investor knows that laws will evolve over time. What is prohibited however is for a State to act unfairly, unreasonably or inequitably in the exercise of its legislative power.'

this Article generally brings anything to the existing limitations under the FET standard in international customary law.

The situation may be somewhat different, however, with respect to the 'legitimate expectations' concept developed by the jurisprudence. Under this line of arbitral decisions, a change in a state's policy can be both justifiable and non-discriminatory and yet breach past undertakings to a specific foreign investor. It is possible for a measure adopted today to be motivated by reasonable policy considerations relating to human or plant health or life and yet be contrary to past undertakings made by a state applying different policies. Here, GATT Article XX could, as regards legitimate expectations, alter the current international investment regime.

III.   Full protection and security

Investment treaties often contain clauses promising 'full' or 'constant' or 'adequate' protection and security to the investors of the other contracting party. Irrespective of the language, such clauses essentially assure reasonable protection to foreign investors against violence or harassment.

At the same time, '[t]here is broad consensus that the standard of full protection and security does not provide an absolute protection, be it against physical or legal infringement'.[35] It only requires the state to exercise due diligence in the protection of foreign investments.[36] International law has interpreted this due diligence to impose an objective standard of vigilance and thus to require the state to afford the degree of protection and security that should be legitimately expected to be secured by a reasonably well-organised modern state.[37] This protection must be afforded to investments against private as well as public action.

The general exceptions in GATT Article XX exclusively encompass measures that are 'not applied in a manner which would constitute a means of arbitrary or unjustifiable discrimination … or a disguised restriction on international trade'. Accordingly, if a measure is not reasonable, it cannot be excepted by Article XX of the GATT. The full protection and security standard can be violated only if the state did not accord reasonable protection to foreign investors. There are, therefore, no

[35] R. Dolzer and C. Schreuer, *Principles of International Investment Law* (Oxford University Press, 2008), p. 149.

[36] *Asian Agricultural Products Ltd.* v. *Republic of Sri Lanka* (Award), ICSID Case No. ARB/87/3, 27 June 1990, ICSID, *ICSID Review – Foreign Investment Law Journal* 6 (1991), 601, para. 50.

[37] *Ibid.*, para. 77.

circumstances in which an act or omission breaching the full protection and security standard would appear to be excepted by GATT Article XX. For this reason, GATT Article XX has little or no relevance with respect to this standard.

IV. Free transfers

The liberalisation of financial transactions around the world is reflected, inter alia, in the numerous BITs that provide for the free transfer of investment-related funds, profits and returns into and out of the host state. There is a multitude of such provisions, which vary as to the scope of the obligation imposed on the host country to permit the payment, conversion and repatriation of amounts relating to an investment.

An overview of state practice shows that an increasing number of investment agreements provide for limitations, exceptions and temporary derogations from the 'free transfers' obligation. Thus, certain BITs indicate that the transfer provision does not prevent contracting parties from ensuring compliance with other measures relating to matters such as bankruptcy, trading in securities, criminal acts or compliance with resolutions of courts or tribunals. Other agreements contain exceptions aimed at providing flexibility for host countries properly to administer financial and monetary policies.[38]

An example of a treaty providing for exceptions from the 'free transfers' obligation is Article 7, paragraph 4, of the 2004 US Model BIT, which provides that:

> Notwithstanding paragraphs 1 through 3, a Party may prevent a transfer through the equitable, non-discriminatory, and good faith application of its laws relating to:
>
> (a) bankruptcy, insolvency, or the protection of the rights of creditors;
> (b) issuing, trading, or dealing in securities, futures, options, or derivatives;
> (c) criminal or penal offenses;
> (d) financial reporting or record keeping of transfers when necessary to assist law enforcement or financial regulatory authorities; or
> (e) ensuring compliance with orders or judgments in judicial or administrative proceedings.

---

[38] See UNCTAD, *UNCTAD Paper on Bilateral Investment Treaties 1995–2006: Trends in Investment Rulemaking* (New York: United Nations Publications, 2007), available at: www.unctad.org/en/docs/iteiia20065_en.pdf, 56ff.

Yet many older BITs have no such exceptions or have more limited exceptions to the 'free transfers' obligation. This is notably the case of investment agreements concluded with third states by Western European countries before their accession to the European Union (EU). The European Court of Justice considered the lack of any provision in those BITs allowing the EU Member States concerned to impose restrictions on the free transfer of capital as inconsistent with treaty provisions empowering the Council of the European Union to take restrictive measures against third states in certain circumstances.[39]

Moreover, the majority of IIAs do not contain an exception clause dealing with a balance-of-payment crisis. For example, only very few of the nearly 3,000 bilateral investment treaties in existence[40] specifically allow for temporary balance-of-payments derogation.[41] Of the regional agreements in force, notably the North American Free Trade Agreement (NAFTA) contains such a provision.[42]

GATT Article XX does not address the policy concerns reflected in the exceptions to the 'free transfers' obligation (except perhaps with respect to those restrictions concerning imports or exports of gold and silver). GATT Article XIV, for example, has much more relevance in this respect to the extent that it specifically addresses restrictions on payments and transfers.[43] Including a GATT Article XX-type of clause would therefore

---

[39] See European Court of Justice (ECJ) judgments of 19 November 2009 in Case C-205/06, *Commission* v. *Austria* [2009], ECR 2009, 1301; Case C-249/06, *Commission* v. *Sweden* [2009], ECR 2009, 1335; and Case C-118/07, *Commission* v. *Finland* [2009], ECR 2009, 10889, available at: http://curia.europa.eu/jcms/jcms/j_6.

[40] According to the UNCTAD World Investment Report 2011, at the end of 2010 the IIA universe contained 2,807 BITs. Report available at: www.unctad-docs.org/files/UNCTAD-WIR2011-Full-en.pdf, 100.

[41] See *UNCTAD Paper on Transfer of Funds* (New York: United Nations Publications, 2000), pp. 36–8, available at: www.unctad.org/en/docs/psiteiitd20.en.pdf.

[42] NAFTA Article 2104 provides that, subject to certain conditions, 'nothing in this Agreement shall be construed to prevent a Party from adopting or maintaining measures that restrict transfers where the Party experiences serious balance of payments difficulties, or the threat thereof.'

[43] GATT Article XIV: '1. A contracting party which applies restrictions under Article XII or under Section B of Article XVIII may, in the application of such restrictions, deviate from the provisions of Article XIII in a manner having equivalent effect to restrictions on payments and transfers for current international transactions which that contracting party may at that time apply under Article VIII or XIV of the Articles of Agreement of the International Monetary Fund, or under analogous provisions of a special exchange agreement entered into pursuant to paragraph 6 of Article XV. 2. A contracting party which is applying import restrictions under Article XII or under Section B of Article XVIII may, with the consent of the CONTRACTING PARTIES, temporarily deviate

not be particularly useful in addressing concerns specifically associated with transfers. Instead, exceptions tailored to the 'free transfers' obligation, such as those listed in Article 7, paragraph 4, of the 2004 US Model BIT or in NAFTA Articles 1109(4) and 2104, would be more relevant. For the transfers discipline, GATT Article XX appears to have little to contribute.

V. Performance requirements

Performance requirements are conditions imposed by a host country on investors in connection with the establishment and the operation of their investments on its territory.

> For example, a host State wishing to ensure that a major foreign-owned manufacturing plant benefits the local economy may require the manufacturer to buy a set amount or percentage of local goods for use in assembling the final product. A State wishing to protect a weak local industry from an efficient foreign investor in that industry may require the foreign investment to export everything it produces.[44]

In recent years an increasing though still limited number of investment agreements have included provisions expressly restricting the state's discretion in applying performance requirements. One of the most relevant – and the most elaborated – clauses is NAFTA Article 1106. This Article

from the provisions of Article XIII in respect of a small part of its external trade where the benefits to the contracting party or contracting parties concerned substantially outweigh any injury which may result to the trade of other contracting parties. 3. The provisions of Article XIII shall not preclude a group of territories having a common quota in the International Monetary Fund from applying against imports from other countries, but not among themselves, restrictions in accordance with the provisions of Article XII or of Section B of Article XVIII on condition that such restrictions are in all other respects consistent with the provisions of Article XIII. 4. A contracting party applying import restrictions under Article XII or under Section B of Article XVIII shall not be precluded by Articles XI to XV or Section B of Article XVIII of this Agreement from applying measures to direct its exports in such a manner as to increase its earnings of currencies which it can use without deviation from the provisions of Article XIII. 5. A contracting party shall not be precluded by Articles XI to XV, inclusive, or by Section B of Article XVIII, of this Agreement from applying quantitative restrictions: (a) having equivalent effect to exchange restrictions authorized under Section 3 (b) of Article VII of the Articles of Agreement of the International Monetary Fund, or (b) under the preferential arrangements provided for in Annex A of this Agreement, pending the outcome of the negotiations referred to therein.'

[44] See B. Legum, 'Understanding Performance Requirements Prohibitions in Investment Treaties', in A. W. Rovine (ed.), *Contemporary Issues in International Arbitration and Mediation: The Fordham Papers 2007* (Leiden: Brill, 2008), pp. 53–4.

prohibits a NAFTA party from imposing or enforcing certain performance requirements, such as export requirements and domestic content
rules, in connection with the establishment, acquisition, expansion, management, conduct or operation of investments. It also prevents the parties from using the specified performance requirements as a condition for
granting advantages or incentives, such as tax incentives.[45] Nonetheless,
NAFTA Article 1106 also provides for specific exceptions. Paragraph 6
reads as follows:

> Provided that such measures are not applied in an arbitrary or unjustifi-
> able manner, or do not constitute a disguised restriction on international
> trade or investment, nothing in paragraph 1(b) or (c) or 3(a) or (b) shall be
> construed to prevent any Party from adopting or maintaining measures,
> including environmental measures:
>
> (a) necessary to secure compliance with laws and regulations that are
>   not inconsistent with the provisions of this Agreement;
> (b) necessary to protect human, animal or plant life or health; or
> (c) necessary for the conservation of living or non-living exhaustible
>   natural resources.

The parallel to GATT Article XX is apparent. The NAFTA, like some other
agreements, allowed contracting parties to make specific reservations to
the performance requirements obligation at the time of the negotiation,
thus excluding in annexes existing nonconforming measures or a particular sector from the scope of application of the discipline on performance requirements.[46]

---

[45] See www.sice.oas.org/trade/nafta/chap-111.asp.
[46] See NAFTA Article 1108 (paras. 1–3): '1. Articles 1102, 1103, 1106 and 1107 do not apply
to:

(a) any existing non-conforming measure that is maintained by (i) a Party at the federal
level, as set out in its Schedule to Annex I or III, (ii) a state or province, for two years
after the date of entry into force of this Agreement, and thereafter as set out by a Party
in its Schedule to Annex I in accordance with paragraph 2, or (iii) a local government;
(b) the continuation or prompt renewal of any non-conforming measure referred to in
subparagraph (a); or (c) an amendment to any non-conforming measure referred to in
subparagraph (a) to the extent that the amendment does not decrease the conformity of
the measure, as it existed immediately before the amendment, with Articles 1102, 1103,
1106 and 1107. 2. Each Party may set out in its Schedule to Annex I, within two years
of the date of entry into force of this Agreement, any existing nonconforming measure
maintained by a state or province, not including a local government. 3. Articles 1102,
1103, 1106 and 1107 do not apply to any measure that a Party adopts or maintains with
respect to sectors, subsectors or activities, as set out in its Schedule to Annex II.'

Performance requirements are at the meeting point of investment and international trade disciplines.[47] Of all the investment disciplines, therefore, Article XX of the GATT is the most relevant to that of performance requirements as recognised by NAFTA Article 1106, paragraph 6. To the extent that it is not clearly spelled out in a specific provision like Article 1106(6), a GATT Article XX-like 'general exceptions' clause would appear to be useful with respect to this discipline.

VI. Expropriation

Under customary international law, and in almost all investment treaties, the taking of a foreign investor's property entails the obligation on the part of the state to offer compensation.

Most investment treaties also expressly address indirect or de facto expropriation, in which there is no formal act of expropriation or nationalisation.

In practice, what effectively constitutes an indirect or de facto expropriation, and where the line of separation from legitimate governmental regulatory measures should be drawn, depend upon the specific facts and circumstances of each case.[48]

As stated in section 3 above, the customary international law doctrine of police powers limits the list of legitimate purposes to public order, morals and health. On the other hand, GATT Article XX refers to additional justifications, especially the protection of 'human, animal or plant life or health', which is sometimes assimilated to the protection of the environment. Here, a distinction should be made between public health measures (such as limiting pollution, or regulating the treatment, storage and transportation of toxic materials) and conservation measures (such as the creation of a wildlife reserve by setting aside plots of land owned by private

---

[47] See Legum, 'Understanding Performance Requirements Prohibitions', p. 56, explaining that 'the prohibition of performance requirements squarely addresses trade in goods and services, although it does so at the cusp where the disciplines of trade in goods, trade in services, and investment intersect'.

[48] *Saluka Investments BV* v. *the Czech Republic* (Partial Award), Permanent Court of Arbitration/UNCITRAL, 17 March 2006, para. 263: '[I]nternational law has yet to identify in a comprehensive and definitive fashion precisely what regulations are considered "permissible" and "commonly accepted" as falling within the police or regulatory power of States and, thus, non compensable. In other words, it has yet to draw a bright and easily distinguishable line between non compensable regulations on the one hand and, on the other, measures that have the effect of depriving foreign investors of their investment and are thus unlawful and compensable in international law.'

persons). If the first category can be said to be covered by both customary international law rules on states' police powers and by GATT Article XX, the second category does not seem to come under any of the customary international law categories.

To the extent that a 'general exceptions' clause exempted conservation measures from the obligation to compensate for expropriation it would materially modify the present investment law regime. Such a result is not necessarily required by the text of GATT Article XX. It would be incompatible with the underlying policy of expropriation obligations – to require the public purse to pay for the taking of private property for the public good.

With the exception of this perhaps unwarranted concern with respect to conservation measures, and given the content of the customary international law justification of police powers, a GATT Article XX exception would not appear to add much to the analysis on expropriation, except for the possible benefit of codifying in a treaty a customary international law rule that could be subject to interpretation.

F.   Conclusion

In conclusion, a 'general exceptions' clause similar to GATT Article XX appears not to be particularly well suited to the investment law regime. With respect to the national treatment standard, there would be little room for application of GATT Article XX given its exception for discriminatory measures, and Article XX's exception for 'justified' discrimination would not appear to be appropriate in the investment context. With respect to the disciplines of fair and equitable treatment and full protection and security there would, with the exception of the legitimate expectations doctrine, be little application for Article XX because of the congruence of these disciplines with the exception to Article XX for justified measures. With respect to the disciplines of transfers and performance requirements, specific exceptions to these disciplines appear to be desirable but not necessarily in the precise form of GATT Article XX. With respect to expropriation, GATT Article XX largely corresponds to the existing police powers exception (with the concern as to conservation measures noted above) and so would add little other than the benefit of codification to this discipline.

23

The inclusion of GATT Article XX exceptions in IIAs: a potentially risky policy

CÉLINE LÉVESQUE

A. Introduction

In their chapter, Barton Legum and Ioana Petculescu question whether general exceptions of the General Agreement on Tariffs and Trade (GATT) Article XX variety should be included in international investment agreements (IIAs).[1] On the face of it, such exceptions would appear to provide (more) balance between investment protection and other goals of public policy.

States seem to seek this balance, as they are increasingly including general exceptions in their IIAs.[2] Take the example of Canada, which has long been a supporter of this approach. Since 1994 Canada has included general exceptions in over twenty of its foreign investment promotion and protection agreements (FIPAs) and its recent free trade agreements (FTAs).[3] Even when Canada revised its Model FIPA in 2003, it kept the

---

[1] See the contribution by B. Legum and I. Petculescu, 'GATT Article XX and International Investment Law', Chapter 22 in this volume.

[2] See *ibid.* See also A. Newcombe, 'General Exceptions in International Investment Agreements' in M.-C. Cordonier Segger, M. W. Gehring and A. Newcombe (eds.), *Sustainable Development in World Investment Law* (Alphen aan den Rijn: Kluwer Law International, 2011).

[3] Sixteen of those foreign investment promotion and protection agreements (FIPAs) originally date from the 1994–1997 period. Interestingly, when some of the early FIPAs concluded with countries that later became members of the European Union were renegotiated, the provision was included. See, e.g., Canada–Czech Republic FIPA, 1990 and 2009. Other FIPAs including general exceptions were concluded after the publication of the 2004 Model FIPA. See, e.g., Canada–Jordan FIPA 2009. See also Canada's free trade agreements (FTAs) respectively with Peru, Colombia and Panama. All international investment agreements (IIAs) available at: Department of Foreign Affairs and International Trade (DFAIT), www.international.gc.ca/trade-agreements-accords-commerciaux/agr-acc/index.aspx?lang=en&view=d.

general exceptions.[4] On the government's website one finds the following statement: 'General exceptions to the disciplines of the Agreement are included *in order to meet several important policy goals*: the protection of human, animal or plant life or health, as well as the conservation of living or non-living exhaustible resources' (emphasis added).[5]

However, as with Legum and Petculescu, I am not convinced that the inclusion of general exceptions clauses of the GATT Article XX variety is the best solution to improve the balance in the IIA regime between investment protection and other public policy objectives. I will go as far as to say that there is a risk that such provisions could reduce rather than improve this balance.[6]

While I generally agree with the analysis provided by Legum and Petculescu, I would respectfully disagree with or present a different perspective related to the potential application of Article XX in relation to national treatment and expropriation.

B. National treatment

On the role of general exceptions in relation to the national treatment obligation, Legum and Petculescu conclude that: 'Hence, a GATT Article XX-like provision would appear unnecessary in IIAs because the application of the national treatment obligation in the investment context prohibits any differential treatment between investments owned by domestic and foreign investors, subject only to such measure- and sector-specific

---

[4] See Canada's FIPA Model at Article 10 (General Exceptions):

> 1. Subject to the requirement that such measures are not applied in a manner that would constitute arbitrary or unjustifiable discrimination between investments or between investors, or a disguised restriction on international trade or investment, nothing in this Agreement shall be construed to prevent a Party from adopting or enforcing measures necessary: (a) to protect human, animal or plant life or health; (b) to ensure compliance with laws and regulations that are not inconsistent with the provisions of this Agreement; or (c) for the conservation of living or non-living exhaustible natural resources.

Copy on file with the author.

[5] See DFAIT, Canada's Foreign Investment Promotion and Protection Agreements (FIPAs) Negotiating Programme, Canada's FIPA Model, under 'Article 10: General Exceptions', copy on file with the author.

[6] See C. Lévesque, 'Influences on the Canadian model FIPA and US model BIT: NAFTA Chapter 11 and Beyond', *Canadian Yearbook of International Law* (2006), vol. XLIV, 249–98, where arguments that an investor is likely to make in order to argue for a narrow interpretation of the general exceptions clause are considered (at 274–7). See also Newcombe, 'General Exceptions in International Investment Agreements', pp. 358, 366, 369–70.

exceptions as may be negotiated for a particular agreement.'[7] In other words, they argue that 'the investment regime does not generally permit "justifiable" discrimination'.[8]

With respect, I would ask a different question: once two states include in their IIA a general exceptions provision (of the GATT Article XX variety) and a foreign investor makes a claim of breach of national treatment against one of them, how might a *tribunal interpret* the exception clause in relation to the national treatment obligation?

This is where I see a risk. In such a case (following the language of Article XX) justifiable discrimination would be permitted, but presumably within the constraints set by the Article. Following the rules of interpretation laid out in Article 31 of the Vienna Convention on the Law of Treaties, the tribunal would interpret the treaty 'in good faith in accordance with the ordinary meaning to be given to the terms of the treaty in their context and in the light of its object and purpose'.[9] As such, the tribunal would consider the limited list of objectives, the 'necessity' (or 'relating to') requirements and evaluate compliance with the '*chapeau*' requirements.[10]

It is useful to compare this approach to the one used by tribunals interpreting Chapter 11 (Investment) of the North American Free Trade Agreement (NAFTA).[11] Tribunals, when they had to interpret Article 1102 (national treatment), did not consider the general exceptions provision because, while it exists in the NAFTA, it does not apply to Chapter 11.[12] Rather, it is through their interpretation of the 'like circumstances' language, that tribunals arguably found balance between investment protection and other goals of public policy.[13]

---

[7] Legum and Petculescu, Chapter 22 in this volume.

[8] *Ibid.*

[9] Vienna Convention on the Law of Treaties (VCLT), Vienna, 23 May 1969, in force 27 January 1980, 1155 UNTS 331.

[10] It is likely that tribunals would be influenced by the method of interpretation of GATT Article XX in the World Trade Organization (WTO). See Newcombe, 'General Exceptions in International Investment Agreements', pp. 358, 363–6.

[11] North American Free Trade Agreement between the Government of Canada, the Government of the United Mexican States and the Government of the United States of America (NAFTA), 17 December 1992, in force 1 January 1994, 32 ILM 289.

[12] See NAFTA, Article 2101.

[13] Article 1102 of NAFTA states: 'Each Party shall accord to investors of another Party treatment no less favorable than that it accords, *in like circumstances*, to its own investors with respect to the establishment, acquisition, expansion, management, conduct, operation, and sale or other disposition of investments' (emphasis added).

While the approaches vary, in cases where tribunals found a difference in treatment between national and foreign investors (or investments), they considered whether reasons existed for the measure that were not discriminatory. In evaluating the reasons provided for the difference in treatment, tribunals have looked for: 'a reasonable nexus to rational government policies';[14] 'legitimate public policy measures that are pursued in a reasonable manner';[15] 'a rational justification' or reasonable distinctions;[16] 'a plausible connection with a legitimate goal of policy'.[17]

Tribunals proceeded in this way for at least two reasons. First, tribunals generally consider that they cannot require investors to submit proof positive of discriminatory government intent. Tribunals have recognised that short of a 'smoking gun' this proof may be impossible to provide.[18] As a result, tribunals have looked for proxies. Simply put, if a tribunal finds a difference in treatment (between national and foreign investors) that cannot be 'justified' by government, then it must be discrimination based on nationality. Second, tribunals arguably felt a need for balance, but did not have another mechanism to implement it.[19] So – they build it in.

The difference in approach, as compared to the application of a 'general exceptions' clause, is striking.[20] Here, there are no limited or closed lists of topics covered by the exception, no necessity requirements and no *chapeau* to constrain the interpreter.

As a result, a tribunal tasked with interpreting an IIA that includes both a national treatment provision and a general exceptions clause would arguably have less leeway –and not more – to balance investment protection and

---

[14] *Pope & Talbot Inc* v. *Government of Canada* (Award on the Merits of Phase 2), NAFTA Arbitration under the United Nations Commission on International Trade Law (UNCITRAL) Arbitration Rules, 10 April 2001, para. 78 (*Pope & Talbot*). All awards mentioned herein are available at: http://italaw.com.

[15] *S. D. Myers Inc.* v. *Government of Canada* (Partial Award), NAFTA Arbitration under the UNCITRAL Arbitration Rules, 13 November 2000, para. 246 (*S. D. Myers*).

[16] *Marvin Feldman* v. *Mexico* (Award), NAFTA Arbitration under the ICSID Add. Fac. Rules, 16 December 2002, paras. 170 and 182 (*Feldman*).

[17] *GAMI Investments, Inc.* v. *Government of the United Mexican States* (Final Award), NAFTA Arbitration under the UNCITRAL Arbitration Rules, 15 November 2004, para. 114.

[18] *Feldman*, paras. 181–183; *Pope & Talbot*, para. 79. See also *International Thunderbird Gaming Corporation* v. *United Mexican States* (Arbitral Award), NAFTA Arbitration under the UNCITRAL Arbitration Rules, 26 January 2006, para. 177.

[19] See *S. D. Myers*, paras. 246–250 and Schwartz opinion, paras. 72–75, 173–174.

[20] See N. DiMascio and J. Pauwelyn, 'Nondiscrimination in trade and investment treaties: worlds apart or two sides of the same coin?', *American Journal of International Law* 102 (2008), 48–89 at 76; Newcombe, 'General Exceptions in International Investment Agreements', pp. 366–8.

other goals of public policy.[21] Specifically, I do not believe that tribunals could give the expression 'in like circumstances' as broad an interpretation as NAFTA Chapter 11 tribunals have because it would make the exception provision redundant. In other words, there is no need for recourse to the exception clause if legitimate objectives are fully considered as part of the interpretation of the primary obligation.[22] Such an interpretation would go against the principle of effectiveness in treaty interpretation.[23]

In this light, general exceptions clauses would certainly appear better in principle than in practice.

C. Expropriation

On the relationship between expropriation and general exceptions provisions, Legum and Petculescu conclude the following:

> With the exception of this perhaps unwarranted concern with respect to conservation measures, and given the content of the customary international law justification of police powers, a GATT Article XX exception would not appear to add much to the analysis on expropriation, except for the possible benefit of codifying in a treaty a customary international law rule that could be subject to interpretation.[24]

With respect, I would argue that GATT Article XX exceptions in IIAs do not function as a police power doctrine equivalent or codify this international customary law doctrine in IIAs.

It is important, first, to be clear as to the consequences of such an interpretation. If a measure falls within the police power of the state, no compensation is due to the investor even though a deprivation of property has occurred.[25] If a GATT Article XX exception had the same effect, it would mean that whenever a government adopted a measure 'necessary for the

---

[21] Newcombe, 'General Exceptions in International Investment Agreements', p. 366.

[22] See, e.g., *In the Matter of Cross-Border Trucking Services*, Final Report of the Panel (6 February 2001) under NAFTA Chapter 20, paras. 259–260, available at: www.worldtradelaw.net/nafta20/truckingservices.pdf.

[23] It is not a coincidence that the International Institute for Sustainable Development (IISD) did not include a general exception provision in the Model Treaty. It also feared the potential restrictive interpretation. See Newcombe, 'General Exceptions in International Investment Agreements', p. 366.

[24] See Chapter 22 by Legum and Petculescu in this volume.

[25] On expropriation and the police power doctrine, see C. Lévesque, 'Distinguishing Expropriation and Regulation under NAFTA Chapter 11: Making Explicit the Link to Property' in K. Kennedy (ed.), *The First Decade of NAFTA: The Future of Free Trade in North America* (New York: Transnational Publishers, 2004).

conservation of living or non-living exhaustible natural resources', for example, it would not have to pay compensation – even though the measure is in effect expropriatory.

I respectfully disagree with this interpretation – for three reasons. First, the wording of the exceptions clause 'nothing in this Agreement shall be construed to prevent a Party from adopting or enforcing measures necessary for ...' (or something equivalent) does not imply that the government does not have to pay compensation for an expropriatory measure. It would be surprising (to say the least) if governments that have included general exceptions in their bilateral investment treaties (BITs) and FTAs (including Canada, Japan, Singapore, etc.) meant to provide their investors less protection than what is provided by customary international law.[26] This would result from the broader scope of Article XX GATT-type exceptions, as compared to the coverage of the police power doctrine.[27]

Second, other agreements and draft agreements have excluded the expropriation provision from the ambit of the general exceptions clause. Legum and Petculescu mention the case of the Energy Charter Treaty.[28] But there is also the draft Multilateral Agreement on Investment (MAI) at Article VI (exceptions and safeguards), which provides that general exceptions do not apply to expropriation.[29] A similar exclusion is provided for

[26] Newcombe, 'General Exceptions in International Investment Agreements', p. 369. Also, in some Canadian FIPA language used is not 'necessary' but only 'relating to' – which would make the potential for uncompensated expropriation even higher.

[27] The difference in scope is acknowledged by Legum and Petculescu, Chapter 22 in this volume.

[28] Legum and Petculescu, Chapter 22 in this volume.

[29] Multilateral Agreement on Investment (MAI), Article VI, available at: www1.oecd.org/daf/mai/pdf/ng/ng987r1e.pdf. See also Newcombe, 'General Exceptions in International Investment Agreements', p. 369. Although this provision is different in coverage from an Article XX GATT exception: 'Subject to the requirement that such measures are not applied in a manner which would constitute a means of arbitrary or unjustifiable discrimination between Contracting Parties, or a disguised investment restriction, nothing in this Agreement shall be construed to prevent any Contracting Party from taking any measure necessary for the maintenance of public order.' Footnote: 'The public order exception may be invoked only where a genuine and sufficiently serious threat is posed to one of the fundamental interests of society.' See also the Commentary on the text which states: '2. The question is whether certain obligations of the agreement are considered so central to investor protection, for example compensation in case of expropriation, that a provision should limit the right of a Contracting Party to invoke this Article [General Exceptions] for actions that would be inconsistent with its obligation to pay compensation in the case of an expropriation. 3. The majority view was that the MAI should provide an absolute guarantee that an investor will be compensated for an expropriated investment.' See Commentary to the MAI Negotiating Text (as of 24 April 1998), 40, available at: www1.oecd.org/daf/mai/pdf/ng/ng988r1e.pdf.

in the 2009 FTA between Switzerland and Japan.[30] I would argue that this position better reflects the intention of IIA parties.[31]

Third, this interpretation is not consistent with the inclusion (in some IIAs) of an Annex on expropriation that includes what arguably is a police power exception *in addition to* a general exceptions provision. Again, take the example of Canada. Since the publication of the 2004 model FIPA, Canadian IIAs include an Annex to the expropriation article that aims to guide tribunals ruling on cases of indirect expropriation. The last provision states:

> Except in rare circumstances, such as when a measure or series of measures are so severe in the light of their purpose that they cannot be reasonably viewed as having been adopted and applied in good faith, non-discriminatory measures of a Party that are designed and applied to *protect legitimate public welfare objectives, such as health, safety and the environment*, do not constitute indirect expropriation.[32]

I would argue that it is not logical to have both provisions *if* the general exceptions provision was already meant to act as a 'police power' exception. From that, I would conclude that Canada never meant the general exceptions provision to apply to expropriation. As it happens, other agreements include both a general exceptions clause and an Annex on expropriation similar to the Canadian version.[33]

---

[30] The investment chapter of the FTA provides at Article 95 for General Agreement on Trade in Services (GATS) Article XIV and XIVbis exceptions, but specifies at paragraph 3 that '[t]his article shall not apply to paragraph 1 of Article 86 [General Treatment], and Articles 91 [Expropriation] and 92 [Treatment in Case of Strife]. See Agreement on Free Trade and Economic Partnership Between Japan and the Swiss Confederation, Tokyo, 19 February 2009, in force 1 September 2009, available at: www.mofa.go.jp/region/europe/switzerland/epa0902/agreement.pdf.

[31] This point raises a key interpretation difficulty related to IIAs. When states realise that their intentions are not reflected in tribunal decisions, they often opt to clarify wording in later treaties. This change in language opens the way for tribunals to later reason that different formulations must mean different intentions. This difficulty explains the use of expressions such as 'for greater clarity' that seek to clarify while not undermining previous formulations. See Lévesque, 'Influences on the Canadian model FIPA and US model BIT', 258–63.

[32] 2004 Canadian Model FIPA, Annex B-13(1) Expropriation (emphasis added). Copy on file with the author.

[33] See Agreement establishing the ASEAN–Australia–New Zealand Free Trade Area, Cha-am, Phetchaburi, Thailand, 27 February 2009, in force 1 January 2010, Chapter 11 at Article 9 (expropriation) and Annex on expropriation and compensation and Chapter 15 at Article 1 (general exceptions), available at: www.asean.fta.govt.nz/assets/Agreement-Establishing-the-ASEAN-Australia-New-Zealand-Free-Trade-Area.pdf.

D. Conclusion

Overall, I would agree with the conclusions reached by Legum and Petculescu to the effect that general exceptions have a limited role to play in international investment law.

In regard to the national treatment obligation, I took a different approach and demonstrated the risk that the combination of national treatment and general exceptions provisions present – a risk of less, not more regulatory space.

Regarding expropriation, I argued that general exceptions clauses do not modify the obligation of states to compensate in case of takings. In other words, it is the police power doctrine at customary international law (or the modified version included in some treaties in an annex on expropriation) that provides for the cases that are *not* expropriations, and, as such, do not call for a duty of compensation.

Where does this leave countries, like Canada, that include general exceptions clauses in their BITs and FTAs 'in order to meet several important policy goals'? First, I would say that clarifying the interpretation of primary obligations has more potential than general exceptions to improve the balance in the regime between investment protection and other public policy objectives. Second, I would argue that other exceptions – better suited or tailored to the balance sought in the international investment law regime – would be more appropriate than the GATT Article XX variety exceptions.

24

Managing expectations: beyond formal adjudication

SUSAN D. FRANCK

A. Introduction

Recognising that the proper balance of international investment law is an area of normative concern, the World Trade Institute (WTI) organised a panel to explore considerations related to the appropriate equilibrium. Scholarship by Anne van Aaken and Bart Legum offered an opportunity to look at investment law more systematically, namely by considering different ways to achieve regulatory and commercial balance, to apportion discretion appropriately and to manage expectations. This commentary offers exploratory remarks that use latent ideas from the chapters by van Aaken and Legum to offer a means for thinking systematically about managing stakeholder expectations of the international investment system.

A critical issue for international investment law relates to cognitive psychology and how to manage the expectations of differently situated stakeholders, particularly when reality does not conform to presumed pre-existing baselines. It is appropriate to think critically about what the baseline expectations should be in international investment. Although there will be overlapping interests and opportunities for joint gains, the expectations and needs of all stakeholders will not necessarily always be in perfect alignment. This means that stakeholders must manage their expectations to avoid dissatisfaction when there is a possibility of either inevitable or unexpected divergence.

There are different methods to manage stakeholder expectations and investment treaty conflict. One element of expectation management involves education, which offers basic information about international

The author is grateful for the research assistance of Washington & Lee University Law Library and Anaeli Sandoval.

investment and its derivative legal regime. Presumably, such information can be used to make evidence-based normative choices that are more informed about the relative costs and benefits.[1] Another element involves recognising different doctrinal opportunities to manage investment treaty conflict and related regulatory discretion. To borrow concepts from administrative law for exploratory purposes, regulation of international investment law can occur either through rule-making procedures or adjudicative processes.[2]

Both authors explore this administrative law model, albeit in different ways. Legum offers a formal rule-making perspective on international investment law that considers opportunities for textual specification. Van Aaken, by contrast, explores how to capture regulatory discretion by focusing on formal adjudication. Despite the differences, the commonality is that both chapters focus on formal regulatory activity.

Yet state regulatory activity is nuanced. Regulation can involve conduct that is more complex than a simple model of formal adjudication and formal rule-making. Rather, a sophisticated view of state regulatory activity involves formal *and* informal conduct. This suggests that there

---

[1] Evidence-based approaches to legal norms and regulation are gaining in popularity given the tangible value of the benefits. See, e.g., J. C. Oleson, 'Risk in sentencing: constitutionally suspect variables and evidence-based sentencing', *Southern Methodist University Law Review* 64 (2001), 1329–404 (using evidence-based approaches to create greater legitimacy in criminal sentencing); S. M. Stern, 'Residential protectionism and the legal mythology of home', *Michigan Law Review* 107 (2009), 1093–144 (using an evidence-based approach to understand normative choices in property law); T. S. Jost, 'Our broken health care system and how to fix it: an essay on health law and policy', *Wake Forest Law Review* 41 (2006), 537–618 (encouraging an evidence-based approach to health care reform to ensure ideology advances policy objectives); B. Trujillo, 'Patterns in a complex system: an empirical study of valuation in business bankruptcy cases', *UCLA Law Review* 53 (2005), 357–404 at 363 n. 17 ('[A]n evidence-based law approach to doctrine can move us past anecdote and unexamined path dependence, and perhaps toward a systematization and verification of knowledge about legal doctrine.') In international investment law, it behoves scholars and stakeholders to take methodologically sound empirical evidence seriously.

[2] See C. H. Koch, Jr, *Administrative Law and Practice*, 3rd edn (Eagan: West Publishing Company, 2010), § 2:11 (describing the difference between the adjudication and rule-making processes); J. W. Yackee, 'Controlling the International Investment Law Agency', *Harvard International Law Journal* 53(2012) 392–448 (discussing administrative law and conceptualising international investment law within that framework); see also B. Kingsbury, N. Krisch and R. B. Stewart, 'The emergence of global administrative law', *Law and Contemporary Problems* 68 (2005), 15–61 at 15–18 (proposing that global governance can be understood by looking at administrative processes such as rule-making and adjudication); R. B. Stewart, 'U.S. administrative law: a model for global administrative law?', *Law and Contemporary Problems* 68 (2005), 63–108 (discussing the convergence of US administrative law and 'Global Administrative Law' and the application of administrative law to international regulatory regimes).

are untapped opportunities for managing stakeholder expectations and regulatory discretion through structured informal mechanisms – including informal rule-making and informal adjudication.

The international investment system has thus far depended heavily on international arbitration as a formal adjudicative system to provide guidance and clarification on the standards contained in international investment agreements (IIAs). There has been dissatisfaction with this state of affairs that has led to calls for the wholesale abandonment or for a radical overhaul of the international investment system. To prevent the baby from being thrown out with the proverbial bathwater, it is critical to think about the evidence in a realistic and balanced manner. This involves first unpacking stakeholder expectations to promote rational consideration of the evidence by: (a) recognising where expectations may have been over-optimistic, and then (b) thinking thoughtfully and systematically about the mechanisms through which to capture and manage regulatory discretion. In an effort to do so, the remainder of this commentary will first consider the empirical and causal links identified by van Aaken to consider how to encourage the purported benefits of IIAs. Second, the commentary considers the inevitable tension among incentives for rent-seeking by investors, the different regulatory goals of states and the hopes of civil society.

This commentary ultimately suggests that formal adjudication has a critical place in the judicialisation[3] of international investment law, yet there is value in moving beyond primary reliance upon formal adjudication. Put simply, there is real value in expanding the acceptable – and necessary – methods of investment regulation. There should be increased attention to formal codification of investment rules at the front end and the express prioritisation of competing investment values. Meanwhile, there should be greater focus on the untapped value of structured – yet informal – regulatory activity, including informal rule-making and informal adjudication.

---

[3] See R. E. Hudec, 'The Judicialization of GATT Dispute Settlement' in M. M. Hart and D. P. Steger (eds.), *In Whose Interest? Due Process and Transparency in International Trade* (Ottawa: Centre for Trade and Policy Law, 1992); D. M. Trubek, 'Transcending the ostensible: some reflections on Bob Hudec as friend and scholar', *Minnesota Journal of International Law* 17 (2008), 1–6 at 3–4; A. K. Schneider, 'Not quite a world without trials: why international dispute resolution is increasingly judicialized', *Journal of Dispute Resolution* 2002 (2006), 119–30 at 119–24 (arguing that certain international disputes are increasingly judicialised).

B.   Managing expectations about investment

The Washington Consensus was based upon the premise that international investment and development objectives were necessarily aligned. A corollary assumption was that foreign investment would yield a net positive benefit for both the investor and the state.[4]

Yet there have been concerns that the purported benefits of international investment are not supported by the data. Whether the disjunction between the expectation and outcome derives from either a lack of information or cognitive processing errors that lead to the overestimation of positive outcomes,[5] the effect is the same. It is unrealistic to assume that a causal chain will function every time, whereby: (1) signing an IIA will lead to investment, (2) the investment will lead to growth, and (3) growth will lead to better quality of life for the population. At each step of that causal chain, problems can arise.

There is not necessarily a single uniform monolithic narrative of international investment that always results in a happy outcome. Van Aaken is correct to urge caution lest one be overly optimistic about the benefits of international investment, and thereby be disappointed when reality diverges from expectation. There are inevitably narratives of success, horror stories and still other situations where outcomes are mixed. In other

---

[4] See generally N. Serra and J. E. Stiglitz, *The Washington Consensus Reconsidered: Towards a New Global Governance* (New York: Oxford University Press, 2008); see also J. W. Salacuse, 'The emerging global regime for investment', *Harvard International Law Journal* 51 (2010), 427–73 at 470 ('The Washington Consensus – the shared belief … that increased investment, open economies, privatization, and economic deregulation would result in increased global prosperity and economic development – was a powerful force for the spread of investment treaties and the development of the regime that they created'); T. Sharot, *The Optimism Bias: A Tour of the Irrationally Positive Brain* (New York: Knopf Doubleday, 2011); T. H. Moran, *Harnessing Foreign Direct Investment for Development: Policies for Developed and Developing Countries* (Baltimore: Brookings Institution Press, 2006), pp. 72–4 (proposing a 'build-up' approach that involves greater liberalisation of the economy and can be used by poorer developing countries to harness foreign direct investment (FDI) and development).

[5] See C. Jolls, C. R. Sunstein and R. Thaler, 'A behavioral approach to law and economics', *Stanford Law Review* 50 (1998), 1471–550 at 1524–5 (identifying over-optimism as a common feature of human behaviour that leads people to think that their probability of a bad outcome is far less than that of others); D. Kahneman, *Thinking, Fast and Slow* (New York: Farrar, Straus and Giroux, 2011) (exploring cognitive biases and their effects in increasing people's perceived positive outcomes); D. Ariely, *Predictably Irrational: The Hidden Forces That Shape Our Decisions* (New York: HarperCollins, 2008) (discussing the role cognitive biases play in everyday decision-making, counteracting the presumption that individuals make decisions based on rational choice).

words, risks related to international investment are complicated and stakeholders would do well to first think in a more nuanced way so as to better manage expectations and promote better decision-making.

Understanding the causal link between IIAs and investment

Data is a critical element of managing expectations and disrupting the cognitive biases that lead to poor predictive conclusions. This section therefore considers the value that data can offer in evaluating the causal link between the value of an IIA and derivative investment flows.

The first link in Van Aaken's causal chain requires assessment of the value of entering into a treaty. The existing empirical literature suggests there is a binary choice, with two competing narratives, namely: (1) IIAs do facilitate foreign investment,[6] and (2) IIAs do not facilitate foreign investment.[7]

Yet recent research suggests the intriguing possibility that the merits of signing an IIA are more nuanced than an either–or dichotomy. Scholarship by Tobin and Rose-Ackerman[8] suggests that there is sometimes a positive relationship between IIAs and investment flows; but the story is typically complicated and without a universal narrative. In particular, these authors suggest that IIAs are a complement to – not a substitute for – the domestic regulation that facilitates investment.[9] Their empirical scholarship indicates that: (1) political risk can moderate the efficacy of an

---

[6] See D. L. Swenson, 'Why do developing countries sign BITS?', *University of California at Davis Journal of International Law and Policy* 12 (2005), 131–55 at 152–5 (evaluating statistical information on BITs throughout the 1990s, and concluding that countries that signed BITs were rewarded with increased levels of foreign investment); United Nations Conference on Trade and Development (UNCTAD), 'World Investment Report 2011: Non-Equity Modes of International Production and Development', UNCTAD (2011), www.unctad-docs.org/files/UNCTAD-WIR2011-Full-en.pdf (detailing the year-to-year growth of FDI flow around the world, and the increase of foreign investment dollars being invested among various states).

[7] See K. P. Sauvant and L. E. Sachs (eds.), *The Effect of Treaties on Foreign Direct Investment: Bilateral Investment Treaties, Double Taxation Treaties, and Investment Flows* (New York: Oxford University Press, 2009) (analysing data from prominent studies, in order to determine whether IIAs are effective legal instruments in attracting foreign investors and concluding that IIAs vary from having a strong effect on international investment flow to IIAs having no effect at all).

[8] J. L. Tobin and S. Rose-Ackerman, 'When BITs have some bite: the political-economic environment for bilateral investment treaties', *The Review of International Organizations* 6 (2011), 1–32.

[9] *Ibid.* at 28.

IIA,[10] and (2) the presence of other IIAs can affect the benefits of a treaty.[11] Similarly, recent scholarship by Jason Yackee analysed whether the presence of an IIA motivated international investors' investment decisions. He explained that 'grandiose claims about the historically demonstrated ability of [IIAs] to promote investment should be consumed with caution. [IIAs] may influence certain investment decisions.'[12]

This recent and nuanced research provides credible evidence that the value of IIAs is not monolithic. Rather, IIAs must be evaluated in a nuanced way. Using a particularised country-by-country and dyad-by-dyad understanding will aid states in making more realistic and evidence-based assessments of the value of IIAs. While this necessarily means more complexity, it reflects real-world variance that stakeholders ignore at their peril. Put simply, while IIAs can lead to investment in certain circumstances, stakeholders may need to lower their expectations about the degree and potential effect of IIAs so that they do not end up unnecessarily disappointed. They need to consider the likely net benefit of 'the grand bargain'[13] and then consider how to strategically maximise the benefits.

C.   Alignment of interest in investment

Even assuming all IIAs are reliably linked to increased investment flows, it is not guaranteed that investment will result in a positive development

[10] As political risk decreased, there were increases in investment. See *ibid.* at 21 ('Across all of the specifications, decreased political risk (a higher risk indicator) has a positive impact on FDI flows … for each one point that a country improves on the political risk scale, the impact of an additional BIT equates to a 1.1% increase in FDI flows'). In the examples Tobin and Rose-Ackerman offered, this translated into increased capital flow of US$1–1.2 million for every IIA signed; *ibid.* at 22.

[11] In the global competition for capital, the overall number of IIAs in a country and worldwide may suppress the positive investment flow that might otherwise be expected from an IIA. See *ibid.* at 17 ('As a country enters into greater numbers of BITs, if other countries do so as well, any positive impact is moderated by those other countries' actions').

[12] J. W. Yackee, 'Do bilateral investment treaties promote foreign direct investment? some hints from alternative evidence', *Virginia Journal of International Law* 51 (2010), 397–441 at 400; see also T. Allee and C. Peinhardt, 'Delegating differences: bilateral investment treaties and bargaining over dispute resolution provisions', *International Studies Quarterly* 54 (2010), 1–26 (exploring how different variables, particularly treaty dispute resolution mechanisms, can have implications for investment decisions).

[13] J. W. Salacuse and N. P. Sullivan, 'Do BITS really work?: an evaluation of bilateral investment treaties and their grand bargain', *Harvard International Law Journal* 46 (2005), 67–130 at 77.

Table 24.1. *Matrix of potential investment outcomes for different stakeholders*

Investor	State	Civil Society
Positive effect	Positive effect	Positive effect
Positive effect	Positive effect	Neutral or negative effect
Positive effect	Neutral or negative effect	Neutral or negative effect
Neutral or negative effect	Neutral or negative effect	Neutral or negative effect
Neutral or negative effect	Neutral or negative effect	Positive effect
Neutral or negative effect	Positive effect	Positive effect
Neutral or negative effect	Positive effect	Neutral or negative effect
Positive effect	Neutral or negative effect	Positive effect

outcome. Another element of managing expectations to avoid unnecessary dissatisfaction involves systemic evaluation of the permutations of the potential investment outcomes. While outcomes can theoretically be positive for host state development, the interests of all stakeholders are not always in perfect alignment.[14]

Investors, states and civil society groups all have important roles to play in the evolution of international investment law. As relevant stakeholders, their positions should be evaluated to consider the scope of potential variations. Even a simple model that considers: (1) the experience of the three key sets of stakeholders,[15] and (2) the potential outcomes of investment,[16] demonstrates the realistic probability for divergence. Table 24.1 provides a visual representation of this possibility. Presuming

[14] See generally E. Albæk, 'Knowledge, interests and the many meanings of evaluation: a developmental perspective', *International Journal of Social Welfare* 7 (1998), 94–8, 97 (discussing economic growth in the United States and acknowledging the 'increased awareness of the many stakeholders' divergent substantial interests as well as institutional interests').

[15] Future scholarship might undertake a more considered discussion about the nuances of different types of stakeholders in the international investment system. For the limited purposes of this exploratory essay, these three key groups have been identified as making significant contributions to international investment law.

[16] For the limited purposes of this exploratory essay, this variable is discrete in that it creates a binary variable to demarcate a distinction between: (a) positive investment outcomes, and (b) either neutral or negative investment outcomes. Future scholarship might create a more nuanced categorical variable or even a scaled range of possible outcomes.

these different permutations are all equally weighted, in only *one* of eight options is there perfect alignment between the effects of all interested stakeholders.

This should be sobering to those who assume that international investment is always a positive development for all stakeholders. It might even suggest that one should expect systemic dissatisfaction with investment outcomes.

This is not to say that there will not be success stories. Indeed, one would hope that investment choices are made with the objective of providing sustainable commercial opportunities for businesses, states and citizens. Yet that hope must be tempered with reality. Human beings have cognitive predispositions to be over-optimistic and overconfident about the success of their ventures.[17] After all, if 75 per cent or more of the population presumes that they are better than average drivers, at least 25 per cent of the population must be wrong.[18] If studies regularly demonstrate the risk of error in estimating something as basic as driving skill, consider the degree of error that may be involved in something as complex as international investment.

It is entirely possible that the mismanagement of expectations related to investment, normal cognitive biases and information-processing errors are part of the current dissatisfaction with the international investment regime. This dissatisfaction, in turn, contributes to the efforts to reclaim state regulatory authority and 'policy space', which José Alvarez has called, 'The Return of the State'.[19]

Unitary characterisations might require unitary solutions. Yet the reality is: international investment flows and development outcomes are complex and require complexity to provide constructive solutions. Dissatisfaction with investment outcomes may not necessarily require

---

17 See K. Schweizer, A. Beck-Seyffer and R. Schneider, 'Cognitive bias of optimism and its influence on psychological well-being', *Psychological Reports* 84 (1999), 627–36 (describing experiments demonstrating individuals' optimism bias and its effect).

18 The classic study by Baruch Fischoff found '[Seventy-five to ninety per cent] of drivers believe that they are better than the average': B. Fischhoff, 'Cognitive liabilities and products liability', *Journal of Products Liability* 1 (1977), 207–20 at 212; see also D. Kahneman, P. Slovic and A. Tversky, 'Judgment under uncertainty: heuristics and biases', *Science* 185 (1974), 1124–31; O. Svenson, 'Are we all less risky and more skillful than our fellow drivers?', *Acta Psychologica* 47 (1981), 143–8 at 146–7 (evaluating perceived driving skill and finding a self-serving bias where people viewed themselves more favourably, i.e. as less risky and more skilful).

19 J. E. Alvarez, 'The return of the state', *Minnesota Journal of International Law* 20 (2011), 223–64.

simple rejection or abandonment of the current IIA regime. There may be more subtle and tailored opportunities to redress dissatisfaction. Stakeholders might be better served by first recognising that perfect alignment with the social good of development will not necessarily be achieved in equal measures for all groups. Beyond this, stakeholders should consider that, more often than not, some of them will be dissatisfied at some point in the investment lifecycle. The question then becomes: (1) how can stakeholder expectations best be managed, and (2) what should be done to redress dissatisfaction with the process given the continuing need to facilitate both investment and economic development?

The next section explores these two related areas. First, it considers how we might manage expectations by conceptualising the regulation of IIAs and development in a more nuanced way. Second, it identifies additional areas for structuring regulatory authority. Finally, it suggests that strategic use of these different opportunities will create better institutional balance in international investment law that more appropriately manages expectations, promotes stakeholder choice and hopefully increases satisfaction with international investment and its regulation.

D. Systemic regulatory opportunities

Global administrative law, or global regulatory law, posits that there is a new administrative legal space that exists beyond the traditional nation-state boundaries. Rather than the traditionally public bodies exercising regulatory conduct, a confluence of public, private and public-private hybrid actors perform key regulatory functions.[20] Scholarship has

---

[20] S. Montt, *State Liability in Investment Treaty Arbitration: Global Constitutional and Administrative Law in the BIT Generation* (Portland: Hart, 2009); see also N. Krisch and B. Kingsbury, 'Introduction: global governance and global administrative law in the international legal order', *European Journal of International Law* 17 (2006), 1–13 at 3 (providing a detailed explanation of global administrative law – how administrative and regulatory functions are performed in a global context – and providing examples of a number of different forms in which regulatory functions of global governance take place); A. Mills, 'Antinomies of public and private at the foundations of international investment law and arbitration', *Journal of International Economic Law* 14 (2011), 469–503 at 485–6, 489 (exploring how investment law's use of arbitration can be viewed as a law-making administrative process); S. W. Schill, 'System-building in investment treaty arbitration and lawmaking', *German Law Journal* 12 (2011), 1083–110 at 1101, 1107–8 (investigating regulatory functions outsourced by treaties and its implications).

begun to apply these concepts to international investment law.[21] Thinking about investment law through this framework provides an opportunity for systemic evaluation.

I. The framework of global administrative law

Administrative law operates primarily through rule-making or adjudication. Both forms of regulation involve a state policy choice that has a normative application to the lives of individuals. Adjudication is a more specific application of law to an individualised context. Adjudication can involve, for example, a judge or other neutral third-party adjudicating the facts before him or her in light of the applicable legal regime. Rule-making, by contrast, is more generalised. It does, however, require the articulation of legal rules and, potentially, interpretive guidelines or examples to guide the application of the broader principles. These forms of administrative regulation can happen through both formal and informal mechanisms.[22] In theory, this means that there are at least four categories of regulatory activity: (1) formal rule-making, (2) formal adjudication, (3) informal rule-making and (4) informal adjudication.

Currently, international investment law functions almost exclusively through a formal paradigm. Regulation starts through the context of formal rule-making. This limited formal activity involves treaty-drafting. It can also take the shape of treaty renegotiation or the drafting of interpretive statements issued by entities with designated authority.[23] These

---

[21] See G. V. Harten and M. Loughlin, 'Investment treaty arbitration as a species of global administrative law', *European Journal of International Law* 17 (2006), 121–50 (explaining four key features of investment treaties and how, together, international investment arbitration best exemplifies global administrative law); see generally Montt, *State Liability in Investment Treaty Arbitration* (recognising investment arbitration as a form of public law adjudication while trying to fill in the gaps regarding the political and legal consequences of developing countries in investment treaties).

[22] In the United States, for example, regulatory discretion operates through the rubric of the Administrative Procedure Act (APA) that sets the standards through which regulatory discretion operates. See Administrative Procedure Act, 5 U.S.C. §§ 500–596 (2000); see also Koch, *Administrative Law and Practice*, §10:1 (providing a brief overview of the four fundamental processes of administrative law – formal and informal adjudication and rule-making); D. Zaring, 'Informal procedure, hard and soft, in international administration', *Chicago Journal of International Law* 5 (2005), 547–604.

[23] For example, the North American Free Trade Agreement (NAFTA) Free Trade Commission has issued an Interpretative Note. See NAFTA, 'Notes of Interpretation of Certain Chapter 11 Provisions', *Foreign Affairs and International Trade Canada* (31 July 2001), available at: www.international.gc.ca/trade-agreements-accords-commerciaux/disp-diff/NAFTA-Interpr.aspx?lang=en&view=d.

processes have created an international law regime with broad standards concerning the treatment of investment. Despite the formality of the rule creation framework, there have been few clear articulations of individualised rules or textual explanations of how the regulatory regime should be applied. Given this gap, it is perhaps no surprise that – to date – the majority of regulation in international investment law has occurred within the context of formal adjudication. By virtue of both the creation of broad standards and the treaty's outsourcing of the adjudicative function, international arbitrators have become the de facto regulators of international investment law.

This focus on formal regulation has benefits. First, it is a move beyond the violence associated with gunboat diplomacy.[24] Second, it provides a check on the unfettered discretion of diplomacy and creates standards for evaluating the merits of economic rights.[25] Third, it promotes judicialisation of economic rights and provides a chance of enhanced predictability.[26] Finally, placing regulatory decisions into the hands of neutral parties can prevent undue politicisation.[27] Focusing on the expedient resolution of economic rights in a neutral forum has the potential to decrease

---

[24] See generally J. Cable, *Gunboat Diplomacy 1919–1991: Political Applications of Limited Naval Force*, 3rd edn (New York: St. Martin's Press, 1994) (giving background information and the history of gunboat diplomacy); F. MacErlean, 'Argentina Launches Naval Campaign to Isolate Falkland Islands', *Telegraph*, 5 December 2011, available at: www.telegraph.co.uk/news/worldnews/southamerica/falklandislands/8936750/Argentina-launches-naval-campaign-to-isolate-Falkland-Islands.html (discussing the naval campaigns Argentina launched to isolate the Falkland Islands, which symbolise a present-day example of gunboat diplomacy).

[25] See C. N. Brower and S. W. Schill, 'Is arbitration a threat or a boon to the legitimacy of international investment law?', *Chicago Journal of International Law* 9 (2009), 471–98 at 480–1 (explaining why it is difficult for investors to enforce promises made by host states as well as the drawbacks that weaken diplomatic protection in forcing host states to comply with those promises); A. K. Bjorklund, 'Sovereign immunity as a barrier to the enforcement of investor-state arbitral awards: the re-politicization of international investment disputes', *American Review of International Arbitration* 21 (2010), 211–41 (discussing how the sovereign immunity laws of a specific state play a role in preventing investors from enforcing a judgment against the host state).

[26] See Hudec, 'The Judicialization of GATT Dispute Settlement', p. 9 (discussing the legalisation in international economic law).

[27] See I. F. I. Shihata, 'Toward a Greater Depoliticization of Investment Disputes: The Roles of ICSID and MIGA' in K. W. Lu, G. Verheyen and S. M. Perera (eds.), *Investing with Confidence: Understanding Political Risk Management in the 21st Century* (Danvers World Bank, 2009) (discussing how international investment disputes have evolved through the years, from politicised disputes requiring the exercise of diplomatic protection and use of force, to the formation of organisations that offer a forum for conflict resolution and depoliticisation of investment disputes).

economic risk and increase investment – hopefully with the concomitant objectives of development.

Nevertheless, exclusive reliance on formal regulation has costs. Such reliance ignores the value potentially derived from thinking systemically about informal regulatory regimes. This means that value is either potentially left on the table or otherwise lost. Moreover, the current system is heavily skewed towards only one form of regulation – formal adjudication. This has certain negative implications. First, as arbitrators are not necessarily from the state or states involved in the IIA, this creates concerns related to a potential democracy deficit.[28] Second, the fragmented nature of the adjudicative regime can create challenges in generating a stable and predictable system.[29] This lack of predictability may, in turn, create negative externalities for the efficacy of investment law and the economic value derived from IIAs. Third, the abundance of discretion in the adjudicative process can give rise to concerns related to abuse of discretion or improper interpretation.[30] Finally, the nearly exclusive outsourcing of regulatory authority to non-state actors raises concerns about the proper balance of state authority and the rights of individuals or corporations.[31] These concerns are no small matters and are, perhaps, contributing to the current backlash against investment treaty arbitration.[32]

---

[28] See I. Lee, 'Practice and predicament: the nationality of the international arbitrator (with survey results)', *Fordham International Law Journal* 31 (2008), 603–33 at 604 (discussing how the practice of national neutrality is widely followed and parties commonly insist that the arbitrator be a national of a country other than those of the parties).

[29] C. N. Brower, 'The evolution of the international judiciary: denationalization through jurisdictional fragmentation', *American Society of International Procedure* 103 (2009), 171–86 at 184 (illustrating the potential for the fragmentation of the international legal system through the example of the conflict between the International Criminal Tribunal for the former Yugoslavia (ICTY) and ICJ over legal doctrine, giving rise to disparate results depending on which tribunal was viewing the problem).

[30] See D. Schneiderman, 'Judicial politics and international investment arbitration: seeking an explanation for conflicting outcomes', *Northwestern Journal of International Law and Business* 30 (2010), 383–416 at 405 (discussing inconsistent Argentinian arbitration awards, based upon identical or similar facts, in order to try and shed light on the process of arbitral decision-making); J. Paulsson, 'Moral hazard in international dispute resolution', *ICSID Review* 25 (2010), 339–55 at 343–7 (illustrating the possibility of improper arbitrator activity by reference to anecdotal information).

[31] See S. A. Spears, 'The quest for policy space in a new generation of international investment agreements', *Journal of International Economic Law* 13(4) (2010), 1037–75 at 1072–3 (discussing the new generation of IIAs and the attempts to balance private adjudication and public policy).

[32] See M. Waibel *et al.*, *The Backlash Against Investment Arbitration: Perceptions and Reality* (Alphen aan den Rijn: Kluwer Law International, 2010) (discussing the current backlash, both procedural and substantive, against investment arbitration, from a multitude of

II. *Exploring untapped value*

The focus on formal adjudication has consequences. It both undervalues the possible role for formal rule-making and leaves the potential value of informal regulatory activity untapped. This outcome suggests three things. First, the status quo may necessitate a rebalancing of the regulatory pendulum to focus on complementary or complete alternatives to capture regulatory discretion and manage investment-related conflict. Second, it necessitates stakeholders making more informed and systematic choices about where they choose to place regulatory discretion. Finally, any adjustments in stakeholders' approaches to the management of investment risk have the capacity to more adequately manage expectations about the role of investment and the role of state authority. Put simply, in the investment context, optimism must be met with realism; realism requires reassessment of the most appropriate method(s) for regulating international investment; and stakeholder expectations should be tempered accordingly.

III. *Formal rule-making*

One of the most critical areas of untapped value is formal rule-making. Utilising formal rule-making capacity could take a variety of forms.

In the first instance, it could require greater particularisation of international investment rules. In their current shape, the broad standards in international investment treaties provide minimal guidance on the law and its application. Given the academic quagmire of the rules versus standards debate[33] and vague treaty standards outsourcing

viewpoints concerning the present state of investment arbitration within the larger international legal regime); see also A. Kaushal, 'Revisiting history: how the past matters for the present backlash against the foreign investment regime', *Harvard International Law Journal* 50 (2009), 491–534 (giving a historical perspective on the backlash against international investment law and arbitration).

[33] See, e.g., L. Kaplow, 'Rules versus standards: an economic analysis', *Duke Law Journal* 42 (1992), 557–629; see also A. van Aaken, 'International investment law between commitment and flexibility: a contract theory analysis', *Journal of International Economic Law* 12 (2009), 507–38; D. A. Crane, 'Rules versus standards in antitrust adjudication', *Washington and Lee Law Review* 64 (2007), 49–119; D. Bodansky, 'Rules vs. standards in international environmental law', *American Society of International Law Proceedings* 98 (2004), 275–80; J. P. Trachtman, 'The domain of WTO dispute resolution', *Harvard International Law Journal* 40 (1999), 333–77; J. Braithwaite and V. Braithwaite, 'The politics of legalism: rules versus standards in nursing home regulation', *Social and Legal Studies* 4 (1995), 307–41; D. Kennedy, 'Form and substance in private law adjudication', *Harvard Law Review* 89 (1976), 1685–778.

interpretation, the adjudicative capture of regulatory authority is not surprising. States may, therefore, do well to reclaim their regulatory space by providing greater detail in the text of their investment treaties. Such detail need not only include more specificity regarding the text of substantive investor rights. It may also include: (1) specific defences, exclusions and non-precluded measures in the text of treaties, (2) clear guidance to tribunals as to how they *must* interpret the substantive text of the treaty, (3) express statements about procedural matters, including any requirements about pleading damages with specificity in the request for arbitration or articulating the methodology for calculating damages, (4) identification and definition of the values that underlie that interpretative guidance, such as sustainable development, or (5) an express prioritisation of the rights contained in the treaty. In other words, states should consider how best to recapture their own discretion and then precisely outsource discretion to arbitrators. This, in turn, offers arbitrators a greater degree of guidance as to how they should and must apply the law. It also sets the expectations of stakeholders before, during and after the dispute.

A higher degree of specificity in the text of treaties is not the only answer. Much like NAFTA Free Trade Commissions,[34] states may derive value from constituting an inter-state panel or other agency that is delegated the task of providing greater clarity about the meaning and application of international investment law. Overall, the objectives of such formal rule-making and the codification of international investment law are to avoid delegation problems, decrease the risk of principal–agent problems and provide clarity to manage stakeholder expectations.

IV.   Informal rule-making and informal adjudication

The other critical untapped opportunities are related to informal regulation. Simply using the term 'informal' does not mean that such regulatory conduct is completely without reference to standards. Rather, it would simply provide an opportunity to offer regulation but without the comprehensive formality of treaty negotiation and ratification.[35] Such

---

[34] See n. 23 (examining the ability of NAFTA's Free Trade Commission to engage in interpretative rule-making, in clarifying the meaning of the treaty).

[35] The ideas in this chapter are preliminary and would require additional details to avoid problems such as an entity being deemed to have impermissibly amended a treaty through its own regulatory authority.

informal activity could include, for example, informal rule-making and informal adjudication.[36]

In the context of informal rule-making, one might imagine the creation of a Lead Government Agency (LGA) within a host state that has been delegated the task of ensuring the state is in compliance with its international law obligations. Such an LGA might even consider how best to create rules and internal protocols that are designed to facilitate conflict resolution, as well as manage and promote dispute prevention.[37] Likewise, although possibly more formal, this might also take the form of negotiated rule-making to bring together different stakeholder groups to fashion rules or investment law guidance. These options can aid the preservation of state discretion and 'policy space', the promotion of state regulatory flexibility and the creation of opportunities to provide legal clarity.

In the context of informal adjudication, there are a myriad of options. Whether in the form of an LGA or an ombudsman service, it is possible to create an entity that helps resolve investment conflicts informally and prevents them from becoming full-blown formal disputes. Examples include early neutral evaluation, expert determination, evaluative mediation or other less formalised conflict management mechanisms. The United Nations Conference on Trade and Development has

---

[36] Another benefit of informal regulation involves the minimisation of 'regulatory fatigue' that is created by more formal processes. See R. B. Stewart, 'Administrative law in the 21st century', *New York University Law Review* 78 (2003), 437–60, at 446–7.

[37] See A. Joubin-Bret and J. Knörich, 'Investor–state disputes: prevention and alternatives to arbitration', UNCTAD Series on International Investment Policies for Development (2010), 77–9, available at: www.unctad.org/en/docs/diaeia200911_en.pdf (hereinafter ADR I) (examining the programme launched by the Ministry of Commerce and the Government of Columbia creating a lead agency that would be the centralised authority for all matters related to investor–state disputes); J. H. Kim, 'Republic of Korea's development of a better investor-state dispute resolution system', UNCTAD, Investor–State Disputes: Prevention and Alternatives to Arbitration II (2011), 69–70, available at: www. unctad.org/en/docs/webdiaeia20108_en.pdf (hereinafter ADR II) (explaining how the Republic of Korea's efforts included the formation of a committee which is responsible for establishing policies regarding investment treaties); *ibid.*, 97 (elaborating on the Republic of Korea's creation of the Foreign Investment Promotion Law whose Article 1 established The Office of the Foreign Investment Ombudsman with the purpose of resolving issues faced by foreign-invested companies in Korea); *ibid.*, 63 (developing four areas for states to evolve including '(1) putting trained officials into central posts of the administration, (2) implementing mandatory consultations, (3) establishing new types of investment treaty practice and (4) implementing continuing legal education of civil servants in investment related matters').

already identified early successes in this area[38] as it permits flexibility and the retention of state policy space. With the requisite degree of capacity-building and protocols, it may be possible to move beyond formal adjudication to a more nuanced approach to the regulation of international investment law.

One size may not fit all when it comes to the regulation of international investment. Overreliance on formal adjudication breeds dissatisfaction, particularly where the regulatory question can be addressed more directly and effectively through an alternative process. To manage expectations better and maximise the value of investment regulation, more than one process may be necessary. Perhaps more likely, a series of processes may be essential to promote a nuanced use of regulatory authority while promoting choice and values of procedural justice.

E.   Conclusion

This nuanced approach to managing the regulatory process, and a recognition that international investment will not normally have a positive result for all stakeholders all the time, can help to manage expectations related to international investment. In turn, this can start to alleviate dissatisfaction with the system and promote a more realistic and balanced basis for regulating international investment.

Overall, the international investment system is neither wholly evil nor wholly good. False dichotomies and overly simplistic characterisations hide the complexity of international investment and promote an overreliance on inaccurate caricatures. Rather, an evidence-based, nuanced analysis is preferable. This permits consideration of specific dynamics relating to stakeholder objectives in light of particularised cost–benefit

---

[38] See ADR I, note 37, 68–74 (examining, in detail, how Peru has set up a government agency to distribute information on IIAs to their governmental agencies, including the creation of an alert system, as well as standardising information and responses to potential and actual IIA disputes); *ibid.*, 88–93 (discussing how the Republic of Korea set up an independent ombudsman programme to monitor IIAs, and assist foreign investors in navigating Korea's business environment, while working to increase the overall investment environment); see also ADR II, note 37, 97 (giving additional historical background on the development of the Republic of Korea's ombudsman programme and explaining some of the remarkable success the programme has experienced).

analysis of an individual IIA regime. This should promote informed choices about where regulatory discretion is best placed and avoid distortion caused by inadvertent cognitive biases. The ultimate goal is to use a flexible and nuanced approach to regulatory choices to foster a more realistic assessment and utilisation of the international investment regime.

PART VI

From an uneven international investment regime towards a coherent international investment system: the way forward

25

Coherence and consistency in international investment law

CHRISTOPH SCHREUER

A. The role of nationality

Coherence and consistency are desirable qualities in any legal system. A legal system is coherent if its elements are logically related to each other and if it shows no contradictions. A legal system is consistent if it treats identical or similar situations in the same way and if it gives equal treatment to the participants in the system. These properties are most easily achieved through rules of general application administered by decision-makers with general jurisdiction.

International investment law lacks coherence and consistency in several respects. In large measure this is a consequence of its legal foundations. There are a large number of bilateral treaties (notably bilateral investment treaties or BITs). There are regional treaties such as the North American Free Trade Agreement (NAFTA) and the Energy Charter Treaty (ECT). And there are some widely applicable multilateral treaties such as the International Centre for Settlement of Investment Disputes (ICSID) Convention. These treaties accord various degrees of protection to the nationals of the states participating in them.

A closer look at this network shows that it does not offer a coherent system of protection. Rather, it is a fragmentary patchwork that favours some investors while ignoring others. The decisive criterion is usually the investor's nationality or, more precisely, the existence of favourable treaty relations between the host state and the investor's home state.

The investor's nationality is relevant for several reasons. The substantive standards guaranteed by a treaty will only apply to nationals of the states parties to the treaty (although permanent residents are sometimes included). In addition, the jurisdiction of an international tribunal is determined, inter alia, by the claimant's nationality. In particular, if the host state's consent to jurisdiction is given through a treaty, the offer will only apply to nationals of a state that is a party to the treaty. Access to ICSID arbitration is limited to nationals of states that are parties to the ICSID Convention. In addition, the ICSID Convention contains a negative nationality requirement: host state nationals are generally excluded.

Similar considerations apply to regional treaties. Only nationals of Canada, Mexico and the United States may rely on the NAFTA against one of the other two states parties. Only nationals of states parties to the ECT benefit from that treaty vis-à-vis any of the other states parties to that treaty.

In the absence of the right treaty relations of their home states, investors will find themselves without protection. But even investors who can rely on a BIT may find that they do not enjoy the same protection as a competitor who has a different nationality. BITs vary considerably. Some provide more comprehensive protection than others. These differences can arise from variations in the level of substantive protection offered. A particular treaty may not include all the substantive standards offered by other treaties. Alternatively the differences can also arise from variations in the treaties' clauses on dispute settlement. Some cover any dispute arising from an investment. Others are restricted to claims arising from breaches of the treaty. Yet other clauses are restricted to disputes relating to expropriations. In addition, access to international arbitration is often subject to a variety of conditions and procedural requirements.

It follows that investors enjoy different levels of protection in relation to the same host state depending on their nationality. Identical or similar fact situations may lead to different outcomes depending on the investors' nationalities. The existence, absence or variation in contents of treaties for the protection of investments is an important cause of inconsistency in the system. But, as will be seen below, it is not the only one.

This preoccupation with nationality in international investment law leads to a paradoxical situation. Nationality is extremely important for the purpose of gaining access to investment arbitration, or generally for protection under treaties. In actual cases, much time and effort is spent in proving or disproving a particular nationality.[1] But when a case reaches the merits, strangely enough, discrimination on the basis of nationality is prohibited: an expropriation that discriminates between investors

---

[1] See, e.g., *Hussein Nuaman Soufraki v. United Arab Emirates* (Award), International Centre for Settlement of Investment Disputes (ICSID) Case No. ARB/02/7, 7 July 2004; *Waguih Elie George Siag v. Arab Republic of Egypt* (Decision on Jurisdiction), ICSID Case No. ARB/05/15, 11 April 2007.

of different nationalities is illegal.[2] There are rules against arbitrary and discriminatory treatment, which includes discrimination on the basis of nationality. Also, discrimination on the basis of nationality would be a violation of the fair and equitable treatment standard.[3] In order to forestall differentiations on the basis of nationality, most treaties contain national treatment and most-favoured nation (MFN) clauses. Discrimination on the basis of nationality constitutes a violation of these clauses.

Distinctions on the basis of nationality are therefore illogical: they are mandated in some contexts and prohibited in others. This leads to conflicting results and affects the system's coherence.

Apart from legal logic, distinctions on the basis of nationality are also unsavoury from an ethical standpoint. Why should individuals and corporations have widely differing rights depending on the accident of their nationality? Unequal treatment of investors that are in like circumstances offends our sense of justice. Yet we seem to be trapped in a paradigm of treaty law that appears to require discrimination based on the accidents of treaty relations.

A number of remedies have been devised to tackle this form of unevenness in the system. Some of these remedies are widely available but are limited in their effectiveness. Other possible remedies would be highly effective but appear unattainable, at least for the time being.

B. MFN clauses

MFN clauses are widely available. An MFN clause in a treaty will extend the better treatment granted to a third state or its nationals to the beneficiary of the treaty.[4] Most BITs, and some other treaties for the protection of investments, contain some form of MFN clause.[5] But there are considerable variations in detail. For instance, some MFN clauses specify whether they include or exclude dispute settlement.[6] However, most

---

[2] See, e.g., *ADC Affiliate Limited and ADC & ADMC Management Limited* v. *Republic of Hungary* (Award), ICSID Case No. ARB/03/16, 2 October 2006, paras. 441–443.

[3] See, e.g., *CMS Gas Transmission Company* v. *Argentine Republic* (Award), ICSID Case No. ARB/01/8, 12 May 2005, para. 290.

[4] See also R. Dolzer and T. Myers, 'After *Tecmed*: Most-favored-nation clauses in investment protection agreements', *ICSID Review – FILJ* 19 (2004), 49–60.

[5] See Article 1103 of North American Free Trade Agreement (NAFTA); Article 10(7) of Energy Charter Treaty (ECT).

[6] The bilateral investment treaty (BIT) between Austria and Kazakhstan specifies in Article 3(3) that most-favoured nation (MFN) treatment extends to dispute settlement.

MFN clauses are worded in general terms and just refer to the treatment of investments.

MFN clauses have considerable potential for the achievement of coherence and consistency. If applied rigorously they could lead to the levelling of differences based on nationality.[7] Yet their effect is limited. Practice shows that they are often approached with trepidation and applied in a half-hearted manner. The applicability of MFN clauses is uncontested as far as the substantive standards of protection are concerned. If an applicable treaty does not contain a clause on fair and equitable treatment (FET), the treaty's MFN clause will usually close the gap. It will be possible to import the FET clause from a treaty between the host state and a third state.[8]

The situation is different when it comes to questions of dispute settlement. The usefulness of an MFN clause to amend the basic treaty's arbitration clause is hotly contested. Most tribunals have allowed the application of MFN clauses to overcome procedural obstacles. These would often require resort to domestic courts for a certain period of time before arbitration became available.[9] By contrast, where claimants tried to import more generous offers of consent to arbitration from other treaties by invoking MFN clauses they usually failed.[10]

---

[7] See S. W. Schill, 'Multilateralizing investment treaties through most-favored-nation clauses', *Berkeley Journal of International Law* 27 (2009), 496–569.

[8] *Bayindir Insaat Turizm Ticaret Ve Sanayi A.S.* v. *Islamic Republic of Pakistan* (Award), ICSID Case No. ARB/03/29, 27 August 2009, paras. 148–167.

[9] *Emilio Augustín Maffezini* v. *Kingdom of Spain* (Decision on Jurisdiction), ICSID Case No. ARB/97/7, 25 January 2000, paras. 38–64; *Siemens A.G.* v. *Argentine Republic* (Decision on Jurisdiction), ICSID Case No. ARB/02/8, 3 August 2004, paras. 94–110; *Gas Natural SDG, S.A.* v. *Argentine Republic* (Decision on Jurisdiction), ICSID Case No. ARB/03/10, 17 June 2005, paras. 24–31, 41–9; *Suez, Sociedad General de Aguas de Barcelona S.A., and InterAguas Servicios Integrales del Agua S.A.* v. *Argentine Republic* (Decision on Jurisdiction), ICSID Case No. ARB/03/17, 16 May 2006, paras. 52–66; *National Grid PCL* v. *Argentina* (Decision on Jurisdiction), United Nations Commission on International Trade Law (UNCITRAL), 20 June 2006, paras. 53–94; *Aguas Cordobesas S.A., Suez, Sociedad General de Aguas de Barcelona S.A., and Vivendi Universal S.A.* v. *Argentine Republic,* ICSID Case No. ARB/03/18; *AWG Group Ltd.* v. *Argentina* (Decision on Jurisdiction), United Nations Commission on International Trade Law (UNCITRAL) ad hoc, 3 August 2006, paras. 52–68; *Impregilo S.p.A.* v. *Argentine Republic* (Award), ICSID Case No. ARB/08/14, 21 June 2011, paras. 51–109; *Hochtief AG* v. *Argentine Republic* (Decision on Jurisdiction), ICSID Case No. ARB/07/31, 24 October 2011, paras. 12–111. But see *Wintershall Aktiengesellschaft* v. *Argentine Republic* (Award), ICSID Case No. ARB/04/14, 8 December 2008, paras. 158–197.

[10] *Salini Costruttori S.p.A. and Italshade S.p.A.* v. *Hashemite Kingdom of Jordan* (Decision on Jurisdiction), ICSID Case No. ARB/02/13, 29 November 2004, para. 119; *Plama Consortium Limited* v. *Republic of Bulgaria* (Decision on Jurisdiction), ICSID Case

To make the situation even more confusing, tribunals have adopted broad statements either embracing or rejecting the use of MFN clauses in the context of dispute settlement.[11] Therefore, the distinction between procedural issues and questions of consent for purposes of MFN treatment is not supported by the reasoning of tribunals.

The usefulness of MFN clauses as instruments for achieving a more coherent system presupposes three elements:

1. There must be an applicable basic treaty upon which the investor may rely containing an MFN clause.
2. There must be another treaty of the host state providing for the better treatment that is desired.
3. The tribunal must be persuaded that the MFN clause should be applied to the issue in question. This is often not possible when it comes to dispute settlement.

C.   Nationality-planning

A more radical approach is nationality-planning. In relation to a particular host state nationals of some countries may be unable to benefit from a BIT or other treaty. Others may find that an available BIT does not offer the desired protection. Yet other nationals may be able to rely on a treaty that offers the required level of security. Nationality-planning consists in the deliberate acquisition of a nationality that gives access to the desired protection. Most often this will be done through the creation of a corporate structure that allows the investor to rely on a favourable treaty.

If the treaty in question accepts incorporation as a sufficient basis for corporate nationality, all that is required is the establishment of a corporation in the state that has the favourable treaty with the host state. That

No. ARB/03/24, 8 February 2005, paras. 183, 184, 227; *Vladimir Berschader and Moïse Berschader* v. *The Russian Federation* (Award), Arbitration Institute of the Stockholm Chamber of Commerce (SCC) Case No. 080/2004, 21 April 2006, paras. 159–208; *Telenor Mobile Communications A.S.* v. *Republic of Hungary* (Award), ICSID Case No. ARB/04/15, 13 September 2006, paras. 90–100; *Tza Yap Shum* v. *Republic of Peru* (Decision on Jurisdiction), ICSID Case No. ARB/02/8, 19 June 2009, paras. 189–220; *Austrian Airlines* v. *Slovak Republic* (Final Award), UNCITRAL, 9 October 2009, paras. 109–140. But see *RosInvest Co. UK Ltd.* v. *The Russian Federation* (Award on Jurisdiction), Stockholm Chamber of Commerce (SCC) Case No. 079/2005, October 2007, paras. 124–139.

[11] Contrast *Gas Natural SDG, S.A.* v. *Argentine Republic* (Decision on Jurisdiction), ICSID Case No. ARB/03/10, 17 June 2005, para. 49 and *Plama* v. *Bulgaria, Plama Consortium Limited* v. *Republic of Bulgaria* (Decision on Jurisdiction), ICSID Case No. ARB/03/24, 8 February 2005, para. 223.

corporation may serve as a conduit for a new investment or as a holding company for an existing investment.

Nationality-planning or treaty-shopping is neither illegal nor unethical as such; but states may regard such practices as undesirable and take appropriate measures against them.

A strategy employed in some treaties to counteract nationality-planning is to require a bond of economic substance between the investor and the state whose nationality is claimed. Such an economic bond may consist of effective control over the corporation by a national of that state. Alternatively, it may consist of genuine economic activity of the company in that state. Another strategy is the insertion of a so-called denial of benefits clause into the treaty that provides for jurisdiction. Under such a clause the states reserve the right to deny the benefits of the treaty to a company that does not have a genuine economic connection to the state whose nationality it claims.[12]

In the absence of treaty clauses designed to block nationality-planning, tribunals have accepted deliberately structured nationalities in some situations[13] but have dismissed them in others. They have accepted provident nationality-planning that was designed to put investments under the protective umbrella of investment treaties,[14] but they have limited this acceptance to prospective planning. Prospective means that the corporate arrangements must have been in place before the facts that led to the dispute occurred, or at any rate before the dispute arose. They have rejected *ex post facto* corporate restructuring to create a remedy after a dispute had occurred.[15]

---

[12] ECT, Article 17(1).

[13] *Autopista Concesionada de Venezuela* v. *Bolivarian Republic of Venezuela* (Decision on Jurisdiction), ICSID Case No. ARB/00/5, 27 September 2001, paras. 83, 89–91, 110–134, 142; *Tokios Tokelés* v. *Ukraine* (Decision on Jurisdiction), ICSID Case No. ARB/02/18, 29 April 2004, paras. 18–71; *Aguas del Tunari* v. *Republic of Bolivia* (Decision on Jurisdiction), ICSID Case No. ARB/02/3, 21 October 2005, paras. 206–323, 329–332; *Saluka Investment BV* v. *The Czech Republic* (Partial Award), Swiss Federal Tribunal Decision, 4P.114/2006/bie, 17 March 2006, paras. 229, 241; *ADC Affiliate Limited and ADC & ADMC Management Limited* v. *Republic of Hungary* (Award), ICSID Case No. ARB/03/16, 2 October 2006, paras. 334–341, 350, 357–9; *Rompetrol Group N.V.* v. *Romania* (Decision on Jurisdiction and Admissibility), ICSID Case No. ARB/06/3, 18 April 2008, paras. 71–110.

[14] *Mobil* v. *Bolivarian Republic of Venezuela* (Decision on Jurisdiction), ICSID Case No. ARB/07/27, 10 June 2010, paras. 142–206.

[15] *Banro American Resources, Inc. and Société Aurifère du Kivu et du Maniema S.A.R.L.* v. *Democratic Republic of Congo* (Award), ICSID Case No. ARB/98/7, 1 September 2000; *Phoenix Action Ltd* v. *Czech Republic* (Award), ICSID Case No. ARB/06/5, 15 April 2009, 135–145; *Cementownia Nowa Huta S.A.* v. *Republic of Turkey* (Award), ICSID Case No. ARB(AF)/06/2, 17 September 2009, paras. 116–7, 122–3, 136, 153–7.

The success of nationality planning therefore depends primarily on the timing of the corporate structure's creation in relation to the relevant facts. If the restructuring is undertaken early on, that is before the adverse acts or at any rate before the occurrence of the dispute, the newly acquired nationality will be honoured. But a last-minute change of nationality in the face of an existing dispute will be rejected.

It follows from the above that nationality-planning as an instrument for achieving coherence and consistency has serious limitations:

1. It requires careful forward planning.
2. The administrative effort involved is typically realistic only for major investors.
3. It requires the existence of a favourable treaty that accepts incorporation as a sufficient connecting point for nationality.
4. It is subject to preventive measures embedded in the treaty such as the requirement for a real economic activity or a denial of benefits clause.

D.   A Multilateral Agreement on Investment (MAI)

An effective method to achieve coherence and consistency would be the creation of a multilateral treaty to replace the multitude of diverse bilateral and regional treaties. Such a treaty could grant identical substantive and procedural rights to investors from all participating countries. A treaty of this nature, if widely ratified, would make nationality largely irrelevant. It would offer the same level of substantive and procedural protection to all investors.

A MAI, while technically feasible, is not a realistic possibility under present circumstances. Repeated efforts to draft such a treaty have all failed for a variety of reasons. At present, the chances for the success of such a project are slimmer than ever. Negotiations for the drafting of such an agreement would open a veritable Pandora's Box of discord. In the unlikely event that agreement on a text were to be achieved, universal or near universal acceptance is unlikely.

E.   Rights for nationals of non-contracting states

The limitation of benefits arising from treaties to nationals of participating states is not a necessary consequence of the law of treaties. It is entirely possible to extend rights arising from treaties to nationals of non-contracting states. Treaties for the protection of human rights are a case in point. For instance, the European Convention on Human

Rights guarantees rights and freedoms to everyone within the jurisdiction of the participating states regardless of nationality.[16] Similarly, applications to the European Court of Human Rights claiming violations of rights set forth in the Convention may be submitted by 'any person'.[17]

The limitation of rights under investment treaties to nationals of participating states is based on a conscious decision. Human rights are accepted as having universal application. Their observance is accepted as an indispensable guarantee of human dignity. By contrast, economic rights of foreigners are regarded as a matter of economic policy. States are only willing to offer treaty guarantees to investors on the basis of reciprocity.

F. Conflicting interpretations

Gaps and discrepancies in treaty relations are not the only cause of problems with the coherence and consistency of international investment law. At times, similar or identical treaty provisions in BITs are interpreted in different ways. Sometimes one and the same treaty provision is interpreted differently by different tribunals. For instance, in the application of the clause on emergency in the BIT between Argentina and the United States, tribunals have reached widely divergent results even in relation to the same facts.[18]

Discordant interpretations of this kind are a consequence of the nature of investment arbitration. Each tribunal is put together on an ad hoc

---

[16] European Convention for the Protection of Human Rights and Fundamental Freedoms, Article 1.

[17] *Ibid.*, Article 34.

[18] *CMS Gas Transmission Company* v. *Argentine Republic* (Award), ICSID Case No. ARB/01/8, 12 May 2005, paras. 332–378; *CMS Gas Transmission Company* v. *Argentine Republic* (Decision on Annulment), ICSID Case No. ARB/01/8, 25 September 2007, paras. 101–150; *LG&E Energy Corp. and others* v. *Argentine Republic* (Decision on Liability), ICSID Case No. ARB/02/1, 3 October 2006, paras. 201–266; *Enron Corporation and Panderosa Assets, L.P.* v. *Argentine Republic* (Award), 22 May 2007, paras. 322–342; *Enron Corporation and Panderosa Assets, L.P.* v. *Argentine Republic* (Decision on Annulment), 30 July 2010, paras. 347–405; *Sempra Energy International* v. *Argentine Republic* (Award), ICSID Case No. ARB/02/16, 28 September 2007, paras. 364–391; *Sempra Energy International* v. *Argentine Republic* (Decision on Annulment), ICSID Case No. ARB/02/16, 29 June 2010, paras. 106–221; *Continental Casualty Company* v. *Argentina* (Award), ICSID Case No. ARB/03/9, 5 September 2008, paras. 160–236; *Continental Casualty Company* v. *Argentina* (Decision on Annulment), ICSID Case No. ARB/03/9, 16 September 2011, paras. 104–143.

basis. Differently composed tribunals will inevitably not always agree on all points. Even competent and impartial arbitrators may reach conflicting results. In addition, arbitration, more than other forms of litigation, is driven by the arguments presented by the parties, which may differ from case to case.

In commercial arbitration such diversity of outcomes is usually not perceived as a major problem. Most awards are not published and the settlement of the dispute at hand is seen as more important than the development of a *jurisprudence constante*. By contrast, investment arbitration attracts much attention, and discrepancies in the application of the law are widely discussed.

Several solutions are feasible for the promotion of a more harmonious case law. One such solution would be a faithful adherence to precedent.[19] Tribunals have emphasised on many occasions that they are not bound by previous decisions. At the same time they have also stated that they will take due account of previous cases when making their own decisions.[20] Tribunals frequently refer to and rely on earlier decisions but this has not always secured consistency.

An institutionalised solution carrying a high probability of uniformity of interpretation would be to create a centralised international investment court. At present there is no indication that such a dramatic step is under serious discussion. Even in the unlikely event of agreement on a comprehensive MAI, it is unclear whether this would involve the creation of a centralised form of adjudication.

Another idea that has been canvassed repeatedly is the creation of an appeals procedure.[21] Although the idea has appeared in a number of documents, it has not been implemented in practice. Any harmonising effect would require an appeals body with wide competence that transcends individual treaties and covers proceedings under the ICSID, United Nations Commission on International Trade Law (UNCITRAL), International Chamber of Commerce (ICC) and Stockholm Rules.

---

[19] See A. R. Sureda, 'Precedent in Investment Treaty Arbitration' in C. Binder, U. Kriebaum, A. Reinisch and S. Wittich (eds.), *International Investment Law for the 21st Century. Essays in Honour of Christoph Schreuer* (Oxford University Press, 2009).

[20] See, e.g., *Saipem S.p.A.* v. *People's Republic of Bangladesh* (Decision on Jurisdiction), ICSID Case No. ARB/05/07, 21 March 2007, para. 67; *RosInvest* v. *Russia* (Final Award), 12 September 2010, paras. 281–286.

[21] See A. Reinisch, 'The Future of Investment Arbitration' in C. Binder, U. Kriebaum, A. Reinisch and S. Wittich (eds.), *International Investment Law for the 21st Century. Essays in Honour of Christoph Schreuer* (Oxford University Press, 2009).

An obvious obstacle to the establishment of an appeals procedure is Article 53(1) of the ICSID Convention, which specifically excludes any form of appeal against an award.[22] An amendment of the ICSID Convention would require the acceptance by all states parties to the Convention, which is close to impossible to achieve.[23] An appeals procedure also presupposes a decision that has been made already, that will be attacked for a perceived flaw and that may be revised and repaired.

G.   Preliminary rulings

The most effective way to achieve judicial coherence and consistency is not submitting decisions to review and reversal. An alternative to an appeals procedure would be to introduce a system of preliminary rulings.[24] Rather than repair the damage after it has occurred, it is more sensible to address the problem of inconsistency through preventive action. The coherence of case law may be achieved more effectively and economically through an interim procedure while the original proceedings are still pending. Under such a system a tribunal would suspend proceedings and request a ruling on a question of law from a body established for that purpose.[25]

Such a mechanism would require the establishment of a central and permanent body that would be authorised to give preliminary rulings. A permanent body of this kind would be less ambitious than a permanent court for the adjudication of investment disputes. It would not do away with the basic structure of the current investment arbitration consisting of a multitude of individual tribunals. But, if successfully used, it could guarantee a large measure of harmonisation without depriving the tribunals of their basic competence to adjudicate the cases submitted to them.

---

[22] Article 53(1) of the ICSID Convention provides in relevant part: 'The award shall be binding on the parties and shall not be subject to any appeal or to any other remedy except those provided for in this Convention.'

[23] ICSID Convention, Article 66.

[24] The idea has been put forward by G. Kaufmann-Kohler, 'Annulment of ICSID Awards in Contract and Treaty Arbitrations: Are there Differences?' in E. Gaillard and Y. Banifatemi (eds.), *Annulment of ICSID Awards: A New Investment Protection Regime in Treaty Arbitration* (Huntington: Juris Publishing, 2004). See also G. Kaufmann-Kohler, 'In search of transparency and consistency: ICSID reform proposal', *TDM* 2(5) (2005).

[25] For more detailed discussion see C. Schreuer, 'Preliminary Rulings in Investment Arbitration' in K. Sauvant (ed.), *Appeals Mechanism in International Investment Disputes* (Oxford University Press, 2008).

Preliminary rulings would not affect the principle of finality. They would leave Article 53 of the ICSID Convention untouched.

H. Summary and conclusions

International investment law suffers from a deficit of coherence and consistency. To a large extent this is caused by differences in treaties applicable to the relationships between host states and investors of different nationalities. This leads to different treatment of investors depending on their nationality. This de facto discrimination on the basis of nationality stands in marked contrast to the prohibition of discrimination reflected by substantive standards of protection.

MFN clauses may offer relief in some situations, but they require the existence of a third-party treaty that offers better treatment. In addition, many tribunals have approached MFN clauses with some trepidation. In particular, they have refused to apply them to provisions on the settlement of disputes.

Some investors have tried to avoid disadvantages based on nationality through appropriate corporate structuring. This technique requires foresight and advance planning. In addition, it will only work in the presence of treaties that accept incorporation in a contracting state as a sufficient basis for protection.

An extension of investors' rights beyond the current system of mostly bilateral treaties is possible, at least theoretically. This could be achieved through the creation of a widely accepted multilateral treaty. Alternatively, states could follow the example of human rights treaties and grant substantive and procedural rights to investors regardless of nationality. Both solutions, while technically feasible, are not a realistic possibility in the near future.

Even in the absence of divergent treaty provisions, tribunals have at times reached conflicting outcomes. Reliance on precedents, while useful, has not always been successful in achieving uniformity of interpretation. The creation of a centralised investment court would be conducive to consistency. But under present circumstances this is not a realistic possibility. Appeals procedures have been discussed but never implemented. One of the reasons for this is a provision in the ICSID Convention that rules out appeals against awards.

The most realistic way to achieve consistency of interpretation would be the introduction of a preliminary rulings procedure while proceedings are still under way before the original tribunal. This would require the creation of a permanent institution to which tribunals would turn for guidance when confronted with a contentious question.

There are several techniques to overcome inconsistencies in current international investment law. Some are more promising than others. All of them require a political will to do away with current inequalities. However, the techniques with the highest potential for harmonisation are also those that are least likely to be implemented.

26

Perspectives for investment arbitration: consistency as a policy goal?

RUDOLF DOLZER

A.   Diversity: an institutional and substantive choice?

Since the beginning of the twenty-first century we have not known whether the current approach to international investment arbitration is in need of overhaul and reform. What we do know is that, if it is needed, such a reform will only succeed if backed by a broad consensus of states from all regions; academic discussion on the point is useful, but the call must come from states around the world.

Of course, for a meaningful discussion there must first be agreement on the relevant policy and on the nature and substance of an intended reform. Indeed, occasional contributions from governments and from academia have asked for a reform without defining its contours.

So, the first task in the endeavour to discuss continuity and reform is to specify the area under review. Which areas have been under scrutiny and discussion? On the substantive side, fair and equitable treatment, the rule of necessity, or the 'investment and … issues' (labour, environment, social policies) come to mind. On procedural matters, issues regarding the selection of arbitration bodies (highest priority!), time and cost of arbitrations or (less often discussed, but crucial) compliance with awards may require attention. On the institutional side, the International Centre for Settlement of Investment Disputes (ICSID) is at the forefront, still attracting more cases than other fora; with good reason, therefore, ICSID has been at the centre of arbitral practice and the debate surrounding it. Which aspects of ICSID's rules and practice have given rise to debate, and may therefore be the most obvious candidates for reform? Answers may differ here. In my view, there is little doubt that the call for more con-sistency forms the front line; exchanges with practitioners and academics seem to confirm this view.

On this topic of consistency, the current state of the debate, however, is far from representing international agreement on a need for reform. This appears to be partly because there is no agreement on the reality of the degree of consistency or inconsistency in recent actual practice. Few, however, would deny that divergence of jurisprudence does exist, even taking into account differences in substantive law to be applied in different cases and differences in factual scenarios submitted. Even a cursory review of recent jurisprudence on critical standard clauses (such as fair and equitable treatment, the most-favoured nation rule, full protection and security, emergency provisions or application of standards for annulment) will clearly point in this direction.

In consequence, the more central issue today is not so much the existence of diversity, but the assessment of the desirability and the need for more uniformity and harmony in the evolution of jurisprudence. Outside observers may be surprised that consistency is not generally accepted as a policy goal; insiders, however, are aware of the elusiveness of this goal in investment arbitration.

Notwithstanding the centrality of this point for the evolution of jurisprudence as well as for its overall assessment and its bearing upon the need (or lack of need) for reform, it would be difficult to pinpoint a broad debate on this matter. Stress on the system has become apparent. The most visible sign of discomfort with the current situation has appeared in the past five years from arbitrators who go beyond deciding their particular cases and explicitly emphasise the need to respect the role of precedent; at least fifteen awards (i.e. forty-five arbitrators) have emphasised that previous decisions should be considered in the formulation of new decisions. Of course, all tribunals are aware that international rules for arbitration do not recognise the role of precedent in the same way as do the Anglo-American legal systems. And yet the apparent common concern of those pointing to the necessity for consideration of precedent is that a set of common rules applied and interpreted by tribunals without concern for consistency is undesirable. Taking an aspirational tone, *AES* v. *Argentina*[1] spoke of ICSID de facto case law as a contribution 'to the development of a common legal opinion or *jurisprudence constante*'.

If it is true that so many actors within the system call for a measure of unity, is it also true to say that the international community has been inclined to work towards a concept that promotes this goal? The answer

---

[1] *AES Corporation v. the Argentine Republic* (Decision on Jurisdiction), ICSID Case No. ARB/02/17, 26 April 2005, para. 33.

may be ambivalent, but it could also be phrased more in the negative. What is the evidence for this assessment? It is simply that states have not attempted to change the current system so as to promote more unity and consistency of jurisprudence. When in 2003 ICSID raised the question of an appeals facility, with the goal of promoting a reform for more unity, the dominant response from the states was lukewarm (in diplomatic phraseology) or on the whole negative (in reality), even though the United States has concluded bilateral treaties allowing (not mandating) an appeal mechanism on the bilateral level. Having received these responses from the Member States to its questionnaire, ICSID de facto shelved the project, and so far has never put it back on to the official agenda.

Indeed, and more fundamentally, the argument has been made, in a most convincing manner, that concern for consistency in arbitral jurisprudence was deliberately not built into the *modus operandi* of ICSID either when it was created in 1965 or as it exists today. This position finds ready support: if jurisprudential homogeneity had been a major concern, the states would not have aimed at a scheme that requires, in principle, that each case is decided by three different arbitrators, with no formal obligation based on the principle of precedent. In such a setting, consistency is not institutionally promoted and, therefore, it is argued, to expect a jurisprudentially homogeneous output must be considered as unrealistic.

Divergence of jurisprudence is not just embedded into an institutional scheme such as the one for which the states opted in the ICSID. In a broader sense, it also underlies the approach to the formulation of the substantive investment law that states have chosen in recent decades. Reference is made here to the negotiation of nearly 3,000 bilateral investment treaties (BITs), with no institutional provision for coherence of rules. It is true that many of these BITs contain similar provisions. Nevertheless, they differ in detail and, sometimes, as a matter of principle. Hundreds of South–South BITs, concluded in the past few years, fall under the same bilateral scheme. In this sense, institutional arrangements for investment arbitration and the formulation of substantive law converge into a scheme based on pluralism, heterogeneity and inconsistency.

In 1996 an effort to create a multilateral regime for investment failed. When an attempt was made to bring the international investment regime into the realm of the World Trade Organization (WTO), this initiative would also have been suitable to promote consistency. Remarkably, at about the same time as ICSID's proposal for an appeals mechanism was made and failed, the effort to fold the investment regime into the WTO also fell apart.

It would be difficult to show evidence that supports the view that states consider inconsistency as desirable in principle; the better, more balanced, view is that states perceive the downsides of any scheme promoting consistency as being so substantial that they would rather accept inconsistency than promote consistency by adopting a solution with a single, standing investment tribunal or an appeals mechanism along the lines of the WTO Dispute Settlement Mechanism.

Why is it that the current international trade regime consists of a single set of rules and a dispute settlement mechanism promoting unity on the one hand, while the investment regime of rules, on the other hand, is embodied in almost 3,000 treaties and has been applied without concern for consistency? Experts may point to structural difference between trade and investment, but most shrug their shoulders and simply refer to historically different patterns of evolution. Should the state-to-state-oriented WTO learn from the more innovative ICSID or the other way around?

The following brief remarks are not intended to explore the full tableau of issues and arguments which have influenced the debate on consistency in investment arbitration in the past and which may surface in the future. The approach here is more modest. It is an attempt to identify the currents and undercurrents which have been articulated so far or which underlie the current amorphous state of the debate.

The working assumption here is that there are essentially three different lines of argument. These arguments are different in nature and lead to different solutions, namely embracing the status quo, calling for a major overhaul or improving the current regime. The claim is not that the debate can be neatly divided according to these three lines or that the arguments are phrased in the way they are presented here; in reality the three lines may overlap. The main point here is that arguments of the kind presented below have been articulated formally and informally, and may, or may not, shape the debate in the future.

B. Line one: embracing the status quo

This line of argument stands for a staunch defence of the status quo resisting change and reform. It is based on the notions:

- that states have deliberately created the current system with all its characteristics, strengths and weaknesses;
- that consistency will not be considered as the primary objective of a regime such as that of ICSID, for which the founders provided that not

even a manifestly incorrect application of the law is grounds for an annulment, and in which the annulment process in general is not in any way concerned with the consistency of jurisprudence;

- that consistency of jurisprudence is at best one value to be observed within ICSID: the appropriate outcome for each case, as presented and argued by the parties before the arbitrators chosen by these parties, is the primary objective of the ICSID arbitral process, and not the concern for an aesthetically attractive jurisprudential architecture;
- that states have now been participating in, or observing, the operation of the system for a significant length of time and have not expressed a wish to change the regime;
- that states deem the current regime to be useful, and that any change would have negative consequences that would outweigh any advantages of change or reform;
- that the states that criticise the current regime are mostly states that have recently lost important cases;
- that the more fundamental criticism comes from academic observers with their own desire for order, based on values and characteristics that are not germane to the approach adopted by states and who insufficiently reflect upon the downsides of the changes they propose;
- that it may therefore be assumed that the regime functions satisfactorily in practice, as intended by the states, and that a crisis exists only in academic writings and not in reality;
- that there is no indication that a majority of states, let alone all groups of states, have embarked on a course of reform or will do so in the foreseeable future;
- that the regime will continue to function as it has done in the past, academic criticism and folklore notwithstanding;
- that, to paraphrase Winston Churchill, the only thing worse than the current regime would be to reform it for the sake of consistency.

C. Line two: a call for serious overhaul

Those who support an overhaul argue that the current regime is in urgent need of serious reform because it allows cases to be decided, but does not permit them to be decided in accordance with an internationally agreed set of rules. The proponents of this line submit:

- that the fundamental deficiency of the current approach is that by design it stands in the way of consistent jurisprudence;

- that a legal system devoid of consistency cannot be called a system of justice;
- that the current rules by their nature are opposed to predictability and to stability of their application;
- that the need for predictability and stability is inherent in particular in the field of investment law in which this need stands at the apex of the system;
- that a serious and thorough analysis of the interpretation of standard clauses in investment treaties points to inconsistencies, to incoherence and to a lack of respect for the decisions of previous tribunals;
- that the international investment arbitral regime was never designed to promote coherence, but it is also true that it was never intended to foster disharmony and heterogeneity of jurisprudence;
- that now the issue of coherence has come to the fore to its full extent, it is the right time to take corrective action;
- that the rule of law is opposed in essence to a legal regime that inherently fails to promote equal justice for all;
- that the international community expects (or at least should expect) ICSID, as a central global institution dedicated to the rule of law within the investment regime, to promote an international legal order built on firm principles that apply in a uniform manner;
- that the role of the ICSID regime, as a permanent global institution, cannot be compared to that of an arbitral tribunal set up to decide on a single case;
- that whereas a one-time tribunal's task is to decide the individual case, an ICSID tribunal must recognise that it is part of the continuous process by which the law is applied and, in consequence, must be concerned about consistency as a condition for the long-term viability of the system;
- that a simple reference to ICSID decisions as manifestations of arbitral process is therefore misleading: ICSID functions as a hybrid between an individual arbitral tribunal and a permanent legal institution charged with the application of the law;
- that, for these reasons, in the long run the investment regime as it has evolved is not viable and will ultimately be set aside one way or another.

D.   Line three: improving the current regime

Those who adopt this view consider that the current system has worked reasonably well, but needs some adjustment as it continues to evolve and mature. This position is based on the arguments:

- that it is not correct to assume that, on the whole, the existing jurisprudence is essentially flawed or inconsistent; often the legal texts applicable and the facts submitted differ significantly from those in other cases, and casual observers overlook these differences;
- that it is possible to work towards more coherence within the current system;
- that, while predictability in an individual case will always be difficult or impossible to achieve, stability in the identification and application of the broader legal framework must remain a concrete goal of any legal system based on the rule of law;
- that a key problem to be resolved lies in the selection of arbitrators who lack sufficient expertise in investment arbitration law, substantive and/or procedural;
- that arbitral practice shows that experience in investment matters must not be substituted by an outstanding reputation as a lawyer in areas other than international investment when nominations for arbitrators are made;
- that this issue has been raised primarily not due to choices made by the appointing authority (such as the ICSID Secretary General), but because the states nominate their arbitrators and thereby limit the choices to be made by the ICSID;
- that it is useless to speculate about a reform that is not yet on the horizon and that would presumably not enter into force for an even longer time;
- that awards that openly ignore relevant decisions of previous tribunals should be appropriately stigmatised;
- that annulment decisions that, in their first part, proclaim that they will not act as appeals courts, and in their second part proceed in the opposite direction should be stigmatised;
- that annulment decisions that decide de facto on the basis of their own view of the merits should be stigmatised;
- that stigmatisation should imply, inter alia, that the arbitrators in the case concerned would be placed on an informal blacklist and not be appointed in future cases;
- that arbitrators who consistently and ostentatiously take one-sided positions should be stigmatised;
- that ICSID should issue a statement, in an appropriate form and context, to the effect that arbitrators are expected to take into account seriously the substance of previous rulings.[2]

---

[2] After publication of early annulment awards with a freely roaming approach to annulment, the ICSID Secretary General informed the ICSID Administration Committee of his serious concern and went ahead with publishing his statement.

E.   Conclusion

Which of the three lines, or which variation of one of them, will prevail in the coming years is impossible to predict. The future course will depend on the degree of international attention paid to the subject, on the priorities of the international investment community and, primarily, on the course of consistency or inconsistency to be followed by future tribunals.

Has case law developed in an inconsistent manner, broadly speaking? An initial useful step would be to clarify, in a sober, detached and transparent analysis to what extent it is correct to assume that tribunals have gone off in different directions in their interpretation of major areas of the law. Any consensus on this point would be a major step towards clarifying the current situation and the debate on the need for a reform; in this respect, studies and seminars initiated and supervised by relevant international organisations would be the appropriate way to go ahead. At the moment, views on this point differ dramatically.

In addition, states should openly discuss the pros and cons of promoting consistency. At the moment, the debate remains unfocused, with broad assertions, in various directions, on the functioning and viability of the regime and correspondingly broad statements on the need for reform.

It is true that the lingering discussion on the future of investment arbitration has led to a widespread sense of discomfort and uncertainty about the viability of the future regime. For all sides in the debate, a major effect of taking stock in the way indicated above would appear to be useful. An informed debate on the contours of the future regime initially presupposes answers to the current state of affairs regarding consistency or inconsistency in international arbitration and, equally important, the significance attached by states to the topic of consistency. Once the answers to these issues have become clearer, it will be possible to steer the ship of international arbitration into calmer waters.

27

Towards a coherent international investment system: key issues in the reform of international investment law

PETER MUCHLINSKI

A. Introduction

'International investment law' has become an increasingly significant element in the process of economic and social development over the fifty years since the signing of the first bilateral investment treaty (BIT) between Germany and Pakistan in 1959. This area is based not only on BITs but on the myriad international investment agreements (IIAs) at the bilateral, regional, plurilateral and multilateral levels.[1] More recently IIAs have been subjected to extensive interpretation in arbitral awards as a result of the sharp increase in investor–state disputes under such treaties in the first years of the twenty-first century.[2] This has led to the development of a new 'international investment law'.[3] Concerns have been expressed regarding the adverse effects of such agreements, how they

---

[1] On which see generally P. T. Muchlinski, *Multinational Enterprises and the Law*, 2nd edn (Oxford University Press, 2007), Part IV. For a general introduction to the history of international investment law see A. Newcombe and L. Paradell, *Law and Practice of Investment Treaties* (Alphen aan den Rijn: Kluwer Law International, 2009), Chapter 1. This introduction is based on and develops P. T. Muchlinski, 'Holistic Approaches to Development and International Investment Law: the Role of International Investment Agreements' in J. Faundez and C. Tan (eds.), *International Economic Law, Globalization and Developing Countries* (Cheltenham: Edward Elgar, 2010), pp. 180–1.

[2] For details see United Nations Conference on Trade and Development (UNCTAD), 'Latest Developments in Investor–State Dispute Settlement', *IIA Monitor* No. 1 (2009), available at: http://unctad.org/en/docs/webdiaeia20096_en.pdf; UNCTAD, 'Latest Developments in Investor–State Dispute Settlement, *IIA Monitor* No. 1 (2011), available at: www.unctad. org/en/docs/webdiaeia20113_en.pdf; and UNCTAD, *World Investment Report* (New York: United Nations Publications, 2011) pp. 101–2.

[3] This has led to the production of many recent works on international investment law. Prior to 2007 there was in effect only one major text dedicated to this subject: M. Sornarajah, *The International Law on Foreign Investment*, 3rd edn (Cambridge University Press,

have been interpreted, and on the balance of rights and duties between investors, host and home countries and the local communities affected by foreign investors and their investments. In particular it has been argued that investor's interests are too readily protected at the expense of other significant social values and interests that can only be secured through effective governance. Indeed it is arguable that investors' legitimate expectations need to be delimited by reference to the social context in which they operate.[4] Accordingly, new generations of IIAs may have to provide for a revised balance of rights and responsibilities for investors alongside the already existing responsibilities of host states. In addition home states may have responsibilities to ensure adequate flows of investment to developing states and to police the behaviour of their investors. A new approach to IIAs is becoming evident in some more recent model treaties and in the Canadian-based International Institute for Sustainable Development (IISD) Model International Agreement on Investment which illustrates how the above concerns can be placed on a more legal footing.[5]

2010), which first came out in 1994; and a section in the author's first edition of his treatise: P. T. Muchlinski, *Multinational Enterprises and the Law* (Oxford: Blackwell Publishers, 1995), Part III; see now second edition: Muchlinski, *Multinational Enterprises and the Law*, 2nd edn. Since 2007 we have, among other more specific works: C. McLachlan, L. Shore and M. Weiniger, *International Investment Arbitration: Substantive Principles* (Oxford University Press, 2007); R. Dolzer and C. Schreuer, *Principles of International Investment Law* (Oxford University Press, 2008); S. P. Subedi, *International Investment Law: Reconciling Policy and Principle* (Oxford: Hart Publishing, 2008); P. T. Muchlinski, F. Ortino and C. Schreuer, *The Oxford Handbook of International Investment Law* (Oxford University Press, 2008); C. F. Dugan, D. Wallace Jr, N. D. Rubins and B. Sabahi, *Investor–State Arbitration* (New York: Oxford University Press, 2008); Newcombe and Paradell, *Law and Practice of Investment Treaties*; C. Binder, U. Kriebaum, A. Reinisch and S. Wittich, *International Investment Law for the 21st Century: Essays in Honour of Christoph Schreuer* (Oxford University Press, 2009); Z. Douglas, *The International Law of Investment Claims* (Cambridge University Press, 2009); S. Schill, *The Multilateralisation of International Investment Law* (Cambridge University Press, 2009); J. Salacuse, *The Law of Investment Treaties* (Oxford University Press, 2010).
[4] See further P. T. Muchlinski, 'Corporate Social Responsibility' in P. T. Muchlinski, F. Ortino and C. Schreuer, *The Oxford Handbook of International Investment Law* (Oxford University Press, 2008), pp. 640–1.
[5] See the IISD *Model International Agreement on Investment for Sustainable Development. Negotiators Handbook*, 2nd edn (Winnipeg: International Institute for Sustainable Development, 2005, revised 2006), available at: www.iisd.org/pdf/2005/investment_model_int_handbook.pdf. The Model Agreement is reproduced in 20 ICSID Rev-FILJ 91 (2005); see also H. Mann, 'Introductory Note', *ibid*. 84. For a detailed analysis of the IISD Model Agreement see further Muchlinski, 'Holistic Approaches to Development and International Investment Law' and M. Malik, 'IISD Model International Agreement

In recent years debates on the future of BITs have taken place in a number of major home-country jurisdictions. Of particular note have been the debates in Norway, South Africa and the United States.[6] While none of these debates appears to have led towards a major rethink on the content of the national Model BITs used by these countries, they have highlighted certain themes that need to inform the evolution of BITs if they are to remain relevant to a world of changed investment conditions and changed expectations as to the relationship between markets and governance. In particular, these debates have shown that there is rising concern about the ability of investors to gain an apparent procedural advantage over local investors and communities by access to international investment dispute settlement mechanisms, and that these challenge the finality and legitimacy of domestic legal rules and remedies. Equally there is anxiety that the balance of BITs favours investor protection over legitimate state regulation.

In the light of the above, the following three themes stand out for consideration: revisiting the conceptual aims and purposes of IIAs in the light of recent ideas of development and social justice; ensuring the constitutional legitimacy of BITs; and recalibrating BITs to offer a more balanced type of agreement that ensures all the main actors in the investment process share rights with responsibilities. Each of these themes will be examined in this chapter with a view to offering a more relevant and contemporary approach to BITs.

B.   Reconsidering the conceptual basis of IIAs

The aims and purposes of IIAs are often assumed to be narrowly economistic: to ensure that investors are protected against governmental maladministration so that the economic operation of the investment can go ahead with as little undue regulatory interference as possible.[7] IIAs were

---

on Investment for Sustainable Development' in M.-C. C. Segger, M. Gehring and A. Newcombe (eds.), *Sustainable Development in World Investment Law* (Aalphen aan den Rijn: Kluwer Law International, 2011). See also UNCTAD, *World Investment Report 2003* (New York: United Nations Publications, 2003), Chapter VI.

[6] See P. T. Muchlinski, 'Trends in International Investment Agreements: Calls for Reforms of Model Bilateral Investment Treaties in Norway, South Africa and the United States' in K. P. Sauvant (ed.), *Yearbook of International Investment Law and Policy 2009–2010* (New York: Oxford University Press, 2010).

[7] In *Azurix* v. *Argentina* (Award), ICSID Case No. ARB/01/12, 14 July 2006, para. 372, the tribunal states in relation to the fair and equitable treatment standard: 'The standards of conduct agreed by the parties to a BIT presuppose a favorable disposition towards

never intended to perform only such a function. The idea of an IIA is a cooperative one. The tribunal in *Saluka* v. *Czech Republic* summarised this approach well by saying:

> The protection of foreign investments is not the sole aim of the Treaty, but rather a necessary element alongside the overall aim of encouraging foreign investment and extending and intensifying the parties' economic relations. That in turn calls for a balanced approach to the interpretation of the Treaty's substantive provisions for the protection of investments, since an interpretation which exaggerates the protection to be accorded to foreign investments may serve to dissuade host States from admitting foreign investments and so undermine the overall aim of extending and intensifying the parties' mutual economic relations.[8]

This approach arguably exemplifies the values enshrined in Article 55 of the United Nations (UN) Charter of a cooperative approach to the improvement of the economic situation of the host country in line with Article 55(a).[9] Equally, investors and their investments do not operate in a social vacuum. They are a constitutive part of the wider community in which they operate and from which they take their profits. Thus IIAs exist in the context of a 'social contract' between the investor and the host community.[10] From these premises three issues appear to offer a foundation

---

foreign investment, in fact, a pro-active behavior of the State to encourage and protect it. To encourage and protect investment is the purpose of the BIT. It would be incoherent with such purpose and the expectations created by such a document to consider that a party to the BIT has breached the obligation of fair and equitable treatment only when it has acted in bad faith or its conduct can be qualified as outrageous or egregious.'

[8] *Saluka Investments BV* v. *Czech Republic* (Partial Award under UNCITRAL Rules 1976), 17 March 2006, para. 300.

[9] By Article 56 of the United Nations (UN) Charter, 'All Members pledge themselves to take joint and separate action in co-operation with the Organization for the achievement of the purposes set forth in Article 55.' Article 55 of the Charter states:

> With a view to the creation of conditions of stability and well-being which are necessary for peaceful and friendly relations among nations based on respect for the principle of equal rights and self-determination of peoples, the United Nations shall promote:
>
> a. higher standards of living, full employment, and conditions of economic and social progress and development;
> b. solutions of international economic, social, health, and related problems; and international cultural and educational cooperation; and
> c. universal respect for, and observance of, human rights and fundamental freedoms for all without distinction as to race, sex, language, or religion.

The UN Charter is available at: www.un.org/en/documents/charter/chapter9.shtml.

[10] See P. T. Muchlinski, 'International Business Regulation: An Ethical Discourse in the Making?' in T. Campbell and S. Miller (eds.), *Human Rights and Moral Responsibilities of*

for reconsidering the conceptual basis for IIAs and BITs: the concept of development, 'sustainable development' as an extension of the concept of development to environmental concerns and the role of human rights in the evolution of investment law.

I. Development and IIAs

In general IIAs do not refer to the concept of development in any detail.[11] IIAs that do refer to development usually do so in the Preamble. For example the Preamble of the United States–Rwanda BIT of 2008 recognises: '[t]hat agreement on the treatment to be accorded such investment will stimulate the flow of private capital and the economic development of the Parties.' The context is clearly that of stimulating investment flows and it stems from the greater economic cooperation between the contracting parties under the BIT itself.[12]

The treaty is silent on any social aspect of development as such. However, the Preamble does stress the need to achieve the economic objectives of the treaty in a manner consistent with the protection of health, safety and the environment and the promotion of consumer protection and internationally recognised labour rights. This is backed up by 'best efforts' clauses seeking to not lower environmental and labour standards as an inducement to investment.[13] Some agreements link technology transfer with human development,[14] while others stress that development should be sustainable, but there are few examples.[15] Indeed one of the most significant examples, the draft Norwegian Model BIT of 2007, has been

---

Corporate and Public Sector Organisations (The Hague: Kluwer Law International, 2004); T. Donaldson, *The Ethics of International Business*, UK Paperback E (Oxford University Press, 1992), Chapter 4.

[11] This section draws upon; Muchlinski, 'Holistic Approaches to Development and International Investment Law', pp. 181–3.

[12] United States (US) Rwanda BIT, 19 February 2008, available at: www.unctad.org/sections/dite/iia/docs/bits/US_Rwanda.pdf.

[13] *Ibid.*, Articles 12 and 13.

[14] See Brunei–Darussalam–Republic of Korea BIT, 14 November 2000, in force 30 October 2003: 'Recognising the importance of the transfer of technology and human resources development arising from such investments', cited in UNCTAD, *Bilateral Investment Treaties 1995–2006: Trends in Investment Rulemaking* (New York: United Nations Publications, 2007), p. 4.

[15] One such reference can be found in the Preamble to the Common Market for Eastern and Southern Africa (COMESA) 'Investment Agreement for the CCIA: Legal tool for increasing investment flows within the COMESA' December 2004, in force 2007, available at: http://vi.unctad.org/files/wksp/iiawksp08/docs/wednesday/Exercise%20Materials/invagreecomesa.pdf: **REAFFIRMING** the importance of having sustainable economic

abandoned.[16] Thus IIAs say little about development save for generally accepting that a quantitative increase in foreign investment equates with development.

This stress on the quantitative aspect of investment for development is reinforced by the predominant use of a broad, asset-based definition of investment in IIAs. There is no reference to development concerns in such definitions.[17]

On the other hand, some recent arbitral awards have considered whether development concerns should affect the interpretation of whether an 'investment' has taken place for the purposes of establishing the jurisdiction of an arbitral panel under the International Centre for Settlement of Investment Disputes (ICSID). According to certain decisions on jurisdiction, for an arrangement to qualify as an 'investment' it should have 'a certain duration, a regularity of profit and return, an element of risk, a substantial commitment and that it should constitute a significant contribution to the host State's development'.[18] The contribution to development requirement may be open to criticism as it introduces an element of motivation into the definition. This may not be relevant if the given definition of 'investment' in the BIT is asset-based.[19] Nonetheless, some

---

growth and development in all Member States and the region through joint efforts in liberalising and promoting intra-COMESA trade and investment flows' (emphasis in original).

[16] The Preamble to the Norwegian Model states inter alia: '*Recognising* that the promotion of sustainable investments is critical for the further development of national and global economies as well as for the pursuit of national and global objectives for sustainable development, and understanding that the promotion of such investments requires cooperative efforts of investors, host governments and home governments' (emphasis in original), available at: http://italaw.com/investmenttreaties.htm. The Draft Model Agreement was abandoned due to the polarisation of views upon it with business interests fearing it did not protect investors enough and civil society groups fearing that it would restrain governments' ability to regulate in the public interest: see D. Vis-Dunbar, 'Norway Shelves its Model Bilateral Investment Treaty', *Investment Treaty News* 6 June 2009, available at: www.investmenttreatynews.org/cms/news/archive/2009/06/08/norway-shelves-its-proposed-model-bilateral-investment-treaty.aspx.

[17] For examples of such definitions see further UNCTAD, *Scope and Definition: A Sequel. UNCTAD Series on Issues in International Investment Agreements II* (New York: United Nations Publications, 2011), pp. 21–8.

[18] *Joy Mining* v. *Egypt* (Award on Jurisdiction), ICSID Case No. ARB/03/11, 6 August 2004, 44 ILM 73 (2005), para. 53; *Salini Construction* v. *Morocco* (Decision on Jurisdiction), ICSID Case No. ARB/00/4, 23 July 2001, 42 ILM 609 (2003), para. 52; *Bayindir* v. *Pakistan* (Decision on Jurisdiction), ICSID Case No. ARB/03/29, 14 November 2005, paras. 122–138; all available at: http://italaw.com.

[19] See *Saluka Investments BV* v. *Czech Republic* (Partial Award under UNCITRAL Rules 1976), 17 March 2006, paras. 209–211.

tribunals have used the development element to deny jurisdiction over a dispute on the ground that the transaction involved failed to make a significant contribution to the development of the host country.[20] In general the development element should be met in most cases where the first three elements are shown to exist.[21]

The discussion of 'development' in arbitral awards is thus very limited. By reason of the narrow economic scope of the treaties that tribunals have to apply, they inevitably focus only on economic development.[22] However, a wider, socially rooted conception of development is needed to understand the true impact of IIAs on the communities to which these agreements relate.[23] That this approach should be taken can be justified by reference to contemporary thinking on the meaning of 'development'. According to Amartya Sen a distinction can be made between two attitudes to development:

> One view sees development as a 'fierce' process, with much 'blood sweat and tears' – a world in which wisdom demands toughness. In particular, it demands calculated neglect of various concerns that are seen as 'soft-headed' [including] social safety nets that protect the very poor, providing social services for the population at large, departing from rugged institutional guidelines in response to identified hardship and favouring – 'much too early' – political and civil rights and the 'luxury' of democracy ... This hard-knocks attitude contrasts with an alternative outlook that sees development as essentially a 'friendly' process. Depending on the particular version of this attitude, the congeniality of the process is seen as exemplified by such things as mutually beneficial exchanges (of which Adam Smith spoke eloquently), or by the working of social safety nets, or of political liberties, or of social development – or some combination or other of these supportive activities.[24]

---

[20] See *Malaysian Historical Salvors* v. *Malaysia* (Award on Jurisdiction), 17 May 2007 (annulled on this point by the Annulment Committee: ICSID Case No. ARB/05/10, Annulment Decision, 16 April 2009) and *Mitchell* v. *Congo*, Decision on Annulment, 1 November 2006, paras. 25–33 and 39, all available at: http://italaw.com. See further M. Jezewski, 'Development Considerations in Defining Investment' in M.-C. C. Segger, M. Gehring and A. Newcombe (eds.), *Sustainable Development in World Investment Law* (Aalphen aan den Rijn: Kluwer Law International, 2011).

[21] Dolzer and Schreuer, *Principles of International Investment Law*, p. 69.

[22] Muchlinski, 'Holistic Approaches to Development and International Investment Law', p. 186.

[23] *Ibid.*, p. 187 on which this paragraph draws. See too A. van Aaken and T. A. Lehmann, 'Sustainable Development and International Investment Law: A Harmonious View from Economics', Chapter 21.

[24] Amartya Sen, *Development as Freedom* (Oxford University Press, 1999), p. 35.

Sen is persuaded by the latter approach, from which he builds his thesis that development can only occur as a process of expanding 'the real freedoms that people enjoy'.[25] Such freedoms include the provision of elementary capabilities for life but also run to political freedoms, access to economic facilities, social opportunities such as access to education or health care, transparency guarantees allowing for freedom to deal with one another in conditions of disclosure and lucidity and protective security based on essential welfare support against abject misery.[26] Not only Sen but others, including Joseph Stiglitz and Jeffrey Sachs, see development as a holistic process including not only economic growth but also societal transformation along the lines suggested by Sen.[27]

If this is indeed the basis of the idea of 'development', it is clear that IIAs cannot continue to be drafted and interpreted as if this concept were invisible. A development-oriented approach to IIAs demands, as a minimum, a flexible perspective that balances investor protection rules with the rights of host countries and communities to regulate in the public interest including in relation to the development of the host country. This approach is advocated by United Nations Conference on Trade and Development (UNCTAD).[28] It requires a sensitivity in IIAs to development issues including development-oriented preambular statements, a degree of special and differential treatment for developing country parties to the agreement, substantive provisions drafted in a manner that allows for the recognition of special considerations for developing countries, including the use of exception clauses, variations in the normative force of certain obligations and by the introduction of mechanisms through which development concerns can be articulated, such as intergovernmental commissions and interpretative mechanisms.

---

[25] *Ibid.*, p. 36.

[26] *Ibid.*, pp. 38–40.

[27] See J. Stiglitz 'Towards a New Paradigm for Development: Strategies, Policies and Processes', 9th Raul Prebisch Lecture, Palais des Nations, Geneva, UNCTAD, 19 October 1998, available at: www.unctad.org/en/docs/prebisch9th.en.pdf and J. Stiglitz, *Globalization and its Discontents* (London: Penguin Allan Lane, 2002), especially Chapter 9, 'The Way Ahead'; J. Sachs, 'Tropical Underdevelopment', National Bureau of Economic Research (NBER) Working Paper 8119, 2001.

[28] See further UNCTAD, *World Investment Report 2003*, Chapter V and UNCTAD, *International Investment Agreements: Flexibility for Development* (New York, United Nations Publications, 2000), Part Two, also found in UNCTAD, *International Investment Agreements: Key Issues* (New York: United Nations Publications, 2004), vol. I, Chapter 2. See too van Aaken and Lehmann, Chapter 21 in this volume.

II. Sustainable development and IIAs

A further element in the development debate is its environmental dimension. The Rio Declaration on Environment and Development asserts, as Principle 1, that '[h]uman beings are at the centre of concerns for sustainable development. They are entitled to a healthy and productive life in harmony with nature.'[29] It goes on to list a number of responsibilities for multinational enterprises (MNEs) regarding the furtherance of sustainable development through the transfer of environmentally sound technology and management practices. This approach is also echoed by the Organisation for Economic Co-operation and Development (OECD) Guidelines for Multinational Enterprises.[30] Such responsibilities could be specified in IIAs as an aspect of the host country's right to regulate environmental matters.[31] For example, the North American Free Trade Agreement (NAFTA) prohibits the imposition of performance requirements as a condition of entry and establishment, including a requirement for technology transfer in paragraph (1)(f). However, Article 1106(2) of the NAFTA provides that, 'a measure that requires an investment to use a technology to meet generally applicable health, safety or environmental requirements shall not be construed to be inconsistent with paragraph (1)(f)'. This approach is further developed in the most recent US BITs, where the imposition of performance requirements, including environmental measures necessary to protect human, animal or plant life or health, or related to the conservation of living or non-living exhaustible natural resources, is permitted provided such measures are not applied in an arbitrary or unjustifiable manner and that they do not constitute a disguised restriction on international trade or investment.[32]

The possibility of mandatory legal obligations being imposed on the activities of MNEs, through governmental regulation based on

---

[29] United Nations Conference on Environment and Development (UNCED), *Rio Declaration on Environment and Development 1992* (United Nations, 1992), p. 9, available at: www.un.org/esa/sustdev/documents/agenda21/english/agenda21toc.htm.

[30] OECD Guidelines for Multinational Enterprises (2011 revision), Chapter VI 'Environment', available at: www.oecd.org/dataoecd/43/29/48004323.pdf.

[31] See generally the papers in M.-C. C. Segger, M. Gehring and A. Newcombe (eds.), *Sustainable Development in World Investment Law* and van Aaken and Lehmann, Chapter 21 in this volume.

[32] See, for example, the United States–Uruguay BIT, 4 November 2005, in force 1 November 2006, Article 8 (3) (c): 44 ILM 265 (2005).

international environmental standards established in binding treaties, may give rise to clashes with investor protection provisions.[33] As the tribunal famously noted in the case of *Compania del Desarrollo de Santa Elena SA* v. *Costa Rica*:

> While an expropriation or taking for environmental reasons may be classified as a taking for a public purpose, and thus may be legitimate, the fact that the property was taken for this reason does not affect either the nature or the measure of compensation to be paid for the taking. That is, the purpose of protecting the environment for which the property was taken does not alter the legal character of the taking for which adequate compensation must be paid ... where property is expropriated, even for environmental purposes, whether domestic or international, the state's obligation to pay compensation remains.[34]

This approach has been criticised for failing to give sufficient weight to the essential public interest purposes behind a regulatory act, which may justify its characterisation as a non-compensable measure,[35] and to the risk that the threat of compensation may give rise to 'regulatory chill' and discourage entirely legitimate interference with foreign-owned private property rights in the public interest.[36]

To avoid such clashes, IIAs may include provisions that privilege multinational environmental agreement (MEA) obligations.[37] Thus NAFTA Article 104 states that MEA obligations, listed in that provision 'shall prevail' provided that, where there is a choice of policy options to fulfil the obligation, that party chooses the least NAFTA-inconsistent option.

---

[33] See Muchlinski, *Multinational Enterprises and the Law*, 2nd edn, pp. 571–2 and 591.

[34] *Compania del Desarrollo de Santa Elena SA* v. *Costa Rica* (Award), ICSID Case No. ARB/96/1, 17 February 2000, available at: www.worldbank.org/icsid/cases/santaelena_award.pdf or 15 ICSID Rev-FILJ 169 (2000), paras. 71–72. See also *Metalclad* v. *Mexico* (Award), ICSID Case No. ARB (AF)/97/1(NAFTA), para. 111, available at: www.nafta-claims.com or 40 ILM 36 (2001): 'The Tribunal need not decide or consider the motivation or intent of the adoption of the Ecological Decree.'

[35] Sornarajah, *The International Law on Foreign Investment*, p. 374.

[36] See UNCTAD, *World Investment Report 2003*, p. 111.

[37] See Muchlinski, *Multinational Enterprises and the Law*, 2nd edn, pp. 571–2, on which this paragraph is based. See also for a discussion of similar provisions in the Canada–Peru Free Trade Agreement (FTA), J. Kammerhofer, 'The Theory of Norm Conflict Solutions in International Investment Law' in M.-C. C. Segger, M. Gehring and A. Newcombe (eds.), *Sustainable Development in World Investment Law* (Aalphen aan den Rijn: Kluwer Law International, 2011). See further M. Hirsch 'Interactions Between Investment and Non-Investment Obligations' in P. T. Muchlinski, F. Ortino and C. Schreuer (eds.), *The Oxford Handbook of International Investment Law* (Oxford University Press, 2008).

In addition, an IIA could make clear that ordinary environmental regulation based on MEA standards will not constitute a regulatory taking, building on general provisions of this kind already in existence in certain BITs. These refer only to non-discriminatory regulatory actions applied to protect legitimate public welfare objectives such as environmental protection.[38] It can be said that where an MEA requires discriminatory action, this may be compatible with such a provision as this might not amount to a case of 'like circumstances' between domestic and foreign investors. The environmental threat in question may require differences in treatment between various foreign investors and/or between foreign and domestic investors.[39]

III. Human rights and IIAs

A further element related to the issue of development concerns the role of human rights in IIAs. In this regard it should be noted that the UN Special Representative of the Secretary-General on Business and Human Rights (the SRSG), Professor John Ruggie, has made clear that the failure of companies to meet their responsibility to respect human rights:

> [c]an subject companies to the courts of public opinion – comprising employees, communities, consumers, civil society, as well as investors – and occasionally to charges in actual courts. Whereas governments define the scope of legal compliance, the broader scope of the responsibility to respect is defined by social expectations – as part of what is sometimes called a company's social licence to operate.[40]

John Ruggie clearly sees a social context for the operations of corporate investors in host countries. It is on this basis that he and his team developed the new UN Framework for Business and Human Rights, which was

---

[38] See, for example, the USA–Uruguay BIT, 4 November 2005, in force 1 November 2006, Article 8(3)(c): 44 ILM 265 (2005), Annex B, para. 4.

[39] But see S. D. Myers Inc v. Canada (First Partial Award, NAFTA Arbitration under UNCITRAL Rules), 40 ILM 1408 (2001), 13 November 2000, para. 255, where Canada was found to have discriminated against a US investor contrary to Article 1102 (national treatment) by imposing a temporary trade ban on certain chemical waste products. This favoured Canadian waste processing firms in competition with the US claimant, who was unable to export the waste in question to its US waste processing facility during the ban. The Tribunal held that Canada could have taken a less investment-restrictive approach to achieve its environmental protection goals.

[40] J. Ruggie, 'Protect, Respect and Remedy: a Framework for Business and Human Rights', UN Doc. A/HRC/8/5, 7 April 2008, para. 54.

adopted by the UN Human Rights Council by way of Guiding Principles in March 2011.[41] The Guiding Principles assert that:

> [s]tates must protect against human rights abuse within their territory and/or jurisdiction by third parties, including business enterprises. This requires taking appropriate steps to prevent, investigate, punish and redress such abuse through effective policies, legislation, regulations and adjudication.[42]

The Guiding Principles exhort states to maintain adequate domestic policy space to meet their human rights obligations under investment treaties and contracts and to use their membership of multilateral institutions to ensure that they do not hinder Member States from meeting their duty to protect, nor that they hinder business enterprises from respecting human rights and that they encourage business respect for human rights.[43] Thus the Guiding Principles clearly envisage a need for IIAs to avoid regulatory chill in relation to human rights concerns.

The state duty to protect is supplemented by a non-binding responsibility to respect human rights on the part of business enterprises.[44] This is seen as a 'responsibility' rather than a 'duty'. The SRSG does this so as to underline the fact that, as a result of the international legal doctrine that non-state actors, such as corporations, are not subjects of international law, there is currently no general legal requirement for corporate actors to observe human rights under international human rights law. Thus the responsibility to respect under international law remains 'a standard of expected conduct acknowledged in virtually every voluntary and soft-law instrument related to corporate responsibility'.[45] To call this a 'duty'

---

[41] See United Nations (UN) Human Rights Council Seventeenth Session, *Guiding Principles on Business and Human Rights Implementing the United Nations 'Protect, Respect and Remed' Framework*, 21 March 2011, available at: www.ohchr.org/documents/issues/business/A.HRC.17.31.pdf (Guiding Principles). See further J. D. Taillant and J. Bonnitcha, 'International Investment Law and Human Rights' in M.-C. C. Segger, M. Gehring and A. Newcombe (eds.), *Sustainable Development in World Investment Law* (Aalphen aan den Rijn: Kluwer Law International, 2011).

[42] UN Human Rights Council Seventeenth Session, *Guiding Principles*, Principle 1.

[43] *Ibid.*, Principles 9 and 10.

[44] This summary is taken from P. T. Muchlinski, 'Implementing the new UN corporate human rights framework: implications for corporate law, governance and regulation', *Business Ethics Quarterly* 22(1) (2012), 145–78 at 147–50.

[45] UN Special Representative of the Secretary General on the Issue of Human Rights and Transnational Corporations and Other Business Enterprises, 'Business and Human Rights: Further Steps Toward the Operationalization of the "Protect, Respect and Remedy framework"', 9 April 2010, UN Doc A/HRC/14/27, para. 55, available at: www.reports-and-materials.org/Ruggie-report-2010.pdf.

would be to misrepresent the extent of the obligation to respect human rights that a corporate actor has under international law. This does not mean that no binding legal duties can arise for corporate actors under the Framework. There is nothing to stop a state, in the exercise of its duty to protect human rights, from imposing legally binding duties upon business enterprises operating in its jurisdiction or even outside, as in the case of claims made under the US Alien Tort Claims Act. Thus the SRSG can say that the Framework is not 'a law-free zone' to the extent that state action under domestic law can create legal duties for corporations.[46]

A key element in the corporate responsibility to respect is the concept of human rights due diligence. In particular, Principle 17 states that due diligence:

(a) Should cover adverse human rights impacts that the business enterprise may cause or contribute to through its own activities, or which may be directly linked to its operations, products or services by its business relationships;
(b) Will vary in complexity with the size of the business enterprise, the risk of severe human rights impacts, and the nature and context of its operations;
(c) Should be ongoing, recognizing that the human rights risks may change over time as the business enterprise's operations and operating context evolve.[47]

Due diligence is normally associated with the buying or selling of company assets, the lending of finance for a specific project, the assessment of a potential joint venture partner, the listing of a company on the stock exchange to verify its ability to carry out its prospectus and the privatisation of state enterprises or state bodies.[48] In all these cases investment risk is involved and due diligence seeks to minimise that risk through a thorough investigation of the assets and liabilities of the firm or investor in question. Thus its extension to human rights risks appears to be a novel departure as this is not a normal aspect of what is generally understood as commercial risk, in that, as the SRSG points out, it requires a shift from considering the risk to the company to the risk to potential victims of corporate action.

---

[46] SRSG, 'Business and Human Rights', para. 66.
[47] UN Human Rights Council Seventeenth Session, *Guiding Principles*, Principle 17.
[48] See generally L. S. Spedding, *Due Diligence Handbook: Corporate Governance, Risk Management and Business Planning* (Amsterdam, CIMA, 2009).

The third element of the UN Framework concerns access to remedies.[49] The SRSG is positive in his view that national legal remedies should be strengthened and made more accessible to claimants.[50] Equally the barriers to effective remedies must be identified and removed. The 2010 Report of the SRSG stresses the value of proper and effective corporate-level grievance mechanisms and argues for a strengthening of the involvement of national human rights institutions as well as a strengthening of the OECD Guidelines on Multinational Enterprises National Contact Points.[51] However, as the Report notes, relatively few states have either type of institution and this absence encourages reliance on lawsuits against companies.[52] As for judicial mechanisms the 2010 Report recommends clarification of the laws relating to corporate group liability and the rules relating to the exercise of extraterritorial jurisdiction over foreign elements of a multinational group so as to reduce barriers to litigation against such groups. In addition the need for solutions to the practical obstacles to such actions are highlighted, including costs, the bringing of class actions and financial, social and political disincentives for lawyers to bring such claims.[53] These issues are echoed in the Guiding Principles.[54]

The UN Framework has been highly influential in the adoption, for the first time, of a human rights chapter in the 2011 revision of the OECD Guidelines for Multinational Enterprises. By Chapter IV of the Guidelines:

IV. Human Rights
States have the duty to protect human rights. Enterprises should, within the framework of internationally recognised human rights, the international human rights obligations of the countries in which they operate as well as relevant domestic laws and regulations:

1. Respect human rights, which means they should avoid infringing on the human rights of others and should address adverse human rights impacts with which they are involved.
2. Within the context of their own activities, avoid causing or contributing to adverse human rights impacts and address such impacts when they occur.

[49] Muchlinski, 'Implementing the new UN corporate human rights framework'.
[50] SRSG, 'Business and Human Rights', paras. 83–91.
[51] *Ibid.*, paras. 91–102.
[52] *Ibid.*, para. 101.
[53] *Ibid.*, paras. 109–113.
[54] UN Human Rights Council Seventeenth Session, *Guiding Principles*, Principles 25–26. The *Guiding Principles* also consider non-judicial state-based grievance mechanisms (Principle 27) and non-state-based grievance mechanisms (Principle 28).

3. Seek ways to prevent or mitigate adverse human rights impacts that are directly linked to their business operations, products or services by a business relationship, even if they do not contribute to those impacts.
4. Have a policy commitment to respect human rights.
5. Carry out human rights due diligence as appropriate to their size, the nature and context of operations and the severity of the risks of adverse human rights impacts.
6. Provide for or co-operate through legitimate processes in the remediation of adverse human rights impacts where they identify that they have caused or contributed to these impacts.[55]

Space limitations prevent a detailed discussion of the new Guideline, save for noting that it reflects closely the thinking of the UN Framework, which is expressly referred to in the Commentary on the Guideline.[56] However, these significant developments within the UN and the OECD cannot but affect the future development of IIAs and their interpretation. How they should do so will now be briefly discussed.

So far human rights issues have not made much headway in investor–state arbitrations. Nonetheless a number of human rights-based arguments have been put to tribunals over recent years in relation to the legality of an expropriation, and human rights case law has been considered by tribunals as a guide to their analysis of the proportionality of the respondent state's actions towards the investor.[57] Equally, in several awards arising out of the Argentine Peso crisis of 2001, the Argentine government sought to defend its emergency legislation, which caused significant financial losses to foreign investors, on the grounds that these measures protected the human rights of citizens by ensuring basic order and/or access to those services that are instrumental to public health and welfare. Thus, measures taken in response to the financial crisis were deemed necessary to uphold Argentina's constitutional order, as well as basic rights and liberties of the Argentine public.[58] This argument met with mixed responses from tribunals, none of which made any significant

---

[55] OECD Guidelines for Multinational Enterprises (2011 revision), Chapter VI 'Human Rights', available at: www.oecd.org/dataoecd/43/29/48004323.pdf. See for analysis P. Muchlinski, 'Human Rights, Supply Chains and the "Due Diligence" Standard for Responsible Business' (London A4ID, November 2011), available at www.a4id.org/resource/article/human-rights-supply-chains-and-%E2%80%9Cdue-diligence%E2%80%9D-standard-responsible-business.
[56] *Ibid.*, p. 29.
[57] See generally UNCTAD, 'Selected Developments in IIA Arbitration and Human Rights', UNCTAD IIA Monitor No. 2 (2009), available at: www.unctad.org/en/docs/webdiaeia20097_en.pdf.
[58] *Ibid.*, p. 8.

contribution to answering the question whether human rights issues were integral to BIT interpretation.

A further issue that has arisen in at least one case concerns the state's duty to promote and protect various individual human rights obligations and the impact of such action on investor rights. In *Biwater v. United Republic of Tanzania* the tribunal accepted, at the procedural stage, that human rights considerations might be raised by the dispute, in that it concerned the operation of a privatised water company and that this involved significant public interests in relation to the right to water and to health.[59] However, when making the 2008 award, the tribunal noted that, while the public interest issues surrounding the right to water in this case were admissible,[60] the tribunal did not explore the United Republic of Tanzania's human rights law obligations in further detail. It decided the case against the claimant on the basis that the claimant had not shown that the actions taken by the Tanzanian authorities in breach of the United Kingdom (UK)–Tanzania BIT had actually caused the losses complained of.

Human rights issues are virtually non-existent in IIA provisions. Few if any IIAs do more than refer to human rights in the Preamble.[61] In the light of this limited practice, any serious response to the UN Framework

[59] See *Biwater Gauff (Tanzania) Ltd.* v. *United Republic of Tanzania* (Procedural Order No. 5), ICSID Case No. ARB/05/22, 2 February 2007, para. 52.

[60] *Biwater Gauff (Tanzania) Ltd.* v. *United Republic of Tanzania* (Award), ICSID Case No. ARB/05/22, 24 July 2008, para. 358.

[61] See Norway Draft Model BIT 2007 Preamble, available at: http://italaw.com/investment-treaties.htm: '*Reaffirming* their commitment to democracy, the rule of law, human rights and fundamental freedoms in accordance with their obligations under international law, including the principles set out in the United Nations Charter and the Universal Declaration of Human Rights' (emphasis in original). See also Article 7.2.d. of the Investment Agreement for the COMESA Common Investment Area (CCIA Agreement), cited in H. Mann, *International Investment Agreements, Business and Human Rights: Key Issues and Opportunities* (Ottawa, International Institute of Sustainable Development, February 2008), p. 10. This enables the COMESA Committee for the Common Investment Area to consider and make:

> recommendations to the [COMESA] Council on any policy issues that need to be made to enhance the objectives of this Agreement. For example the development of common minimum standards relating to investment in areas such as:
>
> (i)   environmental impact and social impact assessments
> (ii) labour standards
> (iii) respect for human rights
> (iv) conduct in conflict zones
> (v)   corruption
> (vi) subsidies.

This is the first time that any investment agreement has expressly included human rights issues related to investment as a possible future working item under the Agreement.

and the Human Rights Chapter of the OECD Guidelines will require new treaty-drafting with the inclusion of a human rights clause. A possible model for such a clause is presented here:

- First, such a clause should make clear that both the Contracting Parties and the investor have a responsibility to respect human rights in the conduct of investment regulation and promotion, and investment operation, respectively.
- More specifically, the host country has the existing international law duty to protect the human rights of its citizens and communities and of all individuals present within the jurisdiction. Thus:
  - It will observe its commitments under international human rights treaties when undertaking the regulation of foreign investment and investors.
  - In relation to foreign investors the host country must therefore observe their human rights, so far as they apply given the legal nature of the investor.
  - Some allowance must be made for the differences in the enjoyment of human rights that can be expected in relation to an investor who is a natural person and one who is a legal entity.[62]
- The home country has the same international obligations as the host country and so:
  - It must ensure that it does not use its foreign outward investment policy as a means of undermining the human rights of host communities and individuals and must ensure that its own citizens' and communities' human rights are respected in this process.
  - Equally it cannot act towards its own investors in a manner inconsistent with the enjoyment of their human rights in the home jurisdiction.
  - In addition, the home country may be required to provide adequate domestic remedies to claimants whose human rights are alleged to have been violated by investors from the home country.[63]
- As for investors they should be subject to the same responsibilities as are demanded by the UN Framework and the OECD Guidelines mentioned above.

---

[62] See further Muchlinski, *Multinational Enterprises*, 2nd edn, pp. 509–11.
[63] On which see UNCTAD, *World Investment Report 2003*, p. 156 and see further P. T. Muchlinski 'The provision of private law remedies against multinational enterprises: a comparative law perspective', *Journal of Comparative Law* 4(2) (2009), 148–70.

- This may follow the non-binding responsibility approach of these instruments.
- On the other hand, the investor may be subjected to a legally binding duty to observe human rights should the Contracting Parties decide that this is appropriate.
- In all cases the investor will conduct a human rights due diligence analysis of the investment as a continuing process in line with the above instruments.[64]

In addition the dispute settlement provision may be made subject to a requirement upon the investor to observe human rights as a precondition to the right to bring a claim under the treaty. This could act as a more specific extension of the existing arbitral interpretation of the 'in accordance with the law' clause contained in many IIAs. Certain investment agreements contain a specification that investment is covered only if made in accordance with the laws of the host country.[65] Thus Article 1(9) of the COMESA Common Investment Area Agreement (COMESA CCIA) states that, '"investment" means assets admitted or admissible in accordance with the relevant laws and regulations of the COMESA Member State in whose territory the investment is made'. In agreements that apply this limitation, investment that is not established in accordance with the host country's laws and regulations will not fall within the definition of 'investment' as used in the agreement. In effect this determines that only investments made in accordance with host country laws and regulations are to be given protection under the agreement. Illegal investments deserve no such protection.[66] Failure to comply with such laws and

---

[64] See for a similar approach based on a 'human rights audit' comprising a review of the likely impact upon existing human rights norms in international law of a proposed investment: B. Simma, 'Foreign investment arbitration: a place for human rights?', *ICLQ* 60 (2011), 573–97. See also the International Finance Corporation, *Guide to Human Rights Impact Assessment and Management (HRIAM)*, available at: www1.ifc.org/wps/ wcm/connect/Topics_Ext_Content/IFC_External_Corporate_Site/Guide+to+Human +Rights+Impact+Assessment+and+Management and see UNCTAD 'Investment Policy Framework for Sustainable Development', note 28 above.

[65] See, e.g., China–Cuba BIT, 20 April 2007, in force 1 December 2008, Article 1(1), available at: www.unctad.org/iia.

[66] See *Salini Construction* v. *Morocco* (Decision on Jurisdiction), ICSID Case No. ARB/00/4, 23 July 2001, 42 ILM 609 (2003), para. 46; *Tokios Tokeles* v. *Ukraine* (Decision on Jurisdiction), ICSID Case No. ARB/02/18, 29 April 2004, 20 ICSID Rev-FILJ 205 (2005), para. 84: 'The requirement in Article 1(1) of the Ukraine–Lithuania BIT that investments be made in compliance with the laws and regulations of the host state is a common requirement in modern BITs.' The purpose of such provisions, as explained by the Tribunal in *Salini Costruttori S.p.A and Italstrade S.p.A v. Morocco*, is 'to prevent the

regulations could result in a tribunal refusing jurisdiction over any subsequent claim made by the investor.[67]

Equally, international public policy may be invoked by a tribunal to bar claims. Thus in *World Duty Free* v. *The Republic of Kenya* the Kenyan government was permitted to oppose a claim made under the investment contract between the claimant, a company that ran the duty free concession at Nairobi and Mombasa airports, and the relevant government agency, where it was shown that the concession had been procured by the bribery of the then President of Kenya.[68] After an extensive examination of national and international legal sources the tribunal held that:

> 157. In light of domestic laws and international conventions relating to corruption, and in light of the decisions taken in this matter by courts and arbitral tribunals, this Tribunal is convinced that bribery is contrary to the international public policy of most, if not all, States or, to use another formula, to transnational public policy. Thus, claims based on contracts of corruption or on contracts obtained by corruption cannot be upheld by this Arbitral Tribunal.

Such public policy based reasoning may apply also to claims tainted by evidence that the claimant has failed to respect the human rights of persons and communities affected by their investment.

C.   IIAs and constitutional legitimacy

In relation to the issue of IIAs and sovereignty two main strands of opinion can be discerned. One strand claims that IIAs and, in particular, BITs form the basis of a new global administrative law which can control governmental maladministration by reference to generally accepted principles of administrative law. This is achieved through the review function carried out by arbitral tribunals in the exercise of their jurisdiction in investor–state investment disputes. Another strand of opinion sees BITs as an unwarranted interference with state sovereignty that has limited national policy space and the state's right to regulate in a manner inconsistent with the original aims and purposes of BITs. This criticism has

---

Bilateral Treaty from protecting investments that should not be protected, particularly because they would be illegal'. See *Salini Costruttori S.p.A. and Halstrade S.p.A.* v. *The Hashemite Kingdom of Jordan* (Award), ICSID Case No. ARB/02/13, 31 January 2006.

[67] See *Fraport AG Frankfurt Airport Services Worldwide* v. *The Philippines* (Award), ICSID Case No. Arb/03/25, 16 August 2007; *Inceysa Vallisoletana SL* v. *El Salvador* (Decision on Jurisdiction), ICSID Case No. ARB/03/26, 2 August 2006.

[68] *World Duty Free* v. *The Republic of Kenya* (Award), ICSID Case No. ARB/00/07, 4 October 2006.

been fuelled by the perception that arbitral tribunals provide an excessively investor-friendly reading of the protection standards and rights of access to dispute settlement contained in BITs. Each approach will be examined in more detail.

The 'global administrative law' approach begins by identifying a growing range of activities in the international sphere that require some form of legal control.[69] These range from international security, environmental protection, banking and finance, trade in products or services to the cross-border movement of persons, to name but a few.[70] The rise of internationalised areas of intergovernmental activity is said to have created 'an accountability deficit in the growing exercise of transnational regulatory power'.[71] In response it is argued that a new type of 'global administrative law' is needed. This is defined as follows:

> the mechanisms, principles, practices, and supporting social understandings that promote or otherwise affect the accountability of global administrative bodies, in particular by ensuring they meet adequate standards of transparency, participation, reasoned decision, and legality, and by providing effective review of the rules and decisions they make. Global administrative bodies include formal intergovernmental regulatory bodies, informal intergovernmental regulatory networks and coordination arrangements, national regulatory bodies operating with reference to an international intergovernmental regime, hybrid public–private regulatory bodies, and some private regulatory bodies exercising transnational governance functions of particular public significance.[72]

International investment law fits into this model through the vehicle of investor–state arbitration. This creates an international review mechanism for national regulatory activity that occurs 'with reference to an international intergovernmental regime'. The aim is to provide 'checks for coordinated domestic administration' where domestic regulators act as participants in a global regime.[73] International investment arbitration

---

[69] This passage is taken from P. T. Muchlinski, 'Corporations and the uses of law: international investment arbitration as a "multilateral legal order"' (5 May 2011), *Oñati Socio-Legal Series* 1(4) (2011), 1–25 at 6–7, available at: SSRN: http://ssrn.com/abstract=1832562.

[70] See B. Kingsbury, N. Krisch and R. B. Stewart, 'The emergence of global administrative law', *Law & Contemp Probs.* 68 (2004–2005), 15–62 at 16; B. Kingsbury, 'The administrative law frontier in global governance', *American Society of International Law Proceedings* 99 (2005), 143–53.

[71] Kingsbury, Krisch and Stewart, 'The emergence of global administrative law'.

[72] *Ibid.,* 17.

[73] *Ibid.,* 36.

is not just a system of dispute resolution but is also 'a structure of global governance'.[74]

> Through publicly available and widely studied awards, investor–State arbitral tribunals are helping to define specific principles of global administrative law and set standards for States in their internal administrative processes. Similarly, investor–State arbitration functions as a review mechanism to assess the balance a government has struck in a particular situation between investor protection and other important public purposes, for example by using proportionality analysis. In addition, decisions made *ex post* by tribunals with regard to such balances may influence what later tribunals will do, and may influence *ex ante* the behavior of States and investors.[75]

In performing this function tribunals 'reflect general principles for the exercise of public power that are applicable not only to State conduct, but likely will be applied over time, mutatis mutandis, to the activities of arbitral tribunals themselves. Investor–State arbitration is thus developing into a form of global governance.'[76] That these principles should also apply to the tribunals themselves is required to ensure the legitimacy of this system.

By contrast, what may be termed the 'state rights' perspective sees this system as the opposite of what is claimed by the 'global administrative law' position. The use of private arbitration run by the very same lawyers who represent investors is seen by some as an illegitimate use of private power to restrict the legitimate exercise of public regulatory power by the state in the public interest. According to Yves Dezalay, the practitioners of international business law are engaging in an age-old process of 'double dealing, by guiding their clients through the regulatory maze they know all the better for having been, to a great extent, its designers'.[77] In particular, national systems of regulation are being disrupted by the 'competitive

---

[74] See B. Kingsbury and S. Schill, 'Investor–State Arbitration as Governance: Fair and Equitable Treatment, Proportionality and the Emerging Global Administrative Law', New York University School of Law Institute for International Law and Justice, Working Paper 2009/6 (2009), p. 1.

[75] *Ibid.*

[76] *Ibid.*, p. 2. See further Schill, *The Multilateralisation of International Investment Law*, pp. 372–8.

[77] Y. Dezalay 'Professional Competition and the Social Construction of Transnational Regulatory Expertise' in J. McCahery, S. Picciotto and C. Scott (eds.), *Corporate Control and Accountability: Changing Structures and the Dynamics of Regulation* (Oxford University Press, 1993), p. 203. This passage is taken from Muchlinski, 'Corporations and the uses of law', 15–16.

pressure exerted by forum shopping for regulatory regimes to which multinationals of expert services incite their clients'.[78]

The resulting regulatory space can be filled by lawyers who offer a
means for international businesses to navigate through the complexities of the transformation of the state from a protective regulatory order,
that seeks to limit the impact of international competition upon national
markets, to one that eliminates barriers to such competition.[79] Thus the
lawyer's knowledge of how to deal with these regulatory spaces becomes
a key element in the process of globalisation of business. That knowledge itself creates the resources for the development of new structures
of regulation and helps to develop a 'vision of the social world or of the
technical-political stakes' that allows international business lawyers to
ensure for themselves a 'situational rent' based on their self-developed
normative system.[80]

This process is at work in international investment law. International
investment lawyers are highly adept at taking BITs and reading into their
vague and general language meanings that ensure the most client-friendly
outcome. In this case the clients are foreign investors – who can range
from large multinationals to small and medium-sized enterprises with
overseas investments, or even passive shareholders in foreign investment
ventures – and the aim is to ensure that national regulatory action is
kept under as tight a control as possible so as to reduce investment risk
to a minimum. That aim is backed up by an expansive reading of the jurisdiction of investor–state tribunals both as regards subject matter and
personal jurisdiction. The system of arbitration itself is the engine of this
growth. In particular, it is well understood that the arbitrators are themselves drawn from the pool of international investment law practitioners that represents clients in such procedures. Thus conflicts of interest
arise in that arbitrators may need to ensure the development of interpretations of BITs that are client-friendly. Since the main clients will be
foreign investors who seek redress under a BIT against the host country,
it is not possible to maintain independence with any confidence in such
cases. The temptation to read the general wording of the BIT in favour of
investor rights, and in favour of widening jurisdiction over more types of
transactions and wider classes of claimants, must be irresistible, indeed

---

[78] Dezalay, 'Professional Competition and the Social Construction of Transnational
    Regulatory Expertise', p. 202.
[79] *Ibid.*, pp. 207–8.
[80] *Ibid.*, p. 211.

natural.[81] It conforms to the liberal market view of the global economy and the need to 'keep government small'.

That is not to say that all arbitrators take this line or that it is indefensible. Indeed it is entirely legitimate to find a host country liable for serious maladministration that leads to unjustifiable economic loss to the foreign investor. Rather, the argument is that the system, as developed by private practitioners, cannot be expected to work as if it were an impartial court system applying rules of global administrative law in an objective and balanced way. Indeed, the inadequacies of the arbitral process are acknowledged by the advocates of a global administrative law approach to investor–state disputes, who accept that tribunals can consider state's rights to regulate as part of their balancing function.[82]

Their hope is that the system will introduce better reasoning methods, use stronger administrative law principles based on the proportionality of governmental action to the regulatory aims, to create a proper system of precedent and make investor–state arbitration more democratically accountable.[83] These are laudable aims if the current system is to continue and is to be more legitimate. But they cannot resolve the basic problem of the privatisation of the review of national administrative action. It is the private challenge to national regulatory space that causes the legitimacy crisis of international investment arbitration and law in the first place.

An important lesson of the debates on the reform of BITs in Norway, South Africa and the United States is that the domestic constitutional effect of the BIT matters.[84] This aspect is seen in relation to the legitimacy of the process of negotiation, conclusion and ratification of the treaty and, subsequently, of its substantive and procedural effects on fundamental principles of national constitutional law and practice. Naturally one can respond by saying that national law, even constitutional law, cannot form the basis of an argument defending a breach of an international obligation. But this is to confuse substantive and procedural issues. A fundamental legal prerequisite for the operation of the regulatory functions of the BIT, the source of the right of the investor to invoke its terms as the

---

[81] See for a fuller exposition of this argument Y. Dezalay and B. Garth, *Dealing in Virtue: International Commercial Arbitration and the Construction of a Transnational Legal Order* (University of Chicago Press, 1996) and G. Van Harten, *Investment Treaty Arbitration and Public Law* (Oxford University Press, 2007), pp. 172–5.

[82] Kingsbury and Schill, 'Investor–State Arbitration as Governance', p. 51.

[83] *Ibid.*, generally.

[84] On which see further Muchlinski, 'Trends in International Investment Agreements', pp. 82–3.

basis of a claim against the host country, is that the BIT is the result of a legitimate exercise of sovereign power to limit state sovereignty. If the treaty is not so constituted then it is hard to defend its effect. In strict legal terms it is not the concern of the claimant whether the BIT it relies upon is properly and constitutionally in order under the laws of the contracting state parties – the claim can be made if the treaty is in force – but it points to the need for a major provision in future agreements, which could be termed the 'Constitutional Conformity Guarantee'.

Such a provision should make clear that the treaty is binding only upon the express acceptance, based on appropriate proof, by both contracting parties that it has been properly and constitutionally adopted by each of them. This could be the first function of any Cooperation Commission set up by the parties to administer the treaty (an institutional innovation that was contained in the Norwegian Model and seems a very useful addition to all BITs, even those already in existence). Where this is done, many of the arguments concerning the preservation of policy space and the right to regulate fall away and the BIT can be seen as a legitimate source of controls over host country maladministration that causes significant loss to the investor.

D.   Recalibrating the balance of rights and responsibilities

The need for a recalibration of the substantive content of IIAs can be illustrated by reference to two recent cases brought before investment tribunals. The first is the case of *Foresti and others* v. *the Republic of South Africa*.[85] This claim was brought before the ICSID by Italian mining investors, who had invested after the fall of apartheid, and who argued that their investment had been indirectly expropriated as a result of South Africa's post-apartheid equal opportunities and land rights policy. Since the end of apartheid, comprehensive efforts have been made to promote Black Economic Empowerment (BEE) in South Africa, so as to transform the economy and overcome the socio-economic legacy of apartheid.[86] In the mining sector the Minerals and

---

[85] *Foresti and others* v. *the Republic of South Africa* (Award), ICSID Case No. ARB (AF)/07/1, 4 August 2010.

[86] See further L. E. Peterson, 'South Africa's Bilateral Investment Treaties Implications for Development and Human Rights', Dialogue on Globalization Occasional Papers of the Friedrich-Ebert-Stiftung, Geneva, November 2006, 16, available at: http://library.fes.de/pdf-files/iez/global/04137–20080708.pdf on which this summary draws. According to this study, 'BEE measures include traditional affirmative action measures, such as employment equity and preferential procurement policies, as well as sector-specific charters

Petroleum Resources Development Act (MPRDA) converted existing mining rights into 'new order' mining rights and required 26 per cent of mining assets to be transferred to black owners over the next decade.[87] The Italian claimants were major holders of mining rights in the South African granite industry. They argued that their rights in a number of quarries could be expropriated and also that as foreign investors they were being subjected to more onerous BEE requirements than domestic firms in breach of the fair and equitable and national treatment principles.[88] The government of South Africa passed the MPRDA as part of its constitutional obligations to put right the injustices of the apartheid era. As such the act represents part of a wider policy to observe human rights in the development of the new post-apartheid era. Is it therefore open to an investor to use the narrow terms of a BIT to require compensation for the effects of such a policy?[89]

The claimants informed the ICSID of their wish to discontinue proceedings in 2009. The reason given was that although they had not been provided with full relief for their alleged injuries, the claimants sought discontinuance because, pursuant to a December 2008 agreement with the respondent, they had been granted partial relief. The claimants also asserted that they had tried to settle the case with the respondent, but to no avail. Therefore, the claimants argued, given that they had received partial relief, and given the costs of the arbitration and current economic conditions, it was now appropriate to seek discontinuance of these proceedings.[90]

---

which gauge the progress of companies in meeting specific indicators and targets, and in meeting targets for divestiture of minority equity stakes to BEE partners.' See further the Department of Trade and Industry's Strategy Document, 'A Strategy for Broad-based Black Empowerment', available at: http://apps.thedti.gov.za/bee/complete.pdf.

[87] Economist Intelligence Unit, 'Country Commerce Report: South Africa', February 2005, p. 10.

[88] See Claimants' Request for the registration of arbitration proceedings in accordance with Article 2(1) of the Arbitration (Additional Facility) Rules of ICSID's Additional Facility, dated 1 November 2006. Not publicly available but summarised in Petition for limited participation as non-disputing parties in terms of Articles 41(3), 27, 39, and 35 of the ICSID's Additional Facility Rules, Case No. ARB(AF)/07/01, para. 4.2, available at: http://ita.law.uvic.ca/documents/ForestivSAPetition_000.pdf. See too *Foresti and others* v. *the Republic of South Africa* (Award), ICSID Case No. ARB (AF)/07/1, 4 August 2010, paras. 54–78.

[89] Claimant's request for arbitration proceedings, *Foresti and others* v. *the Republic of South Africa* (Award), ICSID Case No. ARB (AF)/07/1, 4 August 2010, paras. 4.6–4.18.

[90] See *Foresti and others* v. *the Republic of South Africa* (Award), ICSID Case No. ARB (AF)/07/1, 4 August 2010, paras. 79–80.

Given the very sensitive policy issues raised by the *Foresti* case, and the involvement of a coalition of non-governmental organisations (NGOs) and the International Commission of Jurists as third parties, perhaps there were other reasons for discontinuance as well. South Africa objected to the claimants' request for discontinuance and filed an application for a default award.[91] The tribunal awarded the default, ordering a partial recovery of fees and costs by South Africa from the claimants on the basis that, 'while claimants in investment arbitrations are in principle entitled to the costs necessarily incurred in the vindication of their legal rights, they cannot expect to leave respondent States to carry the costs of defending claims that are abandoned'.[92]

The second case involves a claim made by Philip Morris, the US tobacco products manufacturer, against Uruguay. Philip Morris International (PMI) has initiated an ICSID arbitration against Uruguay over new rules requiring that 80 per cent of cigarette pack surfaces be devoted to graphic warnings of the dangers associated with smoking and over increases in tobacco taxes. The company alleges that the labelling requirements and recent tax increase harm its investments and infringe on its trademarks in violation of the Switzerland–Uruguay BIT. PMI has its international headquarters in Lausanne, Switzerland, and has used the Switzerland–Uruguay BIT to launch its arbitration. Uruguay is a member of the World Health Organization's (WHO) Framework Convention on Tobacco Control. Under this Convention warnings on tobacco packages 'should be 50% or more of the principal display areas but shall be no less than 30% of the principal display areas'. The measures can be seen as a policy to implement the WHO Convention.[93]

Philip Morris is also using the same tactic against the government of Australia. It has threatened to bring a claim under the Australia–Hong Kong BIT through its Asian holding company alleging that the Australian government's plans to bring in plain, brand-less, packaging for cigarettes in January 2012 violates the protection of intellectual property rights under the BIT. The company argues that this policy amounts to a confiscation

[91] *Ibid*, para. 81.
[92] *Ibid.*, para. 132.
[93] *FTR Holding S.A. (Switzerland), Philip Morris Products S.A. (Switzerland) and Abal Hermanos S.A. (Uruguay)* v. *Oriental Republic of Uruguay*, ICSID Case No. ARB/10/7, registered 26 March 2010 and see F. C. Diaz, 'Philip Morris initiates arbitration against Uruguay over new labelling requirements, taxes', *Investment Treaty News*, 11 May 2010, available at: www.investmenttreatynews.org/cms/news/archive/2010/05/11/philip-morr is-initiates-arbitration-against-uruguay-over-new-labeling-requirements-taxes.aspx.

of their trademark rights and that the Australian government has failed to show that plain packaging will reduce smoking prevalence. This claim is currently in the process of negotiation. It is being followed closely by other tobacco firms as they too are considering similar BIT-based claims. British American Tobacco has indicated that it will take out a legal claim after the legislation is in force. The Philip Morris claim has generated concern internationally as Britain, Canada and New Zealand are considering similar measures while the USA has new packaging rules that will compel tobacco firms to print harrowing images of the health consequences of smoking on cigarette packages.[94]

These cases show how the regime of BITs can be used to challenge regulatory action that is not only the outcome of domestic policy developments but which may also be sanctioned by international public policy standards. Although it is clear that investors have the right to defend themselves against uncompensated losses arising out of regulatory interference with their assets, should this right go as far as challenging public policies that are the outcome of legitimate governmental action based on an international consensus as to what an appropriate policy should be?[95] Here the protection of the property rights of the investor may simply be politically unacceptable and governments will seek to oppose such challenges and possibly to question the value, in political terms, of being constrained by BITs. Indeed, even prior to the Philip Morris claim, in April 2011 the Australian government announced that it would no longer support the inclusion of investor–state arbitration in its free trade agreements, explicitly linking its new position to the attempts to 'limit [Australia's] capacity to put health warnings or plain packaging requirements on tobacco products'.[96]

---

[94] See G. Robinson, 'Philip Morris Threatens Australia with Lawsuit over Brand-less Cigarettes', *Financial Times*, 28 June 2011, p. 21; 'Philip Morris Threatens to Sue Australia over Plan to Strip Branding from Cigarettes', *Guardian*, 28 June 2011, p. 26; 'Shock Law Angers Cigarette Firm Philip Morris', *Independent*, 27 June 2011, available at: www. independent.co.uk/news/world/australasia/shock-law-angers-cigarette-firm-phili p-morris-2303423.html.

[95] For an argument that Philip Morris has a weak case in relation to uncompensated expropriation see T. Voon and A. Mitchell, 'Time to quit? Assessing international investment claims against plain tobacco packaging in Australia', *Journal of International Economic Law* 14 (2011), 515–22, also available at: http://ssrn.com/abstract=1906560.

[96] See M. C. Porterfield and C. R. Byrnes, 'Philip Morris v. Uruguay: Will Investor–State Arbitration Send Restrictions on Tobacco Marketing up in Smoke?', *Investment Treaty News*, 12 July 2011, available at: www.iisd.org/itn/2011/07/12/philip-morris-v-uruguay-will-investor-state-arbitration-send-restrictions-on-tobacco-marketing-up-in-smoke/, citing Gillard Government Trade Policy Statement: Trading our Way to More

In the light of such concerns some tentative suggestions are made here as to how to recalibrate BITs so that they are more sensitive to such concerns and offer a more balanced mix of rights and responsibilities for all actors in the foreign investment process.[97] The substantive content of the BIT should now reflect the fact that the rigid division between capital-exporting home countries and capital-importing host countries is breaking down, at least in relation to the main players in the world of foreign direct investment (FDI). Today the main types of investment are likely to be of a wider range and composition than the traditional resource-seeking and market-seeking investments that dominated the mid twentieth-century investment scene when the original model for current IIAs was developing. Equally, investments are being made in increasingly well-governed countries that respect property rights and are interested in increased inward and outward FDI flows.

A fundamental rethink is required as to what types of claims have to be preserved in order for investments to work with certainty, predictability and on a level competitive playing field in modern host countries. The debates to date have not done this but have tinkered with existing concepts that are distinctive for their vagueness and lack of detailed legal content. In this regard the 2004 US and Canadian Models point the way forward, at least in so far as they attempt to define more clearly the scope of coverage of specific guarantees, if not their actual content.

In this regard the substantive and procedural content of the BIT should reflect the actual need for internationalised remedies. Such remedies must, by definition, be exceptional and rare, as it must be assumed that most disputes will be determined within the host country legal order and mostly by negotiation. To prioritise international remedies over national remedies as a matter of course is commercially and practically irrational especially in relation to well-governed host countries. In addition, that the contracting parties to IIAs are limiting their sovereign national control over legal relations with foreign investors under the agreement reinforces the fact that such remedies are exceptional. This exceptionality must be reflected in the types of substantive claims that are open to the investor. That issue requires decisions on a number of questions raised in

Jobs and Prosperity, 14 April 2011, available at: www.dfat.gov.au/publications/trade/trading-our-way-to-more-jobs-and-prosperity.pdf.

[97] The remainder of this section builds on ideas first published by the author in Muchlinski, 'Trends in International Investment Agreements', pp. 83–5.

the debates as to the proper scope of claims both at the substantive and the procedural levels.

In relation to substantive standards, the first key issue is how far the property rights of investors should be preserved, so as to ensure sufficient stability for a reasonable return to be expected from their investment, while at the same time allowing for legitimate regulatory controls over such rights. Is it, for example, acceptable that intellectual property rights be invoked to prevent public health legislation from being passed and applied? Equally, given the controversy over indirect expropriation and regulatory takings, should expropriation be limited to cases of illegal confiscation in the absence of fair market value compensation and in the absence of effective local remedies rather than having a broad general standard that can be creatively expanded to cover almost any type of state interference with the economic value of foreign-owned and controlled property regardless of the reasons for this interference?

The second key issue is how to preserve a 'level playing field' between foreign investors and other foreign and domestic investors. This is at the heart of the most-favoured nation and national treatment standards. Does the current definition of these standards identify adequately the situations in which differences in treatment adversely affect the competitive conditions on the market for foreign investors and should the market power of foreign investors also play a part in the application of this standard when dealing with 'like circumstances'? Furthermore, should non-discrimination standards in BITs only come into operation in the absence of prior national competition law claims being exhausted?

A third key issue concerns the future of the fair and equitable treatment standard. Given the controversy over its precise scope – whether it is a standard limited by the customary international law minimum standard of treatment and whether it includes a notion of legitimate investor expectations – should the current vague format be replaced with a more specific failure of due process standard based on customary international law and specifically detailing acts of maladministration by national administrative or adjudicative bodies that could base an international claim?[98] Again the need is to control an expansive, investor-friendly reading of this very general standard and ensure that legitimate regulation is

---

[98] See further UNCTAD, *Fair and Equitable Treatment: A Sequel*, UNCTAD Series on Issues in International Investment Agreements II (New York: United Nations Publications, 2012) and UNCTAD *World Investment Report* 2012, note 28 above at p. 139 and p. 147.

not impugned. Here the conduct of the investor may also be an important factor to consider.[99]

A further issue has arisen out of the recent global economic crisis: should free transfer of funds be subject to economic crisis exceptions? During the US debates on the revision of the 2004 Model BIT the joint submission of the Center for International Environmental Law, Earthjustice, Friends of the Earth US, Oxfam America, Sierra Club (Civil Society Coalition) to the State Department review asserts:

> We are deeply concerned that the provisions on capital transfers in the model BIT would limit governments' ability to use legitimate measures designed to restrict the flow of capital in order to protect themselves from financial instability. The severe financial crisis experienced by the United States and the world in 2009 should lead to a serious re-thinking of these provisions. Without adequate measures to prevent and respond to severe financial instability, broad sustainable development will remain out of reach for many developing countries. The increased frequency and severity of financial crises also hurts U.S. economic interests, as crisis-stricken countries devalue their currencies and flood the U.S. market with underpriced exports in order to recover.[100]

This led to calls for a strengthening of the prudential supervision measures in Article 20 of the 2004 Model BIT and for the introduction of capital controls in BITs.[101]

As to procedural issues, the exceptionality of international measures would appear to lead to the conclusion that some prior exhaustion of local

---

[99] See P. E. Muchlinski, '"Caveat Investor"? The Relevance of the Conduct of the Investor Under the Fair and Equitable Treatment Standard', *International and Comparative Law Quarterly* 55 (2006), 527–58. See too *Biwater Gauff (Tanzania) Ltd.* v. *United Republic of Tanzania*, Amicus Curiae Submission of: The Lawyers' Environmental Action Team (LEAT), The Legal and Human Rights Centre (LHRC), The Tanzania Gender Networking Programme (TGNP), The Center for International Environmental Law (CIEL), The International Institute for Sustainable Development (IISD), 26 March 2007, available at: www.iisd.org/pdf/2007/investment_amicus_final_march_2007.pdf.

[100] See Center for International Environmental Law, Earthjustice, Friends of the Earth US, Oxfam America, Sierra Club submission of 31 July 2009, pp. 5–8; Civil Society Coalition Submission, p. 10, available at: http://ciel.org/Publications/BIT_Comments_Aug09.pdf.

[101] See 'Reforming International Investment Agreements', Testimony by William Waren, Forum on Democracy and Trade, Hearing on Revision of the Model US Bilateral Investment Treaty US Department of State, 29 July 2009, pp. 3–6; Testimony of Todd Tucker, Research Director Public Citizen's Global Trade Watch Division For Public Meeting of the Administration Review of the US Model Bilateral Investment Treaty Program, 29 July, 2009, US State Department, pp. 6–7. These testimonies are discussed in *International Investment Perspectives*, 2006 edn (OECD, 2006), p. 168, available at: www.oecd.org/investment/internationalinvestmentagreements/40072428.pdf.

remedies is required. Again the absence of this requirement in existing BITs fits where the host country is an unreliable or weak governance zone and where such a requirement could lead to unnecessary delays in the vindication of claims. But where the host country has a reliable system of domestic dispute settlement then there is less reason to allow the investor to choose international over local remedies. Accordingly where the Contracting Parties are happy that their respective systems are adequate to deal with the legitimate and effective resolution of claims (again something that could be verified and periodically monitored by a Cooperation Commission of the Contracting Parties set up under the relevant IIA), the BIT should reflect this. Thus the investor–state dispute settlement provision could be excluded altogether, or included in a form that requires prior exhaustion of local remedies. Equally, a no U-turn clause such as that found in US Model BITs could be more widely used. Such clauses deny the right to the investor to start international investment arbitration proceedings if they have already elected to use domestic dispute settlement procedures unless they waive their right to continue those proceedings.[102] This allows the investor to seek redress in the local courts of the host state without prejudice to a subsequent reference of the dispute to an investor–state tribunal if the investor feels that the local courts and/or the local authorities have not met treaty standards in the conduct of the dispute at the local level.[103]

Equally the exceptional nature of international dispute settlement could be furthered by an end to the use of unilateral offers to accept international dispute settlement upon the election of the investor – the so-called 'arbitration without privity' principle – and through the use of denial of benefits clauses to exclude treaty-shopping. Whether such an approach could become generalised depends very much on how the main players in the world of FDI perceive the quality of each other's dispute resolution systems. However, the main point is that the BIT will remain in place for due process failure claims where the local system has not worked. It is hard to see what more is actually needed to reduce investment risk to levels that are compatible with the normal demands of due diligence and commercial responsibility when undertaking a foreign investment.

---

[102] See, for example, the USA–Rwanda BIT 2008, Article 26(2), available at: www.unctad. org/sections/dite/iia/docs/bits/US_Rwanda.pdf.
[103] See C. Mclachlan *et al.*, *International Investment Arbitration*, p. 107, para. 4.85.

E.   Concluding remarks

This chapter has sought to highlight certain key issues for the reform and reinvigoration of IIAs that seek to balance the rights of investors with the right of the state to regulate the economy in the public interest and the rights of stakeholders who might be adversely affected in certain circumstances by the operations of foreign investors and their investments. Naturally such a recalibration will be dismissed by some as undermining IIAs and their essential function of protection of investors and investments by offering an uncontainable privileging of the right of the state to act as it wishes under a wide notion of the 'public interest'. Indeed it would be highly irrational to replace 'investor protection treaties' with 'sovereign discretion protection treaties'.

That said, IIAs were never only about the protection of investors and investments but also serve a cooperative function as instruments of economic development. In turn, economic development cannot by itself fulfil the aims and purposes of a truly liberal society. This has been recognised for a long time in domestic laws that both facilitate business and control its undesirable social and economic impacts. Nothing more is claimed for here. It is time for IIAs to enter the twenty-first century and recognise the complex interactions of private, public and human rights involved in the process of just and sustainable development in a world where pure 'economism' is an insufficient answer to social problems and where the environment itself is straining to sustain continued growth.

28

Less may be more: the need for moderation in international investment law

MARINO BALDI

A. Introduction

My comments here are based on my experience as a trade and investment negotiator and also on my activities as a Swiss representative to international organisations dealing with trade and investment. Apart from negotiating bilateral and multilateral legal instruments, my activities in the investment field also related to aspects of corporate social responsibility and business ethics.

Following up on the chapters by Schreuer, Dolzer and Muchlinski, I should like to concentrate my comments on two issues:

- investor–state arbitration in respect of investment protection;
- how to approach future work with a view to more coherent and more comprehensive investment rules, encompassing not only disciplines on investment liberalisation, but also rules responding, for instance, to environmental and social concerns.

In both respects, I see rather serious problems with the present 'system'. They lead me to think that the big question of how to improve the existing regime might in the end turn out to be the question of how to save at least parts of it.

B. Investment protection and investor–state dispute settlement (ISDS)

Let me start with some comments on investment protection and investor–state dispute settlement (ISDS). The growing uneasiness of countries worldwide with ISDS on bilateral investment treaties (BITs) is well documented. The policy statement by the Government of Australia that it will stop including ISDS clauses in its BITs highlights the problem.[1] I have a critical view myself, for the reasons discussed below.

The International Centre for Settlement of Investment Disputes (ICSID) – and thus ISDS – was not conceived with a view to settling disputes arising out of BITs. It was created for the purpose of adjudicating *investment contracts* between individual investors and their host countries and not – certainly not in the first place – for solving problems of the framework agreements between *states*, which is what BITs *are*. However, probably without giving much thought to the question of whether BITs and ISDS fit well together, from around the beginning of the 1980s countries started to include ISDS clauses in their BITs.

These countries, or their BIT negotiators, presumably had lost sight of the basic rationale for concluding BITs. This rationale was – and largely still is – to prevent countries not having sufficient tradition of applying concepts such as 'the rule of law' and 'due process of law' from taking *discriminatory or arbitrary measures* vis-à-vis foreigners and their property. Protecting investors and their investments from discriminatory or arbitrary state measures – in other words from 'maladministration' – by the investor's host country is also the essence of what is known as 'customary international law' in the field.

The overall purpose of BITs – which are *bilateral* treaties – has never been and cannot be anything other than to provide a framework for protection against so-called political risks, namely measures by states that are considered to be incompatible with concepts such as the 'rule of law' and 'due process of law'. *BITs can never provide the world with refined rules of international economic law as may be desirable in an increasingly globalised economy.* It amounts to inadmissibly stretching the purpose of BITs if investors – in invoking BIT clauses on 'fair and equitable treatment' or against 'indirect takings' – claim, for instance, large amounts of compensation for damages allegedly caused by measures of general application dealing with public health or environmental concerns – as seen in a series of cases since the end of the 1990s.

Tribunals that decided in favour of the claimants in such cases of 'regulatory takings' basically argued that the challenged measure had

---

[1] Australia provided the following reasoning for this step: 'The Government does not support provisions that would confer greater legal rights on foreign businesses than those available to domestic businesses. Nor will the Government support provisions that would constrain the ability of Australian governments to make their laws on social, environmental and economic matters in circumstances where those laws do not discriminate between domestic and foreign businesses.' See American Society of International Law, available at: www.asil.org/insights110802.cfm.

the same effect as an expropriation – in that the measure largely devalued an investment – even though it had in no way the characteristics of an expropriation. I think that in these cases the term 'indirect taking' has been interpreted in too mechanical a manner, and yet arbitrators could have known that at the Organisation for Economic Co-operation and Development (OECD) there had been extensive discussions on the subject, particularly in the context of the Multilateral Agreement on Investment (MAI) negotiations, and that these had yielded clear results. No OECD country has ever contested the 'right to regulate' in terms of regulatory measures that are non-discriminatory and, according to the concrete circumstances, whose purpose is not that of taking any property, even though, incidentally, the effect may be exactly that.

Let us assume for a moment that a case of the kind in question – I am thinking, for instance, of the *Methanex* facts as a prototype case[2] – came up in a state–state proceeding. Could one imagine a state challenging de facto the right of another state to regulate under the aforementioned circumstances (i.e. non-discriminatory regulation adopted according to democratic procedures)? The answer, I think, is obvious. But accepting that countries in their relations between themselves would be much more hesitant to challenge the right to regulate, practically amounts to saying that investor–state arbitral tribunals have often *not been up to their task*. This is also my view with respect to some other types of decisions by investment and securities (IS) arbitral tribunals. I am thinking, for instance, of arbitral statements on the interpretation of most-favoured nation (MFN) clauses, or of certain decisions in relation to the Argentine financial crisis.

What is then my overall assessment of the present situation? Let me make three points:

First, the conviction seems to be growing that IS arbitration has exceeded its limits, that is its legitimate role. Arbitration panels have, over time, taken on functions they initially were not meant to have. States

---

[2] The *Methanex* case was about the banning of a fuel additive by the State of California, because of the water contamination risks the additive posed. A Canadian investor producing a component of the banned product – i.e. methanol – challenged the measure under the North American Free Trade Agreement (NAFTA) investment provisions, arguing that it was a 'regulatory taking', i.e. a measure tantamount to an expropriation, and claimed compensation of nearly one billion US dollars. After lengthy proceedings before different arbitral tribunals, the claim was finally dismissed, mainly on procedural grounds specific to the NAFTA. However, in a number of other, very similar, cases – i.e. legislative measures dealing with public health or environmental concerns and, incidentally, devaluating an investment – arbitral tribunals decided in favour of the claimants.

would never accept their legitimate policy space being substantially narrowed down by judicial action of other *states*, if merely based on 'creative interpretation' of relatively vague treaty provisions. It is obviously even less acceptable for them to see their policy space limited in such a way by private sector arbitrators.

Second, the question therefore arises whether IS arbitral tribunals will in the future have to step back and accept a more modest role? What could this mean in practical terms? Here are a few indications.

International public law provisions may in certain circumstances be 'directly applicable' in national legal orders ('self-executing' character of treaty provisions). Any such direct application presupposes, inter alia, that the rules to be applied are 'sufficiently clear and precise'. In other words: individuals may invoke international public law rules before national courts only if the rules are sufficiently clear. BIT provisions, however, even if they are anything but sufficiently clear, are often used without any hesitation as a basis for IS arbitral decisions – sometimes in a truly adventurous manner.

I am not arguing that the IS arbitration system as such should be abandoned. IS arbitral tribunals should, however, focus on rules where they are on safe ground, such as when the application of BITs fits into the body of principles that is known as 'international customary law'. Beyond that, the judicial application of BITs, in view of their frequent lack of precision, becomes problematic. In such cases arbitrators have to show self-restraint, lest the system in the end should collapse. Also, using as an interpretative principle 'in case of doubt in favour of national sovereignty' might in the long run benefit the system, that is help to save it.

With a view to future treaty-making, Muchlinski's suggestion to provide – at least in certain cases of IS arbitration – for some requirement of 'exhaustion of local remedies',[3] is worth considering. In this context, in my view we should also give some thought to his statement that 'to prioritise international remedies over national remedies as a matter of course is commercially and practically irrational'.

Lastly, it has been argued that the work of IS arbitrators may be an important part of an emerging international administrative law. From the above, it should be clear that I see relatively narrow limits to this. With what legitimacy should private sector arbitrators be allowed to take

---

[3] See Muchlinski, Chapter 27 in this volume.

a leading role in the development of international public law, particularly under the aforementioned circumstances? In this respect, too, I concur with Muchlinski's critical remarks.

C. Investment protection v. investment liberalisation

Let me turn now to the subject of how to approach future work on *more comprehensive investment rules* that would include liberalisation disciplines as well as rules on other important policy issues, such as consideration of social and environmental concerns. In this context of broader investment rules, the possible interaction between investment protection and investment liberalisation plays a key role.

Traditional BITs focus on investment protection, largely along the lines of relevant customary international law. In recent times, however, investment agreements have increasingly been supplemented with investment liberalisation rules, and also with best-efforts clauses, for example on key personnel, labour rights and sustainable development. Such provisions have notably become part of modern free trade agreements (FTAs). This trend started with the NAFTA, continued with the (unsuccessful) negotiations on an MAI, and has since 2000 increasingly characterised FTAs throughout the world. As to modern FTAs, I should add that the rapid increase in the number of these treaties has, in the investment field, unfortunately been accompanied by a trend towards a lowering of quality. In fact, a good number of these treaties contain such wide-ranging exceptions and vaguely formulated safeguard clauses that their regulatory value is called into question, particularly as such agreements potentially harm the application of core *protection* principles. What is the reason for this?

I am fully convinced that the world needs more comprehensive investment rules. But an important preliminary question for me is how best to achieve this from the point of view of 'treaty design'. Is it advisable to have all the elements under discussion in one instrument (which would be the NAFTA approach), or would it be preferable to have separate instruments for different subject matters (which would be the traditional OECD approach)? I am aware that, from a viewpoint of *negotiating tactics*, the single-treaty approach may have certain advantages. However, experience shows that a *multiple-instruments solution* helps to avoid problems that in a single-treaty approach are extremely difficult to overcome. Based on my experience with the MAI negotiations – and also a number of FTA negotiations with investment chapters – I am convinced that the single-treaty approach – which closely connects investment *liberalisation* and investment *protection* issues – has, in the end, negative effects on both areas. This has to do with the different legal and economic characteristics of the two areas.

Investment *protection* rules have clear characteristics of *property law*. As a matter of principle, provisions of this kind ought to have a broad scope – as basically any kind of asset is worth protecting. Traditional BITs therefore usually feature comprehensive, asset-based definitions of the term 'investment'. Extensive exceptions to the broad coverage of investments are neither necessary nor desirable. Contrary to the property-oriented provisions on protection, investment *liberalisation rules* have a trade-policy character[4] where sector exceptions to the basic rules are a normal feature. Also, from a pure trade-policy perspective, free market access is mainly, if not exclusively, of importance for *direct* investments – and much less for short-term capital movements.

If we now have a single instrument combining protection and liberalisation elements and providing for only one set of definitions (which is normally the case), we almost inevitably run into virtually insurmountable problems. Let us take the case of *portfolio investments*: from a protection point of view, it may be desirable to use an asset-based definition of 'investment' also covering portfolio investments; from a liberalisation angle you might, however, wish to restrict the definition to direct investment. In practical treaty terms, the most frequently chosen way out of this dilemma is to have a broad investment definition together with some kind of a safeguard clause allowing the host country to intervene more or less at its own discretion in the free flow of capital. This solution, however, clearly undermines legal security, whereas the main purpose of investment agreements is precisely to enhance such security.

The problem in question is by no means a theoretical one. In the MAI negotiations we were grappling with it throughout the negotiating process without arriving at a satisfactory solution, as we were never able to decide on an investment definition supported by all sides. I would not say that this was *the* reason for the breakdown of the negotiations. Yet, I do contend that the combination of investment protection elements with liberalisation and other regulatory features in *one* treaty, together with – and

---

[4] Direct investments are often a substitute for trade – a way of doing business internationally which is of increasing importance in a globalised economy, and truly characteristic of the globalised economy.

this is the decisive point – *strict investor–state dispute settlement* (broad 'prior consent'), was the real reason for the failure of the negotiations – and not one or more of the other, rather superficial reasons that are often purported.

Let me finally – and still within the context of my remarks on treaty design – make some comments on the very important issues concerning 'investment and development', which include aspects of sustainability, employment and human rights, among others. It should be clear from my presentation that these issues are much closer to the liberalisation aspects of investment treaty-making than to protection. Moreover, such policy issues are mainly relevant in the context of 'direct investment'. This should be kept in mind when talking, from a global economic perspective, of the need to *rebalance investors' rights and the sovereign interests of host states* (there is not much to be rebalanced in the protection field). Still on rebalancing efforts, it seems to me obvious that they should, given their political and, in a way, systemic nature, mainly take place on a *multilateral* level.

D. Conclusions

I think it is advisable when working towards a more coherent international investment regime intellectually and practically to separate investment protection issues from the broader policy issues. On investment protection and IS dispute settlement, let me reiterate that the issue at stake is ultimately the 'system' as such.

As to the broader policy issues under the catchphrase 'investment and development', they essentially come into the realm of multilateralism. This does not mean that I am thinking of another attempt to negotiate a comprehensive international treaty of the MAI type. Today, this would not be realistic. More modest approaches should now be tried, such as the formulation of voluntary guidelines, benchmarks and the like. The OECD Policy Framework for Investment adopted in 2006 is a welcome step in this direction.

My overall 'motto' with a view to working on an improved international investment regime would be: more modesty and more seriousness!

29

The way forward for the international investment regime: lessons from the past – perspectives for the future

RAINER GEIGER

At the end of this collection of stimulating and thought-provoking contributions, I would like to draw some conclusions and show some avenues for the future. The conclusions and suggestions are nourished by long experience as a senior official and teacher on international investment law and represent my personal views.

I. Areas of convergence

Looking at the present landscape of international investment laws and policies, the observer may sense some disarray: an amazing puzzle of bilateral agreements, the proliferation of dispute settlement and a long string of inconclusive attempts to come up with multilateral rules.[1] But digging below the surface an unexpected wealth appears: lessons that can be drawn from past success and failure and above all a new paradigm putting investment at the service of sustainable development. We will detect a new balance between home and host countries, investors and government and an emerging convergence of interests that can become a basis for renewed efforts of international rule-making.[2]

---

[1] See R. Geiger, 'The Multifaceted Nature of International Investment Law' in K. Sauvant (ed.), *Appeals Mechanisms for International Investment Disputes* (Oxford University Press, 2008).

[2] See generally R. Geiger, 'Coherence in shaping the rules for international business: actors, instruments and implementation', *George Washington International Law Review* (2011), 295–324.

First conclusion: the shift of wealth and power in the international economy

We can observe today that there is no longer a one way street of investments flowing from Organisation for Economic Co-operation and Development (OECD) industrialised countries to the developing world. Investment relations today transcend the old North–South context where the North was on the demanding side for protection of its outward investment – sometimes to the detriment of host countries that have been fighting rearguard battles to preserve their sovereignty. Emerging (or more correctly 'emerged') economies like China, India, Brazil, Russia and South Africa find themselves today in the role of home and host countries with an increasing role in outward investment. Multinationals from these countries have become a common phenomenon and many of them are state-owned or state-controlled enterprises.[3]

Sovereign wealth funds accumulating huge surpluses from exports of resources and goods have become significant actors in the South–South and the South–North context. All of a sudden OECD countries that are the targets of such investment have become concerned about sovereignty and national interests to the point that the OECD had to create a freedom of investment group in order to allay their concerns and to protect the investment environment against defensive if not openly protectionist trends.[4]

Second conclusion: convergence of key provisions in international investment agreements

There are two categories of agreements which offer areas of convergence:

- The traditional North–South BITs are characterised by a quasi-uniform incantation of investor's rights and a range of approaches to investor-state dispute settlement. Sovereignty was cheap at the time they were agreed, and big multinationals were imposing their views, with the support of their home governments. We find extensive provisions for

---

[3] See generally K. Sauvant (ed.), *The Rise of Transnational Corporations from Emerging Markets: Threat or Opportunity* (Cheltenham: Edward Elgar, 2008).

[4] See Organisation for Economic Co-operation and Development (OECD), *Investment Perspectives 2007: Freedom of Investment in a Changing World* (Paris: OECD Publishing, 2007).

investor protection: wide definitions of the taking of property ('measures tantamount to expropriation') and the Cordell Hull trilogy 'prompt, adequate and effective' for compensation. And there were far-reaching most-favoured nation (MFN) and national treatment provisions. The power relations were – and in many cases still are – such that resort to dispute settlement was hardly needed for companies to prevail against host states.

- With the North American Free Trade Agreement (NAFTA) and the negotiations for a multilateral investment agreement new concerns emerged: while the substantive provisions still reflected strong investor protection, developed host states found themselves exposed to investor–state dispute settlement. For NAFTA treaty partners a sudden surge in litigation brought by investors led to a reconsideration of traditional provisions of investment agreements culminating in a new model treaty in the United States.[5] The key features of this trend are interpretative joint statements by treaty partners, which are binding on arbitrators, as well as the possibility of introducing an appeals mechanism in investor–state dispute settlement. At the same time, new treaty elements such as protection of the environment and labour standards appeared. It is interesting to note that the new US model which was heavily criticised at home, is now considered quite appealing by Chinese treaty negotiators and treaties concluded by China, in particular with partners from the developing world, are showing patterns close to the US model.
- Finally the new European Union (EU) investment competence established by the Lisbon Treaty is opening avenues for more balanced provisions in international investment agreements to reflect shared interests between Europe and its main trading partners.[6]

Third conclusion: the broadening of the objectives of international investment agreements

Traditionally investor protection has been at the centre of bilateral investment treaties (BITs). Liberalisation of investment flows has also become an increasingly important objective as witnessed by the growing number

---

[5] For an illustration of the new model see the 2004 United States–Uruguay BIT, signed 25 October 2004, available at: www.sice.oas.org/TPD/URY_USA/Negotiations/signatureBIT_e. pdf.

[6] See European Commission, 'Towards a Comprehensive European International Investment Policy', at 2, COM (2010) 343 (Final), July 2010.

of free trade agreements that contain investment provisions. Finally, investment has been recognised as a tool for sustainable development and this has led to a broadening of the scope of agreements introducing in a number of the more recent agreements provisions on environment, social standards and investors' responsibilities.[7]

Fourth conclusion: the current financial crisis has demonstrated the systemic importance of investment as a driver for growth and competitiveness

If measures to restore financial and budgetary stability are not to stifle economic growth, private and public investment need to be promoted. At the same time, the financial system has to be reshaped to reflect the needs of productive investment in the real economy. This means that investment, more than ever, has to play a key role in economic recovery. In this context the general business environment for both domestic and international investment has become crucial. This includes policies that are of equal importance to both national and foreign investment, such as taxation, competition, corporate governance, infrastructure development and human resources.

Fifth conclusion: the current system of investor–state treaty arbitration has serious deficiencies and needs to be remodelled

Arbitrators and many academics as well as parts of the business community support the existing system of ad hoc arbitration through the International Centre for Settlement of Investment Disputes (ICSID), United Nations Commission on International Trade Law (UNCITRAL), the International Chamber of Commerce (ICC) Court and other mechanisms. They argue that the system in place, while not perfect, is the best possible solution to depoliticising conflicts and establishing legal certainty for investors. In their view the international landscape, which is fragmented by a large number of bilateral agreements, does not permit any solution other than ad hoc arbitration.[8] These arguments are not

---

[7] See International Institute for Sustainable Development (IISD), *Model International Agreement on Investment for Sustainable Development Negotiators Handbook*, 2nd edn (Winnipeg: IISD, 2005).

[8] B. Legum, 'Options to Establish an Appellate Mechanism for International Investment Disputes' in K. Sauvant (ed.), *Appeals Mechanism in International Investment Disputes* (Oxford University Press, 2008).

convincing. First, there is the issue of legitimacy: is it really acceptable to entrust adjudication on public policies and general interest regulations to private arbitrators selected by the parties and operating under procedures of their own choosing? And there is a problem of coherence: there have been disturbing instances of inconsistent awards dealing with the same facts and legal issues.[9] The present system does not lend itself to the development of judicial authority, which in itself is a factor for legal predictability in investment relations.

The argument that the diversity of bilateral agreements requires ad hoc arbitration is simply wrong: as demonstrated by a large number of studies conducted by both the United Nations Conference on Trade and Development (UNCTAD) and the OECD, bilateral treaty provisions show many common features that require consistent legal interpretation.[10] The absence of appeals procedures for investment disputes is being increasingly criticised. Even if the current ICSID Treaty mechanisms are maintained, nothing in the Treaty prevents arbitrators from submitting key prejudicial questions of legal interpretation to a permanent body of adjudication, which could be established by a special protocol.[11]

Within the EU, legal integration is a common good and should be defended against intrusion from ad hoc panels. If future EU investment treaties provide for investor–state dispute settlement, it would be necessary to submit any interpretation of Community law arising in such proceedings to the European Court of Justice for a binding opinion.

---

[9] The issue of consistency is illustrated by the Argentine arbitrations, most of which related to the effects on foreign investors of the measures taken by Argentina in the wake of its 2001 financial crisis. Although many of these instances arose under similar facts involving claims by foreign controlled public utilities, none of them had been subject to consolidation. Of four awards, three have found in favour of the investors with respect to the crucial question of Argentina's defences of necessity, while one rendered a decision favourable to Argentina. An annulment panel that examined one of the original decisions severely criticised the award under review but concluded that it lacked the power to set it aside. For a survey of the relevant decisions, see J. E. Alvarez and K. Khamsi, 'The Argentina Crisis and Foreign Investors, A Glimpse into the Heart of the Investment Regime' in K. Sauvant, *Investment Yearbook 2009* (Oxford University Press, 2009).

[10] See OECD, *International Investment Law: A Changing Landscape* (Paris: OECD Publishing, 2005).

[11] See C. Schreuer, 'Preliminary Rulings in Investment Arbitration' in K. Sauvant (ed.), *Appeals Mechanism in International Investment Disputes* (Oxford University Press, 2008).

Sixth conclusion: the failure of the Multilateral Agreement on Investment (MAI) should not deter renewed efforts towards international rule-making

The collapse in 1998 of the negotiations on an MAI was a dramatic setback in international rule-making. Yet the lessons drawn from this incident are not entirely negative. The MAI was the victim of conceptual flaws, excessive ambition, lack of balance and poor political management. On the positive side, innovative features appeared: a differentiated approach to 'regulatory takings', reference to the environment and social standards and a strong link to responsible business conduct. The final report of the chairman of the negotiation group remains a source of inspiration for establishing a new balance in international investment agreements.[12]

Seventh conclusion: investment and development – a new paradigm

Confronted with global challenges relating to food security, climate change, renewable energies and infrastructure, a new paradigm is emerging based on good economic governance and responsible behaviour by economic operators. Investment – both national and international – is part of this paradigm and this requires a new approach to rules and policies for both national and international investment. Liberalisation and protection alone are not enough to guarantee positive outcomes.[13] An integrated approach is needed to encompass all policies that are crucial to a positive investment environment and good public governance has to go hand in hand with corporate governance and responsible business conduct.

The Policy Framework for Investment adopted at the OECD in 2006 goes in the right direction: it is not prescriptive but authoritative, and sets the markers for policy formulation and evaluation.[14] It is the result of a participatory approach between Member and non-Member countries, governments, business, trade unions and civil society. And it has served as a framework for the development of successful investment policy reforms

---

[12] See OECD, 'Report of the Chairman of the Multilateral Agreement on Investment (MAI) Negotiation Group', available at: www1.oecd.org/daf/mai/pdf/ng/ng989fe.pdf. For the history of the MAI negotiations see generally R. Geiger, 'Towards a Multilateral Agreement on Investment', *Cornell International Law Journal* 31 (1998), 466–75 at 467

[13] OECD, *Foreign Direct Investment for Development: Maximizing Benefits, Minimizing Cost* (Paris: OECD Publishing, 2002).

[14] OECD, *Policy Framework for Investment* (Paris: OECD Publishing, 2006).

in different regions such as South East Europe and the Middle East and North Africa.[15]

II.   Avenues for action

Under the pressure of the present crisis, 'business as usual', that is pursuing the traditional approach to BITs, is no longer an option. A new multilateral approach is needed to use investment as a driver to restore confidence and growth.[16] This requires joint efforts by international economic institutions to promote a favourable investment environment, on the basis of agreed rules and policies. New actors in international investment such as the 'emerging economies' have to be fully integrated in the process and share the responsibilities. As a first step, before engaging in another rule-making exercise, the possibility of building consensus needs to be explored. This could be done through a group of eminent persons operating under the aegis of a joint task force constituted by OECD, UNCTAD and the World Bank to restate the key elements of international investment law.

As pointed out above, investor–state dispute settlement needs reform – both within existing frameworks like the ICSID and through institutional innovations. First, preventive mechanisms such as mediation and conciliation should be developed, as suggested by the contributors to this volume. Second, work should start on the institution of permanent adjudication bodies. Finally, a reference manual for arbitration proceedings, which covers issues such as consolidation of claims, third party intervention, due process, transparency of proceedings and motivation of awards, would help improve the present system.

Creating capacity for successful legal and economic reform remains a major challenge in many countries. Efforts to strengthen the rule of law and the effectiveness of enforcement are crucial for a positive investment climate. Collecting information, exchanging experience, transmitting expertise and building regional and international networks are important steps for capacity-building. This should include the creation of regional resource centres to encourage the development of successful policies and to provide platforms for dialogue between decision-makers, experts, private sector participants and civil society.

---

[15] See OECD, *Investment For Development: Investment Policy Co-operation with Non-OECD Economies*, Annual Report (Paris: OECD Publishing, 2007).

[16] See more generally R. Geiger, 'Multilateral Approaches to Investment: the Way Forward' in J. E. Alvarez and K. Sauvant (eds.), *The Evolving International Investment Regime: Expectations, Realities, Options* (Oxford University Press, 2011).

INDEX